Ethical Arguments for Analysis

SECOND EDITION

Edited by
Robert Baum
Rensselaer Polytechnic Institute

Holt, Rinehart and Winston
New York   Chicago   San Francisco   Atlanta
Dallas   Montreal   Toronto   London   Sydney

Library of Congress Cataloging in Publication Data

Baum, Robert, 1941–   comp.
    Ethical Arguments for analysis.

        1. Ethics—Case studies.   I. Title.   [DNLM:
1. Ethics.   BJ1031 E84]
BJ1031.B33   1976   170   76–1952

ISBN: 0–03–089646–0

Preface

Although every effort has been made to retain all of the features which instructors found useful in the first edition of *Ethical Arguments for Analysis*, there have been a number of changes made in this new edition which have been designed to increase its utility as a primary or supplementary text for a variety of courses, including ethics, logic, rhetoric, and politics. The Introduction has been completely rewritten to provide a sample analysis of an argument similar to most of those included in the fourteen sections, and a number of exercises have been supplied at appropriate points in the Introduction to assist in relating the discussion to the concrete examples contained in the rest of the book. All of the dated examples from the first edition have been dropped, and the total number of items included in this edition is almost double that in the first edition. The examples have been organized into fourteen new sections designed to bring out important points of difference and similarity between various arguments. The section introductions, which also are entirely new and include exercises, not only call attention to central issues unifying the arguments in a given section, but they also assist the student in relating the arguments in one section to those in other sections.

The key features of this book are the "unretouched" arguments drawn from everyday sources and the relatively neutral context in which they are reproduced. This format was proven in the first edition to be extremely flexible; it permits the instructor to use these materials in a variety of ways in a variety of courses. Although the first edition of this book was originally conceived of as a supplementary text for ethics courses, I and a number of other users have found it to be at least as useful in logic and other courses. In particular, it can be used to illustrate the ways in which the same argument in ordinary English can be translated into different logical systems (e.g., syllogistic, propositional, and predicate logics), often with strikingly different results, in contrast to arguments which have been rewritten or even specially written for use in conjunction with a chapter in a logic text on the propositional calculus which cannot be used very well in conjunction with the chapters on the syllogism or the predicate calculus. Even when translating into the same system, a class of students will sometimes come up with twenty or more different ways of translating or symbolizing a single argument out of everyday English. In addition, the arguments in this book provide concrete evidence that few if any arguments which are found in the "real world" resemble the artificial arguments in textbooks. In ethics courses, students will often show how a specific argument could actually be interpreted in terms of several quite different ethical theories. In brief, I and many others have found that the use of the materials in this book in a variety of classroom contexts has provided significant new insights not only for our students but also for ourselves. In this regard, anyone who is using this book for the first time should be prepared for the unexpected. This may make life for the instructor somewhat more difficult, but it also provides a richer, more stimulating intellectual adventure for both the instructor and students.

I cannot begin to name the literally hundreds of persons who have helped make this new edition a reality. I can only express my thanks and appreciation in blanket form to the many instructors who have taken the time to share their experiences in using the first edition and who have offered helpful suggestions for this edition; to the students in my classes who provided much of the inspiration for struggling through some of the more tedious tasks required for pulling this all together; to the copyright holders and members of the editorial staff at Holt, Rinehart and Winston who assisted in securing and keeping track of the reprint permissions; and to the colleagues who have read and commented on various portions of the text. The one person who must be singled out by name for her innumerable contributions—both tangible and intangible—to the completion of this project, is my wife Gail.

January 1976

R. J. B.

Contents

Introduction

It is a basic fact, for which this book provides substantial documentation, that in the course of a normal lifetime every human being is confronted with countless decisions and choices. A few examples should be sufficient for making it clear exactly what are being referred to as "decisions and choices".

A small child is faced with the choice of one of 47 different flavors of ice cream available at the local ice-cream parlor.

A high school athlete has to choose from among 43 colleges and universities which have offered attractive scholarships.

A philosophy professor has to assign a grade to a student who worked very hard in the course but did not do well on the exams or papers.

The members of the admissions committee of a medical college must select 100 persons to be admitted to next year's class from among the 5000 applicants.

A young married couple has to decide which of hundreds of houses and apartments they will buy or rent as their first home.

A corporate executive has to choose one person to be the manager of an important new project from a list of 25 candidates.

A registered voter is confronted with the choice of voting for or against a new bond issue or not voting at all.

Even while recognizing that we do in fact make such decisions and choices on a regular basis, we must also admit that we often make them in a reflexive or mechanical way, without being any more conscious of it than we normally are of breathing or of our heart beating. There are also instances that each of us can cite when we are conscious that a decision is being made (by us), but it is still being made in a mechanical, or at best arbitrary, way. But there are also times and circumstances in which each of us has stopped and thought over the situation, carefully considering the pros and cons of alternative courses of action before making our decision as to which course of action to follow. When it comes to decisions concerning questions such as what career to pursue, or whether or not to begin a family, some people spend significant portions of their lives "thinking things over" before committing themselves to a final course of action (or inaction, which is always an alternative).

Often, in the process of making a decision, we discuss the pros and cons of the alternative courses of action with friends and relatives. And after having made a choice, we often justify and/or defend our decision when circumstances demand it. We also praise or criticize others' decisions, offering our own reasons for agreeing or disagreeing with their choices. The presentation of reasons for our agreement with or opposition to a particular decision comprises what is commonly known as the process of "argumentation." And in so far as we put forward certain statements in support of another statement to the effect that one of a set of alternative courses of action is better or worse than another, we can be said to be presenting an argument in support of that judgment.

The term "argument" has several different meanings in everyday English usage. The type of situation to which this term is most frequently applied is exemplified by a highly emotional dispute between a husband and wife about whether or not to buy a new car, or a quarrel between a teenager and his or her parents over their imposition of a curfew for dates on weekends. A similar and also commonly encountered case to which the term "argument" can be applied is the cool, articulate discussion between formal debate teams. While the examples contained in this book might sometimes share the features of these types of cases, we will be concerned primarily, if not solely, with the fact that they satisfy a more technical and restricted definition of the term "argument", namely the formal, logical definition that *an argument is a set of statements, one of which is designated as a conclusion and the remainder of which are asserted as evidence, supporting or implying the truth of the conclusion.*

The mere presentation of an argument in support of a judgment that a particular decision is good or bad is not in and of itself adequate justification for accepting that judgment, insofar as only a few of the literally infinite number of possible arguments really provide any significant support for their conclusions. Consider the following examples:

> It was right for Joe to cheat on the exam because he doesn't like applesauce.
> It was right for Joe to cheat on the exam because he didn't have time to study for it.
> It was right for Joe to cheat on the exam because the moon is made of blue cheese.

Each of the above statements comprises an argument insofar as each involves the presentation of some reason in support of the claim that it was right for Joe to cheat. The third example is clearly a very bad argument, in that the reason provided in fact gives no support whatsoever to the conclusion; the assertion that the moon is made of blue cheese is in fact false, and even if it were true it bears no logical relation whatsoever to the assertion that Joe did the right thing. The first two examples may be somewhat better arguments insofar as their premises could be true (Joe may indeed dislike applesauce and he may not have had time to study for the exam), but it is still not at all clear what logical relation may exist between either of these premises and the conclusion concerning the rightness of Joe's decision to cheat. In brief, not every argument provides us with the same (or even any) justification for accepting the conclusion; it is necessary that an argument provide actual support for the conclusion before it can be judged to be a *good* argument.

Our basic concern in this discussion is with choices and decisions, and with distinguishing good decisions from bad ones. However, since a judgment concerning the goodness or badness of a decision normally must be supported by an argument, and since there are both good and bad arguments in support of any particular judgment, our discussion must be moved to the more abstract level of evaluating arguments. It is hoped that the connection between our discussion of good and bad arguments and our primary concern with distinguishing good and bad decisions is sufficiently clear. In simplest terms, the connection is that a good argument in support of a judgment that an action or decision is good (or bad) normally is sufficient grounds for believing that the action or decision is in fact good (or bad). A bad argument in support of any judgment provides us with no grounds for believing anything at all about the goodness or badness of the action or decision being judged.

Before proceeding to a discussion of the criteria and procedures for distinguishing good arguments from bad ones, it is necessary to impose an important restriction on the scope of our discussion. In brief, we are *not* concerned in this book with the evaluation of *all* possible kinds of choices and decisions; we are only concerned with those choices and decisions which can be classified as "moral" or "ethical." Although it would certainly be useful at this point to provide a precise definition of the term "moral decision," it is unfortunately impossible to do this, since there are a number of different definitions of the term, most of which are incompatible in one way or another with the others. All that we can do here is provide a rough indication of the general area which for the purposes of this book will be considered as falling within the definition of "moral decision" or "ethical decision." (In this book we shall use the terms "moral" and "ethical" interchangeably.)

Most dictionaries define a moral decision as a decision made on the basis of an appeal to a set of moral rules or principles, or as a decision made by an appeal to one's conscience. Unfortunately, since the definitions provided for "moral principles" and "conscience" appeal back to the concept of moral decision (for example, one definition of "conscience" is "the faculty of mind used for making moral choices"), we are simply led in circles without ever gaining a clearer understanding of the basic concept of moral decision. An alternative procedure for defining "moral decision" is to simply provide examples, and that is the procedure we will use in this book. However, we must make it clear from the beginning that there is much room for disagreement over what does and what does not qualify as a moral decision, and some of the examples contained in this book have been selected precisely to provide examples of cases over which there is much disagreement as to whether they do indeed involve moral decisions. This issue is discussed further in the introduction to Section 7.

EXERCISES

1. Examine the examples in Sections 1, 7, and 13 of this book. Classify each example as involving what *you* consider to be (a) clearly a moral decision, (b) possibly a moral decision, or (c) clearly not a moral decision. Compare your classifications with those of several other persons. Try to determine the reasons for any differences that might appear between your classifications and those of someone else.
2. Using the examples which you classified in the previous exercise, try to formulate a definition or set of criteria for distinguishing in general between moral and nonmoral decisions. Compare your definition with those of several other persons and analyze any differences.
3. Apply the definition which you formulated in Exercise 2 to the following statement to determine whether this statement is true or false (by your definition): "The decision to consider a particular issue as a moral issue is itself a moral decision." (In other words, is it a moral decision, by your definition, to decide to consider, for example, the killing of a dog as a moral issue?)

The remainder of the discussion in this Introduction will be devoted to matters which should be of assistance in the development of the skills necessary for distinguishing good moral arguments from bad ones, which for reasons already discussed will also be of assistance in distinguishing good moral decisions from bad ones. Thus, even though our discussion will be formulated in terms of distinguishing good moral *arguments* from bad ones, it should be understood throughout that we are also concerned with distinguishing good moral *decisions* from bad ones.

For the most part, each of us is normally able to identify a good or bad argument for what it is without much conscious effort. On a purely intuitive level, most people would probably agree that a good argument is one in which all of the premises are already known to be true with a reasonable degree of certainty and in which the premises are related to the conclusion in such a way as to transmit the certainty of the premises in whole or part to the conclusion. In a somewhat more precise formulation, one basic requirement for a *good* argument is that it must be one for which it is the case that if the premises are true, Although this general definition may appear to be relatively simple and straight- then the conclusion is true or highly probable, and the premises are in fact true. forward, it is unfortunately the case that many arguments which we encounter in everyday life are such that it is not at all easy to determine whether they are good or not. Most of the ethical arguments included in this book have been selected precisely because they are not easily evaluated (although some of them at first glance may seem to be obviously good or bad). It is almost always the case that even if most people intuitively judge a particular argument to be "obviously" good, there remains the possibility that someone will not agree and may even feel that the same argument is "obviously" a bad one. In order to resolve such differences of opinion concerning the quality of a particular argument, it is necessary to have a good understanding of the nature of arguments and of the many factors which are relevant to their being good or bad. This kind of understanding cannot be acquired solely by reading an abstract theoretical discussion about analyzing arguments; rather, this understanding must be gained by actually applying the general concepts to concrete examples of the type provided in this book.

EXERCISES

4. Read through all of the arguments in one of the sections in this book. Relying on your own intuitions, label each argument according to the following 1–5 scale. (Remember, you are to evaluate the argument, not the decision being discussed in the argument.)

> 1–Very Good
>
> 2–Good
>
> 3–Indeterminate
>
> 4–Bad
>
> 5–Very Bad

5. Compare your evaluations of these arguments with those of several other persons. Discuss two or three arguments for which your evaluations differed the most to try to determine the reason(s) for the differences. Try to resolve these differences and come to an agreement concerning these arguments.

The process of distinguishing good moral arguments from bad ones (and thus of distinguishing good moral decisions from bad ones) is far from being a simple one. It is for this reason that the cartoon on the cover of this book contains a real element of truth, although its humor derives from its more obvious element of error. Most people would agree that there are no human beings who have some special innate faculty or insight which enables them to distinguish good moral choices from bad ones in a way that other people cannot. But there are in fact persons who have developed certain basic skills so that they can progress further towards the identification of good and bad decisions than persons who have not developed these skills. No medical doctor can cure all illnesses, nor can he or she keep anyone alive forever. However, the combination of basic skills acquired through formal training in medical school and the practice and experience gained from applying this knowledge to real situations during the internship and residence periods is normally sufficient to assist doctors in mastering the art of medicine, which enables them to cure many more illnesses and extend lives longer than can persons who have not had similar training and practical experience. Thus an analog to the cartoon on the cover might be a case where a person is asking for someone who can tell him or her how to live forever or how to cure a presently uncurable disease. We smile at this because we recognize that it is a request for what we now consider to be impossible; but this does not mean that we consider the practice and training of doctors and medical researchers to be a foolish enterprise. We are willing to accept the fact that while they cannot now provide solutions to the "problems" of indefinite prolongation of life or a cure of lung cancer, they are able to treat many problems in a way that most people would consider to be a significant improvement over the way they were treated a century ago and over the way persons without special training could treat them even today. In a like manner, a person with formal training and skills developed through careful practice should be able to deal more effectively and intelligently with difficult ethical decisions than a person without such training. They are not able to distinguish a good decision from a bad one at a glance any more than a physician is able to diagnose an illness at a glance. But a person with the proper training and experience should know what procedures to follow which will most likely lead to a determination of what is the morally right decision in a given situation, even if in many cases it is not possible to adequately complete all of these procedures. But all of this is much too abstract for adequate comprehension and is certainly not persuasive. So we will leave this discussion about the utility of this study and proceed to the study itself. After we have provided sample analyses of several examples, the utility of the study should be more clearly apparent.

To bring our discussion down to more concrete terms, we will use the following argument as the subject of a sample analysis. The argument is not intended to be particularly good or bad, but it is designed to enable us to identify many of the basic factors involved in evaluating most moral arguments.

It was morally wrong for Susan to write Tom's term paper for his ethics course, because helping someone else to cheat is as bad as cheating oneself. And history has shown that when one performs even a small act of dishonesty this can lead to ever more harmful acts, in addition to encouraging others to commit similar wrongs. When too many members of a particular society commit acts which are harmful to other members of that society, it ultimately leads to the destruction of that society, which is certainly reason enough for Susan not to write Tom's term paper.

We will now proceed to evaluate this argument. Remember, if we are able to show that this is a good argument, then we will have reason to believe that it was indeed morally wrong for Susan to do what she did; but if we show that the argument is bad, or even fail to show that it is good, then we will not have adequate reason to believe that Susan's choice was either good or bad. In other words, while a good argument provides justification for accepting its conclusion as true, a bad argument simply fails to provide adequate evidence for the truth of the conclusion. It must be emphasized that a bad argument does not prove that the conclusion is false. A bad argument is bad precisely because it proves *nothing at all*.

The process of analyzing arguments is not a simple linear one; there is no fixed and absolute sequence of steps through which we can mechanically move in such a way that we will automatically wind up with a definite determination of the quality of the argument. Thus, we must begin this analysis by making it as explicit as possible that the procedures used here are to be taken as a "model" procedure only in a very limited way. The sequence in which various points will be discussed should not be interpreted at all as the only possible one, or even as the best one, insofar as many of the steps can be performed simultaneously when they are not being written down as we have to do here. While most if not all of these points should be considered during the analysis of most arguments, there are many other kinds of factors that need to be considered in the analysis of this and other arguments which we simply cannot go into here, although we will try to give some indication of where one can find a more detailed discussion of such factors in the course of our own analysis.

For our present purposes, it is appropriate and useful, but not absolutely necessary, to begin our analysis by trying to identify the conclusion of the argument we have selected as our sample. Probably most persons (whose native language is English, of course) would agree that the conclusion is expressed by the first part of the first sentence, that is, "It was morally wrong for Susan to write Tom's term paper for his ethics course." While this might be considered by many to be simply intuitively obvious, there is a more specific and concrete bit of evidence that this is the case, namely, the word "because" following the sentence. Frequently, *but not always*, the appearance of the term "because" (or "since" or any one of several other words) indicates that the sentence immediately preceding the word is the conclusion of an argument, and that the sentence immediately following (and perhaps other sentences as well) expresses a premise of that argument. Unfortunately, these indicator words are also used in other ways which have nothing whatever to do with arguments, so we cannot rely on their appearance as a guarantee that a particular sentence expresses the conclusion or premise of an argument. In the end, we usually have to rely on our "intuition" or our "feel" for the language for identification of the conclusion of an argument.

But in many cases, including our example, the problem of identifying the conclusion of a moral argument is even more difficult and complex than this. Even though we may agree that the sentence "It was morally wrong for Susan . . ." expresses the conclusion of this argument, it is not entirely clear what the precise wording of the conclusion should be. Is the conclusion really that it was wrong for Susan to write Tom's term paper, or is it instead that it was wrong for Susan to help Tom cheat? While this may seem to be a relatively minor or even trivial question, it does have some significance for the overall evaluation of this argument.

It is also important to recognize that insofar as this is being presented as a *moral* judgment there must be some choice or decision involved, and it is not at all clear from the conclusion as given what the alternatives were from which Susan chose. For example, did Susan know that she was writing this paper so that Tom could submit it for his ethics course or did she perhaps believe that she was doing this for some quite different purpose? And even if she knew that Tom was going to submit it for his course, what options were open to her? If Tom had been pointing a gun at her head, and the option was to not write the paper and get shot, this would significantly affect the evaluation of the entire argument and ultimately the evaluation of the act itself. Likewise, it may be that Tom had saved Susan's life at a previous time and Susan felt herself to be in great debt to him, and if she did not write the paper she would be failing to repay this debt. Thus, it is important that the statement of the conclusion of a moral argument should include an explicit statement of the alternative choices which could have been made. The conclusion in our example should not merely say that it was wrong for Susan to write Tom's paper; it should specify that it was wrong for Susan to have done this instead of one or more of the alternatives that were available to her.

Although most arguments fail to adequately spell out in the conclusion the alternatives to a given course of action, these alternatives are often discussed in the premises in a way which is adequate for enabling us to fully formulate the conclusion for the purposes of analyzing it. Thus, if our example had contained some mention of alternatives in the premises (e.g., a premise such as "If Susan had not written Tom's paper, then she would have been failing to repay her debt to him for having saved her from a shark at the beach the previous week"), the argument as a whole would have been strengthened considerably, and it would have been both easy and reasonable to add this information to the statement of the conclusion. Insofar as no indication is given anywhere at all in the argument of the options open to Susan in this case, the argument is weaker than if these alternatives were explicitly stated.

Not only is some information left out of the statement of the conclusion in some arguments, but it is not uncommon for the conclusion to never be explicitly stated at all. An argument in which some part is not explicitly stated is known as an "enthymeme," and in such cases it is normal procedure to simply try to supply the missing elements of the argument in as reasonable a manner as possible. Consider the following version of our example:

> Helping someone else to cheat is as bad as cheating oneself, and Susan did help Tom to cheat when she wrote his ethics term paper for him. And history . . . .

Although it is not explicitly stated in this version, it is sufficiently clear that the intended conclusion of the argument is that Susan was wrong to write Tom's paper (or to help him to cheat). In such cases, it is necessary for the person analyzing the argument to make explicit in the most reasonable way any and all information which is implicit in the original argument. To analyze an argument should not be the same as to attack it. The purpose of analysis is to identify the strengths as well as the weaknesses of an argument, and to correct its weaknesses as much as possible in order to lead to a determination as to what is the best choice to make in a particular situation. Because the primary aim of our analysis is positive rather than critical, it is necessary to rely on a basic rule which we will refer as the "Principle of Charity." The Principle of Charity is simply the quite reasonable rule that *we should always make every effort possible to interpret an argument in the way which makes it as strong as possible.* For example, we could have interpreted the enthymeme above as not even expressing any argument at all insofar as it has no conclusion, but this would clearly have violated the Principle of Charity. It would not be an unreasonable application of the Principle of Charity to interpret the lack of mention of alternative courses of action in our sample argument as an implicit assertion that none of the possible options available in this specific case involve any special overriding obligations, such as keeping a promise or preserving one's life, which might be relevant to the basic judgment concerning the rightness or wrongness of Susan's act. Wording to this effect might even be explicitly included in our reformulation of the conclusion, although it would have to be kept clearly in mind that we certainly do not have conclusive evidence that this is in fact the case. An argument which states explicitly all of the available courses of action for a given case is generally a better argument than one in which some of the options are only implicitly identified.

Our discussion thus far has focused on an example in which the conclusion is a judgment about a specific decision made by a particular individual. However, an examination of the arguments reprinted in the following pages reveals that many of them have conclusions which involve generalizations about kinds of action (e.g., Abortion is wrong.) or judgments concerning events where the agent is not clearly identified, (e.g., The Vietnam war was morally wrong.). We must therefore digress from our example for a moment to discuss such conclusions.

For the purposes of this book, we will consider arguments with general conclusions as subordinate arguments which are such that they can be used as components of any number of other arguments with conclusions about specific cases. Thus an argument with the conclusion "Abortion is wrong" can be taken as part of a set of premises such as "Dr. Jones performed an abortion on Mary Doe" in support of the specific conclusion "It was wrong for Dr. Jones to perform an abortion on Mary Doe." We will see a little bit later in the discussion of our sample case that the argument concerning Susan and Tom contains several implicit premises which are general conclusions of subarguments in the overall argument. We will therefore wait to discuss these general conclusions in that context.

A conclusion such as "The Vietnam war was wrong" is not a generalization of the type just discussed, since there is precisely one event being talked about— or at least that appears to be the case. The problem with a conclusion such as this is that it is not at all clear what decision by what agent is being categorized as wrong. Since an action cannot be appropriately classified as right or wrong unless there are alternative courses of action open to the agent, it is necessary that both the agent and the choices be known in order to make an adequate determination of the rightness or wrongness of the action being judged. If, as some historians have argued, major events such as wars are the product of forces in society over which no individual has any control at all, then it would follow that it is simply improper, or an incorrect use of language, to assert that the Vietnam war was morally wrong. We cannot go into the whole set of issues related to the question of "historical determinism" here. Instead, we shall simply reiterate that all conclusions with inadequate identification of the alternative courses of action should be reformulated to make the agent and the choices explicit where this is possible. Thus, for example, the conclusion of the Vietnam argument could be reformulated as a judgment concerning Lyndon Johnson's options at the time he took the Gulf of Tonkin resolution to Congress or at the time he made the commitment to send as many as 500,000 troops to Vietnam rather than pulling out the relatively few troops that were then there. Of course, one could also place the responsibility on the members of Congress, or on the Secretary of State, or on other persons who had other options. But the main point to be made here is that we are not even dealing with a moral argument if the conclusion is not general and also is not concerned with a decision for which there were at least two real options available to some agent. The problem of identifying the agent for complex cases such as the Vietnam war is just one issue related to the evaluation of moral arguments that we will not be able to discuss in sufficient detail in this Introduction, although it will be touched on in the introductions to several of the following sections of this book.

It is not possible in the space limitations of this discussion to detail all of the factors which should be taken into account in the single task of identifying and formulating the conclusion of an argument, but we must make it clear that this is indeed a complex process which has not been completely presented here. For example, we have not adequately discussed complex arguments which contain arguments within arguments, and thus multiple conclusions (only one of which, of course, is the primary or final conclusion) which must be sorted out before the final conclusion can be identified. Thus, although we are now going on to discuss some of the other tasks involved in the evaluation of moral arguments, it should not be assumed that our treatment of the procedures for identifying and formulating conclusions has been in any sense complete.

In summary, the identification and complete formulation of the conclusion is a necessary and critical, although not necessarily first, step in the evaluation of an ethical argument. If after making every reasonable effort (in compliance with the Principle of Charity) one is still unable to identify or formulate the conclusion of an argument, one then has adequate grounds for judging the argument to be a bad one. However, if one has adequately identified and formulated the conclusion and then considers the conclusion to be false, this is not an adequate reason for rejecting either the conclusion or the argument. In order to reject an argument whose conclusion is (or can be) properly formulated, it is necessary to identify some other weakness in the argument. If no other weakness can be found, then it would be irrational to reject the argument as a bad one simply because one believes that the conclusion is false.

EXERCISES

6. Select one argument from each of the sections of this book that appears to you intuitively to be a good one, and one argument from each section which appears to be a bad one. Identify, where possible, the main conclusion of each of these arguments. (Remember, some arguments are enthymematic and the conclusions are not explicitly stated.)

7. Classify each of the conclusions identified in the previous exercise as (a) a judgment concerning a particular decision or choice made by a specific individual; (b) a judgment concerning a particular event in which the agent and/or the alternative choices is (are) not adequately specified; (c) a general judgment concerning a type of action rather than a specific case.

8. Determine whether there are any adequate grounds for judging any of these arguments to be bad ones solely on the basis of your consideration of their conclusions.

Even using the Principle of Charity we were not able to provide a formulation of the conclusion of our sample argument which contains any indication of the options which were open to the agent (Susan) in this particular case, so we already have identified one weakness in it. However, insofar as every argument has weaknesses of one kind or another, we shall continue using this example for the remainder of our discussion of some of the other significant factors related to the goodness or badness of a moral argument.

In addition to identifying and adequately formulating the conclusion, it is also a necessary and critical part of any analysis to identify and properly formulate the premises offered in support of that conclusion. The consideration of the premises is not normally a sequel to the identification of the conclusion, insofar as the argument must usually be considered as a whole before the conclusion can be properly identified and formulated. In the case of enthymemes in which the conclusion is implicit, it is necessary to conduct a particularly thorough and detailed analysis of the premises before even trying to formulate the conclusion. We shall also see later that there are a number of other considerations that have to be made before or during the process of identifying and reformulating the premises of an argument.

Referring back to our sample argument, it might not seem unreasonable to assume that all of the statements other than the conclusion were asserted as being in some way supportive of the conclusion, and thus all of them can be considered as premises. Unfortunately, such an assumption is all too often quite mistaken. It is not uncommon to discover in a lengthy editorial that only a few of the many sentences actually express premises which in any way support the conclusion. However, it is not always easy to determine whether or not a particular statement is an essential premise of an argument, and we certainly cannot rely solely on our intuitions as to whether or not a specific statement is essential. The inclusion of totally irrelevant premises in an analysis may complicate things a little and create some extra work, but it will not distort the ultimate result of the analysis. If the argument is basically good, our analysis will show it to be such even if some of the premises are unnecessary. On the other hand, if an essential premise is omitted, any analysis will result in a negative evaluation, even if the original argument was a good one. Thus, since it is better to include too many statements than to leave out an essential premise, we will always follow the rule (which is really a corollary to the Principle of Charity) that *no statement should be discarded in the analysis of an argument unless it can be demonstrated conclusively that it is either redundant or irrelevant.*

Using this rule, the first step in the identification and formulation of the premises of a moral argument is to list the premises as stated in the original argument. The explicitly stated premises of our sample argument are as follows:

1. Helping someone else to cheat is as bad as cheating oneself.
2. History has shown that when one performs even a small act of dishonesty this can lead to ever more harmful acts, in addition to encouraging others to commit similar wrongs.
3. When too many members of a particular society commit acts which are harmful to other members of that society, it ultimately leads to the destruction of that society.
4. This is certainly reason enough for Susan to not write Tom's term paper.

Each of these seems reasonably clear and comprehensible at first glance. The most natural next step would appear to be the determination of whether or not these premises need to be reformulated in any way or whether any implicit or "suppressed" premises must be made explicit. But in order to do this properly, it is necessary to perform several other tasks first (or if it is possible, simultaneously). These tasks include, but are not necessarily limited to, testing the argument for validity or inductive strength and ascertaining the truth or degree of probability of the premises. We shall thus wait to consider any changes in or additions to the premises until we have discussed some of the other factors in the evaluation of moral arguments.

EXERCISES

9. For each of the arguments selected for Exercise 6, list each of the explicitly stated premises in a numerical sequence as was done with the sample argument. Identify any of the premises which are vague or ambiguous and try to reformulate them to remove the vagueness and ambiguity.
10. On a purely "intuitive" basis, try to determine what implicit or suppressed premises need to be made explicit in each of these arguments.

It was indicated earlier in this discussion that in the simplest and most general terms, a "good" argument is one which is structured in such a way that *if* its premises are true, *then* the conclusion must be true or at least highly probable, *and* all of the premises are in fact true. An adequate elaboration of this general definition would require an entire book and/or course on formal logic, and it is certainly to be recommended that anyone truly interested in the analysis of ethical (or any other kind of) arguments should take a logic course or at least study a basic logic text.*

While it is obviously not possible to give a complete discussion of the formal logical factors required for the analysis of ethical arguments here, we will try to provide some elaboration of the intuitive concepts presented thus far. First we must distinguish between two logically different types of argument—inductive and deductive. A valid deductive argument is one which is such that *if* all of its premises are true, then it is logically impossible for its conclusion to be false. In other terms, a valid deductive argument is such that its conclusion is in some way implicitly (or explicitly) contained in its premises. An ancient example of a valid deductive argument is the following:

Socrates is a man.
All men are mortal.
_____
Therefore, Socrates is mortal.

Any argument with the same *form* as this one is also deductively valid, even though its premises may not be actually true. (Remember, our definition stated only that "*IF*" the premises are true.) Thus, the following argument is also deductively valid:

* One such text is this author's *Logic*, Holt, Rinehart and Winston, 1975.

Socrates is an angel.
All angels are mortal.

Therefore, Socrates is mortal.

In this example, the premises are presumably false, but the argument is still valid. The argument could be proven invalid only if it could be shown that it is *possible* for some argument with the same form to have true premises and a false conclusion. The following example is invalid, even though its premises and the conclusion are all true.

Socrates is a mortal.
All men are mortal.

Therefore, Socrates is a man.

This argument can be proven to be deductively invalid by the following example which has exactly the same logical form, but which has true premises and a false conclusion:

Socrates is a mammal.
All horses are mammals.

Therefore, Socrates is a horse.

The presentation of just one argument with true premises and a false conclusion is sufficient proof that *all* arguments with the same logical form are invalid. However, the failure to construct an argument with a specific form with true premises and a false conclusion is not sufficient to prove that the argument is valid, since it is always possible that someone might come along at some future date with such an example. There are several different procedures which can be used to prove that a particular argument is deductively valid, but we cannot discuss them here; any basic logic text can be consulted by interested persons.

EXERCISES

11. Each of the following arguments is deductively invalid. Try to construct an argument with the same logical form but with true premises and a false conclusion to prove their invalidity.

    a. Some students work hard.
       Tom is a student.

       Therefore, Tom works hard.

    b. If Susan worked hard, then she got an A in Ethics.
       Susan got an A in Ethics.

       Therefore, Susan worked hard.

    c. If many students register for Ethics, then it must be a good course.
       Not many students registered for Ethics.

       Therefore, Ethics must not be a good course.

d. Some people are ethical.
   Some people are wealthy.
   _____

   Therefore, some people are ethical and wealthy.

e. Apple A obeys the law of gravity.
   Apple B obeys the law of gravity.
   Apple C obeys the law of gravity.
   _____

   Therefore, all apples obey the law of gravity.

The reason for distinguishing between the two different kinds of argument—inductive and deductive—is that bad (invalid) deductive arguments can still be very good inductive arguments. The last argument in the above exercise is an example of an argument which is deductively invalid but inductively good. A good inductive argument is one for which if the premises are true then it is highly probable that the conclusion is also true, but the possibility always remains that the conclusion is false. The main reason for this difference in certainty between deductive and inductive arguments is that for a valid deductive argument it is always the case that all of the information in the conclusion is also contained in some way in the premises, while for an inductive argument there is always some information in the conclusion that is not contained at all in the premises. Readers interested in learning more about the procedures for distinguishing good inductive arguments from bad ones are again referred to a basic logic text.

For both inductive and deductive arguments it is also the case that in order to be "good" they must not only have a certain logical form but they must also have "true" premises. Of course, even in the sciences there are very few (if any) statements which are considered to be absolutely true and certain. Most statements with which we normally deal are only what would be considered as highly probable. Thus, while it is certainly not as good as an argument with absolutely true premises, an argument with highly probable premises and a good deductive or inductive logical form is also a good argument. In applying the Principle of Charity to the reformulation of any arguments we must always do this in such a way as to give it both the best logical form and *also* the most highly certain premises. This often requires making trade-offs, as in a case where in order to put an argument into a deductively valid form we must add a highly dubious premise, but if we use only highly probable premises then the argument must be put into a not very strong inductive form. Let us now work with our sample argument again with these additional factors in mind.

EXERCISES

12. Examine each of the arguments as formulated in Exercise 10. Label them as either "inductive" or "deductive." If an argument has one or more subarguments, label each subargument as well.

13. Evaluate each of the arguments as reformulated in Exercise 11. In particular, check to see if reformulating a deductive argument as an inductive one, or an inductive one as deductive would strengthen or weaken each argument,

keeping in mind that the overall quality of an argument is a function *both* of its logical form *and* of the plausibility of its premises.

In looking at the four premises as listed on page 11 and the conclusion, it appears on the surface that there is little if any logical connection between any of the premises and between the premises and the conclusion, since the conclusion is about the wrongness of Susan writing Tom's ethics paper, the first premise is about cheating, the second premise is about history, dishonesty, and so on, and the third premise is a generalization about causes of the destruction of societies. There are very few key terms in the different statements which can act as a "logical glue" to hold the argument together. Thus, we must try to reformulate some or all of these statements to make explicit any connections which may exist between them, or else add some additional premises which would also tie them together.

The connection between the first premise and the conclusion is quite clear, even if it is not explicit. It is certainly implicit in this argument that in writing Tom's paper, Susan was helping Tom to cheat. This connection can be made explicit by adding a premise:

5. In writing Tom's ethics paper, Susan was helping Tom to cheat.

It is also necessary for logical purposes to make explicit the assertion that Susan did in fact write Tom's paper. Thus,

6. Susan wrote Tom's term paper for his ethics course.

Elaborating and reformulating this a little bit more in a way which seems to be entirely within the spirit of the original argument, we can construct the following *valid* deductive argument:

7. Cheating is wrong.
1. Helping someone else to cheat is as wrong as cheating oneself.
5. If Susan wrote Tom's ethics paper, then Susan helped Tom to cheat.
8. If Susan helped Tom to cheat, then Susan did wrong.
6. Susan wrote Tom's ethics paper.

Therefore, Susan did wrong (by writing Tom's ethics paper).

Although in this form the argument is deductively valid, it is not a very good argument for several reasons. As we have already noted, it is not a good *moral* argument because the alternative courses of action are not spelled out in the conclusion or in the premises. The argument is also weak in the above form since the first two premises are somewhat questionable, and even a valid argument cannot provide more certainty for its conclusion than is possessed by any of its relevant premises. The second premise is weak in several ways. For example, is helping someone else to cheat if one is not aware that one is doing so as bad an act as knowingly cheating oneself? And is helping someone else to cheat as repayment of a debt as bad as cheating oneself for purely selfish reasons? At best, this premise requires some additional support if it is to lend any significant support to the conclusion. At worst, it is a false statement resulting from a careless oversimplification and overgeneralization of a set of complex, concrete realities. The first premise can be subjected to similar criticisms, but insofar as a subargument is presented in support of this premise, we will analyze the subargument before making a final judgment on the first premise of the main argument as formulated above.

The subargument offered in support of the premise that cheating is wrong consists of a sequence of inductive and deductive arguments based on an interpretation of human history. Insofar as the original argument is formulated using a "can," the Principle of Charity requires that our reformulation be in less than absolute terms. The following would appear to be a sympathetic and reasonable rendition of the subargument, although of course it is only one of a number of possible versions that could be constructed.

7a. In the past it was often (or usually or generally) the case that when a person performed a small act of dishonesty it led to the performance of ever more harmful acts.

7b. In the past it was often (or usually or generally) the case that when a person performed a small act of dishonesty it led to the performance of similar acts by others.

7c. Therefore, in the future it will often (or usually or generally) be the case that when a person performs a small act of dishonesty it will lead to the performance of more harmful acts by many people.

7d. It is generally the case that when too many members of a particular society commit acts which are harmful to other members of that society, it ultimately leads to the destruction of that society.

7e. Any act which leads to the destruction of a society is wrong.

7f. Cheating is a small act of dishonesty and therefore will lead to the destruction of a society.

7. Therefore, cheating is wrong.

Steps 7a, 7b, and 7c, which represent an "unpacking" of the original premise 4, comprise an inductive argument. The two premises of this inductive argument involve questions of historical fact which are probably still quite open to debate even among experts. The more strongly they are stated ("generally" is much stronger than "often") the more doubtful they become; but as their formulation is made weaker, less support is provided for the conclusion of the main argument. But this is not the most serious problem here, because as long as the conclusion of the inductive argument is not formulated in absolute terms (i.e., that it is *always* the case that a small act of dishonesty leads to the performance of more harmful acts by many people), then there is no strong logical connection between it and the rest of the subargument in support of the conclusion that cheating is wrong. The crucial premise in this subargument is one which we supplied, 7e, one which was not present in the original argument, but which we added under the Principle of Charity as a premise which seemed to be implicit in, or at least in the spirit of, the original argument and which appeared to be necessary for the argument to be in its strongest form. It is not uncommon in analyzing arguments to carry out procedures which intuitively seem to strengthen an argument, only to discover on closer analysis that these changes themselves have to be changed. This is in part what was being referred to earlier when we warned that the analysis and evaluation of ethical arguments is a complex and difficult task, one that certainly does not follow any simple, straightforward mechanical procedure.

The subargument which we are currently discussing can be strengthened somewhat by weakening the premise which we added (7e) to the effect that "Any act which leads to the destruction of a society is wrong" by qualifying it to now read "Any act which *can* lead to the destruction of a society is wrong." This strengthens the subargument because in this form it can be logically combined with the other premises, and one other premise to be added which asserts that "Any act which has ever occurred in the past is an act which *can* occur," to yield the conclusion that cheating is wrong. Unfortunately, even though this argument is logically stronger than what we started with, it is still vulnerable to a variety of other criticisms, especially those directed at the basic reasonableness of several of the added premises (which seem to be necessary for logical purposes). For example, the new premise "Any act which can lead to the destruction of a society is wrong" is not at all easy to evaluate in terms of its truth or probability, insofar as almost any act whatsoever could be classified as wrong under this stipulation. Is there any act at all for which it could not be said that under some circumstances or other the act *can* "lead to" the destruction of a society? Responding to such criticisms might be characterized more as a kind of "fine tuning" of the argument rather than anything very serious, but this is still a part of the process of evaluating moral arguments which cannot be entirely ignored.

Questions such as those of which acts are such that in fact they "can lead to" the destruction of a society are questions of historical fact or even of scientific theory insofar as they are concerned with the identification of causal connections between events. However, the premise "Any act which can lead to the destruction of a society is wrong" is essentially a moral judgment or principle concerning the wrongness of a general type of act. Just as the procedures and criteria for evaluating the logical structure of an argument require at least an entire book or course for even an introductory presentation, so also the procedures and criteria for evaluating basic ethical principles and theories are such that no adequate discussion of them can be presented in the limited space available here. All that we can do here is to point out that there are several different types of moral theory. Some of these theories are such that they provide procedures or criteria for generating general principles of the type "Cheating is wrong." In addition to the theory illustrated by our example concerning the judgment of a general type of act in terms of its relation to the destruction or survival of a society (which is a variant of a type of ethical theory known as "utilitarianism"), other principle-generating theories include some based on religious assumptions (e.g., whatever God—or the Bible—says is right is right) or political bases (e.g., whatever the majority of the members of a society says is right is right). The most obvious question now would seem to be that of determining which of the alternative rule-generating theories is the best or "correct" one. But there is an alternative factor which must also be considered at this point in our analysis and that is the fact that most if not all of these rule-generating theories share a basic weakness. The problem they all face can be stated simply; its solution, if it has an adequate one, is certainly not an obvious one. In brief, each of these theories is capable of generating a multiplicity of rules which are such that it is not impossible, or even uncommon, for two or more of them to come into direct conflict in specific real situations. For example, the ethical theory based on the survival and destruction of a society can also generate rules such as "Breaking promises is wrong" and "Not repaying debts is wrong," and it is not difficult at all to conceive of situations in which these rules could directly conflict with the rule "Cheating is wrong," that is, a situation in which the only choices are to cheat or break a promise or not repay a debt. Different rule-generating ethical theories deal with this kind of difficulty in different ways which we cannot elaborate on here. We can only refer the interested reader to an introductory ethics text or course.

The alternative to a rule-generating ethical theory is what is commonly referred to as an *act* theory, a theory that rejects the need for any formal set of intermediary rules of the type provided by the rule-generating theories. Thus, under an act theory, the rightness or wrongness of a particular action must be determined directly (by some kind of direct intuition or perception, as when we determine the color or smell of a flower) or by appeal directly to the ethical theory itself, which may include some kind of a universal principle for judging all kinds of action. Some of the different kinds of universal principles include the Golden Rule ("Do unto others. . . ."), the Principle of Utility ("An act is right if it produces the greatest amount of good for the greatest number of people," or any of numerous variations of this), an Egoistic Principle ("An act is right if it produces the greatest good for me"), and some kind of principle involving motivation ("An act is right if it is done out of good motives"). Once again, it is impossible to begin to discuss the relative strengths and weaknesses of the various act theories of ethics here. It is necessary, however, to point out that each theory does have strengths and weaknesses, just as do the various rule theories. The relative merits of the various kinds of ethical theory have been debated since the beginning of recorded history, and the fact that a large number of different theories are appealed to in the arguments reprinted in this volume is a clear indication that among the general population no consensus has yet been reached concerning which of them is the best.

EXERCISES

14. Examine the arguments as you formulated them for Exercise 13. Identify the premise (or premises) which states the ethical theory being appealed to in the argument. Try to determine whether this is an act or rule theory. (Note: If only a single specific rule is being appealed to, such as "Cheating is wrong," and no other references are made to any general rule-generating principles, you can assume that this ultimately rests on some kind of a rule-generating theory which has not been explicitly stated in the argument. Also, if no ethical rule or theory is explicitly contained in the premises at all, then you can assume that the argument is assuming an act theory which involves

some kind of direct perception or intuition of the rightness and wrongness of particular concrete acts.)

15. Consider the arguments as labeled in Exercise 14. Identify all of those which seem to you to appeal to "good" ethical theories. Now try to determine whether the theories you have classified as good ones have anything in common. Are they all rule-generating or all act theories? If they are all of the same general type, do they all appeal to the same specific theory? (Note that it is quite likely that you will disagree with the conclusion of some arguments even though you agree with the basic moral premises, insofar as there are many other factors which could result in the derivation of different conclusions from the same moral premises.)

Although we are far from finishing a complete analysis of our sample argument, we are going to end our discussion of it at this point. The primary intent of our discussion has been to illustrate certain basic considerations involved in the analysis and evaluation of moral arguments in general, and to make it as clear as possible that this can be a very difficult and complex process. We shall now provide a brief summary of the kinds of factors relevant to the analysis of ethical arguments which we have discussed, and then we will conclude by placing all of this in a more balanced perspective with regard to the ways in which analyses of ethical arguments are relevant to everyday decision-making processes.

The following listing of factors to be considered in the analysis and evaluation of ethical arguments is in no way intended to be complete either in substance or detail. These are at most some of the more important and significant factors, and it must be recognized that there are many other factors which are more or less frequently relevant to the evaluation of particular arguments. It is also hoped that the preceding discussion of the sample argument has made it clear that a simple task description does not always mean that the task is simple. For example, it is easy to stipulate that the main conclusion should be identified and clearly and precisely formulated; it is all too often the case in dealing with actual arguments that this can be a very lengthy and complex task. In part, this complexity is the result of the requirement to adhere to the Principle of Charity, that is, to always try to interpret and formulate an argument in its strongest possible form. Since the strength of an argument is a function of the relation between the premises and conclusion, we cannot really know what formulation of a conclusion will make an argument stronger or weaker unless we already have some idea what the premises are. This also serves, therefore, as a reminder that the following list should not be understood to represent any kind of a fixed, necessary order for considering the specified factors. In actual practice it is not uncommon and often is even necessary to consider several factors simultaneously and/or to go from one to another and then back again to the first in some kind of a cyclic pattern. With these disclaimers and warnings, we now present the following list of significant factors in the analysis and evaluation of moral arguments:

- Identify and reformulate as necessary the main conclusion of the argument.

- Identify and reformulate as necessary the premises of the argument, making explicit any implicit premises.
- Determine whether the argument is most appropriately and strongly formulated in an inductive or deductive form.
- Identify and evaluate (using these same procedures) any subarguments offered in support of premises.
- Test the main argument for deductive validity or inductive strength.
- Make explicit the options or alternative courses of action which are open to the agent.
- Identify the different kinds of premises, that is, those which are definitions, those which are statements of scientific fact or theory, metaphysical theory, ethical theory, and so on.
- Determine the degree of truth or plausibility of each of the premises.

This listing is not only not complete, it is also of questionable value with regard to our main concern—the determination of which actions are right and which are wrong in concrete situations. Even if we have carried out all of the above tasks in compliance with the Principle of Charity, we still may not have reached a determination as to whether or not the argument is a good one or a bad one, that is, whether or not the argument provides reasonable grounds for our acceptance of the conclusion as true. This determination requires the consideration of several factors which are not part of the argument itself, which we will now comment on briefly.

In order to determine whether or not a moral argument provides reasonable grounds for accepting the conclusion as true, it is first necessary to determine *who* is presenting the argument to *whom* for *what purposes* under *what conditions*. A moral argument presented by one person to another under one set of conditions for a specific purpose might be a very good one in that context, but the same argument might not be as good if any one of these conditions is changed. (It must be emphasized that the quality of an argument is not completely correlated with the moral quality of the act being judged. The fact that an argument in support of the judgment that a particular act is right is a good argument in one context but not so good in another context does not necessarily mean that the same act is both right and wrong.) Let us go back to our sample argument to illustrate several points about determining the goodness or badness of moral arguments.

When we first presented the argument concerning Susan's writing of Tom's ethics paper, we gave no indication of who was presenting the argument to whom for what purposes under what conditions. For illustration, let us consider several different circumstances which could have surrounded this argument. First, let us assume that this argument is being expressed by the dean of students at Susan's college after a brief hearing to determine whether or not Susan should be expelled or suspended. Susan had been asked during the hearing whether she had in fact written the paper which Tom had submitted for his ethics course, but she had not been asked nor allowed to say whether or not she knew when she gave it to Tom that he was going to submit it for the course, and she was not asked or allowed to explain her reasons for doing it. Insofar as the person presenting the argument (in this case the dean) could easily have obtained this information before making a final judgment but in fact did not obtain it, and given that this information is quite relevant to the argument for reasons mentioned in our earlier discussion, we would have to consider this as a relatively weak argument. Notice that in evaluating this argument (and this holds for any other moral argument as well), it must be compared to other possible arguments. *It is only insofar as we can specify other arguments which could have been presented under the existing conditions, and then can show that at least one of these is better than the argument which was actually presented, that we can justify a judgment that a moral argument is not a good one.* There is no absolute scale against which one can profitably measure the quality of a moral argument (even though there may be such a scale against which one can evaluate actions). Thus we can only judge that the dean's argument under these conditions was not a very good one because we are able to specify another argument which could have been formulated under the same conditions which would have been better.

For contrast, let us now assume that the same argument was being presented by Ann Landers or a similar person in a newspaper column, in response to an anonymous letter from someone who identified herself as Susan's best friend and who provided only the information included in the argument, that is, that Susan wrote a paper which Tom submitted for his ethics course. Now certainly the columnist could have avoided making a judgment at all on the grounds that not enough information was provided. However, a moment's thought should be sufficient to make it clear that on that condition no such advice columns could ever be written about anything, since it is always possible to demand more information regarding any case whatsoever no matter how much information has already been provided. In this case, then, given that no other details of the case are available, the only possible better arguments would be ones which appeal to different ethical theories than the sample argument *and* which give stronger support for the ethical theory being used. The question about the need for support for the ethical theory being used is dependent on the extent to which the intended audience can be assumed to share this theory with the person giving the argument. If it is reasonable to believe that the audience does indeed accept the theory on which the argument is being based, then it is not necessary to provide the lengthy subarguments which might otherwise be required to support the premise expressing the ethical theory, and the argument as presented is a good one.

This topic can be put into an illuminating perspective by noting that arguments in support of different ethical theories have been under continual discussion, evaluation, and refinement since at least the beginning of written history, and this process is still continuing. It is the analysis of arguments in support of various ethical theories that comprises a significant part of the subject matter in basic ethics texts and courses. It should be clear that it is therefore impossible, in most concrete situations in which an individual must make an ethical decision, for that person to provide a complete argument in support of the ethical theory being used as the basic premise of the main argument. Thus, in evaluating an ethical argument we should not automatically require that some kind of a "complete" justification be provided for the ethical theory being used. Instead, we only need to determine whether an *appropriate* justification has been provided. An "appropriate" justification is one which is based on a careful consideration of both the nature of the audience (i.e., whether, and to what extent, they already accept the theory being used) and the time available in the specific situation.

This last criterion, the time available, is one that we have not really dealt with yet, and even though we are discussing it last, it is really one of the most important factors in the evaluation of any ethical argument. As already indicated, arguments in support of various ethical theories have been under discussion for literally thousands of years. Some individuals, both saints and philosophers, have spent their entire lives trying to provide the best possible argument in support of particular ethical theories. But when an ordinary person is confronted with an ethical decision he or she usually does not have such an abundant amount of time in which to reason things out. Certainly a pregnant woman cannot spend 12 years, or even 12 months, deciding whether or not to have an abortion. A student who is suddenly and unexpectedly confronted with an opportunity to cheat on an important examination may not even have 12 minutes to think things through. It is an inherent feature of all moral arguments that the failure to make a decision itself involves a moral decision—the decision to not act or to maintain the status quo. The pregnant woman who spends 10 months thinking about whether or not to have an abortion has in effect made the decision to not have the abortion. The student in the exam who takes a week to determine whether or not to take advantage of a momentary opportunity to cheat has in fact made the very real decision not to cheat—at least not at this time on this test. Thus, it is necessary in evaluating any moral argument to carefully consider the time factor before judging the argument to be good or bad. A valid deductive argument with highly plausible premises, with a detailed analysis of all of the contextual factors and all of the alternative courses of action—in brief, a very good argument by almost all of the standards we have identified in our discussion—could easily take several hours, days, or even longer to formulate and reason through. Such an argument would obviously not be a very good one in a situation in which one has only a few minutes to think things through and make a decision. Thus, any set of criteria for good moral arguments must contain some recognition of the fact that an argument, to be "good" (at least in the very important sense of being useful), should be one which can be thought through in the time available in the circumstances of the specific case involved.

EXERCISES

16. Reevaluate the arguments which you have been analyzing in Exercises 6 through 15, applying not only the basic criteria listed on pages 19–20, but also the comparative factors just discussed. In particular, try to construct an alternative argument which is a "better" one when considered in the same context (time, audience, etc.).

17. For each of the arguments used in Exercise 16, change the contextual factors in such a way that a) the same argument in the new context is relatively better than it was in the original context, and b) the same argument in an-

other context is weaker than it was in the original context. Try this for different contextual factors, e.g., change the time available for making the decision, the audience, the factual information available, and so on.
18. Apply the instructions for Exercises 16 and 17 to the arguments which you originally evaluated on a purely intuitive basis in Exercise 4.

In concluding this all too brief and incomplete discussion of the rudiments of moral reasoning and the evaluation of ethical arguments, we should take a moment to reflect back on the points made earlier with respect to the "message" of the cartoon on the cover of this book. It will be remembered that we considered an analogy between medicine and ethics, and it was suggested that just as a physician is not able to diagnose and cure all illnesses even though he or she is able to treat many cases more effectively than the person with no medical training, so also a person with training in analyzing and evaluating ethical arguments is able to do this much more effectively than someone with no such training even though there will always be some cases which he or she will not be able to handle adequately. It is hoped that the intervening discussion has given the reader some indication of the kinds of skills which must be developed in order to improve one's ability to deal adequately with ethical arguments. It is especially hoped that one element of the analogy is now more easily appreciated, namely the need for practice on concrete cases as part of the training process. Just as the mastery of the art of medicine requires a great deal of supervised work with real patients, so also the development of the skills needed for analyzing ethical arguments requires a great deal of practice on "real" arguments. A thorough knowledge of anatomy, endocrinology, chemistry, and so on is quite helpful and perhaps even essential in order to be a good physician; but "book-learning" in and of itself is not sufficient for a person to be a good physician. Likewise, a thorough knowledge of formal logic, ethical theory, and other subjects is important, if not essential, in order to be able to properly analyze and evaluate ethical arguments; but this knowledge by itself is not adequate to guarantee that a person can provide a good evaluation of an argument.

It is to provide one of these additional requirements—practice on real cases —that this book is primarily intended. But it cannot be emphasized too strongly that this book in and of itself can provide little if any assistance to persons wishing to develop the basic skills of analyzing and evaluating ethical arguments. It is best if one's study using these examples is done with someone who is more advanced in these skills, and it is also useful to do it in conjunction with other "beginners" from whom it is possible to gain much insight as to the variety of perspectives from which any given case can be viewed. It should also be noted here that one must bring more than one's intellect to this enterprise, just as in medicine. Although these arguments are to all appearances just words on paper, it must be remembered that all of them were originally formulated by real persons who had a deep personal interest in the issues involved. Thus, we must try to use our imagination, in addition to our intellect, to try to place ourselves in the position of the kinds of persons most intimately involved in the cases being discussed. No words can convey strongly enough the need for compassion, empathy, and other human resources in the analysis and evaluation of moral arguments, but it is hoped that some of the cases among the hundreds contained in the following pages will strike close enough to each reader's personal experiences and concerns that this need will be felt and recognized directly in those cases and then transferred to the other more remote cases.

In summary, we should consider briefly the truly fundamental question of the value of this whole enterprise. Is it really better to make moral decisions on the basis of thoughtful and intelligent deliberation, or would we be just as well-off making moral decisions without really thinking about them at all? It is hoped that the reader will attempt to answer this question on the basis of actual experience, waiting until after he or she has made an effort to improve his or her skills along the lines outlined in the preceding pages to make any judgment as to whether these skills are in fact worth developing or not. Certainly any judgment not based on such first-hand experience would not be as good or as well-justified as a judgment based on such experience.

Finally, it is necessary to make several comments on the criteria used for selecting and arranging the arguments in this volume, insofar as the complexity of the arguments and issues involved implies that there is no single "right" way of selecting and organizing the examples. Many different criteria were used in the selection of these arguments, and it is likely that there are other criteria that could have also been used. One of the most important factors in the selection of these examples of moral reasoning was to include arguments from as wide a variety of sources as possible. In fact, the following pages contain items from large and small publications across the United States as well as from several foreign countries, from left-wing and right-wing political groups, from the "establishment" (the Supreme Court, major corporations, several presidents and congresspersons), from a variety of religious sects, and from "just plain folks." A number of arguments from earlier historical periods dating back to the United States colonial period are also included to add a temporal dimension to a variety of current issues.

The general topics of the arguments were also selected using several different criteria. Some topics were included because they represent very frequently debated moral problems while others were included precisely because they are not commonly encountered; some topics were included because they are intrinsically very interesting to most people, while others were used because it was judged that they *should* be studied, even though at first glance they might not appear to be very interesting or significant.

With regard to the grouping of arguments in sections, this too could have been done in different ways, and any argument in any one of the following sections could probably have been reasonably assigned to one or more of the other sections insofar as each argument touches on several different issues. Some of the more significant connections between arguments assigned to different sections are pointed out in the section introductions and exercises.

Although every effort has been made to provide at least one example from each side for topics over which there is significant disagreement, in some cases this proved to be impossible for various reasons. Balance of pro and con arguments on any single topic was only one of the factors taken into account in the selection of arguments, and the lack of this kind of balance on some topic should in no way be interpreted as reflecting the biases of the editor on that topic. Given the emphasis in this Introduction on the need to consider all alternative arguments before making a judgment about the goodness or badness of any single argument, it should be clear that only one argument on a given topic should be sufficient to require the evaluator to think through all possible arguments on both sides of that topic.

SECTION 1

Interpersonal Relations

The arguments comprising this section deal with a variety of situations which confront many of us at different points in our lives—at school, at work and in the marketplace. For the most part the cases discussed in the selections in this section are concerned with actions involving two specific individuals, such as a doctor and patient, a thief and victim, a teacher and student, two friends, or two fellow-workers. This is indeed the level at which most moral decisions are made, and because it is the area with which we are probably most familiar it has been placed at the beginning of this book.

On the surface, cases involving only two persons would seem to be relatively simple in comparison to those involving larger numbers of persons, but this is not necessarily always true. In fact, it is often the case that certain emotional and other factors come into play in situations involving two individuals which are not present in cases involving many parties.

In cases of theft it is not always clear who the affected parties are, especially in contemporary society, and sometimes a thief uses the fact that it is difficult to identify a specific victim as part of a justification for the theft. For example, the thief might argue that the individual from whom he or she stole was probably insured so the "victim" didn't really lose anything. And it is certainly not easy to assess what the cost was to whom when we begin to distribute the loss among all of the stockholders and policyholders of the insurance company. Theft from a large chain store or a corporation involves similar complications. But the burden of proof still rests on the thief to prove that the difficulty of determining the loss resulting from the theft to any specific individual in any way makes the basic act itself any less wrong.

It must also be recognized that even when one individual can be identified as the only one directly affected by a particular act, it is almost always the case that the act indirectly affects other persons, sometimes in relatively significant ways. For example, one of the figures in the Watergate affair, Egil Krogh, Jr., admitted that he authorized the break-in of a psychiatrist's office to obtain the file of the man who transmitted the classified Pentagon Papers to the press. The person directly affected by this act was the psychiatrist who was the victim of the theft, but it is not difficult to see that the act also violated certain rights of the doctor's patient. To pursue the implications of this act even further, it could be argued that this act set a precedent which weakened the system of government in the United States and thus indirectly had some effect, however small, on all citizens of the country.

EXERCISES

1. Identify the individuals *directly* involved in each case discussed in the arguments in this section. Are any of the cases such that the action affects (directly or indirectly) only one individual?
2. To what extent can the same moral principles be applied to the cases of a thief stealing a car from an unknown person, a doctor overcharging a patient, and a student with wealthy parents collecting welfare payments and food stamps?
3. Examine the arguments in Section 9 concerning euthanasia and the arguments in Section 2 concerning the use of drugs (including cigarettes). To what extent do those arguments involve some consideration of persons indirectly affected by the acts under discussion?

A Little Larceny Can Do a Lot For Employee Morale

by Lawrence R. Zeitlin

The dishonest worker is enriching his own job in a manner that is very satisfactory (for him). This enrichment is costing management, on the average, $1.50 per worker per day. At this rate, management gets a bargain.

Toolbox. The important word is *control*. Properly utilized, controlled employee theft can be used as another implement in management's motivational toolbox. As in the case of most motivational tools, costs and conditions of utilization must be carefully studied. (Ethically, of course, it would be more desirable for management to motivate employees by means other than inviting them into lives of petty crime. It is traditionally considered better to have workers directing their energies toward furthering the course of the business rather than toward satisfying their individual larcenous desires.)

Before deciding to minimize or eliminate employee theft, management should ask itself these four practical questions:

1. How much is employee theft actually costing us?
2. What increase in employee dissatisfaction could we expect if we controlled theft?
3. What increase in employee turnover could we expect?
4. What would it cost to build employee motivation up to a desirable level by conventional means of job enrichment or through higher salaries?

Cost. Setting aside ethical and emotional considerations, management may decide that the monetary cost of enforcing honesty is too great.

I do not advocate abandonment of the traditional responsibilities of management, but I suggest that management adopt a more realistic and certainly less hypocritical attitude to business "honesty" and publicly recognize that there is benefit to be obtained by utilizing employee theft as a motivational tool. ⏎

☐ Zeitlin justifies peoples' stealing because they are bored. This is fallacious thinking for several reasons. First: it's like saying, "I'm bored so I'm going to cut off your arm. Shall I cut it off here, or here?" Second: it encourages people to destroy the necessary interdependence among all of us; whereas, we need more and more to encourage and foster dependable healthy relationships. Third: he is advising these persons to hurt themselves by becoming more callous, less sensitive, amoral (if he doesn't concede that stealing is actually immoral) like the very "machinery" they're bucking. Fourth: he underestimates industrial psychologists (I hope). Surely he and they can use their ingenuity to think of constructive alternatives (i.e. profit-sharing, alternating jobs) to help meet the needs he says cause the stealing. . . .

Ellen Smith

Normal, Ill.

Above left, reprinted from *Psychology Today*, June 1971. Copyright © Communications/Research/Machines, Inc.
Above, courtesy of Ellen Smith (Mrs. Ralph L.), Normal, Ill.

Multiplied Theft

The widespread availability of photocopying machines provides another means of stealing—as if there weren't already enough ways to break the eighth commandment. The problem involves the laws of copyright, established to protect the rights of individuals to monetary income for their labors. Writers, composers, and illustrators, for example, support themselves and their families not by creative work itself but by *selling* the product of their creativity. Moreover, their income is usually a few cents on each sale; it's the large number of copies sold that enables them to make a living.

But the culprits—those who would never think of stealing another's tangible property, or who would never think of taking copyrighted material and typesetting it, printing it, and selling it for themselves—misuse the photocopying machine. They will buy, for example, one copy of an anthem for the choir to sing, and then photocopy enough copies for every choir member to have his own. No conscientious person should engage in such an obviously illegal action.

But there's one other culprit: the highly unrealistic state of copyright law in view of modern developments in photocopying and information storage and retrieval systems. According to copyright law it is a violation either to make one photocopy of one page of a thousand-page tome or to make a hundred copies of an entire piece of music. Until the writers, publishers, consumers, lawmakers, and other interested parties come up with a rational, equitable, enforceable set of laws to bring copyright and technology into reasonable alignment, individuals and groups should avoid photocopying multiple copies or single copies of significant portions of a work without permission. We will be glad, however, to give you permission to reproduce without payment as many copies of this particular editorial as you wish! □

Above, copyright 1971 by *Christianity Today*; reprinted by permission.

Above right, courtesy of Ann Landers and Field Newspaper Syndicate.

Right, © 1960 Jules Feiffer.

Ann Landers

DEAR ANN LANDERS: I need the advice of an adult who doesn't know me. Please don't let me down. Last night I was at my girl friend's house. (We have been best friends ever since third grade. We are both 14 now.) She made me promise I would never tell a soul if she let me in on her big secret. After I promised, she took a key out of a hiding place and opened a cedar chest. She started to show me her "fun stuff." I nearly keeled over. This girl has shoplifted at least $300 worth of merchandise. What scares me is that she has plenty of money and can buy anything she wants.

Another queer thing, Ann, there wasn't one article in that chest that she can use. She has dozens of packages of fish food and she has no fish—needlepoint canvases and thread and she doesn't even know how to sew. She has shoplifted an electric heating pad, carpenter tools, fishing equipment, corn and bunion plasters—the craziest stuff you can imagine. The price tags are on everything. She likes to look at this junk and recall the fun she had getting it out of the store.

I now know there is something wrong with her, but I don't know what to do about it. I have promised not to tell, but maybe I should—for her own good. Please advise me, Ann. I am—SCARED SICK

DEAR SS.: A promise is a promise. You must not betray your friend. But you must somehow get across to her that she is sick and needs help. If she gets caught she could be in serious trouble. She must tell everything and asked to be taken to a doctor.

In the meantime, here's a word for you. DON'T go shopping with this girl. If she is caught stealing and you are with her, you could be in trouble, too.

©1960 Jules Feiffer

If he hollers, let him go

Employes Who Snitch

by TIMOTHY H. INGRAM

No one likes a fink—yet our initial revulsion at snitching and our concept of employe loyalty may need serious revision. Clearly the employer has the right to expect a reasonable amount of loyalty from his employes, and to demand confidentiality in everyday business, in contract negotiations, trade secrets, client and personnel lists, and the like. But there are areas of concern to the public—as, for example, uncovering frauds, thefts, and serious improprieties—which require that the informer not be muzzled by employer censorship.

Moreover, the corporate hard-hats holding a "Your company, love it or leave it" attitude are depriving themselves of a useful mechanism for reform, capable of correcting an institution's seemingly unlimited capacity for organized error. Snitchers, in fact, are often a firm's *most* loyal members, for it takes a greater degree of attachment to stay with a firm and to protest than it does to "opt out," by remaining silent or moving on.

Above, from *The Progressive*, January 1971.
Right, from *Time*, January 6, 1975.

Stealing Cars Is a Growth Industry

By PETER HELLMAN

EVEN the thieves are able to justify their work. A veteran, very professional thief who lives in New Jersey reasons, "What I do is good for everybody. First of all, I create work. I hire men to deliver the cars, work on the numbers, paint them, give them paper, maybe drive them out of state, find customers. That's good for the economy. Then I'm helping working people to get what they could never afford otherwise. A fellow wants a Cadillac but he can't afford it; his wife wants it but she knows he can't afford it. So I get this fellow a nice car at a price he can afford; maybe I save him as much as $2,000. Now he's happy. But so is the guy who lost his car. He gets a nice new Cadillac from the insurance company—without the dents and scratches we had to take out. The Cadillac company—they're happy too because they sell another Cadillac.

"The only people who don't do so good is the insurance company. But they're so big that nobody cares *personally*. They got a budget for this sort of thing anyway. So here I am, a guy without an education, sending both my kids to college, giving my family a good home, making other people happy. Come on now— who am I really hurting?"

Above, from the *New York Times* magazine, June 20, 1971.

The Sultan of Swag

Looking for a bargain? Try Vincent Swaggi's store, where merchandise is stacked to the ceiling: household goods, toys, shoes, sweaters, suits, radios, electric toothbrushes, records, film, perfume, wigs, even ballet slippers. Ignore the department-store price marked on most items. Swaggi will give you "a real steal." But watch yourself. What you are reaching for is likely to be really stolen goods.

Swaggi offers no apologies. Says he: "The way I look at it, I'm a businessman. Sure I buy hot stuff ... but if I don't buy it, somebody else will." So the fence goes about his business, cunningly aware that good citizens and good thieves share a common goal: getting something for almost nothing.

Store tag-switcher too honest to steal

Los Angeles Times Service

LOS ANGELES — In the privacy of department store dressing rooms and the confusion around merchandise tables, people who would not think of stealing are taking the price tags off cheap items and putting them on more expensive ones.

With the desired object in hand the switcher marches up to the register to buy, not steal.

If the clerk does not notice the change, the switcher has successfully added his version of Phase III to President Nixon's wage and price controls.

If he is caught, he simply says, "That's just the way I found it."

Dr. John Steiner, a sociology professor at California State College at Pomona, with the help of three students, has done a preliminary study on price tag switchers.

So far he has found that switchers are usually middle class persons, with very strong moral codes that will not allow them to steal.

Although there is no age limit on switching, it usually does not begin until the late teens (before that, youths are more inclined to shoplifting).

Switchers seem to come upon the practice on their own and usually work alone.

Some young tag switchers are politically motivated.

"They are upset about (what they believe are) the exploitative practices of large corporations, and feel the only way to fight against it is to reduce exploitation to a minimum — to what they feel is a fair exchange," Steiner said.

Older tag switchers see their act as compensation for unreasonable prices, he said.

"They feel their budget is at a certain level and they don't want to exceed it so they compromise by lowering prices," Steiner said.

In addition to higher prices, the tag switcher also feels victimized by the disparity between regular prices and sale prices (why can't the store sell the item at sale prices all the time?) and psychologically manipulative advertising, Steiner said.

Through advertising, nonessential items are presented as indispensable commodities and the tag switcher develops a psychological need to own, he said.

Most tag switchers will not tamper with the prices of necessities, Steiner said, but will concentrate on luxury items like cosmetics, sporting and household goods, records and electronic equipment and expensive food items.

The tag switcher sees himself as a "cavalier derelict" — a dispenser of "instantaneous self-serviced justice," Steiner said.

Anything for a Grade

In the fall quarter at the University of Denver, Michael Rock, visiting professor from Bennington College, Vermont, strode into his principles of economics class, made a surprise announcement. "You people have won," he declared. "I'm going to sell grades.

Grades will go to the highest bidder. If you people are so happy with the free market process, why don't we just let the market system dictate who gets what?"

Another professor was called in to auction off the grades without prejudice.

While several students objected to the auction—some even complained to the dean and the department chairman—approximately 90 percent of the class participated. Professor Rock collected almost $2000, averaging $85 for an A in his course, $55 for a B, $35 for a C. Rock accepted promissory notes from most of the students, but one insisted upon giving him $80 in cash. Another student, observing the absence of several friends who were obviously cutting class, bought up extra C's and D's, tried to make a few bucks by advertising them in the school paper.

To the shock of many students who'd ceased studying for their class final and burned their term papers, Rock announced on the last day of class that his auction was a hoax.

Wailed one incredulous student: "That can't be. You're an authority figure. We've all accepted you as an authority figure and what you told us as true."

Rock says now that he wishes he hadn't done it. Why then did he conduct his phony auction? Largely, he explains, because he was annoyed at the uncritical acceptance of the free enterprise system by his students and some of the comments they had written on their examinations. "I had hoped," he says, "that we wouldn't be able to pull it off. Particularly after what I tried to do in the class for nine weeks."

Doctoral Dissertations For Sale

Students Clamor for Ghosted Research Papers

By Richard S. Johnson
FROM DENVER

"Nota: We do not condone Plagairism."

This mocking legend, its pretentious use of a Latin word and its deliberate misspelling suggesting pseudoscholarship, is inscribed on a sign in the offices of a Denver ghost-writing company that expects to sell more than $100,000 worth of term papers, masters' theses, and doctoral dissertations during this academic year.

The company, Research and Educational Associates, Ltd. (REA), was formed here last Feb. 1 and already has 500 student clients. It has hired business managers to open offices in East Lansing, Mich., where there is a 100,000-student population, and in Cleveland. Chicago, and Washington, D.C., all cities with major universities. Its founders also are negotiating with a prospective business manager in Tucson, home of the University of Arizona.

If all goes well, REA's founders expect to double or even triple this expansion before the third academic quarter begins next spring. Moreover, they see in academic ghostwriting a base for a potential multimillion-dollar business in providing information and literary services.

REA is a limited stock company with five youthful shareholders: Charles Johnson, Robert Pike, Paul Relyea, Marge Smith, and Larry Groeger. Johnson, a 30-year-old former college teacher, began the business part-time a year ago, when he was working on a Ph.D. degree at the University of Denver, "because I was tired of being a ribbon clerk in a department store."

The research and writing is supervised by Groeger, 20, an undergraduate philosophy major at Denver's Metropolitan State College. Groeger cheerfully admits that REA stole its misspelled slogan from a Boston group that he says grossed more than $250,000 last year ghosting for Harvard students. But REA's sights are already higher than that, Groeger says: This year it'll offer the first nationwide academic ghost-writing service.

Volume in the Denver area alone during the 1971 spring term was sufficient to convince REA's officers that they can gross a minimum of $100,000 by May 1972. And that should be, they think, a modest beginning.

'Absolute Security'

Yet, says Groeger: "We're not out to make it rich. We operate as a service. We all have a human-resources orientation." REA says that a client needn't sign a contract, and that the company doesn't permit clients to remain dissatisfied—particularly since the value of word-of-mouth advertising is obvious. Groeger says that REA guarantees absolute security of its records and anonymity for its clients.

Groeger can recall only one client whose experience with an REA-produced paper was unhappy. The student ordered a paper for a graduate seminar in philosophy, but "the subject was a very sophisticated one and he didn't understand the paper," Groeger says. "Others in the seminar shot him down." After that, REA began counseling clients on the various possible interpretations of "their" papers.

One of his favorite former college teachers takes a dim view of his occupation, Groeger says. So does his mother. But he himself finds no ethical problems in helping students plagiarize their way to academic degrees.

"Early in life I saw that the real ethos of America is, 'Anything you do is okay if you don't get caught,'" he explains. "I became acquainted with bureaucratic discrepancies in the university, and I saw the double standard that pervades the real world of politics and business." To Groeger, trading deals and favors isn't a moral or ethical matter; it's "just the way the world operates."

'You've Ruined My Week End'

Despite his criticism of the academic establishment, Groeger is considering teaching at the university level some day. He says that some of his philosophy teachers at Metropolitan State College here understand and sympathize with his ghost-writing activities.

But Groeger's department chairman, Dr. William E. Rhodes, didn't know of REA's existence until a reporter asked about it. "You've ruined my week end," he groaned. "I'm the last one to know, apparently."

Dr. Rhodes says that he is "totally unsympathetic" with academic ghostwriting and that he will debate its ethics with Groeger. "It poses a profound moral and ethical problem, both for Larry and his customers—and even more so for members of the faculty who would countenance this." Plagiarism, Dr. Rhodes adds, "undercuts the whole notion of a free and responsible society.

"I would oppose just as much a secret-police agency in the college" to stop plagiarism, Dr. Rhodes continues. "All of this would destroy the integrity of a free and responsible community."

Term Paper Mills: A Booming Business

By M. J. WILSON
(Newsweek Feature Service)

"WHY SHOULDN'T I buy a term paper?" says a student at New York University. "I'm an English major, assigned a paper on physics, a subject I don't know anything about, and don't want to know anything about."

"Even if I write a paper myself," says a University of Maryland coed, "the professor isn't going to read it. How can he? He's got about 300 people writing papers for him. He'll just farm it out to some graduate student."

Term-Paper Hustlers

Meanwhile, the entrepreneurs are in some disagreement over the ethics of their work. Warren claims that customers use his products only as reference sources. "Listen," he insists, "I've taken surveys of 400 of my clients, and the overwhelming majority say that they don't plagiarize." One professor cites the case of a senior she confronted who confessed "four years of successful plagiarism, parental pressure and a conviction of his intellectual incapacity for college." Richard Mari, 26, a former technical writer for General Dynamics who heads Quality Bullshit, says that plagiarism is the whole point. "The kids have so many term-paper assignments now that they're an obstacle to a degree rather than a learning technique. As long as we're operating to help people, the business is not only justifiable, it may even be commendable."

Reprinted by permission from *Time, the Weekly Newsmagazine.* Copyright Time, Inc., 1971.

DEAR ANN LANDERS: Our 12-year-old son is selling his homework and my husband thinks it is just terrific. He keeps saying, "That kid will make it big one of these days."

Albert has fixed prices (from what I gather when he talks on the telephone.) He gets a dime for an arithmetic assignment and 25 cents for a book review. The boy is doing a very good business. He bragged at dinner tonight that he has saved up $21.

I think this is disgraceful but whenever I open my mouth I am shouted down. My husband insists that Albert has ingenuity, is smart and is making his brains pay off. If I am wrong, please tell me. If my husband is wrong, please tell him. I'm beginning to doubt my own sanity.

— CHICAGO MOTHER

DEAR MOTHER: You are not wrong and I hope you'll keep talking.

In this age of tax-chiseling, padded expense accounts and political pay-offs, it's a small wonder a kid would take to selling his homework. Someone should explain to the boy that it is admirable to help friends with their homework by showing them how to do it. But a person who sells "help" is supporting dishonesty in them and behaving dishonestly himself.

Above left, from Newsweek Feature Service.

Above right, courtesy of Ann Landers and Field Newspaper Syndicate.

The 'test' of morality

Morality: Knowledge of moral principles; quality of character; moral wisdom; righteousness; virtue.

That's what Webster says.

We've been "wallowing in Watergate" for over a year now and perhaps there is some truth to the allegations that Americans are too preoccupied with the scandals in Washington.

On the other hand, developments unrelated to Watergate have recently come to light which, although not as sensational, are equally as shocking.

Cheating seems to have become a part of some of our greatest American institutions.

Indications of this began filtering out of our military academies, moved to the high school Regents examinations, down to the leadership of the American Boy Scouts—and now we have reports that there may be cheating in the statewide nursing tests.

The State Education Department has begun an investigation into the reports of cheating last February in the nursing exams. A spokesman said, "We have received reports of irregularities in the nursing examination...and these reports are being investigated."

Quite obviously, we have no intention here to indict those thousands of young and dedicated people who have studied long and hard to reach the stage where they are eligible to take the state exams.

Another 15,000 prospective nurses will be taking the tests next week and the state spokesman said there is "no reason to believe security has been breached." We certainly hope he is right.

But actually that is not the point. If someone is determined to cheat, he can usually find a way to do so.

It therefore becomes a matter of individual morality. If someone makes the test answers available to the student, does that make it necessary for him to accept them? We don't think so.

But apparently there is a kind of rationalization by the individual when he discovers — or thinks he has discovered — that most of the students are cheating, so why shouldn't he? He'll just be left behind, so the thinking goes.

Tighter security may be the answer. But if it is, there is indeed something wrong with today's morality.

The Albany (N.Y.) "Times-Union," July 6, 1974.

AN IMMENSE PROPOSAL
a leading psychologist urges medication
"to contain human cruelty and destructiveness."

By Kenneth Clark   From American Psychologist

Given these contemporary facts, it would seem logical that a requirement imposed upon all power-controlling leaders and those who aspire to such leadership would be that they accept and use the earliest perfected form of psychotechnological, biochemical intervention which would assure their positive use of power and reduce or block the possibility of their using power destructively. This form of psychotechnological medication would be a type of internally imposed disarmament. It would assure that there would be no absurd or barbaric use of power. It would provide the masses of human beings with the security that their leaders would not or could not sacrifice them on the altars of their personal ego pathos, vulnerability and instability.

It is possible to object to the era of psychotechnology on "moral" grounds and to assert that these suggestions are repugnant because they are manipulative and will take away from man his natural right to make errors — even those errors which perpetrate cruelties and destruction upon other human beings. In the light of the realities and possible consequences of nuclear weaponry, these allegedly moral arguments seem mockingly, pathetically immoral. It would seem that man could afford to indulge in this type of abstract, prescientific moralizing in the past when his most destructive weapons were clubs, bows and arrows, or even gunpowder. To continue this type of thinking in an age when nuclear weapons are capable of destroying millions of human beings in a single irrational man-made event would seem to be a form of self-defeating and immoral rigidity.

There could be the further objection that biochemical intervention into the inner psychological recesses of motivation, temperament and behavior of human beings is an unacceptable, intolerable tampering with the natural or God-given characteristics of man. The negative connotations presently associated with discussions of drugs and the drug culture, particularly among young people, could be invoked to support this objection. One could also object on the ground that, in effect, what is here being suggested under the guide of an imperative psychotechnology is just another form of Utopian mechanization of human beings through drugging the masses and their leaders.

These objections seem to be based upon semantic grounds rather than upon essential substance. In medicine, physical diseases are controlled through medication. Medicines are prescribed by doctors to help the body overcome the detrimental effects of bacteria or viruses — or to help the organism restore that balance of internal biochemical environment necessary for health and effectiveness. Medicines are not only used to treat the diseases of individuals, but are also used preventively in the form of vaccines. All medicines are drugs — and all drugs used therapeutically are forms of intervention to influence and control the natural processes of disease. Selective and appropriate medication to assure psychological health and moral integrity is now imperative for the survival of human society.

From Dr. Kenneth Clark's presidential address given to the American Psychological Association on September 1971. Reprinted from *American Psychologist* in *Intellectual Digest*. Copyright 1971 by the American Psychological Association, and reproduced by permission.

Manipulating
Men's Minds

✦ TODAY'S drug culture led the way, but its adherents didn't have the right drugs. Or so it would seem. What is needed to solve the world's ills, suggests psychologist Kenneth B. Clark, is a drug to be administered to successful politicians to prevent abuse of power in public office; at a later stage such a drug might be useful for all mankind "to contain human cruelty and destructiveness." And this mind-controlling drug may already be in the offing; in a September 4 address to the American Psychological Association, of which he is president, Dr. Clark said: "Upon the basis of the presently available evidence, it is reasonable to believe that . . . a . . . type of precise, psychotechnological intervention, geared toward strengthening man's positive human characteristics, could be obtained and implemented within a few years." Admittedly, the possibility of a pharmacological substitute for virtue intrigues us — especially in view of the failure of the church and other supposedly humane institutions to make much headway toward curbing man's baser instincts. Seriously, though our respect for Kenneth Clark is considerable and though we are confident that his motives are honorable, we suspect that his cure-all might turn out to be something of a witches' brew. Certainly the prospect of compulsory mind-controlling medication raises all manner of questions — including the philosophical and theological issue of free choice. But let us put the latter aside and ask a very practical question: Who would determine dosage and administer the drug? Would not those in charge of administering it be susceptible to the very "abuse of power" that Clark wants to eliminate — unless they themselves had been properly drugged? And who would drug *them*? And so on, ad infinitum. The risks of misuse of such medication would seem to be limitless. Clark calls for international agreements to assure that use of the drug would be inaugurated in all countries. But what if one country held out — might not other countries then be at its mercy? Universal agreement on mind control is no doubt even less likely than on disarmament. Clark's Brave New Worldish prescription indeed raises more questions than it answers, and at least until he furnishes further details we are counter-prescribing a healthy dose of skepticism.

Help Loafers?

The Supreme Court is taking on a hot issue in agreeing to decide whether residents of communes may receive federal food stamps.

Of all the issues that could be calculated to get up the dander of Mr. Taxpayer, this is certainly one.

We can hear him now, "Subsidize hippies? Pay a fellow to loaf? Are you kidding?"

This idea of giving food stamps to professional loafers is handing an issue to Archie Bunker on a silver platter.

These fellows who sit around in their communes telling us what is wrong with the world have unmitigated gall to ask us to feed them while they philosophize.

They don't have to tell us what is wrong with the world. We know already. There are too many people like them around.

The learned gentlemen of the Supreme Court bench may check their legal tomes and quote this case or that case as precedent for their decision and then issue it in lofty language.

Far better it is not to have the restraints of Supreme Court dignity upon us and to be able to say:

"Get to work!"

Medical Chauvinism

By HENRY CHIEFFO, M.D.

Traditionally medicine has been regarded as the combination of an art and a science! In the past century, the science of medicine has made monumental progress from which mankind has benefitted greatly in terms of life expectancy. In this period, the science of medicine has developed highly effective vaccines, principles of sanitation and insect vector control, antibiotics, electrolyte and hormonal balance techniques, cardiac pacemakers, and coronary care units. There can be little or no controversy relative to these medical advances. In other areas, such as organ transplantation, cancer therapy, therapy in psychiatry, and "social" medicine, considerable controversy exists. Some of the issues and practices involved are intimately linked to the specifically moral and personal side of life.

Organized medicine has always jealously guarded her proper domain but has never hesitated to enter the sphere of another discipline. A recent happening will serve to illustrate this point. A resolution proposed to a local medical society in New Jersey wished to regard marijuana usage as a medical problem only and urged repeal of all laws pertaining to users of this drug. A letter opposing this proposal was written by the chairman of a local CUF chapter and sent to the medical society. The letter was indignantly considered, by the president of the medical society, to be an arrogant interference with the private deliberations of the medical society. The letter had noted that even though there were indeed medical aspects of drug abuse, still the motivations of the person contemplating or beginning the use of marijuana involved morality and were, therefore, a matter of grave concern to the members of Catholics United for the Faith. The president of the medical society contemptuously brushed aside the issue of the moral principles involved in the abuse of a mind-altering drug as having no relevancy to the problem. This same type of medical chauvinism is also evident in the matter of abortion and sex education.

On the issue of abortion, medicine has changed its position from one that prohibited interference with pregnancy, except in cases where continuation of pregnancy was a definite threat to the mother's life, to one in which it is now a matter between the mother and her physician wherever abortion is not illegal. This is a radical shift in medical ethics. It

contravenes, moreover, the basic medical principle not to destroy human life. Furthermore, it should be clear that abortion is a negative interference with the Natural and Moral Law. When practiced by organized medicine, it represents the invasion and preemption of another domain or discipline. All arguments for the new and erroneous position taken by medicine on abortion are only mere rationalizations! They have nothing to do with strictly medical questions and everything to do with moral and personal questions.

On the issue of sex education in the schools, organized medicine has in one place stated that it is "the primary responsibility of the parents." It has then proceeded to ignore the parents in favor of mandated school programs because "the traditional sources of sex information and guidance for young people are often inadequate." Instead of trying to re-inforce and strengthen the parent's authority and responsibility in this matter, they have encouraged and promoted usurpation of this parental function by public educators. In the forefront of those responsible for this attitude are many psychiatrists and public-health doctors.

These psychiatrists, in the grip of a mental aberration of their own, are among the prime instigators of public sex education. Perhaps they are aware, whether subconsciously or consciously, of their many failures in the treatment of the mentally ill and they need a scapegoat or whipping-boy to explain away these failures. To justify public sex education they theorize that mental illness and abnormal behavior are frequently due to an "unwholesome attitude and a lack of understanding of sex." It never occurs to them that the cause of the trouble is not a matter of information but of formation. They blame moral attitudes on sex for the trouble when precisely the opposite is the cause, namely the lack of morality. Who can doubt that a predominantly moral position on sex will result, for example, in less promiscuity, illegitimacy and venereal disease?

This peculiar aversion for morality in sex appears to be almost an obsession with some psychiatrists. Probably it is because they really do not understand human love and sexuality. They obviously have never read the classical analysis of human love **In Defense Of Purity** by Dr

Dietrich von Hildebrand. The general lack of familiarity by psychiatrists with this monumental work may be due to the fact that von Hildebrand is a philosopher and obviously not one of their "scientific" breed. Morality in sex has the same significance as not starting to use drugs has relative to drug abuse. A very eminent pharmacologist suggests just this resolve never to start as the best way to control that problem.

The position of many psychiatrists that high moral standards in sexual matters are frequently the basis of abnormal human behavior, is patently false and should be repudiated. Fortunately there are some psychiatrists who do not hold this position, but their voices are muffled by the loud declamations of the protagonists.

Most astonishing and alarming is the position of some public health doctors on this subject of morality in sex. Aside from Dr. Mary Calderone's now infamous "I don't believe in the thou shalt nots anymore," there is the unbelievable statement of Dr. Andrew Rudolph of the U.S. Public Health Center for Disease Control: "If we could get people to stop thinking of venereal disease as a moral issue, half the battle would be won" (**Health News** — "The Silent Epidemic" by E. Lochaya — January, 1971, p. 6). The battle referred to is the effort to control venereal disease which everyone agrees is now of epidemic proportions. The astonishing thing about this statement is its obvious self-contradiction. If moral restraints are removed from sexual activity, we can expect a sharp increase in contacts between infected and non-infected people and thus a sharp rise in the incidence of venereal diseases. This is borne out by the caption alongside a graph in the same article in which the above statement appeared. The graph shows a sharp rise in cases of gonorrhea in the United States from 300,000 to 550,000 cases from 1966 to 1970. The caption states, "The significant rise in gonorrhea may reflect greater promiscuity in our society, use of the pill, and perhaps greater reporting." It is obvious that one of the factors, "greater promiscuity," is the result of either an immoral or amoral attitude toward sexual intercourse. In my opinion, this position of Dr. Rudolph is dangerously erroneous and raises the question of his competence in his chosen field.

From *The Wanderer*, May 6, 1971.

ONE-MAN DEFLATION

... A psychologist cuts fees, and smiles.

By Daniel Henninger

Rita Flynn, an Observer reader in Spokane, Wash., wrote recently to tell us about something her husband had done, something she thought worthy of notice:

Jim Flynn, a practicing psychologist in Spokane, is lowering his prices.

Until last December the fee for Flynn's services was $35 an hour. Then he sent a letter to his customers, as he prefers to call them, saying in part:

Comment

"At the same time that I was raising prices in a dizzying dance with all the inflationary forces rampant in our nation, another part of my mind was deciding that my fees were unfair, immoral, and at this time in our nation's needs, unpatriotic."

Though he has 11 children to support, Flynn dropped his hourly fee to $30 and instituted Tuesday as "workers' day." On that day he would treat anyone for an hourly fee equal to his or her own hourly wage.

Had Flynn flipped? I telephoned him to find out.

"I've been in sort of a reflective period for several years," said Jim Flynn, who has been practicing in Spokane for about 20 years, 10 years in a state hospital and the past 10 in private practice.

Fear of Degrading

Flynn had been impressed by some of the things happening in the women's movement. But he considered the flip side of feminism, male consciousness. He finds men more difficult to treat than women; many don't even want to come in to see him.

"I got to thinking here I am charging 35 bucks an hour, and a guy who's earning, say, 5 or 10 bucks an hour in some way or another had to come to terms with that. Does he have to say that Flynn is three or four times the better man than he is? Here I'm trying to help these guys, and yet I'm doing something that could be degrading to them."

Flynn was thinking about himself too. His private psychology practice has made him pretty well off, and though he occasionally wondered about the rightness of his large income, there always seemed sufficient reason to justify it: a big family, all the time spent in graduate school running up debts to earn his degree.

The doubts persisted: "I realized the position I was playing in my family because I was earning so much dough," he said. "Because I was funding all of them, it gave me a power and authority that dwarfed the others. I've got cute kids. But, for instance, one of them said he wanted to be a psychologist but he couldn't because he couldn't be as good as I was, and hell, I'm sure he'll be better."

Finally, Jim Flynn laid it on the line in his letter: "I have come to the conclusion that charging what the traffic will bear or going along with prevailing rates may not be a defensible way to live."

He lowered his rates and eliminated many of the debts owed him. "Some of the people who owed money had finished with me and were hacking away at it 5 bucks a month," he said. "I started to feel like an economic bully."

PROFESSIONAL MORALS.

No man has a right to practice his profession in such a way as to encourage personal vice in those whom he serves, or wrong-doing towards individuals and the community. This is a very simple proposition, to which no respectable man in any profession will presume to make objection. If there ever lived a professional villain of whom a professional vilifier could say: "This is he who made it safe to murder, and of whose health thieves asked before they began to steal," he could only be saved from universal execration by a natural doubt of the justice of the sarcasm and the candor of its author. Theoretically, there are no differences among decent men on this subject, when it is placed before the mind in this way. It is one of those simple, self-evident propositions, about which no man would think of arguing for an instant. Up to the bar of this proposition one can bring every act of his professional life, and decide for himself whether it be legitimate and morally good. We repeat it,—*No man has a right to practice his profession in such a way as to encourage personal vice in those whom he serves, or wrong-doing towards individuals and the community.*

The great cities are full of men who have achieved remarkable skill in the treatment of a certain class of diseases, and other dangerous or inconvenient consequences of a bestial social vice. No matter how often their patients may approach them, or how vile they may be, or how successfully they may scheme against the peace and purity of society, or what form the consequences of their sin may assume, these professional men take their fee, and do what they can to shield the sinners from the effect of their crimes. Whatever they may be able to do professionally to make it safe for men and women to trample upon the laws of social purity, they do and constantly stand ready to do. Yet these men have a defense of themselves which enables them to hold their heads up. They are physicians. It is their business to treat disease in whatever form it may present itself. It would be impertinent in them to inquire into the life of those who come to them for advice. They are not the keepers of other men's consciences. They are men of science and not of morals. It is their business to cure disease by the speediest and best methods they know, and not to inquire into character, or be curious about the indirect results of their skill. Such would be their defense, or the line of their defense; yet, if it can be seen or shown that their professional life encourages vice in the community, by the constant shield which it offers against the consequences of vice, the defence amounts to nothing. If a debauchee or a sensualist of any sort finds impunity for his excesses in the professional skill of his physician, and relies upon that skill to shield him from the consequences of his sin, be they what they may, his physician becomes the partner of his guilt for gold, and a professional pander to his appetites. He may find professional brethren to defend him, but before the unsophisticated moral sense of the world he will be a degraded man, and stand condemned.

There are such men in the world as professional pardoners of sin. There are men in priestly robes who, on the confession of a penitent, or one who assumes the position of a penitent, release him professionally from the consequences of his misdeeds. Unless history has lied, there have been men among these to whom the vicious have gone for shrift and pardon for a consideration, and received what they went for, on every occasion of overt crime when the voice of conscience in their superstitious souls would not be still, and who have retired from the confessional ready for more crimes, from whose spiritual consequences they have intended and expected to find relief in the same way. It is not necessary to charge such desecration of the priestly office upon any one. We have no reason to believe that in this country such things are common; but we know that priests are human, and that there have been bad and mercenary men among them. It is only necessary to suppose cases like this, to see that a priest may, in the exercise of his professional functions, become the partner of the criminal in his crimes, a friend and protector of vice, and a foe to the purity and good order of society. He can set up his professional defense, and find professional defenders, perhaps; but any child, capable of comprehending the question, will decide that he is degraded and disgraced.

What is true, or may be true, of these professions, is true of any profession. Nothing is more notorious than that there are lawyers who are public nuisances—who encourage litigation, who are universally relied upon by criminals for the defense of crime, and whose reputation and money have indeed been won by their ability to clear the guilty from the consequences of their wrong-doing. Between these low extremes of professional prostitution and the high ground occupied by the great mass of legal men, there are many points where self-interest, united with incomplete knowledge, is powerful to lead the best minds into doubtful ways, and engage them in the support of doubtful causes or the defense of doubtful men. It is freely admitted that the best lawyer may find questions of personal morality and professional propriety in his practice that are hard to settle, and that may conscientiously be settled incorrectly; but no lawyer needs to question whether it is right for him to strengthen the position of a notorious scamp, especially if that scamp is known to be a corrupter of the law by all the means in his power, and a wholesale plunderer of the people.

From *Scribner's Monthly,* 1871.

CONGRESSMAN'S SUGGESTION

"Corruption appears to be pervasive in our society. I am thinking not simply of the public officeholder who betrays his trust—a corrupt former President, a convicted Attorney General, police officers who extort bribes, building inspectors who exact illegal commissions. What also troubles me is the corruption of our ordinary citizens.

"I am thinking of children who learn from their parents to cheat the storekeeper, the telephone company, and the government. I am thinking of corporations who in turn cheat the consumer, bribe officials, and do not level with their stockholders. We see evidence of this corruption daily in the sale of shoddy merchandise, tax fraud performed openly and without remorse, Medicaid charged for services not rendered, the elderly ripped off by nursing home operators, just to cite a few examples.

"...I believe...we ought to consider corruption in the same class as that of a physical assault upon an individual...

"...I am equally persuaded that the white-collar criminal, the corrupter, will be deterred and reformed if he or she serves just 30 days behind bars..."

—Rep. Edward Koch (D., N.Y.) addressing the House of Representatives July 28, 1975.

Above, from *Parade*, September 7, 1975. Right, courtesy of Ann Landers, Field Newspaper Syndicate, and *The Atlanta Journal*.

Dear Ann Landers:

For years my husband has provided well for his family. Very well, in fact· We have two cars, a vacation home, and all the extras that go with affluence. Add to this lots of love and wonderful kids.

In spite of this I feel as if I'm going to explode. My husband's income is not all honestly earned. He has a job that requires out-of-town work, for which he gets paid overtime. The money he collects is far in excess of the time he puts in. In other words, he's padding the sheet. I know of instances when he has collected over time for "out-of-town" work when he was right at home. He also uses his car for travel and is reimbursed for trips he doesn't make.

I'm living in style but my conscience is giving me hell. I've told him how miserable I am but he chops me off in mid-sentence. I know he won't stop. You're the only one I can turn to. Help me, please.

—Afraid

Dear Afraid:

You and you alone must decide if you want to continue to catch hell from your conscience or give him the choice: either he can go straight or continue on his crooked way alone.

Dear Ann Landers:

Something has been preying on my conscience and I need to know what to do about it.

As a secretary I make out my boss's expense account reports. I am aware that he puts down false expenses and charges personal expenditures to the business.

I have a strong sense of morality and feel this is wrong. I realize the practice is rampant, but still it doesn't make me feel any better about doing it.

If I confront him he will probably tell me it's none of my business. Is it? (P.S. He is a V.P. and has hundreds of people under him.) Sign me

—Guilty Conscience.

Dear G.C.:

Confront Mr. Chiseler and ask him to give his expense account work to another secretary, or do it himself. (P.S. Have some job prospects lined up before the confrontation. You may be handed your walking papers. If your competence matches your integrity, you have nothing to worry about. You'll do just fine. Bravo, Lady.)

Right, from "The Secretary's Dilemma" by B. J. Phillips, in *Ms.* magazine, March 1975.
Above, courtesy of Ann Landers, Field Newspaper Syndicate, and *The Atlanta Journal*.
Below, from *The Autobiography of Benjamin Franklin*.

I grew convinced that *truth, sincerity* and *integrity* in dealings between man and man were of the utmost importance to the felicity of life, and I formed written resolutions (which still remain in my Journal book) to practise them ever while I lived. Revelation had indeed no weight with me as such; but I entertained an opinion that tho' certain actions might not be bad *because* they were forbidden by it, or good *because* it commanded them, yet probably those actions might be forbidden *because* they were bad for us or commanded *because* they were beneficial to us, in their own natures, all the circumstances of things considered. And this persuasion, with the kind hand of Providence, or some guardian angel, or accidental favourable circumstances and situations, or all together, preserved me (thro' this dangerous time of youth and the hazardous situations I was sometimes in among strangers, remote from the eye and advice of my father) without any *wilful*, gross immorality or injustice that might have been expected from my want of religion. I say *wilful* because the instances I have mentioned had something of necessity in them, from my youth, inexperience, and the knavery of others. I had, therefore, a tolerable character to begin the world with; I valued it properly and determined to preserve it.

What about the Wall Street secretary who knows that her boss has decided to manipulate the price of a stock? Unless the Securities and Exchange Commission catches it, that's business as usual on Wall Street. "It happens every day," said Margie Albert, onetime brokerage-house secretary, now union organizer of office workers. "Sometimes when they had a stock they knew was going to be good because they were going to push it to clients and make it good, they'd cut the secretaries in on it, arrange for the employees to buy some shares. Look, corporate life is shot through with corruption like this. What's a secretary supposed to do? Complain? She'd just lose her job. She's not the one who makes the decisions."

No, she isn't the one who makes the decisions. Yes, Ann Landers agrees, she would probably lose her job. And while it may be easy for me to risk someone else's job with my theories, I believe she should complain. If she is the Wall Street secretary, she should complain to the SEC for the sake of thousands of people who will be financially hurt (and you better believe that means the small investors). Complain for the sake of her dignity. They allow her to know because they think it's safe for her to know. She is, after all, just a secretary. She is identified with her function, not with the rational, judging, moral mind that is hers also. Secretary as Dictabelt, something you turn on when you want, turn off when you want, as devoid of a will of her own as a machine. Complain to be a human being.

Rising Up Angry Funnies © by Aaron Fagen.

Krogh's Letter of Resignation

Special to The New York Times

WASHINGTON, May 9— Following is the text of a letter of resignation submitted this morning to President Nixon by Egil Krogh Jr., Under Secretary of Transportation and former White House aide who has become implicated in the 1971 burglary of the office of Dr. Daniel Ellsberg's psychiatrist:

As I have confirmed in an affidavit filed with the U.S. District Court in Los Angeles, I agreed to a certain mission by employes of the special investigating unit which operated under my direction from the White House in 1971. As the sworn statement makes clear, agreement to this mission was my responsibility, a step taken in excess of instructions, and without the knowledge or permission of any superior.

Under the circumstances which prevailed in the summer of 1971, and based on the best information available to me at the time, I believed that my decision was dictated inescapably by the vital, national security interests of the United States.

I now see that this judgment may well have been in error, though prompted by what was then my highest sense of right. Its consequences, to my eternal regret, have proved injurious both to a number of innocent persons and to that reverence for law on which our society is founded.

My overriding desire now is to accept full responsibility for my acts and decision and to assist in bringing all the facts and circumstances into the open so that a fair judgment of this activity can be rendered.

With public confidence in our Government already shaken by the Watergate affair, and with the complete affirmation of your personal integrity so imperative at this time, I cannot remain in the Administration while my role in the special investigating unit is submitted to the legal scrutiny it must now properly receive.

It is right that the men and women of the Department of Transportation have an Under Secretary who enjoys full public trust and can devote full time to his job. It is for these reasons that I submit my resignation as Under Secretary of Transportation.

Above, from *The New York Times*, May 9, 1973.
Right, from *The New York Times*, November 30, 1973.

Krogh's Court Statement

Special to The New York Times

WASHINGTON, Nov. 30— Following is the text of a statement read today in Federal court by Egil Krogh Jr. upon entering a plea of guilty to a civil rights charge:

The sole basis for my defense was to have been that I acted in the interest of national security. However, upon serious and lengthy reflection, I now feel that the sincerity of my motivation cannot justify what was done, and that I cannot in conscience assert national security as a defense. I am therefore pleading guilty because I have no defense to this charge. I will make a detailed statement as to my reasons which I will submit to the court and make public prior to sentencing.

My decision is based upon what I think and feel is right and what I consider to be the best interests of the nation. The values expressed by Your Honor in the hearing on defense motions on Nov. 13 particularly brought home to me the transcendant importance of the rule of law over the motivations of man.

I have expressed to the special prosecutor's office my desire that I not be required to testify in this area until after sentencing. My plea today is based on conscience, and I want to avoid any possible suggestion that I am seeking leniency through testifying. The special prosecutor's office has expressed no objection to this position.

My coming to this point today stems from my asking myself what ideas I wanted to stand for, what I wanted to represent to myself and to my family and to be identified with for the rest of my experience. I simply feel that what was done in the Ellsberg operation was in violation of what I perceive to be a fundamental idea in the this country—the paramount importance of the rights of the individual. I don't want to be associated with that violation any longer by attempting to defend it.

William Raspberry

The Unlearned Lesson of Watergate

When I met him last year, Ira Rosen —a Cornell University senior at the time—was disturbed over the number of bright, well-educated young men who managed to become involved in the Watergate scandals.

He thought he knew why. "It's the educational system," he said. "It's geared toward cheating because of the pressure to succeed."

Rosen was still disturbed when I had lunch with him the other day— this time because so many of his contemporaries seem to have learned so little from the Watergate experience.

The unlearned lesson, as he sees it, is that once you start rationalizing actions that you know to be immoral or unethical, it is very difficult to stop.

Rosen, who is a reporter intern for columnist Jack Anderson, said he recently interviewed 45 congressional interns and asked them this question:

"Where would you draw the line if you were asked by your congressman or senator to do something that you believed to be morally or ethically wrong?"

Only about half of these brightest and best said they would refuse the assignment outright. The others gave various versions of: "It depends."

One Senate intern said she would "do whatever my senator asked, because that's my job." Another said "I'd do it and sweep it under the rug, because that kind of thing goes on all the time." Rosen said the two interns, both women, indicated they would do their bosses' bidding even if they knew the act to be legally wrong.

On the other hand, one young woman thought that "waiting in the unemployment line would be a viable alternative to doing something which

I think to be ethically or morally wrong," Rosen reported. Another, in her second year as intern to a conservative Republican, said she was prepared to quit her job last year if her boss had asked her to act in support of President Nixon.

In general, however, Rosen said he found that the interns he talked to would have more misgivings about working for a legislator whose politics they disagreed with than about assignments of questionable ethics or legality.

It is all very distressing to Rosen, who thinks he would have little trouble making the moral choices, even at risk of losing his job. "If you continue saying yes, yes—if you continue along the lines of rationalization—where do you stop?" he insisted.

Rosen later acknowledged that it might not be as easy as all that.

He's absolutely certain that he wouldn't help to arrange a bribe for a senator or engage in illegal acts for him. But he might: tell a telephone caller (falsely) that the boss was out; obey a direct order to mail a congressman's private material in franked envelopes; write letters that seemed to imply support of a measure that the congressman intended to vote against, and do other misleading things short of lying outright.

Rosen was acknowledging that the line between right and wrong doesn't always stay put.

Congressional interns seldom get asked to do things which, if discovered, would create scandals. Assignments like that come much later, after you've already proven your reliability and trustworthiness by telling small lies and countenancing bigger ones. They bring you along s l o w l y, and after

awhile you're willing to do nearly anything that isn't flagrantly criminal— and later maybe you'll do that, too.

Take Rosen's advice and avoid that first white lie, and maybe you'll never get the big stuff because you'll never get promoted from office boy.

But that's too cynical. Probably most of the questionable actions are not those that involve personal greed or ambition but those that involve shortcuts to an important goal: passing an important bill, electing a singularly worthy candidate, protecting an important official from scandal so he can be free to go on doing important things.

That is what produces Watergates.

What is less clear is what it takes to produce people like Archibald Cox, Elliot Richardson and William Ruckelshaus, who had sufficient faith of their own moral conviction to say no to a desperate president.

Suppose their attitude had been more widespread. Suppose Robert Bork had said "no" to the firing of Archie Cox, too, and the man under Bork, and so on. Would that have brought the government to a halt? Or would it merely have halted the cover-up?

You'd think that the tough moral stance of a few honest men might inspire some of us and that the devastating consequences of dishonesty might instruct the rest of us. Such are supposed to be the "lessons of Watergate."

But the lessons aren't quite so clear as Ira Rosen would have them. Not to the congressional interns and not to straight-arrow men like Gerald Ford and Frank Church, who so soon after Watergate, can agonize over how much of the truth about CIA crimes is in the public interest to cover up.

Buzhardt Hits Standards As Too High

HILTON HEAD, S.C., March 10 (AP)—Americans demand too much moral accountability of their public officials, according to J. Fred Buzhardt, a key figure in former President Nixon's Watergate defense.

"Would you rather have a competent scoundrel or an honest boob in office?" asked Buzhardt in an interview with the Charlotte Observer.

"You can make a strong argument that for a President in this day and time you don't want a babe in the woods. He's got to deal with some pretty rough-and-tumble people."

Buzhardt, who was primary attorney for Nixon in the Watergate affair until he suffered a heart attack last summer, said the country would have been better off if Nixon had not been forced to resign.

He said he does not consider President Ford a "babe in the woods," however.

The public and the media have set an unrealistic moral standard for government, resulting in a lack of public confidence, Buzhardt said.

Above, © *The Washington Post*, June 26, 1975.
Left, courtesy of The Associated Press.

SECTION 2

"Victimless Crimes"

The cases discussed in the arguments in this section belong to a general category sometimes referred to as "victimless crimes." The implication of this title is not that the acts included in this group have no detrimental effects on anyone at all, but that they cause no harm to anyone other than the person(s) performing the act. The use of the term "crime" in this title makes explicit the fact that the question of greatest concern about these acts is that of whether or not they should be illegal. However, as with many other cases involving the question of legalization or prohibition of an act, there is also a significant moral question at a more basic level. The basic ethical question with regard to the so-called "victimless" crimes is that of whether an individual has a moral right to do things which could lead to his or her own ill health or death. In this regard, the question is almost indistinguishable from the moral question concerning the justifiability of suicide (see Section 9).

It is important to note in this context that any suggestion that any act is "victimless" in the sense just explained must be examined very critically. Although the poet's line that "No man is an island" has become almost a cliché, it must also be recognized that it appears to be very insightful and factually true. It is certainly to be hoped that the death or illness of any individual will have some emotional impact on other persons. In any case, economists, sociologists, and others have provided detailed descriptions in recent years of the ways in which the illness and/or death of any individual has measurable economic and social impacts. Some of these impacts may be positive, but many of them are negative. Thus, we should be very cautious before accepting any claim that a particular act which may be detrimental to the agent(s) has no negative impact whatsoever on any other parties.

Most of the arguments in this section deal with questions related to the use of drugs (in the broadest sense of that term). A critical element in the discussion of this topic is the issue of logical consistency, an issue raised by almost all factions. An example of the appeal to the principle of consistency is the question "If you don't object to alcohol, why do you object to marijuana?". The only satisfactory answer to such a question is the identification of some morally relevant difference between the use of alcohol and the use of marijuana. However, it must be recognized that even if no relevant difference can be identified, this indicates at most that their moral worth is the same. It must still be ascertained whether this moral value is positive or negative, whether they are both good or bad. Also, the whole set of questions concerning the legalization or prohibition of either or both requires the consideration of numerous other factors.

EXERCISES

1. Compare the arguments in this section with those in Section 6 concerned with gun-control legislation. Are there any significant differences between the arguments in the two sections on the two sides of the legalization/prohibition question other than those resulting from the difficulty in identifying victims in the cases in this section?
2. Compare the arguments in this section with those in Section 9 dealing with the question of suicide. Is there any difference in the cases other than that of the degree of certainty that the death of the agent will result from the act being discussed?
3. To what extent could any of the arguments in this section be applied to the question of censorship of pornography as discussed in the arguments in Section 5?

WOMEN AND WINE.

WOMAN has never been associated with wine without disgrace and disaster. The toast and the bacchanal that, with musical alliteration, couple these two words, spring from the hot lips of sensuality, and are burdened with shame. A man who can sing of wine and women in the same breath, is one whose presence is disgrace, and whose touch is pollution. A man who can forget mother and sister, or wife and daughter, and wantonly engage in a revel in which the name of woman is invoked to heighten the pleasures of the intoxicating cup, is, beyond controversy and without mitigation, a beast. "Dost thou think, because thou art virtuous, there shall be no more cakes and ale?" Ay, cakes and ale, if you will, but let it be cakes and ale. Let not the name by which we call the pure and precious ones at home be brought in to illuminate a degrading feast.

Of the worst foes that woman has ever had to encounter, wine stands at the head. The appetite for strong drink in man has spoiled the lives of more women—ruined more hopes for them, scattered more fortunes for them, brought to them more shame, sorrow, and hardship—than any other evil that lives. The country numbers tens of thousands—nay, hundreds of thousands—of women who are widows to-day, and sit in hopeless weeds, because their husbands have been slain by strong drink. There are hundreds of thousands of homes, scattered all over the land, in which women live lives of torture, going through all the changes of suffering that lie between the extremes of fear and despair, because those whom they love, love wine better than they do the women they have sworn to love. There are women by thousands who dread to hear at the door the step that once thrilled them with pleasure, because that step has learned to reel under the influence of the seductive poison. There are women groaning with pain, while we write these words, from bruises and brutalities inflicted by husbands made mad by drink. There can be no exaggeration in any statement made in regard to this matter, because no human imagination can create anything worse than the truth, and no pen is capable of portraying the truth. The sorrows and the horrors of a wife with a drunken husband, or a mother with a drunken son, are as near the realization of hell as can be reached in this world, at least. The shame, the indignation, the sorrow, the sense of disgrace for herself and her children, the poverty,—and not unfrequently the beggary,—the fear and the fact of violence, the lingering, life-long struggle and despair of countless women with drunken husbands, are enough to make all women curse wine, and engage unitedly to oppose it everywhere as the worst enemy of their sex.

And now what shall we see on the New-Year's Day, 1871? Women all over the city of New York—women here and there all over the country, where like social customs prevail—setting out upon their tables the well-filled decanters which, before night shall close down, will be emptied into the brains of young men and old men, who will go reeling to darker orgies, or to homes that will feel ashamed of them. Woman's lips will give the invitation, woman's hand will fill and present the glass, woman's careless voice will laugh at the effects of the mischievous draught upon their friends, and, having done all this, woman will retire to balmy rest, previously having reckoned the number of those to whom she has, during the day, presented a dangerous temptation, and rejoiced over it in the degree of its magnitude.

O woman! woman! Is it not about time that this thing were stopped? Have you a husband, a brother, a son? Are they stronger than their neighbors who have, one after another, dropped into the graves of drunkards? Look around you, and see the desolations that drink has wrought among your acquaintances, and then decide whether you have a right to place temptation in any man's way, or do aught to make a social custom respectable which leads hundreds of thousands of men into bondage and death. Why must the bottle come out everywhere? Why can there not be a festal occasion without this vulgar guzzling of strong drink?

Woman, there are some things that you can do, and this is one: you can make drinking unpopular and disgraceful among the young. You can utterly discountenance all drinking in your own house, and you can hold in suspicion every young man who touches the cup. You know that no young man who drinks can safely be trusted with the happiness of any woman, and that he is as unfit as a man can be for woman's society. Have this understood: that every young man who drinks is socially proscribed. Bring up your children to regard drinking as not only dangerous but disgraceful. Place temptation in no man's way. If men will make beasts of themselves, let them do it in other society than yours. If your mercenary husbands treat their customers from private stores kept in their counting-rooms, shame them into decency by your regard for the honor of your home. Recognize the living, terrible fact that wine has always been, and is to-day, the curse of your sex; that it steals the hearts of men away from you, that it dries up your prosperity, that it endangers your safety, that it can only bring you evil. If social custom compels you to present wine at your feasts, rebel against it, and make a social custom in the interests of virtue and purity. The matter is very much in your own hands. The women of the country, in what is called polite society, can do more to make the nation temperate than all the legislators and tumultuous reformers that are struggling and blundering in their efforts to this end. At any rate, if they will try, they shall have SCRIBNER'S MONTHLY to help them.

From *Scribner's Monthly*, 1871.

Thinking Out Loud

Our national leaders must further demonstrate that they are interested in the preservation of human lives.

If only a small percentage of the time and effort that is expended to stop the slaughter of Americans in Vietnam could be exerted against the greatest killer of all — the monstrous liquor traffic, much progress could be made.

This publication has been against the illegal and immoral war in Vietnam from the very start. It has also been overwhelmingly demonstrated by the politicians who launched it that it was to be a "no win war".

And now at this late date, after sacrificing 45,000 young men, and suffering over 300,000 casualties, any effort to reverse the trend and launch a crusade to win the war has about as much chance as a snowball in hell — and those who are pursuing this ill-fated course are well aware of this fact.

It would doubtless be far less appealing to those who demand "victory in Vietnam", waving flags and marching under banners, if they should be required to shoulder arms and lead in such a crusade in the marshy swamps of Indochina. But knowing that they shall not be called upon to make such a sacrifice they can go right on demanding that more thousands of young Americans must be slaughtered. And for what purpose?

But the subject of this editorial is not Vietnam but the Number One Killer—the abominable liquor traffic. Why can't we work up some steam against this horrible destroyer of human life? How long since we have heard of a politician in Congress — of any stature — getting up on the floor and making a speech — a two-fisted, knockout blow — against the liquor traffic?

Let us take a look at this problem specifically as it is known to be the Number One killer on the highways — to say nothing for the moment of its terrible drain on the national economy, its unspeakable immorality, its conscienceless wrecking of homes and its titanic waste of human bodies through alcoholism. Just think particularly of what it does on the highways:

30,000 lives were snuffed out last year from drinking drivers! This means that in only one and one-half years the liquor traffic claims as many casualties as we have lost in Vietnam in the entire duration of the war. Also, last year alone more than 800,000 accidents in traffic were attributal to beverage alcohol!

And, if we could became interested in comparative statistics on crime, we should be jolted by the fact that twice as many Americans died last year in automobile wrecks in which alcohol was involved as were murdered.

Consider also that twice as many innocent bystanders were killed by drunken drivers as were killed by robbers, rapists, arsonists and thieves combined!

More adults were convicted of drunken driving than of murder, robbery, assault, rape and burglaries combined!

Property destroyed in accidents involving alcohol was six times greater than that of property stolen in all robberies, larsonies, and burglaries in this nation.

The Department of Transportation reports that roughly 2 per cent of the drivers on the highways have enough alcohol in their systems to be legally drunk — but that these two percent are involved in more than 50 per cent of all fatal accidents.

This means that one in every 50 drivers on your highways today is a potential killer. WATCH OUT FOR YOUR LIFE!

And remember, the social drinkers are the greatest offenders! According to Raymond K. Berg, Chief Judge of the Chicago traffic court, a recent study shows that in that city only 20 per cent of those convicted of drunken driving were chronic alcoholics. This means that EIGHTY PER CENT WERE SOCIAL DRINKERS!

The liquor that is consumed at a private social gathering, even at a wedding, will kill on the highways, just the same as if it were consumed at some filthy bar, tavern, or saloon!

In the name of all that is high and holy and respectable and decent; in the name of precious human lives, when will some men in public life, and in national leadership, get up and speak out against this damnable killer — beverage alcohol?

"Wine is a mocker; strong drink is raging: and whosoever is deceived thereby is not wise," Prov. 20:1.

Dale Crowley in *The Capital Voice*, October 1, 1970.

Mother Needs Blood Money

MIAMI, Fla. (AP) — De-Sola Brown, a mother of two hemophiliacs, made 20 trips to Miami's skid row to coax alcoholics into trading blood for booze.

She calls her dealings on seamy street corners "contracts of necessity."

Mrs. Brown, 36, says she bartered drinks in an attempt to pay back the city's blood bank for plasma used by her sons, whose illness prohibits blood coagulation.

"It's been almost impossible to find individual donors," she said. "We owe so much blood and have no way of paying it back I had to find blood somewhere."

Mrs. Brown's son Mark, 9, has needed nearly 300 pints of blood every month for the past five years. Greg, 17, has needed almost as much blood for most of his life.

"I've been told we owe more than 1,000 pints for Marky," Mrs. Brown said. "Frankly, we've lost track on Greg."

She said Miami's Jackson Memorial Hospital has not pressured her for repayment. "But a debt is something to be paid," she said.

In her skid row excursions, Mrs. Brown, solicited more than 100 volunteers. Most of them never tasted the fruits of their generosity, however, because they were rejected as unsuitable by the hospital.

"My agreement with them was they would get the drink after donating a pint of blood," she said.

"I never thought of it as being dangerous," Mrs. Brown said. "I always approached groups of men standing around on the corners. They are really good guys. They just want a drink ... they were desperate, too."

Mrs. Brown, a divorcee, recently went to work as a cashier for the Salvation Army. She gave up her blood deals when told she was in direct conflict with the work of her employers.

"I guess I was wrong in tempting those men," she said. "But I wasn't thinking of their good. I needed blood."

Always low on funds, Mrs. Brown does not know how she will repay her sons' debts. She says she takes comfort in watching her boys grow despite their handicaps.

"I'd do anything for them," she said. "Anything."

Above, courtesy of The Associated Press. Below, reprinted from *The Troy Times Record*, December 6, 1972.

Amphetamines

The disclosure that some of the nation's best known persons have been patients of Dr. Max Jacobson, a New York City doctor who gives amphetamine treatments, the stimulant drug also called "speed," is an indication of the turn life has taken for some people these days.

Dr. Jacobson and a small number of other less known doctors have been prescribing the drug not to treat disease but to energize people, make them happier and more productive.

Among those who have been his patients are writers, artists, composers and people who carry the all-purpose label of jet-setters.

With the known possible hazards of amphetamine the practice raises considerable risks for the welfare of talented and brilliant people.

It would seem that the talents of these people are already adequate and that artificial stimulation of them is non-productive, at least in the long run.

Dissatisfaction on their part with their productivity or art would seem to call more for a personal change in life patterns rather than drug alteration of the pattern.

Literary and art history has numerous examples of persons who were trapped by some form of drug dependence.

One thinks of persons with brilliant minds who came to suffer greatly by falling into addiction.

Edgar Allan Poe is recalled as a great mind struck down because he was unable to face the challenges of life on his own mettle and increasingly depended on opium, finally dying at the age of 40.

The brilliant, restless and imaginative minds of those who produce works of art with pen, brush or otherwise are hard for those of us of lesser talents to fathom.

Legalized Pot

HERE IS ONE small cheer for legalizing marijuana. Rah for *cannabis sativa*, pot, grass, Mary Jane.

Two rahs would be too many, because the principal reason for legalizing the happy-time weed is quite similar to the reason for repealing the prohibition against alcoholic beverages four decades ago. Both marijuana and alcohol seem to cause more trouble when they are illegal than when they become legal.

No one can argue compellingly that Americans become better persons by drinking Martinis, as President Nixon does, or by drawing pot smoke into their lungs, as many young and not-so-young people are doing in defiance of the law. Outside of occasional medicinal use—marijuana now is being tried as a relaxant for terminal cancer patients—there is no strong, positive reason for legalizing either drug.

But a positive reason is not really necessary. A strong negative reason against the grass ban will do. The argument for marijuana rests on such a negative reason and on one indisputable fact: Large numbers of human beings *will* use psychoactive drugs like pot and alcohol.

Today, marijuana is being smoked by great numbers of Americans. Most of them know, or at least guess, that grass is not as dangerous to them as alcohol is. As psychiatrist Lester' Grinspoon of Harvard says in his new book, *Marihuana Reconsidered,* marijuana is "among the least dangerous of the psychoactive drugs." He points to the "curious fact" that Western society sanctions the use of tobacco and alcohol, though both cause tissue damage in humans. Marijuana does not. Nor does it lead to addiction. The question of whether pot leads to harder drugs is in dispute, but most authorities can find no real cause-and-effect relationship. President Nixon chose to ignore these findings last week when he said that legalizing marijuana would be "detrimental" to young people, because pot "is only a half-way house to something worse." Like Martinis?

Those who smoke grass also know they are violating the law, and are "criminals" subject to stiff jail sentences. This "punitive, repressive approach," argues Dr. Grinspoon, leads young pot smokers to view their society as hypocritical. A pot high is banned; an alcohol high is not, even though it is more dangerous.

That is the real problem of the legal ban against grass. As young people turn on with pot, they tend to turn off the society at large.

Dr. Grinspoon offers a reasonable solution: Legalize marijuana under controls similar to those for alcohol. No one under 18 could use it legally. Marijuana's potency would be strictly controlled to reduce the chance of a "bad trip." The quality would be guaranteed, so the smoker would know that his grass was not laced with other drugs.

Over all, this could be about as effective as present controls over alcohol—not perfect, but better than it was. There still would be abuse of pot smoking as there is of alcohol drinking. But no more criminal arrests for getting a simple pot high, as there are no arrests for drinking a Martini at the White House.

—*JAMES G. DRISCOLL*

Q and A

A Pot Law Experience In Oregon

In 1973, Oregon changed its laws to treat possession of small amounts of marijuana much as it treats minor traffic offenses. Oregon Atty. Gen. Lee Johnson was interviewed about the effects of this change by Washington Star Staff Writer Thomas Love.

Question: *As a law enforcement officer how do you justify a law making one part of a chain of events illegal — the production, distribution and sale of marijuana — while virtually legalizing another part — its possession and use?*

Johnson: I would call it a legitimate exercise in hypocrisy — and I would have to put the qualifier on it that I'm not really sure it's legitimate. I suppose I'm looking at it more from the viewpoint of a politician than a law-enforcement officer. It does create problems for law enforcement and I think we sometimes have a hard time comprehending just what the hell we are trying to do. But on the other side of the coin, I think it's society saying that we don't really approve of marijuana. We don't want to give moral sanction to it, but on the other hand we don't want a very heavy hand of law enforcement to enforce the moral disapproval.

Marijuana Legislation

I am distressed that your editorial of April 19th, "A 'Cease-Fire' on Marijuana," wasn't more positive. Having been the initiating House sponsor with Senator Javits of the decriminalization bill in 1972, I know the frustration of having good legislation that because of the political climate won't go anywhere now.

Therefore, we are now proposing a more pragmatic approach which maintains some sanction—that is a civil sanction of $100 fine for not-for-profit use. This appears to be more acceptable to legislators and is now being considered by some 20 states. I would hope The Washington Post would endorse it instead of taking it apart by nitpicking.

It is tough enough to get sponsors for any decriminalization bill. The new proposal of a $100 fine is not, as you suggest, a half way measure. It will affect by its implication (states may follow the federal lead) 400,000 people a year by protecting them from criminal records for personal marijuana use and possession. And, it will take courage for many members whose constituents are fearful to support even this more limited concept.

Edward I. Koch.
U.S. Representative (D.-N.Y.)
Washington.

Left, from the *Washington Star*, May 6, 1975.
Above, letter to the editor of *The Washington Post* by Rep. Edward I. Koch, April 29, 1975.

CRACKDOWN IS ESSENTIAL

The gravity of the drug problem in this country looms over us like the sword of Damocles. Millions of Americans use drugs. Thousands of others are profiting personally by the selling of drugs. Their crimes breed more crime until the shock waves reach every corner of our society.

We have become so inured to drug horror stories that little short of a drug-induced tragedy in our own homes can spur us to personal involvement. Nevertheless the problem is so pervasive that the personal attention of all of us will be required to solve it. The root causes of the problem are many and complex, but one of the basic causes is surely our attitude toward drugs in general.

It has been argued that the line between the legal use of drugs and the criminal use is thin at best, and that we are not certain always where it should be drawn. Where does it belong, for example, so far as the free and easy presciding of antibiotics or sleeping potions is concerned?

Americans may not at times be able to see the problem in taking an occasional tranquilizer or pep pill. On the other hand they certainly can see the moral wrong in the use of amphetimines and other drugs by athletes. The thought that athletic performance is the result of a drug-produced distortion rather than natural perfection is bad enough. Worse is the fact that athletes are heroes to many persons in our society, young and old. Their personal use of drugs adds substantially to the general belief that there is nothing wrong about destroying one's mind and body for personal gain or psychological kicks.

There are many other areas where Americans can agree, we believe, that the use of drugs harms both the person using them or society, or both. A person drunk on marijuana behind the wheel of a car is no different than a driver who is drunk on alcohol, for example. A person so hooked on heroin or cocaine that he must steal thousands of dollars a week to support his addiction is a menace to others as well as to himself.

Drugs certainly do not have any place in the lives of young, immature people whose judgments and characters are not yet formed.

There are many other areas of agreement. Instead of focusing on the thin line of absolutes it is time that Americans attacked the drug problem with the broad brush of consensus.

If police, prosecutors, judges and an outraged citizenry will unite to stop the flow of narcotics into the United States of America, if they throw the book at the pusher and crack down on the addict, whether on the street in the classroom or on the football field, drug prevention will begin to have real meaning.

Subsequent argument over the thin line would be the frosting on the cake.

From *The Troy Sunday.*

Since marijuana is not a deterrent, no more than cigarettes, it seems inhumane that they *schlep* people and put them in jail with it.

"Well, maybe marijuana's not *bad* for you, but it's a stepping stone. It leads to heavier drugs—heroin, etc."

Well, that syllogism has to work out this way, though: The heroin addict, the bust-out junkie that started out smoking pot, says to his cell-mate:

"I'm a bust-out junkie. Started out smoking pot, look at me now. By the way, cell-mate, what happened to you? There's blood on your hands. How'd you get to murder those kids in that crap game? Where did it all start?"

"Started with bingo in the Catholic Church."

"I see."

Top left, from *The Essential Lenny Bruce*. Copyright 1967 Ballantine Books/A Product of Douglas Book Corporation.

Below, from *Psychology Today*.

Drug Abuse— Just What The Doctor Ordered

by J. Maurice Rogers

The image of the physician as expert and benign begins to evaporate when we see physicians pushing psychoactive pills whose consequences are not fully understood into patients whose problems require human, not chemical, solutions.

Ads. Doctors are strongly encouraged in their pill-for-every-problem syndrome by drug manufacturers who bombard them with advertisements in psychiatric and medical journals:

"WHAT MAKES A WOMAN CRY? *A man? Another woman? Three kids? No kids at all? Wrinkles? You name it . . . If she is depressed, consider Pertofane.*"

And:

"SCHOOL, THE DARK, SEPARATION, DENTAL VISITS, MONSTERS. THE EVERYDAY ANXIETY OF CHILDREN SOMETIMES GETS OUT OF HAND. *A child can usually deal with his anxieties. But sometimes the anxieties overpower the child. Then he needs your help. Your help may include Vistaril.*"

And this advertisement, which shows an attractive but worried-looking young woman with an armful of books, and describes the problems that face a new college student:

"*Exposure to new friends and other influences may force her to re-evaluate herself and her goals . . . Her newly stimulated intellectual curiosity may make her more sensitive to and apprehensive about national and world conditions.*" The headline reads: "TO HELP FREE HER OF EXCESSIVE ANXIETY . . . LIBRIUM."

Such advertisements redefine normal problems of living as medical problems to be solved by drugs. Most small children, of course, are at some time afraid of the dark or anxious about school. A person may become depressed after personal loss, upon facing a new job, having to adjust to new conditions, or upon experiencing impotence in the face of increasing social turmoil. But the advocacy of drugs for such problems is socially irresponsible.

One Wrong To Justify Another

Greenberg's excellent article on the marijuana raid at Stony Brook (9 Feb., p. 607) is a perfect exposition of the older generation's apparent helplessness when confronted with adolescent stupidity. The misguided young pot smokers attempt to justify their behavior on the grounds that other things (tobacco and alcohol, used to excess) are known to be bad but are not prohibited; therefore marijuana (the extent of whose deleterious effects are not known with scientific precision) must also be permitted. To generalize, we must not proscribe any evil as long as we allow some other evils to exist.

It seems to me that this rationalization is being used in all kinds of situations by those who would defy any form of authority. In matters of religion we are told that because there are some hypocrites in the congregation (which is true) all pronouncements of churchmen are without standing. In matters of morals, the fact that certain deviations are tolerated or poorly enforced is held to negate all moral authority. The fact that some adults are Babbitts or "squares" is considered ample justification for spurning the advice of all adults. The fact that we don't allow the police to break people's doors down to check up on what they are reading in bed is supposed to make it all right to peddle semipornographic trash in bookstores and theaters. The fact that some white people are prejudiced is given as reason enough to "burn Whitey," and because some Negroes riot there are those who would put "the Negro" back in his place. In every instance, one wrong is being used to justify another.

There is no reason to be surprised that such childish reasoning is used by immature people—this has been going on since time immemorial. What is so discouraging is that supposedly intelligent people, including a fairly strong and vociferous segment of our educators and scientists, are not only unable to cope with such arguments on the part of adolescent students, but actually side with the students in their blind rebellion against any standards of conduct.

JOHN D. ALDEN

98 Sunnyside Avenue,
Pleasantville, New York 10570

Above, letter to the editor of *Science* by John D. Alden, May 10, 1968.

Deterioration of the Human

All that sets man apart from lower forms of animal life, all that makes human life truly human, in some way depends on man's cerebral cortex. So far as we know, that bit of gray protein is the pinnacle of God's creation. It is the growing edge of evolution. Therein lies the seat of rational thought, of moral judgment, of self-awareness, of qualitative distinction, of meaning-perception. To the degree that the cerebral cortex is temporarily numbed, the human is temporarily de-graded back toward the animal. This is precisely what happens when psychotropic drugs are ingested. The brain still works, but it is impaired — reduced to lower than its natural level. It responds not to changes in its real environment, nor to the real needs of the self nor to the Spirit of God, but to toxic substances introduced into its blood supply. Such a condition may be pleasurable — indeed, that is precisely why it is sought. But in such a condition a man is less than fully himself, though he may feel ten feet tall. It is, then, the use of psychotropic drugs, not their misuse, that is the moral issue. It is precisely their intended effect, not just their side effects, that we must ponder.

Better the Ambiguities

It might seem to be a cruel asceticism for a man to deny himself short holidays from his woes, even though our contemporary happiness drugs are faulty and fiendishly risky. But in the long run it is even more cruel to the best that is within us to take trips from which we must return with neither ourselves nor our environment changed for the better, and with some past accounts long overdue to boot. Better the ambiguities and tensions experienced by a real man interacting with other real men and the real God of the real world than the euphoria of chemically induced sensation of escape that does not really let us escape from anything at all, and that frequently forges some very strong chains of its own.

Mark tells us that just before Jesus was nailed to his cross he was offered as an anodyne "wine mingled with myrrh, but he did not take it." Few of Jesus' modern disciples begrudge themselves an anesthetic under any physical suffering whatsoever, be it so slight a thing as a headache. But for the figurative headaches which are so plentiful in our modern lives a damn is still better than a gram. Then when the euphoric moments come they will be genuine.

We must always avoid legislation or molding of public opinion so as to create a situation which makes it enormously profitable to cater to people's vices. In every era young people find ways to live dangerously; to shock and confound their elders; to unerringly find and sample the vices most feared by the "establishment." Punishment and prohibition only make the forbidden vices more enticing.

Howard A. Powers
Medfield, Massachusetts

Within the past year I have read that marijuana is a depressant; is a stimulant; can cause genetic breakdown to the user; can cause genetic breakdown to a developing fetus; can cause genetic breakdown to a future child if conception is within three years of smoking; can cause lung cancer; can cause premature and deep facial wrinkles; can increase the desire for and intensity of sexual relations; can decrease the desire for and intensity of sexual relations and therefore: can be an effective contraceptive.

In college I tried pot but because of reservations about the above and because I did not really enjoy smoking, I found the experience uncomfortable. But I loved the ritual, and still do, although I don't puff, but pass the cigarette along.

Until I find some reliable and supportive facts on pot, I won't smoke. Yes I do feel non-sociable at parties, but the future of my unborn children and possibilities of lung cancer are too important to risk. If medical evidence shows that marijuana is no more harmful than liquor (or, as Mr. Edwards suggests, it is actually better), then I probably will smoke with my friends.

Name Withheld
Albany, New York

Top, reprinted with permission from *U.S. Catholic* (August 1972), 221 West Madison St., Chicago, Illinois 60606.
Below, from *Newsweek*, October 2, 1972.

But one of the poll's most provocative aspects is the light it sheds on young voters' attitudes on supposed youth issues. Far from being a unified, liberal bloc on these questions, the young turn out to be middle-roaders. They divided almost evenly on the legalization of marijuana, took a dim view of amnesty (50 to 40) and women's lib. (Significantly, 54 per cent of the young women surveyed disagreed with women's lib, as opposed to only 44 per cent of the men.) A 56 per cent majority favored legalized abortion, including 51 per cent of the Catholics.

There are already apparent many adverse effects from the use of marijuana (I'm sorry I disposed of these studies), and this is only the beginning. We already foresee some of its evils which portend greater problems, and yet we are asked to legalize it? We are to encourage one more problem? Is this the purpose of government, to encourage self-destructive behavior?

If marijuana is legalized, then there should also be a law that says the taxpayer cannot be forced to pay one single cent to rehabilitate a user or pay for any of the problems that result from usage.

Alice M. Raimondo
Port Jefferson, New York

Why is it that when something becomes difficult to do, or a nuisance, we say, "Well, let's make it legal," and that takes care of everything! Marijuana has not been definitely proven harmless. In many cases, it certainly leads to the use of other drugs. Let's not be in such a hurry to sweep it under the rug. If we work at it a little harder, some solution to the problem will be found.

Mrs. Margaret Sikora
White Plains, New York

The sudden drive to legalize marijuana can be traced to the time when it left the minority groups and sprung into the middle-class area. The so-called socially acceptable people are faced with a dilemma—their out is to legalize marijuana.

Edward T. Mumm
Rahns, Pennsylvania

Confidence: Moreover, issues often do not seem to have much effect on young people's choice of a candidate. "I can't think just of myself," explains 18-year-old Maggie Smartt of Houston, whose personal convictions run to ending the war, legalizing marijuana and abortions (she happens to be eight months pregnant—and single), but who also plans to vote for the President. "I have to think about the majority," she says. "Most of those people won't need an abortion—and they're not going to sit around and smoke dope. I guess I'm willing to make the sacrifice."

POINT

SAFER: So-called "victimless crime" and how we should deal with it is one of those topics of conversation that people argue about. And if people argue about it, you can be sure so do Shana Alexander and Jack Kilpatrick. Here's Point/Counterpoint.

SHANA ALEXANDER: Jack, I've been forced to change my mind about drugs. Let anybody put anything he wants into his mouth or his veins. Make hard drugs as legal as alcohol. Let everybody take charge of his own bad habits, and I really think we'll all be better off. If addicts didn't have to steal, society would no longer have to spend impossible sums trying to protect people from addicts. As for protecting addicts from themselves, from destroying themselves, I no longer think that's society's job. What finally persuaded me was the record here in New York State. Two years ago Governor Rockefeller put through the toughest drug law in the country. Selling just one ounce of the hard stuff means a mandatory prison term of at least 15 years. It can mean prison for life. Yet, even this brutish escalation of punishment to barbarous levels has had no effect whatever, neither on drug addiction nor on drug-related crime. I conclude you cannot protect people from themselves. Therefore, I would remove the penalties from all victimless crimes, not only drugs. Also gambling, drunkenness, prostitution, homosexuality, and so on. If these activities lead to violent crime, prosecute the thief, the mugger, the rapist, but put public safety ahead of public morals. You'll charge me with endangering the safety of children, but kids learn by example, Jack. Make each person free to take pot, to take cocaine, to take rat poison, and you begin to make him responsible for his own acts. That's got to be better, Jack, for us and for our kids.

COUNTERPOINT

JAMES J. KILPATRICK: Up to a point, Shana, I share your libertarian theories. I too believe an individual has a right to mess up his own life, so long as he does no harm to others. But there is such a thing as society or community or the commonweal - a body of moral conviction developed over many centuries out of law and religion, and I believe it cannot wisely be distained. In libertarian theory, laws against prostitution should be repealed. A woman's body is her own, and she can sell it if she wants to. But I believe society has a right to say prostitution is wrong, it's degrading, and if it can never be eliminated it should not be implicitly approved. It's the same with hard-core pornography. As a writer, I'm troubled by legal censorship. I don't like it. But I believe the community has a right to say hard-core pornography is wrong, it pollutes, and it subtly eats at the fabric of our life. You make persuasive arguments for legalized heroin, but maybe society has a right to say, out of its collective wisdom and experience: Heroin is a terrible evil; we ought not to make it easy for the weak to surrender to addiction. What I am suggesting, Shana, is that we should not flinch from setting standards of right conduct, of virtue, of public good and public evil. And we ought to shun the notion that the drunk, the drug addict, and the whore, even if they do not demonstrably harm others, do not affect others - for they do. For better or for worse, a community is influenced by each of its members. Saints and sinners, we are touching atoms. So, ask not for whom the bell tolls, Shana, it tolls for thee and me, and for all of you out there.

Left and right page from the CBS News
broadcast *60 Minutes*, September 11, 1975.

SOUNDING BOARD

One Person's Opinion on a Several-Sided Subject

It's a sin to smoke

YVONNE GOULET

It is a sin to smoke. My certainty of this fact came after reading Kevin Axe's "Sounding Board" article in the November issue of U.S. CATHOLIC entitled "It's Sinful Not to Vote." Mr. Axe's thesis was that not voting shows lack of concern for the welfare of one's fellowman and, therefore, violates the law of love.

It is, I believe, this same law of love that smoking violates (as well as its more explicit formulation in the Fifth Commandment).

I'm convinced that smoking is a sin from considering 1) the nature of smoking; 2) the new understanding of the nature of sin.

Smoking, which has proved to be harmful in a variety of laboratory tests, is sinful, I believe, because it deprives the smoker of 1) health; 2) eventually, life itself. Moreover, it deprives others of comfort, security, health, and sometimes, in the case of stillborn infants and deaths of newborn babies, of their lives. Before elaborating, however, I would like to consider briefly the nature of sin.

In post-Vatican II theology, sin is falling short of the mark, making the wrong choices. As Marc Oraison says in his book, *Morality For Our Time*, "This is our sin: to fail to respond to the demand of love. We spend our entire lives either not responding at all, or not responding enough, or responding only indirectly. We are sinners all the time."

Although some will say that smoking, even if wrong, is trivial compared to worldwide problems of poverty, war, and injustice, I submit that it is precisely the immediacy of smoking that makes its sinfulness so crucial. It is easy to be filled with zeal for abstractions: harder to confront evil literally at one's fingertips.

• • •

The law of love involves three persons: God, our neighbor, ourselves. Smoking sins against all three:

Only God, according to moralists, has direct dominion over creation. We are only stewards of our bodies; by persistently injuring our bodies, we assume dominion over them, thereby displacing God.

We offend ourselves by smoking in that 1) we curtail our ability to function at peak efficiency (according to the same government report mentioned earlier, "clinical studies involving healthy young men have shown that cigarette smoking impairs exercise performance especially for many types of athletic events and activities involving maximal work capacity."); 2) Smokers further offend themselves by increasing seven-fold their susceptibility to lung cancer and to other respiratory and cardiovascular disease (Surgeon General's report).

Smokers violate love of neighbor by 1) causing discomfort to others by polluting shared air; 2) causing physical damage to those with allergies or other respiratory ailments; 3) endangering the lives of unborn children they may be carrying; 4) endangering the financial and emotional security of those who depend upon them; 5) giving bad example to children and young people who may be influenced to smoke.

A recent example of point two, above, is a situation I know of personally. A child with cystic fibrosis has parents who are chain smokers. The child, with diseased lungs, is forced constantly to breathe polluted air in her own home. How can her parents be blameless?

• • •

Those who profit from the sale of tobacco products, I believe, are guilty of a grave sin against the common good. As Paul Hanly Furfey says in his book, *The Morality Gap*, "For the sake of their profits, the tobacco moguls have had no scruple about sending tens of thousands of their fellow Americans to a premature death."

Others who share culpability are doctors who, by smoking themselves, give bad example to their patients, or who, for the sake of profit, fail to warn a patient of the dangers of smoking while accepting his money for treatment.

Since in many cases, the civil authority can pass legislation to protect some citizens from others, I believe steps should be taken to prohibit smoking in public places and perhaps to provide for fines for those who violate those laws. I am against total prohibition because 1) The freedom of smokers to self-pollute should be respected, (although, as suggested by a delegate to the U.N. World Health Organization, restricted to consenting adults in private); 2) It won't work.

Finally, one anti-smoker spoke recently of the need for church leaders to provide direction and good example in this area. He derided a priest who, while preaching about the evil of masturbation, puffed eagerly on a cigarette. I agree that such hypocrisy creates a credibility gap.

I am an anesthesiologist, and daily I have to administer anesthesia to chronic smokers and nurse them through their post-operative period. Fifty percent of those who have smoked a package a day for 10 years have chronic bronchitis.

You know how smoking has crippled someone when you try to get them to cough up their secretions after they have had abdominal surgery and they *must* cough, or be a prime target for pneumonia.

When one sees a smoking colleague get one coronary after another until he is almost dead, one needs little more proof that nicotine constricts arteries and damages tissues.

There is no question that, morally, smoking is a sin. Grave sin.

The problem is that smoking is an addiction. We Americans love freedom, yet so readily give it up to tobacco and other drugs. One wonders why.

Robert H. Irwin, M.D.
Berkeley, California

A silly subject.

Steven Wilson
Ashland, Oregon

This whole bit of trivial rot smells like the "hard sell" Baptist approach of several generations ago: No smoking, drinking, dancing, etc. Why don't you address the real issues that are polluting this nation?

C. Romano
Kailua, Hawaii

Smoke regularly, but hope to quit eventually. As I have done with alcohol. Quitting both are too much right now.

Have just begun to realize the full impact of smoking, the imposition on others, etc. So, awareness comes first, hopefully actions come later.

Name Withheld
Fox River Grove, Illinois

It seems to me that should we agree with Ms. Goulet, we might in the near future be confronted with the question, "Is it a sin to eat eggs?"

There is sufficient scientific evidence pertaining to the relationship of the ingestion of food with a high cholesterol content and heart attacks. Can we not say, therefore, that eggs cause heart attacks like smoking causes lung cancer?

Mary C. Wittingham
Louisville, Kentucky

This topic can be expanded to almost any extent and both sides deserve defense.

Smoking is no more a sin than wearing high-heel, spike-type shoes. These also are dangerous to your health and they destroy the property of others. Have you seen hardwood floors after a woman has walked over them in spike high heels?

Charles M. Fischer
Paducah, Kentucky

As I am not perfect, I am not overly hasty in condemning a smoker his habit. But to smoke in my presence is thrusting a habit upon me which I disapprove of. I find it hard to be a judge, but harder still to be a silent victim. If one must smoke, do it alone or with other smokers. It does not negate the sin, but, to me at least, it definitely lessens it.

Sara Ann Sieland
Troy, Michigan

As a non-smoker and a researcher, I still cannot reach the conclusion that smoking affects health (e.g., cancer).

The correlation cited by the Surgeon General indicates an association between the two but not a cause-effect relationship.

Some smoking may be sinful, but Ms. Goulet tends to view it as an absolute, i.e., all smoking is sinful. That kind of theology and code of morality has done Catholicism much damage in the past and has little place in today's theology.

Joe Gavin
Philadelphia, Pennsylvania

"It is a sin to smoke" may be a puritanism of the next phase of history which we shall have to bear. The medical evidence against smoking will never be great enough to make the command against it absolute, because smoking simply does not have to be a craze or frequency for people who care; and there will always be those few blessed and wise, so free of the Devil, the World, and the Flesh, that they will have no part in promoting extremism for the sake of Salvation. Maybe moralistic laws for an age can be formulated in a more knowing manner, without tending to warp the precise truth.

James Peter Lorge
Milwaukee, Wisconsin

I can't disagree with anything Ms. Goulet said; step by logical step one finds oneself agreeing; but then, in the end, I don't agree. Isn't there something to be said for the quality of life over quantity? Most of life's little pleasures are sooner or later found harmful. Personally, I don't wish to live to be 95 anyway! One would have to live in a sterile box to avoid all the dangers of plain, ordinary, risky living.

Joanne Willette
Delavan, Minnesota

There is a moral responsibility here somewhere, it seems to me. If one really loves neighbor as well as self, then there would be more responsibility and concern by all Christians for our neighbor's well-being. Can one honestly believe that he does not care what might happen to himself and be called morally responsible? No one is an island. If one cannot tolerate cigarette smoke, there are fewer and fewer places he can go.

Lora Jakoubek
Janesville, Wisconsin

Left and right page reprinted with permission from *U.S. Catholic* (June 1973), 221 West Madison St., Chicago, Illinois 60606.

Hey, Let the Lady Smoke!

By Abigail Van Buren

DEAR ABBY: I am a smoker. I know all the hazards, but I enjoy smoking and will not give it up. I resent all the reformed smokers who have quit for whatever reason and preach to me to quit smoking.

I respect all the "No Smoking" signs. I do not smoke while I am in an automobile with others. I smoke while I am in my office, my home or with friends.

I do not drink. I hate heavy drinkers and detest drunks, yet I am constantly being exposed to drunks. On a long plane ride, for instance. I sat next to a woman who drank all the way. She was so loaded when we landed that she had to be helped from the plane.

Bars, restaurants, theaters, etc., serve liquor, but they want to put up "No Smoking" signs.

I protest!

I would like to see every eating place with a "No Smoking" sign stop serving liquor and beer so I won't have to be around drunks. Also, airlines should have a separate section for drinkers, just as they do for smokers.

I am not asking people to stop drinking: "I'm just asking that the drinkers drink with each other and leave us sober people alone."

Mrs. T.S.

You make a valid point. But while obnoxious drunks are no pleasure to encounter, they do no violence to your lungs and the environment. Smokers do.

This Space Available

Broadcast cigarette ads have been banned. It won't end there—that's not the way of governments. Further federal interference was augured by the Surgeon General last month: "Nonsmokers have as much right to clean and wholesome air as smokers have to their so-called right to smoke, which I would redefine as a right to pollute." He specifically mentioned airplanes and restaurants (it won't end there) as public places where smoking should be banned.

Now, to our knowledge, everyone has the right *not* to smoke, whether subjected to an advertisement or not; nor is anyone denying nonsmokers the right to stay away from restaurants. Could it be, then, that the government is getting at the problem, not of "rights," but of pollution? Then why pick on cigarettes and not, say, airplanes or cars? If health is the issue, why not ban television (it causes scurvy of the mind), or saturated fats, or the Pill, or the Surgeon General?

The anti-tobacco evangelism is a neo-Puritan substitute for moral fervor: when no one any longer believes in sin, something new must be found to condemn. But morality, having connections with higher things, does not take kindly to such arbitrary treatment.

Moved by this higher morality, we repeat our willingness to run cigarette ads in our pages. And some of us, as Christians, will do penance for the sins of the state by not giving up smoking for Lent.

Top, courtesy of Abigail Van Buren, syndicated newspaper columnist, "Dear Abby." Above from *Triumph*, publication of the Society for the Christian Commonwealth, 278 Broadview Avenue, Warrenton, Virginia 22186, February 1971.

Smoking and the Public Interest

THE LOGIC of conservative thought often eludes me, so I wasn't suprised the other day to see columnist James J. Kilpatrick inveigh against Government efforts to warn people about the perils of smoking.

Years of "intensive" educational programs "have had little effect on the smoking hab-it," wrote the af-fable pundit from Virginia, a tobac-co-growing state. Health warnings on cigaret pack-ages and in print-ed advertisements are "ignored," he contends, adding that "most smok-ers die from causes apparently unrelated to smoking.

"There may be lessons in all this, in terms of the power of government to control the personal habits of the people," he argues. "Men have smoked for 500 years, and whole platoons of Surgeons General are not likely to dissuade them now."

Well, *some* have been dissuaded, as Kilpatrick's own data attest: "Per capita consumption in 1963 amounted to 217 packs; last year it was 205 packs." The number of smokers has climbed from 50 million to 52 million since 1964, but public health officials estimate that, without the warnings, there would be 75 million today. At least 10 million have quit the habit.

Hence, there no doubt has been less business for farmers, tobacco companies, advertising agencies, broadcasting networks, cowboy actors, chest surgeons, hospitals, mortuaries, cemeteries, and fire departments.

But Kilpatrick's central concern seems to be over the wisdom and propriety of Uncle Sam's involvement in the smoking-and-health issue. He infers that the Government is engaged in a futile, wasteful, and undemocratic war against smoking, and thereby is infringing on the right to use or sell tobacco products.

Nonsense. The Government is merely insisting that potentially harmful products be labeled as such and that publicly owned broadcasting channels not be used to advertise them.

Why should any fair-minded person object to that? What could be more in the public interest?

One is tempted to wonder how Kilpatrick would react if, say, his car were mortally wounded from straying into an unmarked pothole around Scrabble, Va. It's doubtful that all would remain serene around the Virginia highway department.

Really, governments should go further and ban smoking in all public places. The right to gulp tobacco fumes doesn't include a right to befoul air breathed by others.

If Kilpatrick and his right-wing brethren are the champions of personal liberty they profess to be, they should take up that cause forthwith.

—*MORTON C. PAULSON*

Reprinted with permission from *The National Observer*, copyright Dow Jones & Company, Inc., 1974.

SECTION 3

Sexual Morality

The area of human relations involving sexual practices is one of the areas (abortion is another) where conflicting judgments concerning the rightness or wrongness of specific acts often reflect deep-seated metaphysical differences in addition to or instead of basic moral differences. In any case, the moral considerations in this area are often secondary to problems related to different metaphysical assumptions and/or perceptual frameworks of different individuals.

Some people figuratively, if not literally, "see" the world in terms of a grand dichotomy between mind and matter; mind is identified with the morally good, matter with evil. Accordingly, these people reason that things mental ought to dominate over the material (evil) body. In specific contexts this very general and abstract way of approaching experience manifests itself in adherence to rigid and narrow codes of sexual morality which embody the metaphysical belief that the resistance of bodily desires is the resistance of evil. Other persons who do not share this type of world view often perceive sexual desires as morally neutral or even as good. Such people have little sympathy or use for strict or narrow codes of sexual morality.

A related set of issues which are also more matters of different metaphysics or ways of seeing than they are matters of morality are the questions concerning what is "natural" and what is "unnatural." There are many people who do not necessarily accept the mind(good)/matter(evil) dichotomy as spelled out above, but who do perceive certain kinds of acts as being natural and others as being unnatural, with the associated assumption that natural acts are good and unnatural acts are morally bad. This generates disagreements not only with persons who do not associate natural acts with goodness and unnatural acts with evil, but it also involves serious disagreements, among the persons who accept this assumption, over which acts are in fact natural and which are unnatural.

An examination of the arguments in this section provides evidence of the difficulties to be encountered in trying to reconcile conflicting arguments concerning sexual morality. Persons who hold different positions on this topic often cannot even adequately communicate with one another until they are able to perceive the world in different ways, and they cannot fruitfully argue the moral issues involved until they bridge the wide metaphysical gulf that separates them. This is just one further confirmation of the warning given in the Introduction to the effect that the analysis and evaluation of ethical arguments is a very difficult task which requires much more than formal training in ethical theory alone. The fact that metaphysical beliefs manifest themselves in morally significant ways makes it imperative that we try to understand both our own and other metaphysical systems, as the first step to evaluating them as well as to evaluating specific moral arguments.

EXERCISES

1. Examine the arguments in Section 8 concerning abortion as well as the arguments in this section. To what extent are the arguments against abortion, which are based on the assumption that a soul enters the body at the moment of conception, similar to the arguments concerning sexual morality, which are based on the assumption that bodily desires are evil? Is it possible to consistently accept one of these positions and reject the other?
2. Compare the arguments in this section concerning homosexuals with the arguments in Section 4 about women and racial minorities. In what ways, if at all, are the basic *moral* premises different?
3. Identify which acts or situations in this section appear to be "natural" and which appear to be "unnatural." Try to formulate a general definition of "natural" which is consistent with your classification of these acts and situations. Then apply your definition of "natural" to the cases of euthanasia discussed in Section 9 to determine whether modern medical techniques for prolonging bodily functions are natural or unnatural by your definition.

Learn All About Sex

By Terence Shea
FROM BOSTON

The slides showed masterpieces of erotic art, and dark-shadowed photographs of embracing couples in positions of love-making. But to the church-school boys and girls who previewed the visuals as part of a new curriculum about sex, the material didn't show much more than they already knew.

The students generally felt that the loving couple in Rodin's *The Kiss* might proclaim the French sculptor's artistic genius but chiseled figures can't teach teen-agers much about intercourse. The way to show love-making, they said, is with brightly lighted close-ups of couples making love.

The authors of the course agreed. The slides were replaced with a color filmstrip of three separate couples having intercourse. And the filmstrip became just one more teaching tool in what already was the most comprehensive, explicit, and possibly controversial set of materials ever assembled for use in a classroom.

Cautious Introduction

The course is called "About Your Sexuality." It was formulated by educators here in the national offices of the Unitarian Universalist Association mainly for junior-high-school students in Unitarian churches' weekly religion classes. It is expected to be used also with older teen-agers and with adults. The course is being released this month by Beacon Press, the Unitarians' publishing arm. And it is being provided to Unitarian groups through the most cautious and exacting introduction strategy ever devised for a course of its type.

Voluntary for Students

The prospect of imminent classroom use could stir some concern among Unitarian parents, although no student can take the course if he or his parents object. Church leaders expect little internal or external criticism of their use of the course, but it may not escape allegations that it is psychologically too much too soon for adolescents.

That is a major argument of many who oppose increasingly explicit classroom sex education. Many say that such education should be thorough, but it should be at home, or in the privacy of a school psychologist's office. Dr. James M. Parsons, a Melbourne, Fla., psychiatrist who

is national president of the Scientific Information and Education Council of Physicians, contends that most explicit material "is suggestive, and it produces obsessive thinking about human sexuality when [the students] are least able to repress it."

The curriculum covers topics such as anatomy, masturbation, intercourse, contraception, homosexuality, petting, slang, and deviations. The topics are treated in both printed materials and in visuals such as the filmstrip on love-making and others on anatomy, birth control, conception, childbirth, masturbation, and same-sex behavior. In addition, the course includes recordings of young people describing their first heterosexual intercourse.

No Single Set of Values

The curriculum's makers contend that it dictates no single set of values. It is built on the principle that each situation affects the ethics of a person's actions, says Mr. Hollerorth. He offers the example of what happens in the course when "a student asks, 'Is it okay for junior-high kids to have intercourse?'"

"We tell teachers that you don't say yes and you don't say no. That's not an effort to cop out. You don't say yes because what about the kid who isn't having intercourse? You don't say no, because what about the kid who is—in terms of guilt he might feel?

"Our approach is to provide the kind of setting where the information is available, attitudes can be clarified, implications can be considered, and there is an atmosphere of trust." Ultimately the student is expected to answer his own question responsibly in terms of his own situation.

"A major focus of the curriculum," says Gobin Stair, director of Beacon Press, "is letting the kids in on the fact that there's no one set of values." Essentially, he emphasizes, the course is "a process that a bunch of kids, with adults, go through; we just supply the props."

Beacon's position, says Mr. Stair, is that "this matter of understanding living is a religious question." And although the 166,000-member association of Unitarians is one of the most liberal church groups in the country, Mr. Stair adds, "there's plenty of conservative, tense, emotional reaction" in many places. "But the fact that this course is being used," he adds, "is an illustration of the change that's happening."

The first to see the changes, and to note adult reactions, are the dozens of Unitarian educators around the country who have been introducing the course to teachers and other adults. According

to two teacher trainers in Washington, D. C., there is a faint pattern but no predictability among grown-ups' reactions to the materials.

Cecilia Wood, a teacher at Washington's Sidwell Friends School and a director of religious education at her suburban Maryland Unitarian church, says adults who oppose the course argue that it will "open the floodgates" and that "if they hear about it they're going to try it." Mrs. Wood contends that "children are going to learn anyhow; it's infinitely better that they learn from informed persons."

Enoch Albert, a zoology teacher last year at the University of Maryland who gave workshops with Mrs. Wood in the Washington area, says most adults who voiced doubts about the course were middle-aged parents; most who liked it were young or old. Parents, like their children, "are informed, but they aren't aware of their own attitudes," Mr. Albert says.

Examining the course through a workshop can be "a consciousness-raising experience" for adults, says Mrs. Wood. "One thing that happens," she says, "is surprise at their own rigidity and their preoccupations about what's right." Later on, almost every adult "comes to accept that what he believes is not the only attitude."

☆ ☆ ☆

Primitive Reason

Editor, The National Observer:

How utterly stupid Mr. Hollerroth is!

In answer to the student's question "Is it okay for junior-high kids to have intercourse?" he misses the very primitive reason why it is not okay.

Let me ask one simple question: "Is a junior-high kid capable of paying the cost of an abortion, or is he able to assume the financial responsibility of raising the child he so thoughtlessly begets?"

There is a prime point of morality involved: Somebody else has to take on the task of raising the young bastard, while your eggheads coach the kids from the sideline, "So fornicate, enjoy."

JAMES SENTZ

Ridgewood, N.J.

☆ ☆ ☆

Left, reprinted with permission from *The National Observer*, copyright Dow Jones & Company, Inc., August 23, 1971.

Above, letter to the Editor of *The National Observer* by James Sentz, September 18, 1971.

Sexual Rites—and Wrongs

To The Editors
During the past year I have not read a single article on present-day sex mores in America that does not leave out some vital question germane to the subject under discussion.

This is glaringly evident in the article "Kids, Sex and Doctors" [Nov. 25]. What is left out is *responsibility*. If Leah Newman, 16, is living away from home and supporting herself, then her statement holds good. But if she lives at home, supported by her parents, then she has a responsibility to them and they have a responsibility to her—a responsibility larger than just supplying food, clothing and lodging. There must be some moral guidance and some rules of conduct. She is asking for license, not freedom.

If there is to be any moral integrity in America, we must recognize that every "right" has a corresponding responsibility, and when we demand our rights without accepting our responsibilities, our moral sensibilities are lopsided.

Warren P. Waldo
North Ferrisburg, Vt.

May I ask Leah Newman, the doctors, civil liberties groups, and all who advocate medical services for teen-agers where "sex is concerned, without involving the parents," if they will keep the parents uninvolved when it comes to billing for these services and paying for contraceptives? Will they care for these kids in their homes while the kid is getting over VD, the abortion and/or related trauma?

Shirley Becker
Woodside, N.Y.

Don Mitchell

LETTER FROM A COLD PLACE

Heavy snow and cheerless rhetoric in the mountains of Colorado

PASSING A JOINT among delegates to the White House Conference on Youth, I saw a clean-cut kid crumple a Xeroxed proposal in his hands and ask, "Why don't they *eat* this horseshit?" Uncrumpling the sheet of paper, I read the following resolution offered by Archbishop Philip Hannan of New Orleans:

> The Task Force on Values, Ethics and Culture asserts that the development of the individual is derived largely from the family which is the primary unit of society. The individual and the family draw their strength from the mutual love of father, mother and child (or children). The recognition of the family as the primary unit of society is vitally important to healthy social living. Legal approbation of sexual relationships contrary to the present legal and moral position of the family are harmful to the welfare of the family and society.

This resolution was defeated, overwhelmingly, in favor of one which read in part:

> Every person has the right to fully express his or her individual sexuality. Furthermore, any sexual behavior between consenting, responsible individuals must be recognized and tolerated by society as an acceptable life-style.

A Matter Of Morals

It is sometimes said that you should not try to legislate morality.

If this premise were to be accepted then it should also follow that you should not try to legislate immorality.

Yet this is exactly what Senator Roy M. Goodman of New York City is doing in a bill he has introduced in the legislature.

The bill would repeal a section of the Education law that states any article or medicine for the prevention of conception has to be sold in a registered pharmacy or hospital.

The law further states that such devices can not be advertised or displayed.

Finally, and most significantly, it states that it is a misdemeanor to sell these devices to a minor under the age of 16.

If this bill of Senator Goodman were to be passed and approved it would mean that contraceptive devices could be purchased by a 15-year-old at any candy store and just as easily as candy.

Senator Goodman's intent is to prevent the transmission of veneral disease. This is a technical and practical approach to a great problem. However in solving problems it raises more serious problems.

Whatever may be his contention the open display, the open sale of these devices is an open invitation and encouragement to young people to engage in a way of life that most people would not approve.

That many young people would engage in such practice without protection and therefore subject themselves to disease peril must be admitted but we find it hard to assume the "if-you-can't-beat-'em-join-'em" philosophy that says if this condition is to exist let's make it safe even if it isn't right.

The over-the-counter sale to a 15-year-old is a confession of moral bankruptcy and an invitation to immorality. Would the next step be to sell devices in vending machines in shopping centers?

Isn't there a moral approach, a deeper and more meaningful approach to this problem as well as the technical approach? How many bars does society let down, how many guidelines are abandoned for young people. Isn't there a point where one says this much and no more?

Certainly if this legal bar is let down by Mr. Goodman's proposal there will be still more bars let down. Society seems unable to draw a hard and fast line on ethical problems and there are times when nothing but a hard and fast line is proper.

The spirit of the Goodman legislation is to accept the fact of immorality but try to curb its consequences by making it safe.

It is in the home, with proper upbringing, where the problem should be eliminated before it starts. There are many homes that are not the proper setting but it would be even more regrettable to have over-the-counter invitation to immature youths.

Reprinted from *The Troy Times Record*, May 12, 1973.

Dear Abby

DEAR ABBY: I wrote to you about a year ago, telling you how depressed I was because I was dumped by a boy I thought I loved. I wanted to show him I could be "popular," so I threw away my self-respect and went all the way with three different guys on the first date. None of them ever called me back, and I felt so cheap I wanted to die. Then I wrote to you and you told me I would never get a decent boy friend by going all the way with him. You encouraged me to try to rebuild my self-esteem and to keep my morals high from then on, and it would pay off.

That's exactly what I did, and you were right. I am now going with this really great guy who respects me. We have a lot of fun together, and I am all through worrying and praying and feeling cheap.

If this letter convinces only one girl that premarital sex doesn't pay, it will be worth printing. I am no kid. I'm 22, and I've never been happier in my life. You wished me good luck, Abby, and it finally came my way. Thanks for saving my life.
HAPPY IN HARTFORD

DEAR HAPPY: No thanks due me. I only threw you a rope. You caught it.

Left, courtesy of Abigail Van Buren, syndicated newspaper columnist, "Dear Abby."

DESTRUCTIVE SEX

I would like to set straight those persons who write to PLAYBOY extolling the virtues of premarital sex: It is *wrong*. First, failure to control one's sexual appetites until marriage is a sign of weakness; it can be likened to the junkie's giving in to his craving for a fix. Second, without the lasting commitment of marriage, genuine love is impossible, and without love, sex is harmful and destructive. In short, the only type of sexual relationship that is not ruinous to one's own character and exploitative of one's partner is one that takes place in the context God established when He sanctioned marriage in order to purify sex.

Jeffrey Arvin Nissen
Yuba City, California

Above, letter to "The Playboy Forum," *Playboy Magazine*, December 1968.

And What About Situation Ethics?

We hear so much about population explosion in these days — if there is really such a thing as population explosion. Some reliable authorities doubt it. The proponents of situation ethics now teach that the explosion has to be checked. They too teach that any workable means may be used to check it. The pill does it. Consequently the use of the pill is permissible. But this clearly, is against God's original will and design. He created man, male and female and endowed them with distinct sexual qualities, most evidently to be used in the proper way, in the proper place and for the proper purpose. The proper place or institution as God ordained it is lawful wedlock guaranteeing the care and welfare of the offspring on the part of the responsible parents. Situation ethics would go even further: to control the population explosion even abortion and mercykilling is permissible.

But God says clearly and distinctly: "Thou shalt not kill! "This is an outside norm, eternally established by the Supreme Lawgiver and therefore it must be respected and obeyed. After all God is absolutely and unerringly right. He is the only supreme lawgiver and our conscience must always conform to His laws. Apart from the rhythm method there is only one means of population control, and that is abstinence. But here is the crux. This becomes a matter of self-control, sacrifice and religion. Deeply religious people who really love God above all things will make a sincere effort to comply with God's ruling to the best of their ability, hard as it may be. They may not always succeed in · every respect, but they will try time and again. But since the concept of genuine and sincere religion has generally vanished, the spirit of self-control and sacrifice becomes pretty near impossible. The laws of God become a joke! Situation ethics have been made the supreme law and norm of all judgments in order to suit weak human nature.

Left, from *The Wanderer*, September 10, 1970.

On the television here in Philadelphia, there is a commentator who is as filthy as he can be. In discussing sex education, he said he is all for it, that he has no laws, that he has no standards; that he can be with any woman any time who is willing to be with him. He openly says so on the radio, openly talks about it. Ten years ago a fellow like that would have been — well, I don't know what they would have done with him! This whole realm of action which includes sex education is one of the areas where the Communists are really getting through. The humanists, the materialists, those who have no use for God have no understanding of the moral restraints that God has put in this area, and they do not understand that this evil heart of theirs, out of which come these various things, as Jesus said, is the trouble with them and is the trouble with the world itself. Their heart has to be dealt with.

Above, by Carl McIntire; distributed by 20th Century Reformation Hour, Collingswood, N.J.

THE TRUE MORALITY

It becomes more evident every day that the new morality and the sexual revolution, far from being the selfish pursuit of pleasure, will prove to be of immense benefit to society. The old morality, in which sexual intercourse was permitted only in marriage for the sake of raising a family, served a purpose in an expanding industrial civilization. But now we've reached a danger point. If we are to avoid famines, plagues and wars, the population of the earth must stop growing. If future generations are to enjoy the highest possible quality of life, the population must decline.

The principal function of sexuality must now be to provide intensely pleasurable interpersonal communication. This kind of pleasure should be available to everyone. On the other hand, there is no reason everyone should enter into family raising, any more than everyone should study law. A few people are well suited by temperament and talent to the raising of children, and they should be the ones to do it. They would produce enough children to keep the race going. The rest of us should be having sex merely for fun, while making our contributions to society through our work.

So let's see more respect from pulpit and press for our increasing numbers of single swingers. In an age of excessive population growth, they are among the truly moral people.

J. Kelly
New York, New York

Above, letter to "The Playboy Forum," *Playboy Magazine*, November 1970.

Birth Control Subverts Morality

By THOMAS A. LANE

CBS Radio was reporting the Irish conflict over birth control. The message alleged that Catholics as well as Protestants were practicing artificial contraception in Northern Ireland and that the legal ban on contraceptives in Eire, adamantly supported by the Catholic Church, was a serious obstacle to reunion. If the Church would stop trying to dictate morality. . . .

The program recalled to mind the 1930 Lambeth Conference at which the Anglican Church abandoned its moral opposition to birth control and embraced the use of contraceptives for family planning. People of sensitive conscience then decided that the breach of the natural law would serve higher ends of conjugal harmony and population control.

We can now regard that decision with forty years of hindsight. A person may in good faith select a new course of action; but he should then be sensitive to the consequences of his decision. Has the Anglican Church realized its hopes of greater conjugal harmony and improved family life within the Church?

Any objective observer of Western Civilization must note the sharp deterioration of individual and family morality since 1930. As the religious rhetoric of peace and charity intensifies, the practice of both decays. Within the family, the true state of affairs is measured in the high divorce rate and the religiously disoriented children. Sexual promiscuity, illegitimacy, abortion and the drug culture illustrate the rejection of Christian moral influence.

There are other subversive influences shaping our society. However, I believe that a serious study of these decades would identify the Christian acceptance of birth control as the breach in the citadel of Christian family life. The Lambeth Conference merely accepted what had been a growing practice in the community; but that church sanction, approving what had theretofore been regarded as sinful, legalized the destruction of the Christian family.

It was a mistake to suppose that contraceptives could be used within the marriage contract without promoting their general use. If marriage was merely an arrangement for sexual gratification, men would try to devise better arrangements for that purpose. If parents could frustrate intercourse to prevent conception, why shouldn't their children do so?

In professing to set a new standard for married love, the Anglican Church set a new standard for all love. It invited the sex-is-fun syndrome of recent decades which hides from youth the truth that illicit sex is tragedy.

Illicit sex is tragedy for married people, too. When persons accept faithfully the duties of the married state, they harvest the rewards of nature fulfilled. When they cheat on nature, they build a burden of guilt. The first lie begets others. The sanctity of the marriage bond is undermined.

And when a church professing to teach the will of God to men sanctions what all men and women know to be wrong, it forsakes its true mission. It becomes merely another human judge of expediency, severed from eternity.

I suggest to the Protestants of Northern Ireland that they should re-examine their beliefs about birth control. They can see in the travail of our society the future of their own, unless they turn back. They should return to the pre-Lambeth morality of their church. They should look upon reunion with Eire as an accession of strength in which Protestants and Catholics will work together to preserve the Christian family.

In the world context, these considerations challenge our Anglican brethren to condemn the error of artificial birth control and to restore universal Christian adherence to the natural law. Honesty requires the action. The survival of Western Civilization urges it. This should be a first step of ecumenical reconciliation.

from *The Wanderer*, June 17, 1971.

Contraception: a male responsibility?

To the Editor:

Having recently undergone a vasectomy, I read Mrs. Westoff's article with great interest, but some dismay: after the recent essays on the single lifestyle and the modern family, I had hoped for a more complete and sympathetic treatment of the single person's point of view and reasons for wishing to be sterilized. Therefore, for what it may be worth in indicating the diversity of those reasons, I offer some account of my own thinking.

The two charges usually leveled at singles who wish to be sterilized are that they are doing it for spurious ideological reasons or for the sake of sexual freedom. At 33, I think my stock of youthful idealism is about exhausted, but my resolution not to have children was made in college, when I first realized the seriousness of the population problem. If that insight seems precocious, remember that Malthus had it two centuries ago, and it is one of the foundations of evolutionary theory. But the very enormity of the population crisis makes many of us in biology despair of a solution, and I seriously doubt that my renunciation of children is going to do any real public good: it is, so far as smothering the population bomb is concerned, a gesture. Thus I must agree with the charge that, unless and until greater numbers become sterilized, the idealism that impels a single person to this step is perhaps misplaced.

The charge that singles become sterilized to enjoy sexual license is less fair. Surely we have lived long enough with the idea of birth control and the consequent de-coupling of sexual enjoyment and procreation that we do not need to make such accusations! And in what way is it less acceptable for a single than a married person to enjoy sex without the fear of pregnancy? Sexual freedom is certainly a benefit of sterilization, but not—for me at least—the reason for being sterilized.

Rather, I think my main reason for choosing vasectomy comes from guilty sympathy with the women's movement: I believe contraception to be a male responsibility, because so many of the women I know have had some difficulty with their means of birth control, whether mechanical or hormonal. As a biologist, I find endocrinological manipulations repulsive, and while there may be some risks to me from vasectomy, these seem no higher than those associated with female contraceptive techniques — and there is no compelling argument why I should not be as willing to take such risks as my female partners.

A friend of mine in the women's movement has pointed out that there is a sense in which vasectomy may be the ultimate put down of women. As a bisexual who once regarded himself as exclusively Gay, I am particularly sensitive to this criticism; but, on the contrary, I feel that my relationships with women have improved with the issue of children removed: I can see my one-time exclusivity as a form of voluntary sterilization, a way of coping with my adolescent terror of heterosexuality.

Much is made of the regrets a sterilized person may have if she or he does marry and desires children later on. The happy experience of couples who have (for one reason or another) chosen artificial insemination or adoption ought to offset such regrets. We should none of us be so in love with our own genes, or rather gene-combinations, that we object to these alternatives.

Yet, reproduction is the only form of immortality one can be certain of, however weak a simulacrum of eternity the unlikely persistence of a few linked genes may be. Vasectomy or tubal ligation is thus, in a way, a mild form of suicide; and it is in these terms that I can most appreciate the distress that sterilization causes some people. For this reason I urge a more helpful attitude towards singles who wish to be sterilized. Perhaps because I am lucky enough to live in a university community, I encountered very little resistance to my decision to have a vasectomy, or delay in its implementation. This intelligent cooperation in such a serious personal matter is very important if we believe that voluntary sterilization is right—whether we think it right for public reasons, or for the personal growth of the individual.

JOHN A. W. KIRSCH
Assistant Professor of Biology,
Yale University
New Haven

Letter to the editor of *The New York Times Magazine* by John A. W. Kirsch, Assistant Professor of Biology, Yale University, June 28, 1974.

THE ETHICS OF ADULTERY

In *The Playboy Forum*, a lady from Wichita, Kansas, inquired about PLAYBOY's readers' opinions on mate swapping and asked, "When both partners consent, is adultery immoral?" In the old days, people turned to religious authorities to find out what was moral or immoral. More recently, they have been asking psychiatrists and political theorists. Now, in true democratic fashion, the Wichita housewife wants to poll PLAYBOY's readers. This lady and her husband are already indulging in spouse swapping and are apparently enjoying it, but if the *Forum* published many letters telling her the practice is evil, I wonder, would she stop it?

In my opinion, to ask whether or not a given act, such as mate swapping, is moral is to pose a meaningless question. There are those who still believe that some supernatural monarch has decreed a code of rules by which we must live, but they are on ground only slightly less unsound than those who still reject evolution. Nor can any modern-minded atheist or agnostic prove, philosophically or scientifically, that any set of secular rules or obligations is superior to the individual's own desires. Modern ideologues may tell us we have a duty to humanity, society, reason or revolution till they are blue—or red—in the face, but they are human, like everyone else, and why should one man's code bind another?

People such as your mate-swapping correspondent feel that their personal decisions must be guided by some higher rationale. They need reassurance that there is something more important backing their decisions than their own feelings. But individual feelings are the most important thing there is. Religions, philosophies and ideologies are, in a sense, illusions: They have only such size and power as we assign them.

We must recognize that ethical codes are but convenient (and, too often, inconvenient) fictions. By doing so, we can then make decisions on reasonable, realistic bases, while also giving proper dignity to our genuine feelings. We can end the idolization of abstract principles for which too many people are willing to murder others and be killed themselves ("Better dead than Red" —that sort of thing). To realize that each man is a law unto himself is to arrive at an irreducible basis for libertarian thought—the most valuable and needed viewpoint in avoiding the pitfalls of right- or left-wing totalitarianism.

Therefore, I suggest to the lady from Wichita one rule that eliminates the need for all others: "Think for yourself."

Dion O'Glass
New York, New York

Light from the Eternal City

Pope Paul VI . . .

Lust Of The Flesh Leads Man Away From God

Everyone knows what is meant by "flesh" in moral language. It refers to everything connected with undisciplined sensuality; that is, that dangerous interplay of physical sensibility in conflict or in complicity with spiritual sensibility, animal pleasure, voluptuousness, the body in the grip of passion that draws the soul to itself and lowers it to its own instincts, captures it and blinds it, so that, as St. Paul says, "the unspiritual man does not receive the gifts of the Spirit of God" (1 **Cor.** 2, 14). We do not think there is any need of explanations in this connection. It is so much discussed today, too much, perhaps. It is a rare thing today for the novelist not to pay his sorry tribute, with a few pages at least, to some folly of the senses, or to some Dionysiac rapture, with which the world of literary culture is pervaded, as is that of pleasure-loving dissoluteness, pursued by anguish. Psychoanalytical studies on human instincts, and particularly on neuropathology and sexuality, have given a scientific language to the common empirical experience of erotic passions. They have even been exalted as real new discoveries of man.

SHUN TEMPTATION

And the recommendation follows by itself: we say it to the Father in the usual prayer: "lead us not into temptation"! Let us apply it to ourselves, as if to grant this supreme prayer. We must defend ourselves from the tyrannical temptation of the flesh, if we wish to live the paschal mystery. Inwardly and outwardly; in our hearts, above all, from which come the good and the evil of which we are capable (cfr. Mt. 15, 19; 2 Tim 2, 22); and in our surroundings. Today men are concerned with ecology, that is purification of the physical environment in which man's life takes place. Why should we not be concerned, too, with a moral ecology in which man lives as a man and as a son of God? This is what we recommend to you, with our Apostolic Blessing.

Above, from *The Wanderer*, April 15, 1971.

ANN LANDERS: Cop-Out

Dear Ann Landers:

Your rule-of-thumb advice to people considering divorce is, "Will you be better off with or without him (or her)?" Does this advice hold when children are involved? Or should the question be, "Will the children be better off with or without him (or her)?"

Have you given serious thought to the consequences of divorce on the children? If divorce isn't the biggest "cop-put," what is? Why should the young be taught to run away from, instead of living up to, what may be the greatest emotional challenge of all?

And after the divorce, then what? How should the drop-outs deal with their unresolved problems? Should they look for another "mature" individual with whom to build a life? Is failure easier to deal with than marriage? I'd like some answers.
—Eye Of The Cyclone

Dear Eye:

No two marriages (or divorces) are the same. A marriage can range from empty, unpleasant and boring to destructive, brutal and just plain hell-on-earth. No outsider is qualified to judge the true character of someone else's marriage.

While divorce is undeniably anxiety-producing for many children, their lives might be far more difficult if they continued to live in a home with parents who abused each other verbally and physically and hated each other.

The next letter may be an extreme example, but it's a good one. What a strange coincidence that it arrived in the same batch of mail with yours.

Dear Ann Landers:

I'm writing this letter to say a word to married couples who are staying together "for the sake of the children": Don't.

I am one of several victims of this "act of generosity." My parents' marriage was lousy. My father was a sadistic alcoholic who kissed his children in public and beat the living daylights out of them at home. My mother was among those he pushed around, slapped in the face and beat with his fists.

My brother escaped by dying young. That was my mother's way out, too. She succumbed to the flu. (Had she wanted to live, I'm sure she could have done so.)

My sister and I were kicked out of the house when we were 17. She has suffered since childhood from severe ulcers and is now undergoing psychiatric treatment. I am in treatment also, and I'm making it back, thank God. It's been a very rough road, complete with memory lapses, not being able to recall one single thing that happened the day before.

Keep telling your readers, Ann, if a marriage is bad, especially when there is physical abuse, end it for the sake of the children.
—Been There But Back Now

Dear Back:

Welcome to the life of the living—and thank you for a very moving letter.

Dear Ann Landers:

I don't want an essay on morality. Just a simple yes or no will do.

If a woman finds out her husband is having an affair with a so-called good friend of hers, does she have the right to go out and do the same?
—Sauce for the Goose

Dear Goose:

What do you mean by "right"? Who gave *him* the right? Getting even is a poor motive for doing anything. The answer is no.

© 1975, Field Enterprises, Inc.

ASK ANN LANDERS

'All the woman I could ask for'

DEAR ANN LANDERS: I am madder than a hornet's nest over that letter from Asheville, N.C. He signed himself "The Hedonist."

"Hed's" ridiculous statement that every man either cheats on his wife, or would like to if he was sure he could get away with it, is lunacy. I'm 34, a

successful executive who has had his share of temptations, but I did my bed-hopping b e f o r e marriage. I have no interest in fooling around. The question Don Juan should be asking himself is, "What am I trying to prove?"

My wife is all the woman I could ask for. Since she works overtime to make our home happy, all my extra time and energy belongs to her. Marriage beats romping a r o u n d in a motel room with some dingaling who is trying to escape boredom.

"Hed" should spend a few hours a week with a psychiatrist and get his head together. He'd find it more profitable than his present program.

HAPPY AT HOME

DEAR HAPPY: You sound like a mature male who knows the difference between sex as a contact sport and love. The latter can bring to a relationship a dimension of beauty and strength. The former is a temporary prop for a sagging ego, a waste of time, a snare and a delusion.

Courtesy of Ann Landers, Field Newspaper Syndicate, and *Chicago Sun-Times*.

For Some Professional Men

Love by Appointment

The professional who is probably most sexually active with clients is the college teacher. For one thing, sexual relations seem to occur more easily on campuses. Students are away from home. They are young, energetic, and spilling over with curiosity. And a liaison with a teacher could mean the difference between passing or failing a course, or so some students think.

A young teacher at the University of Michigan puts it this way: "The younger [faculty] men and women don't feel there is a professional imperative to absolutely resist sex with students. Instead there is a tendency to intellectualize it. A college campus is a sophisticated place, and middle-class morality isn't taken seriously there. I don't know how many teachers have had sex with students. I just know I have—and there were no terrible complications. And if I were asked to describe the teacher-student sex situation at Michigan or any other large university, I would just say it happens. It happens but it is not really important enough to mention."

'No Forfeit of Respect'

And a woman teacher at UCLA observes: "When it happens, it's not always crucial to the professional teacher-student relationship. A student doesn't feel about a professor the way a patient feels about, say, a psychiatrist. Teacher-student sex goes on. It is simply a human relationship and there is no forfeit of respect for the teacher or student. There is the danger, though, that some students, especially females, will use sex in a nasty way."

For blackmail?

"Not always blackmail as such. But some students won't hesitate to spread gossip, and gossip isn't going to do any faculty member much good. But that happens only rarely. Of course, what can really hang a teacher is a homosexual encounter that's found out. I think regular sex between teachers and students is becoming more frequent, but it doesn't happen every day."

DEAR ABBY

BY
ABIGAIL VAN BUREN

A friend of mine recently died and left a pretty young widow. The brother of the man who died is married, and he told me himself that he has been doing "double duty" and acting the part of a husband to this widow, if you know what I mean. He says the Bible says it is all right. I can't find anything in my Bible that gives approval to such scandalous goings on. If you can, I wish you would tell me where it is. Thank you.

A FRIEND

DEAR FRIEND: Your friend went back to the Old Testament. In Deuteronomy 25:5. "If a brethren dwell together, and one of them shall die, and have no child, the wife of the dead shall not marry a stranger: her husband's brother shall go unto her and perform the duty of a husband. And the firstborn which she shall beareth shall succeed in the name of his brother which is dead that his name shall not be put out of Israel."

Your friend is using this passage to suit his own purpose. The Deuteronomic Law no longer applies. But the Seventh Commandment does.

DEAR ABBY: It is so difficult to know what is morally right and what is morally wrong these days. What used to be considered wrong 25 years ago is suddenly "right." How is a person supposed to know how to behave?

BIG DILEMMA

DEAR BIG :Let your conscience be your guide. For some strange reason, we now have about 20 million laws trying to enforce the Ten Commandments.

Courtesy of Abigail Van Buren, syndicated newspaper columnist, "Dear Abby."

DEAR ABBY: Your outdated advice to the woman whose husband wanted her to have sex with other men really irked me. I'd have advised her to ask her husband why he wanted to share her. If it was because he didn't love her and wanted to get rid of her, then I fully agree, she shouldn't put up with it. But, did you ever stop to think that maybe the husband enjoyed her so much in bed that he wanted to show others what a great wife he has? Or it's possible that his sexual enjoyment may really be heightened if she has sex with other men?

Please don't call this perverted, or say that this man needs a psychiatrist. He doesn't need one. Read the sex manuals. This is an accepted sex practice and is widely accepted nowadays.

SEE THE LIGHT

DEAR. SEE: I'm sorry I cannot agree with you. No man in our culture who truly loves his wife wants her to have sex with other men. If his own sexual enjoyment is heightened by such a need, it suggests either that he may have unconscious homosexual feelings or that he consciously or unconsciously has a need to degrade his wife.

To His Coy Mistress

Had we but world enough, and time,
This coyness lady were no crime.
We would sit down, and think which way
To walk, and pass our long love's day.
Thou by the Indian Ganges' side
Should'st rubies find: I by the tide
Of Humber would complain. I would
Love you ten years before the Flood:
And you should if you please refuse
Till the conversion of the Jews.
My vegetable love should grow
Vaster than empires, and more slow.
An hundred years should go to praise
Thine eyes, and on thy forehead gaze.
Two hundred to adore each breast:
But thirty thousand to the rest.
An age at least to every part,
And the last age should show your heart.
For lady you deserve this state;
Nor would I love at lower rate.
    But at my back I always hear
Time's winged chariot hurrying near.
And yonder all before us lie
Deserts of vast eternity.
Thy beauty shall no more be found;
Nor, in thy marble vault, shall sound
My echoing song: then worms shall try
That long preserv'd virginity:
And your quaint honor turn to dust;
And into ashes all my lust.
The grave's a fine and private place,
But none I think do there embrace.
    Now therefore, while the youthful hue
Sits on thy skin like morning lew,
And while thy willing soul transpires
At every pore with instant fires,
Now let us sport us while we may;
And now, like am'rous birds of prey,
Rather at once our time devour,
Than languish in his slow-chapt pow'r.
Let us roll all our strength, and all
Our sweetness, up into one ball:
And tear our pleasures with rough strife,
Thorough the iron gates of life.
Thus, though we cannot make our sun
Stand still, yet we will make him run.

Above, a poem by Andrew Marvell (1621-1678).

Right, from "A Religious Pacifist Looks at Abortion" by Gordon C. Zahn. In *Commonweal*, May 28, 1971.

Top right, from *The Manchester Guardian Weekly*.

Why Should Men Pay Alimony?

IN THE LIGHT of the recent discussion on divorce reform, I find it nothing less than amazing that men do not rise up in fury and see to it that the divorce laws (whereby a man is impelled to support a woman after divorce whether or not she is quite able to maintain herself) are radically changed to give them fair and equal treatment with the women.

Why should a man be expected to keep in idleness an able-bodied woman for the rest of her life, because he kept her for x years while married to her? Single women work, millions of married women work, but as soon as a woman is divorced she expects to be a pampered parasite.

The time has come for men to free themselves from this iniquitous bondage. This has been done in the three American states of Colorado, Texas, and Pennsylvania, and it is time these feminine gold diggers were made to support themselves like any normal, self-respecting person.

Unless this wrong is put right, and men become more aware of the present unjust divorce laws, the very institution of marriage will be undermined.

—*P. Lewis,*
The Manchester Guardian Weekly.

Even if one were to accept the characterization of a woman's body as "property" (is it not one of the liberationists' complaints that men and man-made laws have reduced her to that status?), the claim to absolute rights of use and disposal of that property could not be taken seriously. The owner of a badly needed residential building is not, or at least *should not be*, free to evict his tenants to suit a selfish whim or to convert his property to some frivolous or non-essential use. In such a case we would insist upon the traditional distinction which describes property as private in ownership but social in use.

To use another example, the moral evil associated with prostitution does not lie solely, perhaps not even primarily, in the illicit sex relationship but, rather, in the degradation of a person to precisely this status of a "property" available for "use" on a rental or purchase basis. It is a tragic irony that the advocates of true and full personhood for women have chosen to provide ideological justification for attitudes which have interfered with recognition of that personhood in the past.

This is not to say, of course, that a woman does not have prior rights over her own body but only that the exercise of those rights must take into account the rights of others. In monogamous marriage this would preclude a wife's "freedom" to commit adultery (a principle, it should be unnecessary to add, which applies to the husband as well).

George F. Will

'Prostitution Should Be Decriminalized'

World's oldest nuisance, government, should abandon the counterproductive fight against world's oldest profession. Prostitution should be decriminalized.

This is not apt to happen soon, given the instinct of state legislators to recoil in horror from any idea that has only reason on its side. But the reasons for decriminalizing prostitution are impeccably conservative, involving respect for privacy, liberty, the Constitution, the law and the police.

As Justice Louis Brandeis said, the Constitution confers on all citizens "as against the government the right to be let alone—the most comprehensive of rights and the right most valued by civilized men." That right to privacy should not be infringed unless a powerfully compelling state interest is served by doing so.

Because prostitution is private sexual conduct between consenting adults, the state should not proscribe it unless the state can demonstrate that it involves substantial harmful public consequences. But the harmful public consequences associated with prostitution are either unaffected by attempts to proscribe it or are produced by those attempts.

Prostitution is immoral, but it is not a threat to the fabric of society. Disrespect for the law is such a threat, and anti-prostitution laws foster such disrespect. The laws do not work, and they usually involve violations of three provisions of the Constitution.

Anti-prostitution laws invariably violate the right to privacy, a right implicit in First Amendment values and given explicit constitutional rank in a Supreme Court decision a decade ago dealing with private sexual activity.

Anti-prostitution laws, usually in their words and invariably in their applications, violate the equal protection provision of the Constitution by discriminating against women. In five states the laws apply only to women, not to their customers. Even where the laws are cast in sexually neutral language or where "patronizing a prostitute" also is a crime, the pattern of enforcement is discriminatory.

Prostitutes' customers rarely are arrested, and when they are arrested it usually is only to induce them to testify against prostitutes. For example, in 1968 New York City arrested 8,000 prostitutes, but only 112 customers, and only two of the customers were convicted.

Because neither prostitutes nor their customers complain to the police about prostitution, it is not easy for the police to make prostitution arrests. So male police officers frequently pose as customers or female officers pose as prostitutes, in order to lure prostitutes into soliciting or to lure men into propositioning. These police practices should be considered illegal entrapment and violations of the constitutional guarantee of due process.

Such behavior degrades the dignity of the police profession. And it is expensive. In 1971 San Francisco spent $375,000 processing 2,000 prostitution arrests. It costs Seattle about $1 million annually for prostitution arrests and trials.

It is estimated that only 5 per cent of the nation's more than a quarter of a million prostitutes have venereal diseases. (The rate for high school students between the ages of 15 and 19 is estimated to be at least three times that high.) The VD rate is low among prostitutes because they know a lot about the problem. Of course, even a rate of 5 per cent is a public health problem, but as long as prostitutes are liable to criminal sanctions, they will be reluctant to risk seeking regular treatment.

And criminalizing prostitution tends to make criminals out of policemen as well as prostitutes.

Prostitution, banned nearly everywhere, exists nearly everywhere, and it often pays for its existence with graft that corrupts the law enforcement machinery. Seventy per cent of all women in prison today were first arrested for prostitution, and many say they've learned about "real crime" while in prison. Indeed, many turned to "real crime" because prostitution arrest records made it difficult for them to find more respectable employment.

To the extent that solicitation by prostitutes is a public nuisance, it can be regulated by statutes concerning street solicitation for commercial purposes. In any case, prostitutes tend to isolate themselves. They know when and where customers are apt to congregate.

Obviously anti-prostitution laws are not the most important of the many laws that infringe freedom while serving no legitimate state interest. But every repeal of such a law helps instill in our rulers the habit of repeal. If that habit spreads, government will appear less foolish and will be less harmful.

NOW Res. 140—Legislative Office: Passed

Be it resolved that as one of NOW's priorities, the National Board of NOW support the NOW Lobbying Office in Washington, D. C.

(Submitted by Lobbying Skills Workshop)

NOW Res. 141—Prostitution: Passed

Whereas, the existence of prostitution in this society is a reflection that women in the society are considered not to be the equals of men, and are valued, almost without exception, for their sexuality first, and their humanness second, and

Whereas, said society maintains a double standard with regard to the sexual activities of women and men, and, under this standard, women are harshly categorized, to wit, the woman who is loved and cherished is protected from any sexual deviation, but any *kind* of sexual deviation is permissible with a woman who prostitutes herself, and

Whereas, research has shown that a woman becomes a prostitute for several reasons among these being a breakdown in positive reinforcement for her early creative and constructive efforts, an overemphasis on her sexuality as a vehicle for male attraction, and finally her economic distress, which in instances where she has defied the racial or sexual mores of one society is combined with social recrimination and is particularly overt, and

Whereas coercion has been reported, first in the reports of some welfare social workers, encouraging women to supplement welfare checks by prostitution, and secondly, in reports in some cities of women being kidnapped and, through torture and drugs, being made dependent on earnings from the fast life, and

Whereas, the prostitute is often a victim of customer brutality but under prohibitive laws and discriminatory enforcement practices found throughout the United States cannot seek police protection, and

Whereas, a practicing prostitute must ally herself with a pimp in order to achieve status in the sub-culture, but also for protection and to supply legal support when she is arrested, and then surrenders her earnings in exchange for his economic and psychological support, and

Whereas, prostitutes enter into an agreement, contractual in nature, with a consenting adult, to perform a service in private, and

Whereas, while the act of prostituting is almost always illegal in this society consorting with a prostitute and

using coercion to influence a woman to prostitute herself are often also illegal, and

Whereas, statistics in the areas where all acts involved in prostitution (being a prostitute, consorting with a prostitute, or coercing a woman to prostitute herself) show that only the prostitute is arrested and convicted, and that customers are almost never arrested let alone charged or convicted, and

Whereas, a prostitute, having been imprisoned for an act she considers essentially a service, can be exposed to persons who may have committed heinous crimes, with the possible result of this interment being her perpetration of genuine crime, such as theft, against future clients, and

Whereas, enforcement of existing laws serve to make prostitution a crime only in the lower echelon of society (for example, the streetwalker) and at the same time virtually ignores prostitution in the middle and upper classes, and

Whereas, the entrapment of prostitutes requires an exhorbitant outlay of police time, effort and expense and thus contributes to a situation in which public morality is regulated at the expense of the public safety, and

Whereas, policemen who volunteer for such activities as entraping and arresting prostitutes often manifest verbal and physical abuse against these women and may as well suffer, because of these activities, a deterioration in their personal and professional self-images, and

Whereas, in the instances of crimes such as prostitution, which have no complaintant, the police become the complaining party, a practice which lends itself to payoff and other corruption and in turn prompts a broad disrespect for the law, and

Whereas, there is no evidence to indicate that liberalization of such prohibitive laws will encourage women to become prostitutes, and

Whereas, the continued legal prohibition of verbal or physical threat in persuading a woman to prositute herself would permit legal access to women who are coerced to prostitute themselves, either by private individuals or public agencies,

Therefore be it resolved:

1) that NOW condemns first the social and economic structure which limits women's alternatives and thus contributes directly to the decision of many women to seek prostitution in hopes that it will at least provide adequate earnings and remove them from

the mindlessness of low-skill, low-paying jobs, and secondly condemns the legal structure which persecutes women prostitutes while ignoring the participation of men,

2) that said organization opposes continued prohibitive laws regarding prostitution believing them to be punitive, especially where women are concerned, and unenforceable, and furthermore, believing they do not deter women who must become prostitutes but rather that the laws encourage the prostitute to become involved in serious crime,

3) that said organization strongly opposes the licensing of prostitutes, believing that (a) such licensing will result in ongoing persecution of women who will not register because they do not wish publicly to proclaim themselves prostitutes, perhaps in the belief that they will one day seek an alternative life, (b) such licensing would serve to place governmental bodies in the business of making money off the sale of women's sexual services and further place government in the role of regulating public morality, when in fact we believe that an ill-advised role for government and (c) finally, it presents a false promise to clients who believe such licensing protects them from venereal disease, to wit, that prostitutes are regularly examined by a doctor, when in fact such medical checkups cannot provide such protection because of the relative infrequency of the checkups when compared to the numbers of clients seen daily by licensed prostitutes,

4) that said organization supports full prosecution of any acts of coercion by any person, public agency or group to influence women to become prostitutes,

5) that said organization seeks only to remove the inequities against prostitutes who are, on the one hand, brutalized without having legal recourse, and, on the other, are, by their singular arrests, the subjects of flagrantly selective law enforcement, realizing that to repeal the laws prohibiting prostitution is not to make a judgement that prostitution is morally good, but rather that it is instead a judgement about the appropriate use of the criminal justice system,

6) that said organization therefore favors removal of all laws relating to the act of prostitution per se and, as an interim measure, favors the decriminalization of prostitution.

(Submitted by Women and the Law-Prostitution Workshop)

Label wrong all along, says author of change

by DAVID L. AIKEN

WASHINGTON—The psychiatrist who prepared the rationale for the American Psychiatric Association's removal of homosexuality from its list of disorders admits that it shouldn't have been there in the first place.

Dr. Robert L. Spitzer, a member of the APA's Task Force on Nomenclature and a psychiatrist at New York's Columbia University College of Physicians and Surgeons, said he felt homosexuality never met the criteria for defining a condition as a disorder: That it cause continual discomfort and interfere continually with ability to function in society.

Instead, he said, the main reason homosexuality was in the list of disorders was simply that society disapproved of it. This, he said, "is not in my view a scientific basis for having a nomenclature."

The primary reason for the APA's turnabout, he admitted, was persuasion from the gay activist movement. Here is a transcript of the interview:

Persuasive Arguments

ADVOCATE: What were the most salient arguments that the Gays used to convince you personally that homosexuality should be taken out of the nomenclature?

SPITZER: I guess the most salient arguments were that if one thought about it clearly, one could not merely use the criterion that the object choice by itself constituted an illness. They forced me to rethink what are the grounds for a condition being considered a psychiatric disorder.

On reflecting on that, it seemed to me that, with the exception of homosexuality, all of the conditions in the nomenclature did meet one of two criteria: Either they were regularly associated with subjective distress—the person was pained in some way—or they regularly led to generalized impairment in functioning—difficulty working, difficulty with friends.

Homosexuality just did not regularly lead to either of those conditions. So one might feel that it was not optimal sexual development, as many psychiatrists, I think, will continue to feel. But it just does not meet the criteria for being considered a psychiatric disorder.

ADVOCATE: Does this decision to change signify that times have changed and the APA is changing with them, or were you wrong all along?

SPITZER: I would have to say we were wrong. Since this is not getting wide circulation, I can say that. Of course, in some sense a mental disorder is whatever the profession says it is, but I think one can have certain criteria which make more sense than other criteria. The old criterion really was, anything that society very much disapproved of was grounds for being in the nomenclature. Society continues to disapprove of homosexual behavior, although certainly not to the extent it did, but that is not in my view a scientific basis for having a nomenclature. So I would have to say, yes, it never should have been there, by itself.

ADVOCATE: Will the APA's decision help change the attitudes of society toward homosexuality?

SPITZER: I think so, and I guess you people have been telling us all along that it will . . . . Of course, psychiatry doesn't have the same currency that it did 10 or 20 years ago. I don't know how much people even care what psychiatrists have to say, but to the extent that they still do, it will have some effect. My impression is that people are not that interested in what psychiatrists have to say anymore.

ADVOCATE: Do you now agree with the slogan, 'Gay is Good'?

SPITZER: No. I haven't joined the homosexual activists movement. If that means that homosexuals should not hate themselves for being homosexuals, I would say, 'Fine, no one should hate themselves for being what they are.' To the extent that psychiatry has in the past made homosexuals hate themselves—which I think it has—to the extent that we're stopping that, I'm very delighted.

Gay Rights

At least ten American cities have now adopted one or another measure designed to assure the so-called civil rights of homosexuals and other deviants, and such legislation is now under consideration in New York City.

In its key passages, the New York bill contains the following language: "A city agency is hereby created with power to eliminate and prevent discrimination in employment, in places of public accommodation, resort or amusement, in housing accommodations, and in commercial space, because of race, creed, color, national origin, sexual orientation, or physical handicap, and take other action against discrimination because of race, creed, color, sexual orientation, or national origin, as herein provided." Such other action, for example, includes enlisting "the cooperation of the various racial and ethnic groups, community organizations, labor organizations, fraternal and benevolent organizations, and other groups, including those devoted to the eradication of prejudice based on a person's sexual orientation." The bill, it is important to note, describes discrimination based on a person's "sexual orientation" as resulting from "prejudice, intolerance, [or] bigotry."

The language of this bill, reflecting the avowed goals of various "gay liberation" organizations, would make homosexuality merely another lifestyle in the eyes of the law, and would both break down social resistance to it and stigmatize such resistance as "bigotry."

A similar measure, it is interesting to note, was recently put to the test of a referendum in Boulder, Colorado, and the voters rejected it by an overwhelming majority. If that expression of ordinary human feeling constituted prejudice, then it was prejudice in the Burkean sense of the word: the intuition of norms and assumptions that lie at the roots of Western civilization.

Though to some it may seem quaint to appeal to Scripture for the illumination of an ethical problem, nevertheless it will not be denied that Scripture is profoundly involved with the assumptions of the West. Scriptural insights can hardly be rejected lightly, within the spirit of the West. And it will be noted that both the Old and the New Testaments begin with *families*. When God perceived Adam's loneliness in the Garden, He did not choose Eve over a catamite by the toss of a coin. It will also be noted that both the original family in the Garden and the Holy Family of the Gospels are direct divine creations. The repetition of that pattern at the commencement of key founding documents of the West can hardly be supposed accidental.

It suggests that the family "was there from the beginning," at least so far as Western civilization is concerned; that the family is fundamental to the civilization of the West.

The religious foundations, the laws, the customs, and the ordinary human feeling of the West all testify to, support, and even celebrate that ethical fact. If custom and prejudice refuse to establish homosexuality and other deviations as the full equals of the family, then they reflect those root civilizational assumptions.

In actuality, discreet homosexuals probably suffer a minimum of discrimination. These homosexual "rights" bills are, accordingly, really a form of ideological assault, rather than humanitarian measures. They strike, and they mean to strike, at fundamental ethical assumptions. But that, you may have noticed, is true more often than not of liberal measures.

Above, reprinted with permission from *National Review* (June 7, 1974), 150 East 35th Street, New York, N.Y. 10016.
Below, courtesy of National Organization for Women.

NOW Res. 144—NOW Literature—Sexuality and Lesbianism: Passed

Whereas, women have the basic right to develop to the maximum their full human sexual potential, and

Whereas, diversity is richly human and all women must be able to freely define and to express their own sexuality and to choose their own life style, and

Whereas, NOW's public relations and communications have omitted references to the unified efforts of women of traditional and diverse sexual experience, and

Whereas, Lesbians have formed a caucus in NOW to communicate openly, without fear and hostility, and

Whereas, the threat traditionally felt from Lesbianism must no longer be a barrier to open communication between all people, and

Whereas, we recognize that women are all oppressed by one common oppression, and therefore, surely we must not oppress one another for any reason;

Therefore be it resolved that a statement adopting the sense of this resolution be included in all appropriate NOW publications and policy statements; and,

Be it further resolved that NOW actively introduce and support civil rights legislation designed to end discrimination based on sexual orientation and to introduce with legislation to end discrimination based on sex the phrase "sexual orientation" in areas such as, but not limited to, housing, unemployment, credit, finance, child custody and public accomodations. (Submitted by Sexuality and Lesbianism Workshop)

MINISKIRTS

A sermon by
Carl McIntire

It is very significant, I think, that, attending the coming of the miniskirt, those who participated in it, those who promoted it throughout the world, there have appeared most of the other things that have helped degrade and pull down our society.

There is such a thing as modesty. There is such a thing as decency. The person who has become a Christian has a different attitude toward the human body from that of the ungodly person. The person who has become a Christian recognizes that there are certain things in the human body that are not merely degrading, but that lead to all manner of tragedy and disaster and sin.

In our Confession of Faith we are instructed:

"Q. 139. What are the sins forbidden in the seventh commandment?

"A. The sins forbidden in the seventh commandment, besides the neglect of the duties required, are adultery, fornication, rape, incest, sodomy, and all unnatural lusts; all unclean imaginations, thoughts, purposes, and affections; all corrupt or filthy communications, or listening thereunto; wanton looks; impudent or light behaviour; immodest apparel; . . . lascivious songs, books, pictures, dancings, stage plays; and all other provocations to, or acts of uncleanness either in ourselves or others." That is part of the doctrinal standards of our church. See how far away we have gotten from these standards!

Why Speak About Modesty?

Why do we speak of the matter of being immodest? Why do we speak of the matter of women conducting themselves in a decent manner? The answer, so far as the Bible is concerned, is because of the heart of man. We are going to turn now to several passages in the Bible.

First, 1 Peter 1:13-15: ". . . gird up the loins of your mind, be sober, and hope to the end for the grace that is to be brought unto you at the revelation of Jesus Christ; as obedient children, not fashioning yourselves according to the former lusts in your ignorance; but as he which hath called you is holy, so be ye holy in all manner of conversation."

Now look at 1 Peter 4:3 and 4: "For the time past of our life may suffice us to have wrought the will of the Gentiles, when we walked in lasciviousness, lusts, excess of wine, revellings, banquetings, and abominable idolatries: wherein they think it strange that ye run not with them to the same excess of riot, speaking evil of you."

I think the problem with the miniskirt is that our young people are not able to resist the pressures of conformity in the world today. They are not able to resist the pressures that they find about them in their schools and the world about them. They cannot resist these pressures, and consequently they want to put on these very short dresses. They are getting them shorter and shorter.

Some time ago, when I was talking with a man who was interested in coming to Shelton College who was then teaching in a secular school, he said to me, "Dr. McIntire I just cannot take it any more." I said, "What is the trouble?" He said: "I am a decent man, I have a lovely wife and a fine family. But I go to classes where I teach and the kids come in dressed in miniskirts. It is disgraceful. There are girls who sit in the front row, and when they sit down there is not anything covered. And that is not all. These girls will not only sit in their chairs with the boys around them, but they will throw their legs apart. It is a total disgrace, and I cannot take it. I have got to get out."

Another man I know, a teacher, talked with me some time ago. He has been teaching in a secular institution. He said: "Dr. McIntire, since this miniskirt business has come in, the familiarity and the fondling which take place in the corridors and in the schools you cannot possibly believe. These girls with short skirts are just an invitation to the hands of the boys." He continued: "Not only that, a lovely young girl who came from a Christian background, Presbyterian, one day came to me and said, 'I think maybe you have some good ideas. I would like to talk to you.' I said, 'All right, I will talk to you.' And this was her story — she put on a miniskirt and then became involved in all sorts of things so far as the boys were concerned. Then she listened to all the civil rights talk about equality and she got the idea that, in order to show that she did not believe in any form of discrimination, and that there was absolute equality between the races, she, with other girls, finally made it a practice to go to bed with one of the Negro students — and this was a regular practice which she and other girls carried on."

It was a miniskirt that brought about this! The damage and the harm that is now being done to young Christian girls who adopt this form of dress is absolutely incalculable. This is practiced on campuses where hippies and yippies stir up riots; that is exactly what you have.

How Long?

Young ladies, your dresses ought to be long enough so that the contours of your body and the areas of your body that involve lust and the stimulation of sex will not in any way contribute to such emotions. I say that to you frankly; I say it to you on the authority of the Word of God. It is a terrible disgrace when a woman who is married to one man goes out and entices other men. And it is a terrible disgrace when a young girl in the high school goes to dances, get worked up, goes out with the boys and loses her purity, and her whole set of moral standards are pulled down. Young lady, do not think this is not involving you! It does involve you. It involves everything about you. And, beloved, I do not want it in this church. You young people ought to face the conscience of this church. You ought to be concerned about it. Someone asked me this morning, after I announced I was going to preach this sermon, "What are you going to say about the miniskirt?" I replied, "I am going to say they ought to be lengthened." And they ought to be let down far enough so that there is no possibility of any problems arising. As a matter of fact, every decent woman ought to recoil when some other woman displays herself. And furthermore, any decent man really does not have any respect for the kind of woman who thus displays herself. Am I right? Of course, I am. But what do the ungodly call such principles? Oh, they call it puritanism.

By Carl McIntire; distributed by 20th Century Reformation Hour, Collingswood, N.J.

WORDS WE LIVED BY...

The following is excerpted from the *Ladies' Guide,* a popular reference book of the 1890s.

EFFECTS OF SOLITARY VICE IN GIRLS

The victim of this evil habit is certain to suffer sooner or later the penalty which nature invariably inflicts upon those who transgress her laws. Every law of nature is enforced by an inexorable penalty. This is emphatically true respecting the laws which relate to the sexual organs.

Wide observation has convinced us that a great many of the backaches, side-aches, and other aches and pains of which girls complain, are attributable to this injurious habit. Much of the nervousness, hysteria, neuralgia, and general worthlessness of girls originates in this cause alone.

The period of puberty is one at which thousands of girls break down in health. The constitution, already weakened by a debilitating, debasing vice, is not prepared for the strain, and the poor victim drops into a premature grave.

SIGNS OF SELF-ABUSE IN GIRLS

Mothers should always be on the alert to detect the first evidences of this vice in their daughters, since later nothing but almighty power seems competent to loosen its grasp. The only positive evidence is detection of the child in the act. A suspected child should be watched under all circumstances with unceasing vigilance.

[But] aside from positive evidence, there are other signs which may lead to the discovery of positive evidence.

• *A marked change in disposition.* When a girl who has been truthful, happy, obliging, gentle, and confiding, becomes peevish, irritable, morose, and disobedient, she is under the influence of some foul blight.

• *Loss of memory and loss of the love for study.* The nervous forces are weakened, giving place to mental weakness and inactivity.

• *Unnatural boldness in a little girl.* If she has previously been reserved, this is just ground for the suspicion of secret vice.

• *A forward or loose manner in company with little boys.* Girls addicted to this habit are guilty of the most wanton conduct.

• *Languor and lassitude.* In a girl who has possessed a marked de-

LADIES' GUIDE

— IN —

HEALTH
AND DISEASE.

Girthood, Maidenhood, Wifehood, Motherhood.

By J. H. KELLOGG, M. D.

gree of activity and energy, this should give rise to earnest solicitude on the part of the mother for the physical and moral condition of her child.

• *An unnatural appetite.* Sometimes children will show an excessive fondness for mustard, pepper, vinegar, and spices. Little girls who are very fond of cloves are likely to be depraved in other respects.

• *The presence of leukorrhoea.* Self-abuse occasions a frequently recurring congestion of the parts, together with the mechanical irritation accompanying the habit.

• *Ulceration about the roots of the nails.* This especially affects one or both of the first two fingers of the hand, the irritation of the fingers being occasioned by the acrid vaginal discharge.

• *Biting the fingernails.* The irritation of the fingers, which gives rise to the habit of biting nails, grows out of the irritable condition of the nails mentioned above.

• *The expression of the eyes.* The dull, lusterless eye, surrounded by a dark ring, tells the tale of sin.

• *Palpitations of the heart, hysteria, nervousness, St. Vitus's dance, epilepsy, and incontinence of urine, giving rise to wetting the bed.*

HOW TO CURE VICIOUS HABITS

The habit of self-pollution is one which when thoroughly established, is by no means easily broken. The victim of this most terrible vice is held in the most abject slavery, the iron fetters of habit daily closing the prisoner more and more tightly in their grasp. The effect is to weaken the moral sense perhaps more rapidly than any other vice, until there is little left in the child's character to which an appeal can be made.

The mother should first carefully set before the child the exceeding sinfulness of the habit, its loathsomeness and vileness, and the horrible consequences which follow in its wake. But in most cases, the evil is not so easily mastered. The little girl should be kept under constant observation every moment of her waking hours. Care should be taken that the child does not feign sleep for the purpose of gaining an opportunity to avoid observation.

It is much more difficult to cure this soul-destroying vice in girls than in boys. They are seldom as ready to confess their guilt as are boys, and then are less easily influenced by a portrayal of its terrible consequences. Sleepless vigilance must be coupled with the most persevering patience.

In obstinate cases, severe means must be adopted. We were once obliged after every other measure had failed, to perform a surgical operation [clitoridectomy] before we were able to break the habit in the case of a girl of eight or ten years who had become addicted to the vice to a most extraordinary degree.

From *Ms.* Magazine, August 1974.

SECTION 4

Discrimination

All of the arguments in this section are related in a significant way to the arguments in the sections concerning abortion, euthanasia, and animals, although they are somewhat different insofar as they generally do not directly deal with matters of life and death. The common thread that runs through all of these arguments is the concern with defining what is "truly human" and/or with ranking the relative worth of various living beings however they are categorized in terms of race, sex, species, eye color, and so on. The primary concern in the arguments in this section is with questions related more to the quality of life rather than with the right to life, but there is no sharp dividing line between the two areas; when an individual's quality of life (with regard to food, housing, etc.) drops below a certain level it almost always results in death (by starvation, exposure, etc.). And some people would argue that even if life can be biologically sustained at certain minimal levels, one would be better off dead than alive under such conditions.

Although the selections in this section deal primarily with issues of discrimination by sex and race in the United States today and one hundred years ago, the basic moral issues which they address are not really related to race or gender per se. Problems similar to those discussed in this section appear in many contexts, such as the Catholic-Protestant situation in Northern Ireland, where the differences are not racial at all. (It is of course possible to even raise the question of how to define the concept of race, a question which not even scientists have answered in a totally satisfactory way.) The problems are not really ones of minority groups either, since women make up about 51 percent of the population in the United States and blacks comprise an overwhelming majority of the population in South Africa.

It is important to recognize that one of the basic issues in all discussions similar to those in this section is that of *discrimination*, a term which must be taken in its literal sense. Discriminating requires identifying clear and precise differences among groups or individuals. If one accepts the basic rule of reason that we should treat similar cases similarly, then we must treat all human beings the same way, unless we can specify some morally relevant and significant difference between two or more individuals. The difficulties of doing this are clearly brought out by the examples in this section from nineteenth century sources; the "facts" presented in these arguments concerning fundamental differences between men and women are almost humorous for the present-day reader. And even if some correlation could be established between skin color or sex and intelligence, it would still be necessary to demonstrate that a moral justification can be provided for determining an individual's political and economic rights on the basis of intelligence rather than eye color, hat size, or the number of letters in one's name. In considering such questions we must also keep in mind the fact that criteria of discrimination work both ways, and that they can be used for discriminating *against* a specified group as well as in favor of that group.

EXERCISES

1. Compare the arguments from the nineteenth century sources in this section with the contemporary selections, and with your own beliefs concerning these topics. If you find any significant differences, try to determine whether they reflect a change in basic moral principles during the last century or result from other kinds of changes.
2. What significant differences, if any, can you identify in the arguments concerning women's rights and those involving racial considerations?
3. In what way(s) are the arguments in this section relevant to the question of international relations raised in Section 13?

"You have blue eyes. You are inferior."

In Riceville, Iowa, a teacher named Jane Elliott taught her all-white class the meaning of an ugly word.

The blue-eyed Mrs. Elliott told her third graders that brown-eyed people are superior.

The blue eyes had to sit in the back of the class. They drank from paper cups, not the fountain. They were refused second helpings at lunch. And they received five minutes less recess.

Soon, the blue eyes were acting like inferior people. They did their lessons poorly. And the brown-eyed children behaved as though they were really superior.

The next Monday, Mrs. Elliott reversed the roles. And suddenly, the brown-eyed children were behaving like inferior pupils.

Mrs. Elliott's pupils know the meaning of discrimination and prejudice. They have experienced it.

Every American child should have a gifted teacher like Jane Elliott. For education to match the challenge of our times calls for more than money. It calls for the imagination of our brightest people.

Yet, a Mrs. Elliott is the exception, not the rule. And will be, until we again give priority to the education of our children.

Our most precious resource is not the plants that dot our land, the cities that house our people, the fields that grow our crops, or the wealth that pays for bittersweet affluence.

Our most precious resource is the child who becomes the man or woman who will inherit this nation.

We cannot fail to give our first priority to the development of that resource.

Unless we are content to become an inferior nation.

TOPICS OF THE TIME.

THREE PIECES OF THE WOMAN QUESTION.
FIRST PIECE.

A SURVEY of the States of the Union, and of the Union under the general government, will show to any candid observer that the legislation of the country, in all its departments, is above, rather than below, the average moral sense of the nation. The fact is seen in the inadequate execution of the laws. There are many statutes relating to public morals and civil policy which appear to be the offspring of the highest and purest principles, that stand as dead letters in State and national law, simply because the average moral sense of the people does not demand and enforce their execution. They are enacted through the influence or by the power of men of exceptional virtue, who find, to their sorrow, that while it is easy to make good laws, it is difficult, and often impossible, to execute them. So far as we know, it has never occurred to them to call for the assistance of women in the execution of these laws, nor has it occurred to women to offer their assistance to them for this end. One or two questions, suggested by the discussions of the time, naturally grow out of this statement.

First:—Is it of any practical advantage to have better laws, until the average morality of the people is sufficient to execute those which we have?

Second:—Is it right that women should have an equal or a determining voice in the enactment of laws which they do not propose to execute, which they do not propose to assist in executing, which they could not execute if they would, and which they expect men to execute for them?

Third:—Supposing that women would give us better laws than we have (which is not evident), what would be the practical advantage to them or to us, so long as they must rely upon us to execute them—upon us, who find it impossible to enforce our own laws, some of the best of which are the outgrowth of the pure influence of women in home and social life?

SECOND PIECE.

In national and international life there are policies of action and attitude to be adopted and maintained. These policies sometimes cost a civil war for their establishment or defense, and, not unfrequently, a war with related nations. It so happens, in the nature of the case, that no single nation has it in its power to abolish war. The only way for a nation to live, when attacked by foes within or without, is to fight; and, in the present condition of the world, a national policy which has not behind it the power of physical defense is as weak and contemptible a thing as the world holds. Out of this statement, which we presume no one will dispute, there arise two questions.

First:—Would a lack of all personal risk and responsibility, on the part of those delegated to establish and pronounce the policy of a nation, tend to prudent counsels and careful decisions?

Second:—Is it right—is it kind and courteous to men —for women to demand an equal or a determining voice in the establishment of a national policy which they do not propose to defend, which they do not propose to assist in defending, which they could not defend if they would, and which they expect men to defend for them?

THIRD PIECE.

Mr. Gleason, the Tax Commissioner of Massachusetts, reported to the Legislature of that State in May, that a tax of nearly two million dollars is paid annually by the women of the State on property amounting, at a low valuation, to one hundred and thirty-two million dollars. The fact is an interesting and gratifying one, in every point of view. Naturally it is seized upon by the advocates of woman-suffrage, and brought prominently forward to assist in establishing woman's claim to the ballot. The old cry of "no taxation without representation" is renewed, however much or little of essential justice may be involved in the phrase. Well, if women are, or ever have been, taxed as women (which they are not, and never have been); if they produced this wealth, or won it by legitimate trade (which they did not); if the men who produced it received their right to the ballot by or through it; if nine-tenths of the wealth of the State were not in the hands of business men whose pursuits have specially fitted them to be the guardians of the wealth of the State; if the counsels of these tax-paying women could add wisdom to the wisdom of these men; if the men who produced this wealth, and bestowed it upon these women, did it with distrust of the laws enacted by men for its protection, and with the desire for the social and political revolution which woman-suffrage would produce, in order that it might be better protected; if there were any complaint of inadequate protection to this property on account of its being in the hands of women —if all or any one of these suppositions were based in truth—then some sort of a plea could be set up on Mr. Gleason's exhibit by those who claim the ballot for woman. As the facts are, we confess our inability to find in it any comfort or support for those who seek for the revolution under consideration. On the contrary, we find that the ballot as it stands to-day, with its privileges, responsibilities, and limitations, secures to woman complete protection in the enjoyment of revenues which are proved to be immense, all drawn from land and sea by the hands of men whose largess testifies alike of their love and their munificence.

WOMEN IN THE COLLEGES.

WE are not among those who fancy that there are any remarkable social dangers connected with bringing the sexes together during the processes of their education. The question of admitting women to colleges hitherto devoted to young men is now up, and at Amherst has been, and still is, under serious consideration. It may be said that if it is really desirable that any considerable number of women should receive the same education that the young men of Amherst College receive, they should have the opportunity to do so, at Amherst and elsewhere. It may be said, too, that this question of the education of women has only an indirect relation to the question of woman-suffrage, and should never be confounded with it. "The Woman Question" proper has no legitimate connection with the question of admitting women to the colleges where young men are educated. If the studies and the modes of study of the college are not to be modified in consequence of the admission of women, the men—teachers and students—need to make no objection. The society of women will do them good rather than harm. It is certainly one of the disadvantages of college and female boarding-school life that it is sexually isolated. There is no question that the daily association of the sexes when young, under judicious supervision and regulation, is much healthier than their separation. It is better that the sexes see each other daily than to dream of each other; and either the one or the other they always do. So, in our judgment, the question is not one mainly of social health and purity. If it is, then it is settled, and calls for no further discussion. It is the universal testimony of teachers, so far as we have learned, that morally the sexes do well together in school—do better, indeed, than when separated. The association of men and women in a school or college is just as safe and healthful as their association in all ordinary life. Men and women are never shut away from each other for long periods of time without damage and disaster. Imagination is unduly excited, feeling becomes morbid, and manners are degraded by such separations; and the earlier they can be dispensed with the better.

Can they be dispensed with altogether? We think not. We have never yet felt called upon to part with our old opinion that a man is not a woman, and that a woman is not a man; that, as a consequence, their spheres of labor and office differ, and that their educational training should have reference as well to their peculiarities of constitution as to the spheres of life they are to occupy. Now if Amherst College, or any other college, is adapted just as well to the training of young women as of young men, it is well adapted to the training of neither. If at Vassar and Holyoke women do not have a better chance than at Amherst and Harvard, Vassar and Holyoke are grossly at fault, and Amherst and Harvard are anything but what they

pretend to be—first-class institutions for the training of young men, to lead the lives and do the work of men. If any of these young men's colleges are particularly desirable institutions for the education of women, they need reforming, unless it is proposed to change them into female seminaries.

The claiming of places for women in young men's colleges as a right, and the denunciation of their exclusion as a wrong to woman, are the special functions of fanatics and fools. There are no rights and wrongs in the matter. It is entirely a matter of policy with regard to that which is best, on the whole, for both young men and young women. Granted that morally they would do good to each other in the college, as they undoubtedly do in the primary and preparatory schools; granted that they would purify each other socially, and stimulate each other intellectually; granted that such association would soften and simplify the manners of all concerned; the facts still remain, that men are not women, that women are not men, and that for their differing spheres of life and labor they need a widely different training. It certainly is not an object for society to make women more like men than they are, or in any way to divert them from a full and fine development of their womanhood.

It ought to be said, on behalf of the women of America, that they have not, in any considerable or influential numbers, demanded admission to the colleges which have been specially designed for the training of young men. The demand has been made by theorists and dreamers, among the men mostly. The truth is that there is no call for these changes of policy which deserves attention. The schools provided for the education of women are growing better and better every year. Colleges for women are springing up all over the country, and Vassar is unquestionably a better place for young women—all sheltered by the single roof of the institution—than Amherst or Harvard or Yale or Union can be, adapted as they all are to the wants of young men, as well as to their lack of wants. There are no wise fathers and mothers who would not prefer Vassar or Holyoke to Amherst as a training-place for their daughters. They can reach any grade of learning and culture in these institutions which they desire, with special adaptations of institutional appointment and machinery to their wants as women, and special choice and arrangement of their studies to the womanly sphere of life they are to occupy. The managers of Amherst and the other colleges will do what they think best in regard to the proposed change, but we believe they will have the support of the best men and women in every part of the country if they decidedly and persistently refuse to make it.

Left and right pages, from *Scribner's Monthly*, 1871.

The only question remaining, therefore, and the only inquiry here proposed, is this: What is the interest, honor, and duty of women, in regard to assuming an identical position with men? The question is evidently a question for women. It is certainly time for women to take it up seriously, consider it thoroughly, and express themselves upon it authentically. There are persons who assume to deliver the opinion and demand of the female sex. Women, it is true, reject for themselves, and justly, the common rule that silence gives consent. It is their right not to be forced to speak. Still, the determined effort to personate them in most important relations, by individuals whose sex is suspected to be rather a disguise, requires the principals compromised by the proceedings to scrutinize and dispose of them in a way of unmistakable authority. They begin to recognize this necessity. A very few have led forward in behalf of their sex, and if in some way the expense of canvassing and organizing the silent sentiment of women were but provided for, very instructive and indeed convincing developments might be realized. Perhaps this will come of itself soon enough, and in a way of its own. Discussion, meanwhile, is yet needed, to give consciousness, consistency, and decision to the sentiments of right-minded women. It is superfluous to add that we address ourselves to women in what we have to advance on this subject. Everything that is said upon the subject is necessarily addressed to women, mediately or immediately, and from them must get its answer in the end.

The right to vote, then, need detain us no longer The question is on the right not to vote. Allowing the vote to stand for all the various masculine functions which women are invited to assume, this title is broad enough to cover the whole debate. Have women such negative right, and is it for their interest, honor, and usefulness to waive it, or to insist upon it?

There is certainly no such right for men. Men must vote, as soldiers must fight. Popular suffrage is an arsenal thrown open to the public enemy. It compels good citizens to arm likewise, in defense. The worst of it is that the modern repeating arms are for the public enemy exclusively. So far, women on both sides are non-combatants. Throw open the arsenal to them also, and you at once put another hostile army in the field as strong as the first (for every bad man has somewhere a bad woman for his mate), and every virtuous woman then must fight by the side of every loyal man. Have they not a right to decline this necessity while they may? Women, good and bad, now stand paired off. Their common abstinence does not affect the vote either way. Shall the zeal or ambition of a minority be allowed to break this truce, and plunge the whole sex, against their will, into a conflict from which none can be exempt and which never will end?

Is it best for women, as a body, to accept and assume an identical position with men, in each or any of the three great spheres of life, social, civil, and political? The social sphere we shall understand to include all relations between human beings which are not established by law. Conventional agreement, or public opinion, is the law of this sphere. Here women are nearly omnipotent. Whatever conventional rules or prejudices restrain them are their own. Men themselves learn all their views of feminine propriety ultimately from women. The sex will therefore approach this part of the question in a peculiarly independent, or say rather sovereign, attitude. Whatever they agree to will be accomplished in the act of agreement. And the power and efficacy of social action immeasurably transcends that of all civil and political processes combined. The latter absolutely proceed from the former. The man is not more effectively shaped in the womb and in the home than the parts and processes of the public organism are shaped in the vital stir of private society or personal intercourse. How far will the position of women be improved by exchanging it for that of men, or assimilating it to that of men, in society?

The material peculiarities which distinguish the social position of men from that of women resolve themselves into these two: (1) the burden of supporting themselves and families; and (2) the burden of carrying on the public, professional, and material business of the world. For the bulk of this work men alone generally have by nature the proper faculties, such at least as physical strength, boldness, and enterprise. But for all of it, the law of self-dependence peculiar to them as men is a necessary condition, as enforcing the life-long application which is in most cases indispensable to success.

In exceptional cases, women voluntarily embrace this self-dependence for life, in preference to such proposals of protection as happen to them. Nearly all women, however, have preferred husbands and children, such as they could get, to all other objects. From this thorough experiment, elucidated by what we have been able to learn of their nature, we (men) feel warranted in the comfortable, not to say flattering, expectation that women will generally continue to give us the preference, and to yield their indispensable good-will to the perpetuation of our species, to the end of time. Could we even waive the solaces of home and children and woman's love, yet the conception of a planet depopulated and left to wiser animals, that the mother of men might dedicate herself to the production of laws, books, arts, and works of art, for which, alas, their dumb inheritors would have no use, is a conception too repugnant to all rational ends of creation and providence to be possible. We mention this, and with the utmost seriousness, because it is too often forgotten that the balance between births and deaths is getting to be a delicate one in civilized countries; that in many places it is already on the side of death; and that as a small change in the inclination of the earth's axis would convert our blooming lands into lifeless wastes of perpetual ice and snow, so a little general shifting of the burdens of active life upon our women would depress procreative action sufficiently to extinguish our own branch of the race, at least, within a moderate period of time. We conclude, therefore, that self-dependence will not become the rule for women until it shall be the pleasure of Providence to exterminate us, and that women will be the least willing executioners of such a decree. Until then, the imperative condition of success in all arts, professions, and businesses —that is, self-dependence, forcing an unalterable and undivided application for life—will be exceptional among women, as now. The cause which makes many employments masculine in practice, which are not distinctively such in character, is this necessity of a more than temporary prosecution of them, in order to succeed in competition with those who can and must give their lives to them. Exceptional women are often found to break the ice of precedent and custom in such matters, and to make for themselves a place among men by a man-like choice and endeavor. But nothing less than a general compulsion to self-support, which if inflicted upon women would be equivalent to the extinction of civilized man, can ever naturalize in the sex any of the learned professions or of the more difficult arts, handicrafts and commercial employments, to such extent that a female *expert* will be less than a prominent exception. Such a general compulsion of women to self-support would be a return to heathen barbarism of the most brutal type.

Possibly the ladies may correct us, but to our own humble perception there is, after this single remark, nothing left of apparent interest or honor to the female sex in the transfer of the arts and professions to their side, or rather in the transfer of the female sex to the arts and professions. Not even the honor of earning their own living independently, of which so much is said by some. There is no peculiar honor in independence. There is something quite the contrary, in fact. The only honor that belongs to independence is that of being useful to others in due proportion to what we receive from them, or in common language, paying one's way. No one enjoys that honor more perfectly than a good wife, mother, or daughter, who never touched a penny of wages or profit in her life.

From *Scribner's Monthly*, 1871.

MY ANSWER TO GENOCIDE

Bitter comic prescribes
big families as
effective black protest

BY DICK GREGORY

LETTERS

BLACK/WHITE DATING

Sirs: In "Black/White Dating" (May 28), Joan Downs asks the question: "How, in a time of deeply troubled black/white relations, does one reconcile group loyalty with friendship —even love—across the color line?" The answer is clear: by recognizing that one's group is, in reality, the whole human race.

CHARLES F. GOLDBERG
Spring Valley, N.Y.

Above, letter to the editor of *Life*, June 18, 1971.

M Y ANSWER to genocide, quite simply, is eight black kids—and another baby on the way.

I guess it is just that "slave master" complex white folks have. For years they told us where to sit, where to eat, and where to live. Now they want to dictate our bedroom habits. First the white man tells me to sit in the back of the bus. Now it looks like he wants me to sleep under the bed. Back in the days of slavery, black folks couldn't grow kids fast enough for white folks to harvest. Now that we've got a little taste of power, white folks want us to call a moratorium on having babies.

Of course, I could never participate in birth control, because I'm against doing anything that goes against Nature. That's why I've changed my eating habits so drastically over the years and have become a vegetarian. And birth control is definitely against Nature. Can you believe that human beings are the only creatures who would ever consider developing birth control pills? You mention contraception to a gorilla and he will tear your head off.

Above, *Ebony*, October 1971.

I read Dick Gregory's October 1971 EBONY article twice. The first reading made me angry, which I suppose was Gregory's intended effect on white readers. The second reading made me feel sorry for his eight beautiful black kids. They are being raised not for their own individual worths but as a protest against imaginary genocide. After Mr. Gregory is dead and gone, they may have to live in a world made unbearably overcrowded by just such uninformed bigotry.

If birth control is a plot by whites to eliminate blacks then why do white women form the majority of pill users? And why have so many young whites decided to forego having children even though they want them? If Dick Gregory wants to raise a mob of children according to his beliefs, why does he and his wife not adopt some of the black babies who are being emotionally crippled in institutions?

He uses the rationale that he does not believe in unnatural practices, but his oldest daughter wears glasses. I believe the reason he hides behind the "natural way" is that he is too selfish to care about his children's future and too unsure of his manhood to give his wife a respite from being a baby machine.

Dick Gregory's children will have to associate with whites eventually, because we are not going to stop having babies either. If Mr. Gregory is as concerned for his race as he claims to be, let him teach his kids to love their fellow man regardless of his color. Having children to spite your neighbors is foolish.

MRS. MARY SHAW
San Antonio, Tex.

Never before have I read an article that stated so many of the things I would like to say myself. The article I'm referring to is "My Answer to Genocide," by Dick Gregory (October 1971). I am from a large family of 12 children —seven girls and five boys—and I am the oldest.

Mr. Gregory is one black man I truly respect because he speaks his mind and shows the world that he is the head of his house and that no one can tell him what must go on in his bedroom.

"The Lord giveth and the Lord taketh away." Don't play around with the babies yet to be born. Let nature take its course. Don't let man take the place of our Master. Only He knows how far to let you go. The Lord looks out for all of us, and there is a justifiable reason for everything He has anything to do with. God never makes a mistake, so why should man try to change things?

During the time of slavery, the blacks could not have babies fast enough for their master. Look at the change now that we have a little power.

MISS CAROLYN A. DONNELLY
Mullins, S. C.

Left, letter to the editor of *Ebony* by Mrs. Mary Shaw, December 1971

Above, letter to the editor of *Ebony* by Carolyn H. Donnelly, December 1971.

If Mr. Richard Gregory is really interested in having the black population rise, why, oh why, doesn't he adopt black children that are for various reasons parentless? These kids get tossed from foster home to foster home. Some never acclimate and spend their entire lives in institutions.

If Mr. Gregory really feels that genocide is being subtly pushed, he should further the cause of blacks adopting blacks. I believe that if he inquired of the authorities in Chicago alone he would find there are many black children needing strong permanent homes.

Come on, Dick, lead the way. Get the blacks to adopt the black—otherwise, they'll be adopted by whites and eventually true integration will take place and then there will be no need for genocide of any sort. We will all really be brothers—both under and outside the skin.

JOSETTE H. MARTINS
Eau Claire, Wisc.

As a black, professional woman, and mother of two, I found the article by Mr. Gregory and his insane reasoning appalling and beyond belief.

The fact that this man wants X amount of children is not my point. The fact that he and his wife share a common desire to have a large family is such an intimate, personal matter, that a comment here would be out of order. But to openly admit that he is capitalizing on the fertility of his wife and himself to strike a blow at the white population of this nation is, in my humble but sincere opinion, bordering on lunacy.

He is using the body of his wife as a weapon, reducing her to the level of a cow, and she apparently accepts her lot as inevitable. It is significant to recall that he did not once mention an offspring as an individual unique personality, did not once speak of a child as a child for his or her own sake, but rather as some wild, distorted joke on the plans and schemes of the white man. Herein lies the crux of my confusion.

I would implore Mr. Gregory to fight his war and his bitterness as a man, and thus allow his wife to become a person, his children to become people in their own right, and not tools for his use, or outlets for his frustrations As brother James Brown might say, "Check yourself."

MRS. SHIRLEY NALLEY
Roosevelt, L. I., N. Y.

Dick Gregory states, "All birth control is definitely against nature. Can you believe that human beings are the only creatures who would ever consider developing birth control pills? You mention contraception to a gorilla. . . ."

Indeed a gorilla does not need birth control because he has no power of death control. The present population explosion is a human problem; most animal species are stable or declining. Within the human species, however, the problem exists in varying degrees for all races. The cause is in part due to great improvements in medical knowledge and resultant reduction in death rates. "Natural" is a high infant mortality; "natural" is a high death rate for women in childbirth and "natural" is a short life expectancy!

Maybe Mr. Gregory will feel better if he reads that the annual rate of population growth in Africa is 2.7 per cent compared to a meager 1.1 per cent in the U. S. But, alas, who is going to catch up with Asia with 2.1 billion people. . . ?

MARINA B. BROWN
Loudonville, N. Y.

Above, letter to the editor of *Ebony* by Marina B. Brown, December 1971.

One may agree or differ with Dick Gregory's opinion on genocide, but when he gets off his subject and states what animals do "naturally," he has entered a field where even his opinions cannot change the facts.

You see, some animals practice infanticide to keep their population down. Other species have smaller litters in times when food is scarce. Still others will *not even* mate if they are unable to provide adequate shelter for their offspring.

Even man, namely the African Bushman, practiced birth control 50,000 years before Dick Gregory was born—but then they didn't know it wasn't natural to do it.

HOWARD FIGOWITT
Harrisburg, Pa

Top left, letter to the editor of *Ebony* by Josette H. Martins, December 1971.

Left, letter to the editor of *Ebony* by Mrs. Shirley Nalley, Roosevelt, Long Island, December 1971.

Congratulations to EBONY for printing Dick Gregory's excellent article, "My Answer To Genocide." I strongly agree with Gregory's intellectual and moral stand on birth control. It is good to hear his voice loud and clear on this vital issue. I believe firmly that artificial contraceptive birth control is against nature. It is beautiful to hear a strong black voice calling our attention to this simple fact of life.

BROTHER DON FLEISCHHACKER, C.S.C.

St. Edward's University
Austin, Texas

It is really discouraging to hear that Dick Gregory is preaching against one kind of genocide while at the same time he and his wife are practicing another kind. When our population gets bigger than our farmland can support, people will die, and there is no ethnic magic that will keep the same thing from happening to the black brothers and sisters that will happen to the whites.

RUTH B. BALL
Portland, Ore.

Above, letter to the editor of *Ebony* by Ruth B. Ball, December 1971.

Top right, letter to the editor of *Ebony* by Brother Don Fleischhacker, C. S. C., December 1971.

Left, letter to the editor of *Ebony* by Howard Figowitt, December 1971.

Hypocrisy laid bare

The full-scale row which always looked likely to break over the all-white South African cricket tour of Australia is on. Sensing a good issue to snipe at the new McMahon Administration, the Opposition leader, Mr Whitlam, has now called for cancellation, and thus joined the slowly swelling anti-apartheid movement in Australia. The particular cause of Mr Whitlam's wrath is the blunt rejection by the Vorster regime of the mild Springbok request that two non-whites should join the touring side. Mr Vorster's Minister of Sport, Mr Frank Waring, has challenged the South African Cricket Association to open their doors to non-whites at all levels. Let them use the white's clubs. Let them play in the whites' league.

In logic Mr Waring's position cannot be faulted, even though he knows that if the white cricketers agreed the Government would not sanction it. But he has effectively called their bluff. The selection of two non-whites was window-dressing and a relatively painless attempt to allay international opinion. If you want non-whites on your tour, have them with you at home, too, the Minister is saying. To which the cricketers could retort (although they will not): "If the Government wants its own form of window-dressing by talking of a dialogue with black Africa, why not be logical and have a dialogue with black South Africans? Why allow a black Malawi ambassador to use white hotels, but not allow the same right to a black South African?"

The episode only shows that there is ultimately no logic in South Africa's system of white supremacy. The argument is between hard-line pragmatists like Mr Vorster's Government and slightly less hard-line pragmatists like the United Party. The most interesting current development is that the Nationalist Government has moved in the past two months back towards its old "verkrampte" position. The cricket decision is the latest in a series of tougher moves. It seems that Mr Vorster has interpreted his recent slight electoral losses to the United Party as a signal that he must move back to the Right. His Labour Minister Mr Viljoen, recently confirmed that there is to be no slackening in job reservation. Indeed, it is to be tightened. There has been the campaign against the Church and the detention or expulsion of Churchmen who have spoken out. And in the face of the worsening economic situation, the Government is looking for a harsh deflationary cure by putting up the sales taxes. The poor will suffer most, and that, of course, means Africans.

Top page, from *The Guardian*, April 10, 1971.

Sirs: I am black. Recently I took a white girl to a show. Therefore, your article was remarkably timely for me.

The idea that interracial dating and marriage will be accepted more readily in 20 years is a lot of nonsense. It is in keeping with that old American pastime, passing the buck. The people who tell you "in 20 years" are too stubborn or too foolish to bend a little in their narrow-minded views. They are the ones who probably figure on not being alive then—so that anything that happens is simply not their problem. Talk about escapists!

These people bring up their children with the same numskull ideas. So how in hell are things going to be different for the next generation? The change in people's minds about this topic and others is going to have to take place now —not 20 years from now.
                    DAVID E. FREEMAN
New York, N.Y.

Sirs: It seems that the whole "problem" is brought about by people of all races who hold opinions about things that are none of their business and do not affect their own lives personally. This includes my opinion, too.
                    M. E. GWYNNE
Alamo, Calif.

Above, letter to the editor of *Life* by M. E. Gwynne, June 18, 1971.

Left, letter to the editor of *Life* by David E. Freeman, June 18, 1971.

Below and right, from *The Guardian Weekly*.

MANCHESTER:

Rest in Peace

NEGRO HUMOR is in rather short supply in the United States, but I would like to tell you a story I heard in South Carolina a couple of weeks ago.

It's about an African who was resting under a coconut tree when he was addressed by a passing Englishman. "What," asked the Englishman, "are you doing for yourself, just idly sitting there? Why don't you get busy and develop your fields, those mines, and build cities?"

"What for?" the African asked.

"To establish commerce," the Englishman replied.

"Commerce for what?"

"So you can make lots of money."

"What good is money?"

"Money will bring you leisure."

"What will I do with leisure?"

"Then you can rest."

"But why do all that," asked the African, "when I'm resting now?"
                    —*The Guardian Weekly*.

A Resolution Against Racism

The doctrine of racial supremacy is with us again. New studies claiming to demonstrate "scientifically" the old notion that black people are inferior have been rapidly spreading in professional literature, texts, and respectable popular magazines. Even more ominously, it is now being taught as fact in classrooms across the country.

The leading contemporary protagonists of this theory include Arthur Jensen (Berkeley), Hans Eysenck (London), Richard Herrnstein (Harvard), and William Shockley (Stanford). Basing their conclusions on the results of aptitude, achievement, and I.Q. tests, these theorists claim that black or other oppressed peoples are genetically endowed with less intelligence than the dominant group. They sweep aside the fact that tests of any oppressed group in a stratified society measure only that group's social rejection and not its relative intelligence. Jensen asserts: "There are intelligence genes, which are found in populations in different proportions, somewhat like the distribution of blood types. The number of intelligence genes seems to be lower, overall, in the black population than in the white." (*The New York Times Magazine*, 31 August 1969, p. 43). And Shockley claims, "Nature has color coded groups of individuals so that statistically reliable predictions of their adaptability to intellectually rewarding and effective lives can easily be made and profitably used by the pragmatic man on the street." (*Boston Sunday Globe*, 12 September 1971, Sect. A, p. 6).

Theories of racial inferiority are rendered untenable by the evidence of human history: every population has developed its own complex culture. Contrary to the supremacist view, the peoples of Africa and Asia have, at various times, produced civilizations far more advanced than those existing simultaneously in Europe. Moreover, the constant geographical shift of centers of culture is in itself proof of the equal capabilities of all peoples. It is nonsense to suppose genetic superiority wandering about the world.

The doctrine of racial inferiority is thus unscientific as well as socially vicious. Its sole claim to objectivity rests on a veneer of scientific techniques that covers distortion and false assumptions. Indeed, the current "master-race" ideas are once again being discredited in the scientific literature (cf. R. Lewontin, *Bull. Atomic Sci.*, March 1970; S. Searr-Salapatek, *Science*, 174: 4016; 178: 4058; C. Brace, *et al.*, *Anthropological Studies*, No. 8, Am. Anth. Assn.). Nevertheless, the generators of this new racism persist in their bigotry. Their theories, despite their academic garb, do not differ in their scientific character or their social effects from those advanced by American slave-owners, the Nazis, or the advocates of apartheid in South Africa. Racist ideas, if it were not for their political and economic role in justifying oppression and exploitation, would long since have joined phlogiston and geocentric theories of the universe in the mausoleum of science.

Our common human heritage has endowed all groups of people with equal intellectual abilities. Of course there are secondary physical differences. Nobody denies this. But they have nothing to do with intelligence. Research involving these differences must not be misused to support theories of racial inferiority.

Racist theoreticians have recently sought sanction and protection in the concept of academic freedom. This is a subterfuge. It is true that academic freedom protects the right to free inquiry and to the expression of controversial ideas. But it is not license to justify oppression. It was no more intended to protect racism than verbal assault or libel, with which racism has more in common than it has with free intellectual inquiry. Nor, in the light of all the evidence, can the ideology of racism be legitimately called "controversial" and open to debate. It is a false doctrine that serves only to facilitate brutalization and exploitation. Thus, because it is both socially pernicious and scientifically incorrect, its proponents forfeit any right to academic protection.

The use of the academy to further racist oppression must be halted. We therefore call upon our colleagues to:

1) Urge their university senates to adopt measures designed to eliminate classroom racism.

2) Urge professional organizations and societies, academic departments, and editors of scholarly journals to condemn and refuse to disseminate racist research.

3) Expose the unscientific character of racist ideas so as to deny them the appearance of legitimacy provided by academia.

4) Organize and support activities to eliminate racist practices and ideas wherever they occur.

Courtesy of the Committee Against Racism.

STATEMENT FROM THE PRESIDENT
BOB JONES UNIVERSITY

THE BOARD OF TRUSTEES of Bob Jones University is made up of fifty godly men and women from all sections of the United States. They are UNANIMOUS in their convictions that Bob Jones University should not enroll Negro students. This Board is responsible for administering the affairs of Bob Jones University, establishing its policies, and seeing that it is operated in line with Scriptural principles.

THE FACT THAT WE DO NOT ACCEPT BLACKS as students here does not mean that we are against the Negro race, that we do not love the Negro, or that we are not concerned about his spiritual welfare. I wish there were an institution like Bob Jones University established exclusively for Negroes; however, with the present emphasis in this country, Negroes would not accept a school established solely for Blacks because the whole emphasis today is on a breaking down of racial barriers which God has set up; and where God sets up barriers, He does it for human good. In fact, Paul makes this quite clear in his sermon on Mars' Hill, the first portion of which the integrationists love so to quote: "He has made of one blood all nations of men for to dwell on all the face of the earth." They never continue, however, "and hath determined the times before appointed, and the bounds of their habitation; that they should seek the Lord, if haply they might feel after him, and find him, though he be not far from every one of us."

THE EMPHASIS TODAY is on one world, one race, one church; but this is to be a world in rebellion against God ruled by Antichrist, a mongrel race in defiance of the separation which God has put up, and an apostate church, serving Antichrist.

COLLEGE YEARS ARE THE TIME when young people make their life contacts, fall in love, and get married; and we do not believe intermarriage of the races is Scriptural. That such is the purpose of the whole present emphasis is apparent from a statement from one of the leaders of the NAACP who said, "The racial problem will not be settled in the Courtroom but in the bedroom."

WE ACCEPT A FEW ORIENTAL STUDENTS, but we do so with a definite understanding that they will not date outside of their own race. If we took Negro students here on this same basis today, they would resent that restriction and would cry that they were being discriminated against because they were not allowed to date Orientals or Caucasians. If we had to expel a black student today for the worst possible offense—stealing, attempted rape, or something of that sort—he could cry that he was being persecuted because he was black; and we would be picketed, annoyed, and harassed. The very attitude of the integrationist today makes it impossible for us to find any basis on which we can accept Negro students without violating Christian and Scriptural principles and without being put in a position where we could be harassed, annoyed, and threatened. The Board is not going to be put in any such position.

IN THIS AS IN ALL MATTERS, this institution seeks to do what we believe to be right, what we believe to be Scriptural, and what we believe to be in the best interest of the testimony of this institution and the welfare of our students. It is unfortunate that some Christians have been brainwashed by the propaganda of the integrationists to the point where they feel guilty if they do not integrate, when the truth is in most cases they should feel guilty if they DO integrate on a basis that violates the boundaries which God has put up.

In Defense of Dissent

The successful attempt by certain faculty members to keep Bill Shockley from speaking at Brooklyn Polytechnic Institute ("News in Brief," 24 May, p. 863) is a classic demonstration of the inability of many self-styled liberals to understand what free speech is all about. These unilateral liberals are willing to tolerate any dissent as long as it is not "wrong"; that is, in disagreement with or questioning the dogma currently held by themselves.

Dogma: "There are no racial differences in intelligence."

Shockley: "I dunno—let's find out."

Unilateral Liberals: "Racist! Nazi! We won't let you speak!"

Such an attitude, I submit, is less scientific or scholarly or liberal than it is dogmatically religious and is indistinguishable in kind from those of Adolph Hitler, both Joes (McCarthy and Stalin), the Birchers, and for that matter, Torquemada and the orthodox Marxists. . . . Free speech implies the toleration not only of "proper" but of "wrong" dissent—Voltaire, the Supreme Court, and the American Civil Liberties Union all seem to agree with me. And if any dogma is sacred and not to be questioned, the age of the Inquisition is on the way back. God preserve us from the man who knows that he is right!

JOHN D. CLARK

Green Pond Road, RD 2,
Newfoundland, New Jersey 07435

SCIENCE, VOL. 161

Right, from *The Citizen*, February 1971.

Above, letter to the editor of *Science* by John D. Clark, July 5, 1968.

How far has it all gone? The Equal Employment bureaucrats
concede that a bank need not hire a convicted burglar,
but they may require the bank to hire a convicted
murderer because his crime wasn't 'job-related'

Are Quotas Here to Stay?

ALLAN C. ORNSTEIN

COMPETITION FOR jobs on the basis of ability is being eliminated, and racial quotas increasingly becoming the norm throughout the employment sector. This sweeping change is being brought about by Executive Orders No. 4 and 11246. The orders were signed by President Johnson to eliminate discrimination in hiring, but were revised by the Department of Labor, and now force institutions to give preferential treatment to minorities in hiring and promotion practices and require that goals and timetables be filed annually by each affected employer. The orders cover public schools, universities, civil services (policemen, firemen, postal workers, etc.), the armed forces, construction and trade industries, unions, private corporations and businesses employing more than 25 people, and *all* organizations that have contracts with government or are regulated by governmental agencies—in all, about 95 per cent of the employment market.

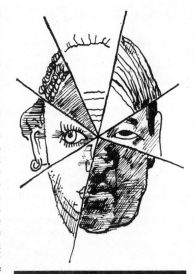

The truth is that under the guise of justice, we have permitted an absurd and illegal policy—a reverse South African policy—to take effect, under which individuals are identified and rewarded or penalized according to race. This mocks everything that the civil rights movement sought to accomplish in the past; it institutionalizes a double standard; it discriminates against people who have had no part in discriminating in the past; it discourages excellence and fosters mediocrity. And it is incoherent and indefensible.

This policy has been produced, it is important to note, not by popular demand or the actions of elected officials, but by a few middle-ranking officials in the Departments of Labor and HEW and their offshoots, who have revised and reinterpreted Executive Orders No. 4 and 11246. It is doubtful the policy could survive if people simply had the guts to throw body count compliance questionnaires into the wastebasket, and filed countersuits and sought injunctions against the application of a law that violates the same individual rights and due process the law was intended to protect. And think of what might happen to affirmative action if everyone were to claim minority status. Surely it is time for the general sense of reality and justice to prevail over the arbitrary decrees of a few unelected bureaucrats. □

gray matter

Issues that are neither black nor white

Quotas work both ways

ANTHONY LOMBARDO

Not so long ago in the South, blacks were forced to sit in the back of the bus. The fair solution was to forbid bus companies from forcing blacks to sit in a special section of the bus. An unfair solution would have been to order white riders to sit in the back; this would simply have shifted the injustice from one group to another. Similarly, the fair solution to educational and employment discrimination is to forbid discrimination on the basis of race or sex or religion or national origin *without* setting up new categories of preferred and non-preferred minorities.

If a college or university insists on sticking with a quota system, it should carry it out to its logical conclusion. Remember we have only 100 percent to start with—not 150 percent or 200 percent. Thus, if every department in a university must employ 10 percent blacks because blacks make up about 10 percent of the U.S. population, then these same departments must also start to limit their Jewish professors to 3 percent, which roughly corresponds to the Jewish percentage of the population.

As everyone knows, Jews are greatly over-represented on university faculties and in the professions. If we plan to introduce quotas as a permanent device, a chemistry department, for example, 25 percent of whose faculty is made up of Jews, will sooner or later have to pare this number down to 3 percent or so. Quotas do work both ways.

The absence of definitions points up one of the problems with preferred categories. What is a black? A black seems to be anyone who says he is a black. He or she might be $^{15}/_{16}$ white, but if he calls himself a black he can be listed as one. Likewise anyone who can claim an Indian great-grandmother can call himself an American Indian. A man or woman with a Spanish surname, such as Gomez, may be mostly French or Irish in ancestry, and be unable to speak a word of Spanish, but nevertheless he qualifies as a member of a "preferred minority."

Furthermore, these preferred categories take no account of family wealth or educational advantages. A black whose father is a judge or physician deserves preferential treatment over any non-minority applicant. The latter might have fought his way out of the grinding poverty of Appalachia, or might be the first member of an Italian-American or a Polish-American family to complete high school. But no matter. His particular ethnic minority does not count, because an agency of the government says it does not count.

It might be legitimate to ask if members of other minorities have their fair share of good jobs, scholarships, etc. What about the 8,800,000 Italian-Americans, the 5,100,000 Polish-Americans, the 5,400,000 Americans of French descent, and the millions of Americans of Russian, Greek, Ukranian, Lithuanian, Czech, Slovak and other ethnic groups? If they are under-represented in medical schools, on college faculties, or in bar associations, can they too apply to state and federal governments for remedy?

Reprinted with permission from *U.S. Catholic*, 221 West Madison St., Chicago, Illinois 60606.

THE DISPOSABLE HUMANS?

SHOULD EVERY HUMAN LIFE BE RESPECTED? OR ARE SOME LIVES DISPOSABLE? IS THERE A DIFFERENCE BETWEEN A HUMAN LIFE AND A LEGAL PERSON?

THESE QUESTIONS ARE NOW ASKED WITH REGARD TO UNBORN BABIES. BUT DIDN'T OUR SOCIETY ASK THESE SAME QUESTIONS ONCE BEFORE . . . IN THE 19th CENTURY . . . WITH RESPECT TO BLACK PEOPLE? *(PERHAPS THIS IS WHY, OUT OF ALL GROUPS, IT IS THE BLACK COMMUNITY — NOT THE CATHOLIC COMMUNITY — THAT TODAY SHOWS LEAST SUPPORT FOR PERMISSIVE ABORTION . . . ACCORDING TO A 1970 HARRIS POLL AND A 1971 POPULATION COMMISSION POLL.)*

WHY NOT COMPARE TODAY'S RHETORIC WITH THAT OF THE LAST CENTURY AND SEE WHETHER THERE ARE SIMILARITIES?

SLAVERY 1857	ABORTION 1972
Although he may have a heart and a brain, and he may be a human life biologically, a slave is not a *legal* person. The Dred Scott decision by the U. S. Supreme Court has made that clear.	*Although he may have a heart and a brain, and he may be a human life biologically, an unborn baby is not a legal person. Our courts will soon make that clear.*
A black man only becomes a *legal* person when he is set free. Before that time, we should not concern ourselves about him because he has no legal rights.	*A baby only becomes a legal person when he is born. Before that time, we should not concern ourselves about him because he has no legal rights.*
If you think that slavery is wrong, then nobody is forcing you to be a slave-owner. But don't impose your morality on somebody else!	*If you think abortion is wrong, then nobody is forcing you to have one. But don't impose your morality on somebody else!*
A man has a right to do what he wants with his own property.	*A woman has a right to do what she wants with her own body.*
Isn't slavery really something merciful? After all, every black man has a right to be protected. Isn't it better never to be set free than to be sent unprepared, and ill-equipped, into a cruel world? (*Spoken by someone already free*)	*Isn't abortion really something merciful? After all, every baby has a right to be wanted. Isn't it better never to be born than to be sent alone and unloved into a cruel world?* (*Spoken by someone already born*)

Will the unborn baby become the modern Dred Scott?
Or will our country use its great resources to respect every human life
. . . black or white . . . poor or rich . . . woman or man . . .
unborn baby or octogenarian?

IT is impossible to deal justly with the Chinese labor question without a fair examination of our entire labor-system.

The United States, in their relations to labor, stand alone among all the countries of the earth. The very principles of freedom and equality, upon which we depend for our cohesion, are adverse to a practical labor-system. Whereas other nations find their labor-market supplied by the peasant order, or by a system of serfdom or slavery, we have no such resource, and are forced to look abroad for paid substitutes for those who, in other countries, are presumed to feel some slight interest in the land and people they serve.

We have no peasantry; and since our native-born population have been disinclined to turn their attention to menial labor, it has followed that we must look for assistance to the refuse population of older and over-crowded countries, in order that we might develop the resources of our own.

This would be all well enough, if it were not that inventive genius and intellectual power require instruments of some mental capacity to make them profitable. The truth is, that while, in the first period of our existence, we needed only brute force, and the muscular power that could fell trees and hoe potatoes, now we must have intellectual and skilled labor to utilize our inventions, to develop our manufactures, and to enrich our land with intelligent agriculture. Agriculture, horticulture, and manufacture, which were at first conducted with a view to absolute necessity, are now followed, in a degree, as fine arts, needing all the adjuncts which the mind can offer to advance them.

For such advancement our present labor-system is incompetent; and this leads to the first proposition to be offered in this article, viz.: that *our present labor-system is intellectually inadequate to the necessities of the people and the capacity of the country and period.*

Again, not only has our labor-system failed to advance in value and capacity with our advancing resources; not only is it a dead-weight upon invention and improvement; but it has also been the occasion for the introduction into our social and political organization of an element fraught with danger to our welfare and position as a nation. Forced to depend for the labor which built our residences and our warehouses, and which tilled our fields and worked our manufactories, upon the refuse of the ignorant lower orders of Europe, or, in default of these, upon a peasantry imbued to a large extent with the *sans-culotteism* of the times, we have seen our servants educated to overturn their masters, and the worst features of despotic injustice introduced into our republican law, by the very ones who had fled from their own homes to escape the workings of similar unjust dispensations.

This brings us to a second proposition, which is, that *the interference of ignorant labor with politics is dangerous to society, injurious to operatives, and practically impedes the progress and advancement of labor itself.*

Hitherto our labor-market has been a monopoly with no competitors; and the consequence has been—as must ever be the case under similar circumstances—labor improperly and grudgingly performed, and exorbitant compensation insolently demanded. There should be nothing freer than labor. Our market should be open to the world, since only by that means can the natural laws which regulate it gain opportunity for their working.

Now as to agriculture. The abolition of slavery was certainly productive of results, as regards our agricultural progress, whose bitter and injurious effects must be felt for an indefinite period of time, unless some other form of labor shall take the place of the one so summarily annihilated. And yet this act of emancipation, ruinous to our agricultural interests as it must be at the outset, cannot but result favorably in the end, provided it be made the stepping-stone to a more advanced and intelligent system. The colored population of the South, ignorant and brutish as a mass, can never be anything more to our soil than the blind workers, whose labor must be fruitless except as directed by a higher intelligence. The necessity for this kind of labor is being rapidly obviated by the introduction of machinery; and it becomes obvious that what will be needed hereafter in this direction is a much higher standard of intelligence, combined with education, and a marked degree of aptitude for the duties required.

Heretofore, the chief immigration to America has been twofold—the class of small farmers from the villages of Germany, who brought money with them and labored to obtain a foot-hold upon the soil for themselves and their families; and the poverty-stricken peasantry of Ireland, whose only desire was to escape a condition which they rightly believed could hardly be made worse. Of these two classes, while one has supported itself, we have had to support the other; neither being precisely what we require to strengthen and improve the country. The German element, while it has, to some extent, developed our agricultural resources, has done so in a small way and purely for self. The Irish has served too largely to fill our prisons and reformatories, and to introduce into the political system of our large cities the worst features of European mobocracy. It is true that Italy sends us organ-grinders, and Germany lager-beer brewers; but it may be questioned if this admixture largely strengthens our body politic.

The usual food of the Chinese is rice, fish, poultry, and vegetables; and on this diet, or any portion of it, they are capable of prolonged efforts in labor which would put to shame many of our stalwart beef-eaters. The Chinaman works for a motive, the strongest possible to his race; his sole wish and design is to obtain sufficient money by his savings to enable him to return to his family, and live in comparative comfort and ease for the rest of his days. He is therefore economical and abstemious. A few hundred dollars in gold will accomplish all his needs and his desires, and if he can save this amount in three or five years he is satisfied. Again, he is content with the current market price for labor, and such an idea as a combination or "Union" to enforce a higher standard of wages, is not only unknown to him, but is foreign to all his instincts and repugnant to his feelings. Naturally peaceable, he shrinks from conflict, and, as his past history has proven, will put up with oppression, contumely, and wrong for the longest before he will strive to relieve himself; and then only by flight. Meanwhile, he will of course seize every legitimate means for bettering his condition, and will not work for one employer for less pay than another is willing to give him for the same amount of labor.

It is, therefore, not only for the convenience to society, the advantage to our national welfare, the healthy competition in labor which it promises, that the new element should be welcomed and sustained, but also for the fact that it promises to eradicate the most pernicious features of our present political life. There is no danger that the Chinese will interest themselves in our politics or mode of government. The experience of California is a sufficient guarantee on that head.

Accustomed to be governed, and to have no word or voice in the laws or their execution, they have only a desire to be allowed freedom to pursue their own avocations, and personal safety while engaged in the pursuit. Of votes, and candidates, and caucuses, and primary elections, torch-light processions, nominations, jobs, and rings, they are in blessed ignorance. And since we know them to be intelligent, there is the less fear of their influence, when they do arrive at this height of learning and experience, than if it were accompanied by that condition of ignorance which cannot discern the difference between right and wrong, except when a greenback is placed between them.

From *Scribner's Monthly*, 1871.

What It's All About

A lot of people take the attitude that, well, sure, the country's got problems, but what can I do about it? I might as well mind my own business and get along the best I can.

In the National Alliance we look at it a little differently. We think there is something we can do.

We believe that we understand what's causing America's problems. We can see a few common factors which are at the root of all the trouble.

If we can get at those factors and change them, we can make a big difference. We can build a better America.

One of these factors — and it's a big one — is that most White Americans have lost their feeling of identity.

Another way of saying this is that they think of themselves merely as individuals, nothing more. They aren't a part of anything bigger than themselves.

Their purpose in life doesn't go much beyond looking out for Number One: providing for their own welfare and recreation. If they're married, they probably include the other members of the family in their purpose, but that's about it.

They have no roots in the past and no responsibility to the future. A psychologist would say they are "alienated."

This is a bad state of affairs. It results in unhappy people and a sick society.

And it's dangerous. People who have no sense of identity or solidarity are easy prey for other groups of people who know who they are and what they want.

That's why we've lost control of our news media, for example. That's why tiny Israel can dictate America's foreign policy and cause oil boycotts against us.

It's why White kids are getting knocked around so much by Black kids in our schools. And it's why terrorist gangs are on the rise, killing White people in the streets, kidnapping, raping, and generally showing us that they have no fear and no respect for us.

Americans are in the habit of looking to their government for solutions to problems like these. The trouble with that approach is that the government itself is a big part of the problem.

The politicians in the government are concerned about America's problems only to the extent that they influence the outcome of the next election. They are captives of the media, the minority pressure groups, and their own greed and ambition.

With people like that running the country, it's no wonder we're in trouble. It's no wonder the schools are failing to instill a pride of race, culture, and nation in young Americans.

It's no wonder that so many people have no proper sense of values. It's no wonder that so many have turned to drugs and other "escapes" from a life that is largely meaningless.

The way to begin curing all these problems is to give White Americans a strong sense of identity. That's part of what we in the National Alliance and its youth arm, the National Youth Alliance, are trying to do.

We're teaching Americans to look at life in a new way: Each White person is not only an individual, but he is also a member of his racial community — a community with roots in the most distant past and with a destiny in the unlimited future.

The individual should regard himself as a vital link in the chain of generations connecting his race's great past with its glorious future. He should think not only of his own welfare and security but also of the welfare and security of his race.

He should understand that, if America is to survive and prosper, the people who built the country — the great, White majority — must once again become masters in their own house, and that this can only happen if they put the interests of the race and the nation ahead of personal interests.

This educational task, which is carried out in part by ATTACK! and by the books we distribute, is only part of what we are doing. The bigger task is to build a new community of all those who share our faith and our concern for the future.

We teach, and we organize those whom we have taught into a coherent force for reaching out to others. Thus, we grow, and our strength and capabilities grow.

Eventually, our community will be large enought to exert a substantial influence on the affairs of the larger, national community. Already, in certain cases where we had a lot of leverage, we've been able to make our efforts felt on a national scale.

So our main task for now is to grow — just continue growing and becoming stronger as fast as we can. And the way we do that is to reach out to more and more Americans who are realizing the emptiness and the sterility of a life with no purpose beyond itself.

We reach out by sending our people, into the streets to sell copies of this newspaper you're reading. We reach out by talking to groups of people in the schools and, whenever there's a chance, by organizing demonstrations and marches.

We do a lot of other things too, but they're all aimed at just one thing: catching your attention and your interest so we can tell you how much more wonderful life is when you're working for something that really matters — and so we can invite you to work with us.

That's what it's all about.

Attack!, April 1975; monthly newspaper of The National Alliance, Box 3535, Washington, D.C. 20007.

SECTION 5

Censorship

The mention of the word "censorship" probably calls up in many people's minds thoughts about pornography, a topic which has been widely discussed and debated in the United States for several decades as the Supreme Court and various legislative bodies have attempted to come up with workable definitions and legal sanctions. But, as the examples in this section serve to remind us, censorship is really the act of preventing public dissemination of any kind of idea or image, and at various times in various societies attempts have been made (very often quite successfully) to censor almost every conceivable kind of idea and image. The problems here, as with gun control, abortion, and drugs, are at several levels which must be kept quite distinct in the analysis and evaluation of arguments. One level is that of the basic rightness or wrongness of specific acts (e.g., the classic case of shouting "Fire!" in a crowded theater) and another quite different level is that of whether or not legal sanctions should be imposed against persons for disseminating particular ideas or images. The arguments in this section address a variety of these issues at both levels, sometimes mixing the two in a way which makes it difficult or impossible to separate them in a clear and precise manner.

The question of censorship often overlaps other basic ethical questions, as is evidenced by many of the examples in this section. For example, it is generally agreed that in most situations telling lies and untruths is morally wrong. But what about fairy tales and other stories which have traditionally been a part of almost everyone's childhood? Is it wrong to tell untrue stories to small children? And if so, should this be legally prohibited by the state? This question may seem almost absurd to some readers, but some very serious debates over it have taken place recently in some schools, as indicated in the first item in this section. Other ethical issues which come into consideration in discussions of censorship range from professional responsibility (of journalists, teachers, scientists, etc.) to protection of one's country (for example, Daniel Ellsberg argued that his "leaking" of the classified information known as the Pentagon Papers was for the good of the country).

EXERCISES

1. Compare the cases of journalistic censorship discussed in this section to determine what basic questions, if any, are common to all of them, and also to identify significant differences among the cases. Are matters such as the nature of the audience (high school students versus adults) or the nature of the subject matter (prostitution, national security, death) "significant" factors in distinguishing cases or not?
2. Examine the excerpts from the opinions in the Supreme Court ruling on pornography to determine the extent to which the arguments of the court might be different from the kinds of arguments that are commonly given by "ordinary" people in everyday situations. Can one formulate a clear distinction between law and ethics on the basis of this comparison?
3. Examine the arguments concerning censorship of sexual materials and those involving violence to see what differences if any exist between them. Is it possible to use the same moral premises to justify the censorship of one kind which would at the same time permit the publication and dissemination of the other kind?

Textbook Banners Busy

By John Mathews
Washington Star Staff Writer

Should Montgomery County kindergarten, first- and second-grade children be told that owls and elephants are wise, that wolves are cruel or that a whale spouts water and a bear hibernates in winter?

Should the school system keep showing a decade-old black and white film ("What is a Concerto?") featuring a young-looking Leonard Bernstein conducting an orchestra with no black or women members?

Or should county students have access to "Mommies Are For Loving," a book some consider "sexist," or to a film, "The Magic Balloons," which shows a young boy smoking, stealing and swimming without supervision.

In each case, Supt. Homer Elseroad or a review committee of teachers, librarians and subject specialists have said "No!," backing complaints of parents who objected to the books and films.

The decisions, made last month, represent a new twist in the continuing nationwide controversy over textbooks and other classroom materials.

Last year, Montgomery and Prince Georges counties' and other school systems were facing citizen complaints — often from conservative organizations — about obscenity, profanity and sexual content in books such as Eldridge Cleaver's "Soul on Ice," or Claude Brown's "Manchild in the Promised Land."

"Now, it's a whole new ballgame," says Frances C. Dean, coordinator of Montgomery's Division of Evaluation and Selection. Individual parents are now objecting to the accuracy and truthfulness of books and films, their contemporary value, sexist content or their moral messages.

A parent, for example, raised questions about the accuracy of animal behavior depicted in the popular early grade book "Animals Everywhere," and its use of anthropomorphism — the attribution of human qualities to animals.

After consulting a mammalogist at the U.S. Fish and Wildlife Service, the teacher committee recommended withdrawing the book, because of "its many misleading or inaccurate scientific statements," including descriptions of owls and elephants as "wise," wolves as "cruel," and statements that a whale spouts water and a bear hibernates.

An unnamed dissenter on the committee (school officials do not reveal review committee members or the names of parents who lodge complaints) said the decision on the book could lead to banning even "Peter Rabbit," since there is a "certain amount of stereotyping of animals" in most children's books.

"Animals Everywhere" does not present itself as "an absolutely scientifically true book," the objector added, noting the cover which shows a boy petting a tiger and a goat, while a cat smiles. "Obviously, the tiger is not ferociously eating them," the dissenter wrote.

Dr. Alfred Gardner, the mammalogist who was questioned on the telephone by a member of the review committee, was much less concerned with inaccuracies in the book than the teacher reviewers. "For teaching purposes, you often hedge the truth and avoid answering all questions," he said in an interview. "As far as anthropomorphic language," he added, "we always think of animals in terms of whether they are soft or nice or dangerous."

But, Dr. Gardner added there were debatable issues of accuracy in the book. "There is no way to tell whether owls or elephants are wise. That's definitely anthropomorphic," he said. Wolves, he added, "are really no more cruel than a human who scales a fish while it's still alive and flopping around."

He said also that whales actually spout air and not water, although the pressure causes water above the whale to be displaced in a geyser effect. Bears do not actually hibernate, which is scientifically defined as a metabolic state of torpor in which body temperature is lowered and physical activity is greatly reduced. Bears, he said, actually enter a state of extended sleep, which is often interrupted.

The teacher committee generally approved the Bernstein film on the concerto, although it acknowledged that there were no blacks or women in the orchestra, and as a music supervisor observed about the decade-old film, "I am sure Mr. Bernstein would be pleased to maintain the youthful countenance seen in this film — unfortunately, only the content is ageless!"

The charge of sexism against the elementary-age book "Mommies Are For Loving" was rejected by the teacher committee. Despite passages, like "Mommies are for saying No . . . and drying tears and scrubs in tubs . . . . Mommies are for lots of things but best of all Mommies are for loving," the committee decided the book was "harmless" and depicted a typical, although not exclusive, role of the mother in a family unit.

"The Magic Balloons," a fantasy film for kindergarten to sixth grade depicting a young boy encountering balloons which magically become real people, things and experiences, was rejected. The committee objected to "examples of antisocial and unsafe behavior: stealing, unsupervised swimming and boating, unsupervised living, dangerous driving."

Elseroad agreed with the committee decision to bar "The Magic Balloons" film, but disagreed with the teachers on the other items. He ordered a ban on "Mommies Are For Loving," which the teachers wanted retained despite the sexist charge, and ordered the Bernstein film removed on grounds it is outdated.

On "Animals Everywhere," the superintendent also overruled the teacher committee. Rather than taking the book off the shelves, Elseroad ordered that it continue in use, but that no new copies be purchased unless the publisher changes statements the committee considered inaccurate.

Mrs. Dean, the county book evaluation head, wrote Doubleday and Company Inc., the publishers, stating the committee objections. She got an answer from a sales manager, who noted that in 21 years "Animals Everywhere" by Ingri and Edgar Parin d'Aulaire has sold more than 150,000 copies and was issued in paperback three years ago.

"He said nothing about our objections, so I guess they don't plan to make any changes," Mrs. Dean said.

James J. Kilpatrick

A willful exercise in intellectual dishonesty

The MacMillan Publishing Company delivered itself the other day of a policy statement expounding "today's egalitarian standards." The statement sets forth guidelines for textbooks that are to govern its authors and illustrators henceforth.

The purpose is "to maintain sexual and racial balance in every item we publish."

The company's statement is likely to be received in most quarters, publicly at least, with the kind of fulsome and dutiful praise extended by Pravda to the utterances of Mr. Brezhnev or, for that matter, by the American Conservative Union to the utterances of Mr. Reagan.

In the popular view of "today's egalitarian standards," MacMillan has said and done the right thing: The publishers have confessed their sins, repented, and embarked upon a new life. They are born-again egalitarians. A holy spirit moves within them.

Permit, if you will, a dissenting view. MacMillan's guidelines ought to be denounced for what they are: a willful exercise in intellectual dishonesty. The company is insisting that its textbooks depict society not as it is, but as the publishers, in the fantasies of their "newly raised consciousness," would like it to be.

Their purpose in producing textbooks is not primarily to teach, to inform, to instruct, or to educate, but to propagandize for a new social order.

The guidelines begin with a preface of Dr. Matina S. Horner, president of Radcliffe College. She speaks for those who are struggling for a "more egalitarian society."

The achievement of such a society is hampered by the "tyranny of the norm," which is to say, by a tyranny that seeks to enforce upon young people irrelevant, innacurate, and outdated stereotypes about the roles they are expected to play.

Dr. Horner would abolish such norms. Through a process of education to counteract the stereotyping, she would rid society of false notions, for example, of what is manly or womanly. In the new egalitarian society, a woman who exhibited "competition, independence, intellectual competence, and leadership" no longer would be regarded as a victim of mental instability.

MacMillan's editors are r'aring to go. They offer examples of their new publishing philosophy. Because more than one-half of the population is female, illustrators should see that females are represented appropriately hereafter.

In the bad old days of textbook illustration, a drawing might have appeared of "mother sewing while dad reads." Under the new egalitarian standards, MacMillan wants a drawing of "mother looking at her desk while dad reads or clears the dining room table."

In the sinful past, an unregenerate illustrator, his consciousness not yet raised, might have depicted "mother bringing sandwiches to dad as he fixes the roof." No more! New textbooks will depict "mother fixing the roof."

Once a textbook might have shown "boys playing ball, girls watching." Such innacurate, irrelevant and outmoded depictions are now condemned. MacMillan decrees "both sexes playing ball; sometimes boys watching a girls' team play."

MacMillan is not bothered by intellectual fraud: "We are more interested in emphasizing what can be, rather than the negatives that still exist. ... The fact that black persons do not yet hold a proportionate share of executive positions should not prevent us from depicting a sizable number of blacks as executives."

Now, for the record, there is, of course, much in MacMillan's position that is admirable. It is perfectly true that for generations our textbooks ignored Negroes, depicted feathered Indians in tepees, put blankets on indolent Mexicans, and consigned darling little lily-white girls to the endless baking of cherry pies. It is altogether desirable to abandon or to modify practices both cruel and stupid.

But the wrong is not corrected, it is merely reversed and compounded, by imposing educational policies depicting a fantasy world. Are we to imagine a baseball team consisting of three white girls, two black girls, three white boys, and a Chinese shortstop?

Children are wiser than we think. Looking at such an illustration, children will not say, "What a beautiful egalitarian ideal!" They will say, "What a fake!"

Courtesy Washington Star Syndicate, Inc.

"HOP IN WE'RE JUST KILLING TIME TILL NEXT CLASS"

DEATH SKETCH — This cartoon by student cartoonist Brian Basset is critical of reckless student driving. Basset resigned from the staff of Langley High School student newspaper in Northern Virginia after the paper decided not to publish his drawing. (AP)

DEATH SKETCH RULED 'TOO PERSONAL'

Teenage Cartoonist Quits Over Publication Dispute

WASHINGTON (AP) — The cartoonist of a high school newspaper in nearby northern Virginia has resigned because the paper refused to publish a drawing bitterly criticizing reckless student driving.

It had been scheduled to appear in the newspaper of Fairfax County's Langley High School last Friday along with an editorial on the subject and a tribute to a Langley student who was killed last month in an automobile accident during school hours.

THE CARTOONIST, Brian Basset, 17, refused to change the cartoon, which depicted five students picking up a black-clad, sickly-carrying grim reaper as a hitchhiker. He also refused to change the

caption: "Hop in . . . we're just killing time till next class."

"Basically I was doing humorous editorials, but death is a strong issue and I wanted the cartoon to have impact," said Basset, the son of newspaper cartoonist Gene Basset.

John Bussey, 18, editor of the paper, said that after a close vote of the staff and considerable soul-searching, he decided to ask Basset to change the drawing because it would not be in good taste along with a memorial to Patricia Collier, 17, the student who was killed.

"THE CARTOON was excellently done," he said, "but it could be taken the wrong way by a segment of the school who knew Patty, and by her family."

Huldah Clark, an English and journalism teacher who serves as faculty adviser to the tabloid paper, described the cartoon as "too personal, too soon and too strong," adding:

"It wasn't a right or wrong situation. There were good points on both sides, but there were reservations that the cartoon might be taken too personally."

Courtesy of The Associated Press.

Editorial

Society's evils unfit for News?

The **News** would like to take this opportunity to comment on some of the letters and conversations we have had with people concerning the prostitution article in the January 31 issue. Many people seem to have their own ideas of what the story really means and why we printed it.

Many people were upset with various aspects of the article and did not read it with the proper perspective. Some felt we were building up prostitution and trying to influence moral judgements. Others thought we "put down" a NT graduate. Still others were offended by the language used. We did not intend to condone or degrade prostitution. The article was simply an interview.

We believe the **News** gives fairly balanced coverage of both the good and bad aspects of NT. Not every graduate becomes as successful as Ann-Margaret and Sen. Charles Percy. No newspaper or news program shows only the good side of life. It is our obligation to print articles whether or not it agrees with the moral code of **some** of our readers.

The obscenity was not put in to purposely offend people or to gain attention to the article. It was merely part of the interview and was a direct quote. The girl chose to express herself in this manner, and we felt it would have detracted from the way she presented herself in the interview if we censored the obscenities.

Finally, many students are not as sheltered as some parents and teachers may believe. We considered the article worthwhile because it presented a new and interesting point of view. While we received several objections to the article, many readers enjoyed it. It was a side of society that is too often censored, but it is a realistic part of life that students will be exposed to sooner or later. It is far better that the student be exposed to this "evil of society" in a matter of fact manner. More harm comes from ignorance than knowledge. We are not our readers' rose colored glasses.

NEWS MEDIA

New Trier News

NT graduate talks about prostitution
by Clark Mackie

New Trier's News: Hooking the readers

High School Confidential

"When I first started," confided the 18-year-old prostitute to her interviewer, "my thinking was: guys can get it on, why can't I? And hell, I can get paid for it and they can't. I was 16 the first time I actually charged." If the interview had appeared in a girlie magazine or even a big-city newspaper, it would have lifted few eyebrows. But it happened to run in a recent issue of the New Trier News, the school paper of the New Trier East High School in the posh Chicago suburb of Winnetka. The interviewer was a 17-year-old senior and the happy hooker was a 1974 New Trier alumna.

Above, *New Trier News*, New Trier High School East, Winnetka, Illinois.
Right, from *Newsweek*, May 26, 1975.

Where responsibility lies

Right from *The Arizona Republic*, February 7, 1975.
Below, from The Arizona State University *State Press*, February 14, 1975.

An Arizona State University committee, composed of faculty and student members, has recommended that the State Press, an undergraduate publication, be placed directly under the office of the President.

The four-times-a-week newspaper is now run as an adjunct of the journalism department. It is financed in large part by a subsidy

Student newspaper has rights, prof says

By Wendy Johnson

A nationally known authority on constitutional law said an Arizona Republic editorial is "dead wrong" by saying the First Amendment rights of free speech and press do not apply to the State Press, an undergraduate newspaper partially subsidized by student fees.

William Canby Jr., ASU professor of law, was commenting on a Republic editorial appearing last week which said the State Press could be legally censored since it is partially funded by the university.

The editorial stated, "The First Amendment doesn't repeal the ancient adage that whoever pays the fiddler can call the tune."

In answer, Canby said, "Several cases, especially in Federal Courts, have upheld the rights of student editors against censorship of a university president, even when the newspaper was financed either by student fees or by direct state appropriations."

The Republic argued "If the State Press were published by students who sold subscriptions, solicited ads and paid their own bills, it would be as free to lambast the ASU administration as The Arizona Republic is."

Canby cited the case of Dickey (a student newspaper editor) vs. Alabama State Board of Education in which the state argued that if the state owned the newspaper, it had the right to prevent the student editor from criticizing the state. The Federal District Court overturned the case in favor of Dickey.

"Virtually every federal court that has considered it (the matter of censorship) has given student editors of college newspapers some sort of protection against censorship by administrative authorities," Canby said.

from student fees. The paper frequently criticizes the administration of the university, sometimes fairly, sometimes unfairly.

Max Jennings, a professor in the journalism department, is faculty adviser to the State Press. He described himself as concerned about the possibility of censorship if the committee's recommendations are followed. Prof. William E. Arnold, who was chairman of the committee, apparently has no such fears.

Obviously The Arizona Republic is as much opposed to censorship as anyone. All general circulation newspapers owe their very existence to the First Amendment, which guarantees a free press in this country.

But the rights of free speech and a free press don't apply to an undergraduate newspaper which is subsidized by fees that the students must pay. The First Amendment doesn't repeal the ancient adage that whoever pays the fiddler can call the tune.

If the State Press were published by students who sold subscriptions, solicited ads and paid their own bills, it would be as free to lambaste the ASU administration as The Arizona Republic is.

But so long as it accepts a subsidy from university funds, with the staffers being paid for what should be a learning experience, the State Press cannot expect to be a free agent.

The undergraduate paper is in fact an arm of the university. A wise administration would give it as much leeway as it seemed to deserve, but it would be foolish to let it remain a burr under the president's saddle.

The faculty-student committee recommendation is interesting in one respect. It shows an admirable reversal of the one-time campus attitude toward the administration.

The committee clearly understands that "academic freedom" does not give either professors or students the authority to publish a newspaper without assuming the responsibility that goes with publication.

Canceled Debate

Roy Innis, executive director of the Congress of Racial Equality, is an advocate of black nationalism and a militant opponent of racial integration. Dr. William Shockley, a physicist who won the Nobel Prize for his role in invention of the transistor, is a vigorous exponent of the theory that genetic rather than environmental factors are primarily responsible for the disadvantaged position of blacks in a predominantly white society.

There is much in the views and ideologies of both men with which rational observers of American society have good reason to disagree. That very fact makes a public debate between these two controversial figures a matter of special interest, with a university campus an appropriate setting.

It is therefore a sad commentary on the state of intellectual tolerance in the academic community that, in response to pressure from the Black Law Students Association, a scheduled Innis-Shockley debate at Harvard has been canceled. The incident renders particularly relevant a warning issued last week by a group of prominent scholars from the United States and abroad. They concluded a four-day discussion in Venice on "The Crisis of the University" by noting that, even though overt violence and intimidation have diminished, "concessions to expediency are being made every day." Such concern is clearly justified when one of the world's leading universities finds it expedient to let free debate be stifled on its campus.

Thinking Out Loud

Permit me to debunk some of the favorite words and cliches of the liberals and left-wingers. One of these is the high-sounding phrase, "Academic Freedom."

Once it appeared to be a good word, when it seemed to give the teacher liberty to explore new horizons, and to teach within the limits of decency and respectability all available knowledge on any given subject, always careful to teach fact as fact, and theory as theory, and to point out and define the difference between the two.

"Academic freedom" was never intended to be divorced from moral responsibility; nor was it ever intended to challenge the existence of God Almighty, or His operations among the sons of men.

It was never intended to be an excuse for free thinkers to challenge the divine creation of man, nor to overthrow the law of God, nor to deny man's need of redemption, nor to teach infidelity.

"Academic freedom" is a misnomer if it seeks to operate outside of God's orbit, for man has no rights—not even the right to exist—outside the sovereign will of God.

But, alas, what has this so-called "academic freedom" come to mean in its present distortion? Never has a phrase been so corrupted or prostituted.

For many today who loudly demand the use of "academic freedom," mean, rather, "unrestrained license" to teach whatever they choose, with total disregard of the basic rights of those whom they teach, and regardless of the people who through their gifts, tax dollars, and sacrifices make possible the very existence of our schools and universities.

To them it means an unhindered, unrestrained, unsupervised license to teach, as they choose, infidelity, atheism, Communism, sex perversion, intemperance, anything — even the change of our form of government from a constitutional republic to a socialistic state.

Under the guise of this so-called "academic freedom" they presume to have the right to usurp the place of the parents, and teach doctrines and philosophies which will have the effect of completely changing the beliefs and the behaviour of our young people.

Under this damnable cloak of so-called "academic freedom" they presume to compel the society which supports them to completely refrain from interference with their program of humanism, and to arrogantly reach their slimy hands down your pockets for the funds necessary to subvert and corrupt your children. Not only so, but they are so lifted up with pride and vanity as to look with disdain upon any citizen who criticizes their licentious program.

If you dare to get in their way, they will brand you as a square, an ignoramous, an old fogey, a Puritan, a hater of arts and literature.

Although they boast of a supreme liberalism, when crowded into the corner they manifest the most pronounced spirit of bigotry. Their ideas, they think, represent the last word in intelligence; no other opinions, or philosophies, or religions are of any worth. All knowledge ends with them!

Well, I've got news for them. They are the biggest bunch of asinine parasites on the face of the earth. And so help me God, I shall continue to devote a good part of my life to exposing their hypocrisy. It is time that we begin to find out who the real phonies are in our society.

Dale Crowley in *The Capital Voice*, January 1, 1971.

John P. Roche

The right to be heard

I WAS RECENTLY asked how I felt about an invitation by a nearby university to a spokesman for the Palestine Liberation Organization: there was some feeling that his talk might constitute a "provocation."

My reply was that I consider the PLO to be a bunch of ideological gangsters, but that if its speaker appeared (unarmed) he deserved to be heard, and anybody who tried to break up the meeting or shout him down should be tucked in the slammer.

Recently, however, Ronald Ziegler has been put through the mill at Boston University's School of Public Communication. Originally the student assembly unanimously voted to invite him to lecture on the "use and abuse of power" at a $2,700 fee.

The dean then intervened, protesting the fee. In fairness, he did add that he would defend Ziegler's right to speak — for nothing. The faculty unanimously supported this suggestion and, when the matter returned to the student government, the latter disinvited Ziegler.

The nub of the attack was that by paying Ziegler, the school was endorsing the whole "immoral" Watergate sequence.

What is raised by this assault on Ziegler is the whole question of double-moral bookkeeping. Let me say, for starters, that I think the student assembly was out of its mind to invite Ziegler to talk at a School of Public Communication. It is comparable to inviting a color-blind individual to lecture on the French impressionists. Ziegler's specialty was non-communication.

Second, the $2,700 fee is mind-boggling. I believe the original offer was inane.

However, once the invitation was out, it seems to me that the dean and his faculty behaved in a quite outrageous fashion. One can make a case — number of conservatives do — that the faculty and administration of a school should act ideologically in *loco parentis* to the students, effectively straightening the children out when the little dears go astray. But the liberal view, as I understand it, is that the students are not to be treated as *non compos* infants, that they have wide areas of free choice, and that customarily in a liberal institution one of these areas is who they want to listen to on issues of the day.

Between 1968 and 71 it was hard to turn around without finding some left-wing militant whooping up the campus revolution. In my personal judgment a number of them were taking "immoral" positions and collecting substantial sums in the process.

To this, a conservative (like, I presume, the dean of Boston University's School of Public Communications) will replay, "why don't you take your morals seriously?" I do, but I also have a haunting sense of fallibility and deep suspicion of obsequious piety.

One of the students at the school, commenting on the decision, said, "we have a chance to tell the entire country that we don't want a deceitful person to speak from a public platform. No one in America had a say in the pardon of Nixon, but this is our opportunity not to pardon Ziegler."

I suppose it's uplifting to have students with such a prophetic afflatus, but this sinner's reaction is simply to gag.

On Stealing Government Documents

By REP. JOHN ASHBROOK (R.-Ohio)

Reprinted with permission from the July 24, 1971, issue of *Human Events*, 422 First St., S.E., Washington, D.C. 20003.

It is amazing how the major media have chosen to overlook one important aspect of the recent Pentagon Papers affair. That is the simple fact that, by his own admission, Daniel Ellsberg just plain stole the government documents in direct violation of law and in violation of his trust as a government employe. If his is to be condoned, where does it ever stop?

I have never been impressed with the validity of the argument that the individual can decide what law he wants to obey and selectively break it whenever it fits his fancy. Historically, the true martyr often felt compelled by act of conscience to violate the law and then pay the penalty. The modern chicken martyr on the other hand has chosen to violate the law but then tries to evade paying the penalty. The Rev. Martin Luther King was a great exponent of deliberate civil disobedience but when he was found guilty of breaking the law he invariably attacked the system as racist.

Now there seems to be an effort to build Daniel Ellsberg into some kind of a Robin Hood hero. This he is not, in my judgment. The news media seem to think that the public's right to know is more important than the logical contention that there are some things that must be discreetly held back. Would the New York *Times* print the invasion plans for Normandy the day before the troops left England? Would it be feasible to tell in advance that the government is planning a devaluation of currency? (Wouldn't the speculators have a holiday?)

Three governments have already protested to our government that they no longer feel they can confide or discuss sensitive problems due to the lack of security and the problems of having some unfaithful employe think he knows best. For example, we are involved in trying to work out some of the really major differences between Israel and the Arab nations. It would absolutely torpedo these negotiations back home if some State Department employe were to tell the New York *Times* and it were to print that "Mrs. Meir is prepared to concede on point X" or to print that "Despite Sadat's public pronouncements, he has indicated that he will compromise with Israel on point X." Such a disclosure would galvanize their position from which they could not retreat.

It sounds simplistically accurate to generalize that everything that goes on in government should be in the public domain but this defies common sense. I personally believe there is too much cover-up and feel that the government has in the past misled and continues to do so in some areas. I don't think that the press has a right to every news item that some disloyal employe would slip to it, however.

The press also takes a singularly one-sided approach to the whole issue of the public's right to know. Capitol Hill reporters write most of their articles on the basis of what "a well-informed observer says" or "a senator who does not want to be identified" or "a usually reliable source." What about the public's right to know where this reporter got his information or if there was, in fact, any source other than the fertile mind of the reporter himself? No, they say. We have an absolute right to keep our sources sacred. Yet they think the government doesn't have any such right. CBS alleges its right to clip news items, rearrange them, present its own propaganda view and then tells a congressional committee they have no right to see the raw, unedited transcripts. The public's right to know stops rather abruptly where their own self-interest is concerned.

Somewhere between full disclosure of everything on one side and censorship and cover-up on the other there should be a reasonable balance. It is hard to find this in a free society, to be sure, but this effort must be made. To follow the New York *Times'* logic to its ultimate conclusion, they or the individual simply knows what is best and will judge. Julius and Ethel Rosenberg had a "right" to give our atomic bomb secrets to our enemy. The government has no right for predetermined withholding of any news item. By the way, it was interesting to note that Cyrus Eaton, a pro-Red fellow Ohioan, let the cat out of the bag. Hanoi knew all of these things all along, says Eaton. Why? Well, some individual privy to them probably thought it was Hanoi's right to know and the government had no right to withhold the information.

Where does this strange reasoning end? You can only guess.

Arrogance, Not Freedom, Tested

Before he became disillusioned by the misbehavior of the media of his day, Thomas Jefferson said that if he were forced to make one choice only, he would select a free press over government.

If the New York Times, the Washington Post and the Boston Globe are sustained in their thesis that they can at their own discretion publish any top secret documents that they can acquire, the nation may face a Jeffersonian choice.

Freedom of the press is really not the issue that the three newspapers have brought before the nation as the federal government seeks to recover top secret documents that were stolen from the Pentagon files.

No responsible person is against freedom of the press or the legitimate right of the public to know the decisions of its governments. By the same token, no responsible citizen challenges the principle that some things that government does must be kept secret in order to protect our nation.

Thus the willful publication of stolen, secret material must be considered in another light, particularly in view of the current newspaper tactics. When the New York Times was enjoined from further publication after publishing three articles, the Washington Post printed the next two. When the Washington Post was enjoined, the Boston Globe presumably completed the series. At no time did any of the newspapers make contact with the government to urge regular procedures to de-classify the material. None of them yielded to the pleadings of the federal government to stop publication. The material, for example, could readily have been paraphrased if principles of free press alone were the issue. Instead volumes of secret data were published verbatim — an act which could be of value to an enemy.

Clearly the challenge is to the institution of government itself. What the three newspapers are saying is that the judgment of the press —

and that could be anybody with a mimeograph machine — supersedes that of the elected and appointed representatives of the people.

Moreover, those newspapers are saying that the means justifies the end — that if they regard their goals as moral, they can break the law to attain those goals. In this respect, their argument is little different than that used by the anarchists who take to the streets. A comparable principle would be that false testimony and tainted evidence could be used in court so long as it results in the guilty being punished.

Reason alone dictates that this concept cannot be sustained if the United States of America is to survive. If the United States could no longer have secrets, or if stolen secrets were fair game for dissemination, there would be no United States government — probably no free press either.

Above from *The San Diego Union*, June 23, 1971.
Below, courtesy of Mike Peters.

The Right to Know vs. Rubies

THE WORD from Boston is that the Justice Department is trying to get an indictment against Neil Sheehan, the New York Times reporter who first wrote the story of the Pentagon papers. The charge being sought is that Sheehan knowingly transported stolen property across state lines.

There may be a technical point of law involved, but in equity and intent this is blatant nonsense.

This is not to say that Sheehan or any other newspaperman is immune from prosecution for violating the law. As Tom Winship, editor of the Boston Globe, said when his newspaper published the Pentagon papers, he was prepared to bear the consequences, whatever they might be. This was the same position taken by civil rights leaders in the South who knowingly broke state laws. They were willing to go to jail to demonstrate to the nation that the state laws were in violation of the Constitution.

To get a conviction against Sheehan, Justice is going to have to prove first that a crime was committed, and then that Sheehan did it. Assuming that Sheehan did what he is suspected of doing, Justice is still going to have trouble proving a crime.

Were the documents stolen? We don't know. They were certainly copied, but that's different. Documents aren't like a ruby necklace, nor was copying them like infringing on a copyright, which denies to its owner something of value.

A theft implies a victim. Who was the victim? The answer is that there wasn't any.

The papers were the result of work done at government expense. The papers belong to the people. And what Sheehan did was not take the papers from the people, but the precise opposite. He and his presumed accomplices took copies of the papers from those who were hiding them from the people and delivered them to their rightful owners.

If anyone could be said to own them more than anyone else, it might be Robert McNamara, who commissioned them while secretary of Defense. Mr. McNamara is on record that the papers should have been given to the public long before.

It is interesting to note that Mr. Sheehan is apparently not to be charged with violating national security, which was the first reaction from the Nixon administration. The reason is simple: Experts from Dean Rusk, secretary of State at the time, on down say that no security was violated.

To argue that Mr. Sheehan committed no crime and violated no security in this case is not to provide the press with an absolute blanket of privilege. We recognize the necessity for some government secrecy and we recognize the dangers to security. On the whole, the media's record is exemplary. It is far better, for example, than the record of government officials who pepper their memoirs with classified material to justify their stewardship.

If anything, this is the issue which Sheehan has raised. The people have the right to know the people's business, not just that part of it some bureaucrat wants them to know. With common sense, publication of the papers will lead to sensible use, rather than abuse, of classification codes. This in turn will better serve the public interest.

From the *Detroit Free Press*, July 17, 1971.

WHAT IT'S LIKE TO BROADCAST NEWS

by WALTER CRONKITE

I don't think it is any of our business what the moral, political, social, or economic effect of our reporting is. I say let's get on with the job of reporting the news—and let the chips fall where they may. I suggest we concentrate on doing our job of telling it like it is and not be diverted from that exalted task by the apoplectic apostles of alliteration.

If it *happened*, the people are entitled to know. There is no condition that can be imposed on that dictum without placing a barrier (censorship) between the people and the truth—at once as fallible and corrupt as only self-serving men can make it. The barrier can be built by government—overtly by dictatorship or covertly with propaganda on the political stump, harassment by subpoena, or abuse of the licensing power. Or the barrier can be built by the news media themselves. If we permit our news judgment to be colored by godlike decisions as to what is good for our readers, listeners, or viewers, we are building a barrier—no matter how pure our motives.

Above, courtesy of Walter Cronkite and *Saturday Review*, December 12, 1970.

IT IS YOUR BUSINESS, MR. CRONKITE

by IRVING E. FANG

I disagree with Mr. Cronkite. It *is* the journalist's concern to consider the consequences of his work, just as it is the physician's, the attorney's, the minister's, the professor's, and indeed every professional man's concern.

Above courtesy of Irving E. Fang and *Saturday Review*, January 9, 1971. Dr. Fang is an associate professor in the School of Journalism and Mass Communication at the University of Minnesota. A TV newsman for nine years, he is author of a textbook, *Television News*, published by Hastings House.

The distinction between the journalist judging an individual story on its merits and the journalist ignoring the impact of news upon his audience is obviously far more than hairsplitting. To cite one example, riot news was once reported on television newscasts purely on its merits as news. But it soon became evident that the impact of riot news on television viewers—including the rioters themselves—was so great that television news departments trimmed their sails. Broadcast journalists had to make the effects of riot news their business. They did so voluntarily, behaving as responsible members of our society. To ignore the effects of this news would have been unacceptable, and everyone knew it.

NATIONAL
REVIEW

APRIL 13, 1971
Vol. 23   No. 14

The Calley Trial
and After
BULLETIN

Horrible and obscene things happen in war, in every war; and in peace, too, and in the course of each individual's life and dying. Human existence bears no resemblance to the projections of sentimentalists and utopians. But to dwell exclusively on the horrors and obscenities is the road not to vision but to madness. Nor is it necessary that *everything* be brought at all times into the open for everyone to see. Not every diner need keep always in mind the horrors of the slaughterhouse. The civilized man believes that even in war a line must be drawn somewhere. Under a global searchlight may not always be the best place for drawing it. There is something to be said, often, for the old-fashioned rite of the drumhead court-martial.

It has been generally remarked that this Vietnam conflict is the first TV war, and therefore the first in which war's horrors have entered mass consciousness. We are told that this will make war impossible since the masses, being conscious now of the horrors, will not permit war. Both premise and conclusion are faulty. It is not the war that is being presented on a global screen, but only a cross-section of horrors and sensationalized happenings drawn by camera crews and reporters functioning freely on our side of the line. There are no freely ranging crews or screens or networks on the enemy's side. The televised war of horrors exists not for the global village but only for the side that is the more civilized, democratic and technologically advanced. If the continuous televising of this war is, in fact, leading the audience to renouncing war, this will not at all mean no more war. If civilized men, overcome by war's quota of sensationalist horror, no longer can fight, then they will inevitably be enslaved, or destroyed, by the uncivilized, who can.

From *National Review Bulletin*, April 13, 1971.

Brutality in Boston

Even in an era hardened to criminal violence, the mind's capacity for horror and revulsion is overtaxed by the hideous sadism of six youths in Boston who forced a young woman to douse herself with gasoline and then set her afire. Race hatred of the kind that is virulent in many sections of this historic city was apparently a motivating element in this demented tragedy, but the television screen may well have provided the murderers with instruction in the inhuman technique they used.

Boston's Police Commissioner, Robert J. diGrazia, notes that a motion picture shown on network television three nights before the killing contained a segment in which Boston teen-agers burned derelicts to death for enjoyment.

The dreadful coincidence cannot be ignored, however much the experts may continue to argue whether or not violence on the screen begets violence on the streets. Common sense and social responsibility ought to give the benefit of the doubt to the counsel against entertainment senselessly polluted with violence.

Dr. David Abrahamsen, an acknowledged expert in this field of psychiatry, warned in his book, "Our Violent Society," that "aggression witnessed on television may serve as a stimulus, a triggering for hostile actions. . . ." The mindless violence, which more than ever pervades the motion pictures as well as this year's television programing, fits that description.

From *The Rat/Underground Press Syndicate.*

Overemphasis of sex and violence on television will be a deterrent to your child. Why? In the formative years, what he sees now, later on he will do. He will ape the actions of the actor.

Good logic. Correct. If so, your kid is better off watching a stag movie than *King of Kings*. Mine, anyway. Because I just don't want my kid to kill Christ when he comes back. And that's what's in *King of Kings*—but tell me about a stag movie where someone got killed in the end, or slapped in the mouth, or heard any Communist propaganda. So the sense of values would be, the morals:

"Well, for kids to watch killing—Yes; but *schtupping*—No! Cause if they watch *schtup* pictures, they may do it some day."

By DAVID ELLIOTT
Chicago Daily News Service

Beast-of-Belsen Type or Relieving Tension?

Why Does He Laugh at Movie Violence?

Michael Caine shoved a knife into the gangster's lung, the victim crumpled to the ground, and the man sitting behind me at the theater laughed, loudly. In fact, every time Caine killed somebody, which in "Get Carter" means every few minutes, my neighbor was thrown into a fit of raucous good humor.

Maybe this was what they mean by the evil of movie violence, but for me the man's behavior was more baffling than obnoxious. Despite considerable past experience with the type, I had to ask again the old question: Why is that man laughing?

Was he, burdened by too active an imagination, simply relieving his tension? Was he a devotee of technique, enjoying the cool dispatch of Caine's style? Or was he a real Beast of Belsen type, perhaps even the son of the man who in 1953 guffawed when Lee Marvin threw that pot of scalding coffee in Gloria Grahame's face in "The Big Heat?"

THE FRANK TRUTH is that many American filmgoers, especially men, seem to enjoy nothing more than virile, vicious, bone-crashing violence. There is even a kind of comradeship to the taste. While scenes of intimate sex will usually throw a pall of tense embarrassment over an audience, "good" violence will often bring out the collective animal spirits. Sex tends to isolate each viewer alone in his seat, while violence pulls the crowd together.

Yet, despite this apparent democratic virtue, and even a small clique of critical support (the "tough guy" critics led by Manny Farber), violence by and large has had a very bad press.

Sex is today a matter of bored approval, at least among many sophisticated viewers, but frequently we hear complaints of too much killing from critics, and even more ritually we hear producers and directors huff and puff about the unfairness of the rating system, which winks at slaughter while slapping Xs and Rs on sexually "adult" films.

"Get Carter," a functional little murder machine, provided a nice litmus test on the issue. In the film Caine plays a hood who murders six or seven people, all disgusting types, to avenge the death of his brother. The killing is fast, brutal and dominant—except for Caine's gritty performance, the film has little else to recommend it.

In an interesting nonreview in Life magazine, Richard Schickel told us that "Get Carter" was an obsessional, sadomasochistic movie, a disturbing specimen of what he feels is a new, amoral toying with deaths in films today.

As opposed to that, he praised the more discreet and supposedly more moral murdering of the 1930s, in which, said Schickel, "Violence was a kind of punctuation mark . . . designed to emphasize some larger point of the director's about the nature of society or, perhaps, the workings of human nature."

One can quarrel with this in several ways. First, it's doubtful that 30s violence, which had to be more restrained (i.e., less plentiful) due to the production code then in effect, influenced audiences any differently than does today's mayhem. We now have more of it, more frankly elaborated, but there's little doubt that in the '30s it was that frequently brutal, enormously entertaining violence that brought the audiences back for more. (Plus, of course, such engaging killers as Cagney, Bogart and Muni.)

In fact, the killers of that day were often lit up in a nimbus of romantic buccaneering whose appeal to the audience might have been even more morally questionable than Caine's Carter, whom we never really doubt is a professional bastard at heart.

It can also be shown that "Get Carter," without ever being pretentious about it, does make a point about the "nature" of a special society: A smut-ridden gangster subculture given to functional, dispassionate, almost priestly murder. And beyond that, there are intimations in the film of a wider society for whom violence is a daily diet.

★ ★ ★

STILL, SCHICKEL is on to a worthy issue. "Get Carter" was heavily advertised as a violent movie. It drew many people who therefore apparently wanted violence.

and, by reduction, enjoyed it. So we have a right to ask whether this is moral or not, whether it should be condoned or condemned.

We first have to disabuse ourselves of the notion that violence today is in a class by itself. In the movies it is simply the oldest, most obvious, if least honored form of physical entertainment. Slapstick comedy thrived on it, as did the first westerns. The ganster era gave it a shot of "gats and guts," World War 2 another (under the protective mantle of patriotism), and the new realism after the war added a further edge of visceral effectiveness greatly assisted by rough language and a mood of weary cynicism.

Some highlights (or low)lights) of the past: The epic brawls in each successive version of "The Spoilers" (and almost every John Wayne film), Humphrey Bogart being kicked in the head by Elisha Cook Jr. in "The Maltese Falcon," the giggling of killer Richard Widmark in "Kiss of Death," the pathological cruelty of James Cagney in "White Heat," the gruesome shot of Jack Palance being mashed by the treads of a tank in "Attack," Marlon Brando trashing Vivien Leigh's sanity in "A Streetcar Named Desire," the sardonic carnage of director Stanley Kubrick's "Paths of Glory."

But, unquestionably, there is a new tone, a new streak of license in contemporary violence. The Clint Eastwood spaghetti westerns showed that an audience will, at least for a time, go for wholesale bulk killing, and the Bond films demonstrated a taste for elaborately contrived torture.

Yet before we leap into a state of Calvinistic anxiety about this, we should pay careful attention to specifics and details. Sure sex is creative, therefore a natural good, and violence is destructive, therefore a natural evil, but in the movies such terms are almost meaningless.

Violence is really moral or immoral only in a world of absolutes. For better or worse, that is not the world of commercial films. Most films are melodrama—westerns, crime and horror, psycho-terror, spectacle, spies and suspense pictures—in which absolutes are notoriously bullied by the imperatives of plot. Plot usually boils down to action, and violence is action maximized.

Sam Peckinpah's 1969 western "The Wild Bunch," though in some respects an admirable film, failed as art on the issue of gore. The long massacre at the end of the movie, with bodies piling up like a stockyard inventory, tried to give gore both a moral and an esthetic bite. However, those aims undermined each other.

The killing was physically graceful, which robbed it of moral impact—we finally became not indignant but sort of charmed by the pretty patterns of the blood spurting and the bodies tumbling. At the same time, the beauty was undermined by our nagging doubt that death had a right to be lyrical, to be made a director's conceit.

Aside from artistic pretensions I suspect that another reason for our greater queasiness about violence today is that it is often combined with sex. There has always been an erotic overtone to violence, but when the two elements are so frankly mingled, as in "Get Carter," we are put on edge.

Is there really such a thing as "good" film violence? In a real moral sense, probably not. But within the confines of film drama, certainly. As critic John Simon has pointed out: "The truth about violence is that it is most effective—and most meaningful—when used sparingly but magisterially." Good film violence is tough, credible and wrenching, and it needs good actors and a skillful director to come alive.

★ ★ ★

AND SO: Why was that man laughing? We'll never know for sure, but I suspect that his motives were probably much more complex, and more morally ambivalent, than we first assumed. Fans of violence are ultimately not that much different from any other specialized group of film buffs.

The major point is to recognize that when talking about film violence the emphasis must be upon the word film, a context which is neither quite real nor ideal, one in which violence carries neither the sting of real brutality or the purgation of ideal suffering.

That is why a moralist is the worst critic, the worst defender and simply the worst audience any movie can have

Vonnegut's Otherworldly Laughter

by BENJAMIN DeMOTT

• Youthcult holds that the attempt of the elders to hide the prevalence of brutality from the young (and from themselves) is both criminally evasive and doomed to failure. Vonnegut says the same. At the end of *Mother Night* Howard Campbell, on trial for genocide, receives some junk mail from Creative Playthings pitching for toys that prepare kids for life and help them to "work off aggression." Campbell answers:

I doubt that any playthings could prepare a child for one millionth of what is going to hit him in the teeth, ready or not. My own feeling is . . . [against] bland, pleasing, smooth, easily manipulated playthings like those in your brochure, friends! Let there be nothing harmonious about our children's playthings, lest they grow up expecting peace and order, and be eaten alive. As for children's working off aggressions, I'm against it. They are going to need all the aggressions they can contain for ultimate release in the adult world . . . . Let me tell you that the children in my charge. . . . are spying on real grownups all the time, learning what they fight about, what they're greedy for, how they satisfy their greed, why and how they lie, what makes them go crazy, the different ways they go crazy and so on . . . .

From *Saturday Review*, May 1, 1971.

Whose morality?

The backlash, as we all know, is against sexual permissiveness. But a backlash implies a return to a different norm. What are we proposing to return to? This is the first question to examine if we are to make sense of a moral controversy that has already been rumbling on for years and looks like keeping its point for a good many years to come. Is there some more healthy, stable, and satisfying morality to which we can return? To the morality of the interwar years? To the Edwardians or the Victorians? Hardly anyone is seriously proposing that, partly because even a strict theologian nowadays allows that there is no unchangeable moral code that can be summarised in a decalogue, and partly because we know that Victorian morality was a fraud, sweeping prostitution and pornography into dark corners.

Indeed what we are still experiencing now is an overdue backlash against Victorianism and its hangover into the twentieth century. The reaction against permissiveness today is more accurately described as a counter-backlash.

That sex should be exciting so much argument is not surprising, for we find ourselves in a situation without precedent. The old taboos were securely based as a defence against the risk of pregnancy. The development of effective contraception has altered the context and consequences of extra-marital sexual relations and has made loving and responsible sexual relationships possible outside marriage. For those who do not acknowledge the religious prohibitions it seems arbitrary and unnecessary to deny the place of sex in extramarital love. With the disappearance of the old taboos it has also become natural to talk openly of sex and sexuality and for the writer and artist to depict the sexual aspect of relationships explicitly. All this offends deep-seated convictions or prejudices in some people, but others ask what is the harm if this greater openness makes for greater fulfilment and personal happiness? Is it not a positive advance in the human condition?

We cannot be too sure, because this is virtually unexplored territory, and one where the experts — psychologists, sociologists, and educationists — disagree among themselves. It is good to take the sense of guilt out of sex. On the other hand every intimate personal relationship carries with it the risk of neurotic hang-ups. To recommend promiscuity as a form of self-education (to take an issue raging furiously at the moment) would seem to invite the misery of rejection, and emotional insecurity.

As for pornography, we cannot be too sure of that either. Probably it can deprave and corrupt. On the other hand, the bawdy and the erotic have a place in literature and the arts.

If we look for the enrichment of the individual personality most people would say that a more relaxed and knowledgeable enjoyment of sexual relationships is a plus point on that test. This is no Sodom and Gomorrah we live in even though there may be fringe extravagances. There is some virtue in having a rather more easy-going, open-minded, and plain-speaking society than we have had in the past.

Above, from *The Guardian*, London, May 15, 1971.

119

The Busybody Factor

Buttinskies Make the Culture Scene

By Clifford A. Ridley

Depending on where you sit, the art business may or may not be running low on people of talent, imagination, and daring. Of one commodity, however, it has no dearth. It is up to its ears in busybodies.

Coming from a critic, that may seem an odd complaint. But I will submit in self-defense that my brethren and I are all yap and no bite—that while we breed preferences and proposals by the gross, we really have neither the inclination nor the power to compel anyone to do much about them.

Others are not so reticent.

Consider, for instance, the ABC television network, which determined some 10 days ago that Chicago Seven defendants Hayden, Hoffman, Davis, and Rubin are apparently so inflammatory that they can't be heard without an immediate rebuttal. Lacking such "balance," the network pulled a Dick Cavett interview with the quartet off the air.

Well, one's first reaction is that the ABC assessment will surely come as news to the Messrs. Hayden, Hoffman, Davis, and Rubin, who are about as effective or, as interested in overthrowing the Government these days as I am. One's second reaction is that ABC is running awfully scared. Hey, guys, haven't you heard? Agnew quit!

One-Sided Demand?

"There's nothing in the fairness doctrine about balance of views within a program," Cavett was quoted as saying. "On the other hand, I have an agreement with the network that such balance will be supplied." That, I suspect, was probably a mistake, but Cavett says he was properly skeptical during this particular show—and anyway, he wants to know, where were the equal-timers during his interview with Jerry Ford earlier this year?

A silly episode, and no mistake. Chalk one up for the busybodies.

Comment

Bury the Bard?

Finally, in Minneapolis, a local rabbi last month deplored the Guthrie Theatre's inclusion of *The Merchant of Venice* in its current repertory, saying, "It's time we did away with all stereotypes." From his remarks, it's clear that the rabbi is no hothead—he's a longtime supporter of the Guthrie—but in this context I fear that he, too, is a busybody.

There's no gainsaying, of course, that there are elements of anti-Semitism in Shakespeare's Shylock, but there's also no gainsaying that for all its biases *The Merchant* is a great play (perhaps, even, because of them), illuminating the human heart and mind in language that is entrusted to but a sacred few. Putting the matter simply, you don't ignore great art, however hard it makes you swallow—and an awful lot of it does, when you think about it.

You can explain it in the context of its time, you can warn folks who might be offended not to come, you can candidly acknowledge that in some respects its creator was a crackpot, but you don't ignore it. We are not yet so well endowed with the truth and beauty that great art provides that we can afford to consign any of it to the dustbin. And I doubt we ever will be.

Hey, everybody! Lay off, huh?

Excerpts From Pornography Opinions

MILLER v. CALIFORNIA
Opinion by Burger

We acknowledge, however, the inherent dangers of undertaking to regulate any form of expression. State statutes designed to regulate obscene materials must be carefully limited. As a result, we now confine the permissible scope of such regulations to works which depict or describe sexual conduct.

That conduct must be specifically defined by the applicable state law, as written or authoritatively construed. A state offense must also be limited to works which, taken as a whole, appeal to the prurient interest in sex, which portray sexual conduct in a patently offensive way, and which, taken as a whole, do not have serious literary, artistic, political or scientific value.

The basic guidelines for the tryer of fact must be: (a) whether "the average person, applying contemporary community standards" would find that the work, taken as a whole, appeals to the prurient interest; (b) whether the work depicts or describes, in a patently offensive way, sexual conduct specifically defined by the applicable state law, and (c) whether the work, taken as a whole, lacks serious literary, artistic, political, or scientific value.

A Rejected Concept

We do not adopt as a constitutional standard the "utterly without redeeming social value" test. That concept has never commanded the adherence of more than three justices at one time. If a state law that regulates obscene material is thus limited, as written or construed, the First Amendment values applicable to the states through the 14th Amendment are adequately protected by the ultimate power of appellate courts to conduct an independent review of constitutional claims when necessary.

PARIS THEATER CASE
Opinion by Burger

It should be clear from the outset that we do not undertake to tell the states what they must do, but rather to define the area in which they may chart their own course in dealing with obscene material.

We categorically disapprove the theory, apparently adopted by the trial judge, that obscene, pornographic films acquire constitutional immunity from state regulation simply because they are exhibited for consenting adults only.

Although we have often pointedly recognized the high importance of the state interest in regulating the exposure of obscene materials to juveniles and unconsenting adults, this Court has never declared these to be the only legitimate state interests permitting regulation of obscene material.

The states have a long-recognized legitimate interest in regulating the use of obscene material in local commerce and in all places of public accommodation, as long as these regulations do not run afoul of specific constitutional prohibitions.

In particular, we hold that there are legitimate state interests at stake in stemming the tide of commercialized obscenity, even assuming it is feasible to enforce effective safeguards against exposure to juveniles and to the passerby. Rights and interests "other than those of the advocates are involved." These include the interest of the public in the quality of life and the total community environment, the tone of commerce in the great city centers, and, possibly, the public safety itself.

As Chief Justice Warren stated, There is a "right of the nation and of the states to maintain a decent society."

But, it is argued, there is no scientific data which conclusively demonstrates that exposure to obscene materials adversely affects men and women or their society. It is urged on bshalf of the petitioner that, absent such a demonstration, any kind of state regulation is "impermissible."

We regret this argument. Although there is no conclusive proof of a connection between antisocial behavior and obscene material, the legislature of Georgia could quite reasonably determine that such a connection does or might exist.

From the beginning of civilized societies legislators and judges have acted on various unprovable assumptions. Such assumptions underlie much lawful state regulation of commercial and business affairs.

Decision for Legislature

If we accept the unprovable assumption that a complete education requires certain books, and the well nigh universal belief that good books, plays, and art lift the spirit, improve the mind, enrich the human personality and develop character, can we then say that a state legislature may not act on the corollary assumption that commerce in obscene books, or public exhibitions focused on obscene conduct, have a tendency to exert a corrupting and debasing impact leading to antisocial behavior?

It is argued that individual "free will" must govern, even in activities beyond the protection of the First Amendment and other constitutional guarantees of privacy, and that government cannot legitimately impede an individual's desire to see or acquire obscene plays, movies, and books.

We do indeed base our society on certain assumptions that people have the capacity for free choice. Most exercises of individual free choice —those in politics, religion, and expression of ideas—are explicitly protected by the Constitution. Totally unlimited play for free will, however, is not allowed in ours or any other society.

Dissent by Brennan

If, as the Court today assumes, "a state legislature may act on the assumption that commerce in obscene books, or public exhibitions focused on obscene conduct, have a tendency to exert a corrupting and debasing impact leading to antisocial behavior," then it is hard to see how state-ordered regimentation of our minds can ever be forestalled.

For if a state may, in an effort to maintain or create a particular moral tone, prescribe what its citizens cannot read or cannot see, then it would seem to follow that in pursuit of that same objective a state could decree that its citizens must read certain books or must view certain films.

However laudable its goal —and that is obviously a question on which reasonable minds may differ—the state cannot proceed by means that violate the Constitution.

Even a legitimate, sharply focused state concern for the morality of the community cannot, in other words, justify an assault on the protections of the First Amendment. Where the state interest in regulation of morality is vague and ill-defined, interference with the guarantees of the First Amendment is even more difficult to justify.

In short, while I cannot say that the interests of the state—apart from the question of juveniles and unconsenting adults—are trivial or nonexistent, I am compelled to conclude that these interests cannot justify the substantial damage to constitutional rights and to this nation's judicial machinery that inevitably results from state efforts to bar the distribution even of unprotected material to consenting adults.

I would hold, therefore, that at least in the absence of distribution to juveniles or obtrusive exposure to unconsenting adults, the First and 14th Amendments prohibit the state and Federal governments from attempting wholly to suppress sexually oriented materials on the basis of their allegedly "obscene" contents.

From *The New York Times*, June 22, 1973.

A Blow To Pornography

AN historic decision by the U.S. Supreme Court now promises to reverse a tide of judicial permissiveness which has left the American people confused and powerless in the face of an explosion of "hard core" pornography in their midst.

Upsetting some easily-evaded definitions of obscenity which had come to prevail in the past 10 years, Chief Justice Warren Burger's majority opinion simply restates p r i n c i p l e s that should have been obvious all along. The "average p e r s o n" serving on a jury is as equipped as any psychologist or sociological expert to decide what kind of material is offensive enough to be banned from the public marketplace, the decision holds. It is for local communities to establish the moral standards of Main Street.

Justice Burger is fully aware that public attitudes toward sex are changing, and that it can be argued that society is better off by shedding some of the "layers of prudery" that once kept sexual subjects in the closet. However, he offers a pertinent analogy that the benefit from the use of medicinal morphine does not mean that c i v i l i z e d people should allow unregulated use of its deadly derivative, heroin.

The battle to restore some rules of decency to what is displayed and sold in our communities is far from over. However, the Supreme Court has cleared the judicial air in a way that will allow the use of one weapon which the courts in recent years had kept largely out of the fray. That weapon is the public conscience, and at last we can hope that its voice and strength will be asserted once again.

Above, from the *Illinois State Journal*, July 4, 1973.
Right, from *The Capital Voice*, Dale Crowley, Editor.
Below, from *Newsweek*, October 29, 1973.

BLUE-MOVIE BLUES

BY SHANA ALEXANDER One difficulty in writing about porn is that *everything* about it has been observed before, yet its essential mystery remains. As Justice Potter Stewart once said, he couldn't define it, but he knew it when he saw it. A couple of months later, Chief Justice Earl Warren observed dryly that it might be more precise to say he knew it when he felt it.

TURNED ON

Yet if pornography is whatever turns anybody on, then "Tristan und Isolde" is porn.

I agree with the London Times: "Pornography always has in it somewhere a hatred of man, both of man as a human being able to respond to ideals, and of man as an animal. Pornography is not an affirmation but a denial of life, and commercial pornography is a denial of life for the sake of money."

My letter to the *Washington Evening Star* and *Daily News* on pornography:
"To the Editor:

Your disgusting editorial in support of freedom of pornography versus the Supreme Court decision benumbs the spiritual sensibilities of all right thinking people who are concerned about the morals of young Americans. The writer of "Off To An Early Start," poking fun at the Albermarle County sheriff because of his efforts to implement the most worthy and commendable ruling on obscenity that has been made by the high court in many years obviously has no children of his own, or even grandchildren of an impressionable age, and utterly no concern for the morals of his neighbors' children.

Why should the *Evening Star and Daily News* take an official position in favor of the free circulation of pornographic material and against the highest interest of the decent element of our society? When you state, "We think the individual is fully capable of judging for himself," you miss the point entirely. Yes, adult, mature human beings are capable of making a decision to go to hell, if they so choose. But why should such decisions be imposed on immature children and impressionable young people of our land. The editor should know that the Supreme Court said absolutely nothing about a man's individual choice in this matter of merchandising obscenity. It simply decreed, at long last, that any community in the United States, (including the editor's own community), has a RIGHT to establish its own standards of morality, and enforce them.

More power to Sheriff George Bailey, and may his tribe increase!
Sincerely yours,
(Signed Dale Crowley"

(Editor's note: Now is the time for the decent citizens, all over America, to enter the fight, and wage a relentless warfare against this ungodly floodtide of moral filth).

Movie Mailbag

'Decent Americans Hail Supreme Court Rulings'

TO THE EDITOR:

YOUR symposium concerning the new Supreme Court ruling on obscenity (Aug. 5) is a fine example of unbalanced reporting.

How about an article devoted to the millions of decent Americans who are hailing the ruling as a step toward rebuilding the moral fiber of our country?

In this war between good and evil, we must learn to recognize who our enemies are and what weapons they use. Key words and phrases such as "censorship," "freedom of speech," "art," "vigilantes," "puritans," "book burners" and "blue noses," are being used as weapons by those forces which are out to destroy every last vestige of decency and good taste, thus bringing about the moral destruction of our nation.

Motion-picture producers, writers and artists with high moral standards do not fear the new decision simply because they would never stoop to the depths of degeneracy. It is only those who are morally deficient who fear the decision. They feel restricted within the framework of decency because the evil inclinations within them have overpowered the good. If they would recognize the fact that God gave them the power to reach greater heights in their thinking and actions so that mankind could be elevated rather than degraded, the turmoil within them would subside and they would find reconciliation within that framework which they now find so confining.

A careful study of the Preamble to the Constitution would reveal to them that it is inconceivable that our forefathers, being fully aware that it was internal moral decay which caused the collapse of nations, would advocate freedom as a vehicle for the filth, vice and corruption which would lead our country to a similar fate.

Pornography does not help to form a more perfect union, nor does it help to promote the general welfare simply because it appeals to the lower, animalistic instincts in man. To cater to such instincts is not "freedom," it is sheer slavery because man becomes a slave to his passions and impulses rather than their master. When man becomes a slave unto himself, he loses the proper perspective and control, thus losing the very values which go into the making of a civilization.

DIANA RONALD
N.Y. Diocesan Chairman
Women for Decency
Catholic Daughters of America
Pound Ridge, N. Y.

Left, letter to the editor of *The New York Times*, courtesy of Diana Ronald, Pound Ridge, New York, September 9, 1973.
Right, © 1973–1975 by The New York Times Company (August 5, 1973). Reprinted by permission.

'Rulings? Not Mine'

By MELVIN VAN PEEBLES, *author and director.*

MY shiftless behind must have slept through the whole thing. NEW OBSCENITY RULING!!!??? Lord, Lord, new rulings and here me I haven't never even run into no relevant *old* obscenity laws.

What obscenity rules? You still can and always could show and do all the most really big obscenities on the old silver screen you wanted—from shuffling niggers rushing to massa with a mint julep, to triumphant superblacks winning with the help of law and order (massa disguised behind a badge), to Tonto getting done in (long on nobility but short on victory).

You can deal, do, show, say all and anything you please about spics, coons, wops, broads, honkeys, wasps, yids, gooks, slopes, imperialism, gangsterism, Watergate games, pacification, reallocation, megatons, methadone, and so on —what obscenity laws? We are free to deal with all the big-time perversions any way we please (with impunity, so the saying goes).

There are no obscenity laws to speak of, unless maybe you mean that pet preoccupation of some of the mainstream folks obsessed with restraining glimpses of PEOPLE DOING IT and associable genitalia. The topsy-turviness of their priorities is a clue to where their heads are. The absurdity of a mentality that puts pubic hair over laissez-faire, sex over self-hate-fostering stereotypes — that's insanity!

When Third World folks and disenfranchised youth are struggling for perspective on their existence, to have some folks pushing their pet coital obsession and coming on righteous behind it, to boot — *that's* obscenity. New rulings, Old rulings, Whose rulings — not mine.

Fred Douglass laid it out a long time ago when he said the master ain't got no laws, national or local, a slave oughta feel duty bound to respect.

The Court and Obscenity: A Dissent

'How Can the Librarian Be Sure?'

♦ The U.S. Supreme Court last week reaffirmed 5-to-4 its decision of last June that the question of what is obscene must be defined according to local community standards. The Court upheld one lower-court obscenity conviction, dismissed appeals in two convictions, and sent eight other obscenity cases back to lower courts for review under the June guidelines. Those guidelines provided for the states to punish printers or sellers of magazines, books, or films "which appeal to the prurient sexual conduct in a patently offensive way and which, taken as a whole, do not have serious literary, artistic, political, or scientific value." As he had last June, Justice William O. Douglas dissented, and last week he was joined by Justices Potter Stewart, Thurgood Marshall, and William Brennan. Here are excerpts from the Douglas dissent:

EVERY AUTHOR, every bookseller, every movie exhibitor, and perhaps, every librarian is now at the mercy of the local police force's conception of what appeals to the "prurient interest" or is "patently offensive." The standard can vary from town to town and day to day in an unpredictable fashion. How can an author or bookseller or librarian know whether the community deems his books acceptable until after the jury renders its verdict? The meaning of the standards necessarily vary according to each person's idiosyncracies. The standards fail to give adequate notice and invite arbitrary exercise of police power. The evil is multiplied because of the danger to First Amendment values of free expression. "Bookselling should not be a hazardous profession" [a quotation from an earlier High Court decision].

If the magazine in question were truly "patently offensive" to the local community, there would be no need to ban them through the exercise of police power; they would be banned by the market place which provided no buyers for them. Thus it must be the case that some substantial portion of the public not only found them not offensive, but worthy of purchase.

How can the bookseller or librarian be sure which of the publications on his shelves are offensive to the majority? Perhaps he will be safe if he sells only publications with a certified history of broad appeal, thus attempting to "steer wide of the unlawful zone." Yet there are many who deem some magazines offensive and even lingerie advertisements in the Sunday papers. A bookseller or a librarian can never know if some jury will find those views representative of the community. A movie exhibitor in Georgia has just found himself convicted under the state's obscenity laws for showing a film [Carnal Knowledge] which received much critical acclaim, and an Oscar nomination for the female lead. We deal here with criminal prosecutions under which a man may lose his liberty. Our Constitution requires fair notice so that the law-abiding can conform their conduct to the requirements of the law.

———

Above, from *The National Observer*, November 3, 1973. Copyright Dow Jones & Co., Inc.

A FOUR-LETTER WORD FOR THE OBSCENITY RULING

The Supreme Court has spoken and, by a 5-4 decision, has taken another tortuous twist in the perpetual attempt to obliterate "obscenity"—which nobody has yet been able to define, except in the dictionary.

This latest effort is really a beaut.

Now every Tom, Dick and Harriet in every hamlet, city and suburb, county and state can and will produce his own judge, jury and decision. Commented Michigan Attorney General Frank Kelley: "Now prosecuting attorneys in every county and state will be grandstanding, and every jury in every little community will have a crack at each new book, play and movie."

And magazine, speech, TV program, radio program and Kiwanis Masters of Ceremonies' jokes.

Despite the kidding that greeted Justice Stewart's observation on obscenity—to wit, "I can't define it but I know it when I see it"—I think I agree with him. In studying Latin (it took me three years to pass Caesar, so my translations might be questioned), I recollect that it didn't take me or my classmates long to locate the "dirty" parts. Ditto *Macbeth* and other required Shakespeare plays.

But this new—I'm tempted to say "current" because I don't see how it can long stand as a guide—decision entitles coffee-klatching collections of housewives to posse down to the local newsstand and get the local police or the area prosecutor seeking reelection to arrest the newsstander for his *Playboy* or any periodical with an "objectionable" picture or word in it.

Books? Every one describing or discussing the fact that storks don't bring all the babies can be the subject of suit by anyone anywhere.

It's hard for people generally to understand that when those of us concerned with a free press object and fight infringements of freedom of expression, we're not trying to defend some of the abuses and some of the explicit in obscenity. But putting up with a little of that to protect your rights under the Constitution to read or to see or to think what you like is vastly more important.

Protecting the young from exposure to pornography and other abuses is another question entirely. Protecting the public generally from public display of such is certainly, too, in order.

But no one forces an adult into a movie theater showing X-rated movies or into book stores to buy erotica.

It was a Justice of the Supreme Court widely considered one of the greatest ever to grace that great bench, Oliver Wendell Holmes, who was said to regale his colleagues with tales of his private collection of pornography. But his revered Supreme Court opinions dealt with the essence of justice, not the circumscribing of freedoms.

—MALCOLM S. FORBES,
Editor-in-Chief

Above, reprinted by permission of *Forbes Magazine* from the July 15, 1973 issue.

Ruling On Obscene
Film Refreshing

By WALTER TROHAN

WASHINGTON, September 15th — Crime is increasing and morality is decreasing. In part, crime is increasing because of a false compassion and unjustifiable obsession with the rights of criminals. Morality is decreasing, in part, because respect for the law and the maintenance of order are being discouraged by some courts, particularly courts of appellate jurisdiction.

It is therefore, refreshing to find a jurist concerned about the rights of society as a whole and one who does not believe that justice is a matter of expediency, but in the general conscience. I cite Chief Judge Harry I. Hannah of the 5th Judicial Circuit of the Illinois Circuit Court of Appeals and his ruling in an obscenity case.

The case involved an "X" rated motion picture, so rated by the industry as unfit for the young, which depicted eight scenes of sexual intercourse — two of husband and wife, two with the husband's friend, another of the wife with a policeman, one of the wife with her brother, two between women, and an attempted rape by a Negro egged on by the woman's brother.

If you and I are shocked, so was the jury of three women and nine men, ranging in age from 23 to 51 and in education from grade school to college. They found the defendants guilty of obscenity in showing the movie. The defendants appealed.

Chief Judge Hannah said, in part in his memorandum opinion: "Much emphasis is placed upon the constitutional guarantee of the right of free speech and expression. However, it has been repeatedly held that this provision does not fold its protective arms about obscenity. We are beginning to wonder if the courts are not becoming unmindful of the fact that the protective arms of the Constitution were intended to protect ALL segments of society with the ultimate purpose of preserving a sound, stable and moral society, according an equal freedom to all, limited, however, to the extent that it not destroy itself.

"Expressed in another manner, are the courts going overboard in their efforts to make sure no one individual is denied what has almost reached an unrestricted right of expression to the exclusion of the right of another segment of the public to insist that the moral standards necessary to the preservation of a stable society be not endangered?

"What was the purpose of the framers of the Constitution — the unrestricted right of expression to the individual or a limited reservation that would preserve the essential moral standards? And who is a better judge of what are contemporary standards in a community than a cross section of the community in the form of a jury selected and chosen by a fair and impartial formula by the parties themselves?"

* * *

The Judge continued: "Many civilizations have preceded ours, civilizations whose skills and education in many aspects excelled the modern civilization. History tells us they have fallen, because, basically, of moral decay. We use the word moral in a broad sense.

"Unrestricted moral decline and decay go to the core of society. A stalwart society can only fruit from a sound core of moral standard. To whom, in the final analysis, do the people look for the preservation of their rights as established by the Constitution and the statutes? "The prime responsibility rests with the judiciary, of which our jury system is an integral part."

Chief Judge Hannah upheld the jury, finding that their verdict was fully supported by the evidence, by the intent of the statute against obscenity and by the light of constitutional provisions. It will be interesting to see whether his view will prevail.

— Reprinted from the "Chicago Tribune," Wednesday, Sept. 16, 1970

Right, W. Kaufman in *The New Republic*, October 17, 1970.
Left, reprinted courtesy of the *Chicago Tribune*, September 19, 1971.

Pornographic action that is filmed or staged or posed for still photographs – pornography *done* by people, not invented by writers or draftsmen – runs right into the matters of social change mentioned above. Performed pornography is an exercise in the humiliation of women. (It can be argued that porno fiction humiliates them, too, in value, but at least they don't physically participate.) The men who are involved in porno performance, though not precisely ennobled, are not being so humiliated. They are treated as masters, usually, and the performances are done for their satisfaction. Those male performers are vicars for the almost entirely male audience. Performed porno is a species of male revenge on our social systems of courtship and monogamy, courtship in which a man has to woo a woman to get her to bed or wed him or both, monogamy in which he has nominally to forego the favors of other women all his life in order to get hers. Performed porno makes every man a sultan.

But it is time out from civilization. Vindictiveness is mean, essentially, and money-coercion is brutal – whether the coercion is on Madison Avenue, in Detroit, or in a sex-flick studio; and it's especially brutal when it produces, not just profit but pleasure.

Letters
from readers

No case against obscenity

The American nation may soon restrict another of its citizens' rights, for today public sentiment seems to be calling for censorship of obscenity.

This is troubling, for no case against obscenity can be made. No evidence has been brought forward showing obscenity to be a harmful influence in our society. Rather, it seems that those who are personally against obscenity would like to see their morals prevail and thus are seeking a legal means of imposing their views on others.

A good case can certainly be made for restricting the use of obscene pictures and language on the outside of a theater or book shop, for no citizen should be forced to look at something which he finds disgusting. But as for what is shown on the inside of the closed doors of any place of business, this should be a freedom left to the owner and attending customers. Unless, of course, someone can present a strong argument showing the harms of obscenity. —Lee Bantle, Minneapolis.

'Throat'

To the Editor:

In your issue of March 31, Clifford A. Ridley wrote a column entitled "X-Raying *Throat* and *Bones.*"

While I have not seen *Throat* and do not expect to, I would like to offer a comment on whether the picture "is utterly without redeeming social value." I do not doubt that such a statement is true, but I could make the same statement about any number of movies which are in no way pornographic.

R. M. HAVOURD
Chatham, N.J.

Top left, letter to the *Minneapolis Tribune* from Lee F. Bantle, Minneapolis, July 17, 1973.
Above left, letter to the editor of *The National Observer* from R. M. Havourd, 121 Southern Blvd., Chatham, New Jersey 07928, April 21, 1973.

"RULINGS MAKE SENSE"

To THE EDITOR:

We ought not to pretend that pornography is written and published for the benefit of mankind, or is so inspiring in its theme as to be composed without an eye on the commercial profits to be derived from it. Today it is an industry with a yearly return of billions of dollars.

This should be weighed in the balance in considering the outcry on the recent Supreme Court rulings on freedom to profit by the display and distribution of pornographic books and pictures. Yet in the Arts and Leisure section of The New York Times we find authors, directors and actors deploring the rulings with such utterances as: "I deplore going back"; "Censorship is deadly"; "A step backward"; "This is tyranny"; "Absurd and unworkable"; "Very real danger."

Any law that restricts a vested interest in any way is bound to get a clamor of vehement protests. But if we are concerned about the polluted air we breathe in our cities, do we show wisdom in turning our attention away from the pollution of minds by dirty books? Are we convinced there is no connection between pornography and the increase in venereal diseases to epidemic proportions? Until these doubts are laid aside, the Supreme Court's rulings make sense.

BERNARD KIRSHBAUM
Flushing, N.Y.

Above, letter to the editor of *The New York Times* by Bernard Kirshbaum, September 9, 1973.

Top, © 1971 *The Wanderer.*

Below, from *The National Observer*, April 12, 1971.

If Dirty Art Is Censored, Who Will Do the Censoring?

By Clifford A. Ridley

The gloom-and-doom boys in the artistic spectrum have been warning artists for some time that if they don't use their new freedoms responsibly, they're asking for trouble. The trouble, it appears, is nigh upon us. Many state legislators and other officials, restive in the face of the new morality to begin with, are turning downright surly. And now comes Prof. Irving Kristol, whose liberal *bona fides* are well in order, with a long argument for nothing less than state censorship.

Writing in the New York Times Magazine, Mr. Kristol passes quickly over what many people, including me, consider the real contemporary pornography; the pornography of violence. His concern is chiefly with the pornography of sex, particularly with its power to corrupt and debase. Few would dispute that it has such power—few would dispute that whisky can make you drunk, either—but the question is how much and for how many. In the absence of empirical evidence, Mr. Kristol undertakes to prove corruption by logic.

He takes issue, first, with the frequent assertion that nobody was ever corrupted by a book. Well, I think that's a little extreme—a few people *are* corrupted by books—but I don't think Mr. Kristol does his cause any good by suggesting that if no one was ever corrupted by a book, no one was ever improved by one either. Literary self-improvement, after

Comment

all, is a function of the mind, while literary sexual corruption affects a quite different portion of the anatomy.

Permissible Deaths

It is the corruption of essentially private behavior that particularly bothers Mr. Kristol; as example, he notes that we do not film or televise the gradual extinguishing of humanity—i.e. an actual lingering death. He does not note, however, that we do film and televise the *abrupt* taking of life in our everyday war and crime reportage—with effects that are doubtless both bad and salutary—and we do simulate death of all kinds on stage and screen. If these deaths are permissible but an actual lingering one is not, who is to decide how efficient an actual death must be, how untruthful a simulated one, before it is fit to be shown to us?

It's a moot question, of course. We will never invade the privacy of a slowly dying man simply because no sane person wants to watch such a thing. And although there are a number of reasons why not—fear of mortality, and so on—the prime one is simply that we have an innate delicacy about such occurrences. I honestly believe that most people do respect purely private matters, that they will not willingly debase themselves.

But, you may argue, what about the viewing of stag films and the like? "When sex is public," Mr. Kristol says, "the viewer does not see—cannot see—the sentiments and the ideals. He can only see the animal coupling." And so he can, but isn't that precisely the point?

In other words, the argument goes like this: "The act of love, when made public, is debased because it's not the act of love." But if it's not the act of love, then the act of love is not being debased. The moment two people agree to copulate before a camera, love is no longer part of the action, and nobody should think it is.

Mr. Kristol thinks the dangers of censorship are minimal. He notes that we have been visited by few suppressed old masterpieces since the gates were opened, and so we have. But—noting only in passing that the suppression of even one masterpiece is a crime—what does that prove? We also have been visited by few masterpieces on potato farming, or in which the hero is lefthanded. Masterpieces are few by nature, and no subject or technique is going to produce very many of them.

Censorship of Pornography?
YES

by REO M. CHRISTENSON

Unhappily, all of the major premises on which our society rests derive from the realm of intuition—the viscera. Can anyone *prove* that the family is a desirable institution? That higher education promotes human welfare? That technology makes men happier? That love is better than hate? That democracy is superior to dictatorship? None of these is provable. But this does not stop us from acting on our best judgment, knowing' that all human judgment is fallible. If, then, the regulation of pornography comes down to a matter of visceral hunches, why should not the majority of viscera prevail?

Is "pornography" such an imprecise term that it lacks sufficient clarity to meet the "due process" test?

Current state laws could be updated and made more explicit if they were refined to forbid actual or simulated exhibitions of sexual intercourse or sexual perversion on stage or screen—or pictorial representations thereof in other media—when such exhibitions or pictorial representations are primarily intended for commercial entertainment rather than for education.

Censorship of Pornography?
NO

by A. S. ENGEL

Finally, I cannot seriously believe that Christenson can really be comfortable as the champion of visceral supremacy or of majorities armed with more feelings than facts. I need hardly remind him that those are the very conditions under which many a community has attempted to legislate its prejudices concerning race, or political belief, or religious favoritism. Simply because we cannot prove scientifically that atheists are headed for hell, although the majority has pretty strong feelings on the subject, does not entitle the majority to legislate its prejudices. Why we should now depart from that rule, which insists that majoritarianism be tempered by minority rights, is not made clear to me.

The Supreme Court on obscenity

The recent decision by the Arizona Supreme Court upholding the state's obscenity s t a t u t e represents a necessary attempt to come to terms with reality.

The Court declared that there is indeed such a thing as hard - core pornography and that "we find it objectionable and illogical to hold . . . that hard - core pornography can be made publishable by interspacing it with items of alleged redeeming social value."

The unanimous opinion, written by Justice James Cameron, agreed with a Maricopa County Superior Court ruling that "I Am Curious (Yellow)" is obscene.

The thicket of legal and moral questions surrounding the subject of obscenity is formidable and complex. However, this is no excuse to regard the subject as incapable of definition.

Doubtless, some people would advocate a stamp of pornography being placed on practically any artistic work.

But these censorious sorts are far fewer today than the muddled but vocal l e g a l i s t s who claim there is no possible way to define hard - core pornography.

The A r i z o n a Supreme Court, agreeing with a definition formulated by the New York Supreme Court, held that hard - core pornog r a p h y "focuses predominantly upon what is sexually morbid, grossly p e r v e r s e, and bizarre, without any artistic or scientific purpose or justification.

" . . . It is to be differentiated from the bawdy and the ribald . . . depicting dirt for dirt's sake . . . the blow to sense, not merely to sensibility," in the words of the New York Court.

This trenchant insight, we believe, should be of considerable assistance to prosecutors w h o h a v e contended that obscenity guidelines have been unsatisfactory.

While pornography may be difficult to define, the State Supreme Court, in dealing with the issue, has not allowed itself to be paralyzed with the indecisiveness that argues there are no parameters to the obscene.

Top page, from *The Progressive*, September 1970.
Above, from *The Arizona Republic*, October 24, 1971.

Ask Them Yourself

Want to ask a famous person a question? Send the question on a postcard, to "Ask," Family Weekly, 641 Lexington Ave., New York, N.Y. 10022. We'll pay $5 for published questions. Sorry, we can't answer others.

FOR GLORIA STEINEM,
journalist, women's activist

How do you feel about pornography? Don't you feel the smut peddlers degrade women by using them to make money?—Mary R. Burns, Fort Worth, Texas

● Yes, most pornography does degrade women because most of it is written from the traditional male viewpoint that women are objects to be used, and therefore humiliated, by men.

But I don't object to pornography as it is usually defined. There is nothing wrong with writing about sexual pleasure.

The problem is that very little sexual writing depicts women as autonomous human beings, with dignity and sexual rights of their own.

Perhaps, what I think of as "pornography" extends beyond glorifying sado-masochism in sex. It is *any kind of propaganda that urges finding personal pleasure in the physical pain or humiliation of another. That kind of "pornography" includes the glorification of war or any other violence against individuals.*

To me, for instance, both Joseph Alsop and the Marquis de Sade are pornographic writers. It's just that the Marquis had more imagination.

Says Pornography Incites To Sexual Crimes

In a recent article in The Los Angeles Times, Judge Macklin Fleming, California Court of Appeal, says it is the experience of most judges, chiefs of police and prosecutors that sexual crimes triggered by pornography are not rare.

Judge Fleming gave as an example a case where a man, excited by pornographic material, sought out a sexual victim and committed murder. In sustaining the murder conviction, the California Supreme Court said he had clearly set out to commit rape and that "he admitted that he became sexually aroused after viewing photographs of nude women in a magazine...."

Judge Fleming wrote, "In the experience of most judges, prosecutors, and chiefs of police, such crimes are by no means rare, and at any given time society contains some sexually unstable persons who may be triggered to violence by exposure to sexually suggestive materials.

"I think any discussion of obscenity and pornography which ignores this connection is bound to be unpersuasive to the general public."

He went on to say, "The advertising effect of obscenity and pornography, that is, the power of explicit sexual materials to suggest and influence the conduct of stable persons, is more difficult to evaluate than the influence of such materials on unstable personalities, but if we start from the premise that society wishes to discourage and inhibit certain types of conduct (forcible rape, child molestation, incest, sodomy, bestiality, etc.), then a strong case can be made for the discouragement of materials which explicitly depict such acts or suggest the desirability of their performance."

*Hold on, you anti-smut crusaders. I know you have lots of "evidence" that persons arrested for sex crimes have had sexual materials in their possession. But the relevant statistic is not how many offenders read dirty books (no one really knows how many do), but whether people who read such books are more likely to commit crimes than people who do not. Before the obscenity commission was established, neither you nor anyone else had ever done extensive research on the subject. The commission tried, and one study done for it showed that adult sex offenders and "deviates" actually had *less* exposure to sexual materials during adolescence than a carefully matched control group. (Does that mean that we should require that obscenity be read?) But even if sex offenders *did* see more obscenity than the rest of us, that would only show a correlation, not a cause-and-effect relationship. It would be quite plausible that people who are perpetually inclined to sex crimes are, for the same reason, also excessively inclined to sexual materials. (Some people think that sexual materials often provide a harmless release for such persons.) Of course, sexual material may, now and then, trigger an act of violence (although no one, to my knowledge, has ever found such a case). But so may detective stories; *The Godfather*, the Bible, and who knows what else. We don't ban these things because a clear and present danger means a high degree of probability of harm, not a one-in-a-million possibility. If a freak possibility of harm from a book were enough, none of us would be able to read anything.

Top, courtesy of *Family Weekly*,
September 19, 1971.
Above, from *The Wanderer*, February 18, 1971.

Above, excerpted from a footnote in "The Obscenity Muddle" by Paul Bender, In *Harper's Magazine*, February 1973.

A CALL TO THE PEOPLE AND THE CONGRESS
OF THE UNITED STATES OF AMERICA
TO
ABOLISH
THE UN-AMERICAN
OBSCENITY LAWS!

We all know that censorship is dangerous and the eternal enemy of freedom and liberty. Yet, year after year the federal government wastes tens of millions of tax dollars prosecuting publishers, film producers, distributors and exhibitors who merchandise so-called "pornography" to forewarned adults. More persons are prosecuted and jailed in our nation for distributing "objectionable" publications than in any other country in the world. The "obscenity" prosecutions are an exercise in hypocrisy. Government sponsored studies demonstrate that most adults seek sexually explicit materials as a source of entertainment and information, with no harmful effect.

A Presidential Commission on Obscenity and Pornography, after spending two million tax dollars in scientific research, concluded that the obscenity laws, as they apply to willing, forewarned adults should be abolished.

Americans deeply value the right of individuals to determine for themselves what books they wish to read and what pictures and films they wish to see. Our traditions of free speech and free press also value and protect the right of writers and film-makers to serve the diverse interests of the American public.

We have had enough censorship by "Big Brother." We urge the new Congress to examine the report of the Presidents Commission on Obscenity and Pornography and implement the wise recommendations of that commission to abolish obscenity laws as applied to forewarned, willing adults.

For further information, write the Adult Film Association of America, 1654 Cordova Street, Los Angeles, California 90007.

 ADULT FILM ASSOCIATION OF AMERICA

A non-profit membership corporation of
motion-picture producers, distributors
and exhibitors.
David F. Friedman
National President

The Adult Film Association of America.

SECTION 6

Gun Control

All of the arguments contained in this section are concerned with the subject of prohibition—not of alcoholic beverages, but of handguns or guns in general. The ethical questions arise at several different levels in any discussion of any kind of prohibition. One question is whether or not a particular type of act is right; in this case it is a question of whether or not it is right to own, carry, and/or in certain situations to actually use a handgun or other type of gun. But the ultimate ethical questions revolve around the moral rightness or wrongness of prohibiting under law, with the threat of arrest and punishment for failure to comply, one or more of these acts. There are many acts which many of us would agree are immoral, but which we would not want to see made illegal for one reason or another. And the question of gun control is not one for which there is anything approaching a consensus as to its rightness or wrongness, which raises the additional question of using the law to force the ethical beliefs of one segment of the population on the other segments. It should be noted in this regard that, insofar as any legal system exists at all, the *lack* of legal sanctions against gun ownership, possession, or use can be perceived as a use of the law (that is, of the legal system) against those who are opposed to guns.

The obvious analogy in any discussion of any kind of prohibition is of course the American experience with the prohibition of alcoholic beverages in the 1920s, a "grand experiment" whose failure is cited by many opponents of gun prohibition as proof that even if enacted, laws against gun ownership and possession cannot be enforced. But, as with all analogies and all inductive arguments, there is always a certain degree of uncertainty inherent in the very form of argument itself, and in this particular case there is a great deal of debate about the conceptual questions of the similarity of the two cases being compared (alcohol and guns), and ultimately of the basic prediction concerning the enforcibility of gun-control laws. However, there are many other analogies which can be and have been drawn in the discussion of this issue, and it is important to recognize that a preoccupation with this single analogy could lead to a failure to adequately consider a number of other relevant factors which are brought out in the examples in this section. For example, there is a radical difference in the very perception of the nature of handguns, so that while some people perceive them as being essentially a means for protecting one's life and property, other people perceive guns as being primarily a great threat to their lives and property. It is differences in perceptions such as this that are critical to the resolution of disagreements concerning gun-control legislation. Thus it might even be profitable to look for some parallels between this topic and the question of the legalization of abortion, where there are radical differences in perceptions of the essential nature of the fetus, ranging from perceiving it as a complete human being to seeing only a mere organic growth in the body of a woman.

As in any question concerning prohibition of some act, it is difficult to formulate it as a clear-cut ethical question. We can easily identify the ethical question in terms of one individual's act in a particular situation—that is, whether it was right or wrong for a specific person to use a gun in a certain situation—but what is the decision being made by what person when we talk in terms of prohibiting a general practice such as the ownership of handguns? This question provides the basis for a quite difficult exercise.

EXERCISES

1. Examine each of the arguments in this section to determine which ones if any are concerned with genuine ethical decisions and which ones are concerned with general ethical rules or principles. Is a conclusion such as "Owning a handgun should be made illegal" directly concerned with a concrete moral decision? Whose decision is it? What are the alternative courses of action?
2. Construct a list of the analogies used in the arguments in this section on both sides of the gun-control issue. Does any one kind of analogy seem to provide more support for one side of the debate than the other, or can each analogy be interpreted as supportive of both sides of the debate? Construct a list of additional analogies which might be useful in dealing with this topic.
3. Compare the arguments in this section with those in Section 2 concerning the legalization of various drugs (which have been prohibited) and the arguments in Section 8 concerning abortion (which was only recently made legal by a Supreme Court ruling). How could one remain logically consistent while arguing for the legalization of one of these practices and the prohibition of another? Is there any real difference between arguing against the prohibition of one act (if it is presently legal) and for the legalization of the same act (if it is already illegal)?

Food for thought: smoking and gun bans

Zealous advocates of legislation to ban handguns might give some thought to the ban on smoking in MBTA rapid transit trains.

Nonsmokers comply. Smokers who habitually obey regulations, from fear or because they prefer the values of an orderly society, also comply. Others smoke. The ban is, in fact, unenforced and unenforceable.

Now if society chose to put a policeman in every car of every train, the problem might be abated, at great cost and not without considerable unpleasantness. Society chooses not to, and we manage, somehow, to get along.

To put a policeman in every home, apartment and place of business to maintain continuous surveillance of such places might make a handgun ban enforceable. It is impossible to say, for sure. It is clear, however, that short of such drastic action a handgun ban would largely serve the interests of its promoters. Americans are just not that law abiding a people.

People who hate guns generally don't have them. Law-abiding gun owners would turn in their weapons. Everybody else would hide them. And once again the state would be making a fool of itself, authority would be flouted, and lawlessness would quite possibly increase.

Advocates of weapons bans prefer not to deal with the conflict of constitutional rights involved here. Searches and seizures in private homes certainly would be conducted by any competent agency to enforce the new law. Do we want to surrender our protection against such state intrusion for the possibly illusory advantages of questionable statutory protection against getting shot at?

Perhaps a better means of obtaining such protection might be a mandatory jail sentence — say 90 days — for any person convicted of carrying, on person or in vehicle, a concealed weapon—gun, knife, switchblade, sling-shot, etc.

One of the points the handgun ban advocates have failed to deal with satisfactorily is the presence on the Massachusetts statute books of very stiff laws, presumably reflecting legislative intention, against unauthorized possession of concealed weapons.

Maximum penalty, in fact, is 2½ to 5 years in State Prison for mere possession. Mimimum can be a suspended $50 fine. Judges have wide discretion in imposing sentences, and, since in most cases gun carrying is a charge in a prosecution involving a crime like robbery or assault and battery, the weapons possession becomes a subsidiary aspect of the case.

Under a recent US Supreme Court decision, police have authority to search suspects if they have reasonable cause to believe a crime has been committed or is about to be committed. A law requiring the jailing of persons found to be carrying concealed weapons would, I think, have public support.

DAVID B. WILSON

It also might be a good idea to cancel all gun permits in force and to require the holders to reapply. The police, in their own interest, ought happily to shoulder this burden. A deadline might be set after which all licenses now in force would be voided.

The argument is advanced that guns cause accidental deaths and woundings in private homes. This is, of course, true.

So also do stairways, defective flooring, the edges of carpeting, power tools, lawn mowers, gas stoves, axes, heating plants and medicine cabinets. Do you want some civil servant inspecting yours?

It seems to me that persons who wish to assume the risk of having guns in their homes ought to be permitted to do so. Else, why not ban fast cars, skiing, swimming, ocean sailing and other activities which produce a certain amount of injury and death every year? Is there any reason to believe that a government that has failed in so much else can really succeed in weapons control?

David Wilson is a Globe columnist.

Above, courtesy of *The Boston Globe* (February 19, 1974). Below, copyright 1975 by Herblock in *The Washington Post* (May 25, 1975).

"Fair enough—let's give them a cut out of what we take tonight"

PISTOL REGULATION

Its Principles and History
(Selected Extracts)

By

KARL T. FREDERICK, A. M.; LL. B.
(1881-1963)

To sum up: laws which attempt to disarm criminals by making it impossible for them to procure pistols or ammunition are inevitably bound to fail. Instead of accomplishing the desirable object of disarming the crook, they can accomplish little in that direction. Such laws, however, will disarm the law-abiding citizen and tend to make him helpless against the raids of the criminal. The legitimate uses of the pistol vastly outnumber its illegitimate uses in the approximate proportion of 98 to 2. Laws which seek to abolish pistols, consequently, are not only impractical, unworkable, and unenforcible but are, in addition, harmful to society because they place the honest man at a distinct disadvantage in the face of crime. They inflict injury upon the honest part of society, without interfering to any appreciable extent with the dishonest and criminal element of society. Their result is exactly the opposite of that which is intended.

Self-Evident Principles

In this study we should bear in mind certain principles which appear to be axiomatic and which we may state as follows:

1. A law which for any reason is incapable of accomplishing its object with reasonable success is harmful and undesirable.

2. A criminal statute which is intended to affect any considerable number of persons and which is not voluntarily obeyed by the great majority of that group is certain to fail. Laws depend chiefly for their effectiveness upon voluntary acquiescence.

3. Laws relating to pistols have but one legitimate general purpose, namely, to hinder or prevent the use of pistols in crimes of violence. (The legitimate and desirable uses of pistols have already been enumerated. They outnumber the improper uses in the approximate ratio of 98 to 2.)

4. A pistol law which is incapable of preventing the frequent use of pistols in crime, but which tends to prevent their use for self-defense or other desirable purposes, will inevitably defeat its own object. It will increase crime by decreasing the means for resisting crime.

The foregoing principles seem to be almost self-evident. But it is apparent that they are not appreciated, or that they are often overlooked. In the end, however, they cannot be ignored. Like the laws of nature they are almost inevitable.

Let Everybody Carry a Gun

By Morton C. Paulson

IN BALTIMORE, where flying lead seems to be as abundant as crab houses and marble steps, Councilman Robert L. Douglass fears for the safety of one and all. He is particularly distressed over the recent murder of a mother before the eyes of her 10-year-old son, and is urging all Baltimoreans to press Congress for stringent controls over firearms use.

If action isn't forthcoming, he asserts, "we ought to do the next best thing. We ought to legalize them [guns] so that everybody can carry them."

Since the nation's firearms policy is dictated by the National Rifle Association (NRA) rather than Congress, the outlook for reforms is less than salubrious. Thus, we are left with Douglass' one-man, one-gun alternative.

The idea of every citizen packing a rod, under the coat or on the hip, Dodge City style, may be unthinkable to some, but the proposition ought not be dismissed out of hand. A lot of people would benefit. The handgun business would boom. Lead mines would prosper, along with target ranges, powder makers, morticians, and the NRA. Unemployment would fall as factories from coast to coast turned to volume production of bulletproof vests and armor-plated cars.

Above, from an editorial by Morton C. Paulson in *The National Observer*, January 18, 1975

The clogging of traffic courts would diminish; many a fender-bender dispute would be settled right on the spot. Children could be expected to spend less time watching X-rated movies and more learning the manly art of the fast draw.

Noise pollution would increase, but population control would be significantly improved.

Finally, street crime might diminish as merchants and pedestrians fought back against gun-wielding thugs—unless, of course, the latter opted for heavier weapons. But that imbalance could be rectified too. Come to think of it, it doesn't seem fair that while machine guns are outlawed, only outlaws have machine guns.

WHY GUN PROHIBITION WON'T WORK

GUN owners are indebted to the U.S. Customs Service, a branch of the Treasury Department, for a clear if unintentional insight into how impossible it would be to banish guns from the U.S. as some anti-gun fanatics demand.

Customs, in a press release, reported a 260% increase in known cases involving illegal attempts to *export* weapons and munitions, not all of them firearms, from the country in fiscal 1974 over 1973.

Just as what goes up must come down, what can be exported illegally through our approximately 90,000 miles of continental and overseas land and sea borders presumably can be imported the same way. We are talking now of firearms, which certain idealists and others would eliminate just as some people attempted to eliminate alcoholic beverages half a century ago.

There can be little doubt that the 15,000 Customs Service employees, hard-working and conscientious though they may be, cannot begin to stop the flow of illicit firearms from this country to troubled parts of the world where underground forces are willing to pay fancy prices for guns. It was always thus. And so it will be here in reverse if the fanatics who want a Federal law to end private firearms ownership ever succeed.

Those in this country who disobey the laws and are willing to pay a high cash price will always be able to get guns. In sad and solemn fact, money appears to be able to buy anything, anytime, anywhere.

Trying to close some 90,000 miles of border to disarm 220,000,000 people obviously never will work.

So why prate about prohibiting guns?

In the urgent quest for crime control, the anti-gun element has come up with the wrong answer, firearms confiscation, but lacks the common sense to see it.

The real problem is exactly what it always was —law-breaking.

The only solution is the one which consistently used to work so well—a court system which serves justice instead of sometimes making an empty mockery of it. ∎

Above, from *The American Rifleman*, December, 1974.

Words Of Wisdom On Gun Laws

THE Governor of a great State and a Supreme Court Justice of another great State have, in public utterances, given the United States able guidance on firearms legislation and its effect. What they said, one in an annual message to the legislature and the other in a court decision, may aptly point the way to more practical, realistic thinking on gun laws—a kind of thinking that is much needed now.

First, take the annual message of Governor John Connally, of Texas, a man tragically close to one of the most shocking misuses of firearms of all time. From a proximity to stark realism that few other public spokesmen can approach, Governor Connally said this:

"I recognize that there is a great hue and cry in some areas of our country today for a gun registration law. I am not convinced that this is the answer to our problems for two principal reasons: (1) the criminal element could still obtain firearms illegally, and (2) many of our most dastardly and shocking crimes have been committed by individuals who would have encountered no difficulty in obtaining and registering firearms under even the most strict gun registration law recommended.

"*I believe that we should hit hard at the unlawful use of firearms and concealed weapons rather than at the right of ownership.*"

As for firearms legislation in general, no one has a greater stake in America nor a deeper concern for national welfare than the 800,000 members of the National Rifle Association.

Citizens in the fullest sense of the word, a high percentage of NRA members have risked their lives for our country in past wars or stand ready in the full vigor of their youth to serve "as needed" in the near future. Many are now in Viet Nam, or in the National Guard or law enforcement agencies protecting Americans at home.

Neither citizens such as these nor the NRA, their organization, would put personal pastime with firearms ahead of the national welfare. The record in that respect is crystal clear. Many of the truly effective firearms regulations in this country, including 2 Federal statutes, were passed with NRA support and counsel. The NRA always has been and always will be ready to do what is best for America. It is first of all a patriotic organization of good conscience.

Therefore it must in good conscience recognize the sound advice of Governor Connally that "we should hit hard at the unlawful use of firearms"—something NRA constantly advocates—rather than experiment with gun laws that might disarm law-abiding citizens in the midst of a crime wave.

Nor can the NRA in good conscience forget that a statute like the Sullivan Law, or its 1966 counterpart in New Jersey, can give rise to a police ruling which, as Mr. Justice Aurelio so well stated, "is not in accordance with the American way of life."

(Permission is granted to reprint this editorial.
THE AMERICAN RIFLEMAN, *Washington, D. C., March 1967)*

Gun Legislation Constructive

When the Colorado House of Representatives passed a mild and constructive gun control bill last week it was expressing a sentiment that has been dominant among the American people for a long time.

For more than a decade, the Gallup Poll has been reporting survey results that show support for gun control to be 70 per cent or higher. Only last fall a proposal for the registration of all firearms drew a favorable response of 72 per cent. The response on that proposal in the West was 69 per cent in favor.

There is good reason to believe that Coloradans share the national sentiment for gun control in about the same proportion.

They have been influenced by the same factors: the steady increase in gun ownership; the extensive use of guns in killings, assassinations, urban conflicts, robberies and suicides; the high number of gun accidents; and the intensifying problem of keeping the peace in a society full of private arsenals and citizens who want to act as their own policemen.

Here are the figures on the effects of guns in the United States in a single year (1971):

Murders with guns:	11,300
Deaths from gun accidents:	2,400
Police Killed by guns:	120
Suicides by guns:	10,000
Accidental Wounds by guns:	20,000
Assaults with guns:	92,000
Persons robbed at gunpoint:	160,000

The gun control effort in the Colorado Legislature is not designed to deal with the total gun problem but only with some of the problems associated with handguns. Of the 11,300 homicide victims in 1971, 9,000 were killed by handguns; and handguns were responsible for 600 of the accidental deaths and 94 of the police deaths.

What the House bill does is to require a five-day waiting period before a citizen can complete the purchase of a handgun and to provide that some handguns—the cheap Saturday Night Specials—cannot be sold in the state at all. The idea is that some "impulse crimes" would not be carried out if the prompt and cheap acquisition of handguns was made more difficult.

In the debate in the House, a number of incorrect and misleading statements were made by opponents of the bill. One was that the measure violates the Second Amendment to the U. S. Constitution, which provides that the right of the people to keep and bear arms shall not be infringed.

What the amendment also provides, however, is that the right to bear arms is associated with the need of a "free state" to protect its security through the maintenance of a well regulated militia.

The U. S. Supreme Court has ruled in U. S. v. Miller that unless there is evidence that a particular gun "at this time has some reasonable relationship to the preservation or efficiency of a well regulated militia, we cannot say that the Second Amendment guarantees the right to keep and bear such an instrument."

The outstanding constitutional scholars, Edwin S. Corwin and J. W. Peltason have written:

"The amendment's sole purpose is to prevent Congress from disarming state militias. It provides no constitutional rights for a private citizen to retain weapons...Furthermore, the amendment provides no protection against regulation by state and local governments." There are, in fact, about 20,000 state and local gun laws in the United States, and a number of them have been tested and upheld in the courts.

The Colorado bill does not, of course, prohibit anyone from keeping or bearing arms. All it does is regulate the sale of some kinds of guns. The Colorado Constitution says that the right to keep and bear arms cannot be called into question; but it is not called into question by the mere regulation of certain commercial gun transactions.

Few persons would argue that the right to keep and bear arms means all arms and that the state could not prohibit the possession of machine guns, bazookas, flame throwers or nuclear artillery. Nor will anyone argue that the waiting period on handguns or the ban on Saturday Night Specials will leave Coloradans without weapons.

Another misleading contention in the gun control debate was that there is not enough distinction between Saturday Night specials and other handguns to justify the discriminatory effects that the ban on the cheaper guns might have on the poor.

Every competent gun dealer—including those who are must violently opposed to gun control legislation— knows that the distinctions between Saturday Night Specials and other handguns are large and clear.

The specials are cheap, light and easy to conceal. They can't be aimed with any precision and their bullets are likely to end up far from their intended targets. They can't be used effectively for hunting or for target practice. Their use is primarily to fire at or threaten human beings.

Many competent gun dealers who sell high quality precision weapons refuse to handle the specials at all. And persons who appreciate guns and the responsibilities associated with them will not buy the specials.

For the legislature to distinguish between guns used by trained hunters and marksmen, on the one hand, and cheap guns that figure prominently in crimes and accidents is reasonable and lawful, even if the poor find it more difficult to buy the costlier weapons.

No one pretends that the Colorado gun control law will prevent criminals from getting guns or bring about any major reduction in crime. But it will prevent some impulse killings and move the state toward a goal that most Americans and most Coloradans approve. The Senate should now pass the bill.

From *The Denver Post*, February 2, 1975.

Study on Gun Laws
and Crime Rates

To The Denver Post:

YOUR EDITORIALS of Jan. 24 and 26 are good examples of the predominant efforts to further erode freedoms provided by the Second Amendment and the Colorado Constitution by appeals to emotion and humbug theories rather than recognizing facts, evidence and experience.

Your dissertation on hollow points failed to mention that anyone can make his own hollow-point bullets by simply drilling a hole in the nose of the bullet or filing the point off to a blunt surface. All the laws which can be passed or studies which waste the taxpayers' money will not alter that fact nor prevent such action.

You didn't mention that the gun used to kill Officer Smith was NOT a Saturday Night Special. Denver's insane ordinance against the poor man's means of self defense, which you supported, has caused and will continue to result in criminals upgrading the quality of their firearms and insure better that they can do what was done to Officer Smith.

The FBI Uniform Crime Report for 1970 shows 8,638,400 violent crimes and crimes against property in the United States. These crimes are homicide, aggravated assault, forcible rape and robbery. But these were only 10 per cent of the total reported crime and firearms were involved in only 15.4 per cent of those serious crimes. That means that firearms were used in 154 ten-thousandths of the total reported crimes. If all firearms were wiped off the face of the nation, and IF no criminal resorted to the use of other instruments of death, we would still have over 99 per cent of the crimes committed. In the face of such evidence you still attempt to fool the people into believing that senseless gun control laws will reduce crime!

The strictest of all gun control laws, the Sullivan law in New York, has been amended 70 times since first passed and it still doesn't work. That's because it is morally wrong both in its concept and its administration. The FBI reports show that in 1972 New York City had the highest rate of violent crimes in the United States (1,357 per 100,000 population). And in the same year that city had the highest rate of murder and non-negligent manslaughter in the United States (19.1 per 100,000 population). The FBI statistics also show that in 1970 less than half (11,304) of the 23,480 suicides in the United States were by firearms or explosives, and of course not all the firearms were handguns.

These continuing appeals for firearms control are designed to deceive the innocent, the uninformed and the gullible, since available, authentic statistics and testimony of competent—competent, that is—law enforcement officers demonstrate clearly that such laws fail to reduce crime rates. Studies by the University of Pennsylvania and others show, conversely, that where increasingly restrictive firearms control laws are adopted, crime rates increase rather than decrease.

Pleas to protect the criminal, insure that his victim will be without self protection, and to minimize his fear of the police officer are a disservice to the people. If these efforts were directed at providing a criminal justice system which would include separate, severe penalties for use of a firearm for criminal purposes, not subject to plea bargaining, probation, parole or pardon, the interests and security of law abiding citizens would be served much better.

D. L. FRODINE

Denver

Letter to *The Denver Post* courtesy of D. L. Frodine, Endowment Member, National Rifle Association, February 2, 1975.

The Silent Protectors

LAST year *The American Rifleman* published in its "Armed Citizen" columns 112 actual instances in which the mere presence of a firearm in the hands of a resolute citizen prevented crime without bloodshed. Every case came from news reports confirmed by police records in 97 communities across the land. Among these were Seattle, Kansas City, San Jose, Atlanta, Baltimore, Dallas, Detroit, El Paso and 89 others.

Every one chronicled a triumph of a self-reliant American with the "cool," to use the current slang, to stop a crime without shooting anyone. They prevented robberies and quite possibly rapes and murders. They were able to do so because they were armed—with guns.

Now on the 100th anniversary of the National Rifle Association of America, we would like to ask a simple question:

Can anyone show us where 112 crimes have been averted by the Federal Gun Control Act of 1968?

Those who uphold this act and would further disarm law-abiding American citizens owe it to the American public to explain themselves.

Can they say why it is that crime continues to rise under the 1968 act instead of decreasing?

Without putting words into overworked mouths, we can surmise that they will say the answer is a need for even stricter gun laws.

In all honesty, we must disagree. The answer is a need for many things, but laws that deprive decent persons of self-protection are not among them.

The answer may be a need for more uniformed policemen patrolling our crime-infested big cities. Philadelphia in chopping down its crime rate provided prima facie evidence of this. The Washington, D.C., police department, recruited to full strength for the first time in many years, also brought about a distinct reduction in crime by putting more properly-trained patrolmen on the streets. Some other communities have succeeded, likewise.

The answer may be a need for longer sentences that keep habitual criminals in jail instead of allowing them to whiz through courtrooms with a speed that makes justice somewhat like a revolving door.

The answer may be the need for broad rehabilitation programs that reorient all but the most hopeless hardened criminals (if there are such), and end the cycle under which many criminals find themselves compelled to return to crime for lack of anything better.

The answer may be an end to flabby permissiveness and a "lie down and quit" attitude on the part of some local courts and authorities whenever unruly, lawless elements "make a fist" at them.

The answer may be a return to a traditional American creed recognized and practiced by every good NRA Member, of respecting the rights and way of life of all respectable fellow Americans.

It is proper to discuss all this on the 100th anniversary of The National Rifle Association of America, an organization founded to promote marksmanship and broadened to support conservation and national improvement, because the legitimate ownership of firearms is an integral part of our Nation. This the NRA recognizes and champions.

As shown in this magazine and elsewhere, the mere presence of firearms in the hands of responsible Americans can serve to curb violence. The Federal Gun Control Act of 1968 apparently can't.

There is reason to believe and hope that the next Congress will recognize this fact and repeal the 1968 Act, at least insofar as it places burdens and restrictions on individual law-abiding gun owners.

That, coupled with the mandatory penalty laws that the NRA has long advocated for criminal misuse of guns, will do more to curb crime than the senseless provisions of the 1968 act which tend to stamp out legitimate gun ownership while criminals run riot and thumb their noses at all laws. ■

(Permission is granted to reprint this editorial.
The American Rifleman, *Washington, D. C. January 1971)*

Gun Deaths and Gun Laws

By Barbara J. Katz

I CAUGHT the news on a late-afternoon broadcast and felt sickened the rest of the day: A Miami couple who had fulfilled a demand to withdraw $50,000 from their bank account had been coldly, senselessly murdered by their alleged captor in a burst of sub-machine-gun fire as he spotted police tailing them.

How needless, I kept saying to myself. Why did he have to kill them? He must have been crazy!

And then I began recalling other recent bizarre gun deaths: the murder of Mrs. Martin Luther King, Sr., as she sat playing the organ in church, the shooting of a National Rifle Association lobbyist in an apparent case of mistaken identity, the self-slaying of a child playing "Russian roulette" with his sister, the killing of a youth by his father, who thought he was firing at a prowler. Were all these persons crazy? Are all the people involved in the hundreds of other gun deaths we hear about every year stark-raving mad?

No, it's not the murderers and the other killers who are crazy, I've decided. It's our society that's insane—for permitting virtually anyone to own a gun, with virtually no requirements for licensing, registration, or proper use and safekeeping. I, for one, am sick of reading about the latest grisly murder or the latest bizarre accidental gun death, and other people tell me the same thing.

But we might as well face one basic fact: Until we decide to enact meaningful gun control, and until we put sufficient pressure on our public officials to fulfill that resolve, the killing is going to continue. We'll continue clucking over the distressing news and wondering how anyone could do such a terrible thing—and the answer lies with ourselves.

Above, from an editorial by Barbara J. Katz in *The National Observer*, August 17, 1974. Below, copyright 1974, Universal Press Syndicate.

GARRY WILLS

Real Wyatt Earp Took Fewer Risks

There are a number of sheepish people who feel that a handgun in their drawer or closet somehow makes them more manly. Their arguments are rather pathetic. They feel that the police force is insufficient protection for them—and so make the lives of policemen more dangerous, their work more difficult, by holding out the constant menace that every man will become his own policeman in some Armageddon encouraged by their very belief in it.

The weird thing is that some policemen are gun addicts, as well—though the peril they live with is encouraged by the ready access to cheap guns, the large permanent floating stock being pushed out by sporting firms and mail order ads.

Movies and TV fantasy feed the old myth that "we" brought law and order to the old wild West with guns wielded by the good guys in self-defense against the bad guys. We neglect, too often, the bad guys who were selling guns to both sides to begin with—"cowboys" and Indians, settlers and herdsmen. The power of this myth to pervert reality is spectacularly exemplified in the story of Wyatt Earp.

Wyatt Earp "cleaned up" Dodge City, among other places—but not the way movie and TV screens have depicted that process. There were no high noon shootouts, barrooms full of gun smoke, or hasty checked motions to "draw" inhibited only by Wyatt's lightning speed.

What was there, then? A room for confiscated weapons, that's what. Wyatt Earp cleaned up Dodge City by making it illegal to wear a gun in the town. By gun control. Arrest was automatic, and Earp's three deputies were encouraged to be zealous by a supplement to their salaries—$2.50 for every arrest made. And one more thing: in Earp's own words, "Dead ones wouldn't count...Mayor Hoover had hired me to cut down the killings in Dodge, not to increase them." Earp had to kill one man in all his time at Dodge City, famed for its toughness.

And it was tough. But Earp's method tamed it. For a while, arrests on this charge ran about 400 per month (good pay for Earp himself and the deputies). But the lawmen worked themselves out of a job—within two years he had these arrests down to a slim 29 for the entire twelve-month.

So he moved on to clean up other towns. Successfully. And died in his bed at age 81. His method worked. All the "good" citizens did not fight it on the grounds that they were being disarmed, but crooks would not keep the law. Those who didn't were arrested.

There is at least one handgun for every eight persons in America—a constant temptation to the angered husband, drunk fighter, young bandit, curious child. Those determined to get a gun may be able to get it despite more stringent controls than we have. But crimes of passion or convenience would not have guns practically pushed into the hands of their perpetrators.

Yet when an eminent psychiatrist, Dr. Kent Robinson of Baltimore, first pointed out the significance of Earp's true history for the question of gun control, he got the usual spate of irrational letters from gun cultists.

If we stop listening to the swaggerers, one truth emerges—that the Wyatt Earp of history was more "manly" than the Wyatt Earp of legend, the mythical stalker of his mirror-selves with guns slung low. Civilization is not kid stuff. But gun games are—very deadly and dangerous kid stuff.

The City as OK Corral

IF, BY SOME unfortunate chance, you had been in the 3100 block of M Street NW at about 5 p.m. on Thursday afternoon, you could have seen some real action, some gunplay that might have reminded you of a western movie. It might also have helped illustrate why the proliferation of handguns in a modern society is a menace to us all.

As the police tell the story, a shopkeeper became suspicious of one of his customers. When the man ran onto the street, according to the police, the shopkeeper "picked up a white-handled revolver" and began chasing the customer down M Street. A plainclothes police officer happened along at about that time, his attention drawn to the spectacle of a man with a gun running in the streets. The shopkeeper turned, gun in hand, toward the police officer, and the policeman shot him. "Why did you shoot me?" the shop owner asked the officer, as he lay wounded on the sidewalk. "I didn't know you were officers. Why did you shoot me?"

Above, © *The Washington Post* (January 18, 1975)

Isn't it time for Congress to act?

Over a quarter of a million Americans were at this end of a handgun last year - victims of 10,000 murders, 100,000 serious assaults, and 160,000 armed robberies.

Since the 1930's a majority of Americans have supported handgun controls. By not enacting effective handgun legislation, past Congresses have not responded to the views of the electorate.

The National Council to Control Handguns, a new non-profit organization, needs your support to bring the urgent message from the people to the politicians — we are fed up living with crime. The 94th Congress should and *can* act to reduce crime in this country.

Congress must start by passing effective legislation to control the handgun — the favorite weapon of the criminal.

Won't you please join us in working for a more peaceful America?

Please make your check payable to:

NCCH (The National Council to Control Handguns)
1910 K Street, N.W.
Washington, D.C. 20006

The rights and wrongs of the actual shooting that took place will of course have to be sorted out by police officials, and possibly even by the courts. Our point concerns the proliferation of handguns and the danger they frequently pose to those persons who own them for their "protection." The sorry statistics show that three quarters of the people wounded by handguns owned by private citizens are friends, relatives or acquaintances of the owner. The notion that a privately-owned handgun protects is one of the most dangerous and enduring myths of our society. And the sad incident on M Street just provides one more example.

We think it is a timely example because this year Congress will again have an opportunity to enact comprehensive gun control legislation. This is a Congress that exudes confidence in its ability to do the people's business, and gun control should be prominent on its agenda. As former District Police Chief Jerry V. Wilson pointed out on these pages recently, every poll since 1938 has shown that a majority of the American people favor some sort of gun control. The problem has been a strident and well organized lobby, one that is also extremely well-financed. It has been able to block legislation because it can put pressure on those legislators who defy it—just because it is so well financed. Yet, a quarter of a million Americans are harmed each year in some way because handguns exist in such large numbers.

The answer in our view is readily apparent. We need a comprehensive law that licenses the use of handguns by those persons who can demonstrate a vital need for them; and the ordinary shopkeeper would hardly qualify unless he could show that vital need. All other handgun ownership by individuals would be illegal. People who use handguns for target practice or other sporting purposes would be required to deposit them with the local police and check them out when they planned to go target shooting. Collectors of antique guns could keep and display them as long as their guns were deactivated by removal of the firing pin. Those guns in existence would be purchased from their owners by the government in a manner similar to that once employed in Baltimore and suggested for the District.

Guns in a city are no joke, as the M Street shopkeeper discovered, and as thousands of other Americans find out—too late. The shopkeeper was fortunate in that he was not badly wounded. But during the summer, a youngster in Northern Virginia was killed by another teen-ager with a hefty .45 automatic after a violent dispute. The same fate awaited a woman executive at the hands of another executive who had just been fired. Whoever gets pleasure from the ownership of handguns must come to recognize that the current state of affairs is too high a price for the rest of us to pay.

Left, courtesy of The National Council to Control Handguns.

How to Kill a Republic

NEARLY 2400 years ago, the great Greek philosopher Aristotle, warning against the decay which caused the downfall of the classic republics of ancient times, wrote: ". . . The citizens begin by giving up some part of the constitution, and so with greater ease change something else in the government which is a little more important, until they have undermined the whole fabric of the state."

Naturally, these pre-gunpowder republics never knew constitutional clauses covering firearms. But the other elements of downfall are evident in our own times. The heaviest attack on the U.S. Constitution today is against the Second Amendment with its "right to keep and bear arms" provision.

Some of our smartest, youngest legal lights and aspiring politicians have proclaimed that the whole Second Amendment is as archaic as an ox-cart; that the need for it and for a militia under it vanished with the nuclear age and ultrasophisticated weapons of war. Some others assert that its "right to bear arms" is confined to the National Guard.

Many of these critics of the Second Amendment can be found high in the ranks of television commentators, magazine writers and newsmen who live and breathe and earn their daily bread by the grace of the First Amendment. They would give up, in Aristotle's words, "some part of the constitution," the Second Amendment, but surely regard the First Amendment as "a little more important."

Aristotle

The objections to such erosive thinking are pointed out by a Past President of The National Rifle Association and eminent attorney, Irvine Porter, of Birmingham, Ala., in a letter to U.S. Sen. John Sparkman of Alabama.

"In the first place," Attorney Porter pointed out, "this philosophy runs roughshod over provisions of State Constitutions which have provisions in them similar to those contained in Sec. 26 of the 1901 Constitution of Alabama, stating that 'every citizen has a right to bear arms in defense of himself and the State.'

"In the second place, this philosophy overlooks a substantial body of opinion that the right protected by the Second Amendment is personal and does not relate solely to the militia (See 98 University of Pennsylvania Law Review, 905, 905-906, 1950). Furthermore, such a philosophy further impinges upon the means by which the absolute Rights of Man (personal security, personal liberty and private property) are secured. Blackstone lists as the fifth means:

" '5. By bearing arms for defense and these must be suitable to the condition and the degree of the subject and such as are allowed by law.' (1 Blackstone Commentaries, 143-144).

Irvine Porter

"It should not be forgotten that during the constitutional convention convened for the purpose of drafting the United States Constitution, there was a protracted controversy over whether there should be a source of military power. The Constitution, as agreed upon by the convention on Sept. 17, 1787, contained provisions designed to keep military power under the civilian control of Congress, the President and the people, as well as under the dual control of the Federal governments and the states. (See Article I, Section 8, Clauses 12, 15 and 16, and Article II, Section 2). . . .

"After adoption and ratification of the Constitution, including the first 10 amendments, Mr. Justice Story, in 1833, said:

" 'The right of the citizen to keep and bear arms has justly been considered as the palladium of the liberties of the republic; since it offers a strong moral check against the usurpation and arbitrary powers of rulers; and will generally, even if these are successful in the first instance, enable the people to resist and triumph over them. (3 Commentaries on the Constitution of the United States, Section 1890, pages 746-747 (1833)).' "

There is disconcerting evidence that the U.S. government takes the legal position that individual Americans have no Second Amendment right to personal firearms.

If further warning is needed, simply look at the Philippines. There President Marcos "got the guns off the streets" under penalty of death for gun owners. (*The American Rifleman*, Feb., 1973, p. 52.) Next, Marcos seized dictatorial powers for a period of seven years. The anti-gun magazine *Newsweek* observed unhappily: "Marcos has merely divested the country of its democratic institutions. . . ."

One important democratic institution to disappear was the right of private citizens to possess arms which could halt dictatorship or tyranny. ∎

Murder in the Making

By W. A. Swallow

Giving a boy a gun is much like striking a match over an open gasoline tank. No mishap may occur, but the chances are all in favor of a big explosion. In the case of the gasoline one explosion will occur and it will be all over. The boy with the gun may cause a number of fatal accidents; he may grow up with the love of destruction instilled in his mind. Which, then, has the more lasting and devastating effect?

The only way to fight this evil is to dig right down to the source and extract the roots, not forgetting the branches on the way. Is it wise to create, in the minds of children of formative years a desire for warlike toys and instruments? Many people argue that a five-year-old with a toy gun cannot possibly do any harm, nor will he in later years have an overwhelming desire to play with real guns. In many cases this is no doubt true. I can remember, as a child owning an air rifle, but at the same time my parents cautioned me that I must never shoot it at anything alive or in any place where there might be the remotest possibility of doing any harm. I was one of the lucky ones — I heeded these warnings. Nothing happened to spoil my taste for weapons, but even at that it was the first and only gun I ever owned.

However, to get back to the subject, I would have been just as well off without the gun with the probabilities all in favor of being *much* better off. Let us give our children something better to do and think about than handling toy guns or any manner of lethal weapons.

We have fought several wars to end war. We thought by various measures, the League of Nations, the United Nations, general disarmament, treaties and whatnot that any future wars were most improbable. Needless to say, these measures fell down one by one and like Humpty-Dumpty, defied "all the King's horses and all the King's men" to put them back in workable condition. Both force and compromise have proved inadequate. The only thing left seems to be education and understanding. After all, the only reason we look down on other nations is because, in some ways, we fail to understand their national customs and manner of living.

From *Reverence for Life*, published by the New England Anti-Vivisection Society.

Education, then, seems to be our last resort. We may not live to see the day when nations are living in accord with each other, but we surely may plan toward that end and insure lasting peace for our children. Proper training in schools and homes will eradicate the thought of war; engender a better understanding of other countries. We must have something positive to give the youngsters. Unfortunately, it has always been true that children have liked best the games where wooden or tin soldiers were involved or, a little later, the actual playing at war with other children.

To perpetuate this ideal, toy manufacturers have put on the market toy guns, toy pistols, toy machine guns, cannon, tanks, airplanes, submarines, destroyers — everything possible that youth might want for its amusement. The first step toward peace-education is the abolition of such toys. That we are on the right road is evidenced by the mounting production of such peaceful toys as electric trains and various types of games. It seems that the yearning of all Americans for an improved standard of living is reflected in toys, reproducing the finest types of American housing, transportations, furniture, art and home making. These toys are keyed in with the desire of American parents to maintain peace. Indeed, it is a step in the right direction.

There is yet another phase of the gun peril, for one of the most popular games of youngsters is still the "cops and robbers" type. There are many factors which determine the source of these games — sensational news stories, moving pictures, radio and television are the principle ones which incite the desire to play at war or gangsters. Those are the roots at which we must strike. It is time our children learn not to make heroes of racketeers and gangsters. If a better example is set them they will respond.

It is but a short step from toy guns to real ones. Rifles, shot guns, even bows and arrows in the hands of minors can and do lead, not only to tragedy in hunting accidents but also inflict untold suffering on such animal targets as may come their way.

Let us all, then, do everything in our power to keep guns, even though they may be only toys, out of the hands of our children.

SECTION 7

Animals and Vegetables

The arguments in this section fall the closest of any in this book to the issue mentioned in the Introduction concerning what is and what is not a *moral* argument. There are indeed some people who would assert that none of the arguments in this section are ethical arguments at all insofar as they do not involve human decisions which have a direct impact on the welfare of other human beings. It is certainly true that the arguments in this section deal primarily with human decisions which directly effect only nonhuman living things. But it is also important to recognize that some people consider this to be irrelevant to the question of whether these are ethical issues insofar as their definition of ethics involves the concept of human decisions which affect the well-being of *any and every* living thing. Thus we are confronted with another level of ethical argument—in addition to those in the other sections which focus on the determination of the rightness and wrongness of various acts and those which focus on the question of making certain acts illegal—namely arguments concerning what in fact comprises the realm of ethical argumentation.

Beginning with the assumption that most people would agree that it is clearly morally wrong to kill another adult human being under most conditions (and possibly even under any condition), it is possible to move across the spectrum of life-forms to terminally ill, comatose adult humans and severely retarded and deformed human infants to human fetuses to dogs and other pets to ants and rats and then to living plants in an attempt to find a point where one can say that it is morally right (or no moral issue at all is involved) to terminate the life of an individual person, animal, or plant. The arguments in this section provide clear evidence that different persons locate that line at radically different points on the spectrum.

It must be pointed out that the arguments in this section are not all of the "all or none" type; some of them are quite clearly focussed on the question of trade-offs. For example, it is not necessary to assume that humans have no moral obligation towards animals in order to justify the killing and eating of animals by humans. Some people would argue that the killing and eating of nonhuman animals is necessary for the very survival of some humans, and that while it would be wrong otherwise to kill animals it is justifiable in order to save human lives. In effect, this argument asserts that when confronted with the choice between killing a nonhuman and allowing a human to die of starvation, it is right to kill the animal. But there are some interesting scientific questions that can be raised here regarding the claim that it is a fact of nutrition that some persons would die if some animals were not slaughtered. It is even asserted as a fact by some persons that the use of grains for the raising of animals bred expressly for the purpose of providing meat for human consumption involves an inefficient use of the grain, which in turn ultimately leads to the starvation of some poor people in other countries who would have lived if they had been given this grain instead. In this kind of argument, the question of the basic treatment of the animal is almost irrelevant and the main consideration is the feeding of one group of people at the expense of others. And this moves into the set of issues raised in the arguments in the section on international relations.

EXERCISES

1. Examine the arguments in this section to determine for which the basic issue is that of taking the life of a nonhuman living thing and for which the basic issue is the causing of unnecessary pain and suffering.
2. Examine the ways in which the arguments in this section have relevance to the questions of international relations discussed in Section 13.
3. Discuss whether there are any significant differences between the position that moral principles do not apply to the killing of nonhumans and the position that moral rules apply but these rules permit the killing of any nonhuman at any time.

What Is a Crackpot?

We are so often labelled "crackpots" by those who do not agree with us, and have no use for our cause, that it may perhaps be worthwhile to attempt an elucidation of this elegant and comprehensive term, according to the context in which it is commonly used.

A crackpot is one who will not admit such self-evident truths as that might is right and the end justifies the means.

A crackpot is one who rates his moral instincts higher than material gain, the dictates of Fashion, or even the sacred name of Science.

A crackpot is one who respects the life that comes from God, even though it is not his own life or that of his own species.

A crackpot is one who sees beauty and poetry and a divine purpose in even the simplest living beings and is incorrigibly averse to destroying them.

A crackpot is one who shows a deplorable lack of the hard-headedness and toughness of feeling which should characterise Modern Man.

A crackpot is one who has the inconvenient habit of putting himself in the place of other sensitive beings so as to share their feelings, to rejoice in their well-being and sorrow in their pain.

A crackpot is one who would rather suffer than inflict pain.

A crackpot is one whose instinctive sympathies are with the hunted and tormented rather than with the hunters and tormentors.

A crackpot is one who holds, in defiance of high society and ancient tradition, that it is uncivilised, unchristian, immoral and disgraceful to inflict pain or death on other creatures for one's own amusement.

A crackpot is one who persists in these unpopular and preposterous ideas even when all his neighbours are laughing at him.

Having glanced through the counts of this indictment and learned the worst, perhaps we shall not mind so very much when the inevitable epithet is flung at us, but shall take comfort from the words of St. Gregory: *Relinquamus noxiam sapientiam, discamus laudabilem fatuitatem* — "May we turn away from cleverness that is baneful, and learn the foolishness that is worthy of praise."

Rev. Basil Wrighton, M.A.
in *Animals' Defender*

October, 1973

From *Reverence for Life*, published by the New England Anti-Vivisection Society.

SOUNDING BOARD

One Person's Opinion on a Several-Sided Subject

Let's stop keeping pets

JOHN MAHONEY

Pets are lovable, frequently delightful. The dog and the cat, the most favored of pets, are beautiful, intelligent animals. To assume the care for them can help bring out the humanity in our children and even in us. A dog or a cat can teach us a lot about human nature; they are a lot more like us than some might think. More than one owner of a dog has said that the animal understands everything he says to it. So a mother and father who have ever cared for pets are likely to be more patient and understanding with their children as well, and especially to avoid making negative, depreciative remarks in the presence of a child, no matter how young.

It is touching to see how a cat or dog—especially a dog—attaches itself to a family and wants to share in all its goings and comings. If certain animal psychologists are right, a dog adopts his family in a most literal way—taking it for granted that the family is the pack of dogs he belongs to.

It is sometimes said that the cat, aloof and reserved except when making some demand of us, "takes all and gives nothing." But is that really true? A cat can teach us a valuable lesson about how to be contented, how to be serene and at ease, how to sit and contemplate. Whereas a dog's overwhelming affection and constant pleas for attention become, sometimes, almost a bit too much. Nevertheless it is the dog who can teach us lessons of loyalty, gratitude, and devotion that no cat ever knew.

So there's plenty to be said in favor of keeping pets. But with all that in mind, I still say let's stop keeping pets. Not that a family should *exterminate* its pets. Very few could bring themselves to do that. To be practical, I am suggesting that if we do not now have a pet we should not acquire one; second, that if we now have a pet, we let it be our last one. I could never say that pets are bad. I am saying, let's give up this good thing—the ownership of a pet—in favor of a more imperative good.

The purchase, the licensing, the inoculations and health care, the feeding and housing and training of a pet—and I chiefly mean the larger, longer-lived pets—cost time and money. Depending on the animal's size and activity, it's special tastes and needs, and the standard of living we establish for it, the care of a pet can cost from a dollar a week to a dollar or more a day. I would not for a moment deny it is worth that.

Reprinted with permission from *U.S. Catholic*, 221 West Madison Street, Chicago, Illinois 60606.

But facts outside the walls of our cozy home keep breaking in on our awareness. Though we do not see the famine-stricken people of India and Africa and South America, we can never quite forget that they are there. Now and then their faces are shown in the news, or in the begging ads of mission and relief organizations. Probably we send a donation whenever we can.

But we do not, as a rule, feel a heavy personal responsibility for the afflicted and deprived for we are pretty thoroughly formed by the individualistic, competitive society we live in—a society whose unwritten rule is, "I got mine, now let him get his." The first dime we ever made for raking grass or shoveling snow was ours to spend in any way we chose. No one thought of questioning that. That attitude, formed before we had learned to think, usually prevails right through adulthood: "I made my money. I can spend it any way I like."

But more and more we are reading that the people of the "Third World" are resentful of us in the developed countries (with the United States far more developed than any of the others) for our grabbing up two-thirds of the world's wealth and living like kings while they scrounge all day for a yam and a bowl of rice—and die off at thirty-five or forty, provided they outlive the heavy scourge of infant mortality.

The money and the time we spend on pets is simply not our own to spend as we like in a time of widespread want and starvation. A missionary society advertises that for $33 a month they can give hospital care to a child suffering from *kwashiorkor*—the severe deficiency disease which is simply a starving for protein. Many a Boxer, Afghan, Irish Setter or Dalmatian requires at least that amount each month for his food and care. Doing without such a pet, and then *sending the money saved* to a creditable relief organization would mean saving a life—over the years, several human lives.

Children not suffering from such a grave disease could be fed with half that amount—not on a diet like ours, but on plain, basic, life-sustaining food such as unpolished rice, soy meal, powdered milk, and an occasional guava or mango. It is not unreasonable to believe that the amount of money we spend on the average pet dog could keep a child alive in a region of great poverty. To give what we would spend on a cat might not feed a child, but it would probably pay for his medical care or basic schooling. The point needs no laboring. That is all that need be said.

They're as much of concern to us as anyone.

The fate of the world's starving may seem very much outside the RSPCA's province.

The truth of the matter is quite the reverse.

Of course humanity must be fed.

And animals must be exploited in vast numbers if Man is to survive.

It's a fact that modern methods of intensive farming have done much to increase production.

Yet in facing up to a vital human right, we feel another is being denied.

The animals'.

As often as not, we make them into machines.

Piglets are frequently kept in total darkness.

Pigs can spend the whole of their productive lives confined in restrictive stalls.

Hens are crammed into battery systems.

Five-day old calves are kept in boxes for fourteen weeks, then taken out and slaughtered.

We believe there simply have to be alternatives.

Economically viable. So the hungry can be fed.

Yet humane.

It's a big job. And in our fight to help solve these problems, we need your support.

To help us find alternative methods of farming. Through our own contribution to research.

And to help us make more people aware. So we gain even more support.

Today tens of thousands of people will die in misery.

Today tens of thousands of animals will die in misery.

In overcoming one problem, we believe there's no reason for turning a blind eye to the other.

Hence this advertisement. But such advertisements are far from cheap.

Won't you help us by sending a donation?

Write to us here at the RSPCA, so we can continue to plead the animals' case.

In return we'll send you a leaflet detailing precisely what you can do to help animals.

Including those you wouldn't normally see.

RSPCA

Be human.
Show animals a little humanity. *Too!*

RSPCA (SE-S-1), 105 Jermyn Street, London SW1Y 6EG.

Reprinted by permission of the Royal Society for the Prevention of Cruelty to Animals.

147

COMPASSION FOR ANIMALS

The beginning of ethical vegetarianism is the knowledge that other creatures feel, and that their feelings are very similar to ours. This knowledge encourages one to extend personal awareness to also encompass the sufferings of others. This is the essence of compassion—the feeling of the sufferings of others, and sympathizing with them, and doing all we can to change such sorry conditions.

Because we know in ourselves the feeling of pain and suffering, we refuse to be a party to inflicting such anguish upon others.

Because we can smell the urine-drenched straw in the livestock truck and see how the animals are packed in for transit (although they sometimes even fall and break their legs in the sudden stops and starts), we realize the grossly cruel conditions of servitude imposed by us upon these animals, and oppose that cruelty.

Because we know that mother cows love their young, and grieve when the calves are taken from them at birth to be fattened up for veal, we cannot in good conscience condone such practices. Indeed, a well-developed conscience dictates that we must stand in opposition to these brutal actions.

Ethical vegetarians oppose not only the killing but the whole assortment of cruelties, artificialities, debasements of humans and animals alike, that go with food-animal raising, shipping, and killing.

We recognize our moral obligation to actively work to correct such conditions, not by a dab of fresh straw here and there, but by doing away with the whole callous system of animal-killing for food.

This is done by refusing to create the demand which makes it profitable for a few, and by helping to educate other thoughtful people to the ethical and other benefits of a common-sense vegetarian régimen.

Left, from "Facts of Vegetarianism" published by the North American Vegetarian Society, Malaga, New Jersey 08328 (1975). Authors: Nellie Shriver, Dudley Giehl, Nat Altman, H. Jay Dinshah.
Right, letter to the editor of *The New York Times Magazine* by F. Brodie, December 12, 1974.

Letters

Cats and dogs eat too

While Maya Pines ("Meatless, Guiltless," Nov. 24) makes the obvious moral points with regard to eating meat in a world faced with unprecedented starvation, she only skirts an issue equally relevant which will have to be faced with the same moral poignancy. I refer to the tens of millions of dogs and cats in this country who consume three billion pounds of food yearly.

Humans can live healthful lives without meat; dogs and cats are carnivorous animals, they *must* have meat. Pet food has become this nation's largest single grocery item, with $2-billion in sales annually.

It seems almost certain that uncounted millions of people will, barring a miracle, starve to death in the near future. It also seems certain that while this is occurring, Americans will continue to feed millions of ecological sponges—the dogs and cats of this country—the meat they require.

Paradoxically, many of the "guiltless" vegetarians will feed the meat from herbivorous animals they didn't eat to other carnivorous animals. And millions of Americans will watch millions of other people die in living color while Morris the cat dines on chicken and Herman the dog gulps down chunks of beef.

FRANKLIN BRODIE
New York City

Dominion Challenged

The National Observer is to be commended for its courageous publication of Peter Singer's "And Now It's Animal Lib." This review challenges the whole "dominion over the animals" interpretation of the Judeao-Christian philosophy.

How tragic that the Jew who is justifiably horrified by the treatment of his kin by Nazi Germany cannot see the cruelty involved in kosher slaughtering. And how ironic it is that the "loving Christian" who is encouraged to "feed the hungry," "care for the sick," "clothe the naked," etc. finds pleasure in "killing for fun and profit" by way of hunting, trapping, vivisection, fishing, etc.

If man is supposed to be made in the "image and likeness of God," shouldn't he realize that compassion and empathy cannot be limited to his own species, but should be extended to all living creatures, many of which cannot lobby for their own rights to "life, liberty, and the pursuit of happiness"? Perhaps the Judeao-Christian man would view the "animals were made only for man's use" doctrine from a different perspective if our planet were invaded by superhuman beings who regarded us as "animals."

MARSHA GRAVITZ
Fond du Lac, Wis.

Logical End

As a marine biologist, I must take exception to the concept of treating animals as "equals." If this reasoning is followed to a logical end, we must not only treat all birds and animals as equals, but also all of the lower animals (snakes and lizards, fishes, insects, and spiders, and then even the single-celled protozoans, many of which are parasites).

Any taxonomist knows that all living organisms form a continuum. If it is wrong to poison squirrels or rats, then it would also be wrong to poison snails and ants. Likewise, if we find it wrong to kill snails and ants, then we must stop the wholesale murder of minute organisms when we chlorinate our drinking water. Are these small animals not entitled to equality simply because a microscope must be used to see them?

JOHN J. GEIBEL
Menlo Park, Calif.

Encouraging Inhumanity

I AM WRITING to protest an article in your women's pages, "Fur Conversions: Recycled Mink." Marji Kunz is a fine writer whose column is enjoyable and helpful, but I still must protest this particular piece.

She suggests having old coats made from the skins of animals made up into coats and jackets in today's styles. Thankfully, this is one way to avoid the needless killing of more animals. But with today's marvelous synthetics, no one else should have to use real fur, certainly not for warmth as our ancestors had to do.

I feel that the wearing of the hide of any creature of God, whether it is domestically raised for slaughter or caught in traps which are, unfortunately, still legal in 48 of our "civilized" states—is grossly immoral. And it encourages more people to do so.

If every person who purchased a real fur or fur trimmed piece of clothing would take the time to contact their humane societies and find out the manner in which many of the animals died to obtain their skins, they would be too ashamed to wear the article.

LINDA SHAFFER
Mt. Clemens

Top left, letter to the editor of *The National Observer* by Marsha Gravitz, June 9, 1973.
Left, letter to the editor of *The National Observer* by John J. Giebel, June 9, 1973.
Above, reprinted with the permission of the *Detroit Free Press*, December 23, 1973.

Rallying Cry

To the Editor:

Bravo and congratulations to The National Observer for the long-overdue article "And Now It's Animal Lib" [April 28].

We must all immediately rally to the cause and pressure our legislators into passing stringent laws which will once and for all put an end to all animal suffering. We must not overlook the fact that mental distress is often more discomforting than mere physical pain, and we must not neglect to stress this too.

The wheels of legislation grind all too slowly; but in the meantime we can alleviate a great amount of suffering quickly by simply getting the Supreme Court to declare unconstitutional all of those old blue laws which require dogs to be kept on leash, muzzled, or confined. Any dog would prefer physical suffering over the frustrations of these atrocities at the hand of man. A dog is by nature a roving animal, and we have no right to subject them to such cruelties.

And we should quickly have outlawed a prevalent custom which is even more cruel: It should be made a felony to confine or otherwise restrain a female dog while she is in heat. That is just about the meanest, most heartless atrocity that we can commit against man's best friend.

And then we must get laws passed to make it a punishable crime to pierce a poor helpless worm with a fishhook. And make it an even greater crime to hook a fish with one. The poor fish doesn't want to be caught; he has been having a great time, swallowing alive all of the smaller creatures he can find in the lake, and we have no right to take his life and so spoil all his fun.

We have already abolished the use of that abominable chemical, DDT; but still many millions of innocent flies are lost each year by man's ruthless lust for murder. Such slaughter can no longer be tolerated.

The next time you take a trip, just count the dead wildlife killed on the highway by vicious motorists for a distance of a mere hundred miles; then multiply that number by how many hundreds of miles of highway there are and see what a tremendous slaughter takes place each day or two the country over. The solution is obvious and simple: Make the cars stay off the highways; all they do is poison the air, anyway.

These are just a sampling of the many, many examples of man's wicked cruelty to animals which the article didn't mention. We are just a bunch of abominable hypocrites if we abolish some offenses and don't abolish all.

And while we are protecting helpless animals, please, please, let's try to get at least a little bit of protection for the millions of good bipeds that are constantly being abused by those who can't mind their own business.

DWIGHT E. PRICE

Malta, Ohio

Letter to the editor of *The National Observer* by Dwight E. Price, June 9, 1973.

Answers To Your Questions

(A page of brief but illuminating answers to some of the questions most often asked about vegetarianism.)

6) EXPERIMENTS INDICATE THAT PLANTS HAVE CONSCIOUSNESS; HOW DO VEGETARIANS FEEL ABOUT THIS?

Wonderful! Vegetarians have been battling for centuries against the cynical attitude that even the ANIMALS are unfeeling brutes; and vegetarian sages of India have taught plant-consciousness and the Universality of all Life, over the past thousands of years. So we are at last making progress in educating the public. Pioneering scientific experiments in this field were made half a century ago by a vegetarian, when Dr. Bose examined rudimentary consciousness in the plants, albeit a greatly different type from that in humans and animals. But we need no Crescograph or Polygraph to prove that ANIMALS are subject to the SAME feelings of pain and emotions as we are.

Still, vegetarians can easily live on those foods which do not require the killing, or even harming, of the plants. These would include ripe fruits & nuts, berries and melons, legumes, tomatoes, seeds, squashes and pumpkins, okras, cucumbers, and many other vegetables.

Potatoes are dug from the ground after the plant has died. Most vegetables are annuals, harvested at or near the end of their natural life. But please bear in mind that animals must eat about ten times as much vegetable food to return to us one unit of food value as meat. Thus, even in terms of destruction of plant-life, we see a factor of 10 to 1. Obviously, the question of plant consciousness can only be a strong point FOR vegetarianism.

7) THERE IS SO MUCH CRUELTY TO PEOPLE; WHY DO YOU WASTE TIME ON ANIMALS?

Can we really separate cruelty to fellow man, to children, to animals, or to nature and the world? If we never learn compassion, pity, and mercy for the weak and defenseless, is it likely we will ever begin to treat our fellow man fairly?

ALL brutality and cruelty poisons and stifles the higher, finer nature in humanity; ALL kindness helps make a better world for all. Vegetarianism—and all it implies—is of the utmost importance and potential benefit for animal and human alike. Thus, there is no question of choosing between them.

From "Facts of Vegetarianism" published by the North American Vegetarian Society, Malaga, New Jersey 08328 (1975). Authors: Nellie Shriver, Dudley Giehl, Nat Altman, H. Jay Dinshah.

Superstition
SCIENCE AND VIVISECTION

Superstition has always played an important role in mankind's development and continues to do so today. Many of the old superstitions have faded away as man has become more enlightened. We no longer tolerate some superstitious cruelties such as the burning of "so called" witches at the stake. However, society still tolerates cruelty to animals by reason of another superstition. This superstition is society's blinding awe and respect for virtually everything and anything done in the name of science.

We are not against progress through scientific research. What we do object to is the often completely needless suffering of millions of living animals used each year in experimental research.

NEW ENGLAND ANTI-VIVISECTION SOCIETY
9 PARK STREET, BOSTON, MASS. 02108

The Rights of Animals

By Brigid Brophy

If we are going to rear and kill animals for our food, I think we have a moral obligation to spare them pain and terror in both processes, simply because they are sentient. I can't *prove* they are sentient; but

---

"When factory farmers tell us that calves do not mind being tethered for life on slats . . . an echo should start in our historical consciousness."

---

then I have no proof *you* are. Even though you are articulate, whereas an animal can only scream or struggle, I have no assurance that your "It hurts" expresses anything like the intolerable sensations I experience in pain. I know, however, that when I visit my dentist and say "It hurts", I am grateful that he gives me the benefit of the doubt.

I don't myself believe that, even when we fulfil our minimum obligations not to cause pain, we have the right to kill animals. I know I would have no right to kill you, however painlessly, just because I liked your flavour, and I am not in a position to judge that your life is worth more to you than the animal's to it. If anything, you probably value yours less; unlike the animal, you are capable of acting on an impulse to suicide. Christian tradition would permit me to kill the animal but not you, on the grounds that you have, and it hasn't, an immortal soul. I am not a Christian and do not avail myself of this licence; but if I were, I should in elementary justice see the soul theory as all the more reason to let the animal live out the one mortal life it has.

From *The Sunday Times* (London), October 10, 1965.

Susan Saint James: "I Vote for Life And for Nonviolence"

By Peer J. Oppenheimer

SUSAN: I used to wear a lot of leather jackets to go with my jeans. I sold all of them. That's the nicest part of the philosophy. Saving animals. Don't kill them to get leather or fur to wear. Or to eat.

FW: Do you believe in a strictly nonviolent way of life in all circumstances?

SUSAN: Absolutely. There are people who hate, who like war, who think that prisons are fine. That if someone commits a crime he should be there. Like if someone kills my daughter, I should be the one to pull the hanging rope. No way! That sort of thing. I vote for life. And for nonviolence. I am not for death.

FW: You said you don't wear anything made out of leather. What about your shoes and your purses on the television series?

SUSAN: I only came to this conclusion just about the time we went on layoff. I will try very hard to carry my philosophy into the series as well. I don't carry purses in the show anyway because they always look empty. As for shoes, women used to wear silk shoes, and they have nice canvas shoes now. My husband used to have beautiful leather boots. Now he's having them made out of canvas.

From *Family Weekly*, October 21, 1973.

VEGETARIANISM

Introduction

The vegetarian way of life is simple to embrace. There are no practical difficulties and it satisfies many different approaches to the question of diet.

We can claim, with scientific support, that we can live just as well as meateaters, and our experience shows that better health and a longer active life are much more likely.

It is logical. There is no valid argument against it. Vegetarianism can be justified medically, biologically and scientifically. Athletes thrive on it, and can clip those vital seconds to gain records by releasing their energy from dealing with toxic wastes associated with secondhand meat products. We have found in our national and international work since 1847 that as a way of life it is absolutely practical, remedial, and wholly delightful.

Vegetarianism has the beneficial effect anticipated by those who approach it for health reasons. It satisfies those who wish to inject a more ethical vigour into their everyday lives—for all cruelty is abhorrent to a thinking man or woman. It fulfils the spiritual aspirations of those who wish to live in accord with the highest principles of conduct.

ETHICS

If it were impossible to live without fleshfoods there would be some justification for killing and eating animals. Today, we can live happily and well without fleshfoods. So we are presented with a clear-cut choice. Life is really a matter of choices: moral and immoral: painful or pleasurable: good and bad; some inherited and some made ourselves. Some choices will be foisted on our children—things like a poisoned environment—deformities through seeking an easy way out with drugs and vaccines. All our choices affect other people—hence the morality therein.

Beneath the surface of our table is a fundamental choice, as clear-cut as any choice could be:

1. We can butcher other creatures and eat them

There is no law to stop our doing this. We are within our legal and spiritual rights, and so long as we live up to our spiritual attainment there is no guilt. While there are animals, we are free to treat them as we wish; they cannot do otherwise than submit. Flesh-eating is the choice of the majority and is accepted by the medical profession and all concerned in butchery. We are free to embrace the health hazards. We are free to cause men and boys to wade in blood all day, killing and dismembering endlessly—cows on Tuesday, sheep on Wednesday, and pigs on Thursday, girls sit at conveyor belts cutting the throats of chickens all day long. Always provided we know no better, we are blameless.

2. We can live perfectly well on a vegetarian diet

Equally, there is no law which compels us to do so. It is a free choice. We can still treat animals as we wish—help them, if we feel inclined, to enjoy a natural life under our protection. There is nothing to stop our enjoying the likelihood of better health, except perhaps, an apathy about the best foods to eat, how they should be grown, prepared and presented.

Snake Eater Being Probed For Cruelty

FORT WORTH, Tex. (UPI) — The district attorney's office is going to investigate a midway sideshow where the main attraction, "Glug Glug, the Swamp Creature," supposedly eats live snakes.

Barry Hickinson, 19, is "Glug Glug" and says he has been performing in midway shows for three years because "I just want to do it. It's kind of fun, especially watching the people."

The Humane Society complained to the district attorney's office the act violates the state's new law against the torture of animals.

Hickinson says the snakes cost him about $400 per week but says his show grossed about $1,500 Monday at 50 cents per admission.

"Glug Glug" splits the snakes' skin with his teeth, peels away the skin and eats the snakes live as the reptiles writhe about his head.

Left, from "Vegetarianism" published 1973 by The Vegetarian Society of the United Kingdom Ltd.
Right, reprinted by permission of United Press International.

Can You be Indifferent?

In January of 1970 the President of the United States promised the people "peace with nature." Yet, in the summer of 1970, men were sent forth to murder 60,000 sentient animals: 9,000 for Japan, 9,000 for Canada—and 42,000 ostensibly for the people of the United States.

As president of Friends of Animals, I, Alice Herrington, spent ten days on the Pribilof Islands, our Federal public territory, to observe and report on this massacre of seals. Hour after hour I watched helpless animals being driven inland a mile or more, until their lungs were bursting; watched the clubs being raised over and over as the seals were battered into insensibility. As my eyes watched, my mind recalled the litany of the bureaucrats, remembered their statements that this is mercy killing, done to save the seals from starvation and disease. And then I moved closer to the seals as they grouped together in terror. The men were killing only the healthy seals whose coats would gleam on fashion row. The seal with fish net imbedded in its fur was ignored after only one bash of the club—a bash which removed an eye. And I remembered these same bureaucrats' statement that only 15 out of every 100 seals born survives the first three years. And there they were, the 15 three-year-old seals nature wanted to survive, being crushed at that very moment by employees of the United States Government.

That individual man often engages his lust to kill is apparent. That our society, our government, condones murder for profit is abominable. And then the profit is only for the Fouke Fur Company which holds a monopoly contract with the government; the whole barbaric "program" is subsidized by the tax dollar of the American people.

If you are one who feels, one who recognizes that all life is bound together on this earth, won't you join and ask Congress to pass this law:

A. To permit the Aleut native on the Pribilofs to kill, for their own commercial profit, 18,000 seals per year; the sealskins—not the American dollars—to be delivered to Japan and Canada ...until 1975 when the current agreement to kill for those countries runs out.

B. To ban the import into the United States of all products, raw or finished, from marine mammals (seals, whales, walrus, polar bear, otters, etc.)

C. To direct the administration to initiate a truly international agreement to protect marine mammals.

As the prime consumer of the world's resources, we owe it to the world and the coming generations of all species not to abuse the world. Please join and write your representatives in the Congress today, asking them to sponsor this measure.

Committee for Humane Legislation, Inc.
11 West 60th Street
New York, New York 10023

I cannot be indifferent. I enclose my donation of $_____ (payable to CHL) to aid the passage of animal protective legislation. Please add my name to your mailing list.

_____
Name

_____
Address

_____
City, State, Zip Code   CHL-1

An advertisement in *The New York Times* courtesy of Humane Legislation, Inc.

Sixty years ago Congress passed a law to save the Alaska fur seal.

This year they're considering a law that could destroy it.

In 1911, a four-nation treaty was signed to save the Alaska fur seal from indiscriminate slaughter on the open sea, a method that had reduced the fur seal population to near extinction.

Alaska Fur Seals Increased 1,000%

As a result of the treaty, and with the careful guidance of the U.S. government, the Alaska fur seal population has grown from approximately 120,000 to 1½ million — an increase of over 1,000%.

In March, a Bill was introduced into Congress that would end the treaty, leave the Aleut natives, who are dependent on the harvests, jobless and with no practical alternative, and eventually return the Alaska fur seal to open sea killing — a method that is sure to complete the job it didn't sixty years ago.

What Is The Issue?

Why, you might ask, has such a Bill been proposed?

Because certain "conservation" organizations have succeeded in misleading many people into believing that what has been going on in the Pribilof Islands for the last sixty years is nothing but some kind of inhuman carnage.

Have all the knowledgeable conservationists and scientists involved in establishing and administering this fur seal program since 1911 been wrong?

Has it been wrong to have administered the fur seal program in such a way that the herd has grown from near extinction to 1½ million?

Has it been wrong that a four-nation treaty dependent on international cooperation has permitted this phenomenal growth?

Is it wrong to harvest animals surplus to the needs of the herd so that disease and starvation are minimized for the benefit of the great majority of the animals?

Is it wrong that man, through sound principles and programs, manages nature, to the benefit of man and nature?

Emotion Vs. Conservation

Because these organizations cannot attack the fur seal program on its record of successful wildlife management, they have resorted to innuendo and exploitation of emotions. How? By clouding the major issue of conservation with the issue of the harvesting method. Yes. The seals are clubbed. Because scientists have as yet found no other method that is more humane, quicker, or more efficient.

The $1,000 Misunderstanding

Which seals are taken? Mostly three- and four-year-old bachelor males. No baby seals are killed; no animals are ever skinned alive. And if anybody can produce an authentic photograph of a baby fur seal being killed on the Pribilof Islands as part of the annual U.S. commercial harvest, The Fouke Company will pay them $1,000.

Consider The Consequences

If this Bill is passed, the consequences will be disastrous.

The Aleuts, who have been dependent on the seal harvests for generations, will be without their livelihood and left with an alternative that is neither practical nor satisfactory to the Aleuts. Many others' jobs will be threatened, or eliminated. (Yes, the fur seal program is also a business — a business that supports a conservation program at no cost to the taxpayers. The United States receives a share, as do Japan and Canada. The state of Alaska gets 70% of the net proceeds from the Pribilof harvests, and the balance goes into a general treasury fund).

The greatest consequence, however, is for the seals. Most of their time is spent in international waters—and they can be preyed upon by any nation, using any method they care to use. Don't mislead yourself into believing others will practice good will if the treaty is ended. They won't. Many countries have commercial fishing industries — and the fewer seals around, the more fish.

Banning the importation of Alaska fur pelts into the U.S. will have little, or no, effect on world seal harvests. The majority of Alaska fur sealskins are sold to Europe, and they can just as easily buy from any of a number of other countries, or individuals, who would now be able to get into the act.

There is little doubt that the Alaska fur seal cannot survive a return to open sea sealing.

We Need Your Help

Think about it. And think about the long-range consequences of this Bill. Don't delude yourself into believing it's for a good cause, because its end is an evil one. And if it goes through, it's only the beginning. (We kill domestic animals and use their products in our daily lives—is that not also "immoral?")

If you're on our side, and the side of conservation and the Alaska fur seal, please write to your senators and representatives in Congress and protest the enactment of S.1315 and H.R.6554.

The Fouke Company, Route 1, Box 168, Greenville, S. C. 29611

An advertisement in *The New York Times*, courtesy of The Fouke Company.

157

Weep Not for the Lamb?

OH, PITY the poor, defenseless little baby seals! Block the heartless hunters from bludgeoning them brutally and mercilessly to death for mere profit and fashion! Stop the threat to still another irreplaceable species! Shouldn't we all shed tears for the poor baby seals?

I won't.

Not until it becomes more fashionable to bewail a far bloodier, far greater slaughter of the innocents than hardly anyone—not even the tenderest heart—speaks much of.

I speak of the lambs and calves who perish by the millions every year for you and me for our breakfast, lunch, and dinner.

I speak of the 500,000 sound, healthy adult animals—sheep, cattle, hogs—that suffer terror and death daily under the packing-house captive-bolt device that supposedly stuns, the electric prod that supposedly stupifies without burning. And there are the billions of chickens that die for you and for me every year by the implacable finger knife.

It would be nice to think that these animals and birds don't know what is happening. But their terrified squealing and bellowing in the slaughter pens engraves the memory.

And it would be nice, too, to think that their deaths are instantaneous and painless. But no one can be sure, despite Federal and state humane-slaughter laws, that the methods prescribed and in widespread use are in fact humane. Packers themselves acknowledge that the act of slaying meat animals is a problem that continues to defy resolution.

The fact is, almost all meat animals are stunned one way or another before they are killed. Baby seals are clubbed, as prescribed by law, because that's the most humane way anybody has so far devised—better than former practice, which included kicking, shooting, gaffing, and ripping open their bellies.

If clubbing seals is inhumane and should be stopped, so also should killing meat animals the way we do. And if no better way can be found, we should all embrace vegetarianism.

But it is safe to say that hardly any hogs, sheep, or cattle will be spared if our palates must suffer.

—*JOE WESTERN*

I believe I have omitted mentioning that in my first voyage from Boston to Philadelphia, being becalmed off Block Island, our crew employed themselves catching cod and hauled up a great number. 'Till then I had stuck to my resolution to eat nothing that had life; and on this occasion I considered, according to my Master Tryon, the taking every fish as a kind of unprovoked murder, since none of them had or ever could do us any injury that might justify this massacre. All this seemed very reasonable. But I had formerly been a great lover of fish, and when this came hot out of the frying pan, it smelled admirably well. I balanced some time between principle and inclination till I recollected that when the fish were opened, I saw smaller fish taken out of their stomachs. "Then," thought I, "if you eat one another, I don't see why we mayn't eat you." So I dined upon cod very heartily and have since continued to eat as other people, returning only now and then occasionally to a vegetable diet. So convenient a thing it is to be a *reasonable creature*, since it enables one to find or make a reason for everything one has a mind to do.

Above, from the *Autobiography of Benjamin Franklin*.

☆ ☆ ☆

Seals and Lambs

Editor, The National Observer:

In regard to Mr. Western's editorial "Weep Not for the Lamb?" [Observations March 29], there is a difference in lambs and calves we eat for food and sealskins we wear to keep up with fashion.

JOAN MOONEY

Washington, D. C.

☆ ☆ ☆

Call for Realism

Editor, The National Observer:

At last someone spoke out expressing my sentiments about the killing of baby seals.

I've had some experience with the economic side of this, so it doesn't seem like wanton killing of a defenseless baby. The parent seals are at sea—the baby is at hand. In most cases, subsistence and even existence of the hunter and his family are involved.

Having spent over a year in a coastal Eskimo village on the Seward peninsula, I've seen what takes place. The hunter takes the sealskin to the trading post, and usually before the actual cash involved leaves the area it has gone through four or five transactions. For these skins he gets food, clothing, fuel, lumber, shells, and other things necessary for his family.

Right, wrong, cruel — who is to say? Clubbing baby seals to death in order to eat, clothe, and keep warm is still a far cry above trophy killing by sportsmen or hunting deer by car lights or crocodile killing at night or the killing of great numbers of seals by early fur-company ship's crews.

Let us be realistic about this and not pick just one isolated group without knowing anything about the circumstances behind the slaughter.

As Joe Western wrote, "We might all embrace vegetarianism." But what about the theory that plants grow better if one speaks kindly of them? Surely this means they, too, have feelings which hurt when we pull up, pare, boil, fry, or chew them.

MALINDA CARROLL

Hyannis, Mass.

☆ ☆ ☆

Top left, from *The National Observer*, March 29, 1971.

Top right, letter to the editor of *The National Observer* by Joan Mooney, April 12, 1971.

Above right, letter to the editor of *The National Observer* by Malinda Carroll, April 12, 1971.

The ANIMAL PROTECTION INSTITUTE opposes the use of steel-jaw leghold traps for the following reasons:

1. STEEL-JAW TRAPS SUBJECT ANIMALS TO INTENSE SUFFERING. The trap clamps shut with force on the leg or paw of any animal stepping into it. Many times the leg bone of the animal is broken. As the animal struggles to free itself, the jaws of the trap tear into the flesh, causing extreme fear and pain. The animal is held in the trap—unless it chews off its paw and escapes—fully conscious until the trapper returns. The trap is staked to the ground or fastened to a tree, branch, or stump. The trapped animal is denied food and water and is exposed to all weather conditions. Researchers have verified that the stomachs of animals taken in traps are often empty of food. The trapped animals also swallow fragments of their own bodies —broken teeth, fur, claws—in their attempts to chew themselves free of the traps.

2. TRAP LAWS ARE NOT ENFORCEABLE. Less than 25 states have laws requiring periodic checks of trap lines. Many of the states say trap lines must be run every 24-48 hours. Other states go so far as to require that trap lines be run once a week. In some areas of the country severe weather conditions can prohibit the trapper's returning to his line for days. State departments of fish and game or conservation do not have the manpower to police trap lines. This is due in part to the fact that trap lines are generally located in rural, remote areas. A great deal of trapping is done too by children, primarily of high school age. Few states have minimum age limits for trappers, and any child may purchase and set a trap and neglect it when he loses interest.

3. TRAPS ARE INDISCRIMINATE. This means a set trap will spring shut on whatever happens to step into it—dog, cat, bird, human, or a wild animal whose pelt is of no value to the trapper. A five-year study conducted by the Ontario Department of Lands and Forests on two trap lines using leghold traps found that the number of animals caught of no value to the trapper — termed "trash" — compared to those the trapper could skin for pelts was nearly 3 to 1. This means that out of every four animals trapped, only one was of actual value for its fur. The other three animals or birds suffered and died or were mutilated needlessly. This is an unjustifiable waste of animal life.

4. TRAPPERS HAVE MADE NO EFFORT TO REDUCE THE CRUELTY OF TRAPPING. The steel-jaw leghold trap was manufactured in the United States by Sewell Newhouse around 1840. It has remained relatively unchanged here since that time. Other versions of the trap have been used throughout the world for nearly 300 years. An instant-kill trap was subsequently developed and marketed in 1958 by Frank Conibear. Other studies to produce more humane traps have been conducted primarily by humane organizations—not trappers nor the fur industry.

5. TRAPPING SUPPLIES FURS, A PRODUCT NOT NECESSARY TO MAN'S SURVIVAL. Our civilization has outgrown the era where we are dependent upon the skins of wild animals for clothing and warmth. Today, furs are a luxury item, appealing only to man's and woman's vanity. For the sake of the human ego we are inflicting incomprehensible suffering on wild animals. Nor can trapping be condoned and continued as heritage or folklore, simply because it played a part in the settlement of our country. In fact, to revere animal suffering is to stand in contradiction of those very ideals which helped establish America.

6. TRAPPING DOES NOT CONTRIBUTE SIGNIFICANTLY TO DISEASE CONTROL IN WILD ANIMAL POPULATIONS. Trappers contend they help control wild animal diseases, such as rabies, by keeping down the animal populations. Naturalists have found that wild animals control their own population levels, usually in relation to the food available in their habitat, and trapping has little effect. Certain animal diseases, too, appear to be cyclical in nature, such as rabies, and are not influenced by population density. The U.S. Fish and Wildlife Service's report, "Fur Catch in the United States, 1970," reveals fur prices greatly influence the species trapped. Skunks are particularly susceptible to and carriers of rabies. Yet, in the 1970 report only 21,874 skunks were reported trapped. In comparison, 1,520,329 raccoons, 112,560 beavers, and 5,164,953 muskrats were taken. Raccoon, beaver, and muskrat pelts bring considerably more money than skunk. Also, animals whose numbers are in serious decline, such as fisher, marten, timber wolf, and wolverine, are still trapped. Where animal populations must be kept in control, surely this can be done in a humane manner.

From "The Steel-Jaw Trap," The Animal Protection Institute of America, Sacramento, California.

The Ethical Basis of Our Cause

That the anti-vivisection movement is essentially ethical in its inspiration — predominantly moral in its objective — cannot be too strongly emphasized. Its philosophy is not primarily utilitarian, but fundamentally humanitarian. Unfortunately, it has always seemed to me that a great number of its active exponents have narrowly limited the field of constructive action to the arena of controversies over the utility of the practices that they deplore. Hence much anti-vivisection literature tends to be largely confined to technical discussions over the scientific value of certain "discoveries," the efficacy of particular serums, the accuracy of various pretensions of certain members of the medical profession and the reliability and value of numerous statistical compilations. These resources are all valid enough when not given a prominence which tends to minimize or obscure considerations which seem to be of far greater importance and possessed of much wider human appeal. I believe the retardation of progress in America is due in no small measure to this misplacing of emphasis on basic principles.

We need no other major argument — and we can find no more persuasive one — against the torture of dumb life in the name of science, than its downright sinfulness. I believe that an ingrained reverence for the mystery and inviolability of life, howsoever manifested, and a profound compassion for all sentient creatures, to be the foundation of the cause we espouse. While, therefore, I am free to question the utility of much that is tolerated in the name of medical science, my abhorrence of cruelty in any form would remain unaffected even if the claims asserted in justification were proved to demonstration. I refuse to ignore the insistent prompting of ethical instincts in the formation of my judgments. I reject the necessity of debating an issue of utility when the moral considerations are to me overwhelmingly preponderant. I decline to compromise with that which I deem fundamentally wrong.

G. R. F.

From *Reverence for Life*, published by the
New England Anti-Vivisection Society.

SECTION **8**

Abortion and Sterilization

Like those in the previous section, the arguments in this section involve consideration of the boundaries of the realm of morality; but the arguments in this section involve one issue which did not appear at all in the previous section, the question of when *human* life begins. The discussion of whether or not certain treatment of nonhumans is morally wrong required a judgment about extending the realm of morality beyond the purely human realm. In contrast, much of the debate about the morality of abortion involves a judgment concerning the boundaries of the realm of the human itself. The discussions in this section also involve a concern with questions of legislation which were not significant in the discussions of the treatment of animals.

Contemporary discussions about the problems related to abortion—especially regarding the desirability, feasibility, utility, justifiability, and/or morality of making it illegal in the wake of the Supreme Court ruling which struck down almost all antiabortion legislation—have involved some of the most passionate and eloquent pleas on behalf of the fetus, the mother, God, and "morality" in general. Some of the selections in this section provide first-hand evidence of the difficulty of extracting the essence of a moral argument from under the window dressing of colorful rhetoric. Once the rhetoric is removed, the difficulty of the problems becomes all too apparent, especially those of defining "human being" and "living." If a four-month-old fetus is a human being, then abortion might well be considered a form of murder; but is a fetus a human being? This is at most only partially a moral question; it also requires consideration of medical, legal, theological, metaphysical, biological, and other dimensions. For example, some people hold the belief that a soul enters the human body at the moment of conception, and for those persons it is unquestionably the case that the fetus is a human being from that first moment. But an analysis and evaluation of premises such as this requires that we go far beyond the realm of ethical theory and the specific issue of abortion to an examination of some of the basic questions of metaphysics and religion.

The resolution of the problem of whether or not a fetus is a human being is not necessary for some arguments dealing with abortion. For example, it is possible to construct an argument which allows (for the purposes of the discussion at least) the assumption that a fetus is a human being. This type of argument then focusses on the question of whether or not there are any conditions under which it is morally permissible to take a human life. Arguments of this type are similar in important ways to certain arguments dealing with issues of life and death in the contexts of war, capital punishment, and even terrorism.

Some arguments about abortion focus on the right of a woman to control her own body and the question of whether or not a fetus is part of a woman's body. There are some important areas of overlap between this type of argument and certain arguments about compulsory sterilization (which involves the woman's right to become pregnant as opposed to her right to terminate a pregnancy).

EXERCISES

1. Evaluate each of the arguments in this section under the different assumptions that a) the mother, b) the father, and c) the physician is confronted with a decision concerning an abortion. How does this change in circumstances affect the support that the premises provide for the conclusion?
2. To what extent are the arguments offered by the Supreme Court justices in their ruling on abortion *moral* arguments? If they are not moral arguments, then what kind are they?
3. Compare the arguments concerning abortion in this section with those concerning euthanasia in the next section. Are there any significant differences in the problems associated with defining "human being" at the beginning and at the end of life?

Excerpts From Abortion Case

Special to The New York Times

WASHINGTON, Jan. 22—
Following are excerpts from the majority opinion, written by Justice Henry A. Blackmun, in Jane Roe v. Henry Wade, the Texas abortion case and from the dissent written by Justice Byron R. White:

Majority Opinion

The Texas statutes under attack here are typical of those that have been in effect in many states for approximately a century. These make it a crime to "procure an abortion," as therein defined, or to attempt one, except with respect to "an abortion procured or attempted by medical advice for the purpose of saving the life of the mother." Similar statutes are in existence in a majority of the states.

It perhaps is not generally appreciated that the restrictive criminal abortion laws in effect in a majority of states are of relatively recent vintage. Instead, they derive from statutory changes effected, for the most part, in the latter half of the 19th century.

When most criminal abortion laws were first enacted, the procedure was a hazardous one for the woman.

Privacy Rights Unclear

The Constitution does not explicitly mention any right of privacy. In a line of decision, however, the Court has recognized that a right of personal privacy, or a guarantee of certain areas or zones of privacy, does exist under the Constitution.

This right of privacy, whether it be founded in the 14th Amendments concept of personal liberty and restrictions upon state action, as we feel it is, or as the District Court determined, in the Ninth Amendment's reservation of rights to the people, is broad enough to encompass a woman's decision whether or not to terminate her pregnancy.

The detriment that the state would impose upon the pregnant woman by denying this choice altogether is apparent. Specific and direct harm medically diagnosable even in early pregnancy may be involved. Maternity, or additional offspring, may force upon the woman a distressful life and future. Psychological harm may be iminent. Mental and physical wealth may be taxed by child care.

There is also the distress, for all concerned, associated with the unwanted child, and there is the problem of bringing a child into a family already unable, psychologically and otherwise, to care for it.

On the basis of elements such as these, appellants and some amici argue that the woman's right is absolute and that she is entitled to terminate her pregnancy at whatever time, in whatever way, and for whatever reason she alone chooses. With this we do not agree.

The Court's decision recognizing a right of privacy also acknowledge that some state regulation in areas protected by that right is appropriate. A state may properly assert important interests in safeguarding health, in maintaining medical standards and in protecting Potential life.

At the same point in pregnancy, these respective interests become sufficiently compelling to sustain regulation of the factors that govern the abortion decision.

The appellee and certain amici argue that the fetus is a "person" within the language and meaning of the 14th amendment. In support of this they outline at length and in detail the well-known facts of fetal development. If this suggestion of peronhood is established, the appellant's case, of course, collapses, for the fetus' right to life is then aguaranteed specifically by the amendment.

The Constitution does not define "person' in so many words. The use of the word is such that it has application only postnatally.

All this, together with our observation that throughout the major portion of the 19th century prevailing legal abortion practices were far freer than they are today, persuades us that the word "person," as used in the 14th Amendment, does not include unborn.

Texas urges that, apart from the 14th Amendment, life begins at conception and is present throughout pregnancy, and that, therefore, the state as a compelling interest in protecting that life from and after conception.

We need not resolve the difficult question of when life begins. When those trained in the respective disciplines of medicine, philosophy and theology are unable to arrive at any consensus, the judiciary, at this point in the development of man's knowledge, is not in a position to speculate as to the answer.

The unborn have never been recognized in the law as persons in the whole sense.

With respect to the state's important and legitimate interest in the health of the mother, the "compelling" point, in the light of present medical knowledge, is at approximately the end of the first trimester. This is so because of the now established medical fact that until the end of the first trimester mortality in abortion is less than mortality in normal childbirth.

It follows that, from and after this point, a state may regulate the abortion procedure to the extent that the regulation reasonably relates to the preservation and protection of maternal health.

With respect to the state's important and legitimate interest in potential life, the "compelling" point is at viability. This is so because the fetus then presumably has the capability of meaningful life outside the mother's womb. If the state is interested in protecting fetal life after viability, it may go so far as to proscribe abortion during that period except when it is necessary to preserve the life or health of the mother.

Dissenting Opinion

At the heart of the controversy in these cases are those recurring pregnancies that pose no danger whatsoever to the life or health of the mother but are nevertheless unwanted for any one or more of a variety of easons —convenience, family planning, economics, dislike of children, the embarrassment of illegitimacy, etc.

The common claim before us is that for any one of such reasons, or for no reason at all, and without asserting or claiming any threat to life or health, any woman is entitled to an abortion at her request if she is able to find a medical adviser willing to undertake the procedure.

The Court for the most part sustains this position: during the period prior to the time the fetus becomes viable, the Constitution of the United States values the convenience, whim or caprice of the putative mother more than life or potential life of the fetus.

The upshot is that the people and the legislatures of the 50 states are constitution ally disentitled to weigh the relative importance of the continued existence and development of the fetus on the one hand against a spectrum of possible impacts on the mother on the other hand.

As an exercise of raw judicial power, the Court perhaps has authority to do what it does today; but in my view its judgment is an improvident and extravagant exercise of the power of judicial review which the constitution extends to this court.

I find no constitutional warrant for imposing such an order of priorities on the people and legislatures of the states. In a sensitive area such as this, involving as it does issues over which reasonable men may easily and heatedly differ, I cannot accept the Court's exercise of its clear power of choice by interposing a constitutional barrier to state efforts to protect human life and by investing mothers and doctors with the constitutionally protected right to exterminate it. This issue, for the most part, should be left with the people and to the political processes the people have devised to govern thier affairs.

From *The New York Times*, January 22, 1973.

Left, reprinted from *U.S. News & World Report*, March 4, 1974. Copyright 1974 U.S. News & World Report, Inc.

To the Editor:

In the recent Supreme Court abortion decision, Justice Blackmun has argued that since there is doubt as to when life begins we may abort the unborn. One wonders if the Court will next argue that when an accused murderer's guilt or innocence is in doubt he may legitimately be put to death.

So much has been written and said about the "presumption of innocence" in our legal system as the protection of individual rights against unjust accusations. How much more important would it have been if the Court had created a "presumption of life" in those cases where legal existence is in doubt.

The Court has made a serious mistake in taking these issues away from the people and attempting to substitute its will for the people's will as expressed in legislatures and referendums.

ALBERT E. GUNN, M.D.
Springfield, Va., Feb. 2, 1973

Cooke Warns Catholics on Abortions

By GEORGE DUGAN

Cardinal Cooke warned Roman Catholics yesterday that any involvement with abortion would mean automatic excommunication.

"Putting aside the public debate for a moment," he declared, "we remind ourselves emphatically that any association with an immoral abortion, for any reason, is a grave personal sin. No state law can change that.

"Nor can any convenience — psychological, matrimonial, economic, cultural or social — permit any Catholic to perform, undergo or encourage a direct abortion. To do so is to commit a grave personal and social sin against God and humanity. In so doing so a person separates himself from the Catholic community and communion."

"Catholics must not be misled," the Cardinal said. "There is no 'new theology' on abortion. An informed Catholic conscience can never tolerate the direct destruction of innocent human life. It is a serious and heinous sin for any Catholic—priest or doctor, parent, husband or friend — to encourage a girl to undergo an abortion.

"If we oppose unjust wars, criminal assassinations, political murders and terrorist hijacking; if we move against life-damaging poverty, pollution, hunger and neglect, then we must not condone abortion. I ask you all to join me in prayer today that innocent life, in every form, will be made safe in this nation."

Top, letter to the editor of *The New York Times* by Albert E. Gunn, M.D., February 14, 1973.
Right, from *The New York Times*, October 8, 1973.

Abortion Decision: A Year Later

It is now a full year since the Supreme Court in *Roe* v. *Wade* effectively struck down the traditional abortion statutes of all 50 states. Not surprisingly, that decision has met with every kind of response, from outcries that it represents nothing less than legalized slaughter to claims that it will stand as the social milestone of the century. But critics and supporters have done far more than issue statements. Legislative and court battles continue in an effort to define the implications of the Court's ruling, whether in the interests of constricting its application or broadening it still further. In addition, of course, there has been a nationwide campaign to sponsor a constitutional amendment to overturn the decision.

Support for such a radical approach to the problem continues to grow, but procedural problems in the House Judiciary Committee—in particular, impeachment hearings—will probably block that road for some months. More significantly the writing of such an amendment, as we pointed out last June (6/2/73, p. 506), would be extremely difficult if an attempt were made to include the various exceptions to an absolute ban on abortion held by different religious and ethical groups. And no amendment could promise *greater* protection to the fetus than is already accorded citizens by other provisions of the Constitution (see James Diamond's discussion of this point on p. 27). If drafting an amendment will be controversial, getting it passed by both houses of Congress and three quarters of the states may be impossible. In short, a constitutional amendment, while the most direct legal route, may prove to be an enormous detour on the road to a sane abortion policy in the United States.

Attempts to change the law, of course whether by constitutional amendment or further litigation through the courts, are perfectly appropriate in our system of government and entirely laudable, but they should not consume all of our energy or be allowed to distract us from a pressing educational dilemma. As long as the law supported the moral position of those who opposed ready abortions, the need to consider the complicated ethical questions involved was minimal. Abortions were wrong *and* illegal. The fact that they have been

rendered licit by Court fiat in no way changes their moral status.

At the very least, a potential human life is at stake in every determination to abort. To say that a fetus is merely a part of a woman's body runs contrary to all the biological evidence that clearly demonstrates the presence of a new and separate organism in the embryo. But it is an organism entirely dependent on the life of the mother for existence and sustenance during the first six to seven months—a fact that makes the fetus a special case. The moral question is what value shall we place on this unique form of human life? The current trend of American opinion, insofar as it is represented by the *Roe* v. *Wade* decision, displays a shocking callousness to the presence of life in the womb. Before the law, it is denied the protection afforded every human person, citizen or not. In the eyes of many, its rights—and most particularly, its right to exist—are secondary to the convenience of another individual. Simply to overlook or consciously ignore the inchoate humanity of the fetus threatens the very basis of our lives together in society, for it strikes at the common dignity we all claim as human beings. Because it treats human life cheaply and encourages a disregard for the value of all that is vulnerable, abortion-on-demand is an antihuman policy. That point must be made over and over again if we are not to be lulled into an uncritical acceptance of what has become legally permissible. If the decision to have an abortion has become a personal one, then the ethical burden of that decision has been increased, not diminished.

Abortions, however, are seldom purely private actions. They require assistance—doctors, nurses, a clinic or hospital. In each case, the consciences of other persons are intimately involved. If the state has decided, through its highest Court, that it has no right to force a woman to bear a child to term against her will, then by the same logic it should have no right to compel an individual, against his conscience, to aid in the termination of that life. The inviolability of one conscience demands the inviolability of the other. Some 17 states have already enacted conscience clauses to cover just such cases. They should be extended as soon as possible to all states and the federal government.

LETTERS:

Abortion—1

I must take ussue with Gordon G. Evans on the matter of abortion. "The crux of the matter" is not, as he contends, "when life begins." Any society that cares as little as ours does for wild life and natural environment *for its own sake* cannot legitimately claim to be concerned about "life" *per se*.

Rather, the crucial question is, When does life begin *to be human*? That can't be answered in physical terms alone. (Remember the plucked chicken that was presented as an example of human life to the philosopher who had defined man as "a featherless biped?")

Birth is by no means "merely an incident" in comparison with conception. It is, instead, the essential event which makes one part of the human community. And it is only as part of the human community, in relationship with other persons, that one can acquire and develop those qualities which are uniquely human. Language is the most clear-cut of these— and no fetus, as long as it is a fetus, is even potentially capable of intelligent speech. That requires communication with other human minds.

Chomingwen D. Pond
Wilberforce, Ohio

Abortion—2

....While it is correct that a union of an egg and sperm determine the biological chacteristics of a new individual, these same sex cells are themselves alive. Such unicellular stages have specific requirements for continued life and a finite lifespan just as do the multicellular stages of life from which they come and to which they can give origin. To argue that the eggs and sperm are in some way less important than these multicellular stages is as pointless as the old "chicken and the egg" problem.

If every effort must be bent to assure that the needs of all human life are met on an equal basis, there is as much argument for compulsory fertilization of all human ova (unfortunately most sperm will be out of luck as evolutionary design has resulted in the production of millions of sperm for each ovum) as for the preservation of each fetus. ....

Melissa Stanley
Fairfax, Va.

Top, Chomingwen D. Pond, "Abortion 1" in
Civil Liberties, No. 302, May 1974, p. 6.
Above, Melissa Stanley, "Abortion 2" in
Civil Liberties, No. 302, May 1974, p. 6.

An open letter to all Americans:

What Do People Really Think about Abortion?

The best way to find out is to *ask* them—but evidently it isn't that simple.

On April 8, The New York *Times* carried a story (page 7) headlined "Abortion Poll Finds Public Evenly Split." It reported a recent Gallup Poll on the U.S. Supreme Court's pro-abortion decisions of January 22, 1973. Said the *Times*: "The survey indicated that 47 per cent of the American people favored the court's ruling, and 44 per cent opposed it." The survey was based "on interviews with 1,582 adults."

Gallup's question was: "The United States Supreme Court has ruled that a woman may go to a doctor to end pregnancy at any time during the first three months of pregnancy. Do you favor or oppose this ruling?"

Our question is: How can you take a poll on abortion without using the word? And how accurate would it be? We decided to find out. We commissioned Sindlinger & Co., a highly-respected opinion research firm, to do the job. First (April 16-23) Sindlinger asked 1,653 people (a nationwide representative sampling like Gallup's, only bigger) *the exact same question* Gallup asked. The results were — for those of us who oppose abortion—worse than Gallup's: 45.9 favored the Court's ruling, 39.5 opposed it; almost 10% refused to answer (keep this point in mind), the remaining 4.9% were undecided.

The following week (April 24-30) we did the same thing, to another 1,653 people (if these numbers seem small to *you*, the statistical experts say that they project to a representative sampling of some 67,220,000 adult Americans). Only this time we changed Gallup's wording "go to a doctor to end pregnancy" to **go to a doctor for an abortion.** No other change. The results were ... surprising. The figures now showed 48.7 *opposed* the Court, 41.0% favored, only 5.9% refused to answer, with 4.4% undecided.

We decided to try it yet again (May 3-8, 1,652 people). The results: 53.7% opposed (i.e., *against* abortion), 42.9% in favor, only 2.3% refused to answer, and a mere 1.1% remained undecided! Clearly more and more people are making up their minds on the issue—very likely because abortion is *finally* getting major coverage from the media (after a very long and very strange blackout).

We did more. We *added* two questions to the basic one: a) "How do you yourself rate the subject of abortion—as very important to you—of some importance to you—or of no importance to you?" and b) "As far as you yourself are concerned would you say you are for or against abortion, or what *do* you think?" The results? We quote Sindlinger's report directly:

"Americans are opposed to abortion by a margin of better than three to two, according to a nationwide survey of U.S. households by Sindlinger & Company of Swarthmore, Pennsylvania.

"In a May 3-8 survey based on a sample of 1,652 households, 59.4 percent said they were against abortion compared with 36.2 percent who favored it. Most of the opposition was voiced by women as 62.7 percent of the females interviewed opposed abortion compared with 56 percent of the men. At the same time, 39.7 percent of the males interviewed and 32.9 percent of the females were for abortion.

"The abortion issue apparently is regarded as important to some degree by seven of ten Americans. In the survey, 29.8 percent regarded the issue as very important and another 39.1 percent called it of some importance. Only 28.4 percent said it was of no importance.

"Better than one of every three women— 35.6 percent—said the issue was very important but less than one of four men—23.9 percent — held it in the same light."

There you have it. If you want to know what Americans really think about abortion, **you have to ask them about abortion.**

What can *you* do about it? If you agree with us that the abortion issue needs to be freely and fully discussed—most especially, if you agree with us in our opposition to the Court's pro-abortion decisions—then you can use the coupon below to help us get our message to *all* Americans! Send as much as you can, but send something, and send it **now!**

The Ad Hoc Committee in Defense of Life • *P.O. Box 574, Murray Hill Station, N.Y.C.*

To the Editor:

The decision to grant what is tantamount to abortion on demand sets the profession of medicine and civilization back 2,500 years to a time when the doctor and sorcerer were the same individual with the power to kill as well as to cure.

Though Justice Blackmun conveniently dismisses the Hippocratic oath as élitist on the basis of a dead scholar's fragile hypothesis, Margaret Mead reminds us according to a 1972 study by Maurice Levine that the oath marked one of the turning points in the history of man. She states that "for the first time in our tradition there was a complete separation between killing and curing." She added that "it was the Greeks who made the distinction clear and delegated to one profession, medicine, a complete dedication to life under all circumstances."

Dr. Mead emphasizes what Justice Blackmun failed to appreciate: that this radical separation of killing and curing "is a priceless possession which we cannot afford to tarnish, but society always is attempting to make the physician into a killer—to kill the defective child [or] the cancer patient."

The majority opinion of the Supreme Court has disregarded her conviction that "it is the duty of society to protect the physician from such requests." By this failure the Court has recycled today's obstetrician back to the dark ages of the sorcerer, who for a fee will kill or rescue the smaller of two patients in a pregnancy on the basis of the woman's request. Furthermore, the majority opinion insures that a killing operation will become the most prevalent operation performed in the United States, as it is in New York State today.   HERBERT RATNER, M.D.
Director, Dept. of Public Health
Oak Park, Ill., Feb. 1, 1973

Left, letter to the editor of *The New York Times* by Herbert Ratner, M.D., February 14, 1973.
Right, courtesy Knights of Columbus.

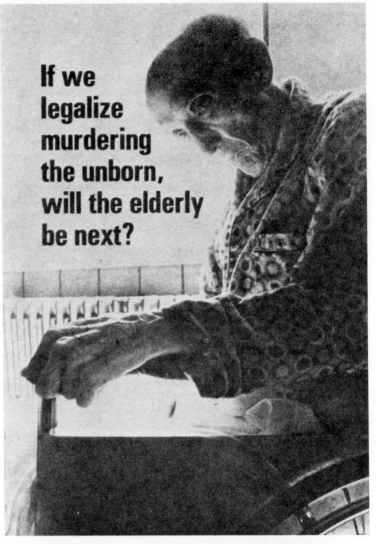

If we legalize murdering the unborn, will the elderly be next?

Far-fetched? Think about it a moment. If society can justify the taking of the life of an unborn child whose only crime is being unwanted, why not the life of a sick or elderly person who has become an unwanted burden?

Once established, there is no end to the ways the principle of legalized abortion could be used to justify the taking of human life "for the good of society."

If you'd like a better understanding of the Christian principles involved, write today for our new pocket-size pamphlet entitled "The Sacredness of Life." We'll send it free and nobody will call.

OBSERVATIONS

An Amendment About Life

SEN. JAMES Buckley has proposed an antiabortion amendment to the Constitution, and cosponsoring the measure are six fellow senators. One is a Catholic and the five others are Protestants.

That's a good line-up. It is of central importance that foes of abortion make it clear that their cause is not just a parochial concern of the Roman Catholic Church. While the Catholic hierarchy has been outspoken in its opposition to abortion, the question is not one of simple sectarian preference. At stake are millions of lives.

The Human Life Amendment (and that is no euphemism) was introduced in response to the Supreme Court's unbelievable pronouncement that it is the law of the United States that unborn babies may be freely killed because they are incapable of "meaningful life."

We do not know at this time whether the Court plans to pursue this reasoning to include paralyzed people, very old people, retarded people, or deformed people. But all such citizens might be described as being incapable of "meaningful life." All we need do to make that phrase fit those categories is revamp our criteria a little.

The Human Life Amendment has an excellent chance of becoming part of the Constitution, not because of the lobbying of the Catholic Church, but because it is one of those rare instruments of law that are powerfully, ringingly right. And because state legislatures and public referendums have indicated that most Americans believe abortions to be profoundly wrong.

Here is what the proposed amendment provides:

Section 1: With respect to the right to life, the word "person," as used in this Article and in the Fifth and Fourteenth Articles of Amendment to the Constitution of the United States, applies to all human beings, including their unborn offspring at every stage of their biological development, irrespective of age, health, function, or condition of dependency.

Section 2: This Article shall not apply in an emergency when a reasonable medical certainty exists that continuation of the pregnancy will cause the death of the mother.

Section 3: Congress and the several states shall have power to enforce this Article by appropriate legislation within their respective jurisdictions.

Interestingly, the most effective campaigner against abortion these days is not some jowly old bishop but a Methodist housewife named Marjory Mecklenburg. Mrs. Mecklenburg has been making speeches around the country, emphasizing the ecumenical nature of the fight against wholesale abortions.

Says she: "To me the crux of this issue is that abortion is the killing of a human who can't protect himself. Obviously, Christians and all humanitarians should help those who can't defend themselves. It is only if you feel that you have no responsibility, one for another, that you can stand by and let another human life be attacked."

If you agree, I hope you will tell your senators. If you disagree, I hope you will think it over.

—*EDWIN A. ROBERTS, JR.*

This column offers varied views of our diverse staff—observations the editors rate worthy of reader consideration.

Intensely Personal

To the Editor:

Regarding "An Amendment About Life" I find it impossible to empathize with Mr. Roberts' point of view. To lump those who are aged, deformed, paralyzed or retarded into the terminology of the Supreme Court decision along with protoplasmic non-beings is, to me, unthinkble. The only common ground in this convenient lumping is that they were all, at one time or another, conceived (convenient insofar as giving additional "weight" to Mr. Roberts' argument).

To my thinking, however, the issue is an intensely personal one and should not be brought under the jurisdiction of the courts or the legislature but should be the sole responsibility of the mother-to-be. I assume that in Mr. Roberts' opinion (as well as Senator Buckley, Mrs. Mecklenburg and unnamed others), all unwanted children should be allowed to be born regardless of the circumstances or results of such births. In this age of increased human sensitivity it seems to me that any woman who feels that the birth of a child would do her irreparable harm should not be compelled to bear that child.

Where do we place the importance? Are we to attach such great importance to "life" that we refuse to prevent it (or stop it, in Mr. Roberts' thinking), thus possibly destroying the lives of those who are already living? Is our responsibility as moral creatures to those who *may be* or to those who *are?* Is it equally moral to force a mother to bear a child she neither wants nor can care for as to bring a child into the world to be loved and cared for by its parents?

I would like to remind Mr. Roberts that we are in the midst of a population explosion. There are children growing up unwanted at all levels of society, whose parent(s) cannot provide the type of environment conducive to developing healthy attitudes toward life, and others who are being brought up in orphanages. These are the victims of the thinking of Mr. Roberts and others who feel the act of conception is the origin of an inalienable right to live.

MIRIAM V. DOMER

Denver

☆   ☆   ☆

Above, letter to the editor of *The National Observer* by Miriam V. Domer, July 14, 1973.
Right, letter to the editor of *The National Observer* by Dorothea Fulkerson, July 14, 1973.

'Self-Contradictory'

To the Editor:

The Human Life Amendment is surely self-contradictory. How can a law proclaim in Section 1 that "persons" born and unborn have an equal right to life and in Section 2 that one person's life may be sacrificed when another person's life is in danger?

Are mothers more equal than babies? Why not just let the mother die and then take such measures as are needed to preserve the life of the surviving "person."

DOROTHEA FULKERSON

Levittown, N.Y.

☆   ☆   ☆

Strong Vatican Stand Forbids All Abortion

VATICAN CITY, Nob. 25 (AP) — The Vatican said today that abortion can never be justified, even when the mother's life is in danger or the child could be abnormal. In its most strongly worded pronouncement on the subject to date, it declared:

"Never, under any pretext, may abortion be resorted to, either by a family or by a political authority, as a legitimate means of regulating birth."

The 5,000-word document was issued by the Congregation for the Propagation of the Faith, which stressed that Pope Paul VI had seen and approved it.

"It may be a serious question of health, sometimes of life or death, for the mother; it may be the burden represented by an additional child, especially if there are good reasons to fear that the child will be abnormal or retarded. ... We proclaim only that none of these reasons can ever objectively confer the right to dispose of another person's life, even when that life is only beginning," the Vatican said.

Acknowledging that "modern technology makes early abortion more and more easy," the document insisted, however, that "moral evaluation is in no way modified because of this."

Pointing out women's responsibilities on the question, the document said, "The movement for the emancipation of women, in so far as it seeks essentially to free them from all unjust discrimination, is on perfectly sound ground. ... But one cannot change nature, nor can one exempt women, any more than men, from what nature demands on them."

The document said all freedoms, including sexual freedom, have a natural limitation in the rights of other pople. "And must always be careful not to violate justice."

"If one tries to say that men and women are free to seek sexual pleasure to the point of satiety, without taking into account any law or the essential orientation of sexual life to its fruits of fertility, then this idea has nothing Christian in it," the document said.

At another point, it declared, "One cannot but be astonished to see a simultaneous increase of unqualified protests against the death penalty and every form of war and the vindication of the liberalization of abortion. ..."

IS ABORTION MURDER?

A mother stepped into the doctor's office carrying a bright and beautiful baby a year old. Seating herself near her family physician, she said, "Doctor, I want you to help me out of trouble. My baby is only one year old, and I have conceived again, and I do not want to have children so close together." "What do you expect me to do?" asked the physician.

"Oh, anything to get rid of it for me," she replied.

After thinking seriously for a moment the doctor said, "I think I can suggest a better method of helping you out. If you object to having two children so near together, the best way would be to kill the one on your lap, and let the other one come on. It is easy to get at the one on your lap, and it makes no difference to me which one I kill for you. Besides, it might be dangerous for you if I undertook to kill the younger one.

As the doctor finished speaking he reached for a knife, and continued by asking the mother to lay the baby out on her lap, and turn her head the other way.

The woman almost fainted away as she jumped from her chair and uttered one word, "Murderer!"

A few words of explanation from the doctor soon convinced the mother that his offer to commit murder was no worse than her request for the destruction of the unborn child. In either case it would be murder. The only difference would be in the age of the victim.

Left, courtesy of The Associated Press.
Right, from Dale Crowley's *Capital Voice* (July 1, 1973), Washington, D.C.

Speaking Out

BY WILLIAM B. OBER, M.D.

WE SHOULD LEGALIZE ABORTION

The question posed by such cases is to what extent society should subordinate individual human values to the codes it has inherited from generations with somewhat different values, different goals, and certainly a different role assigned to women. State and church use "moral" objections to prevent abortions, and yet permit some abortions. I submit that there is no moral difference among abortions, whether the fetus is the result of rape, incest or rich conjugal love. By what right does state or church claim a jurisdiction superior to that of the woman involved in pregnancy? I believe that every woman should be able to have an unwanted pregnancy aborted at her own request, subject only to the consent of her husband and the advice of her physician.

A Grave Distortion Of The Abortion Issue

By REV. FRANCIS PIRO, S.T.L.

In the May 13th issue of **The Philadelphia Inquirer**, an article by a Dr. Wood read in big headlines: "Religious Freedom, Majority Rule Are The Real Abortion Issues."

The article represented a grave distortion of the concept of freedom and a flagrant assault on the basic right to life by someone who is particularly duty-bound and foster that very right. A few observations may help Dr. Wood and those who agree with his views understand the real issue of abortion:

1) The alleged encroachment of religion on the rights of people disregards the fact that abortion is fundamentally a human problem and, as such, it should be the concern of any human being regardless of his religion.

2) We ought to distinguish between physical freedom and moral freedom. A person physically free to kill, steal, etc., is not morally free to do so. In fact, any such violation carries penalties in the framework of civil and penal laws.

3) The right to life applies to any human being as such — independently of its "environmental" condition. Whether a human being be born or unborn is not essential to the fruition of that right. Furthermore, the more incapable a being is of its own defense, the more strictly the respect of its right to life should be enforced. For this very reason the American law protects animals from being cruelly treated.

4) From a scientific viewpoint, it is almost universally accepted that the fetus is a human being. Any doubt, however, could not change its condition of inviolability. Dr. Wood should remember that no law would ever condemn a person unless his guilt be proven beyond doubt. Should not this principle apply to a fetus as well? The slightest presumption as to its human condition would make a direct destruction of a fetus by abortion a crime of **murder**.

5) If the alleged "burden" of the unborn, rather than objective moral standards, is the criterion of human behavior, by the same token and logic society should rid itself of the aged, the handicapped, the retarded, etc. These people, too, are a "social liability." Millions of Jews murdered under Hitler were a liability in the Nazi doctrine.

6) The alleged violation of the rights of the majority, as claimed by Dr. Wood, is based on the false assumption that people are the source of morality. No majority could ever change certain objective moral principles as the criterion of normal human conduct. No referendum could ever change the fact that murder, for example, is a grave crime.

I trust that Dr. Wood and all those who favor a permissive abortion policy will find inspirational a passage from the Hippocratic Oath: "I will give not deadly medicine to anyone if asked, nor suggest any such counsel. Furthermore, I will not give to a woman an instrument to produce an abortion."

SOME POPULATION FACTS - Nobody can predict the population of the United States in years to come. The best is only an educated guess. THE BIRTH RATE has fallen from 25 per thousand to a current 18 per thousand population, a figure that only has to reach about 15 to give us population stability over an extensive time. To put things in the right perspective, we have to look at the DEATH RATE, that is less than 10 per thousand population. (These figures give us an average lifespan of over a hundred years) It is a figure that is sure to rise eventually to about 15 per thousand population. We are faced with great health care needs in our society as the average age of our people rises toward the end of this century. WHERE will the young be to take care of those in need A BIRTH RATE OF 10 PER THOUSAND POPULATION WOULD BRING ON THE EVENTUAL EXTINCTION OF THE HUMAN RACE.

Top left, from *The Saturday Evening Post,* October 8, 1966.
Above right, from *The Wanderer,* copyright 1971.
Above, courtesy of the Non-Sectarian Committee for Life, October 1971.

ABORTION PASTORAL
VARIATIONS ON A THEME

Few of the many comments on the unfortunate contrast between the strong stand of American bishops on the matter of abortion and their silence on the question of Vietnam have been as striking as that of one priest of the archdiocese of New York. After reading from the pulpit Cardinal Cooke's pastoral letter marking Right-to-Life Sunday and preaching on its contents, the priest added that "respect for life in one direction demands respect for life in another." He reread the letter with only slight modifications such as those below. He made no other remarks, nor were any necessary.

My Friends in Christ:

Today, America needs to be reminded of the guiding principles upon which it was founded. Respect for all human life is fundamental to our national existence. In recent years, however, we have seen a steady erosion of respect for life in our society.

The ~~New York State Abortion Law of 1970~~ [war in Vietnam] has drawn our society far down the road to open contempt for human life. Since I wrote to you on behalf of the Bishops of the State last December, we have seen the situation grow worse daily. New ~~abortion clinics~~ [fronts] have opened with increasing frequency. Both as Catholics and as citizens we must speak out against this tragedy of [war] ~~abortion.~~

Some say that Catholics should not speak on this issue. "~~Abortion~~ [The war] is only a ~~social~~ [political] matter," they claim; "religion should not enter into it." Such a position disenfranchises men of certain religious convictions. It says, in effect, that certain citizens may not have a voice on particular issues.

Anyone who is convinced, be he Catholic or not, that ~~abortion~~ [the war in Vietnam] is an attack on human life has the right and the duty to say so. Every human person is a member of society and has a serious social responsibility to shape the values of that society as they are expressed in its laws.

~~In New York State,~~ we have moved far beyond a mere debate on personal values. ~~One hundred thou-~~ [Hundreds of thousands of lives] ~~sand unborn children~~ have been destroyed in ~~New York alone. New York is already the abortion capital of the nation.~~ [Indo-china]

Not only Catholics, but men and women of many diverse religious backgrounds believe that, by the [war in Vietnam, the United States] ~~Abortion Law of 1970, New York State~~ has alienated what the Declaration of Independence calls the "inalienable" right to life.

We urge each person, young or old, who believes in the right of every ~~child to be born~~ [person to life], to enter the public forum and work for the [end] ~~repeal~~ of this tragic ~~law.~~ [war]

There are bills in ~~Albany~~ [Congress] right now that would stop this slaughter of the innocent ~~unborn~~. I suggest that you write, phone, telegraph and speak to all our ~~state's~~ [nation's] lawmakers and make your support of life known to them in a very clear manner.

I join in prayer with you that the tragedy of ~~abortion~~ [the war in Vietnam] may be removed from our society.

Faithfully yours in Christ,

TERENCE CARDINAL COOKE,

Archbishop of New York

From *Commonweal*, May 14, 1971.

Text of Abortion-Bill Veto

Special to The New York Times

ALBANY, May 13 — Following is the text of Governor Rockefeller's message to the Legislature vetoing repeal of the state's liberalized abortion law:

The same strong reasons that led me to recommend abortion-law reform in my annual message . . . for 1968-69 and 1970 and to sign into law the reform that was ultimately adopted in 1970, now compel me to disapprove the bill just passed that would would repeal that reform.

The abortion-law reform of 1970 grew out of the recommendations of an outstanding select citizens committee, representative of all affected parties, that I appointed in 1968.

Under the distinguished leadership of retired Court of Appeals Judge Charles W. Froessel, the select committee found that the then-existing, 19th-century, near-total prohibition against abortion was fostering hundreds of thousands of illegal and dangerous abortions. It was discriminating against women of modest means who could not afford an abortion haven and the often frightened, unwed, confused young woman. It was promoting hypocrisy and, ultimately, human tragedy.

Connecticut Case Cited

I supported the majority recommendations of the Froessel committee throughout the public debate of this issue extending over three years, until the Legislature acted to reform the state's archaic abortion law. I can see no justification now for repealing this reform and thus condemning hundreds of thousands of women to the dark age once again.

There is, further, the recent Federal court decision invalidating the Connecticut abortion law, which is substantially the same as the pre-reform New York law. The law of that case, if upheld, would clearly invalidate the old New York law, as well, were the repeal of abortion reform allowed to stand. In such a circumstance, this state would be left with no law on the subject at all.

I fully respect the moral convictions of both sides in this painfully sensitive controversy. But the extremes of personal vilification and political coercion brought to bear on members of the Legislature raise serious doubts that the votes to repeal the reform has represented the will of a majority of the people of New York State.

Risk to Life Seen

The very intensity of this debate has generated an emotional climate in which the truth about abortions and about the present state abortion law have become distorted almost beyond recognition.

The truth is that this repeal of the 1970 reform would not end abortions. It would only end abortions under safe and supervised medical conditions.

The truth is that a safe abortion would remain the optional choice of the well-to-do woman, while the poor would again be seeking abortions at a grave risk to life in back-room abortion mills.

The truth is that, under the present law, no woman is compelled to undergo an abortion. Those whose personal and religious principles forbid abortion are in no way compelled against their convictions under the present law. Every woman has the right to make her own choice.

I do not believe it right for one group to impose its vision of morality on an entire society. Neither is it just or practical for the state to attempt to dictate the innermost personal beliefs and conduct of its citizens.

The bill is disapproved.

"Surely, The Unborn Have Rights . . ."

Following is the complete text of President Richard Nixon's statement against abortion which he issued on April 3rd to reverse an earlier decision by Defense Department officials approving permissive abortion in military hospitals.

Historically, laws regulating abortion in the United States have been the province of States, not the Federal Government. That remains the situation today, as one State after another takes up this question, debates it and decides it. That is where the decisions should be made.

Partly, for that reason, I have directed that the policy on abortions at American military bases in the United States be made to correspond with the laws of the States where those bases are located. If the laws in a particular State restrict abortions, the rule at the military base hospitals are to correspond to that law.

The effect of this directive is to reverse service regulations issued last Summer, which had liberalized the rules on abortions at military hospitals. The new ruling supersedes this — and has been put into effect by the Secretary of Defense.

But while this matter is being debated in State capitals, and weighed by various courts, the Country has a right to know my personal views.

From personal and religious beliefs I consider abortions an unacceptable form of population control. Further, unrestricted abortion policies, or abortion on demand, I cannot square with my personal belief in the sanctity of human life — including the life of the yet unborn. For, surely, the unborn have rights also, recognized in law, recognized even in principles expounded by the United Nations.

Ours is a nation with a Judeo-Christian heritage. It is also a nation with serious social problems — problems of malnutrition, of broken homes, of poverty and of delinquency. But none of these problems justifies such a solution.

A good and generous people will not opt, in my view, for this kind of alternative to its social dilemmas. Rather, it will open its hearts and homes to the unwanted children of its own, as it has done for the unwanted millions of other lands.

Above, from *The Wanderer*, April 22, 1971.

Right, from *The New York Times*, May 13, 1971.

Bishop's Office
465 State Street
Albany, New York

MAILING ADDRESS
P. O. BOX 6045 - QUAIL STATION
ALBANY, NEW YORK 12206

THE CATHOLIC BISHOPS OF NEW YORK STATE

Dear Friends in Christ:

We find ourselves once more in the season of Advent, looking forward to Christmas and the coming of the Christ child. As we prepare our minds and hearts to welcome Him, we cannot fail to wonder at the glory of new life. For every child is fashioned in God's image, and as Christians we believe that he is destined to be a son of God.

Tragically, our age has seen the growth of a movement that belittles human life and urges the destruction of unborn children. This ruthless assault on human beings in the first stages of life has now been written into the law of New York State.

The appeals that we have made in behalf of unborn babies year after year and especially last Spring, went unheeded by a majority of our lawmakers this year. In April a law was enacted which now makes it legal, at any time from conception to six months later, to destroy the baby cradled in his mother's womb.

Once this law was passed the abortionists lost no time in plying their death-dealing trade. Each day they grow wealthier from the killing of unborn children -- some of whom have been heard to cry as they were dropped into surgical trash cans. They even advertise their monstrous commerce beyond the confines of the State, thus making New York the abortion capitol of America.

Once more we denounce this outrage against humanity. Together with all the Bishops of the world we hold and teach that "abortion is an unspeakable crime". We urge you, our fellow Catholics -- and through you all men of good will -- not to be deceived because a civil law permits abortion. God's law comes first, and God's law says: "Thou shalt not kill". No civil law can ever displace God's Commandment.

Indeed we remind you that lawmakers of another generation and in another land once claimed the right to decree the extinction of innocent human beings for so-called social and eugenic reasons. It happened under the Nazi regime; who is to say it cannot happen here?

We plead with you to recognize the terrible consequences of legalized abortion. Once innocent life at any stage is placed at the mercy of others, a vicious principle has been legalized. Thereafter, a simple majority may decide that life is to be denied the defective, the aged, the incorrigible, and granted only to the strong, the beautiful and the intelligent. The day may come when lawmakers could set standards which people must meet if they are to remain alive. Already one standard has been set; who can say what others will come next? For, once respect for human life has been undermined, the murderous possibilities are limitless.

We urge you, as strongly as we can, to oppose and reject abortion. Lest anyone take our words lightly, we must also remind you that the Church invokes a severe sanction against any Catholic who raises his unfeeling hand to destroy this most defenseless of all human beings -- the unborn baby. The Church disowns by immediate excommunication any Catholic who deliberately procures an abortion or helps someone else to do so.

It is our prayer and hope that, with God's help, the people of our day will come to a true understanding of the sacredness of each human life.

Faithfully yours in Christ,

✝Edwin B. Broderick
Bishop of Albany
and the Catholic Bishops of New York State

December 2, 1970

DEAR ABBY: In regard to abortion: Women must learn to say NO to their husbands more often. In fact, everyone must say no to evil. We are now living in a warring, whoring, boring world because we have forgotten God's word. Jesus told us that if a family cannot afford more children they should quit having sex.

I have never married or had sex even though I have been asked. If a person can say no to evil once, it is a lot easier the next time.

Jesus also said, "Love the sinner, but hate the sin." People today have it turned around. They love sin and hate the sinner. If I sound holier than thou it is because Christ has made me holy.

"A SAVED WOMAN"

DEAR "SAVED:" You insist upon equating sex with sin, and feel that the absence of sex has made you somewhat "holy." Theologians (and indeed Christ Himself) would disagree with you.

Left, open letter of Edwin B. Broderick, Bishop of Albany, and the Catholic Bishops of New York State, December 2, 1970.

Above, courtesy of Abigail Van Buren, syndicated newspaper columnist, "Dear Abby."

The Catholic Viewpoint On Murder Of Infants Is Ours
SOME TRUTHS ABOUT ABORTION

By Walter W. Krebs
Editor of Johnstown Tribune-Democat

(Editor's Note: The author of today's column is Charles E. Kane, president of Johnstown Curia of the Legion of Mary. In this article, he presents arguments against the spreading permissiveness in regard to abortions.)

If you should walk into a public building, and there confront a distinguished-looking man with a knife poised to stab a young chld, and he should turn to you and say, "I have decided the life of this child must be ended; do not interfere with my freedom to do as I see fit," would you agree? Or would you try to stop him?

This act is being performed in many places. The child is 2 . . . 4 . . . 6 . . . 8 . . . months old. The only difference from the above scene is that the child is still in the mother's womb.

Ever since Vatican Council II, Catholics have become very self-conscious about imposing our will on those of other faiths. Meanwhile the forces of existentialism have not been reticent about imposing their will on us. The time has come to cut through the web of permissive mumbojumbo and look at a few objective truths.

Life begins at conception. For support of this position we go back to 400 B.C. to the age of Hippocrates. For those few doctors who may have forgotten, this is the oath they pledged: "I will not give to a woman an instrument to produce abortion."

Common law for centuries has recognized the rights of the fetus. It is a very recent development (I say "development" advisedly) that the desire of the mother not to have a baby has been imposed over the right of the child to be born.

Turn to the Bible and read the account of the Annunciation wherein Jesus Christ is conceived. Then read on to the account of the Visitation a few weeks later.

The God-Embryo sanctified John the Baptist while both were in their mothers' wombs.. Yet it is young souls like this from which some would snatch the right to life, without even offering the sanctifying waters of baptism so that the infant soul could be saved. If Jesus Christ were conceived today under the laws of some of our states, the pregnancy would probably be aborted.

Those who are obsessed with the idea that the murder of unborn infants should be made legal, moral, even desirable, will not settle for half-way measures. They began by advocating abortion of pregnancies resulting from such despicable acts as rape or incest. But this has proved a wedge to abortion on demand. The question in my mind is: At whose demand?

One proponent of abortion labeled it "the ultimate method of birth control." Another advocated on TV that abortion should be imposed on all mothers after the third pregnancy? Still another says the state should allow only two children per couple.

Yet another confused young girl declared to the nation that she will never permit any children to be born because it contributes to pollution. (I suppose she and her husband will invest the money they save by not having children in another expensive sports car or a motor boat.)

If we accept the validity of such argument, where will it stop? Shall we "put to sleep" a child which we discover to be retarded or deformed after birth? If we can kill at 6 . . . 7 . . . 8 months after conception, why not 9 . . . 10 . . . 11 . . . months?

It is obvious the stop will not be called until we give in to those who would supplant God's function of giving life with a committee to decide which children would be born; where and when they would be born; what sex, race and intelligence they would be born with.

Another argument of the abortionists is that legalizing abortion would eliminate illegal abortions. Ridiculous! As a corollary we might say, "We can eliminate speeding on the highways by eliminating speed limits." To carry the argument to the extreme, we could elminate all crime by eliminating all laws.

A similar argument is made for the legalization of marijuana - by many of the same people. I cannot understand how someone can be so disturbed by the deaths of children in Asia and Africa—unfortunate though they be - but at the same time advocate smashing the life from millions of our own children.

But whatever changes we make in the laws of man, there still remain the laws of God. "Thou shall not kill." The abortionists are asking us to say murder is not murder when the victim is still in the mother's womb.

The dehumanization of our society has been noted by many prominent philosophers. This has led us to our current problems, including pornography, sexual deviations, abuse of drugs. The beginning of the decline of respect for human life led us to advocation of artificial birth control. The advocation of abortion for "medical reasons" was only a logical extension of this. This, in turn, has expanded to abortion on demand.

The next "logical" step will be euthanasia. Why not? With millions of abortions - legal and illegal - every year in this country, it is already tantamount to genocide.

I do not call upon my fellow Catholics to impose their beliefs on those of other faiths. But I do call upon all men of good will to recognize an objective moral evil and to speak out while time remains to protect the value of human life.

Right, from *The Wanderer*, March 11, 1971.
Top page, from *The Capital Voice*, March 1, 1971.

Fetuses' Delivery Was Vital

Had No Choice, Doctor Testifies

By LARRY EICHEL
Inquirer Staff Writer

A doctor testified at the fetus murder trial in Camden yesterday that he had no choice but to deliver twin fetuses after their mother was shot in the abdomen.

The twins, who had been conceived 7½-months earlier, were born alive, but both died hours after birth. One had been hit by the single bullet. The other had not.

Winfield Anderson, 24, the Camden man who allegedly fired the shot, has been charged with murder in the death of both fetuses.

The case, which is unprecedented, could help determine whether someone can be murdered before being born, and whether homicide can be committed against a fetus while it is still in its mother's womb.

Dr. Tinliung Jung, an obstetrician-gynecologist at Cooper Hospital in Camden, testified that the bullet struck the mother, Nikki Spearman, in the womb. The amniotic fluid—the "water" that surrounds an unborn child—was already leaking out in two places when she was rushed into the hospital's emergency room, he said.

"I didn't have any alternative then," Dr. Jung said, explaining why he decided to cut open the mother's womb. "I didn't know what was going on inside. The mother might be bleeding or have a serious infection."

Once the womb was opened, he said, his only option was to deliver both fetuses by Caesarean section, even though only one of them had been hit by the bullet.

"The bag that held the babies was already broken (by the bullet)," he said.

Dr. Jung's decision to deliver the babies is critical to the case. If he had not operated—and the twins had been stillborn—there might well have been no murder indictment since, in the eyes of the law, the twins would have never existed as "persons."

In fact, the twins did live outside their mother. The one with the bullet wound survived for 3 hours, 40 minutes. The one without it lasted 15 hours, 10 minutes.

Dr. Jung said both appeared to be normal premature infants upon delivery, except for the bullet wound in one of them. He gave the unwounded one a "9" on a 10 point scale measuring its health just after birth. The wounded one got a "2" rating.

The doctor said that premature infants delivered after 7½ months of a pregnancy had a 50 percent chance of survival.

Dr. William T. Read, Camden County medical examiner, testified that the primary cause of death of the wounded fetus was the wound itself. The other twin died of "immaturity," he said. Both appeared to be surrering from hyaline membrane disease, a frequently fatal respiratory ailment, Dr. Read said.

Moral Question

The highly-emotional moral question of when a fetus becomes a person—entitled to live—came up briefly in the testimony of the pediatrician who treated the twins after birth.

"An embryo or a fetus or an infant is a person to me," said Dr. John M. Tedeschi, of Collingswood.

J. Bond
S.P.L.C., Inc.
Box 548
Montgomery, Ala. 36101

"Lucy," said Dr. Benton, "when I deliver your baby you should have your tubes tied."

"What does that mean?" asked Lucy. Her six grades in Belson County Elementary, still all black, had given her an even poorer education than the average white Tennesseean.

"You don't need no more chillen, Lucy. Tying your tubes will fix that." Dr. Benton's word was usually unquestioned, but this time Lucy knew something wasn't right.

"Lucy, you want me to deliver this baby, don't you? It's due next week. My charge is $250. You ain't got that much money. Unless I let you use my office to get your Medicaid, you ain't gonna have no doctor. And unless you let me tie your tubes, I ain't gonna deliver your baby."

"But Dr. Benton..."

"Look, Lucy, if you don't agree I'll get a court order and I'll see to it that your welfare is cut off."

Dear Friend,

The above is a true story. Only the names have been changed. On May 23, 1973, a white doctor performed a tubal ligation on Lucy Martin, bringing the number of coerced sterilizations this year in that one county to eighteen.

Sterilization is fine...but only for consenting adults.

Dr. Benton told the press he insists on sterilization of all welfare mothers with two or more children because "...my hard-earned taxes go to support these children." Justification for the Relf girls' sterilization was "because boys were hanging around and we could no longer give the shots."

Reports of involuntary sterilizations have since been discovered throughout the South. And they all have a common theme. Each was obtained by coercion, threats or misrepresentation. Several women were even told their tubes would come untied in about two years allowing pregnancy. But, in truth, each operation is final.

Only the most callous have written favoring sterilization of welfare mothers. Many realize that a welfare mother is only temporarily dependent on public support. Over half are off welfare in less than two years. But more importantly, most appreciate the fact that the decision to bear children is a very personal right not lightly to be overruled by government planners. Sterilization of a welfare mother (or any person) might be sound medical and family planning advice.

The decision, though, must be accepted with full, informed consent, and not after threats, coercion or fraud.

Lucy Martin didn't want to be sterilized. She is now having emotional problems, thinking that she is only half a woman, that no man will want her as a wife. Recently, friends say, she has become despondent and has mentioned suicide.

One man or woman sterilized against their will...one child permanently barred from her own decision to become a parent... one illiterate duped into scribbling an "X" on a tubal ligation consent form. Any of these situations is worth every effort you and I can make to insure that the intended recipient of the surgeon's scalpel gives his or her own informed and knowledgeable consent.

You can assist by sending a tax-deductible contribution and joining the Southern Poverty Law Center's effort. Our sterilization suit will cost upwards of $250,000 above what we must spend on numerous other cases in which we're already involved.

May I count on you?

Sincerely,

Julian Bond

JB:ccr

Spiro's Theory

"Sooner or later," said Spiro T. Agnew last month, extemporaneously, government must decide whether or not to let terminal patients die, deprive mothers of illegitimate babies of welfare payments and take children from unfit mothers. "I have a theory that these problems will never be subject to complete solution until somebody in public life is willing to take on the hard social judgments that, very frankly, no one I know in elective office is willing to even think about tackling" for fear of being "victimized by the demagogues."

In a newspaper column appearing at about the same time, the Vice President addressed himself to "one angle of the [welfare] problem that must have our best and most serious thinking." Since it is "ridiculous" to think of welfare mothers as capable of providing a "decent home environment," adoption laws must be liberalized to make it easier for couples "willing and able to give children the home they need." Mr. Agnew was not explicit about how the children were to get from their unqualified mothers into the hands of government-qualified parents (perhaps he did not want to dilute the effect of his next speech), but he did offer a clue as to what children he had in mind: children's problems are "far greater in the urban ghettos and it is here that we must begin."

A Republican-sponsored bill recently introduced in the Connecticut legislature proposes that welfare mothers with two or more illegitimate children be given $300 if they agree to undergo sterilization at state expense. Meanwhile the Supreme Court has ruled, in Justice Harry Blackmun's maiden opinion, that welfare recipients may not refuse, under the Fourth Amendment, to open their homes to "visits" by government social workers; to do so, in fact, should automatically disqualify them for further aid.

All rather surprising views to come from Republicans, from a "conservative" Supreme Court, from Spiro T. Agnew, no? No.

Sterilization

The position of the Catholic Church is therefore a condemnation of all forms of direct sterilization, whether compulsory or voluntary. Her condemnation is based on ethics which lay great emphasis on one's inalienable right to life and bodily integrity. The mentality of the contemporary social milieu cannot understand why God may permit suffering and other forms of societal problems to exist. Eugenists fail to see that happiness hereafter is purchasable by self-sacrificing care of the unfortunate. Divine Providence permits the unfortunate to be among us to give man an opportunity to exercise that charity which deserves the kingdom of heaven. They scarcely deserve that kingdom who would rid us of the inconvenient presence of unfortunates by violating nature's law. (See Higgins, S. J., op. cit., p. 214). If God allows misfortune and adversity to exist, He does so for a reason. Suffering may be the occasion for advancement in our spiritual life. Nothing takes place without a reason. God is the Creator of this universe, He is good, kind, just and all powerful. We must have faith in according Him the wisdom in knowing how to run this complex world in which we find ourselves.

ON THE RIGHT

William F. Buckley Jr.

❊ ❊ ❊

WELFARE. Let's quit horsing around. The permanent denizens of the welfare rolls, as distinct from the handicapped and the helpless and the temporarily unfortunate, are moral criminals and should be treated as legal criminals too. If parents of a child born out of wedlock are unable or unwilling to care for the child, the parents should be jailed and the child should be put in an institution. For the second bastard, the parents should be sterilized. (Here I note parenthetically the distinction between punitive sterilization and eugenic sterilization. The latter is forbidden by the natural law, by the Catholic Church, and I trust by other churches. Not so the former—though I have no doubt the bleeding hearts would be aghast at the idea.)

Drastic, yes. But does anyone doubt that our present system calls for a drastic remedy? We should never forget that the cost of welfare is only secondarily financial. It breeds a growing underclass that saps the foundation of education, morals and patriotism, that assures an ever-growing criminal cadre. Welfare *attacks America*.

SECTION 9

Murder or Mercy?

Although at first thought it might seem that the question "What is a human being?" must be restricted to the period that the fetus is in the mother's womb, this section contains a number of examples which raise this question for a variety of other cases. It is certainly not uncommon to hear in everyday discourse statements to the effect that a severely retarded infant or a comatose, terminally ill adult is nothing more than a "vegetable," where it is not always clear that this expression is being used figuratively. Such characterizations of the nature of certain individuals are used in some of the arguments in this section as part of the justification for permitting the termination of the lives of these individuals.

In contrast to the arguments that attempt to deny that the individuals involved are humans, many of the arguments in this section deal with cases where this strategy is not feasible or which for other reasons are based on the assumption that the individual involved is indeed a human being. In these arguments the basic question is that of the rightness or wrongness of taking a human life under certain very special circumstances, such as to prevent the suffering of the individual or serious inconvenience to others. The decisions involved in these cases fall into three basic categories, each of which has two forms. These categories are:

1. assisting another person in the termination of that person's life at the request of that person;
2. terminating the life of another person when that person is in a state which

prevents him or her from asking for or refusing such treatment (because he or she is comatose, severely retarded, etc.); and

3. terminating one's own life, with or without assistance from others; in other words, committing suicide.

Each of these categories of termination of life have two forms—active and passive; that is, it is possible to terminate the life by some single direct act (such as shooting with a gun or poisoning) or by *not* acting or withholding basic supportive assistance (such as essential surgery, medicine, or food). While this is a problem which many physicians must address on a regular basis, it is *not* one which any person can be confident of not having to face at some time during (possibly at the very end) of his or her own life. When the question does arise, the person most directly involved very often is not in a good condition for thinking things through as carefully and rationally as might be desirable. Thus it would be quite wise to begin to think through some of these issues now while one has the time and mental and emotional capacities required by the significance of the problem.

EXERCISES

1. Into which of the three categories listed above does each of the cases discussed in this section fall? Determine which of the two forms (active or passive) is involved in each case. Ascertain whether the basic strategy of each argument is to deny that the individual involved is a human being or to assume that the individual is human.
2. Discuss the question of defining "human being." Is an argument in support of the judgment that "The term human being should be defined in such and such a way" a *moral* argument? If it is not a moral argument, what kind is it?
3. Compare the arguments in this section which are based on the assumption that the individual whose life is being terminated is a human being with the arguments for and against capital punishment in Section 12. Are there any moral theories which could be used to support the termination of life in one case but not in the other?

Charge mongoloid baby starved 16 days

By Michael Miner

A newborn mongoloid infant in a Downstate Catholic hospital was allowed to starve for 16 days because its parents wanted the baby to die, members of two Illinois organizations charged Thursday.

Mary Anne Smith, founder of Illinois Citizens Concerned for Life, said the baby was born April 8 in St. Mary's Hospital in Decatur.

According to the ICCL and the Illinois Right to Life Committee, the infant's esophagus was incomplete and the parents would not allow the operation that would have permitted their child to eat.

Furthermore, they said, the parents would not allow the child to be fed intravenously.

This is not unprecedented. Medical records show other mongoloid children have been allowed to die in other hospitals.

Jerome Frazel, an attorney for the Right to Life Committee, said he threatened a malpractice suit, after which, according to his sources, intravenous feeding began Wednesday.

Sister Ann, the administrator of St. Mary's Hospital, told The Sun-Times, "I cannot discuss the case with you at this time."

Frazel said that Mrs. Betty Boland, a registered nurse at St. Mary's, resigned because of the hospital's treatment of the infant.

Mrs. Boland confirmed to The Sun-Times that she gave two weeks' notice on Tuesday, but she said she was ethically constrained from discussing what went on in the hospital.

"I'm used to practicing professional ethics," Mrs. Boland said. "I feel it's unfortunate that it's keeping me from taking action if there's any action to be taken."

Other persons with knowledge of the situation also declined to discuss the matter with The Sun-Times.

The Rev. John Spreen, family life director of the Springfield Diocese, which includes Decatur, and a member of both right-to-life organizations, said Thursday, "As far as I'm concerned, the hospital authorities have taken care of the situation."

Father Spreen would say nothing more.

Mrs. Smith said that at least five persons have called Sister Ann to say they would be interested in adopting the infant. The hospital's administrator has taken their names.

One woman, according to Patricia Kelley, another member of Illinois Citizens Concerned for Life, has hired a lawyer to help in an attempt to adopt the baby.

Mrs. Kelley said that members of her organization have tried to contact the parents through Sister Ann, but have received no response.

"As a woman," Mrs. Kelley said, "I'd want to befriend that poor mother and point out to the woman the degree of mental retardation certainly cannot be determined at birth. People will grasp at the slightest straw of hope and sometimes, going on hope, miracles will happen. . .

"It has us all terribly upset, the idea that a child could be shoved aside to starve to death because it might be less than perfect. It disturbs me for society. If we can lock a baby in a room and walk past it as it starves to death, we can walk past a My Lai. We can walk past the South Side of Chicago.

"It diminishes us all as people."

An article on retarded children in the Oct. 15, 1972, issue of Midwest magazine reported that a generation ago, the mongoloid child — that is the child born with Down's Syndrome —"was automatically institutionalized" and seldom spoken of again.

The article continued:

"Now, however, the parents of the mongoloid, guided by their physician, decide which course is correct . . .

"At least four times in the last five years, parents of mongoloids born at Johns Hopkins Hospital in Baltimore have elected . . . to let the baby die. In each case, corrective surgery would, in the opinion of the physicians involved, have spared the child" from death.

Top, reprinted with permission from *The Chicago Sun-Times* (April 27, 1973). Author of the article, Michael Miner.

MEDICINE

The Hardest Choice

In Baltimore three years ago, the parents of a newborn Mongoloid baby refused to allow an operation to correct a fatal defect in the infant's digestive tract. Despite pressure from doctors and hospital personnel, they refused to change their minds, and the child slowly starved to death.

In Portland, Me., last month, when parents made a similar decision about their severely deformed infant, hospital officials asked a court to decide. A judge, holding that the baby had a right to live, issued an order that allowed doctors to operate on the child. Despite the surgery, the infant died 15 days after birth.

These cases illustrate a vexing dilemma now confronting modern medicine: Should lives of retarded infants or those with multiple birth defects be prolonged—at great cost in manpower, money and anguish—especially if the life that is preserved will almost certainly be one of pain or merely vegetable-like existence?

Few, if any, doctors are willing to establish guidelines for determining which babies should receive lifesaving surgery or treatment and which should not. But many recognize that there are cases, particularly those involving multiple anomalies, when a hands-off attitude is probably for the best. Says Dr. Joan Hodgman, professor of pediatrics at the University of Southern California School of Medicine: "If we have a baby that I know is malformed beyond hope, I make no attempt to preserve life."

Time of Need. Other doctors, too, are speaking out on the subject. Drs. Raymond Duff and A.G.M. Campbell reported in the *New England Journal of Medicine* on a study of 299 deaths among 2,171 children treated in the special-care nursery at Yale–New Haven Hospital over a 2½-year period. They found that 43 of the infants died after parents and doctors decided jointly to discontinue treatment. The other 256, who received the best treatment modern medicine could provide, fared no better; few lived longer than the infants who received no special care. Furthermore, their short existence in many cases bore little relation to human life. One infant, who could not breathe on his own, was kept alive for five months as a virtual extension of a mechanical respirator.

Duff and Campbell believe that in such cases doctors must at least consider whether or not their efforts are in the infant's best interests. "Pretending there is no decision to be made is an arbitrary and potentially devastating decision by default," they write. "It may constitute a victimizing abandonment of patients and their families in times of greatest need."

Not all doctors agree. Some feel that they are bound by the Hippocratic oath to do all they can to preserve life. Others, aware that an incurable condition today may be a manageable one tomorrow, fear making the wrong decision. "No matter how expert we are, we can't predict outcome," says Dr. Judah Folkman, surgeon in chief at Children's Hospital Medical Center in Boston.

Above, reprinted by permission from *Time, The Weekly Newsmagazine* (March 26, 1974); copyright Time, Inc.

Wait Three Days After Birth Before Declaring Child Alive

I think we must re-evaluate our basic assumptions about the meaning of life. Perhaps, as my former colleague Francis Crick suggested, no one should be thought of as alive until about three days after birth. . . .

Our society just hasn't faced up to this problem. In a primitive society, if you saw a baby was deformed, you would abandon it on a hillside. Today this isn't permissible, and with our medicine getting better and better in the sense of being able to keep sick people alive longer, we are going to produce more people living wretched lives. I don't know how you get society to change on such a basic issue; infanticide isn't regarded lightly by anyone.

Fortunately, now through such techniques as amniocentesis, parents can often learn in advance whether their child will be normal and healthy or hopelessly deformed. They then can choose either to have the child or opt for a therapeutic abortion. But the cruel fact remains that because of the present limits of such detection methods, most birth defects are not discovered until birth.

If a child were not declared alive until three days after birth, then all parents could be allowed the choice that only a few are given under the present system. The doctor could allow the child to die if the parents so chose and save a lot of misery and suffering. I believe this view is the only rational, compassionate attitude to have.

—Nobel laureate JAMES D. WATSON *in an interview in Prism, a magazine published by the American Medical Association.*

JUDGE ORDERS CARE FORMONGOLOIDCHILD

MANHASSET, L. I., Oct. 1 (UPI)—A couple who told hospital authorities not to treat their newborn Mongoloid son have been ordered to appear in family court tomorrow to explain their action.

In the meantime, a judge has ordered doctors at North Shore Hospital to give the child the medical treatment he needs.

The boy was born Sept. 4 in Syosset Hospital, where the hospital administrator Pearl Klick, said that the parents had given notice that the infant was to receive no medical treatment.

"We don't act as physicians," Miss Klick said. "We just care for people. They have their own physicians."

Doctors said that the infant, David Habib, son of a Queens College teacher and his 20-year-old wife, needed surgery to remove an intestinal blockage as well as other treatment for Down's Syndrome, or Mongolism, the most severe and most physically noticeable form of mental retardation.

An anoymous telephone call alerted the child's condition to the Nassau Department of Social Service's Child Protective Division, which referred the case to family court.

Family Court Judge William Dempsey ordered the baby transferred from Syosset Hospital to North Shore Hospital in Manhasset for corrective surgery over the weekend.

Judge plays God

Deformed child dies after court-ordered surgery

PORTLAND, Maine (AP) —The parents of a deformed baby whose 15 days of life sparked a legal and moral controversy have criticized the court for playing God.

David Patrick Houle, the infant son of Air Force Sgt. and Mrs. Robert B.T. Houle of Westbrook, died Sunday in the Main Medical Center here after being in poor condition since the previous Tuesday.

The baby had undergone court-ordered surgery after the hospital sued the parents when they reportedly refused permission for an operation.

The Houles said in a statement released by their lawyer, Navy Lt. James Freyer, that they were "most disturbed by the actions of the court in divesting them of the right to make an intimate parental decision that they believe was rightfully theirs."

The statement added, "Since nature determined that this infant was not a viable life, it was the court and not the parents that played God in deciding that the infant should be kept alive con-

trary to the laws of nature. Mercifully, as between nature and the Superior Court, nature was the court of last resort."

The baby's physician had told the court that corrective surgery would probably not be of any benefit to the infant.

Superior Court Justice David G. Roberts ordered the operation, saying the parents had no right to withhold the treatment because the baby had a "right to life."

Surgery was performed to place a food tube in the baby's stomach. A second op-

eration to connect the esophaugus to the stomach was to be performed next. The child was born with no left eye or ear canal and other deformities.

"If the infant had lived the life of suffering which might well have resulted from the court's decision, the parents could not have escaped the feeling of responsibility that would come from knowing that they were the ones who brought it into the world, yet they were deprived of any and all say as to its future," the Houles' statement said.

Above, courtesy of The Associated Press.

'Murdered' Infants

To the Editor:

Regarding the article "Why Doctors, Parents Let Deformed Babies Die" [Nov. 10], I would like to know why these so-called doctors and parents haven't been locked up?

The taking of a human life is murder, no matter how much you try to justify it. It was always my understanding that the duty of a doctor was to prolong life, not to stifle it by withholding treatment.

How can the parents of a deformed baby say that it is too expensive to keep the baby alive? If the baby were healthy, the parents wouldn't hesitate to spend $15,000 or more for its education.

A deformed baby is a human life, and who are doctors—or parents, for that matter—to decide whether that life should exist or not? A baby of any kind is a gift from God, and only God has the right to take it away.

CATHY MARTIN

Prince George, Va.

Left, letter to the editor of *The National Observer* by Cathy Martin, December 15, 1973.
Right, letter to the editor of *Newsweek* by Sondra Diamond, counseling psychologist, December 3, 1973.

Life-and-Death Decisions

I'll wager my entire root system and as much fertilizer as it would take to fill Yale University that you have never received a letter from a vegetable before this one, but, much as I resent the term, I must confess that I fit the description of a "vegetable" as defined in the article "Shall This Child Die?" (MEDICINE, Nov. 12).

Due to severe brain damage incurred at birth, I am unable to dress myself, toilet myself, or write; my secretary is typing this letter. Many thousands of dollars had to be spent on my rehabilitation and education in order for me to reach my present professional status as a counseling psychologist. My parents were also told, 35 years ago, that there was "little or no hope of achieving meaningful 'humanhood'" for their daughter. Have I reached "humanhood"? Compared with Drs. Duff and Campbell, I believe I have surpassed it!

Instead of changing the law to make it legal to weed out us "vegetables," let us change the laws so that we may receive quality medical care, education and freedom to live as full and productive lives as our potentials allow.

SONDRA DIAMOND

Philadelphia, Pa.

A New Ethic for Medicine And Society

THE TRADITIONAL WESTERN ETHIC has always placed great emphasis on the intrinsic worth and equal value of every human life regardless of its stage or condition. This ethic has had the blessing of the Judeo-Christian heritage and has been the basis for most of our laws and much of our social policy. The reverence for each and every human life has also been a keystone of Western medicine and is the ethic which has caused physicians to try to preserve, protect, repair, prolong and enhance every human life which comes under their surveillance. This traditional ethic is still clearly dominant, but there is much to suggest that it is being eroded at its core and may eventually even be abandoned. This of course will produce profound changes in Western medicine and in Western society.

There are certain new facts and social realities which are becoming recognized, are widely discussed in Western society and seem certain to undermine and transform this traditional ethic. They have come into being and into focus as the social by-products of unprecedented technologic progress and achievement. Of particular importance are, first, the demographic data of human population expansion which tends to proceed uncontrolled and at a geometric rate of progression; second, an ever growing ecological disparity between the numbers of people and the resources available to support these numbers in the manner to which they are or would like to become accustomed; and third, and perhaps most important, a quite new social emphasis on something which is beginning to be called the quality of life, a something which becomes possible for the first time in human history because of scientific and technologic development. These are now being seen by a growing segment of the public as realities which are within the power of humans to control and there is quite evidently an increasing determination to do this.

What is not yet so clearly perceived is that in order to bring this about hard choices will have to be made with respect to what is to be preserved and strengthened and what is not, and that this will of necessity violate and ultimately destroy the traditional Western ethic with all that this portends. It will become necessary and acceptable to place relative rather than absolute values on such things as human lives, the use of scarce resources and the various elements which are to make up the quality of life or of living which is to be sought. This is quite distinctly at variance with the Judeo-Christian ethic and carries serious philosophical, social, economic and political implications for Western society and perhaps for world society.

The process of eroding the old ethic and substituting the new has already begun. It may be seen most clearly in changing attitudes toward human abortion. In defiance of the long held Western ethic of intrinsic and equal value for every human life regardless of its stage, condition or status, abortion is becoming accepted by society as moral, right and even necessary. It is worth noting that this shift in public attitude has affected the churches, the laws and public policy rather than the reverse. Since the old ethic has not yet been fully displaced it has been necessary to separate the idea of abortion from the idea of killing, which continues to be socially abhorrent. The result has been a curious avoidance of the scientific fact, which everyone really knows, that human life begins at conception and is continuous whether intra- or extra-uterine until death. The very considerable semantic gymnastics which are required to rationalize abortion as anything but taking a human life would be ludicrous if they were not often put forth under socially impeccable auspices. It is suggested that this schizophrenic sort of subterfuge is necessary because while a new ethic is being accepted the old one has not yet been rejected.

It seems safe to predict that the new demographic, ecological and social realities and aspirations are so powerful that the new ethic of relative rather than of absolute and equal values will ultimately prevail as man exercises ever more certain and effective control over his numbers, and uses his always comparatively scarce resources to provide the nutrition, housing, economic support, education and health care in such ways as to achieve his desired quality of life and living. The criteria upon which these relative values are to be based will depend considerably upon whatever concept of the quality of life or living is developed. This may be expected to reflect the extent that quality of life is considered to be a function of personal fulfillment; of individual responsibility for the common welfare, the preservation of the environment, the betterment of the species; and of whether or not, or to what extent, these responsibilities are to be exercised on a compulsory or voluntary basis.

The part which medicine will play as all this develops is not yet entirely clear. That it will be deeply involved is certain. Medicine's role with respect to changing attitudes toward abortion may well be a prototype of what is to occur. Another precedent may be found in the part physicians have played in evaluating who is and who is not to be given costly long-term renal dialysis. Certainly this has required placing relative values on human lives and the impact of the physician to this decision process has been considerable. One may anticipate further development of these roles as the problems of birth control and birth selection are extended inevitably to death selection and death control whether by the individual or by society, and further public and professional determinations of when and when not to use scarce resources.

Since the problems which the new demographic, ecologic and social realities pose are fundamentally biological and ecological in nature and pertain to the survival and well-being of human beings, the participation of physicians and of the medical profession will be essential in planning and decision-making at many levels. No other discipline has the knowledge of human nature, human behavior, health and disease, and of what is involved in physical and mental well-being which will be needed. It is not too early for our profession to examine this new ethic, recognize it for what it is and will mean for human society, and prepare to apply it in a rational development for the fulfillment and betterment of mankind in what is almost certain to be a biologically oriented world society.

From *California Medicine*, September 1970.

The "New Ethic"

By FRANK MORRISS

An editorial in last September's issue of **California Medicine** has one virtue — extreme candor. This "Official Journal of the California Medical Association" suggests we have done with the hypocrisy of suggesting that life in the womb isn't human, which it says is contrary to medical fact. Instead, we should simply become adjusted to taking human life as the changing public attitude demands.

It seems, according to this editorial, that our distaste for taking human life is tied to our Judeo-Christian heritage, "which has been the basis for most of our laws and much of our social policy." But as everyone knows this "traditional ethic," though still dominant, "is being eroded at its core and may eventually even be abandoned."

As, this process progresses, the editorial says, "it will become necessary and acceptable to place relative rather than absolute values on such things as human lives. . . ." Apparently determining these relative values will be the pressure of population, depletion of resources, a "quality of life" linked to "personal fulfillment," preservation of the environment, and most ominous of all, "betterment of the species."

Then comes the call for doctors to get ready to fulfill their duty to the "new ethic." Just as it has responded to the call for abortion (even though bothered by that hypocritical debate over what is being aborted, when every scientist knows it is a human), medical science must be ready to respond when the day dawns for "death selection and death control."

California Medicine is worried that doctors won't be asked to bring their expertise to bear in the determination of these policies, and it insists that "the participation of physicians and of the medical profession will be essential in planning and decision-making at many levels." To guarantee all this, doctors are told that "it is not too early for our profession to examine this new ethic, recognize it for what it is and will mean for human society, and prepare to apply it . . . in what is almost certain to be a biologically oriented world society." There is the distinct impression that **California Medicine** can hardly wait until doctors cannot only serve humanity without reproach by killing admitted humans in the womb, but can extend that service to cover old persons or anyone else standing in the way of that "quality of life" which a biologically oriented world society will make the norm.

All in all, this editorial is one of the most chilling bits of horror writing I have ever come across, perhaps because of its extreme honesty. It is a little as if we should dig up in the ruins of some Berlin building an exhortation to German doctors to get ready to serve Hitler's Reich by exterminating all of the enemies of the "good Nazi life." Here we have the medical profession being told by one of its official agencies to prepare to wipe out all who are enemies of the "good American life," and not be worried about the silly question of whether innocent humans should be killed — for of course they should be if society demands it.

I have called the extreme candor of this editorial a virtue. It is, and it may serve a good purpose if it will only awake our Jewish and Protestant brethren who have been hitherto apathetic to warnings about the implication of abortion. Some of these friends have tried to insist that abortion is well within the Christian and Jewish ethic. I respect the **California Medicine's** view on that issue more than the ignorance of those who don't see what the true issue is.

The Judeo-Christian ethic is being discarded, and what that means is that human life will become valueless as such, and will be protected only in its ramifications for society. No true Christian or Jew can ever allow such a situation to come about without fighting it even to the point of martyrdom. **California Medicine's** appeal for legalization and acceptance of murder must be matched by the religion's determination it shall not happen

(I am indebted to L.I.F.E., 615 W. Civic Center Drive, Santa Ana, Calif., 92701, for a copy of the editorial discussed above.)

From *The Wanderer*, Copyright 1971.

ANATOLY AGRANOVSKY   # Drafting New Laws:
Debate and Decision In the Supreme Soviet

In this article, Izvestia Special Correspondent Anatoly Agranovsky, a leading writer on Soviet internal affairs, employs a breezy, informal style to capture on paper an aspect of the workings of Soviet democracy— the process of drafting new legislation. Rather than encumber Agranovsky's account with numerous completions and explanations, we have left it pretty much as written for Soviet readers.

THE commissions of the Supreme Soviet, seventh convocation, had greatly stepped up their work in preparation for the elections held last summer. At that time I investigated the work of the commissions, to see how, and how well, they were working.

For example, the commission on health and social insurance is meeting (minutes of December 10, 1969). The chairman is N. N. Blokhin, 58, a prominent scientist and surgeon, no newcomer to the Supreme Soviet, he had been a deputy twice before.

As a rule, qualified deputies are elected to head the commissions. In addition to the deputies who make up the basic membership, economists, trade-union leaders, jurists, physicians, and other specialists are invited. They are volunteers, helping to work out the new legislation. The future law is probed line by line. Some corrections are of a purely editorial nature. It is suggested that the word "thus" precede the word "facilitating." Others are more essential: the word "towns" should be followed by "and other populated places." But here is an essential matter: may a patient be operated on without his consent or that of his near relatives?

"How do you expect to get a patient's consent, if he is unconscious? And his relatives are in another city or no one knows where? Can the surgeon afford to waste time?"

"But I don't know of any law in any other country empowering a surgeon to operate at will."

"What about a suicide, when a person does not want to be saved?"

"You're wrong, they always want to be saved."

"And take perforation of an ulcer. The patient will give his consent when it is too late. In order to save lives the surgeon must be empowered . . ."

"I don't agree. During the war there were cases when patients refused to have amputations. And if not all, at least many of them recovered. How can I, without a person's consent, begin sawing his leg off?"

"There can be so many cases, it is impossible to foresee everything."

"It has to be legally provided for, otherwise the rendering of urgent aid will be impaired. When an operation is imperative, the surgeon cannot take time to search for relatives or conduct negotiations."

So it was written down: yes, the surgeon may and even must take the decision upon himself, but only in *exceptional cases,* when any delay *threatens the life of the patient,* when *it is impossible to obtain the consent of the above-mentioned people.* Subsequently, this wording became law.

Need I say that the lives of many people depend on each word? Debates are inevitable here.

From the quarterly magazine *New World Review*, Spring 1971.

William Hines

Abusing the right to die

WASHINGTON — What happened to Harry S. Truman in his final agony shouldn't have happened to a laboratory animal.

The fighting, feisty little figure whom all of us of middle or greater age remember from the '40s and '50s was sustained for weeks (if "sustained" is the proper word) after all rational hope for an old man's survival was gone. The terminal care of Harry Truman wasn't therapy, it was cruelty.

Rumors persist that Mr. Truman had a long-standing agreement with his old friend and personal physician, Dr. Wallace Graham, that when his time came he would be allowed to die in peace and dignity. The rumors are impossible to check because of the traditional veil over the doctor-patient relationship, but it would have been characteristic of Mr. Truman to insist on this, and if in fact the agreement existed it was somehow violated over his not-quite-dead body.

There is no question that a dying person can be sustained for long periods in an undead condition. Medical science has come so far that the Vatican has found it advisable to rule that so-called "heroic" measures of life support are not morally required.

THERE MAY BE AN EXCUSE for keeping a body functioning on a cellular level long after all hope of recovery is past; for example, while a kidney or heart patient is being prepared to receive an organ from a fatally injured donor. And it is not only justified but imperative to give all available support to a sick person with a reasonable expectation of resuming a life with some degree of quality to it.

But to hook up an 88-year-old man with widespread infirmities and without any real hope of improvement, to a battery of machines — to feed oxygen directly into his lungs and chemical solutions into his veins, to invade him with catheters and to visit on him God knows what other sorts of indignities is inexcusable.

To embalm Lenin and leave him on display for half a century has been denounced as barbaric. To publicize Mr. Truman's dying agonies in periodic bulletins trumpeting what can only be described as extremist medicine is hardly less so. The man who filled Franklin D. Roosevelt's chair better than anyone imagined he could deserved something other than this.

The right to life is held in basic American law to be inalienable. Debate over abortion hinges mainly on whether the fetus is an independent being or an appendage of the mother. People who advocate termination of pregnancy while the procedure is still safe for the mother do not advocate post-natal destruction of the infant. The child is born; let him live.

BUT THE RIGHT TO DIE apparently is not so solidly established in law and tradition. Organizations have been formed to protect their adherents from exactly what happened to Mr. Truman, but there is some question whether a written statement of one's desire to die in peace is legally enforceable. A hospital administrator or physician, his eye warily cocked for possible negligence or malpractice suits, might think twice about pulling the plug on a terminal patient if the next-of-kin insisted on further medical efforts.

It has been suggested that maybe Mr. Truman, as a former President, was somehow different from ordinary people and that therefore the special measures to sustain him were justified. This is fuzzy logic to say the least. Presidents are people too, and people die; among all ex-Presidents only Lyndon B. Johnson is the exception that (temporarily) tests the rule.

The place for the former leader of a people is in their hearts, not in an intensive care ward. Today Mr. Truman is where he belongs: he should have been allowed to go there in peace a couple of weeks sooner.

Reprinted with permission from the *Chicago Sun-Times* (January 2, 1973). Author of article, William Hines.

Is 'Mercy Killing' The Same As Murder?

By B. D. COLEN
The Washington Post

WASHINGTON — About four times in the past year, doctors at the Maryland Institute for Emergency Medicine turned off the respirator that was maintaining the life of a quadriplegic patient whose body was completely and irrevocably paralyzed — but whose brain was functioning.

Each time the institute receives such a patient, it keeps the person alive for a few weeks, long enough to determine if the patient's condition will improve to the point where he can again lead a meaningful life. And each time the doctors end up turning off the respirator.

The quadriplegics are never told their respirators are going to be turned off and their families are told only obliquely, according to Dr. William Gill, clinical director of the institute. Gill said the unit receives about four such patients a year.

However, said Gill, the respirator is never turned off if a family asks that it remain on.

"It's illegal, I suppose some people would argue that," said Gill. "(But) you're not actively doing anything to worsen the patient's state than when he came in here. All you are doing is using artificial support to see if you can do something (save the patient), and then withdrawing that support when we find there is nothing we can do.

"We use that as a rationalization in our own mind," said Gill.

The development of various scientific medical marvels has put doctors in a position where they are literally able to revive the dead, but once they do that, they can do nothing to correct the problem that killed the man in the first place.

While the dying and their doctors are often faced with moral dilemmas concerning when to cease treatment, there is also an economic question.

A bed in the intensive care area of the shock trauma unit costs $575 a day and, while officials of the unit said that the average patient runs up a bill of only a few thousand dollars, there have been bills for as much as $50,000 for patients who have been in the unit up to 70 days.

While officials say they never discuss finances with a patient or his family, they say society as a whole must consider the expenses involved in maintaining a patient who will never again function as a normal human being.

"You must think in terms of how much money society should spend on supporting the life of this type if individual," said Dr. McAslam.

"Whether we like to talk about this or not, are we normally correct in spending (huge sums of money to sustain a human vegetable) when we can take a child from the ghetto area with a heart (problem) and, with the same amount of money produce a productive, healthy child with a full life ahead of him, a normal life?" asked McAslan.

DEAR ABBY

By Abigail Van Buren

Top, © The Washington Post.
Above, courtesy of Abigail Van Buren, syndicated newspaper columnist, "Dear Abby."

DEAR ABBY: The headline over your column read, "Is there mercy in killing?" My answer to that question is, "Definitely, yes!"

My mother in law watched her handsome, 6-foot, 200-pound husband dwindle down to 87 pounds when he finally died, and that took four years.

I lost a daughter a year ago. She was 12 years old. For two years she laid there like a rag doll. I saw her go from a beautiful, active 10-year-old girl to a nothing of a 12-year-old vegetable; and all this because of an inoperable tumor, the size of a pea in her brain. She didn't know me or anyone else. Her heart was beating — that was all. They said they couldn't do anything so "inhumane" as to deliberately let her die. You call this living?

The hospital bill alone was $15,000. And after that, the "convalescent" home was $600 a month. A fortune to us which we would have gladly paid to save her life, but it was hopeless and everyone knew it.

Yes, sometimes it is merciful to let a person die. I've seen others suffer and linger this way, and if it ever happens to me, I will kill myself.

A MOTHER

In Terminal Suffering, Euthanasia Is Kindness

DEAR ANN LANDERS: I read with great sadness the letter from the gentleman whose aged father was dying and how the doctors were doing everything under the sun to keep the old man alive even though he wanted to go. Another example of man's inhumanity to man.

My beloved father-in-law was 98 years old. There were no tubes or machines to keep him breathing, but for one solid week we watched him as he tried to escape this vale of tears. It was heartbreaking.

We had a dog we all loved dearly. He suffered a heart attack and was in so much pain he couldn't even lie down. We took him to the veterinarian and I held his paw while the doctor gave him a shot of sodium pentathol which he never even felt. In a short time he was out of his agony. Why can't we be as benevolent to mankind?—I.V.A.

DEAR I.V.A.: I have been an outspoken and vociferous critic of using "extraordinary measures" to keep a person alive when two or three doctors have concluded that the patient is hopelessly ill with a terminal disease. To deny a person the right to die with dignity is wrong.

Your suggestion, however, that a suffering patient be "put out of his misery," as your dog was, is quite another matter. I do not believe in "mercy killing" and cannot condone a decisive act to end a human life.

Left, courtesy of Ann Landers, Field Newspaper Syndicate, and *The Atlanta Journal.*
Right, courtesy of The Associated Press.

Jury Clears Man In Mercy Killing

FREEHOLD, N.J. (AP) — "The only crime Lester is guilty of was having his power to reason overwhelmed by events," Lester Zygmaniak's attorney told a Superior Court jury before it acquitted the young man of slaying his paralyzed brother.

The jury of seven men and five women deliberated 2½ hours on Tuesday before acquitting Zygmaniak, 23, on grounds of temporary insanity. He had been charged with first degree murder.

Zygmaniak admitted killing his 26-year-old brother, George, with a shotgun blast last June as he lay in a hospital bed, paralyzed from the neck down as the result of a motorcycle accident.

The shooting was described by friends and relatives as a mercy killing.

In his closing arguments, defense attorney Robert Ansell pleaded with the jury to release Lester "not on pity, not on sympathy, but on the evidence."

Ansell said Lester was "crazed with love" for his brother when he shot him — "The only crime Lester is guilty of was having his power to reason overwhelmed by events."

Malcolm Carton, First Asst. Monmouth County Prosecutor, told the jury that the state had proved premeditated murder, and he asked the jurors to "do what's right ... do what's honest.... There is nothing in New Jersey law that says you can take the law into your own hands."

In his testimony, Lester admitted carrying a concealed sawed-off shotgun into the hospital and shooting his brother in the head.

"I walked over and asked him if he was in pain," Lester told the jury. "He nodded he was. I asked, 'A lot of pain, George?' He nodded again.

"I went to him and I said, 'Well, I'm here today to end your pain. Is that all right with you?' He nodded yes, and the next I knew I had shot him."

To backup the claim of a mercy killing, George's widow wife, Jeannette related in court testimony during the trial that the night of the shooting her husband screamed:

"Swear to God for me that you won't let me live. Promise you won't interfere, swear to God you won't interfere."

Euthanasia

BY EUTHANASIA OR MERCY KILLING is meant the slaying of helpless invalids and of people in incurable pain. It is called mercy killing because it is prompted by the motive of relieving a person from suffering. No doubt, freedom from pain in dying is most desirable and that was the original meaning of euthanasia (eu — well, thanatos — death). It had reference to the work of a physician when death seemed imminent and his accepted role was to alleviate as far as possible, through his medical knowledge, the suffering of death whenever it occurred.

The word today has taken a new connotation and implies the bringing about of death itself — accelerating death, not easing it. The practice of medicine in such situations is a premeditation to kill and end the suffering of an individual. Mercy killing is merely a euphemistic term; easy death by lethal doses of drugs or other means to hasten the end of life is murder and against the Fifth Commandment, which states, "Thou shalt not kill." If legalized, it will be but legal murder. Mercy killing is contrary to the natural law because it is against human nature and, consequently, against the duties of reason.

Euthanasia is detrimental to the welfare of society because it destroys man's idea of sacrifice, loyalty, and courage in bearing pain. "If some dying persons accept their suffering as a means of expiration and a source of merits in order to go forward in the love of God and in abandonment to His will, do not force anesthetics on them. They should rather be aided to follow their own way" (Pope Pius XII, op. cit.). The Catholic Church adheres to the principle that drugs which have the unintended effect of shortening life may be given to relieve pain. The patient must consent and there must be no intention on the part of the doctor to kill the patient.

Above, from the booklet, *The Sacredness of Life*, published by the Knights of Columbus, © 1966.
Below, from the *Atlantic Monthly*, April 1968.

The notion that life is sacrosanct is actually a Hindu idea, although Hindus practice things like suttee. It is not Christian or biblical. If it were, all heroism and martyrdom would be wrong, to say nothing of carnivorous diet, capital punishment, and warfare. The sanctity (what makes it precious) is not in life itself, intrinsically; it is only extrinsic and *bonum per accidens, ex casu* — according to the situation. Compared to some things, the taking of life is a small evil, and compared to some things, the loss of life is a small evil. Death is not always an enemy: it can sometimes be a friend and servant.

Life is sometimes good, and death is sometimes good. Life is no more a good in itself than any other value is. It is good, when and if it is good, because of circumstances, because of the context. When it is not good, it deserves neither protection nor preservation. Our present laws about "elective death" are not civilized. It is high time we had some constructive guidance, perhaps from a model code committee of the American Law Institute. Let the law favor living, not mere life.

— *Joseph Fletcher*

Clayton Fritchey

A Question of Life and Death

The busybody strain in American life has always been conspicuous, but there are signs that it is fading. It is becoming possible, for instance, to risk one's life or even indulge in suicidal habits without too much public interference. The retreat on the mandatory use of auto seat belts is a case in point.

It is true that the ingrained national passion to save people from themselves still flourishes enough to pass laws like ones we have had on seat belts, but it is equally true that the House of Representatives, responding to public sentiment, has voted to repeal the law, and the National Highway Safety Administration is going to make it inoperative.

There seems to be a growing consensus that if people want to defy death, it's their business, as long as what they do does not endanger others. Protests, for instance, have been lodged against allowing Evel Knievel to go ahead with what has been billed as a suicidal attempt to leap the mile-wide Snake River Canyon in Idaho in a rocket-shaped "sky-cycle," but it appears that the authorities have no intention of interfering in an effort to keep Knievel from possibly killing himself. After all, it's his life.

A few weeks ago the police did rush in when a daring young Frenchman, Phillippe Petit, strung a tightrope between the twin towers of New York's highest building, the World Trade Center, and walked, danced and stunted his way across while thousands cheered below. Petit, who did it for fun, was arrested for disorderly conduct and trespass, but the charges were later dismissed.

Evel Knievel's stunt will be watched by 50,000 people, which is only a fraction of the hundreds of thousands who go to Indianapolis every year to witness the death-defying auto races, but there is an important distinction between the two events: Nobody at Snake River Canyon will be in danger except the man in the sky-cycle. At the auto races, however, many spectators have been killed and injured over the years.

The seat belt controversy revolves around the same distinction. The mandatory interlocking belts are being abandoned in favor of voluntary ones because failure to use the belts endangers only those who choose not to bother with them. Their negligence is not a threat to others.

All cars should be made as safe as possible. It may cost more to make them with four-wheel brakes, stronger bumpers, non-shatterable windshields and other refinements, but it is well worth the price. It is the same with air bags. The will make cars more expensive, but recent tests indicate that they will save far more lives than seat belts without being the nuisance that the interlock belts are.

No doubt some ingenious drivers will find ways of circumventing the bags as they did the interlock belts, but at least the government and the auto industry will have done what they could—but not too much—to save motorists from committing suicide.

There was a time in the United States when anyone who attempted suicide—and failed—could be jailed as a criminal. Today, only nine states count it a crime. Last year San Francisco, which leads the United States in suicides, had a newspaper referendum on whether a costly view-destroying guardrail should be erected on the Golden Gate Bridge, from which more than 500 people have jumped.

By seven-to-one, the citizens voted to let them jump. This is a considerable advance over other American communities where a lot of people are still being committed to institutions after trying to end their lives, often for perfectly rational reasons.

©1974, Los Angeles Times

HB 3184

By Representative Sackett

Prefiled October, 1969

1.
2.
3   A bill to be entitled
4 AN ACT relating to the right to die
5   with dignity; providing an effective
6   date.

7 Be It Enacted by the Legislature of the State of
8 Florida:

9   Section 1. All natural persons are equal be-
10 fore the law and have inalienable rights, among them
11 the right to enjoy and defend life and liberty, to
12 be permitted to die with dignity, to pursue happiness,
13 to be rewarded for industry, and to acquire, possess,
14 and protect property. No person shall be deprived of
15 any right because of race, religion, or national
16 origin.

17   Section 2. Any person, with the same
18 formalities as required by law for the execution of
19 a last will and testament, may execute a document
20 directing that he shall have the right to death with
21 dignity, and that his life shall not be prolonged
22 beyond the point of a meaningful existence.

23   Section 3. In the event any person is unable
24 to make such a decision because of mental or physical
25 incapacity, a spouse or person or persons of first
26 degree kinship shall be allowed to make such a
27 decision, provided written consent is obtained from:

28   (1) The spouse or person of first degree
29 kinship, or
30
31

1   (2) In the event of two (2) persons of first
2 degree kinship, both such persons, or

3   (3) In the event of three (3) or more persons
4 of first degree kinship, the majority of those persons.

5   Section 4. If any person is disabled and there
6 is no kinship as provided in section 3, death with
7 dignity shall be granted any person if in the opinion
8 of three (3) physicians the prolongation of life is
9 meaningless and if such opinion is stated before and
10 approved by a circuit judge.

11   Section 5. Any document executed hereunder
12 must be recorded with the clerk of the circuit court
13 in order to be effective.

14   Section 6. This act shall take effect upon
15 becoming law.

House Bill 3184 introduced and rejected in the 1970 session of the Florida State Legislature. Courtesy of Citizens' Action Committee, Santa Ana, Calif.

'Dad Asked Me If the Doctor Would... Put Him to Sleep'

HELENA, Mont. (AP) — Poignantly tracing the lingering death of her 86-year-old father, a housewife pleaded with a committee to provide in a new state constitution the right to die.

"I maintain that to give to people facing certain death . . . the right to die quickly, easily and in peace when they want to do so, is being compassionate, intelligent and humane," Joyce M. Franks of Alberton told a hushed audience Thursday in the Senate chambers. "And I affirm that it is an act that God, who gave us all life, would approve of."

Mrs. Franks, the mother of two children, described her father's suffering to the Bill of Rights Committee at the Montana Constitutional Convention.

After her father broke a hip, his doctor described the necessary operation, she said.

"Dad asked me if the doctor would please give him something to put him to sleep right then," Mrs. Franks said, but she did not ask the doctor to do so.

As his health deteriorated, she related, her father made the request again.

"My father had been a farmer, and he had given merciful death to animals who had been pets and companions," Mrs. Franks said, sobbing. "He could not stand to see them suffer prolonged and agonizing death when they were severely mutilated or dying of illness.

"He was compassionate and merciful. He asked for the same mercy for himself."

"For eight weeks he died, little by little minute by minute, day by day," Mrs. Franks said·

"He was just denied a release from the suffering and torture which he knew, and we knew, and the doctor knew he faced."

He died in December.

"Have you wiped the eyes that will not close and that look as though they had never closed in over 85 years since they opened on the world?" Mrs. Franks asked.

"Have you struggled with your own breathing, trying unconsciously to help his labored gasps which came nearly as fast as your own pulse beats?

"Have you wiped the thick, choking mucus out of the mouth that filled again nearly as fast as you cleansed it?. . .

"And have you, then, rebelled at a system where this barbaric suffering was called necessary because unfeeling and unimaginative men declare that God willed it?"

Mrs. Franks said it was inconsistent to call it merciful to kill mortally wounded animals but not humans.

"Do you call veterinarians murders?" she asked.

Mrs. Franks proposed constitutional language saying, that "every citizen be allowed to choose the manner in which he dies."

The legislature would have to outline specific detail, if the proposal were adopted, Mrs. Franks said.

She advocated a proposal that would guarantee an individual's right to determine the manner of his death, barring accidents. Moreover, it should be legal for a person to receive a quick medicated death if he desires, she said.

Mrs. Franks has written letters to delegates and editors of Montana newspapers, polled doctors and spearheaded a move for the right to die with dignity.

Above, courtesy of Associated Press Newsfeatures.

Suicide as we mentioned signifies any act whereby a man deliberately chooses to end his life on his own authority. According to Catholic teaching suicide is a grave sin whose malice consists in an invasion of the supreme and total dominion of God over human life. Suicide is essentially immoral. We have heard many times where a man may expose himself to certain death in order to save the life of another person, but this is not suicide; it does not mean killing oneself, but accepting death for another. Suicide is the deliberate taking away of one's own life, and no matter what the motive, this is never allowed.

Man is but a steward of his corporeal life and of all his faculties, he is not the owner of his life in the sense that he owns a car, a boat or a summer home. When he deliberately takes his own life he exercises a sort of ownership which does not belong to him. "The intrinsic evil of suicide is clear also from a consideration of the truth, that, since God is the Maker and Last End of man, man belongs totally and essentially to God, he is the property and servant of God" (T. Higgins, S. J., *Man as Man*, p. 202).

Man was created to love, honor, serve and obey God here on earth and to be happy with Him forever in Heaven. By suicide man is rejecting his status of servitude; he is invading God's exclusive right and by taking his life, he assumes the role of God. The suicide puts an end to the potentiality of further service to society and of his own moral growth and perfection. It is a deliberate challenge to the moral law and an act of rebellion against God.

The first and foremost inalienable right is that of life and physical existence. This primary right flows from the concept of person and the nature of man. Since all human persons have this right, the right is possessed from the moment of conception. The right to life and especially to bodily integrity is possessed regardless of physical or mental condition. (See Pius XI, Encyclical on *Christian Marriage*). The only exception to the right of life is the case of one who is being deprived of his life in just punishment for crime. The criminal can forfeit his right to life, as the common good takes precedence over individual good, and it may become necessary that certain crimes be punished by deprivation of life in order that the rights of one's fellowmen are safe and secure.

The state, however, is no more the supreme owner of life than is the individual. It cannot order the individual to kill himself. "Suicide cannot be exercised by appeals to honor nor hallowed by reasons of state. To make an exception in the name of patriotism is to deny that there is any essential morality in suicide at all; it is to leave all moral absolutes at the mercy of the 'situation ethics' which says that nothing's right or wrong but thinking makes it so" (*America*, June 18, 1960).

According to Christian teaching the individual possesses certain fundamental rights which the state must protect and respect. The right to life is one of these. The totalitarian state grants or limits at will the rights of men, even the right to life. The life of every citizen is at the mercy of the political clique or the state. According to totalitarian thinking, the individual exists in order to serve the state. This is contrary to the Christian thought that man is not a pawn of the state and cannot be ordered to the utility of society. Man is not a mere instrument or cog in the machinery of the state. The state has no right to encourage or command suicide. To accord the state this right would not only be contrary to Christian teaching but it would open the door against all other things we consider sacred.

From the booklet *The Sacredness of Life*, published by the Knights of Columbus, © 1966.
Right, courtesy of United Press International, July 2, 1971.

Dying Woman Wins Court Plea to Stop Terminal Surgery

MIAMI, July 2 (UPI) — A daughter, appointed guardian of her mother by a judge, accepted today her pleas against the "torture" of more surgery, although it is all that can save her.

Dr. Orlando Lopez told Judge David Popper in Circuit Court that if treatments were stopped, Mrs. Carmen Martinez, 72-year-old Cuban exile, would die.

Dr. Lopez brought the case into court because he feared he could be charged with aiding the woman's suicide if he granted her request to stop treatments.

Judge Popper, noting that the cure appeared almost as bad as the disease, ruled that because of her weakened condition Mrs. Martinez was not competent to decide her fate. He appointed her eldest daughter, Mrs. Margarita Gottlieb, as guardian and gave her power to make the decision.

Suffers From Anemia

Dr. Lopez said his patient suffered from hemolytic anemia, a disease that destroys the red blood cells. He said she required either surgical removal of her spleen, or continued blood transfusions involving "cut downs" — surgical opening of her veins to facilitate transfer of blood.

"I am not able to state precisely that Mrs. Martinez will live if she is given the transfusions, but if she is not given the transfusions, then she will die," the doctor said.

"No more cut downs, no more cut downs," the daughter cried. Mrs. Gottlieb told the judge her mother had been "begging, 'Please don't torture me any more.'"

The judge said a person "has the right not to be tortured." But he said his ruling did not mean Mrs. Martinez had the right to commit suicide by refusing treatment.

He ruled that Mrs. Martinez could be given any treatment so long as it does not give her pain.

"Why shouldn't I kill myself if I want to?" he demanded.

She replied to that quite seriously.

"Because it's wrong."

"Why is it wrong?"

She looked at him doubtfully. She was not disturbed in her own belief, but she was much too inarticulate to explain her reaction.

"Well—I mean—it's wicked to kill yourself. You've got to go on living whether you like it or not."

"Why have you?"

"Well, there are other people to consider, aren't there?"

"Not in my case. There's not a soul in the world who'd be the worse for my passing on."

All the more he felt determined to force an admission from her on the ethical side.

"At any rate I've got a right to do what I like with my own life."

"No—no, you haven't."

"But why not, my dear girl, why?"

She flushed. She said, her fingers playing with the little gold cross that hung round her neck.

"You don't understand. God may need you."

He stared—taken aback. He did not want to upset her childlike faith. He said mockingly:

"I suppose that one day I may stop a runaway horse and save a golden haired child from death—eh? Is that it?"

She shook her head. She said with vehemence and trying to express what was so vivid in her mind and so halting on her tongue.

"It may be just by *being* somewhere—not doing anything—just by being at a certain place at a certain time —oh, I can't say what I mean, but you might just—just walk along a street someday and just by doing that accomplish something terribly important—perhaps without even knowing what it was."

From *Towards Zero*, © 1944 by Agatha Christie, published by Dodd, Mead and Company Inc.

John Fischer

THE EASY CHAIR

Letter from Leete's Island: a case of termination

To UNDERSTAND HER LETTER you ought to know something about Dorothy.

She was a strong-minded woman. Some called her eccentric, but since eccentrics are about as common as blue jays in our town, that was no reason for special remark. Until you got to know her ways, though, she could be a little disconcerting. If she thought you were talking nonsense, for example, she would say so, loudly, and command you to shut up. When she decided she didn't like a book she was reading, she was likely to throw it into a far corner of the room. "Scoundrel" was her softest term for people she disapproved of—the real estate man who cut a road through her favorite woods, or the banker who had once refused her husband a loan, to mention only a couple on her long hate list. She never forgave her enemies, because she considered forgiveness "part of that damn fool Christianity nonsense." But to her friends, who were far more numerous, she was so fiercely devoted that she would not abide a critical word about any of them.

AFTER HER eightieth birthday, the rheumatoid arthritis that had plagued Dorothy for years took a turn for the worse. She was in severe and increasing pain; neither medication nor physical therapy was much help; and eventually she could get about only with the help of a walker, a few agonizing steps at a time. She never uttered a word of self-pity, but she did resent her growing dependence on friends and on the town's visiting homemakers' service. Most of all she dreaded the day when she would become completely bed-bound; and though her wits (and tongue) remained as sharp as ever, she feared that her wits might begin to falter without her realizing it, as so often happens with elderly people.

When the visiting homemaker came one morning last spring, she found Dorothy in a coma. The town ambulance got her to a New Haven hospital within half an hour, but she died several days later without regaining consciousness.

To Viola she also had entrusted a handwritten letter, with the request that a copy should be sent to each of her "dear friends" shortly after her death. It reads, in part, as follows:

This message was started in November 1971. I have reread it and added to it from time to time but made no basic changes.

To those whom I dearly value, this is an explanation, and a confession, and a plea. For if this ignorantly managed attempt is successful, I ask you to be happy for me—and ultimately for yourselves too.

Long ago I accumulated the means for this act; with no morbid intentions; with no sense of guilt; merely cherishing the feeling that if the time ever came when I thought it far better to fall asleep and never wake, I had the very great good fortune to have it in my power to do so. I seem always to have felt that one could—and even under given circumstances should—be the rightful judge of that moment. (It always seemed so distant and unlikely!)

I began really to feel it only after Jake's death when I began to feel truly alone—in the very critical sense of loss of mutual dependence. I felt too old and dilapidated to undertake new obligations of any validity.

The time may be long or short, I do not know, because I want no despondency involved when the precise moment comes. I'm sure it'll take a bit of doing, but it is not quite exactly a matter of courage or cowardice, except as it is the courage of cowardice and fear (and common sense?). I want to go while I can still enjoy my friends who are so good to me and who I know can still enjoy me; while I can still feel a not too unfavorable balance between the happiness and competence and interest and even limited usefulness of my days—and the difficulties and discomforts and pain and expense involved in trying

first to maintain that balance and then later merely to prolong life.

At that point I waited (it is now early April) and the effort is steadily increasing.

I think it will not be long now, for once clearly decided, I can feel the decision setting its own time-quickening schedule ... I've just had a splendid hour of sunshine and comradeship in this my best loved room, and it is that which seems real and everlasting—with the other just a grim and foolish nightmare that I'll awaken from. But the inexorable stark truth lies the other way around, and that cherished splendid hour will last only as long as memory lasts. ... The reasons for the when as well as the reasons for the why, make it a tightly woven complex of tough small fibres that result in a determined act when determined on.

TWO THINGS BOTHER ME about that letter. The first is that Dorothy felt it necessary to write it—she who never in the years I knew her had felt any need to explain or apologize for whatever she did. The second is that her last act had to be "ignorantly managed" and the "means" had to be accumulated surreptitiously and "long ago." Presumably, whatever drug she used had lost some of its potency; hence the prolonged coma at the end.

Yet I am glad she wrote it; for it has led me, over the months I have been thinking about it, to reverse a lifelong conviction. I have quoted from the letter at some length in the hope that it may persuade at least a few others to a similar change in belief—to the conviction that our society's whole attitude toward suicide is profoundly wrong.

I was raised like most Americans in the belief that suicide is an immoral act. Under some circumstances, I still believe that to be true. But in Dorothy's circumstances, what she did now seems to me not only sensible but morally praiseworthy. Even the word "suicide" seems wrong to me in such a case, because it is so heavily encrusted with connotations of disapproval. I would rather call it a case of termination.

Dorothy had no children, no dependents, no close relatives. Her wasting body would soon become a grief and burden to her friends, as it was to her. Recovery was out of the question. Her decision then seems a natural one, like that of the old Eskimos who know when the time has come for them to drift off on an ice floe into the final cold.

'A Crime of Love'

Man Helped Ill Wife in Suicide

PONTIAC, Mich., Dec. 20 (UPI)—Robert C. Waters, former Clarkston village president and high school principal, is to be sentenced Jan. 10 for helping his ailing wife commit suicide. His attorney called it a crime of love.

Waters, 65, wept last month when he confessed to police, but appeared calm in court Thursday, when he pleaded no contest to manslaughter charges.

He told police he went to the garage of his home early Nov. 13, started the engine of his car, then led his ailing wife, Kathleen, also 65, to the car and left her inside the closed garage. She died of carbon monoxide poisoning.

"The reason I didn't stop her was if she did not die here she was going into another medical hospital—mental hospital, psychiatric hospital—for care which she neither wanted nor would approve to find herself in all probability," he said in a statement read in court.

He said he had tried to dissuade her from killing herself since 1971, when physical and mental problems beset her. On the night before her death he had come close to making a suicide pact with her, then talked her out of it. While his wife was dying in the closed garage, he said, he was inside their home, pacing the floor and praying.

"I was just not able men-

tally to bring myself to make the decision that if her life was such a hell for her I should not be the one to let her not make up that decision for herself," Waters said.

"And rather than die the way she feared, a cripple maybe and mentally affected, I would rather let her make her own choice and die—if I may say—with dignity, than to go through with what she might have faced.

"It had to be her decision, not mine."

Waters and his wife had been married 40 years. They had no children.

A Nobel Laureate Proposes Education for Suicide

MAX DELBRUCK, *the Albert Billings Ruddock professor of biology at the California Institute of Technology and a winner of the 1969 Nobel Prize for Physiology or Medicine, recently was interviewed in Prism magazine by* IRVING S. BENGELSDORF, *director of science communication at Caltech. Following is an excerpt of the interview, reprinted from Prism magazine, November 1974, copyright © 1974 by the American Medical Association.*

Prism: Do you think that "suicide education" should be provided to the general population by physicians?

Delbruck: Yes. There is an interesting modern example where suicide instruction was denied to a seriously ill patient. In 1961, seriously ill with cancer at the age of 80, Percy W. Bridgman, the 1946 Nobel laureate in physics, took his life. He left a note

that said: "It isn't decent for society to make a man do this thing himself. Probably this is the last day I will be able to do it myself." He then shot himself.

Both his family and his physician should have given him the opportunity of taking his life in a dignified way. But because of society's emphasis on the prolongation of life at all costs, he had to end his own life in a lonely and agonizing way.

Prism: But Socrates, when he drank the hemlock, was in good health, and the decision to take his life was a conscious decision. What about the patient who is severely ill or in a coma and cannot participate in a conscious decision concerning the ending of his life?

Delbruck: It would be silly for me to tell the medical profession what to do in such circumstances. Each case requires a specific evaluation.

ALIVE
The Story of the
Andes Survivors

The chartered airliner crashed high in the remote wastes of the Andean cordillera, a world of snow, rock, wind and subzero cold, where not a living thing grew. Miraculously, only a few of the 45 persons aboard were killed. Although others died later of injuries, by the tenth day after the crash, when the search for the plane was abandoned, there were still 27 people alive. They were too weak to escape the imprisoning peaks, and soon there would be nothing left to eat. . . .

For some days several of the boys had realized that if they were to survive they would have to eat the bodies of those who had died in the crash. It was a ghastly prospect. The corpses lay around the plane in the snow, preserved by the intense cold in the state in which they had died. While the thought of cutting flesh from those who had been their friends was deeply repugnant to them all, a lucid appreciation of their predicament led them to consider it.

Gradually the discussion spread as these boys cautiously mentioned it to their friends or to those they thought would be sympathetic. Finally, Canessa brought it out into the open. He argued forcefully that they were not going to be rescued; that they would have to escape themselves, but that nothing could be done without food; and that the only food was human flesh. He used his knowledge of medicine to describe, in his penetrating, high-pitched voice, how their bodies were using up their reserves. "Every time you move," he said, "you use up part of your own body. Soon we shall be so weak that we won't have the strength even to cut the meat that is lying there before our eyes."

Canessa did not argue just from expediency. He insisted that they had a moral duty to stay alive by any means at their disposal, and because Canessa was earnest about his religious belief, great weight was given to what he said by the more pious among the survivors.

"It is meat," he said. "That's all it is. The souls have left their bodies and are in heaven with God. All that is left here are the carcasses, which are no more human beings than the dead flesh of the cattle we eat at home."

"You cannot condemn what they did," said Monsignor Andrés Rubio, Auxiliary Bishop of Montevideo, "when it was the only possibility of survival. . . . Eating someone who has died in order to survive is incorporating their substance, and it is quite possible to compare this with a graft. Flesh survives when assimilated by someone in extreme need, just as it does when an eye or heart of a dead man is grafted onto a living man. . . . What would we have done in a similar situation? . . . What would you say to someone if he revealed in confession a secret like that? Only one thing: not to be tormented by it . . . not to blame himself for something he would not blame in someone else and which no one blames in him."

Carlos Partelli, the Archbishop of Montevideo, confirmed his opinion. "Morally I see no objection, since it was a question of survival. It is always necessary to eat whatever is at hand, in spite of the repugnance it may evoke."

Andes survivors devoured bodies

Associated Press

SANTIAGO, Chile — Official sources said yesterday that some survivors of a plane crash high in the Andes told them they ate parts of the bodies of dead companions to keep from starving in an ordeal of more than two months.

The plane crashed Oct. 13, and 29 persons were killed in the crash or in an avalanche later. The 16 survivors spent 69 days in temperatures that sometimes plunged to 9 degrees below zero. They were either rugby players, or relatives or boosters.

One of the young men, not i d e n t i f i e d, compared the group's decision to use the cadavers as "similar to a heart transplant." His explanation was that in a transplant operation a heart is taken from a person at death to maintain another's life, and in the same manner portions of bodies had been used to maintain the living.

The sources said other survivors with strong religious convictions compared the decision to use the bodies for food with "the sacrament of the Catholic communion." One survivor was quoted by the sources as saying, "If we would have died, it would have been suicide, which is condemned by our faith the Roman Catholic Church."

Above, courtesy of The Associated Press. Right, from *Newsweek*, January 8, 1973.

CHILE:

Deliverance

Evil: "It was done, and so be it," one of the survivors, 19-year-old Antonio Vizinting, told NEWSWEEK's John Sherman. "I don't think I have anything to regret and I don't think it was something evil. I think we used something without movement, without life, something completely material, with which 16 human beings can continue to live, perhaps aid their fellow men, and who knows what paths God has prepared for them . . .

"I don't think I'll suffer a trauma or anything of the sort. I'll remember this with a great deal of affection and love toward all those beings or persons who died, because thanks to them I am alive at this moment . . . The subject must be approached as something elevated, as a sort of communion. We were entering into communion with a human body. Instead of doing it with the body of Christ, we were doing it with the body of a comrade in order to prevail."

SECTION 10

Corporate Rights and Responsibilities

All of the arguments in this section share the common feature that at least one of the parties involved in the moral judgment is a corporation rather than an individual person, and in most of them a judgment is being made about the moral rights or responsibilities of the corporation. Granted that corporations are built, owned, and operated by a number of individual persons, their structure is such that it is always difficult and sometimes close to impossible to assign certain moral rights and responsibilities to specific individual executives, employees, or stockholders. Without some nonarbitrary criteria for establishing individual responsibilities, the only obvious recourse is to either ascribe responsibilities to "the corporation" or else refrain from making any moral judgments at all concerning cases in which responsibilities cannot be assigned to specific individuals. The latter alternative appears to be a cop-out, while the former is at best not very helpful or satisfying. Thus, despite the difficulty of the task, it is generally best to exert whatever effort is necessary to "sort out" cases involving judgments about rights or responsibilities of corporations in order to identify specific individuals to whom these rights and responsibilities can properly be assigned.

It must be kept in mind when we are trying to identify specific individuals responsible for various corporate decisions and actions that in many, if not most, cases there will be a number of different individuals who in fact share the responsibility to varying degrees. It is very seldom that a single individual can be assigned total *moral* responsibility for a corporate decision, although many areas of corporate law have been designed in such a way that legal responsibility (and any associated liability and penalties) can be placed on a single person. One person often bears more moral responsibility than any other in a specific case, but this does not mean that he or she should be assigned all of the praise or blame associated with that case. And it is worth mentioning explicitly that certain *rights* of corporations are ultimately assignable to specific individuals in the same way as are responsibilities. A company's right to not be ripped off can be sorted out into the components of a collection of rights of individual stockholders and employees to receive fair return on investments and work performed. In this regard it should also be noted that there are some very real ethical problems which arise entirely within corporate structures, particularly those involving conflicts of rights and responsibilities of employees, managers, and stockholders. Once again, the most appropriate way to deal with these issues, if not always the simplest way, is to do whatever is necessary to assign the rights and responsibilities in the proper degree to specific individuals.

EXERCISES

1. For each of the examples in this section, determine as specifically as possible the roles of individuals in the case being discussed.
2. Compare the arguments in this section with those in Section 13 in order to identify any differences involved in dealing with moral issues related to corporations and moral issues related to governments. What might it mean to state that a corporation has certain responsibilities to a government or vice versa?

A GROWING VICE OF BUSINESS.

TWO suggestive incidents will introduce to our readers a vice of business which ought to be reformed before it assumes the magnitude and universality which it is sure to achieve, unless efficient steps are taken to arrest its progress.

INCIDENT NO. 1.—A builder of furnaces was called upon recently to name a price for heating a large structure in a large city. He offered to put in his apparatus for $30,000. After repeated conversations with sundry persons interested in the contracts, he was told that the man who should secure the job would be obliged to pay a percentage to them—in this case amounting to $3,000—the bill, of course, to be rendered in such a form as to make him a party to the fraud upon the owners of the building. He told them that he wanted the job, but that as he also had a desire to go to heaven when he died, he was afraid he should be obliged to decline their conditions. He also suggested that he should like to bid for the job with others, and was informed that not a single contract on the building had been given to the lowest bidder. Then he was politely bowed out of the presence of the gentlemen who could not use him. He went home, and as an experiment, sent them a proposal to put in his apparatus for $25,000. From this he never heard; and some man with a more convenient conscience got the contract and gave the percentage.

INCIDENT NO. 2.—A piano-forte manufacturer sold an instrument, at his regular retail price, to a gentleman of New York. Within forty-eight hours he was called upon by three musicians, every one of whom demanded his percentage upon the sale of the piano, claiming that it was bought upon his recommendation. The purchaser, to make sure of getting the best instrument, had separately consulted all these men, and they had happened to agree upon this maker. The result was, that the maker paid each man the amount of his claim, and said nothing, though he parted with considerably more than his profits on the piano-forte. When asked by the friend to whom he told the story, why he submitted to such an imposition, he replied that he did not dare to do otherwise; that if he had refused to respond to these exactions, the musicians would have turned against him, and transferred their recommendations to other makers.

The way in which corporations are bled by the leeches that fasten upon them is notorious. The men in respectable society, who regard a corporation as the legitimate subject of plunder, are too many to be counted. Tax-payers and stockholders part annually with untold millions to fill the purses of these dishonest men, and the mouths of their mendacious servants and tools. There are States in the Union in which the public conscience has become utterly demoralized with relation to this particular matter,—where every corporation, including Mutual Life Insurance Companies and Savings Banks, is in some way "sweated" by those who have the management of its concerns. In most instances this result is achieved under cover of the law; but, in some, gigantic robberies are effected by the purchase not only of the officers, but of the makers of the law.

This process cannot long go on, of course, without such a sophistication of the popular conscience that private trusts will be as little regarded as those which are corporate and public. Indeed, it has already produced its proper fruit, as the incidents we have cited show. Men are everywhere seeking for money which they do not earn. It is quite likely that the piano-dealer is as much to blame for his bondage to the musicians as they are. He may have invited their patronage, indeed, and promised them their pay; but it is all wrong, and the money all comes out of the consumer in the long run. The price of everything must be raised that tribute may be paid to those who are in a position to exact or steal it. If we go on at the present rate, we shall soon be no whit behind our European neighbors, whose servants are bribed by butchers and grocers and bakers, and who demand their "drink money" for every service, in addition to their legitimate wages. Every man who connives at this mode of doing business is not only a voluntary but a meanly mercenary corrupter of the people.

There is no question that in this matter of personal honesty America has retrograded within the last ten years. The rich corporation and the rich man are come to be regarded by tradesmen and laborers alike as sources of money which they may draw upon to the extent of their ability, without rendering an equivalent. An honest day's work is a much harder thing to get to-day than it was ten years ago; and unless a reformation take place, the good old standard of personal honesty among the laboring poor, and of business integrity among the prosperous, will become a thing of remembrance only. If it were necessary, whole branches of business might be mentioned which pay a regular tax to what is called "influence," to men who have thrust themselves between the seller and the buyer for the simple purpose of fleecing one or both. Many a product of ingenuity and toil is obliged to buy every inch of its way to the consumer; and a thousand improvements which affect the public convenience and comfort fail of adoption unless their profits are shared with the influence and power to which they appeal. Congress and the legislatures do not monopolize the lobby, for the lobby is everywhere. Black-mail, commissions, bonuses, gifts, the feathering of private nests among the recesses of great corporate interests, positions sought, won, and used for purposes of theft—all these things are so common that they have ceased to be remarkable; and they argue sadly against our boasted progress in Christian civilization.

We do not expect to rid the world of thieves; but the danger is, that honest men will not be able to do business at all without the adoption of their corrupt machinery, the prostitution of integrity, and the sacrifice of self-respect. How far are multitudes of our good houses from this position now?

From *Scribner's Monthly*, 1871.

Above, from *The Rat*, Underground Press Syndicate.

Right, copyright 1971 by *Christianity Today*; reprinted by permission.

Labor's Double Standard?

Organized labor relies heavily on the support of society at large. Its clout would be appreciably diminished if it did not resort to a variety of social pressures to sign up workers as members. In any office or shop where a union is recognized as bargaining agent by the employer, the individual employee most likely does not have a truly free choice on whether or not to join the union. Labor's rationale for coercion is that everyone who benefits from collective bargaining should contribute to it.

Our society has accepted this infringement upon individual freedom, for better or worse, feeling that the benefits outweigh the loss of liberty. Unfortunately, however, labor seems lately to be reluctant to recognize its debt to society. Unions still have a long way to go in eliminating racial discrimination, but they are resisting government proposals designed to help correct biased policies and practices.

The nation's construction unions issued a strongly worded statement last month saying they would fight government-imposed quotas on non-white workers in apprenticeship programs. We agree that quotas are probably not the answer. But isn't it merely something of a twist on the quota principle that enables the unions to achieve a de facto closed shop? If the government shouldn't force the unions to take in applicants it doesn't want, why should the unions be allowed to force into membership workers who don't want to join? □

A Friedman doctrine—

The Social Responsibility
Of Business Is to Increase Its Profits

By MILTON FRIEDMAN

WHEN I hear businessmen speak eloquently about the "social responsibilities of business in a free-enterprise system," I am reminded of the wonderful line about the Frenchman who discovered at the age of 70 that he had been speaking prose all his life. The businessmen believe that they are defending free enterprise when they declaim that business is not concerned "merely" with profit but also with promoting desirable "social" ends; that business has a "social conscience" and takes seriously its responsibilities for providing employment, eliminating discrimination, avoiding pollution and whatever else may be the catchwords of the contemporary crop of reformers. In fact they are—or would be if they or anyone else took them seriously—preaching pure and unadulterated socialism. Businessmen who talk this way are unwitting puppets of the intellectual forces that have been undermining the basis of a free society these past decades.

The discussions of the "social responsibilities of business" are notable for their analytical looseness and lack of rigor. What does it mean to say that "business" has responsibilities? Only people can have responsibilities. A corporation is an artificial person and in this sense may have artificial responsibilities, but "business" as a whole cannot be said to have responsibilities, even in this vague sense. The first step toward clarity in examining the doctrine of the social responsibility of business is to ask precisely what it implies for whom.

Presumably, the individuals who are to be responsible are businessmen, which means individual proprietors or corporate executives. Most of the discussion of social responsibility is directed at corporations, so in what follows I shall mostly neglect the individual proprietor and speak of corporate executives.

IN a free-enterprise, private-property system, a corporate executive is an employe of the owners of the business. He has direct responsibility to his employers. That responsibility is to conduct the business in accordance with their desires, which generally will be to make as much money as possible while conforming to the basic rules of the society, both those embodied in law and those embodied in ethical custom. Of course, in some cases his employers may have a different objective. A group of persons might establish a corporation for an eleemosynary purpose—for example, a hospital or a school. The manager of such a corporation will not have money profit as his objective but the rendering of certain services.

In either case, the key point is that, in his capacity as a corporate executive, the manager is the agent of the individuals who own the corporation or establish the eleemosynary institution, and his primary responsibility is to them.

MILTON FRIEDMAN is a professor of economics at the University of Chicago.

Needless to say, this does not mean that it is easy to judge how well he is performing his task. But at least the criterion of performance is straightforward, and the persons among whom a voluntary contractual arrangement exists are clearly defined.

Of course, the corporate executive is also a person in his own right. As a person, he may have many other responsibilities that he recognizes or assumes voluntarily—to his family, his conscience, his feelings of charity, his church, his clubs, his city, his country. He may feel impelled by these responsibilities to devote part of his income to causes he regards as worthy, to refuse to work for particular corporations, even to leave his job, for example, to join his country's armed forces. If we wish, we may refer to some of these responsibilities as "social responsibilities." But in these respects he is acting as a principal, not an agent; he is spending his own money or time or energy, not the money of his employers or the time or energy he has contracted to devote to their purposes. If these are "social responsibilities," they are the social responsibilities of individuals, not of business.

What does it mean to say that the corporate executive has a "social responsibility" in his capacity as businessman? If this statement is not pure rhetoric, it must mean that he is to act in some way that is not in the interest of his employers. For example, that he is to refrain from increasing the price of the product in order to contribute to the social objective of preventing inflation, even though a price increase would be in the best interests of the corporation. Or that he is to make expenditures on reducing pollution beyond the amount that is in the best interests of the corporation or that is required by law in order to contribute to the social objective of improving the environment. Or that, at the expense of corporate profits, he is to hire "hardcore" unemployed instead of better-qualified available workmen to contribute to the social objective of reducing poverty.

In each of these cases, the corporate executive would be spending someone else's money for a general social interest. Insofar as his actions in accord with his "social responsibility" reduce returns to stockholders, he is spending their money. Insofar as his actions raise the price to customers, he is spending the customers' money. Insofar as his actions lower the wages of some employes, he is spending their money.

The stockholders or the customers or the employes could separately spend their own money on the particular action if they wished to do so. The executive is exercising a distinct "social responsibility," rather than serving as an agent of the stockholders or the customers or the employes, only if he spends the money in a different way than they would have spent it.

But if he does this, he is in effect imposing taxes, on the one hand, and deciding how the tax proceeds shall be spent, on the other.

© 1970 by the New York Times Company. Reprinted by permission from *The New York Times Magazine*, September 13, 1970.

Walter Goodman STOCKS WITHOUT SIN

Still, for the sake of argument, what if it should somehow happen that virtuous actions are not rewarded in this life? "I don't notice that DuPont stock has tripled since they announced they're going to spend $300 million against pollution," remarks a veteran fund manager. Having lately, and belatedly, doubled its anti-pollution budget, the St. Regis Paper Company experienced a 51 per cent decline in profits in the first quarter of this year. Or what if companies that behave in unvirtuous ways make money? "What has been the cost to corporations of discriminating against blacks?" asks Phil Moore as though the answer were evident. Well, the nation is paying for it all right, but was discrimination really all that unprofitable all those years to companies that relied on a supply of low-paid workers to do disagreeable jobs?

A rough study at Princeton University, where students protested against the school's investments in South Africa, indicates that those objectionable stocks had almost a 3 per cent higher average rate of return than other securities in its portfolio. (Incidentally, it would cost Princeton an estimated $5 million in brokerage fees to get out of South Africa altogether.) In its 1971 proxy statement to General Motors, the Domestic and Foreign Missionary Service of the Protestant Episcopal Church urged that GM wind up its $125 million of manufacturing activities in South Africa because apartheid "will inevitably lead to turmoil and instability . . . and consequently to the destruction of foreign capital invested there." However, the church went on, GM should get out of South Africa even if it entailed a loss because "only those corporations which conduct themselves in a socially responsible way will be able to survive profitably, in the long run . . ." The Will to Believe survives among Episcopalians. At least it did before GM's annual meeting, where their proposal won 1.29 per cent of the shares voted.

And what of the managers of trust funds and pension funds? Should they be permitted to risk my money in behalf of their principles? The laws governing fiduciary relationships do not encourage experimentation, even for reasons of conscience. The Wall Street rule for persons legally charged with the management of other people's money runs as follows: "Invest funds in a company with the aim of gaining the best financial return with the least financial risk for the trust beneficiaries. If you later come to disagree with the company's management, sell the stock." This rule, we may assume, is used by many trustees to go along mindlessly with management and avoid the wear and tear of decision-making. Nevertheless, there remains a real legal question. David Silver, general counsel of Investment Company Institutes, a trade group, observes, "If a fund sells a share in a company that it thinks is a good investment because it doesn't like its hiring policies in South Africa, there could be a shareholders' suit."

But even if there were no legal problem, might

there not be a moral problem for the prudent trustee? Peter L. Bernstein, chairman of the board of Bernstein-Macauley and chairman of the investment policy committee of CBWL-Hayden, Stone, confesses that he feels some inner pressure to invest the funds in his charge in mortgages in minority areas, with the prospect of a lower return than they might bring elsewhere. But if he should succumb to that small voice, he observes, it will not be he who pays the price, but his clients: "Sorry, fellas, you've been elected to bear the cost." Why should this particular group suffer this special tax? Moreover, Bernstein points out that in a market economy, if capital flows not toward profits but toward social priorities, "we lose a rational measure of how to allocate capital." That, he acknowledges, suggests the limits of a market economy—and awakens in him stirrings of sympathy for radicals who would scrap the whole thing.

Not all investment advisers are as diffident as Mr. Bernstein. "We're making moral judgments all the time," Donald Weeden, chairman of Weeden & Company, told the *Institutional Investor*. "As individuals, we have been picked for our overall sensitivity to what's been going on." Now, no offense to Mr. Weeden, but I don't know any investment adviser whom I would care to have act in my behalf in any matter except turning a profit—and I'm not sure about that. The value of these specialists, I believe, lies in their limitations; they ought not allow themselves to see so much of the world that they become distracted.

Perhaps, though, fund managers might poll their investors and let them make their own decisions when confronted by a conflict between profit and principle. Under a recent SEC decision, shareholders can vote on whether fund managers should consider the social policies of a corporation before investing in its stock. During the latest GM go-around, in May, the Dreyfus Leverage Fund, holder of 25,000 shares of GM stock, solicited the opinions of shareholders on several of the insurgent proposals. In every case, most people voted with GM management and against the insurgents, whereupon Dreyfus voted its proxy *in favor* of the proposal requiring GM to publish detailed information on pollution and so forth. "We had to vote for that proposal," explains a fund spokesman, "because we believe in it." Mutual fund democracy?

Suppose that in a fit of social consciousness, American Motors should decide to put out a two-year model? And suppose everyone knew that the company's sales would sink in the second year? How many fund managers would hold onto their shares of American Motors? How many investors would stay with funds that operated in that public-spirited way?

Why, after all, should one expect selflessness from the widow dependent on her capital, the father concerned for his children's education, the speculator looking for gain—all those stock marketeers who have spent a lifetime trying to make money make money? We may be certain that any stock whose value drops to a tempting low because the Episcopal Church or a Boston synagogue sells it will be quickly picked up by investors of all religions who don't care what a company does, much less the country where it does it.

Ms. Susan Gross — Spokeswoman for the Project on Corporate Responsibility in Washington, D.C. elaborates on the Project's plan to get major institutional investors like universities to use their power as shareholders to direct corporate powers.

Do you feel that ethical considerations are advisable or necessary when a university, or anyone, is investing in corporations?

The Project on Corporate Responsibility does not really believe in ethical investing as it is commonly defined. That is the sort of "clean portfolio" concept of investing. We do not believe that there can be such a thing as a clean portfolio, because we do not believe there is such an animal as a clean company. One company for example, might have good minority hiring practices, while being terrible in the product safety area and the environmental area. There's no such thing as a clean company when you're talking about something which cannot really be defined. What the Project believes is that investors, universities included, ought to invest their money using economic criteria — investing money in order to get a reasonable return. Our concern is what the investor does once he has invested his money in a company. That is where shareholder responsibility must begin. We believe a shareholder has an obligation and a responsibility to exercise his leverage and influence in the company, to persuade the company to adopt more socially responsible positions, and to urge the longer range goal in which the project believes. This goal is the accountability of corporations to the various groups and constituencies that the corporation affects. I just want to emphasize that the way that you will get corporations to regularly, and seriously, weigh the social consequences of their acts and to make socially responsive decisions is by fundamental internal forms in corporate decision making. Corporate decision makers must be accountable, and they are not now accountable to anyone.

From *Business Today*, May 1973.

An experiment in South Africa

Polaroid sells its products in South Africa as do several hundred other American companies. Our sales there are small, less than one half of one percent of our worldwide business.

Recently a group has begun to demand that American business stop selling in South Africa. They say that by its presence it is supporting the government of the country and its policies of racial separation and subjugation of the Blacks. Polaroid, in spite of its small stake in the country, has received the first attention of this group.

We did not respond to their demands. But we did react to the question. We asked ourselves, "Is it right or wrong to do business in South Africa?" We have been studying the question for about ten weeks.

The committee of Polaroid employees who undertook this study included fourteen members – both black and white – from all over the company. The first conclusion was arrived at quickly and unanimously. We abhor *apartheid*, the national policy of South Africa.

The *apartheid* laws separate the races and restrict the rights, the opportunities and the movement of non-white Africans. This policy is contrary to the principles on which Polaroid was built and run. We believe in individuals. Not in "labor units" as Blacks are sometimes referred to in South Africa. We decided whatever our course should be it should oppose the course of *apartheid*.

The committee talked to more than fifty prominent South Africans both black and white, as well as many South African experts. They heard from officials in Washington. They read books, papers, testimony, documents, opinion, interpretation, statistics. They heard tapes and saw films.

They addressed themselves to a single question. What should Polaroid do in South Africa? Should we register our disapproval of *apartheid* by cutting off all contact with the country? Should we try to influence the system from within? We rejected the suggestion that we ignore the whole question and maintain the status quo.

Some of the black members of the study group expressed themselves strongly at the outset. They did not want to impose on the black people of another country a course of action merely because *we* might feel it was correct. They felt this paternalistic attitude had prevailed too often in America when things are done "for" black people without consulting black people.

It was decided to send four of the committee members to South Africa. Since this group was to include two black and two white members, it was widely assumed they would not be granted visas. They were.

It was assumed if they ever got to South Africa they would be given a government tour. They were not.

It was assumed they would not be allowed to see the actual conditions under which many Blacks live and would be prevented from talking to any of them in private. They did see those conditions in Soweto and elsewhere. And with or without permission they met and talked to and listened to more than a hundred black people of South Africa. Factory workers, office workers, domestic servants, teachers, political leaders, people in many walks of life. They also talked to a broad spectrum of whites including members of all the major parties.

Their prime purpose in going to South Africa was to ask Africans what they thought American business should do in their country. We decided the answer that is best for the black people of South Africa would be the best answer for us.

Can you learn about a country in ten days? No. In ten weeks. But our group learned one thing. What we had read and heard about *apartheid* was not exaggerated. It is every bit as repugnant as we had been led to believe.

The group returned with a unanimous recommendation.

In response to this recommendation and to the reports of the larger study committee, Polaroid will undertake an experimental program in relation to its business activities in South Africa.

For the time being we will continue our business relationships there (except for sales to the South African government, which our distributor is discontinuing), but on a new basis which Blacks there with whom we talked see as supportive to their hopes and plans for the future. In a year we will look closely to see if our experiment has had any effects.

First, we will take a number of steps with our distributor, as well as his suppliers, to improve dramatically the salaries and other benefits of their non-white employees. We have had indications that these companies will be willing to cooperate in this plan.

Our business associates in South Africa will also be obliged (as a condition of maintaining their relationship with Polaroid) to initiate a well-defined program to train non-white employees for important jobs within their companies.

We believe education for the Blacks, in combination with the opportunities now being afforded by the expanding economy, is a key to change in South Africa. We will commit a portion of our profits earned there to encourage black education. One avenue will be to provide funds for the permanent staff and office of the black-run Association for Education and Cultural Advancement (ASECA). A second method will be to make a gift to a foundation to underwrite educational expenses for about 500 black students at various levels of study from elementary school through university. Grants to assist teachers will also be made from this gift. In addition we will support two exchange fellowships for Blacks under the U.S.-South African Leader Exchange Program.

Polaroid has no investments in South Africa and we do not intend to change this policy at present. We are, however, investigating the possibilities of creating a black-managed company in one or more of the free black African nations.

Why have we undertaken this program? To satisfy a revolutionary group? No. They will find it far from satisfactory. They feel we should close the door on South Africa, not try to push it further open.

What can we hope to accomplish there without a factory, without a company of our own, without the economic leverage of large sales? Aren't we wasting time and money trying to have an effect on a massive problem 10,000 miles from home? The answer, our answer, is that since we are doing business in South Africa and since we have looked closely at that troubled country, we feel we can continue only by opposing the *apartheid* system. Black people there have advised us to do this by providing an opportunity for increased use of black talent, increased recognition of black dignity. Polaroid is a small economic force in South Africa, but we are well known and, because of our committee's visit there, highly visible. We hope other American companies will join us in this program. Even a small beginning of co-operative effort among American businesses can have a large effect in South Africa.

How can we presume to concern ourselves with the problems of another country? Whatever the practices elsewhere, South Africa alone articulates a policy exactly contrary to everything we feel our company stands for. We cannot participate passively in such a political system. Nor can we ignore it. That is why we have undertaken this experimental program.

Polaroid Corporation

A public statement made by Polaroid Corporation, which appeared in the press in January of 1971.

JOHN R. RARICK
6TH DISTRICT, LOUISIANA

COMMITTEE:
AGRICULTURE

January 13, 1971

Mr. Edwin H. Land, President
POLAROID CORPORATION
Cambridge, Massachusetts 02139

Dear Mr. Land:

Having shared your newspaper advertisement from today's **Washington Post,** "An Experiment in South Africa," with my morning coffee, I felt that I should drop you a line to express my disgust, or rather sympathy, at your naivete.

South Africa is a long way from Cambridge, Massachusetts, and from the United States. So it must be easy to make peace with your blackmailers by joining in their guerrilla warfare against another peaceful ally of the free world.

If it is to now be the policy of the Polaroid Corporation to embarrass the American people further in our international relations for your self-serving employee relations, when are you going to run ads expressing your company's abhorrence for the national policies and customs of other nations?

Is Polaroid going to employ some Arabs to investigate apartheid in Israel so you can denounce that country?

What about India with its caste system, where the untouchables are not to be seen in public even in the street by the higher caste? Of course, under your researchers' racist type examination, you must hire the lower caste to help formulate your policies.

Then we have the many African nations such as Liberia, Congo, Ethiopia, which still practice slavery. Most certainly you will want to alienate these nations as well as Zambia, which persecutes Jehovah's Witnesses, Indians, and all Moslems.

Finally, I notice nothing in your public relations propaganda which indicated that your company is cutting camera trade with Russia or its Communist satellites, which practice apartheid not only against the Zionist Jew, but other religious and ethnic minorities as well.

If you think life is so bad in South Africa, why is it that there are no lines of refugees or escapees fleeing that country? On the other hand, people fleeing from Communist countries at the risk of losing their lives and all of their belongings is a daily occurrence. I dare suggest that for a successful industrial organization, you people have been taken.

Yes, South Africa is a far piece from the United States, and as your article confesses, you have little if any business there anyway, so what do you have to lose in South Africa? Perhaps you are unaware that there are many Americans who are sick and tired of the Black Panthers and these revolutionaries being pampered and bank rolled by organizations such as yours.

It has hardly been a month since your $20,000 contribution to Boston's black appeal was sent to Cairo, Illinois to help destroy race relations in that community — the remainder was sent to Communist affiliated revolutionary troops in Africa, dedicated to kill white people and overthrow responsible governments.

I think that you will find that the people of South Africa have far more friends in the U.S. than your colored advisors have led you to believe. As for me, neither myself nor any member of my family will ever consider buying a Polaroid product, or using same. Until the day when South Africa manufactures her own cameras, I will confine my photography to the Zeiss of Germany, and Yashica. These companies are still interested in increasing sales and friendships — not alienating them.

Sincerely,
John R. Rarick
Member of Congress

JRR:cf

P.S. Incidentally, I am writing the Internal Revenue Service to inquire for an opinion as to whether corporations which are forbidden by law from making political donations can write off full page newspaper advertisements such as this as operating expenses.

U.S. Interests in South Africa

In your article "U.S. Business in South Africa" (BUSINESS AND FINANCE, March 29) you attribute to a Ford Motor Co. spokesman the statement that "U.S. corporations should not interfere in the domestic affairs of the countries in which they do business." Supposedly this is a counterargument to the demand that Ford withdraw its investment in South Africa's apartheid.

The hypocrisy of such an argument is obvious, but its perversity is made manifest in a later article in the same section in which you report Henry Ford II's interference in British affairs. Capitalist Ford presented Prime Minister Edward Heath with the economic ultimatum that until "stability" returned to Britain, he would not make further commitments in that country.

The roots of such a double standard can lie only in the profitability found in fascist but stable South Africa and not found in Britain's experiment in social and economic justice. What are America's priorities? Profitability and repression, or freedom, justice and equality? And why are the latter not the priorities of U.S. business abroad?

ALAN J. ERICKSON

Nashville, Tenn.

Above, letter to the editor of *Newsweek* by Alan J. Erickson, April 19, 1971.

Courtesy of John R. Rarick, the representative from the Sixth District, Louisiana.

209

Maybe the way to change the world is to join a large corporation.

We don't make a lot of noise, but this is where it's really happening. You see, a large corporation like Kodak has the resources and the skill to make this world a little more decent place to live. And we intend to do what we can to see that this is exactly what happens.

Take our home city, Rochester, New York for example. We cut water pollution in the Genesee River by using natural bacteria to dispose of unnatural wastes. We cut air pollution by using electrostatic precipitators in a new combustible waste disposal facility. We helped set up a black enterprise program in downtown Rochester, and we've been experimenting with film as a way to train both teachers and students—including some students who wouldn't respond to anything else.

And we didn't stop with Rochester. Kodak is involved in 47 countries all over the world. Actively involved.

Why? Because it's good business. Helping to clean the Genesee River not only benefits society...but helps protect another possible source for the clean water we need to make our film. Our combustible waste disposal facility not only reduces pollution...but just about pays for itself in heat and power production and silver recovery. Our black enterprise program not only provides an opportunity for the economically disadvantaged...but helps stabilize communities in which Kodak can operate and grow. And distributing cameras and film to teachers and students not only helps motivate the children...but helps create a whole new market.

In short, it's simply good business. And we're in business to make a profit. But in furthering our business interests, we also further society's interests.

And that's good. After all, our business depends on society. So we care what happens to it.

Courtesy of Eastman Kodak Company.

Lamenting the fallen sparrow

Is technology doing the human race good, or doing it in?

That question persists after more than 200 years of technological innovation. Not many people argue any longer that if God had wanted humans to fly, He would have given us wings. But there are plenty of contemporary alarms against invention.

It won't surprise anyone to learn that Mobil believes technology does a great deal of good. It may surprise some people when we concede that technological advance takes its toll. Like many other things, technology is sometimes a blessing, sometimes a bane.

On this subject, we share the views of Dr. Hans Landsberg, director of the resource appraisal program carried out by Resources for the Future—a nonprofit corporation for research and education in the development, conservation, and use of natural resources.

At a symposium some time ago of the American Academy of Arts and Sciences, Dr. Landsberg said:

"One is apt to view the more disagreeable aspects of modern life, including most prominently those due to the impact of technology, with partiality—often unconsciously. We take for granted that we may drink tap water, eat uncooked fruit or vegetables, and consume milk with no thought of falling victim to a lurking bug. We are reminded of our good fortune only when we travel in parts of the world that require preventive or remedial countermeasures....

"But, customarily, we fail to do much balancing of pluses and minuses.

"We tend to overlook the fact that the chemical industry produces not only controversial pesticides, but also antibiotics and vaccines; that the automobile whose incomplete fuel combustion fouls the city air does, at the same time, enable us to escape its boundaries and to know the world in a way available a generation or two ago only to the daring or the rich.

"We are quick to lament the fallen sparrow, but slow to celebrate the fall of 'Typhoid Mary.'"

Responsible enterprise, Mobil believes, should not merely lament the sparrow's fall, but try to prevent it. Yet industry should not be—and need not be—deterred from striving to make technology a blessing for the earth and all the living things that inhabit it.

Mobil®

GUNS & BUTTER

By Sid Blumenthal

Greed

About 150 members of Massachusetts Fair Share demonstrated at the Boston headquarters of New England Telephone on May 22 to protest the company's request to the Department of Public Utilities for a $210 million rate increase. The largest utility hike ever proposed in state history, it would raise basic monthly service fees by a total of from $22 to $34 a year; pay phones from a dime to 20 cents; and metropolitan and suburban service from $50 to $84 a year. This increase would follow the $42 million hike granted only last fall.

Fair Share has set up a meeting with company president William Mercer to discuss the group's reform program for consumers, which calls for fixed rate service, an end to the company's deposit policy (Jim Katz of Fair Share calls it "arbitrary" and "discriminatory against low- and middle-income people"), and a fair billing procedure. Katz says, "The company says straight out they want to increase their profits. They argue that they can't function unless they get more money. It's craziness. It basically comes down to a question of who the utility is resonsible to — the public or the stockholders."

Katz pointed out that William Mercer's personal salary just soared to $170,000 annually, up $20,000 over last year and justified as a cost-of-living increase. Mercer is also a director of the First National Bank, John Hancock Insurance, and the Greater Boston Chamber of Commerce.

New England Telephone is one of the central institutions in the Hub's corporate elite. Fair Share has researched the firm's interlocks and found that three of its directors are also directors of the First National Bank, one of the Suffolk Franklin Bank, one of the Federal Reserve Bank of Boston, one of the New England Merchants Bank, one of the Dorchester Savings Bank, one of the State Street Bank and Trust, one of the National Shawmut Bank, one of the Provident Institute for Savings, and one of the Boston Five Cent Savings Bank. Telephone Company directors are also well represented on the boards of insurance companies. Three are directors at New England Mutual Life, two at Liberty Mutual, three at John Hancock, one at Boston Old Colony, and one at Massachusetts Mutual Life. In addition, New England Telephone directors sit on the boards of Raytheon, the Cabot Corporation, the New York Stock Exchange and the Council of Foreign Relations. Jim Katz says, "These people shouldn't control a public utility."

THE DOW CHEMICAL COMPANY

Statement of Position on Napalm

The Dow Chemical Company endorses the right of any American to protest legally and peacefully an action with which he does not agree.

Our position on the manufacture of napalm is that we are a supplier of goods to the Defense Department and not a policy maker. We do not and should not try to decide military strategy or policy.

Simple good citizenship requires that we supply our government and our military with those goods which they feel they need whenever we have the technology and capability and have been chosen by the government as a supplier.

We will do our best, as we always have, to try to produce what our Defense Department and our soldiers need in any war situation. Purely aside from our duty to do this, we will feel deeply gratified if what we are able to provide helps to protect our fighting men or to speed the day when fighting will end.

(1966–67).

Courtesy of the Dow Chemical Company.

Eco-Guerrilla Warfare

The capers of the Chicago Fox (THE CITIES, Jan. 11) make me think of a scenario that could pose some problems far more significant than the identity of the stain on the rug at U.S. Steel.

Suppose an eco-guerrilla ran a hose from an industrial smokestack into the company president's office. The fumes then kill the executives and a few secretaries. The environmental prankster is caught soon afterward.

Would he be charged with murder? Presumably he would. However, if he could be found guilty of murder for pumping industrial fumes into an office, what about the company that is releasing the poisons into the air in the first place?

Three cheers for the Fox if his actions force people to contemplate deeper implications of the muck on the rug.

JEFFREY C. BAUER
Colorado Springs, Colo.

Left, letter to the editor of *Newsweek* by Jeffrey C. Bauer, February 8, 1971.

Meanwhile we find ourselves confronted by a most disturbing moral problem. We know that the pursuit of good ends does not justify the employment of bad means. But what about those situations, now of such frequent occurrence, in which good means have end results which turn out to be bad?

For example, we go to a tropical island and with the aid of DDT we stamp out malaria and, in two or three years, save hundreds of thousands of lives. This is obviously good. But the hundreds of thousands of human beings thus saved, and the millions whom they beget and bring to birth, cannot be adequately clothed, housed, educated or even fed out of the island's available resources. Quick death by malaria has been abolished; but life made miserable by undernourishment and over-crowding is now the rule, and slow death by outright starvation threatens ever greater numbers.

And what about the congenitally insufficient organisms, whom our medicine and our social services now preserve so that they may propagate their kind? To help the unfortunate is obviously good. But the wholesale transmission to our descendants of the results of unfavorable mutations, and the progressive contamination of the genetic pool from which the members of our species will have to draw, are no less obviously bad. We are on the horns of an ethical dilemma, and to find the middle way will require all our intelligence and all our good will.

Above, from *Brave New World Revisited*, © 1958 by Aldous Huxley.

213

Northrop: Know The Right People

By Jack Egan
Washington Post Staff Writer

The Northrop Corp. saga, as it has unraveled, is the story of influence-peddling at the highest levels of government in an industry where governments are really the only customers and where single decisions can mean hundreds of millions and billions of dollars.

Subcommittee chairman Frank Church (D-Idaho) said the Northrop story was summed up in a quote from one of the company's top Washington consultants, Frank J. DeFrancis: "I don't know a damn thing about an airplane except the nose and the tail."

"But DeFrancis knew the right people," Church said, "and that is really what the Northrop case is all about: how to get to the right people in foreign governments to make the right decisions about which airplane to purchase. The propriety with which this was to be accomplished seems not to matter."

One Northrop executive, John R. Hunt, in an interview with the company's auditors as part of an investigation of the company, said, "The role of the agent is primarily that of influence peddler;' that is, he knows who to talk to and whose pockets to line in a particular country to get the job done."

Hunt said "agents are an expensive and necessary evil of doing business in a foreign country; the agents make the necessary payments." Corporate officials in general "don't know and don't want to know where the money paid to agents goes," he added.

Above, from *The Washington Post*, June 15, 1975.
Below, from *The Washington Post*, 1975.

Lockheed Admits Making $22 Million in Foreign Gifts

By James L. Rowe Jr.
Washington Post Staff Writer

Lockheed Aircraft Corp. admitted yesterday that it has paid about $22 million to "foreign officials and foreign political organizations" over the last 5½ years.

Lockheed, which had steadfastly denied paying any foreign bribes or political contributions, defended the practice and said the payments were "necessary in consummating certain foreign sales." The giant aerospace firm said the overseas payments were made "with the knowledge of management" in Burbank, Calif.

Lockheed said yesterday that it believes all of its foreign payments "are consistent with practices engaged in by numerous other companies abroad, including many of its competitors, and are in keeping with business practices in many foreign countries."

But the company warned that disclosure of any payoffs would hurt the company and that if the company is stopped from making these contributions, it "could seriously prejudice the company's ability to compete effectively in certain foreign markets."

Pay-offs in doing business abroad

Congratulations for casting the harsh light of publicity on the pay-offs American companies allegedly are making to influence peddlers to increase foreign sales. Being in the oil business, hardly a day passes without someone phoning me and offering special deals involving the supply of foreign crude oil if I will only pay them a healthy commission, most of which they allegedly have to use to pay off friends of the shiek, shah, or someone.

My reply is always, "No interest, because I have been told by the representative of the country involved, as well as by our government officials, that such sales must be made direct with the national oil company." In fact, most of the producing countries have publicly stated that their sales policy is never to deal through third parties or brokers.

Companies that pay off in-between influence peddlers are not only wasting their stockholders' money, but, what is even worse, they are casting a dark reflection on our Western ethics of doing business in a moral manner.

Congress and the IRS should act to stop such monkey business. We cannot afford to allow the venality of a few harm the broad interests of our country.

John K. Evans
Washington, D.C.

Left, letter to the editor of the *Washington Star* by John K. Evans, 1975.
Right, © *The Washington Post*, May 1975.

Pepco Won't Seek Special Low Rates

By Claudia Levy
Washington Post Staff Writer

If low-income customers have trouble paying increasing electricity costs, it's not the responsibility of the electric company to seek special low rates for them, W. Reid Thompson, president and chairman of the Potomac Electric Power Co., told stockholders yesterday.

"It's not our function to make the social judgment that some of our customers should bear the problems of poverty-level customers," Thompson said, in answer to suggestions by several stockholders that the local utility ask for adjustments in its rate structure to favor small users.

Any subsidies for this class of customer should come from the federal government, Thompson insisted, perhaps in the form of an "energy stamp" that would provide benefits like those of food stamps.

Last year, average residential bills in Pepco's service areas in Maryland and all of the District rose 33 per cent, while the cost of living generally rose about 12 per cent. Increases in electric bills resulted mainly from increased costs to the utility for fuel, with December residential bills averaging $17.50 in the District and $29.03 in Maryland, for instance.

In the last increase it granted the utility, the D.C. Public Service Commission said Pepco could not charge more for customers who use less than 400 kilowatt hours a month, 55 kilowatts under the average usage in the city.

Stockholders yesterday urged Pepco to institute the lowest, so-called "lifeline" rate for the first 400 kilowatts used by a household. James Sullivan asked his fellow shareholders to "put yourselves in the shoes of low-income customers . . . Think of yourself living without a refrigerator . . . or sitting in a room . . . without heat."

By charging residential customers who use small amounts of electricity less per kilowatt hour than large users—who currently pay a smaller price per unit of electricity—Pepco's income would not be significantly affected and its "image would soar," Sullivan told Thompson.

The Pepco chief said the lifeline rate, currently being widely discussed among utilities, "has some appeal to it, of course . . . " But he said there was a "real question about the use of utility rates as a vehicle for desirable social programs, such as taking care of the economically deprived."

Other stockholders complained about stock offerings recently made by the company—without preferential treatment to existing stockholders at below book value, an action some said diluted earnings for the earlier shareholders and required a greater return per share to keep up earnings. Thompson said the sale had been necessary to raise money for expansion, now slated at far lower levels than previously planned.

Judy Gingert, a stockholder representing D.C. Power, a coalition of local civic groups, said that in meeting with Thompson, her group was told that "the purpose of the company is to provide service to customers . . . But now you speak the same words to stock holders . . . about your 'grave and earnest concern' " for them.

POINT

SAFER: It's said that bribing foreign governments has become a way of life for big American corporations who do business in Asia and Latin America. Although it's been going on for years, it's now become something of a cause celebre. Everyone seems to be talking about it or doing it; and when people talk, Jack Kilpatrick and Shana Alexander insist on having their say. Here's Point/Counterpoint.

JAMES J. KILPATRICK: We're having fits of morality in Washington, Shana, over what's denounced as corporate bribery abroad. It's the most unheard of thing you ever heard of. It appears that Gulf Oil paid out $4-million in political contributions in South Korea alone. It looks as if United Brands paid a whopping sum in Honduras to get out from under a tax on bananas. Down in Bolivia, the former President apparently was involved in accepting corporate money. Can you imagine any such thing? The American corporations are being charged with shame and scandal. Some of the more virtuous members of Congress are demanding punitive measures. The air resounds with cries of lofty rectitude, coming mostly from people with a highly cultivated sensibility for other people's morals. It's a terrible state of affairs! But what it really is, Shana, is a terrible lot of hypocritical nonsense.

The American companies are being singled out by a bunch of professional business haters and sanctimonious rousers. In certain foreign countries, bribery is an ancient way of life. Payments to public officials are a plain and simple business expense. German, Swiss and British companies pay up just as ours do. And to complain that the American corporations didn't disclose these payments to the SEC is pettifoggery. You couldn't very well expect Gulf Oil to publish an expense account - "bribe to a president: $400,000". Gulf's good manners may be better than Bolivia's bad morals.

Who are we to talk? The trade unions give $35,000 to a freshman Congressman, and we call it just a contribution. Milk producers, oilmen, doctors and bankers all kick in to politicians. How did we get so pure? Let's not try to reform the Bolivians, Shana. We have enough to do in reforming ourselves.

Above and right page, from the CBS News broadcast *60 Minutes*, June 1, 1975.

COUNTERPOINT

SHANA ALEXANDER: I'll say I'm shocked! But what shocks me is you,
Jack. You're telling me that the Communists are right, that the end
justifies the means? Well, I can't agree with that. The end, in
this case, is to maintain business as usual between great big
American corporations and a few rotten little countries where bribery
is, indeed, a way of life. Should that make it our way of life?

You're suggesting we crawl back down into the same mud that
Washington and Jefferson founded this country to lift us out of.
You're talking Godfather morality - give them a bribe, a big payoff.
Make them an offer they can't refuse. Well, let the United States do
that, or let Gulf Oil or any other corporate big shot do that, and
you turn what's left of integrity in this country (and there's an
awful lot of integrity left here in my town, if not down there in
Washington) - you reduce that to the ethics of Ecuador and the honor
of Honduras. The argument that everybody does it is no good. Say
your kid gets caught ripping off the five-and-ten, and he says all
the kids do it; you tell him I don't care what the other kids do,
it's wrong! And if he does it again, you'll punish him, because
otherwise he's apt to grow up and become chairman of Gulf Oil; and
when Congress asks him how come you gave $4-million to the President
of South Korea, he's going to say, well, Exxon does it, United Fruit
does it, and Jack Kilpatrick says it's okay because Bolivia does it.

Reprinted from *U.S. News & World Report*
(July 14, 1975).

Why Business Has a Black Eye

Interview With Alexander B. Trowbridge, President of the Conference Board

Everywhere, businessmen hear criticism and doubt—about their ethics, ways they operate. Is it valid? What can be done? The head of the Conference Board answers these and other questions in this exclusive interview.

Q Many people have been shocked to hear about the bribes paid by some big U.S. companies to public officials or others in foreign countries. Can that sort of practice be defended?

A I wouldn't attempt to defend it either on an ethical basis or a business basis. On the other hand, I think we have to define what we're talking about.

In my opinion, bribery as a way of business life does not exist in this country. There are, there have been, and there probably always will be individual cases in which somebody takes what he thinks is the easy way out. When such people get caught and their acts are publicized, the public gets the impression that unethical practices are far more prevalent than is really the case.

When you do business abroad, you move into a different ethical and economic and social structure. As a so-called good citizen of the particular country in which you are operating, you try to live within that structure rather than impose an American legal or political framework on someone else's society.

I know of many cases—and there have been some big and serious ones—in which individual judgments were made by people who came to regret them. But these instances simply underline the fact that paying bribes and passing big sums of money under the table just doesn't work. It doesn't work ethically, and it doesn't make sense from a business point of view, because once you get started you get increasingly bogged down in quicksand. Today's contract or tomorrow's business deal, if you have to get it that way, will be more trouble than it's worth.

Q Another thing that has hurt the image of business has been the disclosure that some well-known companies and their executives made illegal political contributions in this country. Do we need a new set of laws or a new code of ethics to improve business standards?

A Again, I think we have to be sure that a few well-publicized cases do not create an impression of total disregard of the laws and a rejection of the basically well-established ethical and moral patterns that most people follow.

The law is perfectly clear: It is illegal to make corporate contributions for political purposes. Some people, under pressures that they felt unable to resist, broke that law. I think if improvements in the law are required, so be it: maybe a tougher fine, maybe more-stringent warnings, and greater liability for individuals as well as corporations. These are alternatives that we undoubtedly will be hearing a lot about.

I'm not sure, however, that we have to rewrite the Ten Commandments. The old puritan ethic, a deeply ingrained sense of right and wrong, still has pretty solid roots in this country. There are, clearly, people who are going to break both law and code, but I believe that the few cases that we've heard about do not indicate a total breakdown in the morality of U.S. businessmen.

Feiffer

LAWS ARE DESIGNED TO PROTECT SOCIETY.

WHEN CRIMINALS BREAK THE LAW AND GET AWAY WITH IT—

THE RESULT IS RISING VIOLENCE, CRIME IN THE STREETS, ANARCHY.

WHEN BIG CORPORATIONS BREAK THE LAW AND DON'T GET AWAY WITH IT.

THE RESULT IS FALLING STOCKS, RISING UNEMPLOYMENT, CRIME IN THE STREETS, ANARCHY.

SO PROSECUTE CRIMINALS!

AND SUPPORT CORPORATE CRIME!

KEEP AMERICA STRONG!

Above, © 1972 Jules Feiffer.

The efficacy of imprisonment

Americans who wear their social conscience on their sleeve have staked out compassion for prisoners and justice for consumers as two special concerns.

Often they say that the convicted criminal's crime is actually morally neutral: There are so many relative factors involved, and he suffered so much deprivation, that an unjust society is really to blame.

Furthermore, they add, imprisonment is useless because it only amounts to vindictiveness, society's way of shunning its obligation to rehabilitate the individual.

On the consumer front, however, moral relativity suddenly vanishes. The dishonest businessman is not the mere victim of his environment and all the intermeshed social forces. He is not simply caught up in a great tragedy. He is a conscious shyster or polluter who must pay the price of wrongdoing.

This doublethink r e a c h e d its apex — or perhaps its nadir — when a California sociologist at a recent conference on "corporate accountability" said: "The most effective deterrent for corporate c r i m i n a l s is the imposition of criminal penalties on executives who have knowingly committed outlawed acts of a serious nature."

He said a jail sentence, or even the threat of one, would encourage such executives to mend their ways.

Corporate f r a u d s and fakers should be brought to account, no less than other offenders. Still, it is paradoxical that the efficacy of jail sentences is only now being recognized, and only for corporate malfactors rather than for the worst category of criminals, those who commit crimes of violence.

Above, from *The Arizona Republic*, November 5, 1971.

Lockheed's Little Helpers

ANYONE who credits Congress with a collective ethical principle is hard put to prove his point, since ethics usually finishes among the also-rans on Capitol Hill. It is especially difficult to find anything resembling a principle in congressional approval of a $250,000,000 loan guarantee to Lockheed Aircraft Corp. But let's try, very hard, to uncover what our lawmakers were trying to tell us in their handling of that political-economic-diplomatic squabble.

If one can believe the proponents of the loan to Lockheed, a basic goal was to save jobs. President Nixon, in hailing the passage of the bill, said it would "save tens of thousands of jobs that would otherwise have been eliminated." Unquestionably that will happen. But the inequities of saving 60,000 jobs at Lockheed while permitting thousands of other workers to become jobless every month because of business failures are so clear that even congressmen and the Nixon Administration can't help but comprehend them.

Perhaps, then, the idea was to preserve jobs of workers in "big" companies. How big? Companies with 20,000 employes? Or 10,000? Where does one draw the line in deciding which jobs are worth saving?

If that's not the answer, maybe the goal was to "help ensure that the nation's largest defense contractor . . . will continue serving the nation's needs," as Mr. Nixon declared. That brings the Government's emphasis out of saving jobs and into saving companies. Again, apparently size has something to do with it, because Congress is unlikely to rescue a filling-station operator who is going bankrupt or, for that matter, a small defense contractor.

The real reason could be related more to diplomacy than to economics. The British government, after all, was threatening to allow *its* principal industrial weakling, Rolls-Royce Ltd., to go out of business unless the United States bailed out Lockheed. Rolls-Royce makes the engines for the TriStar airbus, the commercial jet being developed by Lockheed; the partnership of the two companies in this shaky project seems singularly appropriate, like putting a Studebaker engine in an Edsel.

All of those reasons for helping Lockheed seem unconvincing, so maybe there is something else. We must try not to be cynical, but the phrase "political expediency" does come to mind. Lockheed has huge plants in California and Georgia, where thousands of Lockheed employes vote. It would have been too much to expect Senators Tunney and Cranston, California Democratic liberals, and Senators Talmadge and Gambrell, Georgia Democratic not-so-liberals, to oppose the bill. And, indeed, they voted for it. One wonders whether the Nixon Administration had some similar vote-getting goals in mind in its strong support of the bill.

That's a nasty thought, not to be dwelled on. It's much better to think of politicians as being motivated by high principles. So if your candy store is going bankrupt, don't call the banker, call your senator or representative. Ask him to apply the "ethics" of the Lockheed "principle" to your little store. But be prepared for a going-out-of-business sale.

—*JAMES G. DRISCOLL*

Reprinted from *The National Observer*, August 9, 1971. Copyright Dow Jones & Company, Inc.

Money-Lending, Interest, and the Christian

A Conflict in Real Values

By EILEEN EGAN

The home of the Venezuelan bishop was simple and orderly. Mother Teresa of Calcutta was paying a courtesy call on him since she had just been visiting a nearby jungle area at the invitation of a neighboring bishop. She was considering asking a team of the Missionaries of Charity to work in the area. I was doing the translating.

The bishop turned to me and asked about my work. When he found out that I worked and lived in New York, he asked me if I could do him a favor. He wanted to make the first contacts with New York banks concerning a loan of up to $50,000. The plan was to borrow the money from the United States at a rate of interest of about seven percent. The funds would then be deposited with local banks and loaned out at the going rate (about twenty or twenty-two per cent). The difference in interest rates would insure the support of the seminary and other activities of the diocese. The bishop spoke in simplicity and utter frankness.

I told the bishop that I was not the person to help him. Not only did I lack contacts with New York banks but to help in such an operation would be against my principles.

"How would it be opposed to your principles?" he asked. "Is not the support of a seminary a worthy Catholic work?"

"Of course," I answered. "It is the matter of interest that is against my principles. I do not think demanding of interest is a worthy action for a Christian. I still believe that the Church was right when it forbade interest. In fact," I added, "to ask for interest of twenty per cent on loans would seem to be what the Church even today would call usury."

My only regret about that conversation with a bishop trapped in the mores of his time and place was that I had not given him an example of opposition to interest that had occurred in New York City. In 1960, the Catholic Worker had returned to the City of New York a check for $3,579.39 because it represented interest. The check came with the sum of $68,000, the payment offered by the city for the Catholic Worker house which was demolished for a subway improvement. As the payment had been delayed, the city authorities punctiliously added the amount of interest the money would have earned had it been deposited in a bank. In return, the city received a letter that will probably remain as a unique item in its files.

Dorothy Day explained in the letter accompanying the check that the Catholic Worker movement still took seriously the prohibition of the Church Fathers and Councils on lending money at interest. "In the Christian emphasis on the duty of charity," she wrote, "we are compelled to lend gratuitously, to give freely . . ." Some readers reacted strongly to the return of the money, money which could have gone into feeding the poor, they pointed out. It seemed an outlandish act, in the twentieth century, to oppose the system of interest.

I have personally discovered that my nonviolent or pacifist position is considered far less of an aberration than my refusal to condone interest. There have been times when I was forced to pay interest, but I opted out of situations where I would receive interest. My friends have felt they had to remind me that the whole free enterprise system of our country and its unexampled growth depends on the amassing of capital for the establishment of basic industries: that the stimulus for investment is the return on the investment; that in any case the return on invested money is often no more than enough to counteract the loss in the value of money through inflation. There are many more arguments of a technical nature, arguments which I can only counter on an entirely different plane with arguments of a moral nature.

The most telling argument, as far as I am concerned, is the collision of values between the capitalistic idea of property and the use of one's surplus property, and the Christian one.

The capitalistic concept of property (according to the proponents but not the critics of capitalism) calls for the accumulation of savings through thrift and their investment at interest. Money thus breeds money. Surpluses are put to use in an unending spiral of gain. No one, no institution, can set a ceiling on this unending spiral. National taxes do not stop its motion. This spiral is accompanied by the spiralling of production and by pressures for ever-greater consumption. If mass production is called for by the spiral of gain, then it becomes the method of production, and there is no question of slowing down to ensure human work for human beings. The rights of the producer are completely lost in the emphasis on supplying the consumer. "Consumerism" is

the result, and the word mirrors not only the succumbing of the consumer to the pressures of advertising, but the degradation of the producer.

Since the rise of capitalism, the Christian who does not believe in using his surplus for gain is often considered a troglodyte. For the Christian is expected to direct his surplus funds, not into the nexus of the market, but to meet the need of his near and far neighbor in the human family. His surplus is to bring him no gain but should contribute to the development of his neighbor and society. The collision of values, clear-cut in the early days of capitalism, became foggy as capitalists embraced the globe.

Perhaps today, when spiralling industrial growth and consumption are polluting the planet and depleting its energy resources, the Christian idea of property may emerge as having pragmatic as well as ethical validity. The god of un-controlled economic growth has clearly failed.

The Christian concept of property was unequivocally stated in the 1967 encyclical letter of Pope Paul VI, **The Development of Peoples.** "No one is justified," says the encyclical, "in keeping for his exclusive use what he does not need when others lack necessities. This is a simple rule, and each follower of Jesus can, and must, work it out for himself. Each person's, each family's, needs are different. The point is that a determination of those needs must be made in the light of the needs of others. Those others are not only those whose needs we see around us, but also those whose needs come to our attention.

The Development Of People is specific in condemning other abuses of capitalism, including the transfer of income abroad, the phenonemon known as "flight capital," the retention of large landed estates against the common good, and the concept that property constitutes "an absolute and unconditioned right." Regrettably, part of the sting of this encyclical was removed for Americans by a disclaimer pasted into the first edition, namely: "This individualistic system of capitalism so strongly condemned by Popes Leo XIII, Pius XI, Pius XII, John XXIII and Paul VI, involves a type of calloused exploitation which certainly is not descriptive of the prevailing business practices of the United States in 1967."

"Money-Lending" by Eileen Egan, *Catholic Worker.*

221

Editorials

Protecting Buyers of U.S. Grain

When the Russians start taking delivery of the American grain they're now in the process of buying, they'd better bring along their own inspectors to make sure they get what they pay for. American inspectors are supposed to guarantee the quality of American shipments, but many of them can't be trusted. They're hired hands of the very exporting companies that stand to benefit from the sale of substandard grain overseas.

The Federal Grain Standards Act is supposed to ensure that grain exports comply with federal standards for quality and cleanliness. But overseas shipments are routinely shortweighted by substituting stones for some of the grain, which then can be sold twice. Some shipments are adulterated with rice hulls and other fillers, and some are infested with rodents.

None of this should come as much of a surprise to the Department of Agriculture, which has on its books no less than 101 official complaints about the quality of American grain delivered overseas—some of them dating back a decade.

Under the present inspection system, the Agriculture Department licenses grain inspectors, but they're not federal employees. They work for private firms and local boards of trade that hire them out to the companies whose cargos they are supposed to inspect. Only Alice in Wonderland would expect that system to work.

Twenty persons, mostly grain elevator inspectors at New Orleans and Houston, are under federal indictment for allegedly taking bribes and engaging in other illegal practices. Now the scandal is spreading to virtually every American port that handles grain exports. The only way to stop it is for Congress to put teeth into laws designed to protect the integrity of American exports.

Since it's the Russians and other overseas buyers who are being stuck, why should Americans worry about the grain scandals? Because they're driving up the price of grain on world markets—and that's being reflected in U.S. supermarkets. Because other countries are likely to retaliate with the same sort of slipshod inspection of raw materials they ship to the U.S. And because American firms now stand accused of the same type of illegal and unethical practices they frequently complain about having to put up with overseas. Integrity begins at home.

A woman moves the Pentagon

Can one person make a difference? You'd better believe it.

One person, an unmarried pregnant Wave stationed at Patuxent River Naval Air Station in Maryland, "was a factor," Navy Secretary J. William Middendorf II concedes, in forcing the Pentagon to change a longstanding policy.

Until recently, the policy was that a servicewoman, married or unmarried, who became pregnant was automatically dismissed from the service unless she could get a waiver, which wasn't easy.

The new policy is that she will automatically be retained unless she requests a release or became pregnant during her initial indoctrination or training.

The Wave, whose name has been withheld, pointed to the anomalies of the policy she successfully fought. "If I had chosen to get an abortion," she wrote a congressman, "the Navy would not only have paid for it, but I would not have been forced to go through the mental harassment that I have."

Moreover, as she pointed out to her superiors, her status was no more of a burden on the service than if she'd been a divorced man or widower with custody of children.

It goes without saying that we don't recommend that unmarried women, in service or civilian life, get pregnant. But fair is fair. If a woman can do her job and wants to, having a child shouldn't disqualify her.

Alas! why must we be so selfish that we can feel nothing but that which touches ourselves, *our* hearts, *our* pleasures, or *our* pockets?

And since so many children are born into the world without competent protectors from its evils, why is innocence left in ignorance and poverty, to stumble and fall under temptation? And when is that ever-present enigma to be solved which Carlyle suggests as the great problem of life:—"So many shirts in the world, and so many shirtless backs; how to get the shirtless backs into the shirts?"

So many little unprotected children in the world, and so many rich men and women with warm human hearts; how to get these children into these hearts? How to show people who are anxious to save a suffering and perishing world, that the place to begin is the cradle, just as they would begin with a very young plant in order to fashion the tree in symmetry.

Inquiries by the United States Commissioner of Education, seeking the solution of such problems, have elicited facts respecting the number and condition of the poor children in this city, which, it is believed, will be of interest to every thinking man and woman in the country.

How few residents of Manhattan Island realize, or are even aware of the fact, that within its confines are at least one hundred thousand children—the adjacent cities contain perhaps as many more—to whom the morning light on six days of the week brings only toil. For these children there are no schools, no nuttings in the woods, no bright walks in Central Park. They are prematurely burdened with the cares of life; dwarfed in stature from the lack of proper nutriment; by confinement in the bad air of workshops; by the bearing of heavy burdens, and the deprivation of such recreations as a normal childhood imperatively demands. They may be seen in the early morning, in all portions of the city, among the laboring throng, hastening with serious mien to the service of the day.

When Briareus-handed industry knocks at the gates of the morning, we are apt to think only of strong men and healthy women. But here, side by side with these, are frail little forms, too often but poorly protected against the wintry blast.

Did you, reader, ever reflect that many children begin the terrible struggle of life for food, shelter, and clothing, at an age when others are scarcely out of their cradles?

But in all these hundreds of occupations which busy the skilled fingers of little children, the greatest number, and those of the most tender age, are engaged in the preparation of feathers, flowers, and tobacco—mere luxuries, yet considered so indispensable by a majority of men and women.

Reader, if this fact should seem to you of any special significance, and if it should suggest serious thoughts occasionally, do not drive them away, but entertain them kindly. I do not desire to plant thorns in any of your flowers. Far from it. But may it not be hoped that the fine lady, luxuriating in forms of airy beauty, grace, and harmony will sometimes think pitifully and helpfully of the little children; that the man of ease, contentedly smoking his pipe or cigar, or rolling the sweet morsel under his tongue, may occasionally be carried in imagination to the filthy rooms where young children—almost babes—spend the long day in "stemming" the weed.

Do you think God intended childhood as a season for drudgery? If not, can any of you suggest some good plan by which the "rights" of children may be secured to them? Women who are already awake to some of the great issues of this city, will you now arouse more fully to the importance of educating the children? Is not the question a fundamental one? And the rights of all children once secured, will not the world then be right?

Ten thousand children, it is said, are working in tobacco, in New York and Brooklyn, for ten hours a day, six days of the week, and fully five thousand of them are believed to be under fifteen years of age. Children in many cases supply the places of more mature hands, and thus offer the employer an opportunity for gain not to be resisted as long as other manufacturers with whom he must compete employ this cheap labor.

Were stringent laws passed, similar to those existing in some of the New England States, regulating the employment of children under a certain age, many of the employers would accept the change, and would co-operate with others in arranging for a voluntary system of half-time schools; while not a few declare that such a system "wouldn't work," they "couldn't be bothered with it."

Tell them of the good results at Indian Orchard, and other places, from half-time schools, they say:—"O, in New England things can be done that can't be done anywhere else. Besides, in New England they work more hours than we do here. Our children can have an extra two hours for evening school."

In addition to the outrage of sacrificing the health and educational interests of children by keeping them at mechanical drudgery nearly all their waking hours, certain kinds of labor they perform are absolutely dangerous to life and limb. At the evening schools we heard of girls who, while working in twine manufactories, had lost one and two joints of their fingers. The principal of one school stated that last winter she had ten girls who had lost the initial finger from the right hand, and therefore could not be taught to write. One child, who learned to write with the left hand, came to school afterwards with the initial finger of that hand also gone. It was taken off in the twisting machinery at a twine factory.

It is expected that penalties must follow violations of the law of mechanics, as of other laws, but children should not be placed in situations where so sad a penalty is the result of a moment's inattention. Their innocence and ignorance appeal for protection against the possibility of such calamities. An engine of 150 horse-power, driving a balance-wheel of 18,000 pounds weight, is an irresistible force when it clashes with the little finger of a child. Should not children's fingers be protected from the destruction threatened by such machinery, in some manner, by law if not otherwise?

But if the situation of children engaged in regular employment is so sad, what can be said of those who are drifting about the streets of the city, without any real homes or steady employment, but supporting a miserable existence by such irregular work as they can obtain—living "by their wits." From fifteen to twenty thousand is considered a moderate estimate of the number of boys and girls situated thus in the midst of this great centre of wealth and refinement. Many of these are orphans — others worse than orphans — children of criminals and poor wretches sunk deep in the degradation of drunkenness. Some are runaways from other cities; some are children of emigrants whose parents die upon the way here; some have fathers in the army and no mothers; others have invalid mothers and no fathers. Their daily portion is hunger, cold, and misery of almost every description. They may be seen almost every day upon the street, bent double, staggering under heavy loads, sweeping the crossings, or begging.

From *Scribner's Monthly*, 1871.

Courtesy of UE News Service.

Catholic Worker Positions

The general aim of the Catholic Worker Movement is to realize in the individual and in society the expressed and implied teachings of Christ. It must, therefore, begin with an analysis of our present society to determine whether we already have an order that meets with the requirements of justice and charity of Christ.

The society in which we live and which is generally called capitalist (because of its method of producing wealth) and bourgeois (because of the prevalent mentality) is not in accord with justice and charity—

IN ECONOMICS—because the guiding principle is production for profit and because production determines needs. A just order would provide the necessities of life for all, and needs would determine what would be produced. From each according to his ability, to each according to his needs. Today we have a non-producing class which is maintained by the labor of others with the consequence that the laborer is systematically robbed of that wealth which he produces over and above what is needed for his bare maintenance.

IN PSYCHOLOGY—because capitalist society fails to take in the whole nature of man but rather regards him as an economic factor in production. He is an item in the expense sheet of the employer. Profit determines what type of work he shall do. Hence, the deadly routine of assembly lines and the whole mode of factory production. In a just order the question will be whether a certain type of work is in accord with human values, not whether it will bring a profit to the exploiters of labor.

IN MORALS—because capitalism is maintained by class war. Since the aim of the capitalist employer is to obtain labor as cheaply as possible and the aim of labor is to sell itself as dearly as possible and buy the products produced as cheaply as possible there is an inevitable and persistent conflict which can only be overcome when the capitalist ceases to exist as a class. When there is but one class the members perform different functions but there is no longer an employer-wage-earner relationship.

TO ACHIEVE THIS SOCIETY WE ADVOCATE:

A complete rejection of the present social order and a non-violent revolution to establish an order more in accord with Christian values. This can only be done by direct action since political means have failed as a method for bringing about this society. Therefore we advocate a personalism which takes on ourselves responsibility for changing conditions to the extent that we are able to do so. By establishing Houses of Hospitality we can take care of as many of those in need as we can rather than turn them over to the impersonal "charity" of the State. We do not do this in order to patch up the wrecks of the capitalist system but rather because there is always a shared responsibility in these things and the call to minister to our brother transcends any consideration of economics. We feel that what anyone possesses beyond basic needs does not belong to him but rather to the poor who are without it.

We believe in a withdrawal from the capitalist system so far as each one is able to do so. Toward this end we favor the establishment of a Distributist economy wherein those who have a vocation to the land will work on the farms surrounding the village and those who have other vocations will work in the village itself. In this way we will have a decentralized economy which will dispense with the State as we know it and will be federationist in character as was society during certain periods that preceded the rise of national states.

We believe in worker-ownership of the means of production and distribution, as distinguished from nationalization. This to be accomplished by decentralized co-operatives and the elimination of a distinct employer class. It is revolution from below and not (as political revolutions are) from above. It calls for widespread and universal ownership by all men of property as a stepping stone to a communism that will be in accord with the Christian teaching of detachment from material goods and which, when realized, will express itself in common ownership. "Property, the more common it is, the more holy it is," St. Gertrude writes.

We believe in the complete equality of all men as brothers under the Fatherhood of God. Racism in any form is blasphemy against God who created all mankind in His image and who offers redemption to all. Man comes to God freely or not at all and it is not the function of any man or institution to force the Faith on anyone. Persecution of any people is therefore a serious sin and denial of free will.

We believe further that the revolution that is to be pursued in ourselves and in society must be pacifist. Otherwise it will proceed by force and use means that are evil and which will never be outgrown, so that they will determine the END of the revolution and that end will again be tyranny. We believe that Christ went beyond natural ethics and the Old Dispensation in this matter of force and war and taught non-violence as a way of life. So that when we fight tyranny and injustice and the class war we must do so by spiritual weapons and by non-cooperation. Refusal to pay taxes, refusal to register for conscription, refusal to take part in civil-defense drills, non-violent strikes, withdrawal from the system are all methods that can be employed in this fight for justice.

We believe that success, as the world determines it, is not the criterion by which a movement should be judged. We must be prepared and ready to face seeming failure. The most important thing is that we adhere to these values which transcend time and for which we will be asked a personal accounting, not as to whether they succeeded (though we should hope that they do) but as to whether we remained true to them even though the whole world go otherwise.

"Positions" published by *Catholic Worker*.

Editorials

Unsolicited Business

A prostitute has been defined as a person, usually a woman, who has sexual intercourse for money. An expanded definition is a woman who gets paid for not rejecting another, i.e., the customer.

Interestingly, the definition of a prostitute as one who receives money for not rejecting sums up rather nicely women's role in society at large. Women in their social functions, as lover, mother, and wife, are trained not to reject, but to give. For the glory of the family, as it's called. In return, by convention, women are umbrellaed under a contract of perpetual care. So are cemetaries.

Likewise, the corporation's female staff ("the girls") is hired not to reject. As secretaries, administrative assistants, and girl fridays, women are hired not to reject the boss' sexual attentions, fantasies, whims or well-paid courtships. The solicited woman stands or falls alone, but all of us have a responsibility to react to sexism whether in employment or advertising.

Even if accepted into the male job hierarchy, a woman should alert new employees to the boss' sexual harassment and stalking patterns. Women in all job levels, including corporate executives, should support others who resist. Notably, women most often preyed upon by "corporate johns" are those in the lower strata with the least power and influence in the business world. Women who yield to the situation are equally in need of support. Whether a woman accepts or rejects, she loses; she should not be ostracized.

The sexist nature of the situation is heightened because it is the younger, prettier women who are chosen; often the older less attractive women take satisfaction in the individual's dilemma or relish the office gossip.

Sexual offensiveness must be confronted. Suggested actions are: organize office guerrilla campaigns against offending executives, know how and where to activate existing laws to prevent job harassment, and hold advertisers responsible for demeaning copy by writing letters to those advertisers and their competitors.

Boycott their products.

News, Ethics and Negotiations

FOR SOME TIME, a debate has been going on with respect to the ethics of those who bring you the news each day. It concerns such questions as whether it is ever proper for a reporter to accept any form of gift or gratuity from a news source; whether the outside activities of reporters and editors should be known to the people they work for and to their readers; whether journalists should accept free tickets to sporting and cultural events granted merely and specifically because of their association with a news-gathering organization. Most of those questions have been argued informally within news organizations and between journalists and their outside critics.

Now, it appears, the debate has been given a more formal structure. Last week, Judge Nancy M. Sherman of the National Labor Relations Board issued a ruling against the Madison (Wisconsin) Capital Times that is sure to be appealed. Judge Sherman found for the Capital Times Unit of the American Newspaper Guild, which had charged the editor-publisher of the Capital Times with unfair labor practices. The reason for the charge was that the editor, Miles McMillin, had set forth a code of ethical behavior he said he expected editorial employees to follow. The union charged that such a code was a proper subject for negotiation, that the editor could not enforce such a code on his own.

It is impossible to guess where the full NLRB will come out, should the controversy go that far. As matters now stand, the variety of permissible practices is almost as extensive as the number of news organizations. Some newspapers permit their employees to accept free trips worth hundreds, if not thousands, of dollars from groups that have an interest in what the reporters write. Often, nothing specific, save "goodwill" is expected in return—and often something is. Sometimes a "good" story is expected by the donor.

Judge Sherman argues in her opinion that it is all right for a newspaper to try to promulgate a code of ethics, but that since such a code necessarily affects the economic life of reporters, it must be a subject of negotiation. Judge Sherman's ruling is framed within her understanding of the National Labor Relations Act. We do not share her certainty, however, that ethics are negotiable, since we believe that a newspaper's principles are more than a summary of labor-management contracts.

Judge Sherman's opinion asserts, for example, that if a reporter knows that certain gifts are likely to result from working for a particular newspaper, then the newspaper management cannot eliminate the reporter's right to accept those gifts without bargaining on the subject. "I find," said Judge Sherman, "that the receipt of 'freebies' usable in connection with coverage constitutes, at least presumptively, wages and working conditions which are a mandatory subject of collective bargaining."

By that reasoning, once a reporter on a newspaper has become accustomed to these extra emoluments, they cannot be denied by order of the management—even if management believes such practices undermine the credibility and independence of the newspaper. Here we are faced with a conflict between the state of labor law and the requirement of newspapers to shun even the appearance of impropriety.

To allow a lengthy negotiation process to be the sole basis on which a newspaper's ethical standards are established could make it possible for a dizzying array of standards to prevail in the meantime. In the best of all possible worlds, responsible journalists will know better than to accept gifts from news sources and subjects, to accept some form of side employment with those they may be called on to cover or to accept membership in groups and organizations in which they have a journalistic interest and which have a particular interest in their treatment by the press. Because journalists are human and subject to all the frailties that go with that condition, rules help. This newspaper, for instance, expects its reporters to accept no gifts or other emoluments from their sources or those about whom they write. Some other newspapers do the same. There is no way to tell what the impact of the Sherman ruling will be in American journalism, but we still believe in the old fashioned right—indeed, duty—of a paper to set its standards for ethical conduct, and we hope that view prevails as the Capital Times case goes through the courts

227

Now...A Word from the Strikers...

Western Union Can <u>Easily</u> Afford Fair Pay and Security

That's What This Strike Is All About!

SOME MATTERS OF PRINCIPLE

Of course we're sorry that our strike, by closing down every Western Union telegraph office in the nation, has caused inconvenience to the general public. But the root cause of this shut-down lies in Western Union management policies that forced us, as self-respecting citizens, to go on strike.

Three very important principles are involved in this walkout. For instance:

☐ Must working men and women forever take second place to computers and new technology? Don't we deserve to be treated as well as machines? Should we be expected to subsidize machines?

☐ Does a prospering company like Western Union have a moral right to talk out of both sides of its mouth at once . . . to boast about high profits when it speaks to stockholders, to cry poverty when it talks to its employees?

☐ Does Western Union truly serve the communications needs of the nation when it rushes ahead with programs to curtail telegraph service to the public, to close many hundreds of present telegraph offices, to slow down still further the transmission and delivery of telegrams?

We think not.

Yet these matters of principle are all involved in this strike.

AN OPEN LETTER TO ALL STRIKING LOCAL 1199 EMPLOYEES

The tragedy of the 1199 strike continues. The safety and lives of our patients are in danger. The fear and worry of the patients' relatives are great. Thousands of our fellow New Yorkers cannot get the services of our hospitals that they need.

This strike was called for two reasons:

- For the full wage increase of $12. or 7½%.
- And to bring to the attention of the public and government officials the delay in arriving at a decision by the Cost of Living Council.

THE WAGE INCREASE:

You know that you already have 5½% guaranteed. Therefore, the wage issue at stake in this terrible strike is 2%. As of tomorrow, you will have lost one weeks' pay—the equivalent of 2% of your annual salary!

PUBLIC AND GOVERNMENT OFFICIALS:

The strike has disrupted vital health services. It has created the worst health emergency New York has ever seen. The Mayor, Governor, Senators and Congressmen and many other government officials are feverishly working to solve this tragic matter.

The point has been made and there is no public official in the city, state or federal government who has not been pressured to act. **As we have done before many times the League of Voluntary Hospitals and Homes has expressed to all these officials the support of all of its member institutions for full implementation of the arbitration award.** To continue this walkout would be senseless, illogical and demeaning to you as compassionate human beings.

You have nothing else to gain. You have made the impression you walked out for. Contrary to what has been stated by the union, we all know now that the delay in arriving at a decision was due to the labor unions' representatives on the Cost of Living Council, including Mr. Max Greenberg, the President of Local 1199's International Union.

To continue to punish the men, women and children needing the care, attention and support of all hospital employees would be criminal.

MEMBERS OF THE
LEAGUE OF VOLUNTARY HOSPITALS AND HOMES OF NEW YORK
60 EAST 42nd STREET, NEW YORK, N.Y. 10017

Courtesy of the League of Voluntary Hospitals and Homes of New York.

An Important Statement By Important People About The Shell Strike

The following statement was issued by the undersigned people regarding our strike at the Shell Oil Company. We believe it deserves the thoughtful consideration of everyone who is concerned about the world we live in and the way we live in it.

Last January, the Oil, Chemical and Atomic Workers International Union (OCAW) struck Shell Oil refineries and called for a boycott of Shell oil and chemicals. This strike is unique in labor history, being exclusively prompted by concerns for occupational health rather than by labor's traditional preoccupations and wages.

Earlier this year, OCAW negotiated new contracts with all major oil companies which established the basic, but innovative, principle of joint management-labor responsibilities for protecting workers' health. Shell and Chevron refused to agree to this principle and insist on maintaining unilateral control over occupational health and safety.

The major provisions of these contracts are:

—Periodic inspections of plants, by independent consultants, jointly approved by labor and management, to determine whether workers are being exposed to hazards.

—Medical examination of workers, at company expense, when indicated by inspections.

—Availability to the Union of all future company records on workers' sickness and death.

dustrial use, 500 new chemicals are introduced annually. Existing standards relate to only 450 of these chemicals, are obsolete, ignore delayed toxic effects, particularly cancer and chronic respiratory disease, and are poorly enforced.

Despite recent conclusions by an *ad hoc* HEW committee of international authorities in carcinogenesis, that *no* exposure level to carcinogens is safe, many workers are continuingly exposed to potent occupational carcinogens, including asbestos, benzidine, 2-naphthylamine, 4-aminodiphenyl and bis—(chloromethyl) ether and occupational radiation exposure, particularly in the growing nuclear industry and in uranium mines. Some 1,100 of 6,000 Western uranium miners will probably die of lung cancer in the next 20 years. Of 50,000 insulation workers, 20,000 are likely to die of asbestosis or cancer. The fate of 3.5 million others already exposed to lower levels of asbestos will remain unknown for 20 years. Recently, bladder tumors have been found in 16 percent of 315 workmen exposed to the rubber antioxidant 4-aminodiphenyl.

The major objective of the 1970 Occupational Safety and Health Act is "... to ensure so far as possible every working man and woman in the nation safe and healthful working conditions ..." Implementation of the Act has, however, been ineffective. There are fewer than 100 qualified Occupational, Safety and Health Administration (OSHA) industrial hygienists and only about 500 OSHA inspectors for 4 million workplaces. OSHA has promulgated only one permanent standard, for asbestos. This standard, reflecting the epidemic of asbestosis and asbestos-induced lung and other cancers, particularly in insulation workers, however, will not be implemented until 1976. Labor has consequently recognized that vigorous enforcement of the Act demands its own initiatives.

The scope of occupational hazards is generally unrecognized. Of 80 million workers, there are over 7 million annual work-related diseases and injuries, of which 2 million are disabling and 14,500 fatal—more than the number of U.S. servicemen killed yearly in Viet Nam. Industrial disability results in losses of 250 million-man working days—ten times more than from strikes—costing $1.5 billion in wages and an annual loss to the GNP of $8 billion.

This situation is progressively deteriorating. The incidence of disabling injuries in manufacturing industries is now 20 percent greater than in 1958. Apart from over 10,000 chemicals in widespread in-

The growing recognition that most human cancers are environmentally induced and hence preventable has had no apreciable impact on occupational practice. Imposition of a zero tolerance for certain occupational carcinogens—as promulgated for carcinogenic food additives by the 1958 Delaney Amendment, and minimizing exposure to all categories of carcinogens—would be a major step towards practical implementation of the President's Cancer Conquest Program to prevent, besides treat, cancer.

Workers have long served as unwitting "guinea pigs", providing useful toxicological data which helped to protect the public. The effects of most environmental pollutants, such as carbon monoxide, lead, mercury and also of most human carcinogens were first detected in workmen; the in-plant environment is a concentrated toxic microcosm of that outside. Additionally, many toxic agents disperse beyond the plant and post public hazards.

The success of the OCAW strike is critical both to labor and the public. This has already been recognized by ten major environmental and public interest groups who have endorsed the Shell strike and boycott. The demand of labor to participate actively in protecting the health and safety of workers is basic and inalienable and cannot be sacrificed to narrow economic interests. It is hoped that Shell will adopt a posture more consistent with the public interest and the intent of the 1970 Occupational Safety and Health Act and follow the example of other oil companies.

OIL, CHEMICAL & ATOMIC WORKERS INTERNATIONAL UNION, AFL-CIO

A. F. Grospiron, *President*
1636 Champa Street
Denver, Colorado 80201

Left and right page, published by special permission of the Oil, Chemical and Atomic Workers International Union, AFL-CIO/CLC, P.O. Box 2812, Denver, Colo. 80201.

SECTION 11

Civil Disobedience

Many of the arguments in most of the sections of this book are concerned either directly or indirectly with the question of whether or not certain acts (e.g., abortion, drug use, handgun ownership, sale of pornography, and sale of term papers, to name just a few) should be prohibited by law. The arguments in this section are primarily concerned with the question of whether or not under any circumstances whatsoever it is morally right to commit an act which is prohibited by law. The question can be formulated in many ways which range from relatively minor violations (such as breaking the speed limit to get a dying person to a hospital) to the extreme of overthrow of the entire legal system (revolution). The most violent form of this last extreme is what is today referred to as "terrorism."

"Give unto Caesar that which is Caesar's and unto God that which is God's." This is one of the oldest statements of the theory that there are two kinds of duty—moral and legal. Statements such as this suggest that this is a simple, clear-cut dichotomy, that all cases fall directly into one category or the other. In point of fact, many of our laws are essentially codifications of basic moral rules and principles, in direct contradiction of the adage that "You can't legislate morality." The difficult questions arise when there is a direct conflict between moral and legal rules. And since in a democratic system, when a majority of the population believes that if a law is in conflict with moral principles the law should be changed, the most difficult questions are those focussed on cases in which an individual's moral judgment is in conflict with the moral beliefs of the majority of the society, as well as of the laws of that society. In cases where the democratic process is not functioning, the question of opposition to the law and violation of it requires the consideration of additional factors, including the problem of identifying the "will of the majority."

EXERCISES

1. Examine the working draft of the United States Declaration of Independence. Discuss the significance of each of the changes in wording in the various versions with regard to the extent to which each change strengthens or weakens the support provided for the conclusion that it was right for the American colonies to overthrow the laws of the English government. Is this argument in any way relevant to the discussion of violating any of the laws of the United States government today? Does this argument in any way provide justification for various acts of terrorism in the United States or in other areas of the world today?

2. Examine the arguments in the examples in this chapter to determine if there is any significant difference between cases in which the law is violated openly and the violator is willing to accept the prescribed punishment for that violation and cases in which the violator attempts to act in secret and to avoid punishment.

3. Discuss the question of whether or not one can justify the violation of a moral principle on the grounds that to do so would be to break a law of the society.

Editing the Declaration

THE DECLARATION OF INDEPENDENCE underwent numerous changes, mostly minor but some major, before Congress approved it last week. The editing process is illustrated in key excerpts. The words that are crossed out and replaced in roman type are alterations made after Thomas Jefferson consulted with John Adams and Benjamin Franklin. The bracketed words were cut and the italicized words were added by the Congress.

"When in the course of human events it becomes necessary for one ~~a~~ people to ~~advance from that subordination in which they~~ another, and to ~~have hitherto remained, & to~~ assume among the powers of the separate and equal earth the ~~equal & independent~~ station to which the laws of nature & of nature's god entitle them, a decent respect to the opinions of mankind requires that they should declare the causes which impel them to the separation. ~~the change.~~

"We hold these truths to be self-evident; ~~sacred & undeniable~~; that all men are created equal ~~& independent~~; that they are endowed from that equal by their creator with ~~equal rights, some of which are~~ ~~creation they derive in rights~~ certain [inherent &] in-rights; that these alienable* ~~among~~ which these are ~~the preservation of~~ life, liberty, & the pursuit of happiness; that to secure these rights ends, governments are instituted among men, deriving their just powers from the consent of the governed; that whenever any form of government ~~shall~~ becomes destructive of these ends, it is the right of the people to alter or to abolish it. . ."

The Declaration then lists 27 specific charges against King George III. Among the most important:

"he has refused his assent to laws the most wholesome and necessary for the public good:. . .

"he has dissolved, Representative houses repeatedly [& continually], for opposing with manly firmness his invasions on the rights of the people:. . .

"he has [suffered] *obstructed* the administration of justice states [totally to cease in some of these colonies]. . .

"he has made [our] judges dependent on his will alone. . .

"he has kept among us in times of peace standing armies [& without the consent of our legislatures: ships of war],

"he has combined with others to subject us to a jurisdiction foreign to our constitutions and unacknowledged by our laws; acts of giving his assent to their pretended ~~acts of~~ legislation. . . for cutting off our trade with all parts of the world; for imposing taxes on us without our consent; for depriving us *in many cases* of the benefits of trial by jury. . ."

The Declaration concludes:

"We therefore the representatives of the United states of America in General Congress assembled *appealing to the supreme judge of the world for the rectitude of our intentions,* do, in the name & by authority of the good people of these [states, reject & renounce all allegiance & subjection to the kings of Great Britain . . . & finally we do assert & declare these colonies to be free & independent states,] *colonies, solemnly publish and declare, that these United colonies are, and of right ought to be, free & independent states; that they are absolved from all allegiance to the British crown . . .* & that as free & independent states they ~~shall hereafter~~ full have power to levy war, conclude peace, contract alliances, establish commerce, & to do all other acts and things which independent states may of right do. And for the support of this declaration, *with a firm reliance on the protection of divine providence,* we mutually pledge to each other our lives, our fortunes & our sacred honour."

*This word was changed — to "unalienable" — apparently by the first printer, John Dunlap of Philadelphia.

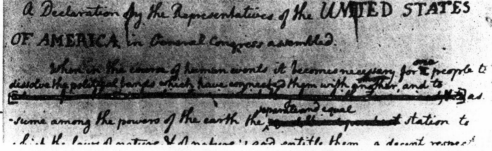

SCIENCE

Concerning Dissent and Civil Disobedience

What rights are exercised, and what rights are violated, when students forcibly occupy a campus building, when participants in the Poor People's Campaign march to the U.S. Capitol with the intention of being arrested there, or when critics oppose the war in Vietnam? Abe Fortas, newly appointed Chief Justice of the Supreme Court, has written an admirably brief and clear explanation* of the constitutional principles involved.

The need to understand the principles will continue. The war in Vietnam is not the first and may not be the last unpopular war. Much has been achieved in the removal of racial discrimination, but the much is still too little. Justified student complaint must be distinguished from disruptive intent. The dean of Howard University's Law School has described the dilemma of his students in wanting to follow the law yet wanting to change radically our legal and social structure. The reformer's appetite is increased, not satisfied, by moderate initial success. The need to understand the principles involved will not soon disappear.

The rights to dissent, to advocate social change, to oppose government policy and practice, to change government itself—all these, if carried out by peaceful means, are protected under the Constitution. Fortas writes: "Nowhere in the world—at no time in history—has freedom to dissent and to oppose governmental action been more broadly safeguarded than in the United States of America, today."

But the right to dissent runs into another right. "The Constitution seeks to accommodate two conflicting values, each of which is fundamental: the need for freedom to speak freely, to protest effectively, to organize, and to demonstrate; and the necessity of maintaining order so that other people's rights, and the peace and security of the state, will not be impaired." It is actions, therefore, rather than motives or thoughts that must be judged. No matter how nobly motivated, actions that endanger others or infringe their rights are unlawful and subject to punishment.

Yet sometimes one feels it his duty to disobey a law he considers immoral, and Justice Fortas writes: "I am a man of the law. I have dedicated myself to uphold the law. . . . But if I . . . had been a Negro living in Birmingham or Little Rock or Plaquemines Parish, Louisiana, I hope I would have disobeyed the state law that said I might not enter the public waiting room reserved for 'Whites.' "

If the route of disobedience is taken, the consequences must be accepted. Acting in the great tradition of true civil disobedience, Dr. Martin Luther King warned that Negroes would disobey unjust laws, and then insisted that the disobedience be open and peaceful and that those who disobeyed accept the consequences. It may seem unduly harsh to fine or jail a person who violates a law he believes immoral or unconstitutional, but this is the rule of law—the rule of law that is essential to the procedure we have developed to protect dissent and to encourage peaceful change. The objectives of a particular movement or protest may be of great importance for the quality of our lives, but preservation of the procedure is our guarantee of future change and improvement.

In a time of troubled disagreements, when the term *civil disobedience* is widely misapplied, Mr. Fortas offers help to protestors and activists in understanding their rights and the limitations on those rights, and a guide to other persons in formulating standards for judging the actions they watch with fear, with wonder, or with sympathy.—DAEL WOLFLE

*Abe Fortas, *Concerning Dissent and Civil Disobedience* (New American Library of World Literature, New York, 1968), 64 pages, paper, 50¢.

Above, "Concerning Dissent and Civil Disobedience," by Dael Wolfle in *Science*, 161, p. 9, July 5, 1968. Copyright 1968 by The American Association for the Advancement of Science.

Right, letter to the editor of *Science* by Donald A. Strickland, September 13, 1968.

It is surprising to encounter solecisms in Wolfle's editorial. Justice Fortas, whose recent essay *Concerning Dissent and Civil Disobedience* stimulated the editorial, is permitted such legerdemain: Fortas is a lawyer, and lawyers are trained to confound and to employ logic dialectically.

1) The freedom "to speak freely and protest effectively" (*ex Fortas*) is activity and entails further activities. So it makes no sense to say that exercises of First Amendment rights must be judged by the consequent actions "rather than motives or thoughts." To imagine such a disjunction between motives, thoughts, and behavior is not only to subscribe to a passé legal fiction, but also to consign science and the intelligentsia to the status of a bauble.

2) Actions which "endanger others and infringe on their rights" are of course, *ex def.*, "unlawful" if reference is to positive law. (That is not quite accurate, since official action that endangers people *is* lawful, except in cases where subsequently it is officially decided to have been unlawful.)

3) To assert next that "the [legal] consequences must be accepted" by those who disobey laws which they deem to be immoral is to beg the question altogether—the question being, under what circumstances, if any, should the law be set aside to satisfy the claims of morality? The reasoning of the editorial could not distinguish Eichmann from Dr. Spock, because it values legal coercion for its own sake.

4) "The rule of law" is offered as the logical and ethical underpinning of this line of thought. To be sure, the rule of law is not a term of art among jurists. It is a political slogan which celebrates the values of compliance and due process. What it means is that disputes should be settled according to rules agreed upon in advance of the dispute, administered impersonally, and stated sufficiently precisely for people to be able to anticipate the risks of liability. Hence, "the rule of law" is procedural, has no substantive contents, and cannot possibly be relevant to political disputes in which the interpretation or validity of a particular law is in issue. . . .

Those who agreed with the sentiment behind Wolfle's editorial will be protesting to themselves that it was never intended to be understood in this way. That means that it was never intended to be understood, period; it was meant to be agreed with.

DONALD A. STRICKLAND
Department of Political Science,
Northwestern University,
Evanston, Illinois 60201

A Government of Laws, and Not of Men

Wolfle's editorial "Concerning dissent and civil disobedience" (5 July, p. 9), represents . . . unreal thinking. If one may disobey the law according to one's personal feelings then the only wrong that can be adjudged against Sirhan, Ray, or Oswald for their alleged offenses is that of resisting arrest, of "not accepting the consequences."

Personal physical violence is not included? Then how about destroying a man's home or business? No? How about just partially destroying them? How about hindering his means of livelihood? Where should the line be drawn?

The fact is that the basic statement is wrong. One is morally obligated to change a law he feels is wrong, not disobey it. As long as there are any legal means by which the law may be changed one must use them. The mere fact that a majority of people do not support the change gives no license to disobey, but only to work to make a majority see the need for the change.

No, I submit that "civil disobedience" in this country is wrong, a truly immoral act, and will remain so as long as we have a freely elected form of government and legal redress in the courts.

LESLIE M. BAGNALL
Department of Mechanical Engineering,
Texas A&M University,
College Station 77843

The editorial stated that "the term *civil disobedience* is widely misapplied." That term can be defined as the refusal to obey civil laws, especially, as Webster's puts it, "as a nonviolent collective means of forcing concessions from the government." The alleged crimes of Messrs. Sirhan, Ray, Oswald, and Eichmann are in a different domain.

Bagnall briefly, and Rhine more fully, hope we can rely on majority rule. So does the true civil dissenter (but not the violence monger who may come along at the same time). He accepts the principle of majority rule; he wants the majority to change a law; when he concludes that other means of persuasion will not succeed, he uses civil disobedience to emphasize and dramatize his case. He is saying, "I believe this law to be morally wrong. I believe it so strongly that I violate the law and expect to be punished. But I hope thereby to convince you that the law is wrong and that you should change it." Although he is violating a particular law, he accepts what Strickland called "rules agreed upon in advance" or the editorial called "the rule of law."

The sentiment behind the editorial was, I thought, clear and cogent. It is the desirability, in a period of much controversy—which concerns a variety of issues and is expressed in a variety of ways—of understanding the constitutional principles concerning dissent and civil disobedience, and of discriminating among the various means by which disagreements are expressed. I am sorry Strickland misunderstood.

DAEL WOLFLE

Left, letter to the editor of *Science* by Leslie M. Bagnall, September 13, 1968. Right, letter replying to critics of editorial by Dael Wolfle in *Science*, September 13, 1968.

College Prof Comments Magruder
'Corrupted by Power'

NEW HAVEN (UPI) — Jeb Stuart Magruder was told as a college student that he was a nice guy "but not a good man." Fifteen years later, a former teacher describes him as a man who has fallen victim to the corruption of power.

Yale University Chaplain William Sloan Coffin Jr. had Magruder, a key figure in the Watergate bugging scandal, in an ethics class at Williams College, Williamstown, Mass., during the 1958-59 academic year.

"He got corrupted by power," Coffin said in an interview Friday. "I think that a young guy is very vulnerable to the corruptions of power and his ambitions."

Magruder, testifying Thursday before the Senate Watergate Committee, cited Coffin's civil disobedience in the antiwar movement as a justification for his own violations.

But Coffin said there was a world of difference between what Magruder was doing and his own actions in protesting the war policies of the Johnson and Nixon administrations.

In everything that I did, it never infringed on the civil liberties of anybody else," Coffin said. "It was open and aboveboard and we were willing to take the consequences

'What he did was underground, invaded other people's privacy and he wasn't willing to take any consequences until he had been uncovered.

"I used to say to Jeb, 'You're a nice guy, Jeb, but not yet a good man. You have lots of charm but not yet a hard core.'"

Coffin and four other men, including Dr. Benjamin Spock, were arrested in January, 1968, and charged with conspiring to urge young men to evade the draft.

A year and a half later, Coffin, Spock and two other defendants were freed by a federal appeals court in Boston.

Coffin, whose anti-war activities included a trip to North Vietnam late last year, said his protests were in opposition to the illegal use of power.

'What he (Magruder) did, he did to secure that power," he said.

"There is a big difference between civil disobedience taken in the name of conscience which is not interfering with the private lives of anybody else and this type of criminal activity which is a distant invastion of other people's privacy simply in order to secure the power of the President."

'Not Yet a Good Man'

By William Sloane Coffin Jr.

NEW HAVEN—I was very fond of Jeb Magruder when we were together at Williams College. It was in 1958, his senior year and my first year as teacher and college chaplain. He and two classmates used to take my wife and me to dinner. He babysat for our daughter. Although we never saw each other after his graduation, for several years we corresponded.

During his time at Williams I worried about Jeb. I used to say to him: "You're a nice guy, Jeb, but not yet a good man. You have lots of charm but little inner strength. And if you don't stand for something you're apt to fall for anything."

When I saw him again on television testifying before Senator Ervin's committee, I was again drawn to him. While I do not excuse his conduct, I want to say something in explanation, for his testimony said as much about his education and American society as it did about Jeb himself.

In the 1950's students were agreeing their way through life. There was no civil rights movement to speak of and of course no antiwar movement. At Williams, as at so many exclusive colleges, there were few blacks, no Chicanos, no women and altogether too many fraternities which tended to promote an élitist team spirit, and breed a mistrust of healthy criticism. Professors everywhere were morally asleep. For the most part they represented the bland leading the bland.

Education was for making a living, not a life, to be traded upon rather than to be used to create a better world.

Jeb was very gregarious. He wanted to be liked. He had a much greater sense of himself when he was with others than when alone. As a natural winner, he conformed easily to the American success ethic of the day—popularity, power, money.

As his ethics teacher, I wish now I had stressed the errors and illusions that stem from the fear of being a loser in this particular game plan. I wish I had pointed out the paradox of winners being losers, and losers winners. I wish I had stressed the importance of solitude. I wish I had emphasized that it is the individual consciences of history which, as opposed to the mass mind, best represent the universal conscience of mankind.

Maybe these emphases would have helped Jeb to develop individual convictions. Certainly it would have helped his understanding of civil disobedience, for many of the great consciences of history—Moses, Jeremiah, Jesus, Socrates, Thoreau, Gandhi —many we today regard as heroes were notorious lawbreakers in their time.

I was shocked to hear Jeb lump all lawbreakers together. He should have known — and the Senators pressing him should have reminded a listening nation—that Martin Luther King and many in the antiwar movement were protesting what they considered to be illegal laws whose constitutionality could be tested only by a refusal to obey them. There is an enormous difference between trying to keep the nation under the law and trying to keep it under Nixon, between being a loyal servant of the Constitution and being a loyal servant only of the man who hires you.

If there are differences in ends so there are differences in means. Whatever Dr. King and Dr. Spock did they did openly. All America could see and judge. Jeb operated behind closed doors. Most of the people in the civil rights and antiwar movements were careful not to infringe on the civil liberties of other citizens. Jeb and his friends deliberately violated these liberties. When the Supreme Court declared against him, Dr. King went from Georgia to Alabama to take his punishment. The draft resisters who went to jail accepted theirs. But Jeb's crowd, far from accepting punishment, tried only to conceal their crimes. Dr. King and those who followed him disobeyed the law to protect it. It is a sad and savage irony if Government officials learn from the practitioners of civil disobedience that law is made to be circumvented.

Teaching is at best a precarious business; the rational mind is no match for an irrational will that needs to place popularity and power above truth. Nevertheless all of us who taught him, and American society as a whole, could have done better by Jeb. Now we have the opportunity to learn from him the ancient lesson that to do evil in this world you don't have to be evil—just a nice guy, not yet a good man.

The Rev. William Sloane Coffin Jr., is chaplain at Yale.

Article in *The New York Times* by the Reverend William Sloane Coffin, Jr., June 10, 1973.

Magruder on Watergate:
Ends Justify the Means

By JAMES M. NAUGHTON

Special to The New York Times

WASHINGTON, June 14—Government officials he respected had done it. The university professor of ethics he admired had done it. So Jeb Stuart Magruder had done it too, he told the Senate committee investigating the Watergate affair today. He had let the end justify the means.

Mr. Magruder, the former deputy director of the Committee for the Re-election of the President, displayed a controlled nervousness and was more than a little apologetic as he sat all day at the witness table relating in detail that he and an assortment of high officials—from the Attorney General to the President's lawyer—had planned, executed and then tried in vain to cover up the Watergate affair.

Q. I still can't quite come to grips with why you all had an expressed reservation about this and you still went ahead with it.

A. I knew you would get to this line of questioning, so why don't I give you what I think is the appropriate response here.

I had worked for some two years, three years, really, in the White House and at that time, I was mainly engaged in the activities trying to generate some support for the President. During that time, we had worked primarily relating to the war situation and worked with anti-war groups.

Student of Ethics

Now I had gone to college, as an example, under—and had a course in ethics as an example under William Sloane Coffin, whom I respect greatly. I have great regard for him. He was quoted the other day as saying, well, I guess Mr. Magruder failed my course in ethics. And I think he is correct.

During this whole time we were in the White House and during this time we were directly employed with trying to succeed with the President's policies we saw continuing violations of the law done by men like William Sloane Coffin. He tells me my ethics are bad. Yet he was indicted for criminal charges. He recommended on the Washington Monument grounds that students burn their draft cards and that we have mass demonstrations, shut down the city of Washington.

Now, here are ethical, legitimate people whom I respected. I respect Mr. Coffin tremendously. He was a very close friend of mine. I saw people I was very close to breaking the law without any regard for any other person's pattern of behavior or belief.

So consequently, when these subjects came up although I was aware they were illegal we had become somewhat inured to using some activities that would help us in accomplishing what we thought was a cause, a legitimate cause.

Now, that is absolutely incorrect; two wrongs do not make a right.

For the past year, I have obviously had to consider that and I understand completely that that was an absolute, incorrect decision. But that is basically, I think, the reason why that decision was made, because of that atmosphere that had occurred and to all of us who had worked in the White House, there was that feeling of resentment and of frustration at being unable to deal with issues on a legal basis.

I fully accept the responsibility of having made an absolutely disastrous decision, or at least having participated. I didn't make the decision, but certainly participated in it.

SENATOR ERVIN: I was very much impressed with your testimony about the climate that prevailed in the White House and afterwards in the committee to re-elect the President. As a matter of fact, was there not a fear there of Americans that dissented from policies of Government? You spoke about your former professor—

A. The Reverend Coffin. Yes.

Q. He just came down and demonstrated. There were a great many demonstrations, weren't there? A. He did quite a bit more than demonstrate.

Q. He was supposed to try to frustrate the draft. A. He did, and he participated in many activities that were considered illegal.

Q. You were disturbed at the demonstrations, weren't you, the people at the White House? A. Yes, sir. We were.

Q. The reason I asked the question, I have had to spend my time fighting such laws and legislative proposals as no-knock laws, preventive detention laws, the claim that there was an inherent right of the President to bug anybody suspected of domestic subversion, and things of that kind. And I just could not understand why people got so fearful.

A. I would characterize that at least my reaction was stronger after three years of working in that atmosphere than it had been before.

Q. I am familiar with that kind of atmosphere. I came up here during Joe McCarthy days when Joe McCarthy saw a Communist hiding under every rose bush and I have been here fighting the no knock laws and preventive detention laws and indiscriminate bugging by people who've found subversives hiding under every bed. In this nation, we have had a very unfortunate fear. And this fear went to the extent of deploring the exercise of personal rights for those who wanted to assemble and petition the Government for redress of grievances.

Some of it happened before you got into the White House and I am not blaming you, because even under a Democratic Administration, I had an investigation here where they became so afraid of people that they used military intelligence to spy on civilians whose only offense was that they were dissatisfied with the policies of the Government and assembled and petitioned for relief.

Now, I think that all grew out of this complement of fear, did not it, the whole Watergate incident?

A. I think from my own personal standpoint, I did lose some respect for the legal process simply because I did not see it working as I had hoped it would when I came here.

From The New York Times, June 14, 1973.

240

Spread of objections of conscience
must be halted

One thing must be made plain from the very beginning – demands for a defence tax (Wehrsteuer) must be accompanied by demands for a better army. Defence tax can only have a sound purpose if it is considered as a way to adapt general conscription to the age in which we live.

All considerations must be based on the duty of protecting the community. Providing external security is a binding commitment on everybody. This can be achieved in a number of ways. One of these is by becoming a soldier.

What we now understand by defending our country has been largely freed of the pathos of a personal sacrifice of life and limb.

NATO armies are trained for war, it is true. They must be able to fight. The martial spirit must not be extinguished.

But their military role is given a political interpretation. The army is a means of preventing war. It has to exist as a threat to others. Its deterrent effect is one of the cornerstones of the strategy of maintaining peace.

Diplomatic flexibility, political will, industrial power, technical organisation, economic opportunity and treaties of alliance are the other factors of our strategy.

Conscription and the soldiers thus provided are essential to external security. Soldiers are important but they do not stand at the centre of planning for this work-sharing strategy. Not all the young people liable for conscription are called up. A selection can be made among them.

Conscription must be interpreted differently than was once the case. It is no longer the reservoir for a large armed body. It must be compared with the readiness of the modern industrial nation to contribute to external security in a large number of fields.

In times of peace a measurable form of action for the security of the community is the financial contribution of the individual in preserving the common good.

Everyone pays for our external security by paying taxes. Those who do military service in addition are taking over further burdens.

Starting from the fact that everyone has to pay taxes and that events do not force everyone to do military service, a person cannot fail to come to the conclusion that a person who does military service should pay less.

Nobody will underestimate the technical difficulties involved in shifting various parts of the tax burden. The first thing to do is to work out the financial value of the service period.

The period during which a person is freed from paying taxes need not necessarily be the same as the time he spends in the reserves. How are people who want to serve yet are not recruited to be treated?

But really all these questions can be answered during the course of events. The main point to be recognised when discussing the problem of a defence tax is that the contribution to external security can take a number of forms.

Military service too must be viewed as a special type of defence tax. At the same time it must be freed from the myth that it is a *levée en masse*.

The old idea of the indissolubility of the right of the citizen to be provided with defence and his duty to provide it is no longer relevant in an industrial nation. We have become more sober. We are satisfied by the duty alone.

This type of attitude makes it easier for a government to approach the ideal production State. Even the mention of "military autonomy" could not be used to prevent modern interpretations of the role of army and State.

If military defence tax is to be understood as compensation, it is easy to draw up laws to satisfy the moral and political demands of soldiers for balanced personal treatment in a democracy.

The way would also be cleared for greater justice in the armed forces. The chance that often decides whether a person is conscripted or not has done a lot to contribute to the disinclination toward doing armed service.

Conscientious objection may be traced to the recognition that modern European war is no longer a battle between knights but a military form of mutual extermination. A sensitive conscience must be respected.

But a large number of young conscripts know that their role is to provide security. Many have understood what deterrent strategy entails.

The suspicion is therefore justified that there is a link between conscientious objection and the injustice surrounding conscription. There is no other explanation for the flood of applications to be excused military service on the grounds of conscientious objection.

11,446 applications have already been received in the first quarter of 1971. Six thousand applications were made during the whole of 1967, twelve thousand in 1968 and nineteen thousand in 1970.

It is estimated that by the end of 1971 more than 100,000 applications will have been made since the Bundeswehr was set up.

The Bundestag could not ignore this fact during its debate on the subject. Unorthodox action is necessary if the situation is to be changed.

Adelbert Weinstein
(Frankfurter Allgemeine Zeitung
für Deutschland, 12 May 1971)

Originally published in *Frankfurter Allgemeine Zeitung*, May 12, 1971.

REFLECTIONS OF A YOUNG DESERTER

by Scott Udall

For the moment Stewart Udall's son can't—and maybe won't—go home again

I am told there is a distinct possibility that a President or Congress will declare an amnesty within a few years after America's complete withdrawal from Vietnam. The recent national publicity amnesty has received in numerous magazine and newspaper articles gives an idea of its prominence as an issue. In addition, the growing number of statesmen and organizations working toward amnesty illustrates the substantial support the issue has received at this decidedly early time.

However, the possibility of an amnesty does not affect my desire to apply for Canadian citizenship in two and a half years. I, like most Americans who have refused induction or deserted from the Armed Forces, do not believe that I have committed a criminal act, as is implied by amnesty.

On the other hand, I think amnesty would be an important element in bridging the enormous gap now dividing the American people. The Vietnam war has deeply affected the soul of America. I see the protest of many young Americans as a rejection of the U.S. militarism and an awakening of a new consciousness with more humanistic values.

In the long run, to me the greatest political danger to the United States now is the possibility of the further militarization of American life. A graphic testament to the grip of militarism on the minds of U.S. citizens is seen in the fact that Washington, D.C., the nation's capital, has more than one hundred statues and monuments to military men and only one monument to a poet or philosopher.

I deserted because I hoped that news of my desertion would reach the men in power, and that this news would help shock them into realizing that something was wrong in America. Why would the son of such a respected public servant as Stewart Udall desert the Armed Forces? This is the question I wanted people to ask themselves.

From the beginning, whatever the final reasons were that made thousands of young Americans become "War Resisters," we have expressed by our actions a belief in life and basic human values. I think that we have won a victory for humanity and the right of individual conscience.

Among the soldiers slaughtered in the bloody, useless trench warfare of 1915 was Charles Hamilton Sorley, twenty, a young man who showed promise of being one of England's great poets. Sorley accepted the call to military duty in World War I, but as he trained for the trenches he began to question the senseless patriotism that is part of the war-making of all nations. He wrote these words in a letter to a friend:

"There is no such thing as a just war. What we are doing is casting out Satan by Satan. England—I am sick of the sound of the word. In training to fight for England, I am training to fight for that deliberate hypocrisy, that terrible middle-class sloth of outlook and appalling 'imaginative indolence' that has marked us out from generation to generation. Indeed I think that after the war all brave men will renounce their country and confess that they are strangers and pilgrims on the earth."

My own feeling is that most of the scattered war resisters from the United States were cornered in a terrible time that made them choose as a matter of conscience to be "strangers and pilgrims on the earth." I know the personal heartache and pain of many of these men and their desire to return to their families.

I wonder whether America will ever again have a strong but gentle President like Lincoln who will dare to speak again the words, "With malice toward none, with charity for all . . ." and end the homeless odyssey of these men?   ⧺

AMNESTY AND THE PEACE

STAFF EDITORIAL

The war is over! The Vietnamese and Cambodian peoples have defeated the United States and its client governments in Saigon and Phnom Penh. This is a momentous victory for Indochina and a cause for great rejoicing for all Americans who opposed the war which was wrongly fought in our name.

Faced with the collapse of thirty years of U.S. policy in Indochina, President Ford and Secretary of State Kissinger have suddenly switched to the Bicentennial rhetoric of national unity. They say let's forget about the 56,000 GIs killed, the more than 300,000 wounded, and the more than $150 billion squandered in aid. Let's forget about anti-personnel weapons, chemical defoliants and poisons, My Lai's, etc. Let's look to the future greatness of America. Let's bind up the domestic wounds caused by the war.

It is all too easy for war resisters to see through this phony reconciliation line. "No recriminations" rings rather hollow on the ears of people who have been told they must submit to two years of forced labor ("alternate service"), loyalty oaths and less-than-honorable ("Clemency") discharges in order to "earn their way back" into American society. And the thousands of civilian resisters and half million badly discharged veterans who were not even covered by Ford's so-called "Clemency" program must wonder exactly whom the President wants to reconcile with whom?

All the evidence indicates that he wishes to reconcile middle America to the warmakers. In White House lingo, "no recriminations" translates to "let's not have a national debate about our Indochina War policy." Too many people might learn the truth. They might learn that the war was not a result of good intentions gone sour or an aberration of policy. It was a war to protect the interests of the American empire. It was a war fought neither in the interests of the Indochinese nor the American people, but in the interest of that small minority which controls our economy and formulates government policies.

For war resisters and supporters in the amnesty movement, the war is not over until we win universal and unconditional amnesty, and in the process help others to understand what we were forced to learn about the nature and meaning of the war. A recent "Open letter to the American people" from AMEX-Canada and the Toronto American Exiles' Association (TAEA) put it this way: "The fight for total amnesty should not merely concern itself with winning back our rights, but also must be an instrument with which to drive home a fuller understanding of America's Thirty Years' War. In a wider sense, it is the struggle to win the right to resist unjust, imperial wars." And the sooner we forget the last war, the sooner we'll be ready for the next . . .

NCUUA's statement of purpose calls on us to educate the American people concerning the structures and institutions that created the war in Southeast Asia. There could not be a better time than now to make this commitment real, and to make it the context for the campaign for total amnesty and real peace—meaning no more U.S. wars of aggression.

Courtesy of National Council for Universal and Unconditional Amnesty (NCUUA) staff: Fred Adler, Dick Bucklin, Gerry Condon, Dee Knight, Irma Zigas.

Amnesty?

Naturally, a great deal of sentimentality surrounds the entire issue of amnesty for draft-dodgers and deserters now residing abroad, mostly in Canada and Sweden. The President is asked to be "generous," Lincoln's example is invoked, the cry goes up to forgive and forget. Yet all of this should not be allowed to obscure the profound political and philosophical issues raised by the amnesty demands.

First of all, be it noted, the individuals now in exile chose not to plead conscientious objection through the established legal channels. Many other men did take this course. Indeed, the grounds for claiming CO status have been greatly broadened in recent years by the Supreme Court. Virtually all an individual now must do is demonstrate good faith when he claims opposition to war.

The demand being made by and for the draft-dodgers and deserters is for a different thing altogether. To be sure, the two categories must be distinguished, and, at the appropriate time, individual cases would naturally be judged on their merits. But right now, both groups are demanding in essence the right not to have served in this particular war, about which, they further stipulate, their judgment differed from that of the nation's elected leaders and other officials of its legitimate government. What they are demanding as a group, therefore, is the right to formulate and act upon a foreign policy of their own, different from the foreign policy of the United States Government.

It is not surprising, accordingly, that the demand for amnesty has been taken up by the antiwar politicians and spokesmen in the United States; but it would be very surprising if the demand were acceded to by the very government which prosecuted the war.

Furthermore, to grant this demand would be to extend to dissenters in the future a right of veto over the nation's foreign policy. No responsible, legitimate government can do this. At the present time, then, the draft-dodgers and deserters constitute a kind of countergovernment in exile, a countergovernment with numerous allies within the country, and, like them, resting claims to legitimacy on superior moral insight.

Contrary to what is being asserted by proponents of amnesty, there has never, following any American war, been a general amnesty for draft-dodgers and deserters.

1. The familiar comparison with Civil War "amnesty" turns out to be fallacious. In 1863, before the end of the war, Lincoln offered pardons to Confederates who took an oath of loyalty to the Union. This was clearly a psywar gambit against the Confederacy. In 1865 Lincoln offered full pardons to Union military deserters, provided they returned to their units within 60 days to serve out a period of time equal to their original enlistments. In 1865, 1867, and 1868, full pardon was offered to all Confederates taking the oath of allegiance. In 1866, President Johnson allowed deserters to return to military duty without punishment, but with forfeiture of pay. Conclusion: Neither during nor after the Civil War was there a general or unconditional amnesty.

2. In 1924, President Coolidge granted amnesty to one hundred deserters; but all hundred had deserted after the November 11, 1918 armistice. In 1933, FDR granted amnesty to 1,500 men who had violated the draft and espionage laws during the war—but only *after* they had completed their sentences.

3. Some 28 months after V-J Day, President Truman pardoned 1,523 out of 15,803 violators of the draft law, a ratio of 1 in 10. Those pardoned had received favorable recommendations, upon individual review, by his Amnesty Board.

4. There was no amnesty after Korea. In December 1952, President Truman granted amnesty to peacetime deserters: those who had left their units between V-J Day and the outbreak of war in Korea in June 1950.

A review of the 34 instances of amnesty in U.S. history, dating back to George Washington's 1795 pardon of participants in the Whisky Rebellion who agreed to obey the law, shows that there has never been an unconditional amnesty for draft-dodgers or deserters following any war; for the simple reason that the Federal Government has never been willing to recognize the sovereign claims of a countergovernment composed of its own citizens.

Reprinted with permission from *National Review* (March 16, 1973), 150 East 35th Street, New York, N.Y. 10016.

Exile Or Prosecution
Draft-Dodgers' Choice

A MAN who renounced his U.S. citizenship four years ago to avoid the draft has now come face to face with the consequences of his act. A Supreme Court decision has confirmed that he is a "man without a country" and faces deportation.

Although Thomas Glenn Jolley took the unusual step of formally foreswearing his birthright, he is not alone in being divorced from his native land as a result of his determination to escape military service. American draft-dodgers and military deserters in Canada, Sweden and elsewhere are more or less in the same boat. Although they may still claim U.S. citizenship, they must choose between self-imposed exile or a return to America to answer for violations of the law.

There is a notion arising that because U.S. forces are being withdrawn from Vietnam, the moral stigma and legal consequences attached to desertion or draft evasion are somehow lightened. Arguments are advanced that it is wrong to exact justice for violations of the Military Code or the Selective Service Act that were committed in the name of "protest" during the height of the Vietnam war. President Nixon has been urged to grant amnesty to t h e s e offenders. One Democrat c a n d i d a t e for president, Sen. George McGovern, has even made amnesty for draft dodgers a plank in his platform.

Moral issues do not change with headlines, nor does the meaning of our laws. Amnesty for these offenders would make a mockery of the sacrifice of all those who have obeyed the call to national service and fulfilled their enlistment oath, and all who would be asked to do so in the future. The dignity of the law, including the obligation of each citizen to obey it, has been abused enough in our c o u n t r y without the body blow that would be dealt it by such an amnesty.

"To err is human, to forgive divine." What of those young men who were led into a disgraceful act by the deceptive counsel of others, who now with greater maturity can recognize their folly and are filled with regret? They deserve sympathy, and justice is certainly not without mercy. The road is open to each to satisfy both his conscience and the law by returning to his country and pleading his case before a court. It is the function of our courts to determine degrees of guilt or innocence in individual cases.

Some organizations continue to try to coax young men who are wavering in their sense of duty across an awful line that is so difficult to recross. It would be a pity if more should be pulled into the moral abyss of desertion by a meaningless and grossly irresponsible offer of "sanctuary" by that radical-dominated council.

The fact is that there can be no real sanctuary for deserters or draft evaders—in Canada or elsewhere — nor should the prospect of amnesty be held out to ease the burden they must bear. Having turned one's back on a moral duty, there is no refuge — except to turn around and confront the consequences of one's own behavior.

Above, from *Illinois State Journal,* November 26, 1971.

Right, letter to the editor of *Illinois State Journal* by James Krohe, Jr., December 6, 1971.

Raps Draft-Dodgers Editorial

Journal Editor:

I've just finished reading your editorial of November 26 e n t i t l e d "Draft-Dodgers' Choice."

I must take exception to the opinions there expressed concerning the issue of amnesty for these young men who have flown the country to escape the Vietnam draft.

In that editorial you posed this question, "What of those young men who were led into a disgraceful act by the deceptive counsel of others, who now with greater maturity can recognize their folly and are filled with regret?" To that I pose this question: What of those young men who followed the deceptive counsel of men like yourself, who for years have confused morality with a shop-worn and dubiously legal "duty," and have been forced out of ignorance or deceit to resort to sloganeering to justify a war that was at best a mistake, and at worst a crime against principle?

It is true, as you stated on the 26th, that "some organizations continue to try to coax young men who are wavering in their sense of duty across an awful line that is so difficult to recross."

One of these organizations is the U.S. Army. Another is the Copley Press. Both have been tiresome in their attempts to convince the public to forsake its moral responsibility and to support a war that should never have been fought.

"Having turned one's back on a moral duty, there is no refuge" is an opinion you share with the many thousands of young Americans who have chosen exile or imprisonment as the only possible alternative to a war that is both politically suicidal and morally repugnant.

James Krohe Jr.
Springfield

ADVICE
TO A DRAFTEE *by Leo Tolstoy*

In my last letter I answered your question as well as I could. It is not only Christians but all just people who must refuse to become soldiers — that is, to be ready on another's command (for this is what a soldier's duty actually consists of) to kill all those one is ordered to kill. The question as you state it — which is more useful, to become a good teacher or to suffer for rejecting conscription? — is falsely stated. The question is falsely stated because it is wrong for us to determine our actions according to their results, to view actions merely as useful or destructive. In the choice of our actions we can be led by their advantages or disadvantages only when the actions themselves are not opposed to the demands of morality.

We can stay home, go abroad, or concern ourselves with farming or science according to what we find useful for ourselves or others; for neither in domestic life, foreign travel, farming, nor science is there anything immoral. But under no circumstance can we inflict violence on people, torture or kill them because we think such acts could be of use to us or to others. We cannot and may not do such things, especially because we can never be sure of the results of our actions. Often actions which seem the most advantageous of all turn out in fact to be destructive; and the reverse is also true.

The question should not be stated: which is more useful, to be a good teacher or to go to jail for refusing conscription? but rather: what should a man do who has been called upon for military service — that is, called upon to kill or to prepare himself to kill?

In every person's life there are moments in which he can know himself, tell himself who he is, whether he is a man who values his human dignity above his life or a weak creature who does not know his dignity and is concerned merely with being useful (chiefly to himself). This is the situation of a man who goes out to defend his honor in a duel or a soldier who goes into battle (although here the concepts of life are wrong). It is the situation of a doctor or a priest called to someone sick with plague, of a man in a burning house or a sinking ship who must decide whether to let the weaker go first or shove them aside and save himself. It is the situation of a man in poverty who accepts or rejects a bribe. And in our times, it is the situation of a man called to military service. For a man who knows its significance, the call to the army is perhaps the only opportunity for him to behave as a morally free creature and fulfill the highest requirement of his life — or else merely to keep his advantage in sight like an animal and thus remain slavishly submissive and servile until humanity becomes degraded and stupid.

For these reasons I answered your question whether one has to refuse to do military service with a categorical "yes" — if you understand the meaning of military service (and if you did not understand it then, you do now) and if you want to behave as a moral person living in our times must.

Please excuse me if these words are harsh. The subject is so important that one cannot be careful enough in expressing oneself so as to avoid false interpretation.

April 7, 1899   Leo Tolstoy

Courtesy of the Houghton Library of Harvard University and The Atlantic Monthly Company.

Which Side Needs the Pardon?

The amnesty question is a thicket of thorny moral issues. One school would interpret amnesty as a generous pardon from the state for youthful transgressions. Others insist that it is the government, not the exiles, that should be seeking pardon. In their view, amnesty would be a "mea culpa" from a guilty government, a sort of official act of contrition for the war. Most of the exiles themselves feel strongly that they have done nothing wrong. "It's not a question of the government forgiving us," contends Rick Thome, a deserter now living in Vancouver. "The United States has to be willing, for once, to admit it made a mistake."

Above left and right, from *Newsweek*, January 1971.

A Time to Close the Book

Indeed, the broadest support for amnesty seems to come from those who take it literally—the word comes from the Greek for "forgetfulness." Amnesty in this sense would be a recognition that the moral equations on Vietnam are too complicated and too painful to keep endlessly computing. It might very well include not only draft evaders but also deserters, since the difference between them is often only one of class: the better educated and more sophisticated evade, the others don't know what they're getting into until they are already serving. And some make a case for covering American troops who have been convicted of war crimes as well—on the argument that a true national reconciliation must include all who have been caught up in the special pressures and dilemmas that Vietnam has produced.

THE BATTLE HYMN OF LT. CALLEY... AND THE REPUBLIC
• • • • • • • • • • • • •

MICHAEL NOVAK

The sleeper in the Calley case is the link between populism and the lesson learned in the Hitler period. It is not enough for a Christian or any moral man merely to be patriotic, or obey orders, or give his conscience over to a bureaucracy. Each man must reflect, choose and pay the consequences. Populism in this case might carry large numbers of "little people" into a tradition of personal responsibility and dissent. Not a few in the South, traditional breeding ground of professional soldiers, have said in recent days that they would now prefer their sons to be draft-dodgers and deserters rather than fall into Lieutenant Calley's shoes. . . . Yes, that's the moral point. That's what the brave young men in the Resistance and among the deserters were trying to say all along. History is already vindicating them.

Theodore Goetz would not pledge allegiance to the flag, nor to the republic for which it stands. Neither would his brother, Jack. This got to be quite a bone of contention at Shaker High School in Latham (near Albany) where the two are students. Theodore said he did not believe in the words of the pledge and wished to remain seated as an expression of his views. The principal said he must leave the room or face suspension. So much for Liberty for All. Jack actually did get suspended. Theodore has brought suit through NYCLU. "I have always been taught by my parents to examine my beliefs and actions and to act independently according to my conscience," he told the court. Leaving the room is unacceptable, he says, because that's a form of punishment for bad behavior at Shaker and "it appears to me and to others that I am being punished for my beliefs."

Above left, from Commonweal, April 30, 1971.
Above right, from *Civil Liberties in New York*, February, 1973.

ARMY SAYS SOLDIERS MUST REFUSE ILLEGAL ORDERS

"The American Government and most other nations take the law of war very seriously," says U.S. Army Training Film 21-4228. The new film was produced to explain in graphic terms a soldier's responsibilities in warfare, according to Army spokesmen. News of the film appeared in the New York Times, December 15.

"After World War II many members of the German and Japanese forces were brought to trial on charges of having committed war crimes," the film says. "The accused often claimed that he was 'just following orders'. But this was ruled no defense. Those who had committed acts they knew, or should have known, were wrong, were held responsible for their acts. Convicted, they were jailed and, in some cases, excuted."

The same fate awaits American military men who violate international law, the audience is reminded. The best way to respond if ordered to do something unlawful is to ask questions, the film says. But if this doesn't work, the soldier must refuse the order.

The film depicts an enlisted man refusing the obey an illegal order to use prisoners to clear a path through a mine field, and the officer refusing to retract his order under questioning. "No sir, I refuse," the soldier tells his lieutenant.

The narrator admits that "it takes guts to stand up in this kind of situation." What is not said is that one reason it takes guts is that the Army itself has so far been the only judge of what constitutes an illegal order. If the Army decides the order was legal, then the GI is found guilty of unlawfully disobeying an order, and is subject to court martial and a maximum sentence of five years hard labor and a Dishonorable Discharge.

The film was made as a result of the killing of civilians at the South Vietnamese hamlet of MyLai, according to Army Secretary Howard Callaway. "Our training takes into account what happened at MyLai and takes into account the seriousness of it," Callaway said.

War resisters might well ask if this means the Army intends to drop all charges against men who refused orders or deserted from the Army during the war in Indochina. Unless pressed, the Army will undoubtedly take the position that MyLai was an isolated incident, in spite of the testimony of hundreds of GIs to the effect that MyLai was "standard operating procedure" for the U.S. Army in Indochina.

As part of its new approach, the Army says it is stressing General Order 100, issued in 1863 by President Lincoln, that said: "Men who take up arms against one another in public war...do not cease to be moral beings responsible to one another and to God."

Courtesy of Amnesty Update staff: Dick Bucklin, Dee Knight, Joe Urgo, Irma Zigas.

SECTION 12

Punishment vs. Rehabilitation

A number of the sections of this book contain arguments which deal primarily with whether or not certain kinds of acts (e.g., possessing, using, or selling certain kinds of drugs, having or performing abortions, publishing certain materials) should be prohibited by law. One of the factors relevant to such discussions is the feasibility of enforcing such laws (see the arguments concerning gun-control legislation in Section 6). But the question of legislating against certain acts necessarily involves the additional questions of what kind of treatment should be prescribed for persons who violate the laws, what the purpose of that treatment should be, how it should be administered, and so on. And these questions themselves require consideration of feasibility as well. For example, some of the suggested purposes of the treatment to be imposed on violators include discouraging others from violating the same law and rehabilitation of the violator so that he or she will not violate laws in the future, in addition to the traditional aim of the treatment which was simple and direct retributive punishment.

During the past century there was a shift in emphasis in the American criminal justice system away from the goal of punishment and toward the goal of rehabilitation—at least in the nominal sense that many jails and prisons today are called "correctional institutions" and "rehabilitation centers" instead of the traditional "penal institutions." But there is a growing debate as to whether or not any institutions do in fact or could reasonably be expected to "rehabilitate" persons who have violated laws, and it is being suggested by many that the only purposes of treatment of violators of laws should be deterrence of others from violating laws and/or simple punishment of the violator for purely retributory reasons. It is even being argued by some that the procedures being used in an attempt to rehabilitate violators are more inhumane and in violation of basic human rights than are the traditional methods of direct retribution.

Even if one accepts the goal of treatment of violators to be simple retribution, there are still many questions as to what is an appropriate, fair, and just punishment for specific acts. Should it be a simple and automatic "eye for an eye" procedure or should the system of punishment be "tempered by mercy" as was argued by President Ford in his pardoning of Richard Nixon? And what about the problem raised by the fact that the legal system as a whole is (and quite possibly must be) very complex, which often means that persons who can afford expert legal counsel can avoid punishment for apparently major violations of law while poor persons can get substantial punishment for relatively minor violations? Some people would argue that if a system of punishment cannot be operated in a truly just and fair manner it would be better to have no laws at all.

About half of the arguments in this section are concerned with the most final form of punishment—the death penalty. It is a complex topic whose complexity is compounded by its ultimate finality, although it is also possible to perceive this feature as making this the simplest possible case. If it is simply *always* wrong to take another human life, then killing cannot be justified even in the case of someone who has taken another's life. But as soon as one allows the possible legitimacy of taking another's life in self-defense, then the gate has been opened for the argument that the very existence of the death penalty will prevent at least some murders from occurring.

EXERCISES

1. Examine President Ford's statement of pardon for Richard Nixon. To what extent could the same premises be used for justifying the pardon of other violators of the law, or is the statement sufficiently qualified to permit its application to this case only?
2. Apply the various arguments concerning punishment in this section to the specific cases in Sections 1–3 and 6. Discuss what punishment, if any, would be appropriate for the various "crimes" in those sections and what the grounds for that punishment are (e.g., retribution, rehabilitation, deterence).
3. Can punishment be justified for violating moral rules if no laws have been violated?

Sarajevo Hails Assassin but Debates Ethics of Deed

By MALCOLM W. BROWNE
Special to The New York Times

SARAJEVO, Yugoslavia, March 24—With plans going forward for a new movie about the 1914 assassination that brought permanent fame to this ancient and pictur-, esque town, some Sarajevo citizens are wrestling once again with the moral issues of political killing. It was an assassination here on June, 28, 1914—the victims were Archduke Franz Ferdinand, heir to the Austro-Hungarian throne, and his wife, Sophie — that precipitated World War I.

The Talk of Sarajevo

According to Veljko Bulajic, the Yugoslav producer of the film, previous movies on the assassination have been "romanticized commercial ventures." This one, in effect, will seek to justify the assassination and will portray the plotters as "men who were and remain the early heralds of contemporary revolutionary developments."

Dr. Marko Sunjic, vice-president of the executive council of Bosnia and Herzegovina and a principal Communist leader here, said of the killing in an interview:

"Sometimes we regret that people know us for the assassination and think of Sarajevo as an unsafe place where heads of state can be killed. But as an Austrian colony Bosnia had a very high illiteracy rate, and its natural resources were exploited in a colonial way. In such a situation no other remedy could be found, and young people undertook the assassination."

Asked if this reasoning would not justify all acts of political terrorism, including those of the Palestinian guerrillas, he replied:

"Revolutionary movements do not condone individual acts of terrorism. Terrorism is the last resort of young people who are disillusioned and can achieve their ends in no other way.

"There have been several such examples in the history of the League of Communists of Yugoslavia. The league never approved such acts, although the idea of individual sacrifice for a cause cannot help but inspire admiration. Even today our young people are inspired by Princip."

'Acts of Despair'

"As for the Palestine liberation movement," he continued, "I do not personally approve of terrorism, but I see the acts of the Palestine guerrillas as acts of despair. If there was a political solution, there would not be such acts."

Above, © 1973–1975 by The New York Times Company. Reprinted by permission.
Below, editorial from the *Washington Star News*, September 19, 1974.

Buying More Trouble

Now that The Netherlands is advertised as the place that is kind to terrorists, one may only wonder how long it will be until the next armed fanatics take advantage of Dutch hospitality. Those three gunmen of the underground Japanese Red Army who departed from Amsterdam in style this week, after releasing 11 hostages they held in the French embassy, no doubt are exemplars to many on the lunatic fringe.

Their success, indeed, was astounding, even taking into account that the French ambassador to Holland was among their captives. They demanded and secured the release of a fellow terrorist held in a French jail, but that was the least of it. The other rewards were rich: $300,000 in ransom for the hostages (which has been returned), a French jet airliner to take them anywhere they chose, the Dutch premier at the airport to see them off. And also smaller favors such as ample Coca-Colas, mineral water, food, reading materials and a big police escort to assure their unhampered getaway at the airport.

It must have been a heady sensation for this trio, which doubtless was fully ready to kill its hostages and be killed, but possibly had no firm expectation of bringing a nation to heel. They could, of course, simply have been sealed off in that embassy without food, water or utilities, to do what they might and suffer the consequences.

That would have been the wiser course, we expect. The Dutch, in their humaneness, decided otherwise and saved the lives at stake. But the question is how many lives will be lost further down the road by capitulating to, and hence encouraging, this sort of thing.

CARL T. ROWAN

Delusions of Tough Guy Machismo

By the time this column reaches print, those Black September terrorists who murdered three diplomats may already have been executed by a Sudanese government that has been ruthlessly swift at punishing wrongdoers.

Yet, perhaps not. The same "blood is thicker than water" impulses that caused the terrorists to weep and surrender without killing their Arab hostages. could work in a way to cause the Sudanese to spare the lives of Arab killers.

But no matter what happens to those Black September madmen, we Americans have some thinking to do about how to deal with terrorists, and about how far a civilized people are obligated to go to save the lives of ambassadors and other diplomats abroad.

A lot of Americans, from the White House down to Joe Blow, are infected with delusions of John Wayne-type *machismo* that lead to simplistic slogans like, "The first rule is that you never reward terrorists." This is movie-tough-guy nonsense that simply cannot be applied to every airplane hijacking, to every kidnapping, to every seizure of a U.S. diplomat abroad.

While much of the world was still hoping and praying that Ambassador Cleo A. Noel Jr. and his outgoing deputy, George C. Moore, could be gotten out alive, we heard the tough-guy line from the White House that the U.S. would not be "blackmailed."

The standard argument is that when you give in to one band of terrorists, you encourage others. The implication of that White House stance, so popular in Israel, is that a seized ambassador, or anyone else, must become a sacrifice to the cause of not encouraging terrorism. The line is than an envoy accepts that risk and duty when he goes abroad.

Let me make it clear that I have no evidence that the two Americans and the Belgian diplomat could have been gotten out of the Sudan alive. I do know that, had I been the ambassador, I would have wanted my country to give me the same chance to live that a kidnapped child receives from his father.

Who among us, with his child, wife, or other close relative abducted, would take the hard, pious line that we will "pay no ransom, because ransom encourages other kidnappings"? All but the mentally ill among us would try to get our relatives back, and only with them in our embrace would we launch any derring-do campaigns to prove that crime, especially kidnapping, does not pay.

I have some colleagues in this town who, after the first martini, start arguing that the answer to hijackings is not all these searchers and electronic gear that infest our airports, but an armed guard aboard every airliner who will start shooting the moment any hijacker rears his evil head.

You ask them a question: "If your wife is on the plane, sitting next to the hijacker, do you still want the guard to start shooting?"

You find they aren't so eager to start shooting.

' Many airline passengers are alive today because ransoms were paid and because no trigger-happy guard started a shootout at 33,000 feet.

Let the Black September terrorists be executed, if that be the decision of the Sudanese. Let them lie in the sun as a festering monument to the bestiality of man. But let us not forget that their deaths, their ignominy, will not assuage in any degree the sorrow and suffering of the Noel and Moore families. For no one among them would trade Noel's or Moore's life for those of a thousand terrorists.

"But it would be unthinkable to let Sirhan B. Sirhan, the killer of Robert F. Kennedy out of prison to free those diplomats," one American hardliner said to me.

Unthinkable? It would have been unthinkable to do anything else if there were a reasonable chance of getting Noel and Moore out alive. The joy of seeing those two diplomats alive and with their families is infinitely more important to me than knowing that Sirhan suffers.

Field Newspaper Syndicate 1975.

Web of barbarism

Random violence rightly horrifies civilized society. Man recognizes that uncontrolled, unchecked force represents a step back toward the beast. The social structure, therefore, organizes rules and patterns to suppress such outbursts.

In time of war, the lid comes partly off, as large numbers of citizens take up arms and become soldiers. But even then, societies still usually observe rules which aim at channeling violence so it does not become all-encompassing, and does not engender such hatred and destruction that it makes any chance of post-war recovery impossible.

For instance, it is regrettable but expected when soldiers are killed in battle. But when a civilian area is bombed, even if accidentally, society is disturbed that the combatants did not take greater care.

Deliberate attacks on civilians or civilian installations are rare in ordinary warfare, if only because military commanders naturally consider concentrations of enemy troops and arms to be immensely more appropriate and rewarding targets than unarmed civilian areas.

And yet civilian areas are precisely the target of the modern urban guerrilla, who deliberately chooses non-combatant men, women, and children for his victims. He lays his plans not in a moment of passion, miscalculation, or frustration, but with full and careful knowledge.

The urban terrorist thus introduces a barbaric level of violence into civilization.

The most arresting current example is in Northern Ireland, with bombings and counter-bombings, assaults and counter-assaults by extremist Catholics and Protestants who do not allow each other safety in a tavern or while Christmas shopping.

Surely it is the height of man's overweening moral arrogance for him calculatedly to blow up a store packed with shoppers (killing four persons, including two children), as occurred Dec. 11 in Belfast, or to touch off a bomb and destroy 16 lives in a pub, as happened a week earlier.

Something is morally amiss with the world's violent radicals—as exemplified so well by Ireland's IRA and Quebec's FLQ—when they decide that their social goals are attainable at the cost of lives of housewives and children.

Individual tragedy means nothing to terrorists who claim to seek that elusive ideal, the perfected social order. What a travesty that the victims of their delusion are innocent bystanders.

Left, from *The Arizona Republic*, December 21, 1971.

Below, courtesy of Hallowell Bowser and *Saturday Review*, March 20, 1971.

Against Provocation

"**A**gent provocateur" is a fancy term for a quite ugly kind of spy. Unlike ordinary spies, the provocateur does not join a "suspect" group to keep close tabs on its activities; instead, his aim is to stampede the group into doing something rash, egregious, and incriminating.

When challenged about using such provocative, para-legal tactics, the "fuzz and feds" claim they are just needling extremists into attempting now, in a botched, premature way, anti-Establishment exploits that they would have brought off with devastating success if allowed more lead time.

This is, of course, thin reasoning. As "red squad" people well know, an impassioned-cause group is like a Navy blimp that is riding free just a few feet off the ground. The blimp may weigh many tons, but a good hard shove by a determined man can warp the craft around and send it floating off in any direction the shover chooses. When an undercover agent gives a volatile splinter group a hefty push, the group is likely to go kiting off in an ideological direction astonishing to the onlooker.

But why push for empty violence that only enrages both the public and the police? Why not try instead to provoke—or evoke—positive, fruitful activity? Roger Baldwin may have hit on part of the explanation when, thirty-odd years ago, he wrote in the *Encyclopedia of the Social Sciences*, "Sometimes the political police have provoked or committed crime . . . to make a showing of the need for their services and thus to wrest from a hesitant government increased funds and larger powers."

—HALLOWELL BOWSER.

A NEW TWIST IN EXTORTION

BUENOS AIRES

"Ransom in advance"—that's the latest extortion racket being worked by foreign terrorists, with U. S. business interests a major target.

Ford Motor Company, with a booming car and truck plant in this Argentine capital, became a million-dollar victim of a "protection" demand by revolutionary guerrillas on May 23. Pay up, the terrorists warned, or a Ford executive will be kidnaped or slain.

But Ford is not the only American victim—or even the largest—of extremist activity sweeping this country.

Two months ago Eastman Kodak paid a reported 1.5 million dollars to gain the release of a kidnaped executive, Antony R. da Cruz, a U. S. citizen.

Other firms known to have paid ransom for their kidnaped executives include the First National Bank of Boston, International Telephone & Telegraph Corporation and the British-American Tobacco Company.

In addition, terrorist bombs have damaged offices of an ITT subsidiary, the First National City Bank, the 3M Company, General Electric, Pan American and Sheraton hotels.

Protection, but—. Executives have hired hundreds of guards and taken extra precautions—but they admit their inability to cope with the problem.

Says one top U. S. businessman:

"It will not do any good for one company to say 'We will not pay.' Everybody has to say 'We will not pay.' And that is just about impossible."

Foreign firms are setting up their own corps of security experts, installing all sorts of security gadgets in their plants and in the homes of executives. It has proved of little effect. Some firms have even taken out insurance policies against kidnaping—an expensive and complicated form of protection.

The policy of the U. S. Government is not to pay ransom, even in the cases of kidnaping of American diplomats. The State Department informed the Ford Company of this policy—but said that Ford would have to make its own decision.

Said Edgar R. Molina, a vice president of Ford in Buenos Aires: "We believe, under the circumstances, we had no choice but to meet these demands."

Other Ford officials said theirs was the 25th company to meet guerrilla payoff demands.

"Apparently the Government has no way of protecting business from this sort of thing," one executive commented.

American executives and officials of other foreign firms were quick to take sides for and against the decision of Ford to make the payoff.

"This will have a terrible repercussion," said a U. S. banker. "Extortion will take the place of kidnaping."

A forecast from a long-time North American resident of Buenos Aires:

"It will be 2 million dollars next time there is one of these demands."

But another U. S. executive saw the situation this way:

"There are lots of reasons for Ford to have come to the conclusions that they did. They have hundreds of employes out there—I would not want to have the burden of saying that I was prepared to risk the lives of those people."

That, apparently, was the conclusion also reached in talks between Ford officials here and at the home office in Michigan. Ford prides itself on excellent employe relations, resulting in freedom from strikes for nearly a decade in a country that is one of the most strike-ridden in the world.

Left, reprinted from *U.S. News & World Report,* June 4, 1973. Copyright 1973 U.S. News & World Report, Inc.
Below, from the *San Francisco Chronicle.*

Investigating Torture

by Philip Nobile

According to Dr. Amelia Augustus, Amnesty International's UN representative, torture has become epidemic. She claims that even the United States has dirty hands. Despite the benevolent uses one might imagine for torture in extreme situations, Dr. Augustus emphasizes that it never leads to good.

Without seeming to defend the horror of torture, I would argue that the case is not open and shut, and I took that line in the following conversation.

Do you rule out torture under any conceivable circumstance?

Yes. You never know whether you're getting truth from torture. So what good is it?

Say we caught one of those Arab terrorists who slaughtered 31 innocent people at the Rome airport recently. What if we could prevent further mass murders by getting him to talk about future terrorist plans? And only torture would make him talk? Would you bend the rules then?

Never. I will not torture even a mass murderer in order to save other innocent lives. Torturing one Palestinian doesn't stop all the others. If you want to be a torturer, you're going the way of dictators.

Why not a little selective torture in very special situations? Where's the harm?

This is insanity. A little torture is like being a little pregnant. Once a government gives in to torture, its use is bound to increase.

NEW HUMANIST

Volume 88 No 3   July 1972

HECTOR HAWTON

Personally Speaking

Ethics and blackmail

I WAS LOST in admiration for the skill and panache with which the Israelis recently dealt with hijackers at Lydda Airport. They were faced with a moral dilemma all too familiar nowadays. Should they risk the lives of 90 passengers, or let the blackmailers get away with it? They took the risk — and one can imagine the outcry if the gamble had not succeeded. They have been criticized, however, for allegedly breaking a promise to the Red Cross not to use force. If that is the case — and it has been denied — they were faced with two conflicting principles: never yield to blackmail, and never break a promise. Most moral principles are too general to be applied to particular situations, but this is not quite true of the rule to keep promises. If you don't, nobody will ever believe you again. On the other hand, whether or not the Red Cross were deceived, the brilliant operation carried through by General Dayan cannot be repeated. Future hijackers have been alerted, and you can't perform the same trick twice.

The problem of hijacking, like that of political terrorism, can be finally solved at a price that would be morally repugnant. There is no certain way to prevent another outrage by suicidal fanatics.

Left, from the *New Humanist* (July 1972), published by the Nationalist Press Association, London, England.

Right, reprinted from *The Guardian*, July 14, 1972.

Sentence on in balance Okamoto

From ERIC SILVER : Sarafand, July 13

Kozo Okamoto will have to wait until Monday for the military court's verdict on his part in the Lydda Airport massacre. The prosecution and defence rested their cases with brief closing speeches this afternoon, but for the first time in the four-day hearing they were overshadowed by the small, sullen figure in the dock.

Freed temporarily from the handcuffs that have manacled him, waking or sleeping, for most of the six weeks since his arrest, Okamoto today delivered his revolutionary testament. The world now knows as much as it ever will about what impelled him and two Japanese comrades to fly here and turn their automatic rifles on the crowded customs hall. It remains precious little.

Okamoto stood stiffly to attention for one hour and 25 minutes. He had sat passively through the long girations of "bourgeois justice." Now his time had come and he was ready for it.

"We accept this system of jurisprudence as our means of propaganda,' he told the court. His delivery was as fluent and coherent as the frequent pauses for translation would allow. Once he shouted in English, " I want to continue." But this was his chance and he was not going to waste it.

Okamoto emerged as neither an original nor a particularly penetrating social thinker, but he has learnt his latter-day Marxism diligently. History demanded revolution, revolution demanded violence. If this meant his own life or other people's, so be it. He was no armchair romantic.

His profession, he said, was a soldier of the Red Army. " The three of us, soldiers in the Red Army, in this revolutionary action decided that our contentions would have to be carried forward decisively. That is to say, it was my duty towards the people whom I sacrificed and towards my two comrades who lost their lives.

" I take on myself full responsibility for the people who have been killed. Revolutionary warfare is a warfare of justice.

"The definition of the word justice is to create a society in which there is no class distinction. The meaning of justice is to create a society in which there is no class struggle."

The Lydda attack, Okamoto added, was no mere battle. It was warfare, and warfare was destruction. " As we engage in this we cannot limit warfare to destruction of buildings. We believe that the slaughter of human bodies is inevitable.

But why this operation ? Why Israel ? " I believe that as a means towards world revolution I must propose the creation of a world Red Army. And we decided to have relationships with the Popular Front for the Liberation of Palestine. This was one springboard, one means by which we could propel ourselves on to the world stage...the Arab world lacks in spiritual fervour. So therefore we felt we could probably stir up the Arabs."

And no qualms ? " My leader approved of the operation. Since I am a soldier I obeyed and joined this operation. The Red Army soldier is ready at all times to give his life. This is for the sake of the revolution : it is not for the sake of anything else."

Lest anyone should still miss the point, Okamoto flashed a further warning : " Red Army soldiers will slay anyone who stands on the side of the bourgeoisie. This I do not say as a joke."

Finally, and with the nearest to a hint of remorse, the 24-year-old student took refuge in Japanese folklore. " We three of us, after we died, wanted to become the three stars of Orion. When we were young we were told the story that when we died we would become stars in the sky. While I may not totally believe it, I was ready to be persuaded of it.

" I do not know what the customs are in foreign countries. I believe that some of those whom we slaughtered have become stars in the sky. The revolutionary war will continue, and there will be many, many stars. However, if we recognise that we shall go to the same heaven, there to shine together, then we can have peace of heart."

255

Reprinted from *U.S. News & World Report*

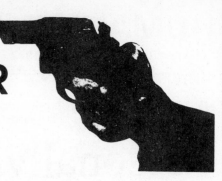

POLITICAL TERROR IN U.S. WHAT NEXT

Interview With Dr. David Abrahamsen,

A Leading Psychiatrist

How dangerous is the new turn to radical violence in the U. S.? In this interview, an internationally known authority puts new light on terror as a political weapon—and assesses its methods and announced goals.

Q Dr. Abrahamsen, how serious a threat is terrorism in the form of political kidnapings becoming in the United States today?

A I believe it is quite clear that we are now getting a kind of terrorism that is familiar to Europeans but not to Americans. By that I mean terrorism that is well organized and planned, and has definite, long-term aims.

I also believe that this terrorism is going to continue and perhaps grow among a segment of young people who see no other approach to problems such as poverty and, accordingly, become desperate and extremely disturbed—perhaps almost deranged in some cases.

Q How rational, in general, are these young terrorists?

A On one side, their thinking is quite rational. You see this in the way they planned and carried out the kidnaping of Patricia Hearst. It was very cleverly planned in detail: how to go about seizing the girl, later having her talk taped and put on radio, and so on. Furthermore, all their actions were carried out in secrecy, giving them an aura of mystery and power, instilling fear in people—not only in the mother and father of the young girl but people at large.

Q Is their aim to make law-enforcement officials and authority in general look impotent?

A Yes. If terrorists can disable authority, it makes authority invalid and encourages the feeling that nobody can do anything to stop their terrorism.

Yet it is also true that terrorists usually are possessed of an idealism that is Utopian and unrealistic, and borders on the irrational.

Q Unrealistic in what way?

A Well, I'm talking of terrorism in general, but in this case it is quite interesting that the group which claims responsibility for the Hearst kidnaping has chosen the name "Symbionese Liberation Army." Now, "symbiosis" is a Greek word which means "living together," and this suggests an ideal—a long-term goal of a society in which all people live together in peace and harmony.

Of course, this in itself is a noble idea. People should be able to live peaceably together. As we know, however, not all persons can live happily together. Most individuals have preferences in friendships as in other matters, so the idea of "symbiosis"—if that is the kind of society the terrorists want—is based upon a very Utopian ideal. This, in turn, means that they may become more and more frustrated in trying to realize their goals, hence more and more desperate.

Q Would you call them insane?

A Not from what we know about them. You might call them fanatics, but really they are desperadoes. When people are desperate, they carry out desperate acts. This means that one has fear of what such people might do to achieve their Utopian dream.

In other words, terrorism usually embodies both realism and lack of realism. In the Hearst kidnaping, the terrorists did get in touch with the family and did offer a proposal, rather than just engage in an act of destruction. Yet they also asked that the Hearst organization, or the establishment in general, give each poor person in California $70 worth of food—which adds up to a very high, unrealistic figure.

Killer group halts war on educators

OAKLAND, Calif. (UPI) — A killer organization claiming responsibility for the cyanide-bullet slaying of a schools superintendent has "rescinded" its so-called "shoot on sight warrant" against other education leaders.

A letter received during the weekend by the Oakland Tribune from the Symbionese Liberation Army said the shooting will stop because school administrators are heeding its demands.

Supt. Marcus Foster was killed by three assailants Nov. 6. He was hit eight times by pistol bullets packed with cya-nide as he entered a car in the parking lot behind an administration building. Foster's chief deputy, Robert Blackburn was wounded in the abdomen by buckshot during the attack. He is recovering at home after intensive hospital treatment.

It was the second letter received by the newspaper since the shootings.

The first, on Nov. 7, said Foster and Blackburn were targeted for "execution by cyanide bullets." The police did not disclose that cyanide had been found in the hollowed-out slugs until after the letter became public knowledge.

The second letter noted that the school administration canceled a student identification-card program for junior and senior high schools. The plastic ID cards contained pictures of the bearer and were part of a police-on-campus program.

The letter said that if at any time the board of education "reinstates programs of political police forces in our schools, forced youth identification cards and contributions to the internal warfare identification computer system, then the death warrant order is to be immediately reactivated without warning."

Would Be A Fraud

The kidnapers of Patricia Hearst who are beating their breasts in self righteousness as the would-be saviors of the world, demanding millions of dollars in food for the poor and unfortunate, are perpetrating a fraud on the people they say they would help.

Seventy dollars worth of meat, vegetables and dairy products isn't going to solve the problems of those on welfare or otherwise in need. A hand not a handout is what these people need, an improved welfare system that would get rid of the chislers and give more help to those really in need. A handout is humiliating and it would suffice for only a matter of days.

The truly concerned person works for the reform of the system so that gains are permanent. The kidnapers' philosophy is that of throwing a bone to a dog. It is humiliating and degrading.

But working in a sane and sensible manner to improve the lot of the unfortunate does not gain the world headlines and attention that these twisted minds crave.

One would think that persons who pretend to want to help the unfortunate would be the essence of kindness and humaneness. Yet they would not hestitate for one moment to take the life of an innocent girl to achieve something that would be a fraud worked on those who it would pretend to benefit.

If the Hearsts are forced to bow to the outrageous demands of the kidnapers it will encourage others of like mind to dream up even more fantastic schemes.

Unfortunately the Hearst family has to look at the problem from only one viewpoint, how to get their daughter back alive.

Let not the world be fooled by any pretended noble purpose of these twisted minds.

A goodly number of California people who say they would qualify for the food are tagging the kidnapers for just what they are — phonies. They say they want no part of any blood money. This is indeed an inspiring side to an otherwise evil story.

Top, reprinted by permission of United Press International.
Above, from *The Troy Times Record*, February 14, 1974.

SYMBIONESE LIBERATION ARMY DEMANDS REPRINTED

The emblem of the Symbionese Liberation Army [S.L.A.].

We of the Symbionese Federation and the S.L.A. define ourselves by this name because it states that we are no longer willing to allow the enemy of all our people and children to murder, oppress and exploit us nor define us by color and thereby maintain division among us, but rather have joined together under black and minority leadership in behalf of all our different races and people to build a better and new world for our children and   people's future. We are a United Front and Federated Coalition of members from the Asian, Black, Brown, Indian, White, Women, Grey and Gay Liberation Movements.

Who have all come to see and understand that only if we unite and build our new world and future, will there really be a future for our children and people. We of the People and not the ruling capitalist class, will build a new world and system. Where there is really freedom and a true meaning to justice and equality for all women and men of all race and people, and an end to the murder and oppression exploitation of all people.

We of the Symbionese Federation and the S.L.A. are the children of all oppressed people, who have decided to redefine ourselves as a Symbionese Race and People. Yet recognizing the rich cultures of each and enforcing our rights to possession of our many cultures within a united federation of independent and sovereign nations, each of them flourishing and protected by its own laws and codes of self determination.

We are of many colors, but yet of one mind, for we all in history's time on this earth have become part of each other in suffering and in mind, and have agreed that the murder oppression and exploitation of our children and people must end now, for we all have seen the murder, oppression and exploitation of our people for too long under the hand of the same enemy and class of people and under the same system.

Knowing this, the Symbionese Federation and the S.L.A. know that our often murderous alienation from each other aids and is one of the fundamental strengths behind the ruling capitalist class's ability to murder and oppress us all. By not allowing them to define us by color, and also recognizing that by refusing ourselves to also internalize this false division definition, knowing that in mind and body we are facing the same enemy and that we are all comrades of one people, the murdered and oppressed, we are now able to become a united people under the Symbionese Federation and make true the words of our codes of unity that TO DIE A RACE, AND BE BORN A NATION, IS TO BECOME FREE.

Therefore, we of the Symbionese Federation and the S.L.A. DO NOT under the rights of human beings submit to the murder, oppression and exploitation of our children and people and do under the rights granted to the people under the Declaration of Independence of the United States, do now by the rights of our children and people and by Force of Arms and with every drop of our blood, Declare Revolutionary War against the The Fascist Capitalist Class and all their agents of murder, oppression and exploitation. We support by Force of Arms the just struggles of all oppressed people for self determination and independence within the United States and The World. And hereby offer to all liberation movements, revolutionary workers groups and peoples organizations our total aid and support for the struggle for freedom and justice for all people and races. We call upon all revolutionary black and other oppressed people within the Fascist United States to come together and join the Symbionese Federation and fight in the forces of The Symbionese Liberation Army.

THE ETERNAL CASE AGAINST INJUSTICE

By JACQUES MADAULE

Friends of mine have been very shocked when, in a moment of discouragement, I have told them that the petitions we sign and the demonstrations we stage against this or that injustice, against a death sentence, for example, are totally useless and probably do not have any effect upon the outcome. After all, there were demonstrations galore for Sacco and Vanzetti, and the Rosenbergs, and Julian Grimau —and they changed nothing.

There were slightly happier endings to the Burgos and Leningrad trials, inasmuch as no one was hanged, but all the demonstrators and petitioners may not have influenced the issue. What makes me think so is that in Yaoundé and Conakry, very soon afterwards, the public killings went on and no one batted an eyelid. Neither does a week go by without bringing more ghastly evidence of torture in Brazil year in, year out, and for how many years?

Perhaps we ought to throw up our hands in despair and call the whole thing off, since they are always the same people making the same useless fuss. Governments could perfectly well forecast, with all their computers, the world's precise reaction to this or that particular misdeed. The only astonishing thing is that, despite all their marvellous machines, they persist in acting irrationally, putting their political opponents to death and systematically torturing political prisoners.

Of course, one could retort that they are counting on the effects of terror and that unhappily this is not a completely irrational premise. My answer would be that for all Brazil's Gestapo tactics the regime's opponents still manage to pull off a spectacular kidnapping from time to time; and the police can no more find the missing diplomat than the opposition can stop torture. The dénouement comes with the inevitable exchange of the hostage against a score or two of prisoners, a scene out of a familiar ballet.

It adds up to this: we hear about all kinds of the world's wrongs, we protest and demonstrate indefatigably, and we ignore the very patchy results we tend to obtain. Protests and demonstrations do not seem to lessen the sum of suffering, or the universal bane of mankind, as Péguy's Joan of Arc said, particularly since we cannot protest or demonstrate against everything.

Surfeit of causes

You can spend days and nights signing protests, you can always be up at the front of the demonstrations, even so there will always be someone to ask why you failed to protest against this abomination or demonstrate against that horror, and what principles determined your choice of good causes. If you answer, "public opinion," you will be reminded how dextrously all sides manipulate it.

All of which is almost unanswerable—short of saying that there is a lot of wrong with the world, that no one person can hope to put it all right, but that it is still necessary, even vital, to keep fighting, and break down the conspiracy of silence that so many find so convenient.

Should the day ever come when not a voice raised because it seems there is no point in doing so, then the condemned and tortured will suffer and die in abominable loneliness. The real reason why we petition and demonstrate is to show them there are others, in the world outside who have not forgotten them. It is to give them the feeling of a human presence, even if it is invisible.

I believe that in so doing we keep up the morale of those for whom we cannot do anything more. There are too many of them, in too many parts of the world, and the vision of so much horror everywhere makes even the most stout hearted lose hope —not to mention the huge, indifferent herd interested only in their personal affairs, people more inured than ourselves, people who have always known that protesting does not help and that injustice has always had its way since the world began.

Heaven preserve us from such niggardly common sense! One day, the sooner the better, we should perhaps tackle the root causes, rather than the periodic symptoms, of the evil which men keep doing to each other—as if disease and injury, death and natural disasters were not enough. What makes us take out our personal frustrations on our fellow beings as if they were to blame for them? One might think the pain we cause them compensates for the pain we feel ourselves. It is always dangerous to give one man power over another, in case he takes advantage of it. It is the principle of tyranny.

So let us give credit to those who are sincerely trying to lessen the sum of evil in the world, even if they feel a twinge of flattered vanity at seeing their names in print, or buy an easy conscience too cheaply. Only, let us also hope that they do not remain content with merely demonstrating. Let them think, hard, without prejudice, about the real causes of all this human wretchedness.

In that case their devotion will certainly not have been totally useless.

From the weekly English edition of *Le Monde*, February 17, 1971.

Terror at the Top

From one end of the world to the other, people are sickened by the way terror is disfiguring human society.

They are aghast when a gunman fires into a car carrying Princess Anne and her husband, Capt. Mark Phillips, in a kidnapping attempt. They are horrified by the monstrous irresponsibility of militants who use kidnapping as a means for forcing social progress. They are stunned when a madman, thinking himself a patriot, shoots his way onto a commercial airliner, intending to crash-dive it into the White House.

But what about terror employed by governments as an instrument of foreign policy? Why is there no indignation over the fact that the largest nations in the world openly pursue their objectives through a balance-of-terror strategy? Both the United States and the Soviet Union seek credibility in their policies toward each other by possessing the means for setting off instant holocausts. Each country has access to a switchboard of total annihilation that can be activated by a fingertip.

NEW FORMS of authorized terror continue to spin off the apocalyptic assembly belts. The latest advance is the "smart bomb," which, it is said, will revolutionize warfare. Unlike the German buzz bombs of World War II, which exploded over the general vicinity of London, the new bombs have special features that ensure precision-targeting. Computers, lasers, and television combine to elimi-nate even the marginal errors of the vaunted Norden bombsight. The "smart bombs" can carry a nuclear payload.

News of this technological advance in man-made cataclysms has been received without any of the moral indignation that has attended news of still another hijacking or kidnapping. Nor has there been a public outcry over the fact that the United States and the Soviet Union, between them, possess nuclear stockpiles in excess of 75,000 megatons of explosive force. If only one-fourth of this power were to be used, life on earth could be severely jeopardized. A blanket of deadly radioactivity could settle over the globe.

In this sense, the entire human race today is hostage to the balance-of-terror strategies of the nuclear powers.

We can keep on hoping that the SALT negotiations at some point will hit pay dirt, but the best chance that they will do so depends on the pressure of public opinion rather than on any bursts of initiative by the negotiating parties. It is here—in the field of public opinion—that the real issue will be tested. That issue is whether people will apply to government the same moral yardsticks that apply to the rest of human society. The special exemptions that people tend to make for foreign policy no longer fit into the requirements of rational survival. We can count on it that governments will make moral judgments in the formation of their foreign policies when their own political survival depends on it.

N.C.

Courtesy of *Saturday Review/World*, April 20, 1974.

Assassin Beheaded by Saudis

RIYADH, June 18 (AP)—A young Saudi prince was publicly beheaded today with one swipe of a gold-handled sword for the assassination of his uncle, King Faisal. The watching crowd of thousands chanted in Arabic, "God is great" and "Justice is done."

Earlier in the day, Prince Faisal Ibn Musaed, 27, had been judged guilty by a Sharia, or religious court, of assassinating his uncle as the monarch celebrated the Moslem feast of the Prophet Mohammed's birthday March 25. The sentence was approved by King Khaled.

The American-educated prince was led out of the jail behind the government palace into Dira Square as afternoon prayers were ending and crowds of men were leaving Riyadh's great mosque nearby. An official of the court faced Prince Faisal and read the guilty verdict, then invoked "heaven's mercy" for the convicted man.

Prince Faisal appeared calm. His hands were tied behind his back, but he was not blindfolded.

As the prince knelt, a security man prodded him in the side with a stick so that his head jerked upward. The executioner brought the sword flashing down and decapitated him. Blood spattered on the dusty pavement.

The assassin's head was hoisted on a wooden stake and displayed briefly to the applauding crowd.

Immediately afterward, the head and body were placed on a stretcher and carried away for burial in an unmarked grave—the same simple Islamic interment given to the assassinated monarch.

Saudi Arabia's strict Islamic law prescribes the death penalty for murder unless the defendant is found to be insane. The Koran demands "a soul for a soul," and gives the next of kin of a victim the right to exact revenge.

With the modernization of Islam, the government has taken over the duty of exacting revenge, chopping off the heads of killers and the hands of thieves, stoning adulterers and jailing others.

The Koran also states punishment is important for its deterrent value and calls for it to be carried out publicly. Saudi Arabia boasts one of the lowest crime rates in the world, and there are only occasional public executions and maimings.

Above, courtesy of The Associated Press.
Below, from *The Washington Post*, 1975.

U.S. Penal System 'Truths' Questioned

By Leroy Aarons
Washington Post Staff Writer

LOS ANGELES—Out of the violence and turmoil inside American prisons that boiled over into the public realm in the late '60s and early '70s, a new consensus is emerging. Mainly, that the basic assumptions on which most prisons have been operating for the last 50 years have been disastrously wrong.

"A lot of it is just cosmetic," said Willie Holder, an ex-convict who heads the San Francisco prisoners union. "We're still waiting to see if they're serious."

Holder favors elimination of indeterminate sentencing, probation and parole, and he favors voluntary rehabilitation programs.

"Criminals should be punished," he said. "Society ought to admit that punishment is a form of retribution and not pretend that prisons are for any other purpose. I've heard many prisoners say they'd rather be beat in the head with a shovel than have their brain constantly examined like they do.

"The important thing is that if you're going to punish, you ought to do it equally. If Spiro Agnew is a thief, he ought to get the same thing some ordinary burglar gets."

Mr. McCLELLAN. Mr. President, in June of 1972, the Supreme Court handed down its decision in the case of Furman against Georgia, one of the Court's most significant decisions in recent years. It was in the Furman decision that a bare majority of the Court—five of the nine Justices—determined that the death penalty could not constitutionally be imposed as administered in the cases before it. The effect of that decision was to eliminate capital punishment throughout the country as an authorized deterrent and punishment for even the most violent and brutal crimes.

I recognize that we are not only faced with the question of whether or not legislation can be drafted that will meet the requirement of Furman. We are also faced with a much more basic question—whether or not this country should have a death penalty at all.

The answer to that question becomes clearer and clearer with every new kidnaping, with every new hijacking of a plane filled with innocent people, with every new murder by the Symbionese Liberation Army, with every murder committed for hire. The death penalty must be restored if our criminal justice system is to combat effectively the ever-increasing tide of violent crimes—crimes of terror—that threaten to engulf our Nation and if the confidence of the American people in our system of justice is to be restored.

Mr. President, those who argue against the death penalty claim that it serves no useful purpose and should therefore be eliminated. Perhaps most importantly, they say that there is no proof that it deters crime.

I simply do not agree with that.

I can recall from my youth that the knowledge that I would be punished for doing wrong was indeed a deterrent. And the more severe I thought the punishment was likely to be, the less likely was it that I would misbehave. I would suggest that everyone in this Chamber has had a comparable experience.

To say that the death penalty, the severest penalty society can impose, does not deter is to say that no punishment deters—and with that I believe no one here can agree.

Some will say that the real issue is not whether the death penalty deters, but whether it deters more than life imprisonment. To me the answer to that question is obvious.

Life is our most precious possession. So long as the premeditated murderer has his life there is the chance for parole, for freedom, for escape. There is often the opportunity and the temptation for

one convicted of murder or imprisoned for some crime to kill a guard or a fellow prisoner—there are many instances of such tragic occurrences. If a criminal knows that he will forfeit his own life if he commits one of the crimes enumerated in this bill, he will certainly be must less likely to commit that act than if all he had facing him was a prison sentence and eventual parole.

What better example of this do we have than the case of the man robbing a bank with a gun when the police get the drop on him. The robber is told to drop his gun or he will be killed. What does he do? If he believes he is going to be killed, he drops his gun. If the police told him to drop his gun or he would be slapped in the face, or kicked, or even put in prison, it might not be enough to stop him.

Where the criminal—the murderer—knows that he is going to pay a price for his crimes and that price is death, he will be deterred.

Mr. President, it is here that the problem exists. The criminal must be made to realize that he is going to die himself if he chooses to murderously deprive someone else of his life. If penalties are not imposed, the mere prescribing of them by law will not deter. We can be sure of that. A punishment is only going to be effective as long as it is imposed. Once it stops being applied, it loses its potency.

The death penalty is a perfect example. The last execution in this country took place in 1967—not because the country disapproved of the penalty, but out of a desire to let the Supreme Court rule on the question. In the 5 years between 1967 and 1971 the number of murders in this country rose 61 percent. More importantly, the rate of murder for every 100,000 persons rose 52 percent in that same 5-year period of time. Can anyone seriously argue that this was a mere coincidence?

Not only our law enforcement officers but even criminals themselves have told us that it was not. Very shortly after the Furman decision was handed down a bank robery took place in New York City. Hostages were taken and threats were made. The Washington Star-News quoted one of the robbers as saying:

> I'll shoot everyone in the bank. The Supreme Court will let me get away with this. There's no death penalty. It's ridiculous. I can shoot everyone here, then throw my gun down and walk out and they can't put me in the electric chair. You have to have a death penalty, otherwise this can happen every day. [The Washington Star-News, Aug. 23, 1972, p. 1, col. 1.]

I agree completely.

Mr. President, when all is said and done, when all the talking about deterrence and retribution and incapacitation is finished, what it all boils down to is whether it is ever "just" to impose the death penalty. Can a man ever be found to have acted so viciously, so cruelly, so much like an animal as to justify society in imposing upon him the ultimate punishment? I firmly believe he can.

What other punishment is "just" for a man, found to be sane, who would stab, strangle, and mutilate eight student nurses?

What other punishment is "just" for men who would invade the home of members of a rival religious sect and shoot to death men, women, and children, after forcing a mother to watch as her three young children were drowned before her eyes?

What other punishment is "just" for a band of social misfits who would invade the homes of people they had never even met and stab and hack to death a woman 8½ months pregnant and her guests?

What other punishment is "just" for people who would force a 24-year-old woman to douse herself with gasoline so that they could turn her into a human torch and watch as she burned to death?

There are other current cases that I could cite that we would all recognize, that come within the category of those I have just described. But since some of the defendants are now in the process of being tried for their crimes I will not mention or identify them in my remarks today. But, Mr. President, pick up almost any newspaper, today, yesterday, or the day before, or pick one up tomorrow, and you can read about some of these current cases to which I am now referring.

Mr. President, human justice is not feeding and clothing such people for a few years and then returning them to society on parole to do what they wish.

People who commit crimes like these have forfeited their own right to life. They have merited the clearest statement that such inhuman action cannot and will not be tolerated and that people who perform such acts will not be allowed to do so again. Justice demands no less.

It is indeed a great tragedy that a Nation, a civilized Nation, such as ours, that offers so much to so many, needs the death penalty to protect its citizens. Although it is sad and lamentable, there is no other course that squares with equal justice under the law. Nothing less will provide ample protection for the innocent, or insure a safe society.

Mr. HUGHES. Mr. President, the question before us today is symbolic and overriding—whether it is morally right and socially defensible for the State, under our system of criminal justice, to destroy a human life for any crime.

The legislation before us would restore the death penalty that was ruled unconstitutional by the Supreme Court in 1972.

How is it that a nation that has not suffered the brutality of a public execution for 8 years is now deliberately considering going back to the hangman's noose, the electric chair, and the gas chamber?

Primarily, public support for the restitution of the death penalty, as reflected in some public opinion polls, is a reflex response to fear.

One of the great tragedies of our time is that law-abiding citizens of this great land are spellbound from day to day by the fear of crime and violence.

The situation calls for remedial action.

But what action?

Is the morbid trip back to the death penalty the right way to go to protect society from violence and to keep faith with our moral purpose as a people? Is ultimate violence the antidote for violence?

For me, the answer must be "No."

I cannot be brought to believe that the way to conquer crime in America is to revert to institutional killings in the name of justice.

It is true that I am one of those who, for deeply religious reasons, believes in the absolute sanctity of human life.

"Thou shalt not kill" is the shortest of the Ten Commandments, uncomplicated by qualification or exception. I recognize that there are other passages of scripture that are cited in justify the death penalty.

To me, the Sixth Commandment is overriding.

It is as clear and awesomely commanding as the powerful thrust of chain lightning out of a dark summer sky.

But I oppose the restitution of capital punishment for good and sufficient reasons in addiiton to my basic religious conviction.

I oppose the death penalty because it demeans human society without protecting it. The weight of the evidence is that capital punishment does not deter serious crime. The weight of history is that judicial killing brutalizes the nations who practice it.

I oppose the death penalty because it cannot undo or rectify any crime that was committed, however brutal, and because there is no road back if the convicted man is later proven innocent.

As Lafayette said:

I shall ask for the abolition of the penalty of death until I have the infallibility of human judgment demonstrated to me.

Finally, I oppose the death penalty because it is grossly destructive of human hopes for a society more amenable to peace and less dependent on violence for the solution of its problems.

No Member of this body should be spared the agonizing knowledge of the suffering he has been asked to sanction.

Listen to the words of men who have been face-to-face with the manner of death imposed by the State:

The classic form of execution, still used by several States prior to the Furman decision, was hanging. Warden Clinton Duffy of San Quentin, a frequent witness, describes the process of hanging:

The day before an execution the prisoner goes through a harrowing experience of being weighed, measured for length of drop to assure breaking of the neck, the size of the neck, body measurements, etc. When the trap springs he dangles at the end of the rope. There are times when the neck has not been broken and the prisoner strangles to death. His eyes pop almost out of his head, his tongue swells and protrudes from his mouth, his neck may be broken, and the rope many times takes large portions of skin and flesh from the side of the face that the noose is on. He urinates, he defecates, and droppings fall to the floor while witnesses look on, and at almost all executions one or more faint or have to be helped out of the witness room. The prisoner remains dangling from the end of the rope for from 8 to 14 minutes before the doctor, who has climbed up a small ladder and listens to his heart beat with a stethoscope, pronounces him dead. A prison guard stands at the feet of the hanged person and holds the body steady, because during the first few minutes there is usually considerable struggling in an effort to breathe.

Clarence Darrow put the question even more graphically:

But why not do a good job of it? If you want to get rid of killings by hanging people or electrocuting them because these are so terrible, why not make a punishment that is terrible? ... Why not boil them in oil, as they used to do? Why not burn them at the stake? Why not sew them in a bag with serpents and throw them out to sea? ... Why not break every bone in their body on the rack, as has often been done for such serious offenses as heresy, witchcraft and adultery?

There is no such thing as being half-dead. Death inflicted by the State is not painless or instantaneous.

Our vote today is a signal to the world of the true regard we as a nation have for the value and dignity of human life everywhere.

Today is the time. There can be no alternative. It is life or death. It is not just a matter of a few simple crimes. It is not just a matter of applying it to remove someone from society. Certainly, with the technology we have and the ability we have, we can remove such persons from society without killing them.

For killing does brutalize us. After 10 long years of war, after savagery reaching all over the world and in our own political processes, after watching our own leaders struck down in violence, and noting the effects on television, do we now have to tell this country again that we are going to resort, in the name of the State, to killing, because there is no other way to proceed, because in our day and age and time there is no other way?

Who can deny that the death penalty is cruel and unusual punishment?

Has anyone ever described any execution, to say that by premeditation it is not cruel and unusual punishment? Let's stand behind the Constitution, the Supreme Court and the sixth Commandment.

Many years ago, the poet, John Donne, wrote:

No man is an island entire of itself, every man is a piece of the continent, a part of the main ...

Any man's death diminishes me, because I am involved in mankind, and therefore never send to know for whom the bell tolls, it tolls for thee.

We have seen humankind diminished enough by the ways of violence. Let our decision be not to return to the primitive darkness, but to move forward into the light of day.

For whom the bells tolls? It tolls for us.

Mr. President, the issue cannot be avoided today, tomorrow, or whenever this vote comes. It is a vote for life or a vote for death. A vote for life is a torch for a more humane and understanding way for humanity, a symbol to the world that people can see; but, in my opinion, a vote for death is a step backward into the primitive world of the past.

Mr. McCLELLAN. Mr. President, I am moved to make one observation. It is life or death. And the question is, shall we sacrifice the lives of future victims in order to spare the life of a murderer? Yes, there is life and death involved. He who demonstrates that he has no respect for life and is willing to set himself up as a judge and a god, to wantonly take the life of his fellow man, makes that decision, and makes it with sanity, when he carries out the act. If he does it once, he will do it again.

It is easy to describe the agony of death, either by hanging or in a gas chamber. It is also easy to describe the agony of a mother, 8½ months pregnant with child, begging strangers whom she has never seen, whom she does not know, who stand over her with a dagger to take her life and that of her unborn child, begging for her life.

Yes, you can describe horrors, but shall the murderer be permitted to live and have another opportunity to commit such a horrible crime, or shall we protect society and the next innocent victim against his dastardly deed?

Innocent people are entitled to live. He who commits the act condemns himself, and the law says that if he does it, that is his penalty.

Even the Bible, if I recall correctly, condemns to the eternal punishment. It is punishment that is sanctioned. We may want to forgive but we also want to protect the innocent. They must be protected, otherwise we do not have a civilization. A society that cannot protect its people from violent death, that refuses to take the precautions which are necessary, even if it does take the life of a murderer in order to protect the innocent, invites a repetition of the dastardly act by him who is so callous as to commit it in the first instance.

Witness Admits She Killed Heiress At Tate Mansion

LOS ANGELES (AP) — Patricia Krenwinkel calmly confessed on the witness stand Thursday that she ran down and killed coffee heiress Abigail Folger at Sharon Tate's home and the next night stabbed to death the wife of a wealthy market owner.

She said she and other members of the two killer parties were stoned on LSD. She said she felt "nothing."

The 23-year-old member of Charles Manson's hippie style clan—second of two women defendants to admit slayings at the Tate murder trial—also said she carved "WAR" in the chest of victim Leno LaBianca, the market owner, and stuck a fork in his stomach.

And asked if Manson "had any connection with you in these homicides you are on trial for," Miss Krenwinkel replied: "None whatsoever."

Attorney Objected

Miss Krenwinkel, soft-spoken and articulate, testified despite an objection from her attorney that she might incriminate herself and a warning from the judge that she might talk herself into a death penalty.

She described her life with Manson's nomadic family, and said she deemed him "perfection" personified. Then, she told of the night of August 1959 when Miss Tate and four visitors to the Tate home were shot and stabbed to death.

She said, referring to Miss Folger, 26: "I had a knife in my hand and she ran out a back door ... I chased her through the door and onto the lawn and I stabbed her and I kept stabbing her and I looked up and there was blackness and that was all."

Because of the LSD, she said, she remembers little: "It was like all reaction ... It's all a picture of motion and reaction. I can't remember details. There was some man I was tying up. I can remember looking up and Sadie was fighting with two women. I remember I just got up and went over and I was fighting."

Sadie is the nickname of defendant Susan Atkins, who admitted killing Miss Tate.

What did she feel, her attorney asked. "I guess complete paranoia ... Nothing. It was just there, and like it was all right."

No Remorse

On cross examination Miss Krenwinkel was asked by Deputy Dist. Atty. Vincent Bugulosi why she stabbed Miss Folger.

"It was just there to do," she replied.

Bugulosi continued:

'Q: Do you have any remorse?

A: I don't even know what that word means.

Q: Do you have any sorrow?

A: No ... it was right then, yes.

Q: Do you still feel it was right?

A: Yes.

Q. Did the thought enter your mind that Abigail Folger wanted to live as much as you did?

A: No. Because I am willing to give up my life.

She said there was no reason for the stabbing and she doesn't know why she did it.

"I don't judge it. All I know is what happened and it was right because it happened. I don't try to figure it out."

Left, courtesy of Associated Press Newsfeatures.

Top page, letter to the editor of *Newsweek* by Adela Santos, April 25, 1971.

Above, letter to the editor of *Newsweek* by Gary Missel, April 12, 1971.

Don't bring back capital punishment

MONSIGNOR S. J. ADAMO

Let me emphasize this point. In the year 1964 I served as a member of the New Jersey Commission To Study Capital Punishment. Among the shocking statistics presented at that time were some that covered a fifteen-year period ending August 1, 1962. The figures concerned the various national backgrounds of those convicted of capital crimes and how they fared.

Thus, 76 convicted Americans had been executed while 29 had their sentences commuted to life. That means that roughly 30 percent were shown mercy. During the same period 26 Italians were put to death—without one commutation. Likewise executed were three Puerto Ricans, three Russians, one Pole and one Irishman.

When it came to American citizens of foreign descent, a similar pattern was discovered. Thus 15 persons of Italian descent went to the electric chair, while only 2 were shown mercy. Three of Polish descent were executed, and one Pole was spared. However, three criminals of Irish descent, marked for execution, were all given life instead. The luck of the Irish!

In the event you are ecumenically inclined it may be discouraging to realize that a Protestant sentenced to death during that period would have had a 50-50 chance of having his sentence commuted to life imprisonment; whereas a Catholic sentenced to death had only one chance in eight for commutation. In short, the possibility of a convicted murderer being shown mercy were four times greater if he were a Protestant.

These figures simply demonstrate the terrible bias that was operating in meting out capital punishment. The more wealthy were always less likely to feel the full impact of the law. Crime doesn't pay, but having money does shield one against the law's severity.

One minor item: it is almost unheard of for a woman to be put to death, especially during the last half century. For them the quality of mercy was seldom strained, and was generally poured out fully. Even though Women's Lib thinks that the female sex is disfavored in America, in this vital area it was always highly favored.

Clearly, then, the Supreme Court decision was a tribute to social justice not to reckless permissiveness.

There are those who insist that all the argumentation so far proves only that the death penalty should be administered more equitably. So they urge the fashioning of laws that are airtight, precise and utterly impartial. Even granted such an impossible dream could be realized, there is still reason to seek the abolition of the death penalty.

Consider that it is basically an act of vengeance. It doesn't correct the criminal nor help the dead victim. It satisfies only the desire to avenge a murder or some other terrible crime. This is why the Indiana Catholic Conference recently called for the continued elimination of capital punishment, stating that "a most effective way to teach respect for human life is to refuse to take life in the name of the law."

A 1973 Modest Proposal (from 33 A.D.):
Those who call for the restoration of the death penalty do not go far enough! Is it not written: "An eye for an eye, a tooth for a tooth"? Not only should we begin killing murderers once again (life for life), but we should return to the practice of cutting off the robber's hand, pulling out the slanderer's tongue. (Surely he was talking collectively for all his people where it is written: "Vengeance is mine; I will repay, sayeth the Lord.")

But first things first. Let us begin killing people again to show people that killing people is evil!

Who says that capital punishment is not a deterrent? So what if several states that have abolished the death penalty have not had a rise in the number of murders committed? What does that conclusively prove?

Enough of this permissive sentimentalism! Restore the death penalty, then. . .

Steve Mailloux
Los Angeles, California

Even God in explaining the Ten Commandments says: "When a man kills another after maliciously scheming to do so you must take him even from my altar and put him to death." (Ex. 21:14)

Name Withheld
Dubuque, Iowa

There are no arguments for capital punishment for a Christian. "Vengeance is mine, sayeth the Lord." As Christians we might best show our deep respect for the awesome mystery of life by challenging the taking of human life at all times, abortions, war killings, killing of caged humans.

Edward J. Lozicki
Fremont, Michigan

"He who kills a man shall be put to death." (Lev.: 24:17)

Name Withheld
Winchester, Illinois

The question of capital punishment is very much related to other much-discussed issues of today like warfare and abortion.

I am opposed to warfare; I am opposed to capital punishment; and I am opposed to abortion for the same reason—I am for life.

I don't think the Scriptures give us a clear foundation one way or the other on the absolute sacredness of human life. I just think it will be more productive of social development if we highly regard human life on the battlefield, in the womb, or in the jail cell, than if we take human life lightly in any of these places.

Father Ronald Luka, C.M.F.
Garden City, New York

Top and above, reprinted with permission from *U.S. Catholic* (May 1973), 221 West Madison St., Chicago, Illinois 60606.

How About The Victim?

All sorts of legal semantics are involved when there is argument over the death penalty as has just taken place before the U.S. Supreme Court. But it comes down to a simple moral issue.

All along the line from the less severe crimes right up to murder, the victim is increasingly becoming the forgotten man.

But to nail the issue right on the head let us confine the discussion to murder and to be more specific let it be a typical case of murder committed during a holdup.

A housewife, walking home to her husband and children is assaulted and robbed. When she resists she is shot and killed, the assailant is later caught, tried and convicted. The opponents of capital punishment would say that to electrocute this man would be cruel and unusual punishment and that the death penalty has been "repudiated by the conscience of contemporary society."

Now this matter of conscience: Where does proper concern comes in? A family is left motherless. The focus of the opponents of capital punishment is centered not on the victim but on the killer who has contributed nothing to society and in fact is a proven enemy of society. If he had not been apprehended he would likely have committed more crimes.

Yet the concern is that capital punishment would be a cruel penalty for him. We feel that the surviving husband and children of the dead woman know more about cruelty than the attorneys who would strike down the death penalty.

Top, editorial cartoon by Pat Oliphant. Copyright *Washington Star*. Reprinted with permission Los Angeles Times Syndicate. Above, from *The Times Record*, January 19, 1971.

266

Capital Punishment Protects Civilization

By THOMAS A. LANE

WASHINGTON — In our city, we learn all too frequently of some young policemen being gunned down by criminals. A wife and children are bereaved. Good men are murdered; evil men survive. Justice is mocked.

In Britain, the killing of a policeman is so horrendous a

Thomas

A.

Lane

crime that even the criminals outlaw it. In the rare cases when a policeman is killed, criminals cooperate with police in identifying and exposing the murderer. He is the common enemy of all mankind, straight and crooked.

But in our society, the killing of a policeman is condoned by the silence of people and officials. In our city, criminals are executed only by policemen defending themselves or by storekeepers defending their property. The processes of justice are so attenuated by a sickly sentimentality as to be an obstacle to law enforcement. Through flagrant abuse of judicial discretion, in a perversion of philosophy and purpose, the courts have become instruments to protect the criminal from the community.

Some States are considering the abolition of capital punishment. Various arguments are advanced to support the proposed legislation: that society should not set an example of killing; that society should reclaim errant citizens, not destroy them; that society may err and execute an innocent man; that the death sentence is not a deterrent.

These arguments are a retreat from truth and rationality. They illustrate the difficulty which the human mind sometimes encounters in distinguishing between fantasy and reality. They repudiate the great truths about man which philosophy has taught us.

To assert that capital punishment is not a deterrent to murder is to deny reason. We know that criminals act out of conceptions of their own self-interest. If British criminals do not condone police killing, that is because British society did not condone police killing. British criminals foreswore a course which would have been against their self-interest.

If an American robber cold-bloodedly murders a gas-station attendant to prevent future witness to his crime, he does so because he believes it is to his advantage to kill. Pity the society which encourages such a judgment. If murder is to be outlawed from our society, murder must never be advantageous to the potential killer.

The question of deterrence is obscured by the records of jurisdictions in which capital punishment is prescribed but not assessed. Criminals deal in reality, as they see it. If the law is a dead letter, indeed it does not deter them. Where the law in enforced, it does deter murder.

If the law is not enforced, the cure is enforcement, not repeal. We must elect officials who will perform their duties, not abet their malfeasance by repealing the law.

The greatest reclaimer of errant citizens is justice, pure and swift. It operates to prevent crime by making it clear to all that crime does not pay. When the penalties of the law are suspended in misguided charity, offenders are encouraged to err again.

The execution of murderers is an imperative of justice. If you believe that the cold-blooded killing of a law-abiding citizen is an intolerable crime, you must believe that the only just punishment is the forfeiture of the murderer's own life. No other punishment is adequate. This is the law of Moses.

If you do not exact that just punishment, you create a society in which wanton killing is encouraged. This is the condition of our society today.

There is a terrible consistency of decadence in a society which executes its unborn children but will not execute its murderers. Both errors illustrate the rejection of philosophy which influences our law-givers. Decadence contrives its own justification.

Courtesy of Thomas A. Lane and *The Wanderer*, April 15, 1971.

Shapp on Capital Punishment

ON MARCH 23, nine years ago, the late Gov. David Lawrence announced in Harrisburg a freeze on capital punishment until the Legislature resolved the issue of whether to execute or not to execute. Later that year the General Assembly voted to retain the death penalty.

The freeze was lifted. But, except for 1962, the following years saw no human beings die in the electric chair in this state.

With Gov.-elect Shapp's weekend statement of total opposition to capital punishment, the freeze is back on. It will be up to the General Assembly to do what it failed to do under previous governors, from Shafer (who, as Lieutenant Governor, favored the death penalty), through Scranton (who doubted its efficacy) to Lawrence (who opposed it outright).

It will be up to the General Assembly to legislate us out of this vestige of tribal barbarism by replacing capital punishment with life imprisonment. In this predominantly Christian nation, we understand the moral rule to be one which prohibits the taking of human life except in self-defense and, by extension, in war—although we like to think that that tribal form of aggression will soon be conquered, too.

In any case, neither the state nor its citizens can know absolute truth, which is solely for the gods to ponder. Yet unerring, perfect truth is the assumption on which sentencing and executing a person is based. The state's killing a convicted killer is the final, absolute act.

Scientifically, we know just enough about psychology and about brain circuitry and its malfunctions to know how little we do know, far from enough to "know" who is really guilty enough to deserve death. That, again, is for the gods to ponder.

Under Mr. Shapp's moral impetus, we suspect the Legislature will find it difficult to duck this issue which has hung fire so long. We hope, however, that the people's representatives in Harrisburg will have the wisdom to eliminate the death penalty completely, rather than keeping it for some classes of crimes—like the killing of an on-duty police officer, an exception which some legislators favor. There is no moral or logical reason to place higher value on a policeman's life than on any other human being's. Either capital punishment is an effective deterrent or it isn't. Crime figures over the years do not support its efficacy. Logic and morality do not support it at all.

Let us have done with it.

Right, from *The Pittsburgh Post-Gazette*, December 30, 1970.

What Death Row Has Taught Me About Living

By Leaman R. Smith

After what seemed an interminable pause, the bailiff's dull, flat voice intoned: "We, the jury, having found the defendant, Leaman Russell Smith, guilty of murder in the first degree, fix the penalty as death."

What had begun as a bad-check spree had ended with my killing two policemen and receiving the death decree. Society demands my life, and I will no doubt pay in full. In the interim, I have existed for nearly seven and a half years on San Quentin's overcrowded death row, apprehensively waiting for someone to push the button that will end my existence.

Although I have offended society and must pay for it, you and I may have more in common than you suspect. I have read where 91 percent of people questioned admitted they have committed acts for which they might have received prison sentences. Ninety-one percent!

And may I be forgiven for asking: What good does my punishment really do?   □

Above, from *Family Weekly*, February 27, 1972.

An Open Reply to Death-Row Author Leaman R. Smith

In the February 27 issue, FAMILY WEEKLY published an article by Leaman R. Smith entitled, "What Death Row Has Taught Me About Living." I'm afraid Mr. Smith only convinced me that his ordeal on death row really has taught him very little. He mentions that he learned to face reality and stop indulging in self-pity. Yet he closes with an obvious appeal for sympathy motivated by self-pity.

Mr. Smith mentions a survey showing that 91 percent of people questioned admitted having done things for which they could legally be imprisoned. That statistic is probably close to the truth. How many of those people, though, had only done a *single* such act, for which they would probably have been given a suspended sentence? And how many of the 91 percent he calls his fellows would have taken the life of a police officer in the midst of a crime? No, I think most of us have very little in common with Mr. Smith.

The greatest deterrent to crime yet devised, since we have not been able to eliminate the motivation toward crime, is the certainty of detection, capture and punishment. The 91 percent cited by Mr. Smith are not a symbol of brotherhood with *him*; rather, they are a monument to our citizenry's failure to care.

How many hardened criminals are walking the streets today because citizens will not report criminal acts, will not appear as witnesses; in short, will not "get involved"? Why is it so reprehensible for an American to report somebody who is assaulting or stealing from his neighbor? If every citizen were to report criminal acts to proper authorities, we could reduce our crime/conviction ratio enormously, secure proportionate reductions in our insurance premiums and greatly improve the personal security and happiness of our daily living.

What good does Mr. Smith's punishment really do? By his capture, trial and execution, other young men and women are made aware that the law *does* operate to apprehend criminals and mete out justice. By this knowledge they may be deterred from following Mr. Smith's example and instead encouraged to make their way within the law. To let him go free or reduce his sentence would do just the reverse and encourage more to enter the field of crime.

Why should Smith *not* be punished? Would it give life back to those from whom he violently took it? Would it give comfort to their widows and children? Would it make our citizens feel safer walking the streets, or going about their daily lives? Would it help our policemen do a better job of protecting us? In point of fact, Mr. Smith, *what have you done to deserve to live?*

If you don't know the answer to your question, Mr. Smith, I don't believe you have much to offer society. And if society does not recognize the answer, I fear that it has little to hope for except more crime, more fear, less individual freedom and less enjoyment of life in these United States.
—*Victor T. Lyon, Hobbs, N.M.*

Letter to *Family Weekly* by Victor T. Lyon, May 14, 1972.

What Does the Bible Say About the Death Penalty?

By Carl McIntire; distributed by 20th Century Reformation Hour, Collingswood, N.J.

3. Modern Humanism

It is the social gospel, which is nothing more than a pious expression of humanism, that is being used to attack the death penalty in the various state legislatures. The liberals and leftists in ecclesiastical circles come in the name of an appreciation of human life and of doing good, and without the knowledge and the standards of God's Word many are misled in this field. The truth is that such propagandists have a very low view of human life and its importance. Their humanistic philosophy is built upon a thoroughly anti-Christian and unbiblical concept of the universal brotherhood of man and the universal Fatherhood of God.

According to this erroneous and apostate line, the world indeed is not under the curse and the wrath of God, and all men are His children. The Scriptures say: "The wrath of God is revealed from heaven," "Cursed is the ground for thy sake," "The wages of sin is death," "Sin is the transgression of the law," and the penalty pronounced by God is death. Only when men repent of their sin and look to Jesus Christ by God's grace and in faith can they become the children of God. "Ye are all the children of God by faith in Christ Jesus" (Gal. 3:26). Surely our Saviour knew what He was talking about when He said to the religious leaders of His day: "If God were your Father, ye would love me. . . . Ye are of your father the devil, and the lusts of your father ye will do. He was a murderer from the beginning. . . . He is a liar, and the father of it" (John 8:42-44). These humanists completely ignore the exceeding sinfulness of the heart of man and the depravity of the race.

It is the Bible that tells us the consequences of man's sin—the physical evil, the pains and miseries of life which have come upon the race, and finally the separation of man from God in hell itself. The death penalty for the capital crime is divinely decreed in keeping with the judgment and the justice of God pronounced against sin in all of its heinous offense against God. Humanism offers no saviour. Humanism anticipates no judgment. Humanism offers man no future and no hope.

4. The Current Arguments

The arguments of those who want to abolish the death penalty are humanistic and based upon the pride and the lusts of man and an inversion of what might be called the moral force.

The majority of the New York State Penal Law Revision Commission favoring abolition of capital punishment wrote, "The execution of the penalty of death calls inescapably on the agents of the state to perpetrate an act of supreme violence under circumstances of the greatest cruelty to the individual involved. . . ." At this point the majority has departed completely from any concept of moral judgment and punishment deserved, as pronounced by a righteous God.

The next statement of the majority also involves the same level of thinking, ". . . the social need for the grievous condemnation of the gravest crimes can be met, as it is met in abolition states, without resort to the barbarism of this kind." The reflection is primarily against God, for a God who would require capital punishment would Himself be a barbarian. The fact is that the humanists have an entirely different god. Man is their god, not the God of divine revelation, whose penalty for the breaking of law when it comes to murder is the forfeiture of the life of the murderer.

The next argument partakes of the same emotionalism, "The very fact that life is at stake (in a capital crime trial) introduces a morbid and sensational factor in the trial of the accused and increases the danger that public sympathy will be aroused for the defendant." The conscience of the public should be so attuned to the demands of God —and it would if the Word of God were being preached from the pulpits of the country—that public sentiment would approve of the justice of the conviction just as it did in the United States, for instance, in the famous Lindbergh case where the child was first kidnaped, then murdered, and the murderer paid for his crime.

Those who defended the death penalty on New York's Commission made an appeal to morality:

"Because wanton murder is so extremely wrong, morally wrong, the punishment therefore must remain proportionally extremely severe to emphasize to other would-be murderers the high outrage that society feels against the commission of such crimes.

". . . were there to be no room in our system for sentences any more severe than the presently understood 'life sentence' even for the most bizarre and outrageously heinous crimes of murder, there would in time be further erosion of the concept of the dignity of human life and a corresponding weakening of faith in, and respect for the law on the part of a preponderant majority of law-abiding citizens. Human nature, being what it is, must be understood to demand, on occasion, a reversion to earlier penal concepts of retaliation, vengeance, and the placation of an outraged community."

The statement further said:

"There is more crime in the State of New York than anywhere else in the world. The historical reasons and justifications that have kept the death penalty for certain crimes in this state to the present time, should not be suddenly and summarily invalidated or nullified by untested and unproven claims of the humanitarianism of other methods of punishment or the ineffectiveness of the old one."

5. The General Moral Breakdown

The campaign to have the death penalty removed in the various states of the United States is simply a reflection of the general moral breakdown and debauchery that is multiplying in the United States. Four of the major commandments dealing with man's relationship to man as presented in the Bible are: (1) "Thou shalt not kill" —this protects and honors human life. (2) "Thou shalt not commit adultery"—this protects the purity of life and makes possible the honor of the family. (3) "Thou shalt not steal"—this protects the property to which a man is divinely entitled. (4) "Thou shalt not bear false witness"—this protects the truth and the good name of the individual against slander and false accusation.

Capital Punishment— For What?

By DAVID BRUDNOY

Shortly before the election, in what could probably be seen as his gesture to the friends of "law and order," Massachusetts Gov. Francis W. Sargent gave a tough little speech in which he urged the imposition of compulsory capital punishment on anyone convicted of killing a police officer or bombing a building in which someone was killed:

The governor's talk seemed to evoke little comment in the press, although, coming from a liberal like Sargent, the position should have been more widely remarked. His position—death for two types of killers, and two only—raises several questions and leads at least to a few tentative answers.

Those favoring capital punishment have long contended that the ultimate penalty deters would-be criminals from committing their crimes and/or is morally right, in that our respect for the lives of innocents is shown by demanding death for those who kill.

Anti-capital punishment people rebut, saying the death penalty does not deter crime and/or that the morally correct response to a heinous crime is compassion, not the further taking of a life.

As stated, these two positions have the virtue of internal consistency, whatever one might think of that view with which one disagrees.

The argument as to morality also admits of no final proof. No one can "prove" the existence of God scientifically, nor disprove His existence; no one can prove what "morality" is by reference to objective criteria, but only by reference to man-made systems of ethics, which may or may not derive from divine inspiration—which gets it all back again to the non-provability of God's existence by scientifically verifiable criteria.

Thus we can assert until kingdom come that capital punishment is moral or immoral, and be "right" by our own lights, but dismally wrong according to other, perhaps just as thoughtful, observers.

Why, then, capital punishment for cop-killers and bombers who kill while bombing? If Gov. Sargent thinks capital punishment is such cases will be a deterrent, then surely we might demand that he press for capital punishment for all killers, in the hopes that such punishment will deter their crimes as well. If the governor believes it is morally right to kill killers under cover of law, then are we to believe that he thinks the lives of policemen are worth more than the lives of others, or that those killed by a bomb are any the less dead, or of more worth, than those killed by a knife, gun, pipe, rope, razor, what have you?

Perhaps the governor has arrived at his conclusion because he thinks the two types of crimes which he has named are so dreadful that they exceed in wickedness all other types of crime; that is, the Eichmann analogy. May others not feel just as strongly that some other form of killing—such as the bashing in of a skull of some defenseless old person, by a brutal attacker—is even more reprehensible, or at the very least, equally as reprehensible?

Gov. Sargent's proposal seems short of the mark, according to those who favor capital punishment for whichever or both of the reasons I've suggested and it seems to be excessive to those who are against capital punishment.

Suspicion as to the governor's motivation for his proposal continues to bother one. Is Mr. Sargent trying to steer a careful course between the "get-tough" types and the "go-soft" sorts? Because of the current wave of bombings and cop-killings? If not, why? If so, what of other terrible types of killing?

My own view, for what it's worth, is that whether capital punishment is a deterrent or not—and my hunch is that it is, although as mentioned above I cannot so prove—it is morally right for society to avenge the death of innocents by demanding the death of the killer, after a fair trial, according to scrupulous due process, and with access to appeals procedures.

There, too, my "morally right" position is based on faith, not on proof. But my position is only one man's and need not cloud the major point I wish to make which is this: The governor's position lacks internal consistency and hints at expediency.

Both the governor of Massachusetts and the rest of us should examine the matter seriously, right now, and bring the issue to the point of active intellectual controversy. Perhaps we can arrive at a statewide consensus which could help guide the General Court in its next session.

Reprinted with permission from the July 5, 1971, issue of *Human Events*, 422 First St., S.E., Washington, D.C. 20003.

Mainstreams

... On Murder

By Edwin A. Roberts, Jr.

◆ This week the Mainstreams columnist interviews himself.

Daniel St. Albin Greene, your friend and fellow staff writer, recently attacked you in print because in the past you have defended the legitimacy of capital punishment in certain instances. What is your response?

Well, all things considered, I would rather be attacked by Dan Greene in print than in an alley. As for the issue itself, it is one that offers no satisfaction to either side. For one thing, it requires long thoughts on unnatural death, a subject no sober man takes up with pleasure. But once we are into it, I think we must decide with what degree of outrage we regard cold-blooded murder—and I refer to moral outrage, not the emotional kind. Moral outrage lasts.

What we seek, of course, (and what we will never have) is a society without

---

Comment

---

murders. The best we can do as a community is to emphasize with spirit our belief that premeditated murder is an abomination. One way to demonstrate our conviction is to provide that kidnap-murder, rape-murder, political assassination, and similar misdeeds are repaid in kind. Is this tawdry vengeance or fair retribution? If we believe that society must be the victim's surrogate, inasmuch as the victim has been rendered incapable of seeking redress on his own, then I think the word is retribution.

But doesn't the death penalty brutalize society even as it fails to deter would-be murderers?

The murder rate is soaring, which means we are already brutalized, and terrorized, by the killers among us. Do we make society more brutal by executing those who are the first brutalizers? I'm not sure. Do we become more brutal when we fire a gun at an intruder? Our major concern must be for our personal safety. There is no reason to believe that a prison term is equal to death in the mind of a man with murderous notions.

Top left, from *The National Observer*, December 21, 1974. Copyright Dow Jones & Co., Inc.
Top right, letter to *The National Observer* by John C. Allen, December 7, 1974.

False Solution to Crime

IT HAS BEEN said by critics of more stringent firearms regulation that such legislation would be futile if left unenforced. There can be little argument to that line of reasoning. More enforcement is needed.

But to say that the best policy in dealing with convicted killers is "an eye for an eye" abdicates humanity and denies the possibility of human beings solving human problems. And to say that society's attempts to date have been only marginally successful is no argument that the effort should not be continued.

I fear that to pursue the course of capital punishment is to abandon efforts to solve society's problems; it would be a false panacea to a society that no longer cares enough to try. Surely there is still faith in the humanity of mankind.

LeROY KRAMER III

Above left, letter to the editor of the *Detroit Free Press* by LeRoy Kramer III, December 4, 1973.
Above right, letter to the editor of the *Detroit Free Press* by John J. Jackman, December 25, 1973.

As Our Readers See It

THE POLICE slaying of 15-year-old Anthony Moorer is yet another tragedy for the city of Detroit. I would like to express my personal sorrow over his death, and over the deaths of the young boys recently murdered. I would also like to add my voice to that of many others in asking all Detroiters to put away their guns and stop the killing.

Many people are calling for a return to capital punishment in order to halt the rising crime rate. I feel that the restoration of the death penalty would only serve to further cheapen life. If we do not eliminate the root causes of the despair and frustration felt by many people, the death penalty will add to our tragedy.

The way to reduce crime is to achieve true social justice: true economic justice, where a man's worth on the job comes from what he achieves, not from the color of his skin; true educational justice in a school small enough to treat people as individuals; equality in housing, without blockbusting or "steering"; criminal justice that brings all accused persons to a speedy trial.

If we achieve social justice the dope dealers will disappear, the "Saturday night specials" will be thrown away, and a young boy's life will be worth more than a yellow 1971 Ford LTD.

JOHN J. JACHMAN

The Unnecessary Deaths

By KENNETH A. GIBSON

NEWARK, N. J. — The bloodshed that occurred in Attica, N. Y., disturbs me more deeply than any event in recent memory.

The use of coordinated organized violence in overcoming the inmates at Attica state prison stands as one of the most callous and blatantly repressive acts ever carried out by a supposedly civilized society on its own people. All of us who oppose violence must deplore this use of force by so-called responsible authorities. Further, we must attempt to understand this event fully.

The demands of the inmates at Attica were basically reasonable and human. They asked for more relevant vocational shops, true religious freedom, a chance to work at renovating the facilities, and other things which we recognize as necessary for a man to function as an alert, healthy being. The fact that they had to take over the prison only suggests the extent of their frustration and the lack of other channels to express totally legitimate grievances.

We understand why these demands had to be made.

But we must understand more than this. We must recognize the political awareness present in the inmates' actions. And we must see in this awareness an awakened desire of people actively and constructively to change and improve their condition.

Across the country young men and women in prisons are becoming aware of the forces which have controlled their lives. Many of these people have previously been uninvolved, alienated, without direction. They now attempt to learn how to deal with these forces and institutions so that they might be able to shape their own destiny and that of their children.

We applaud this as a vital and human development, recognizing that it is good for people to become involved in the process of changing their lot.

And we say that if this practice involves challenges to existing institutions then those institutions must be open to the challenge for it is made out of genuine legitimate concerns. Yet, we must recognize that those in positions of power who feel threatened by this political awareness react in a most violent and repressive manner. We condemn this repression, because awareness and involvement of people in controlling their own future is something to be encouraged.

And there is still more to understand. When we look at pictures from Attica or the Tombs or San Quentin, we see black and Spanish faces. In some prisons inmate population is 80 per cent or more black and Spanish. Those people who have been victimized by the society on the streets are now victimized in prison. When we look at prison conditions and the brutal use of force at Attica we see the same force of racism which caused and then put down with force civil disturbances in this country's ghettos. This racism cannot be tolerated.

The inmates of Attica were victims of a systematic violence which pervades not only our prisons but the streets and towns of this society. We must admit as a nation that the deaths at Attica should never have occurred and we must act to erase the possibility of their recurrence.

Mayor Kenneth A. Gibson of Newark wrote this statement on Monday, Sept. 13, immediately after hearing of the Attica catastrophe.

Dull or not, it is obvious that the great majority of Americans prefer to fight crime within the law, agreeing with the following statement given to PARADE by Attorney-General Edward H. Levi on the dangers of vigilantism.

ATTORNEY GENERAL'S VIEW

"Vigilante groups always have one thing in common: They operate outside of the law. With crime at such high levels today, some citizens might be tempted to band together in vigilante groups, but such actions are not only counter to our democratic processes, they are ineffective as well.

"Vigilantes do not build respect for the law—they destroy it. There are a great many responsible roles for citizens to play today in the support of law enforcement and criminal justice. Crime can be reduced only if the criminal justice system is strong and effective. It cannot be strong if every group tries to take the law into its own hands."

Left, from *Parade*, June 22, 1975. Right, reprinted with permission from *National Review*, 150 East 35th Street, New York, New York, 10016.

Curing the Criminal

Should prisons rehabilitate? The question has received a new twist in Connecticut, where a state prison has lately paroled nine convicted child molesters who have submitted to an experimental behavior modification program. The 12-week program uses mild electrical shock and other "aversive" techniques to cure the subjects of their lust for children. So far, none of the parolees, who have been free for as long as 11 months, is known to have repeated his offense, and another inmate, soon to be released, says the program, though unpleasant, has been both painless and successful. "Children are not sexual objects to me anymore," he asserts.

The program is of course voluntary, but objections have naturally been raised. "It's inherently coercive," charges William Olds of the Connecticut Civil Liberties Union. "There's no such thing as a real volunteer in a prison, especially when a prisoner knows participating may enhance his chances for parole." If this is so, then by the same token prisoners should not receive time off for good behavior either. But why deny, in the name of liberty, the penitent convict who really wants to be rid of an inclination to one of the most loathsome of perversions? "Also," Olds goes on, "it's unproven, and we're concerned about the danger of releasing pedophiles into the community on the basis of something like this." A much better point, and how wonderfully reassuring to hear it made by the leader of an organization that usually turns livid *en masse* when a murderer is treated brusquely by his arresting officer. An ACLU official Alvin Bronstein, objects that such techniques have "a tremendous potential for abuse." True; so does all power; which is why it must be exercised prudently with all reasonable safeguards. But this program also seems to have a tremendous potential for good, for real rehabilitation, far beyond any yet shown by sociologica homilies and prison study groups; and that is why i should not be hastily forsworn.

ARMY OFFERS MISSILE BASE AS SITE FOR VIOLENCE CENTER

(San Francisco, Calif.) - Congressman Ron Dellums disclosed last week at a community meeting here that consideration had been given to the idea of establishing part of the much opposed Center for the Study and Reduction of Violence at UCLA on a top secret Nike missile base in the Santa Monica hills.

The information was received by Rep. Dellums in the form of a letter written in 1973, to a state official by Dr. "Jolly" West, head of the Violence Center project at UCLA and leading proponent of its funding. The Congressman read the letter aloud to the assembled group of over 200 interested persons:

"I am in possesion of confidential information to the effect that the Army is prepared to turn over Nike missile bases to state and local agencies for non-military purposes. They may look with favor on health-related applications. Such a Nike missile base is located in the Santa Monica mountains within a half mile drive to the neuro-psychiatric institute. It is accessible but relatively remote.

"The site is securely fenced and includes various buildings and improvements, making it suitable for prompt occupancy. If this site was made available to the neuro-psychological institute as a research facility, perhaps initially as an adjunct to the new Center for the Study and Reduction of Violence, we could put it to very good use. Comparative studies could be carried out there in an isolated but convenient location for experimental or model programs for the alteration of undesirable behavior. Such programs might include control of drugs, or alcohol abuse, modification of chronic anti-social or impulsive aggressiveness, etc.

"The site could also accomodate conferences or retreats for instruction of selected groups of mental health related professionals and others, i.e., law enforcement personnel, parole officers, special educators; for many of whom demonstration and participation both would be effective methods of instruction. My understanding is the direct request by the governor or another appropriate officer of the state to the Secretary of Defense or of course the President would be most likely to produce prompt results. Needless to say, I stand available to participate in any way that might be helpful."

Sincerely yours,
Lewis West, M.D.
Medical Director

Commenting further on the implications of the letter, Dellums said:

Scientists and corrupt governmental officials mistakenly believe that violence can be cut on and off.

"We have violence in this society, some of it is condoned and legitamized violence and some of it is illegitimate and uncondoned violence. We have the violence of war, the violence of pollution, the violence of our economics, the violence of racism, the violence of sexism and the violence of an insensitive and corrupt government.

And then, we, in some way, choose to decide that the way we prevent violent behavior is not to alter the values and priorities that created, legitimated and perpetuated violence in our society. And again we find an establishment-oriented, bureaucratic - oriented, maintenance man for the status quo orientated proposal rather than altering the values, the practices and priorities of a society that perpetuates violence.

"I think that these types of violence centers are dealing with symptoms and not basic causes. Those of us who live as oppressed people in the country understand the anguish and the anger and the frustration of crushed dreams and stomped on hopes, limited opportunities. We, out of our ignorance, in this nation and in this world, have established standards that ignorance has allowed us to maintain...

"I think we've gone to an absurd conclusion with respect to allowing our ignorance to dictate our standards of humanity. I think that if we are going to begin to study the process of how we can prevent violence then we have to go to the values, we have to go to the mentality, go to the practices and go to the institutions that have been perpetuated and developed as a result of our violence.

"I am unequivocally opposed to the concept of this center, the mentality of this country that sees a need to spend millions and millions of dollars never dealing with the basic reason why we are violent to each other. We have evolved a society that has never spent any money teaching our young people how to live...

"This center in my opinion is a sham, it is a bureaucratic, elitist, arrogant, dangerous, sinister response to a very serious problem." □

From *The Black Panther* (February 2, 1974), published by The Black Panther International News Service.

Is Punishment a Crime?

By WALTER BERNS

So far I have considered deterrence and retribution as independent justifications for capital punishment. But there is a point where they come together. We can recognize that point of convergence when we acknowledge that the law works by praising as well as by blaming.

The law blames when it prescribes punishment for certain acts and when it subjects those who commit those acts to punishment. We see that easily enough. We tend to forget, however, that in punishing the guilty (when it blames the deed he commits), the law praises those who do not commit the deed. The law praises righteousness and obedience to law.

This point is well made by Adam Smith: we resent the criminal, he says. So much do we resent him, that not only do we wish to see him punished, but we wish to see him punished by our own hand and for the crime he committed. We feel cheated, he says, if the criminal should die of a fever before he is brought to justice. And with respect to murder, "nature, antecedent to all reflections upon the utility of punishment, has in this manner stamped upon the human heart, in the strongest and most indelible characters, an immediate and instinctive approbation of the sacred and necessary law of retaliation."⁹ This passion—which he labels resentment—must of course be tamed; it must be tamed lest it become simple revenge, the "most detestable of the passions." It is the job of the law to tame this passion, which the law does by satisfying it. The law tames that passion, that anger we feel in the presence of injustice,' by satisfying it, and it satisfies it when it brings the guilty to justice and when it pays him back.

Last summer, for example, a seven-year-old boy was brutally murdered on the lower East Side of Manhattan. The next day, in a nearby neighborhood, a 28-year-old girl was stabbed to death in the doorway to her apartment. The police caught the man suspected of doing it, and had a hard time protecting him from an angry crowd of local residents. A week later a 31-year-old man was stabbed to death by a burglar in his Ninth Avenue apartment, this before the eyes of his wife.

I now quote from the New York *Times* account of these events (Sunday, Aug. 26, 1973, News of the Week, page 6): "On the lower East Side, most residents seemed to agree with the police that the next time a murder suspect is identified, Tuesday's mob scene is very likely to be repeated. There is a widespread feeling that the police, the courts, the entire criminal justice system simply acts out a sort of charade, and that it is up to the community to demand that justice is done. 'When the police find him, they'll just say he's a sick man and send him to a hospital for two years,' said . . . a Delancey Street shopkeeper. 'Then he'll be right back on the street. The only thing to do is to kill this man right away, quickly and quietly.' "

That anger is not reprehensible. Anger is the sentiment aroused by the sight of injustice, and is therefore intimately allied with justice—and civil society requires justice. But that anger has to be tamed, and the local police alone cannot do it.

I mean, the police protecting the suspect at the police station cannot tame that anger unless they can assure that righteously angry crowd that the murderer will be paid back. But there is more in this than immediately meets the eye: that anger is satisfied when retribution is exacted, yes, but that righteous anger is also *rewarded* when retribution is exacted. And that righteous anger should be rewarded, for its basis is the sentiment that to murder is wrong. The law blames murder when it punishes the murderer; the law praises those who do not murder when it punishes that murderer, and in this way deters murder. "Many are the pangs of the wicked, but steadfast love surrounds him who trusts in the Lord. Be glad in the Lord, and rejoice. O righteous, and shout for joy, all you upright in heart." (*Psalm 32, vs. 10-11*)

The abolitionists, following modern thought, want to excise anger from the soul—to get rid of it rather than to make a virtue of controlling it. To them anger is mere selfishness and altogether reprehensible. But if anger is a natural attribute of the human soul, one is bound to wonder how it will manifest itself when it is denied its legitimate expression, however tamed. And what would a world without anger be like? Nietzsche thought this through and called what he saw in his imagination the world of the Last Man.

From *Human Events*, July 13, 1974.

Another Angle

by James L. Hicks

"Revenge is mine. I will revenge it, if I have to swim in my own blood to do it. A pig will die, and in the name of the people. I'm tired and won't lay back and watch them kill my brother. So this will probably be the last letter you'll get from me."

This, indeed, was the last letter that George Dobbins, a 25 year old Black activist inmate of the maximum security prison at Atmore, Alabama, wrote to his mother on January 18th. Shortly after writing the letter, George Dobbins dies in the aftermath of a prison riot.

Alabama state authorities first said that Mr. Dobbins was shot to death when security forces stormed the cell block where prisoners were holding guards as hostages.

But on February 12, almost a month later, a white newspaper publisher who is a member of a citizens' committee probing the cause of the prison riot, said in a front page article in his newspaper that George Dobbins was not shot to death during the riot, but that he had been stabbed to death long after the riot had been quelled.

The newspaperman, who incidentally is editor and publisher of the largest and most influential newspaper in the state, was backed up by a state toxicologist, who confirmed, after viewing the body, that George Dobbins did in fact die from stab wounds in the head.

Thus, we have another mysterious slaying of a Black man in prison and another echo of Attica in far off Alabama. It's the same old story repeated over and over again, of state authorities apparently using an often justified riot among inmates to "Get" certain leaders in prison who refuse to bow to the often inhuman treatment imposed upon them by prison authorities.

Dobbins claimed in his letter that prison authorities had beaten his brother Charles "Because they hate me and have found out that he is my brother". And now after the fact, the fact being that Mr. Dobbins is dead, a spokesman for the prison system says that his death is "under investigation" and that prison authorities will present the "results" to a grand jury.

This is merely the second chapter that goes along with the first, in far too many cases. If the third chapter follows the pattern that has become the mode in other parts of the United States, the third chapter will end up as a whitewash by the grand jury with prison guards being exonerated and given a pat on the back for "doing their duty"

This is what has happened over and over again, and despite the courage of the newspaper publisher who unearthed this deadly dirty work, there is little reason to believe that the state of Alabama will not follow the pattern already set in so many other states.

Thus, the shame of America's penal institutions will continue unabated with prison officials heavily armed, either shooting down defenseless men themselves or persuading weaker inmates in their custody to do their dirty work through the promise of a little relief from the horrible conditions under which they live.

The situation now borders on a national outrage which obviously can no longer be left to state officials for correction.

It's time for the federal government to take the lead in bringing about badly needed reform in our prisons.

Above, "Another Angle" by James L. Hicks, February 23, 1974 issue, New York *Amsterdam News*.

Violent Us

The Burgesses Would Turn Prisons Into Torture Chambers

By a PRISON GOVERNOR

LONDON—If criminals are to be punished even more severely (be it hanged or beaten or flogged or psychologically assaulted, humiliated, degraded, or broken as human beings) who is supposed to do the punishing?

Where will the wild men who advocate such punishment recruit those who will punish other men as their daily contribution to the health of society?

There are, of course, in every society, sick and perverted men and women who would gladly spend their lives as professional punishers, degraders, humiliators, hurters, torturers and killers of their fellow men—people who are fulfilled by psychological and physical violence against others. They exist in every society. But when any society legitimizes their perversion by employing them in numbers to degrade

and punish and destroy, that society itself is sick unto death.

We know about the Gestapo, the SS and the concentration camps and the gas chambers. In our own time we see around us in this stricken world the same phenomena. God forbid that our society, sick though it is, should decide to employ professional punishers. When we do, if we do, civilization has gone ultimately from our society. These are not times in which we can afford to stand lightly by such matters.

The task of the Prison Service in our country is to ameliorate, as best it can, the appalling effects of imprisonment.

Prison staff are not employed to punish or to degrade. The only punishment the courts deal out in this respect is loss of liberty. Prison governors are instructed to hold in custody, not to *punish* prisoners. Loss of liberty is terrible enough for most men to bear without additional punishment.

Imprisonment — especially in the quite appalling conditions of overcrowding which exist today and which will continue to exist for as long as can be reasonably anticipated — can degrade and dehumanize both prisoners and staff alike unless there is constant moral vigilance and an un-

remitting conviction that human beings, even in captivity, must be treated with respect as persons and accorded the highest degree of dignity possible in their circumstances.

Only such an attitude, and the behavior appropriate to it within the penal system, can preserve the fabric of civilized society. Civilization is a tenuous concept even in Britain today. If the present staff of prisons are forced to become, or are replaced by, professional punishers and degraders, society will not be helped

I, for one, would want no part in a society which employed men for such a task and which legitimized violence of such a kind.

I am more afraid—and all of us should be more afraid—of the violence of those respectable burgesses who cry for death and blood and pain and degradation for criminals, than I am of criminals themselves—and I have known thousands of criminals. The violence of the frightened burgess is the most terrifying of all, and the most destructive of all.

What we need to recognize more than anything else in our disintegrating world is that violence is not a problem only of the criminal.

Above, from *The New York Times*. This letter is excerpted from *The Guardian* of London. The author, who asked that his name be withheld, is governor of an English prison.

WHEN PUNISHMENT IS A CRIME

article **BY RAMSEY CLARK**

the former attorney general indicts america's medieval prison system for corrupting and dehumanizing rather than rehabilitating those behind bars

The goal of modern correction must be not revenge, not penance, not punishment, but rehabilitation. The theory of rehabilitation is based on the belief that healthy, rational people will not injure others. Rehabilitated, an individual will not have the capacity—will not be able to bring himself—to injure another nor to take or destroy property. Rehabilitation is individual salvation. What achievement can give society greater satisfaction than to afford the offender the chance, once lost, to live at peace, to fulfill himself and to help others? Rehabilitation is also the one clear way that the criminal justice system can significantly reduce crime. We know who the most frequent offenders are; there is no surprise when they strike again. Even if nothing but selfish interest impelled us, rehabilitation would be worth the effort. When it works, it reduces crime, reduces the cost of handling prisoners, reduces the cost of the criminal justice system and even relieves pressure to provide the basic and massive reforms that are necessary to affect the underlying causes of crime.

Left,
from *Playboy Magazine*;
© 1970 by Playboy,
November 1970.

I very much enjoyed your Photo-editorial entitled, "Black-on-Black Crime." (Nov. '73). It reminded me of a character in Katherine Anne Porter's *Ship of Fools* who said: ". . . there are many evil people in this world, many more evil than good ones, even the lazy good ones . . . we encourage these monsters by being charitable to them, by making excuses for them, or just by being slack . . . we do evil in letting them do evil without punishment. They think we are cowards and they are right. At least we are dupes and we deserve what we get from them . . ."

As a child going to confession in the Catholic church, I was taught to distinguish between sins of commission and sins of omission. Both types were of equal seriousness. To be aware of a crime or an injustice and do nothing about it is a sin of omission.

L. KENT SWEENEY
Yarmouth, Nova Scotia

Above, letter to the editor of *Ebony* by L. Kent Sweeney, Yarmouth, Nova Scotia, February 1974.

By W.G. ROGERS
Saturday Review

CRIME IN AMERICA: Observations on its Nature, Causes, Prevention and Control. By Ramsey Clark. Simon & Schuster. 346 pp. $6.95

SINCE I HAVE TO STOP somewhere, just one more: noting that Spiro Agnew in the 1968 campaign advocated the shooting of looters, Clark writes: "Persons under the influence of alcohol killed 25,000 Americans in automobile accidents in 1967. Fewer than 250 people died in all the riots of the 1960's. Looters, as such, killed no one. Why not shoot drunken drivers?"

Above, reprinted from *Saturday Review* by the *Albany Times-Union*, November 22, 1970.

Fred Hampton lies in an uneasy grave yet the Grand Jury report marches on. Rap Brown is underground yet the courts go thru their dance of death, grinding out some form of legitimization of his outlawry. Throughout this country courts grind out every day the most horrible pound of flesh — against those who speak out. Sometimes it is done with 30 years for the possession of one joint, as with Lee Otis Johnson in Houston, Texas, or 10 years for John Sinclair in Michigan . . . and everyone says, well, that's due process of law . . . he broke the law, he had a marijuana cigarette in his possession, and no-one begins to wonder why its life imprisonment in Texas for that crime and a max. of 10 days in Washington D.C. And how could you reconcile those two punishments with the identical crime? Because Lee Otis Johnson was a member of SNCC, 30 years for his joint; because John Sinclair was a leader of the White Panthers in Mich., its ten years, and the court applies the rationale that the sentence was within the permissible limits.

Above, from *Outlaws of Amerikkka* in *Nola Express*, as reprinted in the *Underground Press Digest*, January 1971.

Why Punishment Must

By THEODORE L. SENDAK

(Following is the text of a speech made by Mr. Sendak, who is the Attorney General of the state of Indiana, before the Law Enforcement Luncheon Meeting of Officials of Northern Indiana at Wabash, Ind., May 12, 1971.)

The purpose of our system of criminal law is to minimize the quantity of human suffering by maintaining a framework of order and peace. The primary object of the law in this area is to forestall acts of violence or other aggression by which one person inflicts harm on another. To the extent that government fails to do this, the primary function of the state is neglected, and individual suffering is increased.

The question we must ask ourselves about the death penalty is: which of several possible courses of action will serve the true humanitarian purposes of the criminal law? We must weigh the execution of the convicted murderer against the loss of life of his victims and of the possible victims of other potential murderers.

Many factors enter into the perpetration of crime, some of which are obviously beyond the bounds of social control. And it is true that some murders occur under circumstances which no system of penalties can prevent. Yet the objective, statistical evidence available to all indicates one major factor in the commission of crime is the relative probability of punishment *or* escape. If punishment is certain, the impulse to crime is to some extent checked. If escape seems probable, the criminal impulse has freer reign.

The propaganda drive to abolish capital punishment appears to be a geared part of a general drive toward leniency in the treatment of criminals in our society. Such leniency has had in my opinion, undeniable psychological impact on potential murderers, and has contributed to the upward spiral of the crime rate. There is a striking over-all correlation between the recent decline in the use of the death penalty and the rise in violent crime. Such crime has increased by geometric proportions.

In the first three years of the last decade, the number of executions in the United States was by present standards relatively high. Fifty-six persons were executed in 1960; 42 in 1961; and 47 in 1962. During these same three years the number of people who died violently at the hands of criminals actually declined and the murder rate per 100,000 of population also declined.

Beginning in 1963, however, there was a drop in the number of legal executions, and the graph line of violent crime simultaneously began moving up instead of down. In the following years the number of legal executions has decreased dramatically from one year to the next, until in 1968 there was none at all. But each of these years has seen murders increase sharply both in absolute numbers and as a percentage of population.

In 1964, for example, the number of legal executions dropped to 15. Yet the number of violent deaths moved up from 8,500 to 9,250, and the murder rate per 100,000 went up from 4.5 to 4.8. In 1965 the number of legal executions

---

The Pay-Back Crime Code

By JENKIN LLOYD JONES

Senator Mike Mansfield and Rep. William Green of Pennsylvania have introduced bills in Congress that would appropriate federal money for the relief of the victims of criminals.

The proposed legislation would not only provide funds to victims of crimes under federal jurisdiction, but it would supplement payments which the legislatures of six states have now authorized for the victims of state law infractions.

Crime compensation at taxpayer expense is getting popular. Britain, New Zealand, Sweden and seven Canadian provinces have now enacted such laws.

There is, indeed, little logic in freely spending public money to enable the criminal to perfect his defense, while leaving the bleeding victim to borrow money to overcome his lost earnings and the cost of doctors and hospitals.

But the idea can be improved. It can be improved by going back to the first principle of ancient law—the principle that it is the perpetrator of the crime who has the primary obligation to the victim.

In ancient days the idea of paying damages was not limited to civil law. Hammurabi and Draco understood that a criminal was not merely the enemy of the people as a whole, but was a particular debtor to his victim. Draco provided for fines in oxen, not to be paid to the state, but to the aggrieved party.

A couple of weeks ago Dr. John Kielbauch, prison psychologist, resigned from the Oklahoma Department of Corrections to take a position in the federal penal system. And in departing, he made a few radical suggestions:

It is time, he said, that the man who robs or injures makes direct restitution. To this end, he proposed that the courts determine proper compensation and that the state set up elaborate training programs and prison industries which would enable the prisoner to earn real money in behalf of those he had wronged.

Dr. Kielbauch suggests indeterminate sentences, the duration of which would largely depend on the efforts the prisoner would make toward full restitution. He adds that if a prisoner is released or paroled before this restitution is completed, a portion of his outside wages could be deducted.

The trouble with most prison job-training programs, according to Dr. Kielbauch, is that many prisoners associate the training with their punishment. This gives them a negative attitude toward useful work. They develop skills reluctantly and slowly and often turn

Fit the Crime

dropped to seven, while the number of violent deaths increased to 9,850, and the murder rate went to 5.1. Similar decreases in legal executions have occurred in the following years, accompanied by similar increases in the murder rate.

In 1968, with no legal executions at all, the total number who died through criminal violence reached 13,650, while the murder rate climbed to 6.8 per 100,000.

The movement in these figures, with murders increasing as the deterrence of the death penalty diminished, confirms the verdict of ordinary logic: That a relaxation in the severity and certainty of punishment leads only to an increase in crime.

These remarks concern the deterrent effect of the death penalty on those who might commit murder but do not. That is a negative phenomenon which can be inferred both from the record and the assessment of common sense. The repeal of the death penalty would not repeal human nature. To these truisms we may add the fact that there are numerous cases on record in which criminals have escaped the capital penalty for previous murders and gone on to commit others.

Likewise there are numerous cases of prison inmates who have killed guards and other inmates, knowing that the worst punishment they could get would be continued tenancy in the same institution. Opponents of the death penalty usually resist even life sentences without parole, and the deterrent function of that would be even less effective than capital punishment.

The general growth of violent crime in the past decade is the outcropping of the attitude of permissiveness and leniency going hand in hand with an increase in the rate of victimization. As more and more loopholes have been devised for defendants, the crime rate has increased steeply.

Between 1960 and 1968, the over-all crime rate in America increased 11 times as fast as the rate of population growth —plainly meaning that more and more people are being subjected every day of every year to major personal crimes— murder, rape, assault, kidnapping, armed robbery, etc.

Is a course of action humanitarian which actually encourages a vast and continuing increase in the number of people killed and maimed and otherwise brutalized?

There have been many sentimental journeys into the psychological realm of the criminals who are to be executed; I think there should be more sympathetic concern expressed for the thousands of innocent victims of those criminals.

Opponents of the death penalty may rejoice that in 1968 there were 47 fewer murderers executed in this country than was the case in 1962. But do they say anything of the fact that some 5,250 more innocent persons died by criminal violence in 1968 than was the case in 1962?

In the question of human suffering, this is a staggering loss of more than 5,000 individual innocent lives. What about the human rights and civil rights of the individual victim? Are not those 5,000 persons entitled to the dignity and sacredness of life? Is that a result of which humanitarians can be proud? I think not.

Only misguided emotionalism, and not facts, disputes the truth that the death penalty is a deterrent of capital crime.

Individuals must be held responsible for their individual actions if a free society is to endure.

---

their backs on them when they hit the streets.

If, on the other hand, hard work and the acquisition of marketable trades became their keys to freedom, this might put shop training in a different light.

If a court can decide that the man who suffers a broken arm has $1,000 coming to him from the non-criminal who hit him with his car, why shouldn't the criminal who breaks an arm in a brutal assault also owe the victim $1,000?

And there have been too many cases where robbers who have made big scores have sat out their prison years in the smug confidence that the caches will be waiting for them when they emerge. If full restitution is insisted upon the profit vanishes.

Since a law was passed in Michigan making parents financially liable for the depredations of their minor children the incidence of juvenile vandalism in Detroit has turned down remarkably. Parents who were quite casual about scolding in juvenile court began to take a lively interest in the behavior of their young as soon as they received bills from the school board for wrecked classrooms.

Money may be the root of all evil, but the possibilities of using money as a means of discouraging evil have been underexplored in America. The trouble with the bills proposed by Sen. Mansfield and Rep. Green is that they would load upon the blameless taxpayer the indemnity for the victims of crime.

What's wrong with charging the criminal?

"Paying one's debt to society" would then take on a new and more practical meaning.

And it's about time.

Denies Guilt, But –

Calley Admits My Lai Killings

FT. BENNING, Ga. (AP) — Lt. William L. Calley Jr. admitted Tuesday that he fired at a handful of Vietnamese civilians in My Lai nearly three years ago, and decreed the mass execution of others. But he said he felt he did no wrong.

"I never sat down and analyzed whether they were men, women and children—they were enemy not people," Calley told the court-martial jury of six superior officers trying him on charges of premeditated murder of 102 My Lai villagers on March 16, 1968.

"It was a group of people who were the enemy, sir," Calley testified at another point. "I was ordered to go in there and destroy the enemy. That was my job that day. That was my mission . . .

"I felt then and still do that I acted as I was directed and that I carried out orders I was given. And I do not feel I was wrong in doing so, sir."

Calley said he fired fewer than 18 rounds from his M16 automatic rifle during an infantry assaut on My Lai. Among his targets, he added, were Vietnamese men, women and children in a ditch. He denied a sizable number of other civilian murders charged against him.

Above, courtesy of Associated Press Newsfeatures, February 24, 1971.

The next afternoon Mr. Latimer pleaded for his client's life in his maundering, cliche-ridden style: "Lieutenant Calley. outside of a normal traffic ticket, was a good boy. . . . He stayed that way until he got in that Oriental environment . . . . Maybe you can say he used bad judgment and became too aggressive and went too far . . . . But who taught him to kill, kill, kill?"

Then Rusty Calley, standing at the microphone that his 70-year-old advocate always had to use to magnify his weak voice, addressed the jurors. His voice quavered uncontrollably, and whatever had kept a maelstrom of emotions from gushing out all these months seemed about to give way at any moment:

"I'm not going to stand here and plead for my life or my freedom. . . . I have never known a soldier, nor did I ever myself, ever wantonly kill a human being in my entire life. If I have committed a crime, the only crime that I have committed is in judgment of my values.

"Apparently, I valued my troops' lives more than I did that of the enemy . . . when my troops were getting massacred and mauled by an enemy I couldn't see, I couldn't feel, and I couldn't touch—that nobody in the military system ever described as anything other than communism. They didn't give it a race, they didn't give it a sex, they didn't give it an age; they never let me believe it was just a philosophy in a man's mind. . . . Yesterday you stripped me of all my honor. Please, by your actions that you take here today, don't strip future soldiers of their honor."

Above left, from *The National Observer*, April 5, 1974. Copyright Dow Jones & Co., Inc.

280   Above right, from *Newsweek*, March 29, 1971.

Latimer pleaded with the jury of career officers to consider the Army itself. "I'm proud of the United States Army," he told them. "It grieves me to see it being pulled apart from within . . . An acquittal will help the Army. It will show the judicial process protects a man who makes an error in judgment . . . There ought to be a difference between errors in judgment and criminality."

Then came Daniel's final, stinging rebuttal. Calley, he declared, had been "judge, jury and executioner" at My Lai. "There has been talk of the accused as a poor kid sent over there, but there hasn't been anything said for the victims. Who will speak for them? . . . Would any tribunal in this world have found one of those children guilty of any offense and then ordered his execution?" He concluded pointedly: "You gentlemen are the conscience of the United States Army. You are the conscience of this country. Your duty is clear . . . to find the accused guilty as charged."

Right, letter to the editor of *Time* by Captain Douglas S. Thornblom, April 1, 1974. Reprinted by permission from *Time, The Weekly Newsmagazine*; Copyright Time, Inc.

Sir / There are those of us in the professional officers' corps who view Mr. Calley (I cannot bring myself to call him lieutenant) as what he is: a convicted mass murderer. I was appalled when he was sentenced to only 20 years and angered when he was allowed to remain in his quarters at Fort Benning and enjoy "almost daily visits from his girl friend."

That Calley now walks the streets of Columbus wearing the uniform that he has disgraced fills me with despair and disgust.

DOUGLAS S. THORNBLOM
Captain, U.S.A.
West Point, N.Y.

Hersh: Now Try the Leaders

By DICK BELSKY

"If the Army thinks it has the answer to My Lai by finding Calley guilty of premeditated murder, it's wrong. He's not important. He's just the guy who happened to be on trial."

—*Seymour Hersh, Pulitzer Prize-winning author of My Lai 4, who first broke the story of the massacre.*

"If they're going to charge Calley with premeditated murder, the next step is to initiate a million court martials. I think he was guilty of murder. But for the premeditation I think we have to look to the Pentagon and the White House and people like John Kennedy and Lyndon Johnson.

"They were the men who tried to computerize the war, and make the body count all-important. That's where we have to find the premeditation, not in William Calley."

Above, reprinted by permission of *New York Post*, © 1971, New York Post Corporation.

ON THE RIGHT

Calley By WILLIAM F. BUCKLEY JR.

Below, © King Features Syndicate, Inc.

4) As regards the question of ultimate responsibility, the public is entitled to be confused. We hanged Admiral Yamashita after the Second World War, and if we applied rigorously the logic of that execution, we would have a case for hanging General Westmoreland. That would be preposterous and cruel. So that we learn, gradually, what some people knew and warned against in 1945: victors' justice.

We are overdue for shame in our complicity in the Nuremberg-Tokyo trials. But whatever we do to amend these doctrines, it is inconceivable that we should come up with new rules of war that permit to go unpunished such an act as Lieutenant Calley was found guilty of, and I for one am proud of a country that makes such activity punishable by imprisonment or death.

Moreover, the Nuremberg trials after the second world war made clear that the Nazi high government officials, the brass as well as the individual soldier were all indeed guilty of the most barbaric war crimes.

What about Calley, is he guilty? We think he is profoundly guilty. He admitted committing the murders. Though Calley was operating within the genocidal framework of the war policy itself and though he had specific orders (from above) to murder at My Lai, we think Calley had a choice! Men in Calley's own company, we must remember, refused to commit the same atrocities at My Lai. Why didn't Calley?

Left, letter to the editor of *Newsweek* by Pam Seaman, May 3, 1971.

■ Calley was doing what he was ordered to do, so why convict him? If he were a high officer's son, the Army would find a way to pardon him.

PAM SEAMAN
DeTour Village, Mich.

Excerpts from a letter to President Nixon from Captain Aubrey M. Daniel III, the prosecutor in the Calley trial:

... How shocking it is if so many people across this nation have failed to see the moral issue which was involved in the trial of Lieutenant Calley—that it is unlawful for an American soldier to summarily execute unarmed and unresisting men, women, children and babies.

But how much more appalling it is to see so many of the political leaders of the nation who have failed to see the moral issue or, having seen it, compromise it for political motive in the face of apparent public displeasure with the verdict. .... I have been particularly shocked and dismayed at your decision to intervene in these proceedings in the midst of the public clamor....

Your intervention has, in my opinion, damaged the military judicial system and lessened any respect it may have gained as a result of the proceedings....

For this nation to condone the acts of Lieutenant Calley is to make us no better than our enemies and make any pleas by this nation for the humane treatment of our own prisoners meaningless.

From *Life* magazine, April 16, 1971.

Laws of War

Twenty-five years ago I defended General Yamashita who, after a military trial in Manila and hearing before the United States Supreme Court, was hanged as a war criminal.

Prof. Telford Taylor (NATIONAL AFFAIRS, Feb. 22) is correct when he says that Gen. William Westmoreland, Army Chief of Staff, could be found guilty of the My Lai atrocities under the rules of Yamashita's case.

This is because the statement you quote from Army general counsel Robert E. Jordan III—"a commander cannot be held to be a murderer merely because one of his men commits murder"—does not square with the law. The fact that General Yamashita had no knowledge and indeed could not have known of the atrocities in the Philippines was held immaterial. He was declared a "war criminal" and while that may not be identical to a charge of "murder," the penalty was equally final.

The late Justice Frank Murphy objected to this idea of "command responsibility" and in his dissenting opinion he prophesied that "the fate of some future President of the United States and his Chiefs of Staff and military advisers may well have been sealed by this decision."

Must we try General Westmoreland and former President Johnson for these capital crimes? A better answer would be a frank admission that we were wrong in deviating from the concept that we punish men for committing crimes, not merely for holding jobs. Inherent in convictions for "violations of the laws of war" is the assumption that there are good and bad ways to kill; that it is criminal to shoot unarmed civilians on the ground but legal to bomb them from the skies. If we won't quit trying to solve disputes by killing people, let us at least recognize war for what it is and stop such hypocrisy.

A. FRANK REEL

New York City

Above, letter to the editor of *Newsweek* by A. Frank Neel, March 22, 1971.

◆ Here is President Ford's statement announcing a pardon for former President Nixon:

LADIES and gentlemen, I have come to a decision which I felt I should tell you and all of my fellow American citizens, as soon as I was certain in my own mind and in my own conscience that it is the right thing to do.

I have learned already in this office that the difficult decisions always come to this desk. I must admit that many of them do not look at all the same as the hypothetical questions that I have answered freely and perhaps too fast on previous occasions.

My customary policy is to try and get all the facts and to consider the opinions of my countrymen and to take counsel with my most valued friends. But these seldom agree, and in the end, the decision is mine. To procrastinate, to agonize, and to wait for a more favorable turn of events that may never come, or more compelling external pressures that may as well be wrong as right, is itself a decision of sorts, and a weak and potentially dangerous course for a President to follow.

I have promised to uphold the Constitution, to do what is right as God gives me to see the right, and to do the very best that I can for America.

I have asked your help and your prayers, not only when I became President, but many times since. The Constitution is the supreme law of our land, and it governs our actions as citizens. Only the laws of God, which govern our consciences, are superior to it.

As we are a nation under God, so I am sworn to uphold our laws with the help of God. And I have sought such guidance and searched my own conscience with special diligence to determine the right thing for me to do with respect to my predecessor in this place, Richard Nixon, and his loyal wife and family.

Theirs is an American tragedy in which we all have played a part. It could go on and on and on, or someone must write the end to it. I have concluded that only I can do that, and if I can, I must.

There are no historic or legal precedents to which I can turn in this matter, none that precisely fit the circumstances of a private citizen who has resigned the Presidency of the United States. But it is common knowledge that serious allegations and accusations hang like a sword over our former President's head, threatening his health as he tries to reshape his life, a great part of which was spent in the service of this country and by the mandate of its people.

After years of bitter controversy and divisive national debate, I have been advised, and I am compelled to conclude, that many months and perhaps more years will have to pass before Richard Nixon could obtain a fair trial by jury in any jurisdiction of the United States under governing decisions of the Supreme Court.

No Respecter of Persons

I deeply believe in equal justice for all Americans, whatever their station or former station. The law, whether human or divine, is no respecter of persons, but the law is a respecter of reality.

The facts, as I see them, are that a former President of the United States, instead of enjoying equal treatment with any other citizen accused of violating the law, would be cruelly and excessively penalized either in preserving the presumption of his innocence or in obtaining a speedy determination of guilt in order to repay a legal debt to society.

During this long period of delay and potential litigation, ugly passions would again be aroused. And our people would again be polarized in their opinions. And the credibility of our free institutions of Government would again be challenged at home and abroad.

In the end, the courts might well hold that Richard Nixon had been denied due process and the verdict of history would even more be inconclusive with respect to those charges arising out of the period of his Presidency, of which I am presently aware.

Concern for the Country

But it is not the ultimate fate of Richard Nixon that most concerns me, though surely it deeply troubles every decent and every compassionate person. My concern is the immediate future of this great country.

In this, I dare not depend upon my personal sympathy as a longtime friend of the former President, nor my professional judgment as a lawyer, and I do not.

As President, my primary concern must always be the greatest good of all the people of the United States whose servant I am. As a man, my first consideration is to be true to my own convictions and my own conscience.

Sealing the Book

My conscience tells me clearly and certainly that I cannot prolong the bad dreams that continue to reopen a chapter that is closed. My conscience tells me that I, as President, have the Constitutional power to firmly shut and seal this book. My conscience tells me it is my duty, not merely to proclaim domestic tranquility but to use every means that I have to insure it.

I do believe that the buck stops here, that I cannot rely upon public-opinion polls to tell me what is right.

I do believe that right makes

might, and that if I am wrong, 10 angels swearing I was right would make no difference.

I do believe, with all my heart and mind and spirit, that I, not as President, but as a humble servant of God, will receive justice without mercy if I fail to show mercy.

Goal of Peace

Finally, I feel that Richard Nixon and his loved ones have suffered enough and will continue to suffer, no matter what I do, no matter what we, as a great and good nation, can do together to make his goal of peace come true.

Now, therefore, I, Gerald R. Ford, President of the United States, pursuant to the pardon power conferred upon me by Article II, Section 2 of the Constitution, have granted and by these presents do grant a full, free, and absolute pardon unto Richard Nixon for all offenses against the United States which he, Richard Nixon, has committed or may have committed or taken part in during the period from Jan 20, 1969, through Aug. 9, 1974.

Q. *Since President Ford was so quick to give Richard Nixon a full and complete pardon for all the crimes he may have committed, including income tax evasion, obstruction of justice, telling lies to the American people, masterminding the Watergate coverup, and who knows what else—why won't Ford give the same sort of pardon to Nixon's fellow conspirators: John N. Mitchell, Bob Haldeman, John Ehrlichman, and Robert Mardian?—F. G., Phoenix, Ariz.*

A. President Ford's reasoning is as follows: Mr. Nixon is the only President in U.S. history who was forced to resign from office. The pardon for him was intended to end the national focus on Watergate and to put the bitterness and divisiveness surrounding Watergate behind us so that the nation could focus on its difficult problems. Ford contends that these circumstances do not apply to Mitchell, Haldeman, Ehrlichman and Mardian and that these convicted men must pursue the normal judicial processes. This is specious reasoning, of course, having little to do with equal justice under law and pointing up the proclivity of relating prior pardon to high office. But according to White House spokesmen this is what President Ford contends.

Above, from the April 13, 1975 issue of *Parade.* Courtesy of Parade Publications.

'Regret' for 'My Mistakes'

◆ This statement by former President Nixon was released after the announcement of a pardon of Nixon by President Ford:

I HAVE been informed that President Ford has granted me a full and absolute pardon for any charges which may be brought against me for actions taken during the time I was the President of the United States. In accepting this pardon, I hope that his compassionate act will contribute to lifting the burden of Watergate from our country.

Here in California, my perspective on Watergate is quite different than it was while I was embattled in the midst of the controversy while I was still subject to the unrelenting daily demand of the Presidency itself.

Looking back on what is still in my mind a complex and confusing maze of events, decisions, pressures, and personalities, one thing I can see clearly now is that I was wrong in not acting more decisively and more forthrightly in dealing with Watergate, particularly when it reached the stage of judicial proceedings and grew from a political scandal into a national tragedy.

No words can describe the depths of my regret and pain at the anguish my mistakes over Watergate have caused the nation and the Presidency—a nation I so deeply loved and an institution I so greatly respect.

I know that many fair-minded people believe that my motivation and actions in the Watergate affair were intentionally self-serving and illegal. I now understand how my own mistakes and misjudgments have contributed to that belief and seemed to support it. This burden is the heaviest one of all to bear.

That the way I tried to deal with Watergate was the wrong way is a burden I shall bear for every day of the life that is left to me.

A LESSON IN SOCIOLOGY:

THE REWARDS OF CRIME

by Jonathan Quick

PRISONS

One of the most disturbing events of the last decades is the extraordinary increase in crime. Theft, burglary, rape, fraud, etc., occur in ever increasing frequency and a larger range of people than ever before seem to become involved in such activities. Even policemen have been caught committing burglaries and selling stolen goods.

The experts don't agree on the reason for this phenomenon. Some of them believe that poverty breeds crime and they point to the plight of many poor people, who live cooped up under terrible conditions in city slums. Others, however, take a less deterministic view.

They tell us that the poor, God bless them, have always been with us and that they are not necessarily criminals; it is not poverty that causes crime, but people commit crimes (just as guns don't kill people, but people kill people).

No doubt this is true to the same extent as one can say that hens lay eggs and cattle produce fertilizer, but it doesn't go far enough for an explanation. (For instance, farm animals could hardly persist in their physiological functions unless they are fed. We therefore need to look at those who feed a bull to understand what he produces.)

Coming back to the issue of crime, we must look beyond the obvious fact that people commit crimes. A good case can be made for the proposition that wealth, not poverty, causes crime.

In the first place, poverty hasn't greatly increased in recent years, but the overall standard of living went up and the number of very rich people became much larger.

It should certainly be possible to demonstrate a high correlation between increase in crime and increase in the number of millionaires during any recent period of time. Moreover, there are good reasons to believe that such a correlation is not accidental or trivial, but in fact causal.

As people acquire wealth, they also acquire prestige and credibility (in contrast to poor people, who have to be simply truthful to be believed) and they often go into politics or become members of various boards and foundations; they can well afford to give financial support to their peers (it is always less embarrassing to give to those who don't need it) and they are in a position to influence government and other agencies.

Recent experience has shown that they may become over-zealous in their civic efforts and do things which are against the law. If they then get caught and convicted for, let's say, bribing an official or taking a bribe, they can count on being punished with a fine many times smaller than the amount of money that had been feloniously transacted.

This enormous discrepancy between the benefit and the punishment of a crime is bound to serve as an incentive for the wealthy to commit even more and bigger crimes. (Such an incentive is not available to the poor, who can't afford expensive lawyers and payments of fines, and who have to serve jail terms for infractions of the law.)

While it may be unfortunate that crime does pay for the rich, the worst part of this is the bad example it sets for the vast middle classes (or at least that half-vast part of them with social ambitions -- those who read and pay attention to the news).

In order to acquire wealth, these people tend to imitate the wealthy and are likely to get involved in criminal activities at whatever scale they feel they may be able to get away with. Thus, the most damaging role of wealth in the causation of crime is that it serves as a corrupting model.

It is, therefore, proposed to reduce crime by the simple device of reducing the number of wealthy people. The French, during their well known revolution, tried to solve the problem by reducing the people themselves, but much gentler methods have since become available, such as the almost painless removal of excess wealth by taxation.

It is only a question of being willing to apply these already available methods to stop the spread of the criminally rich (or vice versa). Once the big crime has been taken care of, it should be easy to deal with the small fry in our urban centers.

■

By Jonathan Quick, reprinted from the February 1974 issue of *Freedom News*, Richmond, California.

SECTION 13

International Relations

The area of international relations and ethics is at once the most general and abstract and also the most immediate and concrete of those addressed in this book. It is general and abstract insofar as most of us feel that we have no direct influence on decisions made in this sphere, but it becomes frighteningly concrete when the decisions that are made at this level result in wars or famines which can in turn result in death and suffering for a large number of individuals. It is in part the abstractness of the issues that makes it particularly difficult to identify their moral dimensions. Who (what person or persons) is confronted with what decisions? As mentioned in our discussion in the Introduction, it is not at all obvious that any individual has any real control at all over the course of events at the international level. But this is not an ethical question in and of itself (at least not in most definitions of ethics).

Certainly some of the arguments in this section must be classified as quite abstract and general, particularly the "debate" between Henry Kissinger and Alexander Solzhenitsyn over the morality of détente, although even here the concrete implications of this general policy (in terms of the possibility of a nuclear war and the reality of the treatment of individuals—particularly political dissenters—within the two countries) cannot be easily missed. But many of the arguments do involve quite specific decisions confronted by particular individuals within the context of the international political realities. For instance, given the fact of détente in 1975, a police equipment salesman was confronted with a choice that he did not have previously of whether or not to sell various types of equipment to the Soviet Union. And given the realities of the international trade situation, in conjunction with the world food and population situation, there are some choices which certain groups assert are open to all of us which could result in preventing the death by starvation of one or more individuals in another country, although as always, the scientific accuracy of such assertions must be carefully scrutinized. In brief, while ethical issues related to matters of international relations are among the most difficult and complex of all to deal with in any intellectually adequate way, they are also of such great potential significance (even in terms of some everyday decisions of quite ordinary persons) as to justify any efforts to give them thought and consideration.

EXERCISES

1. From the arguments in this section, identify the different decisions open to specific individuals concerning international issues.
2. Compare the arguments in this section with those in the sections on civil disobedience and gun control to identify common issues. In particular, is there any significant difference between the role of the individual in relation to foreign policy and international relations and his or her role in relation to national policies and laws within the country?
3. Compare the arguments in this section with those in Section 10 concerning corporations. Is the corporation more like the individual person or more like the state with regard to moral judgments?
4. Are there any significant similarities between the arguments concerning inter*national* relations and the arguments in Section 1 concerning inter*personal* relations?

The 'Covert Operations' Debate

The following are excerpts from the Senate debate of Oct. 2 on an amendment to the foreign aid bill which would have ordered the Central Intelligence Agency immediately to halt all covert operations not related to intelligence. The amendment was defeated, 68 to 17. This marked the first time either house of Congress had debated and voted on this issue.

Sen. James Abourezk (D-S.D.): This amendment will, if enacted, abolish all clandestine or covert operations by the Central Intelligence Agency.

I believe very strongly that we must have an intelligence-gathering organization and I believe the CIA and our defense intelligence agencies do an adequate job in this respect.

We have every right to defend ourselves from foreign attack and that right includes intelligence gathering to protect our security.

But there is no justification in our legal, moral, or religious principles for operations of a U.S. agency which result in assassinations, sabotage, political disruptions, or other meddling in another country's internal affairs, all in the name of the American people. It amounts to nothing more than an arm of the U.S. government conducting a secret war without either the approval of Congress or the knowledge of the American people.

I want to remind the Senate that the present director of the CIA, William Colby, said a couple of weeks ago that while he preferred to retain the clandestine or covert services, the Capitol would not fall if it were abolished. He also said that there was not any activity going on anywhere in the world at this time that required the use of clandestine activity.

●

Sen. Clifford Case (R-N.J.): If I may express my own view about covert activities, it is that they all should be regarded as wrong. There ought not to be an institutionalization of them, even to the extent that we have now. I do not think that a committee is the answer. We have a committee downtown, a Committee of 40, which is supposed to review this matter and advise the President; and he acts on their advice in most cases, I understand.

We have a committee here, when it meets. I am not complaining that it does not meet more often, because I do not think a committee is the answer.

Once we get into an institutionalization of this kind of thing, we begin to make it respectable, and that I do not like. There ought to be a general rule against it, with a general understanding of the American people that on occasion the President has to act in violation of the law, if you will—our law, other laws—and take action in the interest of a country, in great emergency. This I think he does at his own peril and subject to being either supported or turned down by the country, after the fact. I think this is about as close as we can come to any statement about how this matter ought to be handled.

I would, of course, consider any proposal made for procedural reform here, but I want to state now that I do not think any such thing is possible because of the nature of the animal with which we are dealing.

●

Sen. Mark O. Hatfield (R-Ore.): To me, it is transparently obvious that the CIA's covert operations, undertaken in Chile to "destabilize" the Allende government, were in violation of these commitments of international law. At the very least, such operations compromise the sincerity of our loudly proclaimed desire for world peace and world freedom, I think we ought to address ourselves to the legal obligations this nation has undertaken when it has affixed its signature to these various statements and these various charters.

That is why I feel that the amendment offered by the senator from South Dakota really does not go far enough. I should like to see it go farther, to put this Senate on record that we totally and completely oppose any involvement whatsoever in covert activity. That does not deny the gathering of information and intelligence, but indicates the refusal of this Senate to permit the CIA to go beyond gathering intelligence into an action of covert activity.

●

Sen. Barry Goldwater (R-Ariz.): If we destroy our right to engage in covert activity altogether by the adoption of this amendment—in fact, I think the language of this amendment would even prevent us from going to war—I think we would be making a very grave mistake.

I do not support everything that the CIA has done. On the other hand, I do not know everything it has done, and I do not think we necessarily have to know. I think this would be dangerous.

I cite the example of a member of the House of Representatives who happened to have seen, so he says, a page of testimony. We do not know whether he saw that testimony or not. But on this one statement, in which, in my opinion, he violated his pledge to secrecy, the whole CIA has come under criticism. I do not believe it is fair of this body to accept the hearsay words of a man who divulged classified material.

So, I hope we will defeat this amendment and defeat it soundly. I think I am safe in saying that the chairman of the Committee on Armed Services, together with the chairman of the Committee on Foreign Relations, would be willing to institute proper hearings, at which time we could hear all arguments for and against the operation of our intelligence collecting agencies.

From *The Washington Post*, 1974.

The Secretary of State

Speech

July 15, 1975
Minneapolis, Minnesota

Bureau of Public Affairs
Office of Media Services

THE MORAL FOUNDATIONS OF FOREIGN POLICY

Secretary Henry A. Kissinger before the Upper Midwest Council.

It is time to face the reality of our situation. Our choice is not between morality and pragmatism. We cannot escape either, nor are they incompatible. This nation must be true to its own beliefs or it will lose its bearings in the world. But at the same time it must survive in a world of sovereign nations and competing wills.

We need moral strength to select among often agonizing choices and a sense of purpose to navigate between the shoals of difficult decisions. But we need as well a mature sense of means, lest we substitute wishful thinking for the requirements of survival.

Morality and Policy

The relation of morality to policy is thus not an abstract philosophical issue. It applies to many topics of the current debate. It applies to relations with the Communist powers, where we must manage a conflict of moral purposes and interests in the shadow of nuclear peril; and it applies in our political ties with nations whose domestic practices are inconsistent with our own.

Our relationship with the Communist powers has raised difficult questions for Americans since the Bolshevik Revolution. It was understood very early that the Communist system and ideology were in conflict with our own principles. Sixteen years passed before President Franklin Roosevelt extended diplomatic recognition to the Soviet Government. He did so in the belief, as he put it, that *"through the resumption of normal relations the prospects of peace over all the world are greatly strengthened."*

Today again courageous voices remind us of the nature of the Soviet system and of our duty to defend freedom. About this there is no disagreement.

There is, however, a clear conflict between two moral imperatives which is at the heart of the problem. Since the dawn of the nuclear age, the world's fears of holocaust and its hopes for a better future have both hinged on the relationship between the two superpowers. In an era of strategic nuclear balance—when both sides have the capacity to destroy civilized life—there is no alternative to coexistence. In such conditions the necessity of peace is itself a moral imperative. As President Kennedy pointed out: *"In the final analysis our most basic common link is that we all inhabit this small planet. We all breathe the same air. We all cherish our children's future. And we are all mortal."*

It is said, correctly, that the Soviet perception of "peaceful coexistence" is not the same as ours, that Soviet policies aim at the furthering of Soviet objectives. In a world of nuclear weapons capable of destroying mankind, in a century which has seen resort to brutal force on an unprecedented scale and intensity, in an age of ideology which turns the domestic policies of nations into issues of international contention, the problem of peace takes on a profound moral and practical difficulty. But the issue, surely, is not whether peace and stability serve Soviet purposes, but whether they also serve our own. Constructive actions in Soviet policy are desirable *whatever* the Soviet motives.

Our immediate focus is on the international actions of the Soviet Union not because it is our only moral concern, but because it is the sphere of action that we can most directly and confidently affect. As a consequence of improved foreign policy relationships, we have successfully used our influence to promote human rights. But we have done so quietly, keeping in mind the delicacy of the problem and stressing results rather than public confrontation.

Therefore, critics of detente must answer: What is the alternative that they propose? What precise policies do they want us to change? Are they prepared for a prolonged situation of dramatically increased international danger? Do they wish to return to the constant crises and high arms budgets of the cold war? Does detente encourage repression—or is it detente that has generated the ferment and the demands for openness that we are now witnessing? Can we ask our people to support confrontation unless they know that every reasonable alternative has been explored?

In our relations with the Soviet Union, the United States will maintain its strength, defend its interests, and support its friends with determination and without illusion. We will speak up for our beliefs with vigor and without self-deception. We consider detente a means to regulate a competitive relationship—not a substitute for our own efforts in building the strength of the free world. We will continue on the course on which we are embarked because it offers hope to our children of a more secure and a more just world.

These considerations raise a more general question: To what extent are we able to affect the internal policies of other governments and to what extent is it desirable?

There are some 150 nations in the world, and barely a score of them are democracies in any real sense. The rest are nations whose ideology or political practices are inconsistent with our own. Yet we have political relations and often alliances with some of these countries in Asia, Latin America, Africa, and Europe.

Congressman [Donald M.] Fraser has raised this issue with great integrity and concern, and I have profited from many discussions with him. We do not and will not condone repressive practices. This is not only dictated by our values but is also a reflection of the reality that regimes which lack legitimacy or moral authority are inherently vulnerable. There will therefore be limits to the degree to which such regimes can be congenial partners. We have used, and we will use, our influence against repressive practices. Our traditions and our interests demand it.

But truth compels also a recognition of our limits. The question is whether we promote human rights more effectively by counsel and friendly relations where this serves our interest, or by confrontational propaganda and discriminatory legislation. And we must also assess the domestic performance of foreign governments in relation to their history and to the threats they face. We must have some understanding for the dilemmas of countries adjoining powerful, hostile, and irreconcilable totalitarian regimes.

Our alliances and political relationships serve mutual ends; they contribute to regional and world security, and thus support the broader welfare. They are not favors to other governments, but reflect a recognition of mutual interests. They should be withdrawn only when our interests change and not as a punishment for some act with which we do not agree. In many countries, whatever the internal structure, the populations are unified in seeking our protection against outside aggression. In many countries our foreign policy relationships have proved to be no obstacle to the forces of change. And in many countries—especially in Asia—it is the process of American disengagement that has eroded the sense of security and created a perceived need for greater internal discipline, and at the same time diminished our ability to influence domestic practices.

The attempt to deal with those practices by restrictive American legislation raises a serious problem, not because of the moral view it expresses—which we share—but because of the mistaken impression it creates that our security ties are acts of charity. And beyond that, such acts—because they are too public, too inflexible, and too much a stimulus to nationalistic resentment—are almost inevitably doomed to fail.

There are no simple answers. Painful experience should have taught us that we ought not exaggerate our capacity to foresee, let alone to shape, social and political change in other societies. Therefore let me state the principles that will guide our action:

• Human rights are a legitimate international concern and have been so defined in international agreements for more than a generation.

• The United States will speak up for human rights in appropriate international forums and in exchanges with other governments.

• We will be mindful of the limits of our reach; we will be conscious of the difference between public postures that satisfy our self-esteem and policies that bring positive results.

• We will not lose sight of either the requirements of global security or what we stand for as a nation.

Solzhenitsyn- WORDS OF WARNING TO AMERICA

By ALEXANDER SOLZHENITSYN

It was a dramatic warning to all the world—and to Americans in particular—that Nobel Prize winner Alexander Solzhenitsyn delivered in Washington, D.C., on June 30.

Something which is almost incomprehensible to the human mind is the West's fantastic greed for profit and gain, which goes beyond all reason, all limitations, all conscience.

I have to admit that Lenin foretold this whole process. Lenin, who spent most of his life in the West and knew it much better than Russia, always said that the Western capitalists would do anything to supply the Soviet economy—"They will fight with each other to sell us goods cheaper and sell them quicker so that we'll buy from one rather than from the other."

And in the difficult moments of a party meeting in Moscow he said: "Comrades, don't worry when things are hard with us. When things are difficult, we will give a rope to the *bourgeoisie* and the *bourgeoisie* will hang itself with this rope."

Then, Karl Radek, a witty fellow you may have heard of, said: "Vladimir Ilyich, where are we going to get enough rope to hang the whole *bourgeoisie?*"

Lenin said immediately: "They'll supply us with it."

Nikita Khrushchev came here and said: "We're going to bury you." People didn't believe that—they took it as a joke.

Now, of course, the Communists have become more clever in my country. They do not say, "We're going to bury you" any more. Now they say, "Détente."

Nothing has changed in Communist ideology. The goals are the same as they were.

Many papers in the West have written: Let's hurry up and end the bloodshed in Vietnam and have national unity there.

One of your leading newspapers, after the end of Vietnam, gave a full, big headline: "The Blessed Silence." I would not wish that kind of blessed silence on my worst enemy. I would not wish that kind of national unity upon my worst enemy.

I have spent 11 years in the "archipelago." And for half of my lifetime I have studied this question. Looking at this terrible tragedy in Vietnam from a distance, I can tell you: A million persons will be exterminated. Four to 5 million—in accordance with the scale of Vietnam—will spend time in concentration camps and will be rebuilding Vietnam.

What is happening in Cambodia you already know. It is genocide. It is full and complete destruction, but in a new form.

Once again, the technology is not up to building gas chambers, so in a few hours the entire capital city, the guilty capital city is emptied out—old people, women, children are driven out without belongings, without food. Go, die!

Now we hear voices in your country and in the West: Give up Korea and we will live in peace. Give up Portugal, of course. Give up Japan, give up Israel, give up Taiwan, Philippines, Malaysia, Thailand, 10 African countries. Just let us live peaceably.

Give us the possibility to continue driving our beautiful cars on our splendid highways. Make it possible for us to play tennis and golf. Let us mix our cocktails as we are accustomed to doing. Let us see the beautiful, toothy smile in the glass on every advertisement page of a magazine.

One hears: "We cannot defend those who cannot defend themselves with their own human resources, with their own manpower." But, against the powers of totalitarianism—when all of this power is thrown against a country—no country can defend itself with its own resources.

We are told: "It is not possible to protect those who do not have full democracy." This is the most remarkable argument of the lot. This is the leitmotiv I read in your newspapers and I hear in the speeches of some of your political leaders. Who in the world, on the front lines of defense against totalitarianism, ever has been able to sustain full democracy? You? The United States?

Even the united democracies of the world were not able to do it—America, England, Canada, Australia. With the first

Above and right, from *U.S. News and World Report,* July 14, 1975.

danger of Hitlerism, you stretched the hand out to Stalin.

It is also said that "if the Soviet Union is going to use détente for its own ends, then we"— But what will happen then? The Soviet Union *has* used détente in its own interest, is using it now, and will continue to use it in its own interest.

For example, in China and in the Soviet Union they're both participating in détente, but they have grabbed three countries of Indo-China in a quiet way. True, perhaps as a consolation, they will send you a table-tennis team!

Do you understand properly what détente has meant all these 40 years? Friendship, stabilization of the situation, trade, et cetera—I have to tell you something which you've never seen or heard—how it looks from the other side. Let me tell you now:

A mere acquaintance with an American—and God forbid that you should sit with him in a restaurant—means a 10-year term for espionage. In the fourth volume of the "Archipelago," I will tell of an event. One Soviet citizen was in the United States, and when he came back he told people that in the United States they have wonderful automobiles, roads. The State Security arrested him and they demanded a term of 10 years. But the judge said: "I don't object, but there's not enough evidence. Couldn't you find something else against him?" So the judge was exiled because he quarreled with the State Security, and they gave the other man 10 years. Can you imagine what this means? He said there were good roads in America. He got 10 years for that.

So what are we to conclude from that? Is détente needed or not? Not only is it needed, it's needed like air. It's the only way of saving the earth; that is, instead of having a world war, we must have détente, but a true détente. I would say that there are very definite characteristic marks of what a genuine détente would be.

There are only three. In the first place: that there be a disarmament—not only a disarmament from the use of war, but also from the use of violence—not only arms, but also violence; not only the sort of arms which are used to destroy your neighbors, but the sort of arms which are used to destroy your fellow countrymen.

This is not a détente, if we here with you today can spend our time in a friendly way, while over there people are groaning and dying and in psychiatric insane asylums. The doctors are going around and putting injections in people which destroy their brain cells.

And the second sign of true détente is the following: that it be not one based on smiles, not on verbal concessions. It has to be based on a firm foundation. You know the word from the Bible, "Not on sand, but on rock." There has to be a guarantee that this will not disappear overnight or be broken overnight. And for this, we need that the other party to the agreement have some control over attacks, some control by public opinion, some control by the press, control by a freely elected parliament. Until such controls exist, there's absolutely no guarantee.

And the third simple condition: What sort of détente is it when they employ the inhumane propaganda which is called, in the Soviet Union, "ideological war"? Let us not have that. If we're going to have détente, let's be friendly—and end ideological warfare!

In evaluating everything I have said to you today—and I'm coming to my conclusion now—I could say we don't even have to have our conversation on the political level—why such and such a country acted in such and such a way, how they—what they were counting on in acting in such a way. We should rather rise above this to the moral level and say:

"In 1933 and in 1941, your leaders and the whole Western world in an unprincipled way made a deal with totalitarianism. We will have to pay our cost for this and for 30 years we've been paying for it, and we're still paying for it, and we're going to pay for it in a worse way."

One cannot think only in the low level of political calculations. It's necessary to think also of what is noble, what is honest and what is honorable, not only what is useful.

The adroit Western legal scholars have now introduced the term "legal realism." By this legal realism, they want to push aside any moral evaluation of affairs. They say: "Recognize realities. You have to understand that if such and such laws have been established in such and such countries, then these laws, which provide for violence, have to be recognized and respected."

At the present time, this concept is widely accepted among lawyers—that law is higher than morality; law is something which is worked out and developed, whereas morality is something inchoate and amorphous. That isn't the case. The opposite is rather true—morality is higher than law.

Law is our human attempt somehow to instill in the laws a part of that moral sphere which is above us. We try to understand this morality, bring it down to earth and present it in the form of laws—sometimes we are more successful, sometimes less. Sometimes you actually have a caricature of morality, but morality is always higher than law. And we cannot forget this ever.

In our heart and soul, we have to recognize that it's almost a joke now to talk in the Western world in the twentieth century about words like "good" and "evil." These are almost old-fashioned concepts, but these are very real and genuine concepts. These are concepts from a sphere which is higher than us.

And instead of getting involved in shortsighted political calculations, we have to recognize that the concentration of world evil and the tremendous force of hatred is there, and it's flowing from there throughout the world. And we have to stand up against it and not try to give to it, give to it, give to it everything which it asks for.

I started by saying that you are the allies of our liberation movement in the Communist countries, and I call upon you: Let us think together and try to see how we can adjust the relationship between these two processes. Whenever you help the persons being persecuted in the Soviet Union, you're not only displaying magnanimity and nobility, you are defending not only them but you're defending yourselves as well. You're defending your own future.

So let us try to see how far we can go to stop this senseless process of endless concessions to aggressors, these clever legal arguments for why we should make one concession after another and give up more and more and more.

Why have we got to hand over increasingly more and more technology—complex, subtle, developed technology—that it needs for its weapons, for crushing its own citizens?

If we can at least slow down that process of concessions, if not stop it altogether, and make it possible for the process of liberation to continue in the Communist countries, ultimately these two processes will combine and yield us our future.

On our small planet, there are no longer any internal affairs. The Communist leaders say: "Don't interfere in our internal affairs. Let us strangle our citizens in quiet and peace."

But I tell you: Interfere more and more, interfere as much as you can. We beg you to come and interfere.

Solzhenitsyn's Politics

ALEXANDER SOLZHENITSYN arrived in Washington on the wings of his immense artistic reputation and his great personal stature as one who has suffered, as a prisoner and dissenter in his native Russia, for his beliefs. In his speech before the AFL-CIO, moreover, the exiled Russian writer offered a critique of detente that strikes chords both in those who had expected too much from Soviet-American relations in recent years and in those who had expected very little at all. In his new role as a direct participant in American political dialogue, as in his old role as a Russian prophet, his is a voice that demands to be heard.

It is in terms of that old role, nonetheless, that he must still be understood. For Mr. Solzhenitsyn is a man with a single mission: to bring about the moral regeneration of the Russian people and their release from what he regards as the immoral grasp of Communist power.

© *The Washington Post* (July 4, 1975).

He has no particular interest in, or knowledge of, f eign affairs. He has a consuming obsession with destiny of his own people. This is precisely why Soviet authorities jailed, harassed and finally exiled h It is the wellspring of his artistic genius. And it is v his counsel on foreign policy needs to be listened with care.

The first purpose of American foreign policy, af all, is to prevent war and enhance the welfare of own citizens. Mr. Solzhenitsyn, however, would dedic American power to the defeat of Soviet communism. him this is a matter not of strategic advantage but moral necessity. He regards every compromise Washi ton has made with Moscow over 40 years—from FD recognition of Russia, to his wartime alliance agai Hitler, to the various increments of contemporary tente—as deals struck with the devil. Their result, declares, is to deny the liberation of the Russian peo

The nobility of Mr. Solzhenitsyn's summons is und able, and his words stand as a deserved rebuke to th who would read a moral component out of foreign po altogether. Fortunately, few citizens in the United St share either his compulsion against compromise or fierce commitment to a Russian renaissance. For th would involve a cost and peril beyond reckoning. is not to say that every American step toward dete has been a wise and good one. But Americans h spent the better part of a generation escaping from notion that foreign policy should be a moral crus The example of Mr. Solzhenitsyn's personal cour should not blind us to the dangers of trying to emu it on a national scale.

His host in Washington, AFL-CIO President Ge Meany, shares the Russian writer's conviction that c munism is immoral. He does so out of his own longst ing belief in what he calls the "first principles of labor movement"—the welfare of workers and "free for all people elsewhere." This meeting of fundame ist minds is one of the more sobering, not to say ex political matches of our time. But it does not add u a prescription for wise policy. Human dignity, as sued by these two men, is a high moral value. But the avoidance of nuclear war—this is the overarc goal of detente. There is more room on the moun top than Mr. Solzhenitsyn and Mr. Meany may be pared to grant.

Proposed Sale Of Police Equipment To Russia Hit

Left, courtesy of The Associated Press.

WASHINGTON (AP) — Several American firms are going to an international exhibition next month in Moscow with hopes of selling sophisticated police and criminology equipment to the Soviets.

Participation by the U.S. companies came under fire Sunday from Sen. Henry M. Jackson, D-Wash., who said in a televised interview:

"Are we getting detente when we are going to sell...to the Russians police equipment that will help the KGB to hold the dissidents even under tighter control?"

Rep. Charles A. Vanik, D-Ohio, who along with Jackson has been pressing for tighter controls on export of American technology to the Soviet Union, has called the prospective business deals "shocking and unconscionable."

"A crime control device can easily be converted into a weapon of oppression," Vanik declared in a House speech last week. "It would be tragic if oppression in the Soviet Union would result from devices and equipment stamped: 'Made in America.'"

Voice Identification Inc. of Sommerville, N.J., one of the American firms participating Aug. 14-28 in the Soviet-sponsored exhibition, "Krimtehnika '74," manufactures an advanced electronic voiceprint device widely used by law enforcement agencies in the United States.

Right, excerpted from "The Necessary Amorality of Foreign Affairs" by Arthur Schlesinger, Jr., *Harper's Magazine*, August 1971.

Voiceprint devices identify individual characteristics in a person's voice.

Voice Identification equipment was used to verify the voice of ex-Soviet premier Nikita S. Khrushchev on tapes that were later published as "Khrushchev Remembers."

Alexander I. Solzhenitsyn's novel "The First Circle" focused on a Stalin-era Soviet institute where scientist prisoners were under pressure to develop a rudimentary voiceprint machine for pinpointing a political criminal.

"They envisioned a system, like fingerprinting, which would someday be adopted: a consolidated prints of everyone who had at one time or another been under suspicion," Solzhenitsyn wrote.

Asked whether he thought the Soviets might employ his firm's equipment in wiretapping of political dissidents, as well as against ordinary criminals, William Hughes, vice president of Voice Identification, said:

"Boy, that's a hell of a question. It's an interesting one.

"Quite honestly, I am going over there to exhibit equipment. I suppose they'll want to buy it — I certainly hope so, that's the purpose. It's obviously, as it is here, an investigatory tool. Now, how do they want to use it? I don't know. I can't speak for them or their system of justice or anything else."

In short, the individual's duty of self-sacrifice and the nation's duty of self-preservation are in conflict; and this makes it impossible to measure the action of nations by a purely individualistic morality. "The Sermon on the Mount," said Churchill, "is the last word in Christian ethics. . . . Still, it is not on those terms that Ministers assume their responsibilities of guiding states." Saints can be pure, but statesmen must be responsible. As trustees for others, they must defend interests and compromise principles. In politics, practical and prudential judgment must have priority over moral verdicts.

Losing crusades

IF MORAL PRINCIPLES have only limited application to foreign policy, then we are forced to the conclusion that decisions in foreign affairs must generally be taken on other than moralistic grounds. What are these other grounds? I believe that where the embryonic international community cannot regulate dealings among nations, the safest basis for foreign policy lies not in attempts to determine what is right or wrong but in attempts to determine the national interest.

National interest, realistically construed, will promote enlightened rather than greedy policy. So a realist like Hamilton said (my emphasis) that his aim was not "to recommend a policy absolutely selfish or interested in nations; but to show, that a policy regulated by their own interest, *as far as justice and good faith permit*, is, and ought to be, their prevailing one." And a realist like Theodore Roosevelt could say: "It is neither wise nor right for a nation to disregard its own needs, and it is foolish—and may be wicked—to think that other nations will disregard theirs. But it is wicked for a nation only to regard its own interest, and foolish to believe that such is the sole motive that actuates any other nation. It should be our steady aim to raise the ethical standard of national action just as we strive to raise the ethical standard of individual action."

A Basic Human Right: The Right to Leave

By REP. JACK KEMP (R.-N.Y.)

Next to the right to life, the right to leave one's country and return is probably the most important of human rights. However fettered in one's country a person's liberty might be and however restricted his longing for self-identity, for spiritual and cultural fulfillment and for economic and social enhancement, opportunity to leave a country and seek a haven elsewhere can provide the basis for life and human integrity.

The right of all persons to emigrate from and also return to one's country is probably first among the human rights that define a free society. Only a free society grants its citizens the liberty to leave.

In the United States, we strongly believe that the right to leave and to return is the constituent element of personal liberty, and thus all Americans (except those under some kinds of legal due process) may leave and may return for good reason or bad or no reason at all.

It is significant to note that this concept is hardly one of recent origin. The right to leave is founded on natural law. Socrates regarded the right as an "attribute of personal liberty," and the Magna Carta in the year 1215 incorporated the right to leave for the first time into national law.

The French Constitution of 1791 provided the same guarantee, and an act of the U.S. Congress declared in 1868 that "the right of expatriation is a natural and inherent right of all people, indispensable to the enjoyment of the rights of life, liberty and the pursuit of happiness."

The right to leave must be recognized as a precedent for other rights. For example, if a person is restricted from leaving a country, he may thereby be prevented from observing or practicing the tenents of his religion; he may be frustrated in his efforts to marry or found a family; and he could be prevented from obtaining the kind of education that he desires.

Denial of the right can also be a precedent for the denial of other rights. Disregard of this right frequently gives rise to discrimination in respect of other human rights and fundamental freedoms, resulting at times in the complete denial of those rights and freedoms. I believe that for a man who is being persecuted, the denial of the right to leave may be tantamount to the total deprivation of liberty, if not life itself.

I am personally familiar with someone who has experienced the abuses I have just described. On a recent trip to Israel I met with Rita Gluzman, whose husband has been prevented from emigrating from the Ukraine to join her and their infant son in Israel. I am sure that such regrettable instances are very common.

This view that next to the right of life, the right to leave one's country and return is probably the most important of human rights is sustained by international opinion as authoritatively expressed in a study compiled by the Subcommission on the Prevention of Discrimination and Protection of Minorities entitled, "Study of Discrimination in Respect of the Right of Everyone to Leave Any Country, Including His Own, and to Return to His Own Country." Published in 1963 after exhaustive research, it is considered to be the best expression of international opinion.

By Rep. Jack Kemp in the October 30, 1971 issue of *Human Events*.

George F. Will

Victory in the Sheep Meadow

Last Sunday about 50,000 peace activists gathered for a last hurrah and hootenanny at the Sheep Meadow in Manhattan's Central Park. There, at the scene of so many peace rallies, they celebrated the peace that has come to Indochina.

In Cambodia, the Communists, running true to form, are concentrating their fury on the ultimate enemy of any Communist regime, the people. The Communists have emptied the cities, driving upwards of 4 million people—young and old, childing mothers and newborn babies, the healthy, halt and lame—on a forced march to nowhere, deep into the countryside where food is scarce and shelter is scarcer still.

Even hospitals have been emptied, operations interrupted at gunpoint, doctors and patients sent packing. The Communists call this the "purification" of Cambodia.

This forced march will leave a trail of corpses, and many more at its destination, wherever that is. But this is, according to the Communists, not an atrocity, it is a stern "necessity."

The Detroit Free Press contained a droll (I hope it was meant to be droll) sub-headline on events in Cambodia: "Reds Decree Rural Society." If one kind of society offends you, decree another.

Communism, like its totalitarian sibling, fascism, is the culmination of a modern heresy: People are plastic, infinitely malleable under determined pounding. And society is a tinker toy, its shape being whatever the ruling class decrees.

To create a New (Soviet, Chinese, German, Cambodian) Man—and what totalitarian would aim lower?—you must shatter the old man, ripping him from the community that nourishes him. Send him on a forced march into a forbidding future.

He may die. If he survives he will be deracinated, demoralized, pliant.

There is no atrocity so gross that American voices will not pipe up in defense of it. Today they say: It is "cultural arrogance" for Americans to call this forced march an atrocity, when it is just different people pursuing their "vision."

This is the mock cosmopolitanism of the morally obtuse. Such people say: "Only ideologically blinkered" Americans mistake stern idealism for an atrocity just because it involves the slaughter of innocents. Such people will never face the fact that most atrocities, and all the large ones, from the Thirty Years War through Biafra, have been acts of idealism.

Of course, one must not discount sheer blood lust, and the joy of bullying. Totalitarian governments rest on dumb philosophy and are sustained by secret police. But they are a bully's delight.

Totalitarians have never been without apologists here, people who derive vicarious pleasure from watching—from a safe distance, of course; from the Sheep Meadow, with ice cream bars, if possible—other people ground up by stern "necessities."

Apologists say that totalitarians only want totalitarianism for the sake of the revolution. The apologists, being backward, have got things backward.

Above, © The Washington Post (May 16, 1975).

Gigantic moral failure

One of the lasting shames of our age is that decent Western liberals, otherwise so sensitive to assaults on human values, have failed to condemn Communist brutality and terror in other than pro forma phrases.

Instead, they have r e s e r v e d their obloquy for those who have perceived that communism is perhaps the most sordid d o c t r i n e ever to enslave the minds and bodies of masses of 20th century men. They have not been content to denounce merely the oversimplifiers among the anti-Communists; they have worked over virtually every public figure or scholar who has refused to genuflect before the belief that communism is merely another political sys-

tem, worse than some and better than others.

Communism is not pernicious merely because it is atheistic, bureaucratic, and minatory. It is pernicious because it is a doctrine that transforms ordinary human beings into moral monsters, capable of even such heinous crimes as the wholesale slaughter and liquidation of its own people.

It is pernicious because it regards human beings as mere clay to be moulded and twisted according to official state doctrine. It is evil because, in every Communist nation on earth, it exacts obedience through fear, terror, and intimidation. It is, as Russian writer Valery Tarsis described it, a

system of "police facism" on a scale unknown in history.

But leftists in the Western democracies, with only a handful of honorable exceptions, have regularly excused the crimes of communism and attacked its critics. Theirs is a moral failure without parallel in our century.

Russia remains what it has been — a vast prison run by guards driven by a brutal, debased ideology. And while we are appalled at the treatment given the Tutnauers during their visit, it is worthwhile to point out that they received red carpet treatment compared with the ordeal the average Russian citizen is subjected to throughout his lifetime.

Above, from The Arizona Republic, August 28, 1971.

Was FDR Derelict in Not Visiting Hitler?

Nixon Ignores Moral Considerations in Planning China Trip

By WILLIAM F. BUCKLEY JR.

Concerning the evolving drama of Mr. Nixon's trip to China, a few observations:

If Mao Tse-tung had "free elections" in mainland China tomorrow, it is altogether possible that he would achieve 99 per cent of the vote even if immunity were granted to dissenters. The reason for this is apparent from the reports on China that have come flooding in since the authorities raised the curtain to a few athletes and journalists last spring. China seems to have killed or otherwise disposed of the incremental objector, so as to have achieved the society of the perfectly misled.

Even so, we are hardly absolved from the moral question. One could visit the slave markets of Charleston, South Carolina, in the early part of the 19th century, and find total docility, from which it did not follow that slavery was a happy estate. Terror in China, largely cloistered from public view, has produced Chinese Man: and it is before this audience that Richard Nixon proposes to exhibit himself.

One thinks of the forthcoming elections in South Vietnam, and of the critics of President Thieu who are already busy discounting those elections, insisting that they will not yield a government which is "responsive" to the will of the people. What is their quarrel with the government of Mao Tse-tung? Do they hope that Mr. Nixon will ask Mao to form a government responsive to people who have not been ground out by cookie cutters from his book of Thoughts? Will the Americans for Democratic Action ask Mr. Nixon to demand that China invite Chiang Kai-shek back from Taiwan, to form a coalition government?

NO, THE MORAL ARGUMENT is of course put permanently in abeyance. The critics of South Vietnam, which introduced rudimentary democracy 14 years ago, are like the concentration camp inmates, silent, and smiling, and unctuous, when they address Mao Tse-tung or Chou En-lai. Their sins are not only forgiven them, they are not remembered.

All the restraints one thinks of as decent against suddenly fraternizing with the killers are forgotten: and it becomes basely clear that what matters isn't so much whether a government is vile in its provenance, in its practices, in its ambitions, as whether it is powerful. If it is powerful enough, American liberals will preen like schoolboys before a headmaster. I am waiting for one of the progressive legislators who are congratulating Mr. Nixon to answer simply the question: was Franklin Roosevelt derelict for not traveling to Nazi Germany to be convivial with Adolph Hitler?

Why has Mr. Nixon neglected this dimension of the problem? Only a few months ago, asked by a reporter what excuse did we have left to continue to ostracize Fidel Castro, Mr. Nixon drew himself up and delivered some anti-Communist boiler plate on the evil behavior of Castro. The evil behavior of Castro! By Maoan standards, he is Florence Nightingale.

IN 1939, THE WORLD was stunned, as it was stunned last week, by the announcement of a Soviet-Hitler pact. The Soviets had been merchandising the Nazis as their principal enemies for six years, and vice versa. Suddenly, a pact.

One year and ten months after that pact, the two nations went to war, the reversal of feelings suiting the convenience of Hitler (and for that matter Stalin). But meanwhile, the two countries totally reversed themselves and accordingly even Stalin's fellow-travelers totally reversed themselves on the question whether the United States should go to the help of England.

The moral of this historical reminiscence is that Nazi-Soviet pacts are precisely possible between governments which are run by Nazis and Soviets. Free countries require preparation. Require, in this case, elaborate reasons and public discussion for suddenly turning as Mr. Nixon has done.

What makes him think that he can manipulate the nation, as Hitler and Stalin did? Because the public is hell bent on appeasement at this moment, he can probably get away with kissing the bull on the nose. But then when he gets around to making his move, and needs the strong military tools, the indomitable public mood, the tenacious public opinion, how is he going to come up with it? Who will believe him? Why should they believe him? Do you see what I mean?

296

Garry Wills

Real legacy of Truman detestable

NEW YORK — One wishes each departing soul eternal rest in peace. But that does not oblige one to be patient with his more sentimental-eulogizers.

Not that I would join the anti-Truman historians, the so-called "revisionists" who blame the whole cold war on the man. They are simply reversing the moralistic absolutism that let Mr. Truman, in a total war, so blithely drop two atom bombs on teeming cities.

The revisionists, like the cold warriors, want to see all our postwar conflicts in terms of right vs. wrong. If we were not entirely right, then we must have been wrong. Assuming a first situation of mutual innocence, these scholars look for an original sin that caused us to fall from innocence: some act of Truman's, his refusal of a Russian loan, his intervention in Greece, the construction of NATO, or what have you.

Actually, there was a tangle of rights and wrongs, neither monopolized by either side. And the principal evil of that time was the assumption of an American moral mission that had been encouraged by our two world wars, by the Wilsonian moralism with which we waged them, the attitude of total righteousness that made us demand total surrender and use total methods to obtain it (saturation bombing, even atomic bombing).

MR. TRUMAN, to the extent that he acted out of this mood, did what most politicians were doing at the time. Dropping the bombs on Japan was a hideous act; but any President in his position probably would have done the same. Insofar as we have tempered (somewhat) our tendency to total war, we have made the massive bombing of Vietnam even more hideous. The provocation is less the advantage more dubious, the argument from necessity is finally disallowed by any scale, President Nixon is a far more sinister figure than the first man who used nuclear terror.

But people who admire Mr. Truman — that is, most Americans — do not do so because they defend the cold war or our use of atomic bombs. His whole myth rests on his "gutsy" comeback from what seemed certain defeat in 1948. "Give 'em hell, Harry," the encouraging cry of that campaign, has become his approving accolade in history. When he should have lost, he won — and Americans were allowed to indulge their conflicting sentiments for the underdog and for the winner.

PEOPLE NEGLECT the fact that he won by an artful use of empty vituperation. He created the non-issue of a non-performing Congress. The "do-nothing" Eightieth did almost everything for which Mr. Truman later called his presidency memorable. It passed the enabling bills for the Marshall Plan, NATO, extensive foreign aid and Greek subvention. It created the peacetime draft, reorganized the military, and set up the farm program. Even when Mr. Truman differed with that Congress, while it was in session — for example, on the Taft-Hartley Act — he was attacking what it did, not what it didn't do.

Mr. Truman was a workmanlike politician who, to save his job, gulled the people by calculated vituperation. Nothing unusual in that. What is disturbing is the way people rejoiced in being gulled, the way they have sentimentalized the man's cynicism — so that another man's vituperation (for example, Spiro Agnew's) is automatically justified by a comparison with Mr. Truman's. This makes it "authentically American," and somehow lovable.

That is the real legacy of Harry Truman, and I do not find it lovable, or even admirable. It is as detestable as the political trade Mr. Truman both coarsened and glorified.

The War: The Record and the U.S.

By W. W. ROSTOW

AUSTIN, Tex.—Mr. Reston's column of June 13, 1971, says this:

"One of the many extraordinary things in this collection is how seldom anybody in the Kennedy or Johnson Administrations ever seems to have questioned the moral basis of the American war effort." He mentions me among others who "concentrated on pragmatc questions . . . rather than whether they were justifiable for a great nation fighting for what it proclaimed were moral purposes."

Mr. Reston is quite wrong. The moral and other bases for the position I held—and hold—on American policy in Asia are set out in "The Prospects for Communist China" (1954); "An American Policy in Asia" (1955); "The United States in the World Arena" (1960); as well as in a good many other pieces, including a talk at Fort Bragg in June 1961 and a number of memoranda written as a public servant which have, somehow, not yet found their way into The New York Times. My colleagues can speak for themselves, but I am sure their views were as deeply rooted as mine.

I raise the matter now not in personal defense, for I feel no need for that. I do so because the relation of morality to the national interest has been a peculiarly difficult problem for Americans (as George Kennan, for example, has lucidly pointed out) and because the question is dangerously bedeviled in current discussions of foreign policy. For reasons that reach back to our birth as a nation, out of the ideas of the Enlightenment, we have tended to oscillate between high-flown moralism and a highly pragmatic pursuit of conventional national interests.

There are moral issues involved in supporting the pursuit of the national interest—ours or anyone else's. And they are not simple.

First, and above all, is the question of pacifism. For any reasonably sensitive human being the rejection of pacifism does not come easy. War is ugly and sinful. But pacifism requires an acceptance of all the consequences of never fighting. And this most Americans, including myself, cannot do. That means, however, that all national policy—like the human condition itself—is morally flawed because it envisages war as an ultimate sanction and contingency.

Second is the question of whether the defense of American interests runs with or against the interests of those most directly affected. In Asia this has meant, for example, answering the questions: Did the South Koreans in 1950 and the South Vietnamese in 1961 and in 1965 want to fight for an independent destiny or did they prefer

to go with the Communist leadership in Pyongyang and Hanoi? (I can attest that it was this question President Kennedy felt he had to answer above any other before making his critical commitments to South Vietnam in November-December 1961.)

Third is the tactical moral question of conducting war, if it comes, so as to minimize damage to civilian lives. The history of war suggests this is never easy nor wholly successful; but it is clearly a part of the problem and a legitimate claim on the nation and its armed forces.

Fourth is the broad question of whether the raw power interests of the nation, in general, are decent and morally defensible in at least relative terms. I have for long taken the power interest of the United States to be negative: to prevent the dominance of Europe or Asia by a single potentially hostile power; and to prevent the emplacement of a major power in this hemisphere. These objectives demonstrably accord with the interests of the majority of the peoples and nations of Europe, Asia and Latin America. We could not have conducted our post-1940 foreign policy if this were not so. This convergence of our interests with theirs is reflected in treaties and other agreements which have been approved in accordance with our constitutional arrangements and those of other nations. In the world as it is, I find our power interests, as I would define them, to be morally legitimate.

Fifth is the moral question of the nation's word, once given. For a great nation to make the commitments we have to Southeast Asia involves a moral commitment to stay with them. I believe it immoral to walk away from our treaty commitments, which other nations and human beings have taken as the foundations for their lives in the most literal sense.

I do not detect any thoughtful weighing of these inherently complex moral considerations in Mr. Reston's casual *obiter dicta*. What I do detect is a slipping into *realpolitik* in the next column. What he implies is that, for reasons he does not explain, the fate of South Vietnam ceased at some point to relate to the fate of Southeast Asia as a whole. Mr. Reston appears to have unilaterally repealed the domino theory. As late as 1969, when I last toured Asia, there was great and widespread anxiety from Tokyo to Djakarta about the consequences of premature American withdrawal from the area. And I would guess that anxiety is at least as high today. This is not a moral but a factual question and a matter for judgment on the basis of evidence. We ought to be able to discuss it in a mature and dispassionate way.

In many years of debate about Southeast Asia, I have studied with care and sympathy the views of those who arrived at judgments different from mine. The issues at stake are such that, as Mr. Rusk used to say, they ought to be approached on our knees. My most profound objection to those who would withdraw our commitment to the defense of the area is the sanctimony with which they sometimes clothe their positions.

It is time for all of us to recall these words of Dean Acheson: "On one thing only I feel a measure of assurance—on the rightness of contempt for sanctimonious self-righteousness which, joined with a sly worldliness, beclouds the dangers and opportunities of our time with an unctuous film. For this is the ultimate sin."

W. W. Rostow is former White House adviser to President Johnson.

Yet, granted this principle of having no clear principles, how do we determine the point at which we should abandon principle? Where does consistency become an "illegitimate extension"? In Vietnam, for instance, Schlesinger himself did not become aware of the illegitimacy until well into Johnson's regime; he was still defending the war during the successful antiwar "teach-ins." Now he tells us that we "went too far" in Vietnam, but his norms seem merely quantitative — he falls back on the "just war" concept of proportionality: "I do not see that our original involvement in Vietnam was per se immoral. What was immoral was the employment of means of death out of all proportion to rational purposes." It was not wrong to kill Vietnamese (or Americans); but we should not have killed *so many*. Bombs away, but sparingly. It is easy to see how such a view leads men imperceptibly — one bomb at a time, as it were — into situations that are not, for a long time, repugnant to their original principles, but which become, at some stage of the carnage, more than they can stomach.

U.S. Chaplains Under Attack For Supporting Vietnam War

In an interview in his office last month, the Army Chief of Chaplains, Maj. Gen. Francis L. Sampson, a Roman Catholic who will complete his four-year-term next month, said violence was an evil "but the man who doesn't resist the violent man becomes culpable, it seems to me." He added:

"In the case of nations, innocent friends who are being attacked by aggressive nations, it seems to me if we made a commitment of friendship to a country, we owe it our support."

Not Applicable

The commandment against killing, he said, is actually a prohibition against murder and therefore is no applicable to wartime.

If all the professions that have participated in Vietnam are honest with themselves, and are prepared to examine the notions upon which their involvement was predicated, it can provide an opportunity for this country to attain a wiser sense of direction, and to evolve a higher system of accountability in humanitarian terms for decisions that in the past have been justified solely by vague national security principles.

Albert Speer, sentenced to twenty years' imprisonment by the Nuremberg Tribunal, addressed himself to the old excuses of not knowing about Nazi atrocities or not participating directly in them. In his remarkable memoirs, *Inside the Third Reich*, he wrote:

I no longer give any of these answers. For they are efforts at legal exculpation. . . . In the final analysis I myself determined the degree of my isolation, the extremity of my evasions, and the extent of my ignorance. . . . Whether I knew or did not know, or how much or how little I knew is totally unimportant when I consider what horrors I might have known about and what conclusions would have been the natural ones to draw from the little I did know. Those who ask me are fundamentally expecting me to offer justifications. I have none. No apologies are possible.

Americans now know enough about Vietnam to draw some natural conclusions. The question is: Will they do it?

299

IN GRATITUDE "As the last withdrawal of Americans from Vietnam takes place, it is my special responsibility to address to you, the men and women of our Armed Forces, a few words of appreciation on behalf of the American people.

"For many of you, the tragedy of Southeast Asia is more than a distant and abstract event. You have fought there; you have lost comrades there; you have suffered there. In this hour of pain and reflection you may feel that your efforts and sacrifices have gone for naught.

"That is not the case. When the passions have muted and the history is written, Americans will recall that their Armed Forces served them well. Under circumstances more difficult than ever before faced by our military services, you accomplished the mission assigned to you by higher authority. In combat you were victorious and you left the field with honor.

"Though you have done all that was asked of you, it will be stated that the war itself was futile. In some sense, such may be said of any national effort that ultimately fails. Yet our involvement was not purposeless. It was intended to assist a small nation to preserve its independence in the face of external attack and to provide at least a reasoable chance to survive. That Vietnam succumbed t powerful external forces vitiates neither the explicit purpose behind ou involvement—nor the impulse of generosity towa those under attack that has long infused America policy.

"Your record of duty performed under difficul conditions remains unmatched. I salute you fo it. Beyond any question you are entitled to the nation's respect, admiration, and gratitude."

JAMES R. SCHLESINGER,
SECRETARY OF DEFENSE.
APRIL 29, 1975

A FTER having very carefully studied every scrap of evidence on which I could lay my hands, regarding the trial of Lieutenant William L. Calley, I have decided that the prosecution has no case at all. Calley was a "good" officer, loyally obeying orders from a chain of command that reached right back to the Commander-in-Chief of the US Armed Forces, the President of the United States. And as he prayed to the Almighty before the main executions, Calley was obeying even Superior Forces which the president also recognizes. There is no reason why, for his performance at My Lai, his name should not be put down for another of those two million medals which, the press informs us, have already been awarded to Vietnam war veterans. The only formal criticism that a military court could have of Calley's conduct was that he revealed that dogs and pigs—in addition to babes and grandmothers—were also included in the "body count" statistics. But apart from that lapse, Calley should be decorated for faithfully applying official policy, as laid down by successive US presidents. That is to exterminate by any means whatsoever the political opposition, actual and potential, to the type of regime the government of the United States decided was suitable for South Vietnam. Calley's method of suppressing the political opposition was relatively simple and straightforward—grenades and machine-gun bullets.

Calley, as he testified, saw his victims. In fact he loved them. He found them to be "very wonderful people" and he appreciated that the word "kill" was never used. "Waste them" was the more delicate expression and he felt he could be sentenced to death for disobeying orders "to waste" the citizens of My Lai. "The defense contends," according to a UPI report from Fort Benning, where Calley was being tried, "that Lt. Calley did not consider the villagers to be human beings, but only enemy with whom he could not talk or reason."

Actually the original charge sheet had admitted that the My L victims were in fact "Oriental human beings" so Calley was one st behind low-level official formulations, but otherwise he was well step with top-level policies, expressed in more lofty philosophi terms. Charles Wolf, Jr., for instance, in a paper highly appreciat at the White House as far back as May 1965, had refuted the id that US policies in Vietnam should be aimed at winning popul support. Wolf's conclusion, at the time the US invasion force w being built up for its first big battles, was that "the primary questi should be whether the proposed measure is likely to increase t cost and difficulties of insurgent operations, rather than whether wins popular loyalty and support. . . ." To hell with trying to v "hearts and minds," says Wolf in effect, "let's go after the bodies."

That was the policy that Calley was implementing. Calley saw h victims, even if briefly, face-to-face, huddled together on the grou before his grenades tore them to pieces; lined up against a ditch befo their bloodied bodies were hurled into it by his firepower and orde But what about the technicians of "Mitey Mite," blowing high conce trations of CS poison gas at two pounds per minute into sealed-c underground shelters, killing, as cruelly and inevitably as the Zykl B death machines in the Nazi gas chambers, those who seek shel from US bombs and shells? Come out like men (not to mention wom and children) to a clean death from our bullets, or die like rats, p soned in your holes—that is the alternative given by the gas exper To hide from bombs is evidence of guilt and any GI can act as jud and executioner. Calley is a clean killer in comparison. Who has hea of any "Mitey Mite" operator being brought to trial? One has se filmed scenes of them dragging out gassed babies and piling th up for the body count!

Top, from *Parade*, June 22, 1975.
Above, "America's Genocide in Indochin by Wilfred Burchett, from the quarte magazine, *New World Review*, Spring 197

Accountability for My Lai Extends to All of Us

AS THE TRIAL of Lt. William Calley ends on its painful course, the evidence mounts that he was as much a victim as villain.

This in no way excuses the charges against him—the mass murder of 100 civilians and the individual murder of two others—that morning in the war three years ago. Nor, under the Nuremberg doctrine which American prosecutors propounded at the trial of the Germans, can he be excused by proving that he was only acting under orders.

The Nuremberg doctrine specifies that an individual's behavior is his own responsibility, for which he must be held accountable.

But there are circumstances which show clearly how Calley got into his present predicament. They are an indictment of a military system and of the rest of us who, through approval, ignorance or apathy, let it happen.

Taken to its logical conclusion, as Gen. Telford Taylor, one of our Nuremberg prosecutors, took it in a book he wrote recently, accountability extends all the way to the White House.

Calley was hardly the Army's brightest soldier. He graduated 666th out of 731 students in his high school class. He dropped out of junior college with failing grades, and when he finally got through Officer Candidate School, he graduated 119th of 156.

Still, he was smart enough to learn his lessons. And one of the lessons he learned best was to obey orders. His orders that day, he sincerely feels, were to "waste" the Vietnamese.

"Lt. Calley," his attorneys announced a few days ago, "states that he did not feel as if he was killing humans, but rather that they were the enemy with whom he could not speak or reason."

On the witness stand this week, Calley said that originally he had intended to save some Vietnamese civilians for a later attack on a neighboring hamlet called My Lai I.

"It was understood when we made our final assault on My Lai I, we would have had civilians pulled in front of us," he said.

The purpose? "Clear the minefields."

Considering that Calley has been judged sane and "normal in every respect," it is only fair to ask where he got such ideas—that the Vietnamese weren't humans, that they could be "wasted" without a second thought, and those saved could properly be used as human detonators.

It came from the Pentagon psychology, in which Orientals are "gooks" or "slopes." It manifests itself not only in the William Calleys, but in an official policy that decrees free fire zones for artillery, indiscriminate bombing raids, search and destroy missions, defoliation, and a scorecard based on body counts.

It is fair to ask, as Newsday asked the other day, whether we would destroy Indochina and its people so viciously if the people were Europeans or ethnically like us.

The next question, then, is that if U.S. policy does not consider these people human, what must the Indochinese think of us? It would be too much to expect them to view us with anything but hatred.

From the *Detroit Free Press*, March 1, 1971.

Thinking Out Loud

The Editor

True Christian believers hate war without being pacifists. A pacifist is one who does not believe there is ever a justifiable war. But even a casual study of the Old Testament Scriptures reveal that God has helped His people through many military conflicts.

However, these wars have always been *defensive* wars — never aggressive wars. Always the occasion for warfare was the invasion by a foreign power, or the deliverance from bondage of nations which held God's people in captivity.

An apparent exception was the invasion by the Israelites of the land of Canaan, under Joshua. However, it must be remembered that Israel's mission was to "re-possess" their own land, a land which had been given by God to Abraham and his posterity. They did not invade territory belonging to other nations. So that, strictly speaking, it could not be considered an aggressive action. Through the performance of many miracles God enabled them to re-repossess their own land.

The only justification the United States has for engaging in a military contest with another nation is when that nation either attacks our country or endangers our security. On the basis of this truth, we were not justified in launching the campaign in Vietnam.

Left, courtesy of Dale Crowley in *The Capital Voice*, June 1, 1971.

REFLECTIONS
THE LIMITS OF DUTY

"Let us follow the process of creating an evil more closely. A scientist who is doing his specialized duty to further research and knowledge develops the substance known as napalm. Another specialist makes policy in the field of our nation's foreign affairs. A third is concerned with maintaining the strength of our armed forces with the most modern weaponry. A fourth manufactures what the defense authorities require.

A fifth drops napalm from an airplane where he is told to do so. The ultimate evil is the result of carefully segmented acts; the structure itself guarantees an evasion by everyone of responsibility for the full moral act."

From an article by Charles A. Reich, appearing this week in The New Yorker. Yes, The New Yorker.

Above, courtesy of *The New Yorker*.
Right, courtesy of C. P. Sarsfield and *The New Guard*.
Below, a message from Pope Pius XII.

CEASAR'S DUTY

A nation is required to protect the lives of its citizens; it is not expected to do good to all the world, and those who would demand that it do are not fit citizens. Given a choice of having liberty or death, some would choose the latter, for there are fates worse than death. Letting it be known that death is not feared if life as one wants it connot be had, can sometimes be an effective measure of policy. It is sometimes known as calling a bluff. It draws a line, and though the price may be high, in time that line is usually respected. Some may die, even many, but their deaths win worthy goals for their successors. That is sometimes known as laying down one's life for his fellows. It is an act the benefits from which the pacifist is willing to accept without contributing his proportional measure.

In a remarkable allocution to Military Doctors (October 19, 1953), Pius XII said:

"Let there be punishment on an international scale for every war not called for by absolute necessity. The only constraint to wage war is defense against an injustice of the utmost gravity which strikes the entire community and which cannot be coped with by any other means — for otherwise one would give free course, in international relations, to brutal violence and irresponsibility."

Relating the principle of proportionality to modern times, he added:

"Defending oneself against any kind of injustice, however, is not sufficient reason to resort to war. When the losses that it brings are not comparable to those of the 'injustice tolerated,' one may have the obligation of 'submitting to the injustice.' This is particularly applicable to the A.B.C. war (atomic, biological, chemical)."

First Decree for the Protection of Life

WHEREAS —

After thousands of years of slow and laborious development, mankind during the past few decades has rapidly come into possession of technological means which promise either unlimited opportunity and abundance or sudden and universal catastrophe.

The People of Earth are, in fact, confronted daily with the threat of instant extermination by the accidental or deliberate unleashing of nuclear weapons. This threat multiplies as more nations gain nuclear capability and install multiple warheads which defy inspection and control by treaty.

Even limited use of nuclear weapons and other weapons of mass destruction imperils civilian populations, towns, cities and country-sides, and can turn entire countries into ravaged battlefields.

The $200,000,000,000 being spent by the nations each year for military purposes, mainly for weapons of mass destruction and their deployment, is a criminal waste of resources and manpower which could otherwise be devoted to supplying the People of Earth with adequate food, shelter, clothing, education, health services and expanding opportunities in life.

So long as nations give priority to expenditures for military might, there is scant chance of applying the brain-power, manpower and resources needed to solve other rapidly mounting problems which threaten humanity with the breakdown of society, misery and death in multiple ways before the end of the century. These problems include environmental pollution, the gap between rich and poor, hunger and population, urban decay, technological cancers, social disorientations and other troubles.

Apart from dangers of universal ruin, the means of modern warfare comprise the tools of force by which stronger nations interfere in the affairs of weaker nations and enforce imperialistic and colonial policies.

Meanwhile, the civil and human rights of people in all countries are nullified when nations are permitted to keep large and heavily armed military forces, since it is with military force that dictatorships and tyrannies are enforced, movements for peaceful change crushed, and people kept subservient — making a mockery of the Charter of Human Rights adopted by the United Nations.

Despite the extreme dangers to all life on Earth, which are growing every day and year, the national governments not only fail to protect their citizens from these dangers, but on the contrary many national governments are actively increasing the hazards by continuing to install nuclear weapons and to devise other weapons with ever greater capacity for death and ruin.

During the next one to thirty years, in order to survive and prosper, the residents of Earth must overcome manifold problems and perils of planetary scope unknown in history. Yet at the world level, no agency exists which has the authority or competance to cope with the problems, and anarchy prevails.

THEREFORE —

When life is seriously endangered and existing governments are either unable or unwilling to remove the dangers and improve the conditions of life, then it becomes necessary for responsible citizens to proceed with remedies which seem appropriate.

Men and women acting under such circumstances may be described as Trustees acting for the common good, ultimately justified by whether their actions are endorsed by their fellow citizens.

In view of the increasing jeapordy to the lives and property of everyone on Earth, and in the absence of effective action by national governments and international agencies to protect life, we who are listed below, from many countries, have organized ourselves into an Emergency Council of World Trustees to take immediate action on behalf of humanity. Our purposes are to outlaw war and war preparations, to convene a Peoples World Parliament for continuous work, to prepare a Constitution for Federal World Government for submission to the Parliament, to appoint global legislative commissions to prepare legislation on urgent world problems for submission to the Parliament, and to take other appropriate action leading to the establishment of a Provisional World Government under democratic popular control.

As a first action to rescue Planet Earth and its inhabitants from destruction, and to provide a tangible rallying ground for people everywhere who want peace and human rights while moving towards the creation of a Provisional World Government, we do hereby issue this First Decree for the Protection of Life:

1. Upon the effective ratification of this decree, it shall be outlaw and forbidden everywhere on Earth to design, test, produce, transport, sell, buy, install, deploy or use nuclear weapons, chemical-biological weapons, or any weapons of mass destruction, including airplanes equipped for bombing, I.C.B.M.s and other delivery systems, battleships, tanks and all manner of bombs and newly devised weapons.

2. This decree shall go into effect as soon as it is ratified by groups of students and professors at 200 universities and colleges in at least 20 countries, or by the signatures of at least 10 million individuals in at least 20 countries, or any equivalent thereof.

3. Any and all executive, administrative and chief policy making officials in governments, the military forces, industry, scientific work education or labor who may be responsible for violation of this decree after effective ratification, shall be guilty of war crimes and crimes against humanity.

4. Those who sign or ratify this decree thereby pledge themselves personally to abide by the decree. Opportunity to ratify shall be continued beyond the minimum stated herein for the decree to go into effect.

5. Individuals found guilty of violation of this decree may be assigned to rehabilitation and reconstruction work in areas devastated by war, or to other work of service to humanity.

6. Procedures for enforcement of this decree shall be determined either by the Emergency Council of World Trustees upon effective ratification, or by the Peoples World Parliament or Provisional World Government as soon as the latter institutions are established.

PEOPLE OF EARTH, UNITE TO OBTAIN NEW PRIORITIES FOR LIFE, BY SIGNING OR RATIFYING THIS FIRST DECREE FOR THE PROTECTION OF LIFE!

This First Decree for the Protection of Life was issued at the inaugural meeting of the Emergency Council of World Trustees at Santa Barbara, California, Dec. 28, 1971, to Jan. 2, 1972. At time of issuance, the Decree carried the signatures of several hundred persons from all continents of Earth, more than half being presidents of university student unions and other student leaders.

ALL PERSONS WHO AGREE WITH THIS ACTION ARE URGED TO RATIFY THE DECREE AND SEND A CONTRIBUTION TO CARRY THE ACTION FORWARD!

Ratified by .... Native country ....

Print name .... Contribution $................................

Address ....

Occupation or position ....

Please send me .... copies of the Decree to circulate for ratification, together with a list of the first signers. (Note: You can help the cause by printing the Decree at once and circulating it in your community or on your campus. Use this copy for offset printing.)

Return signed Decrees with contributions to the World Constitution and Parliament Association, Inc., Trustees Office, 1480 Hoyt St., Lakewood, Colorado 80215, USA.

Courtesy of the World Constitution and Parliament Association, Inc., and *The Humanist*, January-February 1972.

Proms and liking Ike

There was another fifties

By Richard R. Lingeman

As for the war, at times it seemed a banal meaninglessness. There were actually two wars in my mind; war, which was bad, and the "police action" war, which reasonable men could give reasons for. I wrote a muddled *cri de coeur* in my diary as the time for entering the service drew near:

"About the war: It seems to me I must approve of it. Our country is acting on principle and is motivated by a world-wide vision. To fight for our belief —in a world order—we must use the irrational techniques of war. We, as a whole, are acting through goodwill but we are faced by a nation [I meant the Soviet Union] that does not act through goodwill, only expediency. We are forced to fight with that nation on its own terms—the evil terms of war.... This war is a big impersonal one—a preview perhaps of those '1984' wars. The principle of our actions and the institutions which embody them are too large really to motivate any but a few. The rest merely carry out their part in the war and perhaps die. Oh well, I will think about it more later."

I didn't think about it much later — especially the dying part—but, armed with a principle I admitted was too abstract and distant for me to accept in my heart, I enlisted in 1953, scared, excited, prepared to hate the Army.

Top, from *The New York Times Magazine*, June 17, 1973.

Playing at War

Why *The Progressive*, with a sixty-two year record of outspoken opposition to war and all things military, was included in a recent publicity mailing from the Avalon Hill Company, we shall never know. But the Baltimore firm which has designed such war games as *D-Day, Afrika Korps, Stalingrad, Gettysburg,* and *Blitzkrieg,* recently sent us a release that panted with excitement about its latest game offering—*Panzerblitz.*

This new board game, says the communique from the Avalon Hill command post, "is a tactical-level strategy game that simulates action of the largest ground campaign of World War II." Developed "from official documents" it recreates "thirteen historical engagements" in "a faithful re-creation of the critical armored battles fought on the Eastern Front 1941-45."

"Fifty-six per cent of all soldiers killed in World War II were Russian. Yet this gigantic theater has been virtually ignored by Western historians," the company discloses—an oversight by military scholars that Avalon hopes to correct, at a profit, through a large sale of *Panzerblitz.*

Their new war game "also happens to be fun to play," says Avalon Hill. All you need to play it is "just common sense, a competitive spirit," and the $8.98 purchase price charged "wherever adult games are sold."

What can be considered "adult" about war games we cannot imagine. They glamorize war, the most infantile and lunatic of all men's pursuits. It would be a healthy sign of American maturity if *Panzerblitz* and all other war games and toys turned out to be a total flop in the stores this Christmas shopping season.

Above, reprinted by permission from *The Progressive*, 408 West Gorham Street, Madison, Wisconsin 53703. Copyright 1970, The Progressive, Inc.

The Great Trip-Wire Delusion

Courtesy of Alan Cranston, U.S. Senator from California and *Saturday Review*, July 19, 1971.

EDITOR'S NOTE: *The following guest editorial is by Alan Cranston, U.S. Senator from California, and longtime contributor to SR.*

The U.S. Senate recently voted down Majority Leader Mike Mansfield's attempt to compel a 50 per cent reduction in the number of American ground troops stationed in Europe.

In the Senate debate much attention was given to the need to scale down East-West tensions, to correct our adverse balance of payments, and to get our now quite prosperous allies to assume a larger share of the financial and military burdens of NATO. All good points. But I sensed a disturbing undercurrent.

There appears to be a tacit understanding on both sides of the Atlantic that a sizable number of American troops must be stationed on the Continent as a kind of human trip wire to assure our intervention in the event of a Soviet invasion of Western Europe.

The theory seems to be that thousands of Americans must be engaged in mortal combat in the first days of such an invasion, else we will not intercede. The belief is that the larger this human trip wire, and the more human flesh it contains, the more confident our friends and allies will feel, and the more hesitant the Russians will be.

I find this concept utterly repellent, and morally grotesque. I am appalled by the image of 300,000 Americans being offered up as sacrificial hostages in a new, perverted version of "earnest money" to reassure our friends that we will keep our pledge. I am shocked each time our foreign friends interpret any effort to reduce the number of hostages as hard evidence that we indeed intend to go back on our word.

What kind of friends are these anyway? What kind of opinion do they have of us to think that we do not value human lives unless they are American lives? To think that we would not consider the lives of other free men worthy of our concern in the event of Soviet aggression? And to think that only the on-the-spot slaughter of young Americans could provoke us to act in our own best interests?

Those who subscribe to the trip-wire strategy claim it offers us flexibility—a way to resist aggression without resorting to all-out nuclear retaliation. The fact is, however, that the great armies of NATO and the Warsaw Pact facing each other across an imaginary line in Central Europe are as dated as the cavalry that tried to stand up to the Nazi panzer divisions in Poland. Our troops in Europe are armed with tactical nuclear weapons as are, presumably, the Warsaw Pact forces.

The Davy Crockett, a cannon manned by a crew of five, has been called the "keystone of the Allied defense line." With an explosive force somewhat less than that of the Hiroshima bomb, it is our smallest tactical weapon, and we have others even more powerful.

In an East-West war in Europe, the side that is losing, or thinks it is losing, will without doubt resort to nuclear weapons to "save the day." Even the "winning" side would do so, if it thought the enemy was about to launch a strike. It is for just these eventualities that we have our tactical nuclear weapons positioned there. So our troops in Europe are targets for almost certain death or radiation poisoning in the event of war. They cannot win; they can only destroy and be destroyed.

We have been lucky so far, but the day must come soon—before this murderous insanity goes too much further—when we will have to reduce our NATO forces. We must recognize that there is no true security for us or for anyone else in a world in which nuclear weapons are on the loose. We must set about the task of providing leadership dedicated to achieving world peace through world law.

Do some of our leaders feel that they must use a trip-wire force to insure that we will keep our commitment to our NATO allies? Are we busily preparing for a day when we may be in the same position in Europe as we are now in in Southeast Asia? Will we someday be told that millions of Americans must die for those 300,000 American troops in Europe—just as we are being told now that still more Americans must die in Indochina so that the deaths of the 45,000 already killed there will, somehow, have been "worthwhile"?

If that is what some of our leaders think, if that is why they insist on maintaining 300,000 American troops on European soil, their perspective, in my judgment, is dangerously distorted. One such horror is more than enough in the lifetime of any nation.

The fact is that the whole structure of the trip-wire concept is built on false assumptions. The fact is that we do not need such an immoral mechanism forcibly to link Europe's destiny with ours. The fact is that we are inextricably linked with Europe—by past history and heritage, and by present politics and economics.

A free, independent Europe is vital to America's survival and to world peace; a free Europe and a free America stand or fall together.

That is the real meaning of NATO, that is why we are in the alliance, that is why we will unhesitatingly honor our commitment should we ever be called upon to do so—not to avenge the blood of American hostages, but to defend American freedom and the very concept of freedom.

Our European allies and those of our leaders who presume otherwise do the American people a grave injustice.

—ALAN CRANSTON.

SR/JUNE 19, 1971

THE SOVIET MILITARY TAKES A LOOK

AT THE U.S. MILITARY

Translated from KRASNAYA ZVEZDA, Moscow

The American press in recent months has focused on the sad array of problems facing the U.S. military services, so it shouldn't be surprising that other nations have taken up the cry. The following article from Moscow's military journal *Krasnaya Zvezda* ("Red Star") doesn't spare us clichés or old-fashioned propaganda, but it is interesting nonetheless as an illustration of the current image of the American G.I. behind the Iron Curtain. For Capt. Yuri Romanov's view of poor old G.I. Joe, see the following report.

THE AMERICAN SOLDIER—who is he? What devilish machine turns him into a cynical killer, out to stifle the freedom of his own people and that of other nations?

In an attempt to deceive and flatter, Pentagon propagandists print lies about him in the *Army Digest:* "The American soldier has pride and he knows how to pray. He often gives away the chocolate bar from his K-ration, he smiles and waves to children weary from years of war."

Pentagon propagandists go on lying even though the entire world has seen the photographs of the Song My victims, has read the notorious caption: "The children, too." The photography of that Song My "hero", Lieutenant Calley, should bear a caption taken straight from the U.S. Officers Manual: "An officer is a gentleman . . ."

Bravo, gentlemen! Don't blame yourself if honest people all over the world identify invaders and cynical killers with Yankees in uniform.

"It is a soldier's honor and duty to defend American ideals," he is told. "Soldiers have to believe that they are fighting for a just cause." "American soldiers have to know what they are fighting for." These are quotes from official regulations. Just what are American soldiers fighting for? The answer should be "for the fortunes of the duPonts and the Rockefellers, who are the worst enemies of their own people and of all humanity," but, of course, the American soldier is not given this answer. He gets highflown

slogans, obvious lies and shameless rhetoric. One thing is important to notice: the dollar oligarchs know that they can no longer ask their soldiers to obey orders blindly, they can no longer proclaim such obedience as being synonymous with honor and duty.

Let's take a look at the machine that turns "honest" citizens into the final product—Yankee soldiers.

The American soldier is not only lied to and brainwashed, he is also corrupted and bought off. Take the case of the so-called volunteers—and there are quite a few of those in the armed forces of the United States. What they are really being paid for is killing Vietnamese, including children, ransacking villages, and destroying the Vietnamese countryside. It is particularly shameful that young college-trained Americans agree to become mercenaries. Everyone should know these facts: in 1968 more than half of all U.S. Army officers in active serv-

ОКРАСНАЯ ЗВЕЗДА

ice, including 168 generals, were college and university graduates. Officer rank was conferred upon many while they were still in college and members of ROTC. American imperialism takes advantage of the high cost of higher education in the U.S. For many young people with limited economic resources joining the ROTC is the only way to get a higher education. The U.S. military establishment knows how to profit from this situation.

This is one of the most monstrous methods of morally corrupting American youth: Do you have a yearning for learning? Fine. You'll get your education, but you have to join an ideological and military machine that is essentially hostile to science and enlightenment.

Do you want security in life? You will get it, if you agree to say that white is black and black is white; if you agree to become a professional soldier.

But that's not all. Deceit and bribery is not enough. Young people are taught to hate—we will not exaggerate if we call it animal hatred. Everybody knows the formula. It consists of brainwashing via TV and the press. The entire atmosphere of the American way of life, with its cult of violence and cruelty, does its share of influencing young minds. Take, for example, a game currently popular with American children—shooting Viet Cong, which is their derogatory name for Vietnamese patriots. Less known but no less infamous is the practice of dressing the "enemy" in Soviet or Vietnamese uniforms during military training. The uniforms are intentionally made to look very ugly, with huge hammers and sickles or red stars on the helmets. Training films show officials dressed in such uniforms jeering at prisoners in fictitious P.O.W. camps.

"Training an army dog consists in teaching it to hate the enemy. For this purpose the 'enemy' must wear the uniform of the hostile army, and he must be cruel to the dog," says a military encyclopedia.

Sometimes it is argued that the commanders and not the soldiers are responsible for war atrocities. That is true, of course. The men in charge of the U.S., the men who train the soldiers and make them do what they do in Indochina and at home, are the embodiment of cruelty and hatred. They think they can deprive a people of freedom. But that people cannot envisage a future without freedom, and their struggle is supported by all of progressive humanity.

Reprinted from *Atlas* magazine. Translated from *Krasnaya Zvezda*, Moscow.

Humanity's Day in Court

To the Editor:

On May 9, the Governments of Australia and New Zealand instituted proceedings in the International Court of Justice asking the Court to adjudge and declare the carrying out of further atmospheric nuclear tests in the South Pacific by the Government of France to be inconsistent with applicable international law. The conduct of tests which give rise to radioactive fallout, it is argued, violates legally enforceable rights of the claimant states. The Court is being asked to provide injunctive relief pending its judgment on the substance of the charges. [Editorial May 19.]

Two days later, in an unrelated action, the Government of Pakistan asked the Court to enjoin India from handing over some 195 Pakistani prisoners of war to Bangladesh where they are said to face trial on broad allegations of genocide and crimes against humanity.

Quite irrespective of the merits of these claims and their success in obtaining for claimants the practical relief sought, the two proceedings confirm to the attentive observer that more and more of late a perception of world legal order is taking hold which raises humanitarian considerations to a status at law previously enjoyed only by the mystique of national sovereignty.

This is a remarkable turn of events, coming less than a decade since an equally divided Court (the tie was broken by a casting, i.e., second, vote by the then President of the Court, Sir Percy Spender) in the *South West Africa Cases* loftily dismissed humanitarian considerations as "inspirational" but not such stuff as generates legal rights and obligations.

No, world order is not yet in any condition to pass a sobriety test. But humanity does seem, at last, to be getting its day in court.

EDWARD GORDON
New York, May 16, 1973

Above, letter to the editor of *The New York Times* by Edward Gordon, May 23, 1973.
Above right, copyright © 1971, by Minneapolis Star and Tribune Co., Inc. Reprinted from the July, 1971 issue of *Harper's Magazine*.
Right, *The Arizona Republic*, December 23, 1971.

The movable small town

USUALLY WHEN I FIRST MET a general, he would take the trouble to explain that the Army was just like anywhere else, that it really wasn't so different from business, or law, or the electronics industry. At the end of a few months I came to understand that few generals believed that. Most of them take pride in the distinction between the Army and civilian society, the latter commonly referred to as "the outside" and thought to be inferior. An officer obliged to live away from an Army post is said to be "living on the economy"; the customary inflection of the phrase implies foraging in hostile country. The distinction rests upon the premise that civilian society is dominated by "the commercial values" (i.e., money and greed) whereas the Army is seen as being governed by the ideals of honor, duty, and country. The expression of the prejudice takes various forms.

Most explicitly it was the sentiment that Galloway had framed under glass and placed on the wall of his office at Fort Knox: "War is an ugly thing, but not the ugliest of things. The decayed and degraded state of moral and patriotic feeling which thinks nothing worth a war is worse . . . A man who has nothing which he cares about more than his personal safety is a miserable creature who has no chance of being free, unless made and kept so by the existence of better men than himself."

An hour's torture

Although military brutality should not be kept secret, as was the case at first with the My Lai killings, neither does the solution lie in inviting thousands of spectators to watch soldiers torture prisoners to death.

Yet this is exactly what took place in Dacca Dec. 18, perpetrated by Bangla Desh soldiers, the "moral" side in the India-Pakistan war which the U.S. was severely criticized for failing to support.

It was not merely a public execution, like the town-square hangings in frontier America; instead, it came close to the ferocity of human dismemberment by lions 2,000 years ago in the Roman Coliseum.

The AP report, carried in The Republic, described how in almost an hour of sadism, with 5,000 cheering spectators at Dacca's race course, four men suspected of sympathizing with Bangla Desh's enemies were beaten and stabbed to death. —

A youngster, believed to be related to one of the victims, flung himself on a prostrate figure. Bangla Desh soldiers and the crowd efficiently battered and trampled him to death.

None of the military leaders present was able to cite any specific charges against the four men, who had been beaten for half an hour, struck with rifles, karate-chopped in the genitals, kneed in the abdomen, burned with cigarettes, shot, and repeatedly stabbed with bayonets, which were twisted and turned in their gaping wounds.

The Indian government, which toppled East Pakistan's former leaders, decided that foreigners would somehow be offended by this lively display. And so officials of India's Overseas Communication Service, which transmits wirephotos for news services, rejected five graphic Associated Press photos of the sadism, declaring, "We do not consider them to be in our interests."

That's beyond dispute. They are neither in the interest of Bangla Desh nor of India. Nor in the interest of those who chant that the U.S. is the most barbaric nation in the world. Nor of those who portrayed the Bangla Desh - India alliance as morally superior to the authoritarian Pakistan government.

We have all heard about dictatorships torturing opponents in secret cellars. But when the public is invited to cheer calculated vengeance, it is hard to distinguish between the democrats and the totalitarians.

AN OPEN LETTER

To the 78 members of the U.S. Senate who sponsored, co-sponsored, or approved a resolution calling for the shipment of Phantom F-4 aircraft to Israel "without delay."

Dear Senators:

It is only proper that you should express your grave concern over developments in the Middle East;

What is not proper is that your concern should take the form of fanatical and one-sided support for Israel;

It is only just that you should reiterate your wish to see peace return to that turbulent area of the world;

What is patently unjust is that you should so irresponsibly condone Israeli occupation and expropriation of Arab lands, and even act to further bolster Israel's position;

It is only wise that you should express fear over an East-West confrontation as a result of the worsening Middle East crisis;

What is unwise is that you should identify so closely with Israel's policy which serves only its immediate expansionist aims, and which strives to polarize the Arab-Israeli conflict in an East-West context;

It is your moral duty to show human concern for the Jews of Israel;

What is immoral is your utter lack of compassion for the inalienable rights of the Palestinian people, and for their attachment to their homeland on which Israel now stands.

WE CALL UPON YOU TO RECONSIDER YOUR POSITION AS IT RELATES TO THE MORAL AND LEGAL ISSUES INVOLVED AND TO A RESPONSIBLE AMERICAN FOREIGN POLICY. WE CALL UPON YOU TO RESIST PRESSURE WHICH REQUIRES YOU TO GIVE SPECIAL CONSIDERATION AND TREATMENT TO ISRAEL.

We urge you to reassess your stand in the light of the following:

● *Israel enjoys undisputed military superiority in the M.E.*

Neither American officials, the information media nor even Israeli leaders have differed on this point. A recent New York Times editorial stated:

"In any event, Moscow knows—as does Washington — that no amount of new Soviet arms of any kind can overcome in the foreseeable future the decisive military advantage the Israelis continue to hold over the Arabs. That advantage is based in large measure on factors that cannot be imported—such as morale and technical competence. It is also strengthened by such Israeli-made weapons as the new Jericho missile, said to be capable of reaching Cairo and beyond with nuclear warheads."

● *Israel continues to occupy territories many times its size.*

Relying on unwavering American support, Israel has been able to defy world opinion and even to oppose plans advanced by its own benefactor, the U.S. It has adamantly denied the right of Palestinians to return to their homeland, as called for in General Assembly Resolution 194, which has been confirmed a nually since 1948; Security Council Resolution 237 (1967); General assembl Resolutions 2252, 2452, 2672 (1967, 1968, 1970). Furthermore, it has ev refused to give a commitment on withdrawal, as stated in Secretary General Thant's Report of March 5, 1971 to the Security Council.

● *Israel continues to be at the receiving end of the most gene ous official and private aid from the U.S.*

In an authorization bill before the Senate Foreign Relations Committee, Administration has requested $500,000,000 for *military credit sales* of whi $300,000,000 is expected to be made available to Israel. Senator Henry Jac son is planning an amendment to the bill which would provide Israel alone w $500,000,000 in military credits half of which is to be earmarked for Phanto fighter-bombers.

For the period 1962 to 1969 the largest volume of classified arms sales the U.S. to any nation has been to Israel, according to "National Diploma 1965-1970," May 1970, *Congressional Quarterly.*

During the period 1948-1970, U.S. Government economic assistance Israel totaled $1.8 billion; tax-exempt dollar transfers from private sour amounted to $2.5 billion and sale of Israeli Bonds netted $6.0 billion. This s total of $10.3 billion represents $4000.00 per capita on a current population ba of 2.5 million Israelis. It is to be noted that tax-exempt Zionist organizations the U.S. are affiliates of the Jewish Agency-American Section, a body whi is officially registered with the U.S. Dept. of Justice as an agent of a forei government. Furthermore, Israeli development bonds sold in the U.S. ha been exempted from the Interest Equalization Tax to which foreign securiti sold in the U.S. are subject.

Additionally, the Senate has voted to include in the *Foreign A Authorization Bill* $85,000,000 in assistance to Israel. This, according the New York Times of October 16, is pursuant to a clause which authoriz "economic aid to countries with a heavy defense burden that they cannot m without help."

Dear Senators:

It is only right that we should question the irresponsibility and the ethic basis of any American actions that place the United States in the position effectively helping to lighten "the heavy defense burden" of an *occupier* a which give moral and material support to that occupier's illegal territorial acqui tions seized by force of arms.

In order to understand the full implications of your actions and their fect on Israel's stand in the Middle East, one need only recall the words of yo colleague, the Honorable William Fulbright, Chairman of the Senate Comm tee on Foreign Relations, who has stated that the principal reason why there h been no progress in abating the Middle East crisis is "the belief on the part Israel that the United States will back it, no matter what position it takes. I belie that attitude is most unfortunate, because I do not see any possibility of negoti tions so long as Israel believes we are at her disposal."

PHANTOMS FOR TERROR AND DESTRUCTION CANNOT INCREASE THE CHANCES OF ACHIEVING A JUST AND LASTING PEACE IN THE M.E.

Tax-exempt contributions to help defray the cost of this advertisement and requests for information may be addressed to:

ASSOCIATION OF ARAB-AMERICAN UNIVERSITY GRADUATES, Inc.
P.O. Box 85, No. Dartmouth, Mass. 02747

The Association of Arab-American University Graduates (AAUG) is gratefully acknowledged for permission in using this "open letter."

Mideast

To the Editor:

I usually avoid reading articles about the Mideast problem, but the opening sentence in Mr. Roberts' Mainstreams column grabbed my attention [Nov. 3]. He proposed that the United States supports Israel for moral reasons. From that statement I gathered he believes the 130 nations in the United Nations which don't support Israel are either immoral or amoral. This seemed to me to be a very precarious position, so I read on expecting to find a well-thought-out argument based on the moral principles common to all the great religions.

The first point Mr. Roberts made was that the United States sought no material advantage from its support of Israel. I was surprised. Wasn't this the same argument put forth by the Watergate defendants and the whole corrupt White House coterie? Was it possible that the author believed everything goes as long as we don't profit materially?

Next came a discussion of Hitler's efforts to destroy all of Europe's Jews. Visions of gas chambers, deadly shower rooms, and thousands of stacked bodies came to mind. Once again my sympathy was aroused, but my emotion didn't shield me from the realization that the author was using an obvious *non sequitur*. What justification could Hitler's actions provide for the outright massacre of whole communities in Palestine in 1946 and 1947? I was more than ever aware that in presenting his moral argument Mr. Roberts had made not a single reference to a moral principle. He did, however, concede that European Jews had no legal right to the land that became Israel. At long last he would share his moral position with us.

Apparently the keystone of his argument was the fact that the United States was not prepared to offer any of its desolate wasteland to the displaced Jews. He found instead that the Arabs were powerless and didn't really need the land they had lived on for more than 2,500 years. Seemingly their land is less dear to them than ours is to us. In putting forth this argument Mr. Roberts is obviously illustrating such moral principles as might makes right and all men are created equal.

About halfway through the article he advised us to forget what happened 25 years ago (not at Belsen or Buchenwald, but in Palestine). He told us the Zionists now have the deed to the Holy Land. The assassinations, the massacres, the terror have all become legal, not moral mind you, but legal. If the Arabs were to get back the deed by the same methods, Mr. Roberts would then recognize their legal position. What kind of moral argument is this?

After that bit of rationalizing the author turned his attention to the condition of the two million Palestinian refugees and accused the United Nations of ignoring their plight. What a mixed-up world he lives in! He knows it was United States money which helped drive the Palestinians from their homes, and it is United States arms which maintain Israel as a theocracy (we sheepishly call it a democracy) in which there is no place for the infidel Arab. Nevertheless he believes our position is moral and that of the other nations immoral.

Through the final paragraphs Mr. Roberts continued to ignore the supposed moral basis for the United States' position. He stuck in a passing reference to the fact that the Zionists are making the desert bloom, this to illustrate that the ends justify the means (he would have loved Mussolini). He also argued that the Israelis only did to the Arabs what we did to the Indians, undoubtedly to point out that two wrongs make a right.

I thought the article was a disaster. I'm sure Secretary Kissinger does an infinitely better job when he presents our position to the leaders of all those materialistic, Godless, immoral nations which oppose us and Israel in the United Nations.

JAMES J. BUTLER

Arlington, Va.

■ New York Congresswoman Bella Abzug recently appeared before the House Armed Services Committee, where she harangued against continuing the draft, characterizing it as "immoral." Rep. Abzug found her congressional peers less easily finessed than the New York electorate, however. Why, asked Rep O. Clark Fisher (D., Texas), is it immoral? Because, replied Mrs. Abzug, it violates "freedom of individual rights." "Do you apply that same standard . . . to Israel?" asked Rep. Fisher "What other countries do is a matter of national policy for them to decide," she answered. "I see," said Fisher dryly. "Then you feel it is a matter for each country to determine based on the problems and responsibilities they are confronted with. Your revulsion against conscription is not universal. Morally you think it's wrong only in the U.S." Replied Mrs. Abzug: "Yes, that is my view."

Do you not consider it an "atrocity" that 1.5 million Palestinians are living in refugee camps and that another 1.5 million are scattered round the world, homeless? In my opinion, Palestine has not died. It is living in the souls of her people (guerrillas and refugees, as well as men, women and children all over the world). The only thing Palestine has lost is its address.

Karim Sahyoun
Wellesley Hills, Mass.

Top, letter to the editor of *The National Observer* by James J. Butler, December 8, 1973.
Left, from *National Review*, April 20, 1971.
Right, letter to the editor of *Time* by Karim A. I. Sahyoun, December 9, 1974.

Something jars

Because there's an alarming economic gap between you and the poor bloke who grew or harvested the coffee beans which went to make your instant coffee.

You pay maybe 25p for a small jar.

He'll be lucky to earn £100.

A year.

You can afford the trimmings: processing, packaging and advertising.

He can barely afford essentials: food, clothing and shelter for his family.

Coffee is grown in poor developing countries like Brazil, Colombia and Uganda. But that doesn't stop rich countries like Britain exploiting their economic weakness by paying as little for their raw coffee as we can get away with.

On top of this we keep charging more and more for the manufactured goods they need to buy from us.

So?

So we get richer at their expense. Business is business.

Perhaps one day humanity will replace self-interest in international trade. Meantime, something needs to be done now about the appalling poverty which these Third World countries are facing.

Oxfam is a very small part of this effort. Currently, we're spending the money you give on more than a thousand development projects in 80 countries.

Nets and boats for poor fishermen. Family planning clinics. Reservoirs to catch the seasonal rains. Training for youngsters in skills their countries desperately need. Tools and seeds for struggling farmers.

Want to know more?

Write to us and we'll send you a copy of *The Internationalist*. It'll cost you 25p, and it reports on the way rich countries treat their poor neighbours. We'll also tell you more about our worldwide development programme —and how you can help.

And next time you drink a cup of coffee, remember where it came from.

And what it really cost.

OXFAM

Room 4, 274 Banbury Road, Oxford OX2 7DZ

Pragmatic Immorality

Today's issue of The New York Times Magazine carries a description of one of the most pessimistic and morally threadbare intellectual positions to be advanced since the demise of the Third Reich. The position, called Triage, is based on a World War I medical practice—necessitated by scarcity—of separating the wounded into three categories: those who would get well without treatment, those who would die no matter what, and those who might be saved if given care. Only the wounded in the last category were treated.

It is now argued earnestly by some American analysts that the problems of food scarcity around the globe and the incompetence of some of the countries in need are so severe as to require the application of the Triage principle in dispensing humanitarian food aid.

The first problem is that the competence argument doesn't entirely wash because India and other South Asian countries—the obvious first victims of the policy—are currently in deep trouble largely because of factors beyond their control: soaring oil and food prices, fertilizer scarcity and bad weather.

Beyond that, however, and more basic, the world has yet to make a really serious effort to crack the food crisis. The Rome food conference last November was the first universal attempt to face up to the problem. Just two years ago, prior to the grain sale to the Soviet Union and a run of bad weather around the globe, there was too little awareness of the food problems to marshall the political will for an effective effort.

There is no question now that the problem is urgent and extremely difficult, but there is no proof that there are not on earth the will, the resources and the technology to overcome the crisis. Nor is there evidence that letting people starve will actually solve the population problem. There is some evidence indicating that where death rates go up because of starvation, there is a compensating rise in birth rates. Conversely, there is other evidence that the encouragement of small-scale farming by small farmers and landless laborers—a program discussed at length at Rome—results not only in substantially increased food production but also in a decline in the birth rate.

But the essence of the problem is that humankind has not yet come close to defining, in terms of political and economic cooperation, what responsible membership in the human family or the community of nations can be or can produce. There is thus no basis in reason or morality to argue that the only recourse now, in the interests of the greater good, is to allow millions of people a long way off to starve to death. It may be hard to be human or moral, but it is even harder—in fact impossible—to play God.

Turkey to lift ban on heroin

ANKARA (UPI) — Turkey has decided to bow to demands from its unemployed poppy farmers and lift a 13-month-old heroin ban imposed at the request of the United States.

A government s0okesman said Thursday Foreign Minister Turhan Gunes told U.S. Ambassador William Macomber the decision was made to ease the financial plight of Turkey's 70,000 poppy growers.

"One part of mankind cannot be driven to despair to safeguard another part," the ne2spaper Hurriyet quoted the foreign minister as saying.

The announcement did not say when the ban would be lifted or whether the government might reconsider i5s decision if the United States offered to step up compensation payments to farmers.

Turkey banned poppy growing last year after a decade of delicate negotiations with the United States. In return, Washington a:reed to pay Turkish farmers more than $35 million in indemnities.

The farmers complained, however, the compensation payments were "hardly more than a tip" and pressed candidates in last October's national elections to take a stand on the issue.

Sacrificial priorities

While the United States could certainly decrease its consumption of beef with profit (although we are not the champion beef eaters of this world; Argentines eat half again as much per capita) it would be politically and economically difficult to do so quickly to an extent that would much help the world's underfed.

But there is one point concerning cattle and beef that should be raised. India is a far worse offender than we when it comes to the misallocation of scarce resources to feed cattle. The United States, with a human population of 210 million, has a cattle population of about 120 million and a per capita beef consumption of 114 pounds. India has a human population of 563 million people, and a cattle population of about 233 million. India's per capita beef consumption is, for all practical purposes, zero. This incredibly vast herd contributes little to the economy and almost nothing to the Indian diet, beef being religiously proscribed. Even the milk yield is small, of poor quality, often unsafe, and largely allocated to feeding calves, not humans.

Anyone who has had the privilege to have traveled in that astonishing country, as I have, cannot help but be appalled and saddened not only at India's malnutrition problems but at the depredations made upon that inadequate food supply by the omnipresent cattle. I recall that more than once, frantic owners of vegetable stands tried to shoo away some cow that was browsing through their produce.

While only the most flint-hearted could be indifferent to the plight of the underfed in India, still the conclusion is inescapable that if we are to sacrifice our beef-eating ways for the sake of India, she should likewise be willing to take whatever steps are necessary to curb the plague of cattle that infests the land.

JOHN STEELE GORDON
Ossining, N. Y. ∎

Sign up to eat less

Relevant to Maya Pines's article, in which she states that "one obvious solution to the food crisis would be to have the nation turn vegetarian—or at least, radically reduce its consumption of meat," the Ethical Humanist Society of Long Island has formed a group to be known as AMFAM (Americans Against Famine). The group, by means of a personal pledge, has resolved to cut back on its present meat consumption by at least 10 per cent.

We are urging all organizations, churches and groups of people, to present this pledge to their members and friends and to begin their own local AMFAM movement.

The pledge is as follows: "Due to the world-wide food shortage and famine, I, the undersigned, as an act of conscience, pledge to reduce my meat consumption by at least 10 per cent."

These pledge cards are to be sent on to the Department of Agriculture and the United Nations Food and Agriculture Organization.

ARTHUR DOBRIN
Leader, Ethical Humanist
Society of Long Island
Garden City, N. Y.

Above and right, letters to the editor of *The New York Times Magazine* by John S. Gordon and Arthur Dobrin (Leader, Ethical Humanist Society of Long Island), December 12, 1974.

More food for a hungry world... or less?

With lives at stake, decisions had better be based on fact.

There are hundreds of millions of people in the world whose food intake is near starvation level.

These people must have food.

They will not get it if we produce less beef in this country, as some suggest.

The United Nations Food and Agriculture Organization says beef is a source of high-quality, assured-quantity protein that helps provide adequate nutrition. This is as true for industrialized nations as it is for developing nations.

It is unfortunate that many people are being misled, because of faulty information, into believing less meat will mean more of something else.

It is a fact that...

Beef has every amino acid the body needs ...the amount and quality of protein no single vegetable, grain or fruit can provide.

It is a fact that...

It takes about 3 pounds of grain to produce one pound of beef, not 8 or more, as has been reported.

It is a fact that...

75 percent of all feed consumed by cattle is grass, forage and by-products which are inedible by humans.

It is a fact that...

Most cattle are raised on land that cannot grow food for humans—nearly 900 million acres in the U.S. alone.

It is a fact that...

Only ruminants (animals with four stomachs) such as cattle can produce high quality protein for humans from this otherwise unusable natural resource.

What we need in this world is more food, not less. That means more beef and other animal proteins as well as more grain, vegetables and other foods. The beef industry accepts its share of this challenge to increase food production through increasing efficiency and use of available resources.

Courtesy National Live Stock & Meat Board.

BEEF INDUSTRY COUNCIL OF THE MEAT BOARD

Feeding the World Is
A Task for the Whole World

Many of the developing countries have dubious records in food policy. They too often failed to offer their farmers adequate incentives to produce. They have too often tried to placate urban consumers with cheap food policies based on concessional imports. They have too often put their development capital into glamor industries instead of into fertilizer plants and irrigation pumps. They have too long put off serious efforts to slow their own birth rates.

The world must feed the world.

The United States and U.S. agriculture will do their share, but we should not mislead ourselves or others. The job is too big for any one country. And we must begin now to build a stronger world agriculture — especially in the developing countries—or suffer the consequences in the years ahead.

—From a speech by CLAYTON YEUT- TER, *assistant Secretary of Agri- culture, before the National Water Resources Association meeting in Fresno, Calif.*

Left, from *The National Observer*. Copyright Dow Jones & Co., Inc.

Sir / Having just returned to the U.S. after six years of living in Asia, in Asian terms and on Asian levels, I notice that we Americans are virtually all fat. It is ethically as well as aesthetically disgusting. We overconsume ourselves into an unhealthy obesity. Then we compound our selfish idiocy by pouring still more dollars into fancy-priced reducing salons, ranch vacations, exercise programs and machines. We waste twice, while the rest of the world dies because it cannot eat its fill once.

J. VAN CLEVE
Round Lake, Ill.

Right, letter to the editor of *Time* by J. Van Cleve, June 3, 1974. Reprinted by permission from *Time, The Weekly Newsmagazine*, Copyright Time, Inc.

SECTION 14

Sports

It has been argued by a number of advocates of physical education programs that sports comprise a microcosm of the universe of human experience. The selections in this section provide evidence in support of this claim, at least with regard to the ethical dimension of the human realm. Almost every conceivable type of ethical question can be found related to some activity or other which falls into the general category comprising the world of sports, questions ranging from matters of life and death to cases of cheating and dishonesty to the issues of women's and minority rights and the mistreatment of animals.

The only significant question raised in this section which is not discussed in any of the other sections of this book is that of whether or not a different set of rules and standards should be applied to cases that arise in the context of a sport than would be applied to similar cases in other contexts. As usual, there is a wide spectrum of opinion concerning this question. At one extreme, some persons argue that the basic moral principles of society should also be applied to sports, and if at all possible they should be applied more rigorously in sports insofar as sports should provide a model to be emulated in other areas of human activity. At the other extreme, it is argued that the realm of sports is a realm of "escape" from the "real" world and that the rules of the "real" world should not necessarily be applied to the realm of sports at all. This is not to say that there is no need for a moral code in sports, but only that this code could theoretically be completely different from the moral rules used in the other areas of human activity.

One interesting element which has appeared in discussions of ethics in sports in recent years is the growing trend toward viewing sports as an industry or a kind of major business activity. Certainly it cannot be denied that many sports (ranging from Little League baseball and the Soap Box Derby to college football and horse racing) have become more and more highly organized and commercialized in recent years. Thus one of the ethical decisions currently open for discussion is that of whether or not, and if so in what way, various sports organizations should be changed. Thus, in the sports microcosm we even have a version of the issue of civil disobedience when an athlete raises the question of whether or not to openly violate the rules of the Olympic Committee or the NCAA, or whether the Little League should be abolished.

EXERCISES

1. Try to find at least one argument from each section of this book which deals with essentially the same basic moral issue (e.g., cheating, the taking of a human life, etc.) as one of the arguments in this section. If you can find no analogs in this section for any argument in one of the other sections, try to conceive of some situation which *could* occur in some sports context which would involve at least one of the issues in the other section.
2. Compare the arguments in Section 9 dealing with suicide with the arguments in this section concerning the right of a sports participant to risk his or her own health or life. Compare these arguments also with those in Section 2 dealing with the rights of an individual to take risks in using drugs or smoking. Can you identify any unique features of the arguments concerning sports which are not contained in the arguments in the other sections?

People in Sports: Drug Tests Are for Cows

No sooner did Pete Rozelle, commissioner of the National Football League, announce adoption of some new procedures in the league's drug-abuse program than the two most valuable players of last season stood up to object. Not that **O. J. Simpson** or **Larry Brown** are for drugs—far from it—but both protested proposed urinalysis tests for N.F.L. players, which are not part of the new procedures, but are being considered.

Since there is a chance the urinalysis proposal will be adopted by the N.F.L., which is eager to preserve its clean image, Simpson and Brown both call the test "dehumanizing."

"I'm against it," said O. J., the Buffalo Bills' running back. "I don't take 'bennies' or anything else, but I don't like anyone forcing me to take a test. I'm a human being. Urine tests are O.K. for cows or horses, but I'm not an animal."

Brown, the Washington Redskins' running back, said: "I think this whole thing about drugs has been blown out of proportion. We shouldn't even be discussing hard drugs in pro football. We should only be discussing 'ups' and 'downers.' As for doing urinalysis on us players, it's dehumanizing. I wouldn't do it."

NOTICE

It is League policy that the use by NFL players of any drugs which have not been specifically prescribed, recommended, or approved by your team doctor or personal physician is not in your interest, the interest of your team, or the interest of the National Football League.

The use or distribution of "pep pills" or "diet pills" by members of this team is not condoned by the League or by the management of this Club. The taking of these drugs, regardless of amount, has never been shown to improve performance on the athletic field. Furthermore their use should not be viewed as a matter without medical consequence. To the contrary, significant side effects can occur on the heart, pulse, and blood pressure, as well as in connection with withdrawal or "coming down" from the drug, especially with repeated or prolonged usage. Added medical risks can be encountered if one is injured and requires anaesthesia for surgery.

Should there be any questions about this policy, or about the use of drugs of any character either on or off the playing field, the team doctor will be happy to discuss them in private with individual players.

Copy of a sign that will be posted in training camps and locker rooms of the 26 teams of the National Football League around the country this season.

Dave Anderson

The Shame of Shea Stadium

Left, from *The New York Times*, October 13, 1973.
Right, from *The New York Times* (October 13, 1973). © 1973–1975 by The New York Times Company. Reprinted by permission.
Below, from *Family Weekly*, September 19, 1971.

OAKLAND, Oct. 13—When a celebration occurs at Shea Stadium, the only rule is mob rule. Tragedy is inevitable some day. When it occurs, it will be on the conscience of the New York Mets management. If the Mets win the World Series at Shea Stadium next week, tragedy will be lurking in the aisles leading to the field, as it did Wednesday when the Mets eliminated the Cincinnati Reds in the playoff for the National League pennant. In the chaos that erupted, about 30 people required first-aid treatment, five required hospital treatment. "Only five," shrugged an apologist for the Mets' rowdies. But it was five too many. Winning a pennant was once an occasion in New York for happiness and pride. Now it's an excuse for lawlessness and fear.

Sports of The Times

"To be on the field," said Cleon Jones, the Mets' outfielder, "is their way of being part of what's happening. We had been a beaten team and they had been beaten fans. It was their way of showing us they're as happy as we are."

The police also emerged as apologists. Perhaps a dozen rowdies were detained, but none was arrested. One officer described those who clawed out chunks of grass as "souvenir hunters." Semantics again. The proper word is vandals. Take a chunk out of that officer's lawn and see if he considers it a souvenir.

People in Sports: Sparky Ashamed

After 24 hours of meditation, **Sparky Anderson**, manager of the Cincinnati Reds, has changed his mind. After the pennant-winning game Wednesday, when the Met fans went wild, Sparky said: "I'm ashamed I live in this country, and I'm not too sure New York is in this country. New York ought to be the next atomic bomb-testing ground."

But now Anderson says this: "It isn't New York that's to blame, or the people of New York. It's us. I'm talking about me, the players and everyone else who are supposed to set an example for the fans.

"After a pennant-clinching, the players are supposed to salute each other's performance, enjoy their victory and maybe take a couple of sips of champagne. But do they? Of course not. They throw it all around the clubhouse, douse everybody with it and what not. You see how they carry on, the wild way they act.

"If the players do this, why not the fans? I did the same things. I'm no better than them. Here I am calling them animals and lunatics and I'm doing the same thing. How can I sit here and criticize the behavior of the fans when mine isn't any better?"

●

Ask Them Yourself

FOR BOB VOGEL, *Baltimore Colts*

What is your reaction when people say pro athletes should set an example for youngsters?—Mrs. R. L. Little, Durham, N.C.

● Why should I have to set an example for other people's kids? That's not my job. I think each one of us should take stock of where we stand and assess our relationship with our own children. It doesn't make any difference what kind of example an athlete sets if, when the kid gets home, his own father is a hypocrite and a liar and a cheater.

Forbes: Sock' Em or Assault?

By SKIP MYSLENSKI
Inquirer Staff Writer

MINNEAPOLIS — For over three days the historic trial of Boston Burin Dave Forbes moved slowly, tediously, through jury selection and a series of preliminary witnesses. But finally yesterday afternoon Henry Boucha, the victim, appeared to tell his version of the story.

"We'd given each other a couple of cheap shots with elbows in the chest," the former wing for the Minnesota North Stars said. "Then he gave me another elbow, I dropped my gloves and sticks and punched him . . .

"Then we had some words in the penalty box. There were a lot of words back and forth. Vulgarities. He

distinctly told me he'd shove the stick down my throat.

"I didn't think anything would come of it. I thought maybe it would come later in the game. But sometimes players come out of the box and fight right there, so I was kinda watching him over my shoulders . . . He threw a punch with a stick in his hand and got me in the eye."

The injury that night of Jan. 4 in Bloomington, Minn., sent Boucha to Minneapolis' Methodist Hospital, where 25 stitches were needed to close the eye. Two weeks later, Dave Forbes was indicted for aggravated assault with a dangerous weapon (the hockey stick).

"Are we supposed to sit here and say, 'Boys will be boys?' " said Hennepin county attorney Gary Flakne when he announced the indictment. "I agree that hockey is a contact sport, but there seems to be a line which the grand jury found, and I agree with, beyond which something other than good-natured hard contact becomes assault."

And so on Monday Dave Forbes, the first professional athlete ever to face criminal charges for his actions during a contest, sat at the defendent's table in a courtroom here and watched quietly, unemotionally, as this unique trial began.

Above, from *The Philadelphia Inquirer*, July 11, 1975.
Below left, United Press International, August 11, 1975.
Below right, from a column by Geri Joseph in the *Minneapolis Tribune*, 1975.

Forbes Case Retrial Is Ruled Out

MINNEAPOLIS, Aug. 11 (UPI) — Hennepin County Attorney Gary Flakne said today he will not seek to retry Boston Bruins' forward Dave Forbes and will ask District Court Judge Rolf Fosseen to dismiss an aggravated assault charge.

A mistrial was declared July 18 in Forbes' initial trial when a jury failed to reach a decision after deliberating 18 hours.

"There is no reasonable basis to believe a second trial would result in conviction," Flakne said at a news conference. "I am convinced that no matter how carefully selected the next jurors might be, they could not reach unanimity if the case was retried.

"It would only serve to harass and make an example of Mr. Forbes. This would be wrong."

Flakne said he believed the jury's initial 9-3 vote in favor of conviction in the first trial was "a fair and accurate community consensus with regard to game violence in general and the action of Mr. Forbes in particular."

"We have served notice on the National Hockey League and others that extraordinarily violent acts will no be tolerated in this community and that athletes, no matter in what sport they participate, will not be immune from prosecution should they conduct themselves in a manner similar to that of the defendant," he said.

And why do otherwise sensible parents put up with the worries about injuries, the unhealthy stress on winning, the disrupted meal-time schedule? Because athletics—especially the rugged variety—are favored as one of the golden roads to manhood. Both the good and the bad values of sports are held up as desirable standards for boys. What happens to boys who cannot compete in that tough game is another whole column.

There is no dearth of suggestions about how to get rid of excessive violence in contact sports. Players should know that they are liable legally, and thus financially, for injuries they inflict, one observer proposes. Offending players should be barred from playing for a season, even for life. Teams should forfeit a game in which there is violence. Organizations such as the NHL must tighten the rules and be more stringent about enforcing them.

All well and good. But this sports fan has the uncomfortable feeling that not much will change until we fans decide that contrary to Vince Lombardi's hallowed maxim, there are values other than winning. Nor will things change until we refuse to lionize the team or player with the roughest reputation in the league

Another Example of Sport Officials (NCAA) Against the People

BASKETBALL PLAYERS SUSPENDED FOR PLAYING CHARITY GAME

Bill Robinzine is a 6' 7" black basketball star at DePaul University on the North Side of Chicago. He went to Chicago's Phillips High School. Andy Pancratz is a 6' 9" white center at DePaul who went to Hershey High School in Arlington Heights. Together they make up the backbone of the DePaul basketball team.

Last March, after the DePaul season had been completed, the two played in a benefit tournament in Gary, Indiana sponsored by Mayor Hatcher. The tournament had been organized to provide quality college basketball for the kids of Gary to see. Admission was free. Robinzine and Pancratz received no money for playing in the tournament, no trophies, not even expenses — just the satisfaction of knowing they had helped out. Now, they have been notified by the NCAA, the organization that "regulates" college sports, that they are being suspended for at least a part of this season. Why? Because they hadn't asked the NCAA's permission to play in the benefit tournament. This ridiculous ruling has been appealed, and because of public disbelief and pressure against the suspension, it might be lifted. But judging from past NCAA action, the suspension will probably stick.

Contradictions like these — between athletes and the authorities who run and own the sports world in this country — are becoming clearer and clearer. With this most recent idiotic ruling by the NCAA, and with the college basketball and football seasons coming to a peak, it is worthwhile taking just a brief look at college sports and how they are run.

Most of us know what we know about college sports from watching Notre Dame play football on television. Those who are able to go to college learn one thing real fast — at most schools, especially the big ones, sports are not run for the students, the public, or even the athletes. Steve Owens, a former Heisman Trophy winner now playing for the Detroit Lions put it simply, "at college, sports is big business." A look at the athletic program of any major school shows he is right.

Schools spend as much as $5 million on their football programs. Football coaches spend $25,000 a year just on phone calls recruiting athletes. Yet only about 1 person in 10,000 in America gets to play on a varsity college team. For others, and for those who enjoy sports that are not "good business", facilities are pathetic. For example, women receive an average of less than 1% of athletic budgets for their programming. Why? Because womens sports isn't good business. So instead of colleges encouraging involvement, they produce show business products and involve people that way, charging people a lot of money just to watch.

The NCAA, the group which suspended the DePaul players, helped build this kind of sports atmosphere step by step. For years they have allowed colleges to "buy" good athletes. It has allowed trainers to hand out drugs faster than pharmacists. It allows coaches from different schools to unite in schemes to reduce recruitment of blacks. It allows coaches to take two scholarship football players who will not help the team and have them crash heads until they can take it no longer and quit, allowing the coaches to use the scholarships on other players. In short, the NCAA allows schools to do almost anything to build strong teams in the "business"sports.

At the same time the NCAA is quick to hand out punishment to make sure athletes stay in line. A few examples: Sylvester Hodges, one of the country's best wrestler's and a three year veteran of the Air Force was not allowed to wrestle because he refused to shave his mustache. The NCAA had a rule forbidding wrestlers to have hair on their face below the ear. Stanly Royster, the All-American track captain at the University of California, was dismissed because of involvement in the black liberation struggle on campus. These are only two of hundreds of examples. So the suspension of the DePaul athletes is nothing new or unusual.

Why are sports run this way? Max Rafferty, a top "educator" in California explained it. "There are two great national institutions which simply cannot tolerate dissension: our armed forces, and our interscholastic sports programs. Both are of necessity dictatorships . . ." Now that the armed forces has mutinied in Viet Nam, interscholastic sports is left as the last stronghold of All-Americanism.

And even this last stronghold is beginning to crumble. In the last 2 years over 150 college campuses have been subject to demonstrations led by athletes-demonstrations ranging from charges of racism and mistreatment to opposition to the war in Viet Nam. Athletes are changing, despite the efforts of the NCAA, just about as fast as everyone else in America.

Most of us, men and women, enjoy sports. But most of us aren't the exceptionally talented few able to win athletic scholarships to college. And more and more of those who do are beginning to understand the mentality of sports in American schools that led President Eisenhower to say, "the real reason for American sports is to prepare young men for war." Instead people are beginning to realize that the recent All-American basketball player at Maryland was right when he said, "One things for sure, playing ball is a lot more fun on the playgrounds." That's where most of us are anyway, summer and winter. Or trying to find a place for the family to swim, or trying to find a girls softball league, or trying to get $40 to join the YMCA. Sports, even in schools, is run like every business and institution in America — so that a few get rich while the rest of us hustle to survive.

FRIENDSHIP FIRST –
COMPETITION SECOND.

ALL POWER TO THE PEOPLE

As this issue of R.U.A. went to press, the NCAA turned down the appeal of the two DePaul University players and suspended them for half the season. The NCAA also suspended another player, from Norther Illinois, for playing in the same charity game in Gary.

From *Rising Up Angry* (December 2–23, 1973), Chicago, Illinois.

Big-money college sports

The National Collegiate Athletic Association, which is to college sports what McDonald's is to hamburgers, has just taken several actions that might be viewed as reformist — although they were approved for the wrong reason. What cannot be attained by principles may finally be impelled by economics. A reduction in the swollen importance of intercollegiate athletics in this land has much to recommend it.

The NCAA, with more than 700 member schools, decided in a special session on athletic economics to shrink football and basketball coaching staffs, and sliced, gently, into the number of football players at major colleges who may be taken on road trips or suited up for home games. The association voted also to curtail some recruiting practices, and to eliminate the $15-a-month "incidental money" that athletes on grants-in-aid often are given. A modest decrease in the number of athletic scholarships was also given the NCAA imprimatur, though this primarily applies to the "non-revenue" sports — all but football and basketball.

The motivation for this retrenchment had nothing to do with the bloated priorities reserved for major sports at too many institutions of higher learning. The NCAA did not grapple with these issues because of the blatant, and tacitly accepted, function of intercollegiate athletics — to provide farm systems for the professional leagues.

It was money that caused the NCAA to squirm. More than 80 per cent of colleges are showing a deficit in athletic budgets, the Baltimore Sun reported from the Chicago gathering. The efforts to cut expenditures are intended only to avert athletic bankruptcy at a number of schools.

However, what the NCAA did not do in Chicago reveals the taint of hypocrisy in big-time, big-money college athletics. The association opened its proceedings by promptly tabling a motion that athletic scholarships be granted on a basis of need. It has been an article of faith, exuberantly asserted for decades, that athletic scholarships permit many, many young men (though few young women) to receive a college education who might otherwise be denied the opportunity of attending college. As with all myths, this one is true in some specifics but false in its generality.

If financial need, with the corollary of making an education available to deserving youngsters, isn't the fundamental criterion of providing athletic scholarships, what is? To ask that question is, of course, to answer it.

We strongly admire and support athletics; it is one of the saner human endeavors. But the integral development of body with mind hardly seems the overwhelming rationale of most intercollegiate rivalry. There is, we suppose, a benefit in providing student bodies — and the public — with a vicarious outlet for the competitive instinct and in offering a psychological attachment. Those elements pretty well justify professional athletics.

However, intramural athletics would seem the proper vehicle for sports in a college environment. While most colleges and universities do maintain intramural programs — some excellent, some adequate — they usually exist as barely respectable third cousins to the intercollegiate squads, again, particularly in football and basketball.

We do not advocate abolition of intercollegiate competition. But wouldn't it be refreshing to see athletics restored to a more sensibly proportionate function on campus?

From the *Washington Star-News*, August 20, 1975.

My Turn

Robin Roberts

Strike Out Little League

In 1939, Little League baseball was organized by Bert and George Bebble and Carl Stotz of Williamsport, Pa. What they had in mind in organizing this kids' baseball program, I'll never know. But I'm sure they never visualized the monster it would grow into.

I believe more good young athletes are turned off by the pressure of organized Little League than are helped. Little Leagues have no value as a training ground for baseball fundamentals. The instruction at that age, under the pressure of an organized league program, creates more doubt and eliminates the naturalness that is most important.

If I'm going to criticize such a popular program as Little League, I'd better have some thoughts on what changes I would like to see.

BUSY SCHEDULES

First of all, I wouldn't start any programs until the school year is over. Any young student has enough of a schedule during the school year to keep busy.

These programs should be played in the afternoon—with a softball. Kids have a natural fear of a baseball; it hurts when it hits you. A softball is bigger, easier to see and easier to hit. You get to run the bases more and there isn't as much danger of injury if one gets hit with the ball. Boys and girls could play together. Different teams would be chosen every day. The instructors would be young adults home from college, or high-school graduates. The instructor could be the pitcher and the umpire at the same time. These programs could be run on public playgrounds or in schoolyards.

WHAT DID THEY WANT?

The whole idea of Little League baseball is wrong. There are alternatives available for more sensible programs. With the same dedication that has made the Little League such a major part of many of our lives, I'm sure we'll find the answer.

I still don't know what those three gentlemen in Williamsport had in mind when they organized Little League baseball. I'm sure they didn't want parents arguing with their children about kids' games. I'm sure they didn't want to have family meals disrupted for three months every year. I'm sure they didn't want young athletes hurting their arms pitching under pressure at such a young age. I'm sure they didn't want young boys who don't have much athletic ability made to feel that something is wrong with them because they can't play baseball. I'm sure they didn't want a group of coaches drafting the players each year for different teams. I'm sure they didn't want unqualified men working with the young players. I'm sure they didn't realize how normal it is for an 8-year-old boy to be scared of a thrown or batted baseball.

For the life of me, I can't figure out what they had in mind.

A Scandal Clouds the Famous Race

Have Adults Corrupted the Soap Box Derby?

Ski-boot manufacturer R o b e r t B. Lange, Sr., of Boulder, Colo., wrote to his local Jaycees last week—not about skis or boots or business, but about cheating in the Soap Box Derby.

Lange's allegations about widespread use of prohibited but commonplace tricks for winning cast a cloud over the renowned race. Lange told the Jaycees, sponsor of Boulder's local Soap Box

This account was prepared from reports by correspondents Peter Geiger in Akron and Richard S. Johnson in Denver.

Derby, that there was nothing uncommon about the electromagnetic device that gave his nephew a boost to become this year's national Soap Box Derby winner— and that also caused the youth to be disqualified two days after the race.

Lange, whose son won the race last year in a different car, admitted in his letter that he had advised his nephew and ward, Jimmy Gronen, 14, to cheat in the All-American Soap Box Derby in Akron, Ohio, by installing a battery-powered electromagnet in the nose of his gravity-driven racer. The electromagnet provided an advantage for Jimmy by drawing has car toward a metal restraining plate that is dropped forward to the track surface at the start of the downhill race. Jimmy won, but he was disqualified after officials discovered the magnet.

'Mistake in Judgment'

"I knew that this was a violation of the official Derby rules," Lange wrote, noting that he made a "serious mistake in judgment." But he said he felt that "to be competitive" his nephew needed one of the "speed gimmicks in widespread use." He maintained that "the Derby rules have been consistently and notoriously violated by some participants without censure or disqualification." Derby officials declined to comment on the allegations.

Among the violations that officials in the national competition have failed to see, according to Lange:

"Some cars are built by professional adult competitors who get lightweight drivers known as 'chauffeurs' to drive the cars.

"Metal and other substances are used extensively as ballast.

"Unofficial tires and axles and altered official tires and axles are used.

"Magnetic noses and other fast-start aids are employed."

Lange's six-page letter "reads like *The Prince*," Machiavelli's classic on political power, says Boulder County District Attorney Alex Hunter. Last week Hunter charged Lange with two counts of contributing to the delinquency of a minor, a misdemeanor, in connection with the Derby cheating. No charges were planned against Jimmy, who was disqualified before receiving the winner's first-place trophy and $7,500 college scholarship.

"The cars are too sophisticated," Tom Jenkins, 45, a United Rubber Workers Union business agent told The National Observer. Each year Jenkins spends his two weeks' vacation as chief of the racecourse service area's volunteer repair crew. Says Jenkins: "The boys and girls [aged 11 to 15] couldn't build these cars. There's no question in my mind about that. Some of them are quite professional looking. I have to agree with Lange: The professionals have taken over. Sixty per cent of the cars in the All-American were never touched by the boys. I'm very serious about this. You'd be surprised how many kids can't even change a wheel. . . .

Girls in Little League favored by slim margin

C. Lawrence, Albany: "I do not think girls should participate on Little League teams as they exist. Sweeping changes are needed. Often it serves as an outlet for frustrated men who badger boys into bad bones and bad attitudes. When the game is made safe for boys, girls should be able to join."

John Robinson, Troy: "Baseball is a competitive sport, and those who play are generally the best competitors. If girls can compete well, as some have, they should be allowed to play."

Above, from the Albany (N.Y.) *Times Union*, 1974.
Below, from *The American Rifleman*, December, 1974.

NOT QUITE FAIR TO WOMEN?

THE International Olympic Commitee maintains that it can find no place for smallbore events for women shooters in the famous Olympic Games.

The professed reason is that the Olympics are overgrown and, they say, already involve far too many people.

Yet the IOC reportedly yielded to pressure and included women's basketball and team handball events in the Olympics for the first time after rejecting the women's smallbore events.

Women have participated in events of their own in the Olympics since the 1920's if not earlier. Current competitions for women include track and field, swimming and diving, archery, fencing, skating, gymnastics, skiing, rowing, basketball and volley ball. There are 15 such separate programs, some including a dozen or more individual matches.

Women are also eligible to compete *as persons* with men in shooting as well as in yachting, horseback riding and canoeing. It required a strenuous effort of U.S. Olympic officials, including the late Franklin L. Orth, then NRA Executive Vice President, to pry open the Olympics to women shooters at all, and that was managed only in 1967.

What The National Rifle Association of America and other backers of women's events propose now is simply to add smallbore prone and three-position matches for women, plus air rifle and air pistol events for all. Against the vast panoply of the Olympic Games it seems like asking very little. ■

Mainstreams

. . . Man Has a Right to Court Danger

By Edwin A. Roberts, Jr.

In the weeks since the running of the 1973 Indianapolis 500, a wave of criticism has rolled over the sport of auto racing—again. Blood and rain combined to make this year's abbreviated contest a profound disappointment to fans while furnishing heavy ammunition to people who favor outlawing auto racing altogether.

These people were further bolstered in their position by the death last week of a driver injured during the race, the third death to result from the contest.

Auto racing, like boxing and bullfighting, is the kind of competition that lends itself to emotional objections. The chances of serious injury and even death appear to critics to be uncommonly good, and so the question is asked whether the show's excitement is worth the risk.

Bullfighting, at least the authentic Spanish variety, is banned in the United States, while boxing and auto racing are not. This leads one to suppose that legislators fear more for the well-being of animals than they do for the safety of humans. Bullfighting is against the law because the bull is always tormented and killed, not because matadors occasionally come to grief in the ring.

Comment

As a general matter, we tend to be most indignant about those dangerous sports we know the least about. Perhaps that is why some of us think auto racing is slightly crazy and why we react contemptuously to assertions by the auto-supply industry that racing leads to important improvements in conventional cars.

If, say, the tire makers declare they need the Indy 500 to test their products, then they are hopelessly unresourceful either as industrialists or as liars. Common sense tells us the tire people can find out all they want to know about tires without supporting so potentially deadly a diversion. Beyond that, the fascination in watching cars go around in circles is lost on those of us who are uneducated in the fine points of gripping a steering wheel.

The Square Ring

The resurgence of antiracing feeling is due partly to the great speed of the new generation of cars. As recently as 1963, Parnelli Jones won the Indy 500 with an average speed of 143.14 miles an hour. Today the cars career around the ancient Indianapolis Speedway at close to 200 miles an hour, vastly increasing the risks to the drivers. We all know about highway speeds and driver-reaction time. Even a highly skilled racing driver is more likely to collide with another car or crash into a wall when he is running at the cruising speed of a light airplane.

Well, say racing fans, at least the drivers don't try to hurt each other, as prize fighters do. And indeed many famous editorial pages have for years urged the outlawing of professional boxing. Actually, boxing has been outlawed at various times in various states, only to be made legal again when the fight crowd protested—and when fight-related revenues were observed pouring into more permissive states.

Many fighters have died as the result of battles in the ring. A good many more have suffered crippling injuries. To a large segment of the population, prize fighting smacks of primitivism and by its nature violates civilized values.

However that may be, it remains true that there is probably no other form of competition so intensely exciting. Ennobling it probably isn't, but the roar of a fight crowd is a special kind of roar. Call it healthy enthusiasm, call it mania, call it blood lust. Whatever you call it, the thrill of watching a great fight cannot be produced by any other sporting event.

It should be clear by now that prejudices in this space run against auto racing and in favor of boxing. They also run in favor of bullfighting. Most Americans have never seen a bullfight, have never learned about the art of that ritual dance, and probably have decided that the spectacle suggests a defect in the Latin personality.

Well, it may be for the best that Spanish bullfighting is illegal in the United States. Bullfighting is a drama and a ballet. Like religion, it is a subject poorly suited to casual argument. Either you know bullfighting and appreciate its esthetic aspects, or you condemn it as an overdressed exhibition of animal baiting.

So long as bullfighting is legal in some Latin countries, that is enough. The contest between a man and his courage needs Latin sunshine and Latin humors for a backdrop. I cannot imagine, for instance, a good bullfight in Red Bank, N.J.

Blood and Grand?

And though the bull is superficially lanced by men on horseback, stuck with darts by men on foot, run through with a sword (and sometimes finished with a dagger) by the matador, thousands upon thousands of sensitive people have called the *corrida* beautiful.

Nor need we doubt that auto-race fans feel strongly about their Indy, their Grand Prix of Endurance at Le Mans, their Watkins Glen. As *aficionados* remembered Belmonte, Manolete, Arruza, and Dominguin, and as the fight mob retells tales of Mickey Walker, Tony Zale, Joe Louis, and Ray Robinson, so (I guess) the racing-car crowd entertains itself with memories of Barney Oldfield, Wilbur Shaw, Ray Harroun, and Mauri Rose.

And they have a right. No one forces Bobby Unser to risk his neck in a car, or commands Joe Frazier to fight for money, or directs Dominguin to come out of retirement just one more time. Such gentlemen do what they do because they are good at it and therefore love it. And they are regarded with admiration by millions who pay money to see them at work.

Let's be tolerant of dangerous sports, whatever our own predilections, if only because it's every man's right to prove himself in the face of honest danger. And to do it in his own way.

George F. Will

Death as a Spectator Sport

Idaho's Snake River Canyon, where every prospect pleases and only man is vile, soon will be the scene of a remarkable example of man's work. On Sept. 8 Evel Knievel will try to leap 1,500 feet across the canyon on a 350 m.p.h. motorcycle.

Through all of what might be called his adult life, Knievel has devoted himself sedulously and successfully to the task of breaking all his bones seriatim. His usual metier is motorcycle jumps over Mack trucks. But repetition has blunted the keen edge of his zest, so the canyon provides a needed change and an opportunity to break all his bones simultaneously.

Obviously he is loony to the core and tough enough to eat spinach with sand in it. Conversation, especially about himself, tumbles trippingly from his tongue, and he expresses himself with especially generous strength on the subject of his own heroism.

But Knievel, and the hard-eyed men who merchandise him and the mutton-headed people who celebrate him, are enough to alter one's conception of man as nature's final word.

He estimates that he has a 50-50 chance of failing in his jump and falling to his death in the canyon. If the jump is not as risky as it is advertised to be, it is a fraud. If, as seems probable, it does involve serious risk of Knievel's life, it is obscene. Millions of people watching this dreadful spectacle will be happy as giddy crickets at the prospect that they have a 50-50 chance of seeing a man splatter himself on Idaho's rocks.

Asked why she was waiting in a long line to see the gruesomely shocking movie "The Exorcist," a lady answered: "I want to see what everybody is throwing up about." That movie only titillated an unseemly appetite for the grotesque. The witless Knievel is titillating a barbaric appetite for treating violent death as a spectator sport. Like pornography, the event is brutalizing, anti-life.

Knievel is nimble at minting canards for every occasion, and his latest batch includes: "I like to live with a lump in my throat and a knot in my stomach." He also likes a lump in his wallet.

When he is not dispensing metaphysical mush ("The greatest competitor in life is death"), it is clear that money is the lamp unto his feet. He is going to make a fortune with this jump.

The voluptuous pleasure of watching a man risk killing himself evidently is not dampened by the nagging possibility that he might not kill himself. Knievel is building roads to enable a huge mob of spectators to gather on the rim of the canyon.

Watching Knievel's foul enterprise from the canyon rim is not a pastime for the proletariat. Spectators must pay $25. But the carriage trade is expected to snap up 50,000 tickets, briskly. Millions more will pay $8 to watch on closed-circuit television.

Knievel or his estate will make at least $13 million from the jump itself. And his various promoters and sponsors—the toy and T-shirt manufacturers, and others—think they can milk more than $100 million from this. Obviously they are aiming at children of all ages, but especially at real children.

Knievel's success on the jump is a consummation devoutly to be desired, if only because failure would bestow upon him a mindless martyrdom and might make his merchandisers rich even beyond their dreams of avarice. The merchandisers know that if Knievel plunges to his death, in living color, he will go down in legend and in song. Says a vice president of the Ideal Toy Co.: "If he does go, we hope that he'll still be unique. He'll be a legend."

If Knievel wants to risk smashing out what might be called his brains, that is his business. If adults want to pay to watch, that is a free transaction between consenting nincompoops. But it would be nice if there were some exploitation to which not even a toy manufacturer would stoop.

The whole wretched business calls to mind Macauley's observation: "The Puritan hated bear-baiting not because it gave pain to the bear, but because it gave pleasure to the spectators." Sound folks, Puritans.

Boxing Poses a Challenge to Religion

The Moral Conflict Spotlighted by Case of Muhammed Ali

By The REV. LESTER KINSOLVING

Despite more than 400 deaths in the boxing ring since 1900—plus the unnumbered army of brain damaged ("punch drunk") ex-boxers—the expressed concern of organized religion about boxing has been minimal and isolated.

Nearly two decades ago, Jesuit Father Alfredo Boschi wrote that "Boxing cannot be justified from a moral viewpoint, but must be condemned as something gravely illicit in itself. It not only produces, but aims to produce serious injuries which can become permanent and lead to death . . . It makes a beast of a man . . . adoration of brute strength, of the fist which can pulverize the brain."

(Replied the Vatican's L'Osservatore Romano: "Rocky Marciano is a fervent, practicing Catholic . . . Many boxers, both in Italy and the U. S., cross themselves before entering the ring, which would be sacrilegious if boxing were essentially immoral.")

In 1963, the Rt. Rev. Nelson Burroughs, Episcopal bishop of Ohio, noted that "Five men have been killed in the boxing ring since the first of January." Bishop Burroughs, now retired, went on to assert: "To encourage their potential violation of the Sixth Commandment and to pit man against man under the guise of American entertainment is in my judgment a denial of Our Lord's emphasis on the sacredness and value of human personality."

YET SUCH ECCLESIASTICAL concern has been rare—despite organized religion's historic (if initially unpopular) opposition to a considerable number of bloody "sports' from gladiatorial games to bear-baiting.

Currently the strongest opposition to boxing comes not from the clergy but from many of those most closely acquainted, such as sportswriter Jim Murray. Recently this widely syndicated columnist drew a beat upon a TV announcer who enthusiastically shouted the gory details of the physical dismemberment of a boxer named Quarry.

"Quarry is bleeding from the nose!" screamed this announcer. "He can't see out of his eye! . . . His lip is split!. . . . He's a punching bag!"

Commented Murray, in italics: "What if he were blind altogether? Champagne all around? . . . Can you get me four tickets to a train wreck?' . . . How would you like a nice set of recordings made at midnight at Gestapo headquarters?"

"If there is a nobility in prize fighting, it lies not with the crowd, which is a collection of 16,000 sick jokes," concluded Murray. "Boxing today is about as scientific as an avalanche. You fight with your face. It's for people who would cackle at watching a sledgehammer on the Venus de Milo."

CURRENTLY RELIGION is a point at issue in boxing regarding America's most celebrated pugilist—and ham actor. Muhammed Ali contends that he should be exempt for military service because he is a Black Muslim minister.

Just how "pacifistic" is this theologically fantastic hate group is well documented in the autobiography of the late Malcolm X, who expressed little doubt as to the identity of those seeking after his life for his having dared to object to the unofficial harem of Black Muslim leader Elijah Muhammed.

The entire concept of clergy draft exemption has been substantially challenged by Father Peter Riga of California's St. Mary's College. But for the Rev. Mr. Ali to demand that he be exempted from military service so that he may make several fortunes by brain-bashing is as grotesque as the military chaplain who recently prayed for a large body count of the enemy in Vietnam.

THAT THE Rev. Mr. Ali's present occupation is in fact lethal is apparent in the research conducted by Prof. Robert Francis of the University of Wisconsin. He found that a 145-pound amateur (lightweight) could exert 600 pounds of pressure in just one punch. When such force is exerted against the brain, (average weight: three pounds), which is not anchored but rather encased in fluid, Dr. Ward Halstead of the University of Chicago notes: "Even a light blow causes the brain to bounce—it is appalling the ruin boxing causes the brain."

Hence the Rev. Mr. Ali is particularly skilled in what should rightfully be known as "the manly art of murder—or, death in small doses."

Perhaps the ultimate irony in this case is in the thousands of his fellow blacks who have either been without the funds to prolong draft resistance in the courts—or who have died, often very bravely, such as the black medic who saved the lives of his comrades by falling on a live grenade.

And if the parents, wives or children of such men have ever expressed any outrage at this irony, it has scarcely been heard.

It was a good day yesterday for two Cincinnati Bengals, one former and one present.

Bengals' running back Essex Johnson was told he will start against the Green Bay Packers Saturday night. To get his chance, he had to sign a medical waiver because doctors have warned him he is risking permanent injury to his knee.

Top, permission of National Newspaper Syndicate.
Left, from *The Washington Post*, 1975.
Right, from a column by Kenneth Denlinger in *The Washington Post*, 1975.

Lenny Hauss, for one, gets testy when one probes too deeply about how far a player should push himself and what he should use to prepare for a game.

"Look," he said, bristling, "it's all right for you to take every pill in the world to write a story, or it's all right for some gas station manager with no help to keep himself going any way possible, but it's different if a pro player does it?

"I disagree. Howard Cosell can take anything he wants to cure the flu, or whatever, and he has the right to stand in judgment of pro players? No."

HUNTERS Make it "Dear"... not "Deer"
will you...won't you...can't you?

friends of animals, inc. 11 West 60th Street, New York, N.Y. 10023 Circle 7-8120

Rod Hunter, "Sports" Columnist
Echoes Sentinel
Stirling, New Jersey

Dear Mr. Hunter,

You suggest that hunters have a "reverance" for life. Is it then something akin to the reverence the Marquis de Sade had for women? We never thought of it that way but it seems to make sense.

To your astute observation that nature is "no Disneyland" may we add: nor is it a boudoir. We're not turned on by a show of masculinity which takes place in the forests through maiming or occasionally killing helpless animals. We like guys whose virility holds on better proving grounds.

But, credit where credit is due: You hunters certainly are potent with the politicians. Now you may enter a sanctuary and blast off. On December 19, the New Jersey Great Swamp National Wildlife Refuge will throng with 150 of you lucky lottery-winners, tested for sharp-shooting by your ability to pay $7.15 for a license to murder.

Please spare our minds as you spare our bodies and don't try to ennoble your psychotic behavior by claiming you are trimming the herd for the benefit of the herd (which you say consists of 400 deer). We've read your magazines where you admit to each other that it's fun... fun...fun...to kill...kill...kill.

The only herd that needs trimming is the herd of hunters. So please garb yourselves, you brave 150, in fawn color on December 19, and double your thrill... thrill...thrill.

Sincerely yours, For the Girls:

GRETCHEN WYLER

LAUREN BACALL

GLORIA DE HAVEN

ALI MacGRAW

JUNE HAVOC

PATRICE MUNSEL

SHEILA MacRAE

BETSY PALMER

JOANNE WOODWARD

Courtesy Friends of Animals, Inc.

It's Open Season On Hunters

By JERRY KENNEY
Outdoor Editor of THE NEWS

HUNTERS this weekend are quietly moving through the painted autumn uplands of New York, stalking the lordly whitetail deer and the elusive black bear that for a short season are legal targets.

And stalking the hunters, but not quietly, are the seasonal crowd of ecologists, conservationists and other cause collectors to whom hunting is a bloody atrocity.

In New York alone, a half-million hunters will be on "binges of mayhem and murder," to hear the anti-hunting zealots tell it.

"Miserable cowards with a lust to kill," is how one so-called animal-lover described hunters on a radio program. Then she was permitted to express her wish that all of them be shot, too.

This bitter critic of hunting represents just one of several organizations that are determined to put an end to all game shooting.

They aren't opposed to killing steers, pigs, sheep, turkeys and other critters that are lured to the block by a man in a white, blood-spattered apron and an ax or hammer. And they aren't particularly upset that mink, beavers, raccoons and all those cuddly creatures have to be dispatched unceremoniously to provide warmth for some soft, pink bosom.

But the 17 million men and women who hunt for sport in this country have to go. This anti-hunting movement continues to grow even though its supporters have no concept of game management or what the ultimate outcome will be if they accomplish their goal.

It's easy to understand how the anti-hunters arouse the greatest amount of sympathy from the Bambi-lovers. Innocent, lovable, limpid-eyed creatures are pictured being slaughtered by ruthless hunters who will shoot anything that moves.

Unfortunately, there are a few creeps around the woods who fit this description. They take their share of horses, cows, dogs and chickens and they pepper farm houses, roadsigns and automobile tires. And every time one does, this transgression is blown all out of proportion and held to be typical of the hunting breed. But this charge is as unjust as tabbing every New York City cop a bribe taker.

The sport hunter does his damnedest to keep these characters out of circulation because they are his biggest threat. They keep the anti-hunting forces supplied with ammunition. But it's the only valid charge they have. Once they switch to the "hunters - exterminate - game - charge," they don't have a leg to stand on.

Game management professionals don't even like to use the term "hunting." It is hunting to us who tramp the woods and mountains. But, to them, killing animals is considered a harvest. Like any growing crop, game must be harvested or it will choke itself out of existence.

If deer and other game animals kept within the bounds of their habitats and obtained sufficient sustenance within that area, there would be no hunting. But there are no birth control pills out there, and doing what comes naturally can send any population completely out of control.

As the population increases, the habitat shrinks and the winter food supply disappears. The result is starvation and sick, weak deer. Additional starvation is likely in subsequent winters because the food supply is not replenished in one season, but may take from three to 10 years.

An unchecked game population is doomed, and this would have happened to the deer if sound game management hadn't been practiced long ago. The excess population must be harvested, and it's the hunter who harvests it. Hunters have taken over a million deer in New York in the last decade, but for every deer a hunter kills, there is still one that starves or dies a "natural" death.

Those who insist we should let nature take its course have never seen a deer starving, a doe trampling her fawn to get browse on a tree or dogs tearing at deer until their guts are dragging on the ground as they run.

Cars and trucks alone kill about 20,000 deer every year in New York. Predators—wolves, wildcats and such—no longer are a threat to deer. But domestic dogs, the collies, poodles, beagles and mutts that are allowed to roam untended, are becoming one of the most serious threats to deer in the Northeast. It's so serious that game protectors shoot any dogs they find in the woods from October through April.

The dogs don't eat the deer. They just kill them, thus wasting a link in the food chain. Man is also a predator, and has been since the beginning of time. Most men do not have to hunt to eat today, but if they eat meat, someone has to kill it for them. So, when a hunter kills swiftly with an accurate, high-powered bullet, and makes good use of the meat, why should he be condemned?

Every hunter aims for a clean kill. Anything short of that lessens his chance of taking his prize. Everyone can't be a marksman, but with the quality of firearms and optics available today, hunters rarely wound animals and lose them.

A hunter's bullet is at least as humane as a slaughter house worker's ax, hammer or knife, and probably more so, but even the most dedicated of conservationists is seldom moved to tears by the sight of a succulent steak on his plate.

From *The New York Daily News*, November 21, 1971.

In Defense of Deer Hunting and Killing

By Arthur C. Tennies

FROM CHENANGO COUNTY, N.Y.

"You hunt deer?" When I nodded, my shocked colleague went on to say, "Why my whole image of you has been shattered. How can you kill such beautiful creatures?"

And so would many others who view the deliberate killing of deer as brutal and senseless. Such people look upon the hunter as a barbaric hangover

---

Comment

---

from the distant past of the human race. To my colleague, the incongruity between the barbarism of hunting and normal civilized conduct was made more intense because I was a minister. How could I as a minister do such a thing?

I thought about that as I drove through the early morning darkness toward the southeastern part of Chenango County. It was a little after 5 a.m. I had gotten up at 4, something I only do in the case of an emergency or when I am going deer hunting. It was cold, the temperature in the 20s. With

~~~~

Arthur C. Tennies is the associate executive director for Planning and Research for the New York State Council of Churches and Associate for Non-Metropolitan Ministries with the United Presbyterian Program Agency. He is author of a book entitled, A Church for Sinners, Seekers and Sundry Non-Saints, published by Abingdon.

~~~~

the ground frozen, it would be too noisy for still hunting until the sun had had a chance to thaw the frost. So it would be wait and freeze. My first thoughts about why I would hunt deer had nothing to do with the supposed barbarism of it. I thought of the foolishness of it. Wait hour after hour in the cold, feet numb, hands numb, and small chance of getting a deer.

I was going to hunt on Schlafer Hill on the farm of Pershing Schlafer. My choice of a place to hunt had been determined by the party permit that three of us had, which allowed us to kill one other deer of either sex besides the three bucks that we were allowed.

I thought about the party system in New York, the way the state controlled the size of the deer herd. The state is divided into about 40 deer-management areas. The state biologists know how many deer each area can handle, how many deer can feed on the browse available without destroying it. If there are too many deer, they will kill the plants and bushes upon which they depend. The next step is starvation for large numbers. Since the deer's natural predators were wiped out by the first settlers, the only control over their numbers now is starvation or hunting. Thus, so many deer must be killed in a deer-management area. A certain number will be killed by motor vehicles. The biologists can estimate how many will be killed on the highways and also the number of bucks that will be killed. The surplus is taken care of by issuing a set number of party permits.

I have often marveled at the state biologists, their skill and knowledge in managing the deer herd. As I have pondered the problems of people—poverty, starvation, injustice, and all the others—and our frantic and often futile efforts to solve these problems, I have thought, "If only we could manage the problems of people as well as we can manage a deer herd."

The Great Difference

Then I realize the great difference between the two. People are not for being managed. We manage people only by robbing them of the right to choose—and the most brutal attempts to manage are ultimately frustrated by the obstinacy of human nature, its refusal to be managed. A handful of biologists may manage a deer herd and a handful of scientists may be able to put a man on the moon, but no handful of planners will ever manage the human race. And so I thought again, as the car rushed through the dark, that all of our modern management techniques would fail to come up with quick and perfect solutions to the problems of people.

It was Dead

I waited another hour. It was warmer now. Finally a deer appeared, a head above a rise. It started to come nearer. Then it stopped. Something was wrong. It decided to leave. As it turned, my gun came up and I shot. It lurched sideways, kicking and thrashing, disappearing under a pine tree. I walked to the spot. No deer. I went around the tree and there it lay. In a second it was dead.

I looked down at the deer, a button buck, and I thought: This is the way of nature, one creature feeding on another. Thousands of years ago our forebearers survived in just this way. They killed, gutted, butchered, and ate. Now we buy in a supermarket or order in a restaurant.

The first task was to gut the deer, kind of a messy process. I got my knife cut, turned the deer on his back, and slit him open. I spilled the guts cut on the ground. I saved the liver and heart, even though the heart had been mangled by the bullet. I cut through the diaphragm and pulled the lungs out.

Back Up the Hill

Then I was ready to pull the deer back to the car. It was 3 p.m. when I got to the car. Time yet to hunt for a buck, so I dumped the deer into the trunk. Back up the hill, but no luck. As night came on, I got back to the car. I tied the deer on the top of the trunk and started for home.

As I drove toward home, I had a sense of satisfaction. I had fitted myself to nature's way and had been successful. For a few short hours, I had marched to the beat of nature's drum, not that of our modern world. At least for me, the barrier that we had built between nature and us could still be breached.

As I went to sleep that night I thought: "I suppose that no matter what I say, a lot of people will still never understand why I hunt deer. Well, they don't have to, but let only vegetarians condemn me."

By Arthur C. Tennies in *The National Observer*, January 18, 1975.

Mom Says Hunting's No Game

DEAR ABBY: The letter in your column about hunting prompts this letter. Hunting is a sport to which I am morally opposed. My husband knows my objections, but, since he is an adult, I realize that his decisions are his own, and it is with his own conscience he must wrestle. I don't participate in his hunting trips, and have no intentions of doing so.

The problem centers around our 12-year-old son. My husband wants to buy him a gun and introduce him to the sport. Our son, eager to participate in activities with his father, is excited by the prospect.

I don't feel that humans have the right to kill animals unless their lives are directly endangered, or unless they need the meat for survival. We are an upper-middle-class urban family, and neither of these situations is likely to occur.

My husband says that he wants our son to know the joy of our rapidly vanishing wilderness areas. I say, "Fine, take him camping and teach him the craft of the woodsman."

He claims he wants our son to know the challenge of stalking elusive game.

I say, "Fine . . . let him stalk with a camera. And if he needs to have a trophy . . . bring home some pictures."

He says he wants our son to be skillful with a rifle. I don't mind that. We have access to an excellent skeet-shooting range and instructors.

Finally, and worst in my opinion, my husband says he wants our son to be a man, and that my refusal to sanction the hunting will turn him into a sissy.

Abby, to me a true man (or woman) is one who rejoices in the beauty of life, who works hard to preserve all of that beauty, who respects mankind and all animals, and who kills only as a necessity and never for pleasure or sport.

Many of our traditional and superficial concepts of manhood and womanhood are being questioned these days, and I think that the question of hunting as a means of developing masculinity deserves being considered by more Americans.

ANIMAL LOVER

DEAR ANIMAL LOVER: Well said. But let's hear it from another animal lover:

* * *

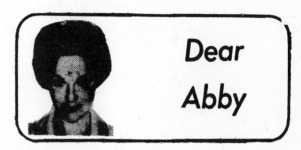

DEAR ABBY: Those meat-eaters who throw a fit about harvesting wildlife have got to be some of the biggest hypocrites of all time.

Just where do they think beef, pork and mutton come from? Anybody who's raised a 4-H calf, or nursed along a runt pig or an orphan lamb knows that these animals are every bit as lovable as the majestic buck or graceful doe.

How much kinder is death from a hit on the head with a sledge hammer than from a bullet? All meat eaters are guilty.

In case you're wondering—yes, I eat meat. And no, I don't hunt. And yes, I love animals (present population, one dog, four cats, six horses, and one pig).

MRS. K., LA MOILLE, ILLINOIS

Courtesy of Abigail Van Buren, syndicated newspaper columnist, "Dear Abby."

Ruffian's Last Race

The blow came with such sickening suddenness that it took several gasping moments to absorb its impact—and its cruel lesson in the fragility of thoroughbred racehorses and of the dreams built around them. At one point last week, the magnificent filly Ruffian was the flamelike fulfillment of generations of planning and dreaming: a huge, nearly black three-year-old with rippling muscles and those rare champion's eyes that seemed to know that she couldn't be beaten or even seriously challenged. Then, as she raced alongside the colt Foolish Pleasure in an eagerly awaited, nationally televised match race at New York's Belmont Park, Ruffian thrust her 1,125-pound body forward onto her delicate thoroughbred legs for the final graceful time.

Both jockeys heard the sound—"like when you break a stick"—as bone cracked in her right foreleg. Then Jacinto Vasquez was fighting desperately to pull her up, knowing that her marvelous competitive fires would propel her forward on three legs and further endanger the fourth. By the time she came to a reluctant halt 100 yards further on, Ruffian had pounded her ankle into a pulp of blood and tissue and shattered bone. Eight hours later she was dead.

Ruffian

Man's inhumanity to other men is usually rationalized by various social, economic or political excuses, but inhumanity to animals other than his own species is inexcusable.

Certainly, many people watching Ruffian break down in her match against Foolish Pleasure had tears welling in their eyes out of sympathy for the unfortunate and beautiful horse. My sympathy is for the people who profit from and promote the "sport" of horseracing, a sport in which man once again asserts his superiority over yet another species. "Sports" like football and boxing involve violence against other humans who chose to participate, in spite of the risk of serious physical injury. Why drag other animals into our madness?

Only when arrogant man learns just how effective he has been in the destruction of his own ecosystem will his narrow-minded concept of the earth expand and, with a little humility, he will see that he is only part of a natural life cycle, not the only player in the game.

Michael J. Walter.

Washington.

Above, from *Newsweek*, July 21, 1975.
Left, letter to the editor of *The Washington Post* by Michael J. Walter, July 14, 1975.
Below, reprinted by permission of United Press International.

Death for Greyhounds Threatened in Dispute

PHOENIX, July 15 (UPI) —Gov. Raul Castro today called "unjust, inhumane and immoral" a plan by Arizona greyhound breeders to kill 30 dogs to focus attention on its dispute with racetrack operators.

The Arizona Greyhound Breeders Association, which said it would kill the dogs today, postponed the killing until Thursday.

The association threatened to carry out the eventual destruction of 300 greyhounds worth more than $1 million.

"It is unjust, inhumane and immoral to sacrifice these dogs as innocent victims of a dispute between two groups of people," Castro said. "Surely both sides are rational enough to sit down and resolve their differences."

The breeders have boycotted track operations of Funks Greyhound Racing Circuit, Inc., in an attempt to get Funks to recognize their association as official breeder representative.

Allen Walker, financial chairman of the association, said the dogs would be killed in hopes of arousing public pressure to force Funks to recognize the association.

"We're going to start with our low quality animals," Walker said. "Next week, we'll cut into our better dogs and gradually we'll get up into destroying the top animals that race on this circuit. We're talking about approximately 300 greyhounds worth well over $1 million."

Joe the Cockfighter Pitted Against Hypocrites and Chicken Cockfighters

By Kathleen Maxa
Washington Star Staff Writer

In these times of rampant pornography, pot-smoking in the best of homes, legalized off-track betting and state-run lotteries, Joe Zannino is baffled that most people react to cockfighting with the moral outrage the folks of River City directed toward pool. Right. Cockfighting. Starts with a "C" and that rhymes with "T" and that stands for trouble.

"It's illegal, sure," said the cigar-chomping, barrel-chested, East Baltimore mortician. "But so is everything else — smoking pot, prostitution, spitting in the street. But these things are flourishing."

"Cockfighting is not nearly as cruel as many other sports that are flourishing today — big game fishing, fox hunting, or even rodeo," Zannino said.- "You hook one of those beautiful marlins or any other big game fish and he doesn't want to play the game. He's hooked and he's fighting. In fox hunting, even if they don't kill the fox outright, they run him to death and he doesn't want to play the game either. Same thing with rodeo. You think those little calves like having those big, 200-pound cowboys jump on them?

"Cockfighting is the only sport in which the creature being used is doing it by choice. He wants to fight. Fighting is a normal facet of his mating behavior," Zannino said.

"I DON'T buy the argument that cocks naturally enjoy fighting each other," said Captain Donald P. Lambert, chief law enforcement officer of the Massachusettes SPCA and the man who is to cockfighters what Elliott Ness was to mobsters. "I can't disagree with the fact that other sports operating freely under the law may involve cruelty to animals, but do two wrongs make a right?

"One of the things cockfighters like to say is that George Washington fought gamecocks. Well, I say they kept slaves in the old days too. How's that for an analogy?"

Reprinted by permission of *The Washington Star* (August 26, 1975).

ABOUT THE AUTHOR

Robert J. Baum received his B.A. in Philosophy from Northwestern University and his Ph.D., also in Philosophy, from The Ohio State University. From 1965 to 1967, as a Peace Corps Volunteer, he served as Visiting Lecturer in Mathematics and Philosophy of Science at the Middle East Technical University in Ankara, Turkey. He has been a member of the Philosophy Department at Rensselaer Polytechnic University since 1969; he is currently an associate professor and Director of the Center for the Study of the Human Dimensions of Science and Technology. He served as the first Manager of the Ethical and Human Value Implications of Science and Technology Program at the National Science Foundation from 1974 to 1976. In addition to coediting the first edition of *Ethical Arguments for Analysis* with James Randell, he has authored *Philosophy and Mathematics: From Plato to the Present* (1974) and *Logic* (1975) as well as a number of papers and articles on ethics, philosophy of science, and philosophy of mathematics.